FOR ORGANS, PIANOS & ELECTRONIC KEYBOARDS

39

THE BEST CHILDREN[...]ER

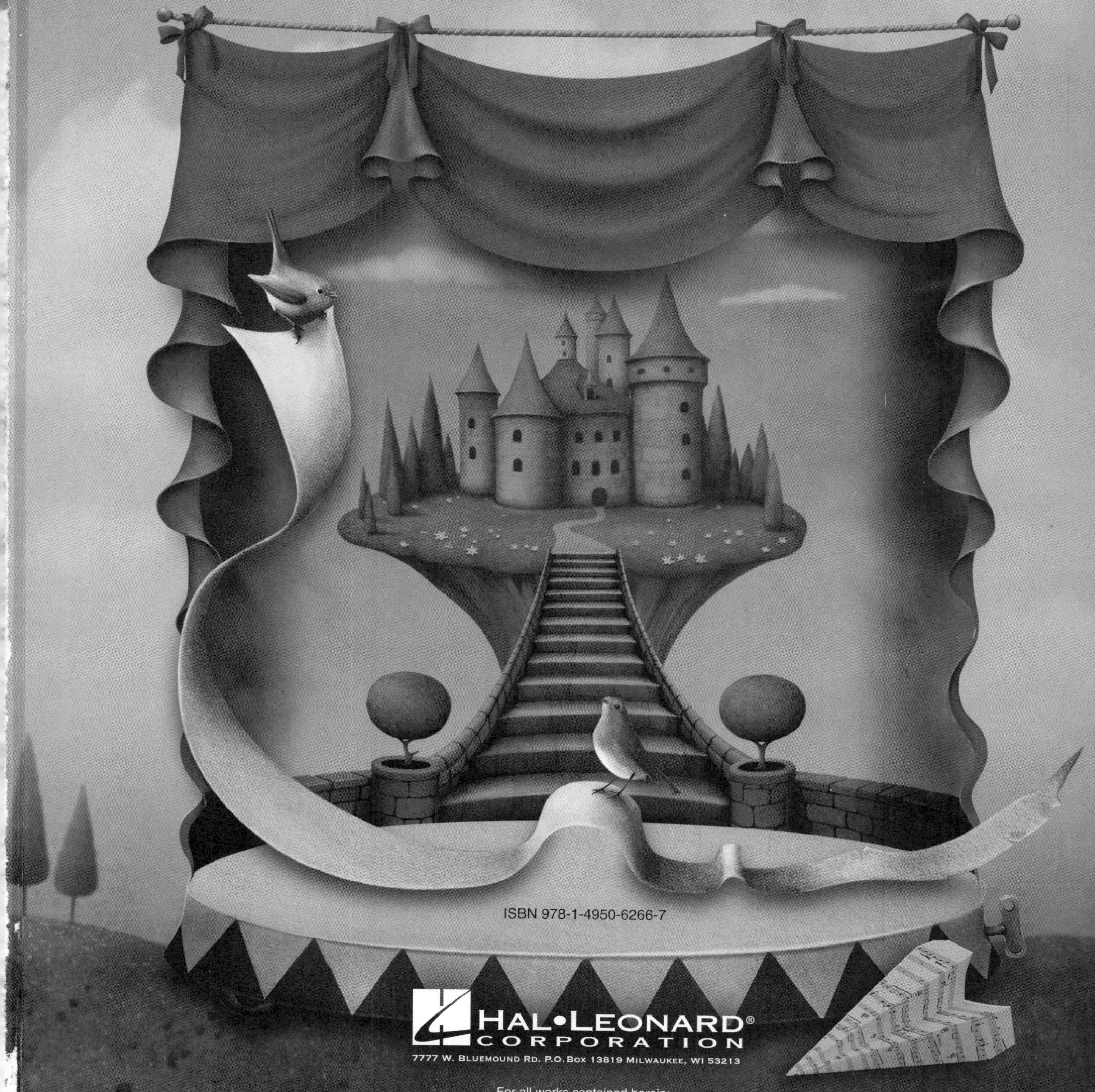

ISBN 978-1-4950-6266-7

7777 W. BLUEMOUND RD. P.O. BOX 13819 MILWAUKEE, WI 53213

For all works contained herein:
Unauthorized copying, arranging, adapting, recording, Internet posting, public performance, or other distribution of the printed music in this publication is an infringement of copyright.
Infringers are liable under the law.

E-Z Play® Today Music Notation © 1975 by HAL LEONARD CORPORATION
E-Z PLAY and EASY ELECTRONIC KEYBOARD MUSIC are registered trademarks of HAL LEONARD CORPORATION.

Visit Hal Leonard Online at
www.halleonard.com

Alouette

Registration 3
Rhythm: Fox Trot

Traditional

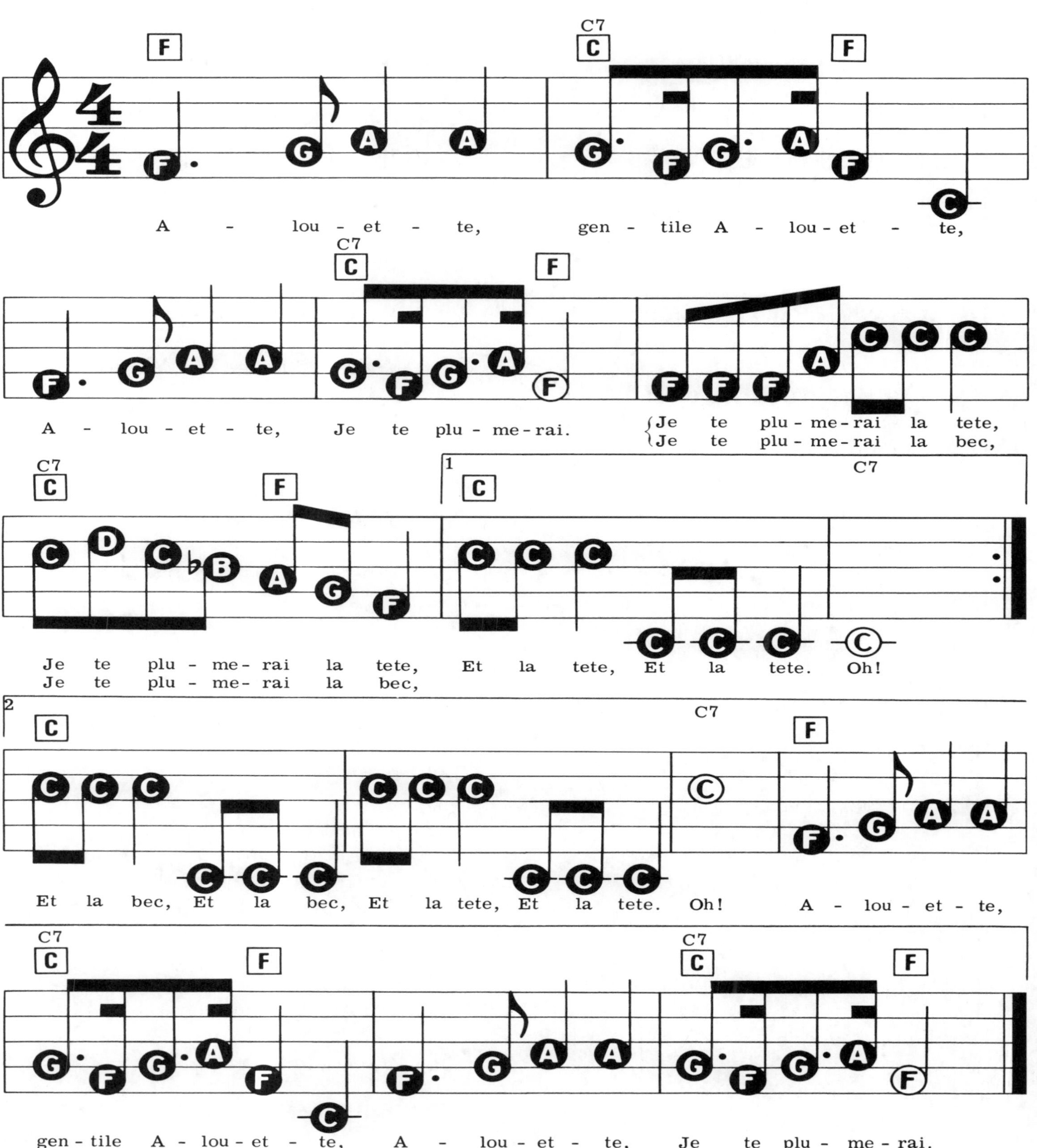

Copyright © 1975 by HAL LEONARD CORPORATION
International Copyright Secured All Rights Reserved

Any Dream Will Do

from JOSEPH AND THE AMAZING TECHNICOLOR® DREAMCOAT

Music by Andrew Lloyd Webber
Lyrics by Tim Rice

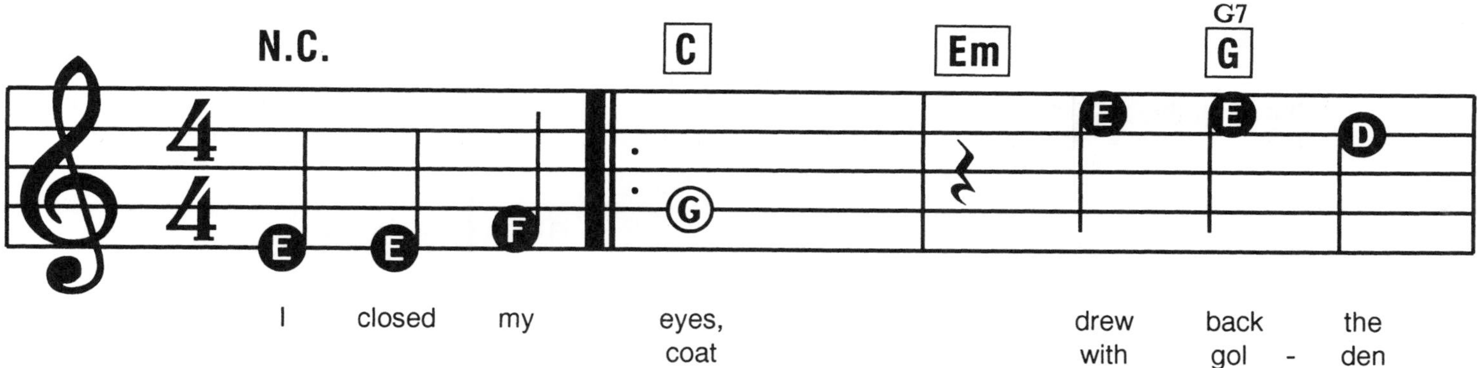

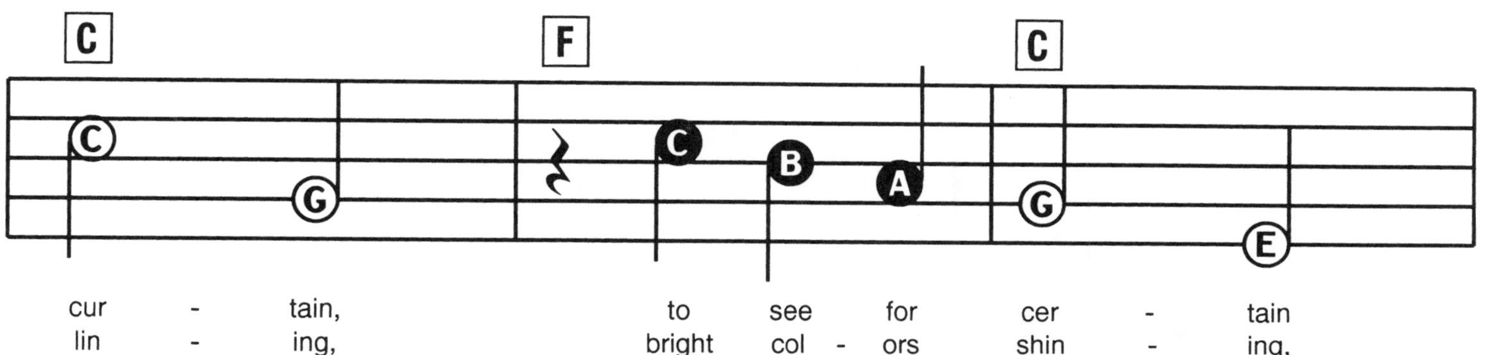

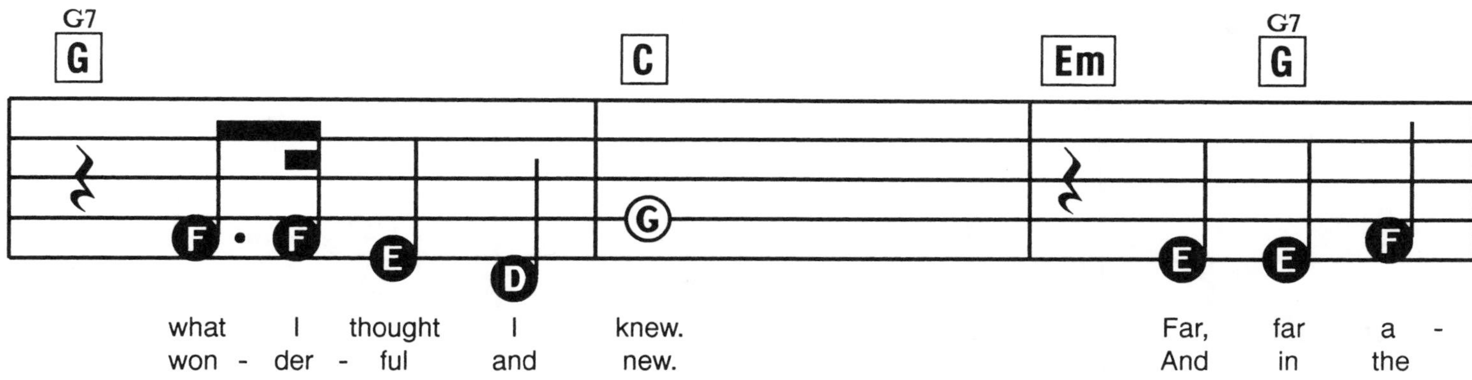

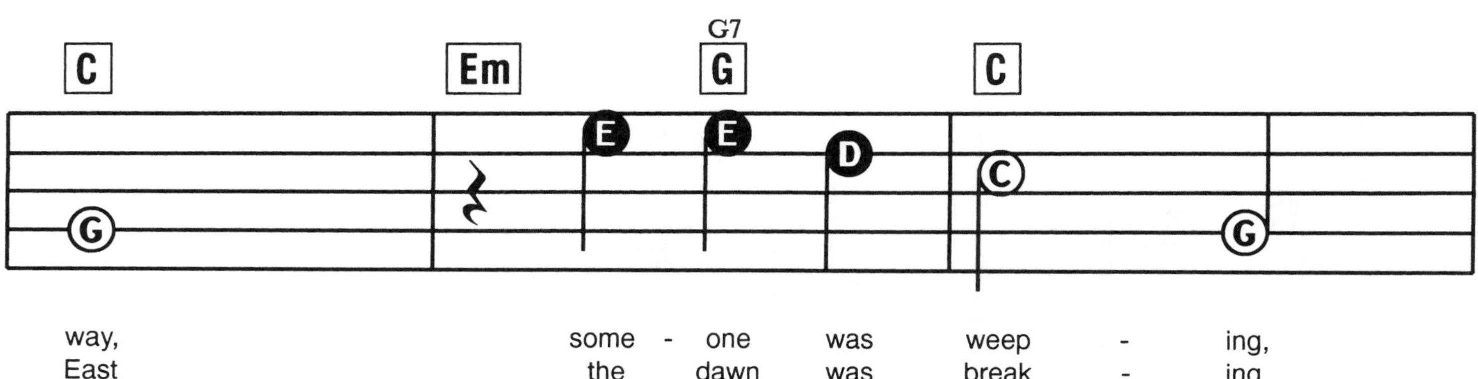

© Copyright 1969 The Really Useful Group Ltd.
Copyright Renewed
International Copyright Secured All Rights Reserved

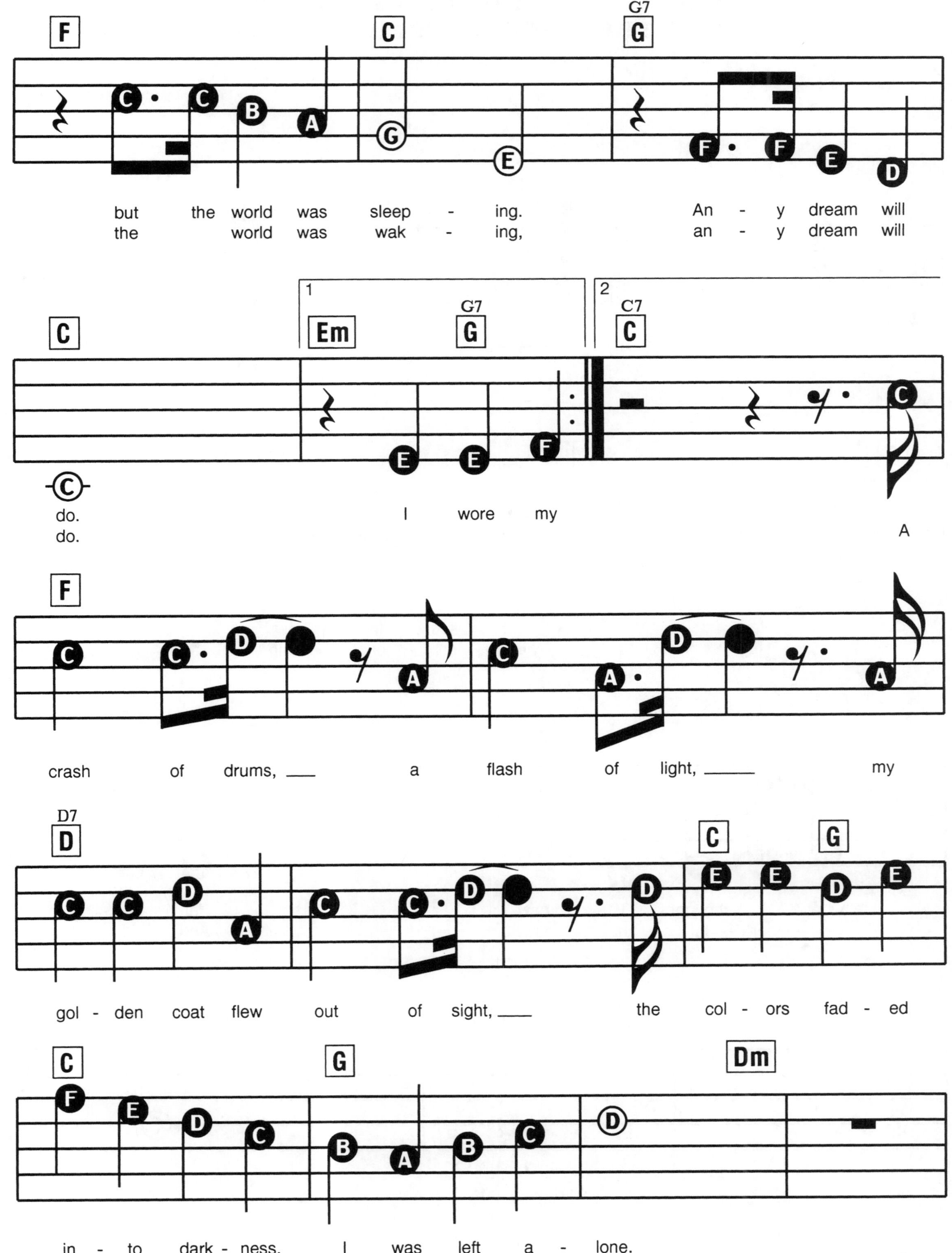
F
C
G7
G
but the world was sleep - ing.
the world was wak - ing,
An - y dream will
an - y dream will
C
1
Em
G7
G
2
C7
C
do.
do.
I wore my
A
F
crash of drums, a flash of light, my
D7
D
C
G
gol - den coat flew out of sight, the col - ors fad - ed
C
G
Dm
in - to dark - ness, I was left a - lone.

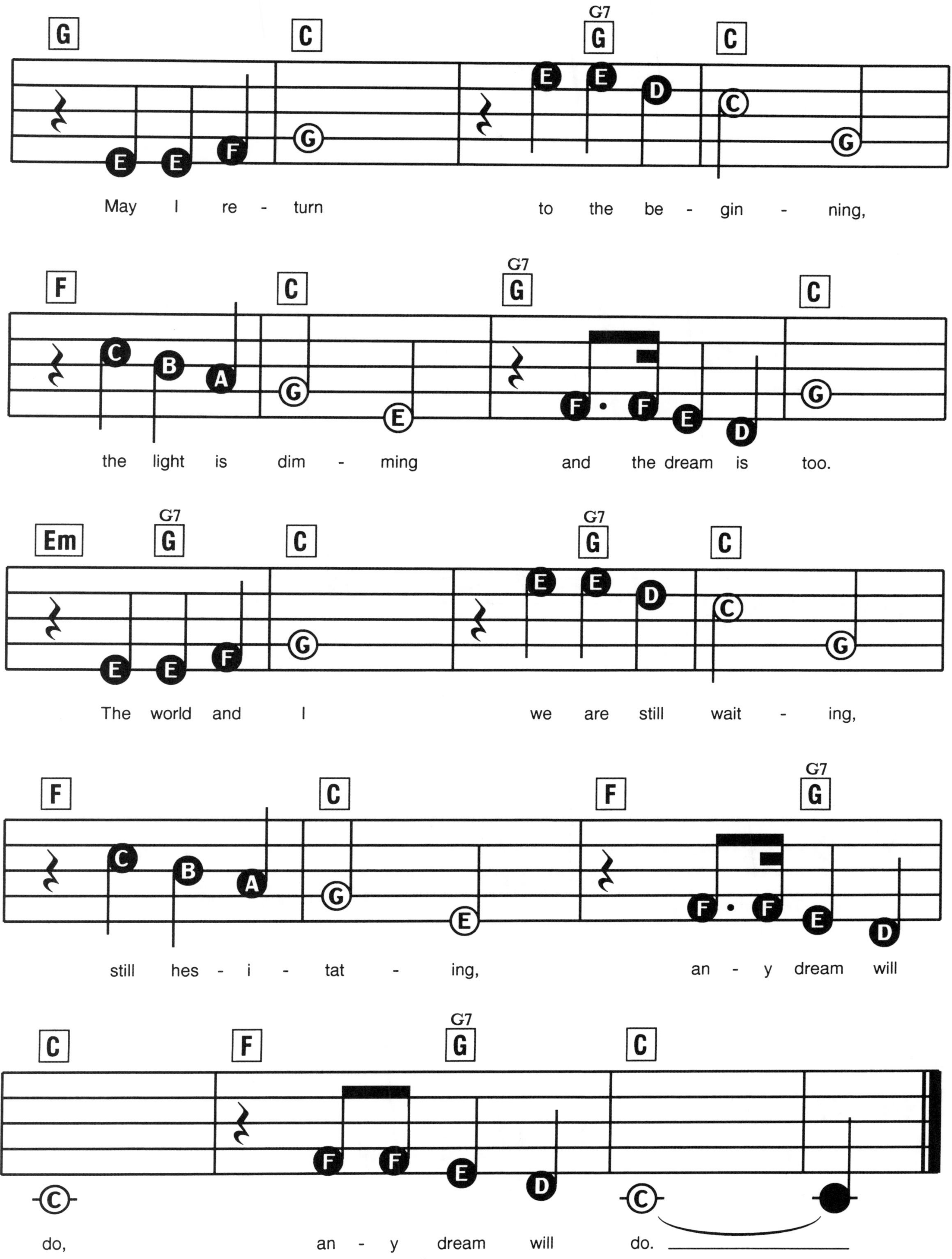
G
C
G7
G
C
May I re - turn to the be - gin - ning,
F
C
G7
G
C
the light is dim - ming and the dream is too.
Em
G7
G
C
G7
G
C
The world and I we are still wait - ing,
F
C
F
G7
G
still hes - i - tat - ing, an - y dream will
C
F
G7
G
C
do, an - y dream will do.

Alphabet Song

Registration 8
Rhythm: Country or None

Traditional

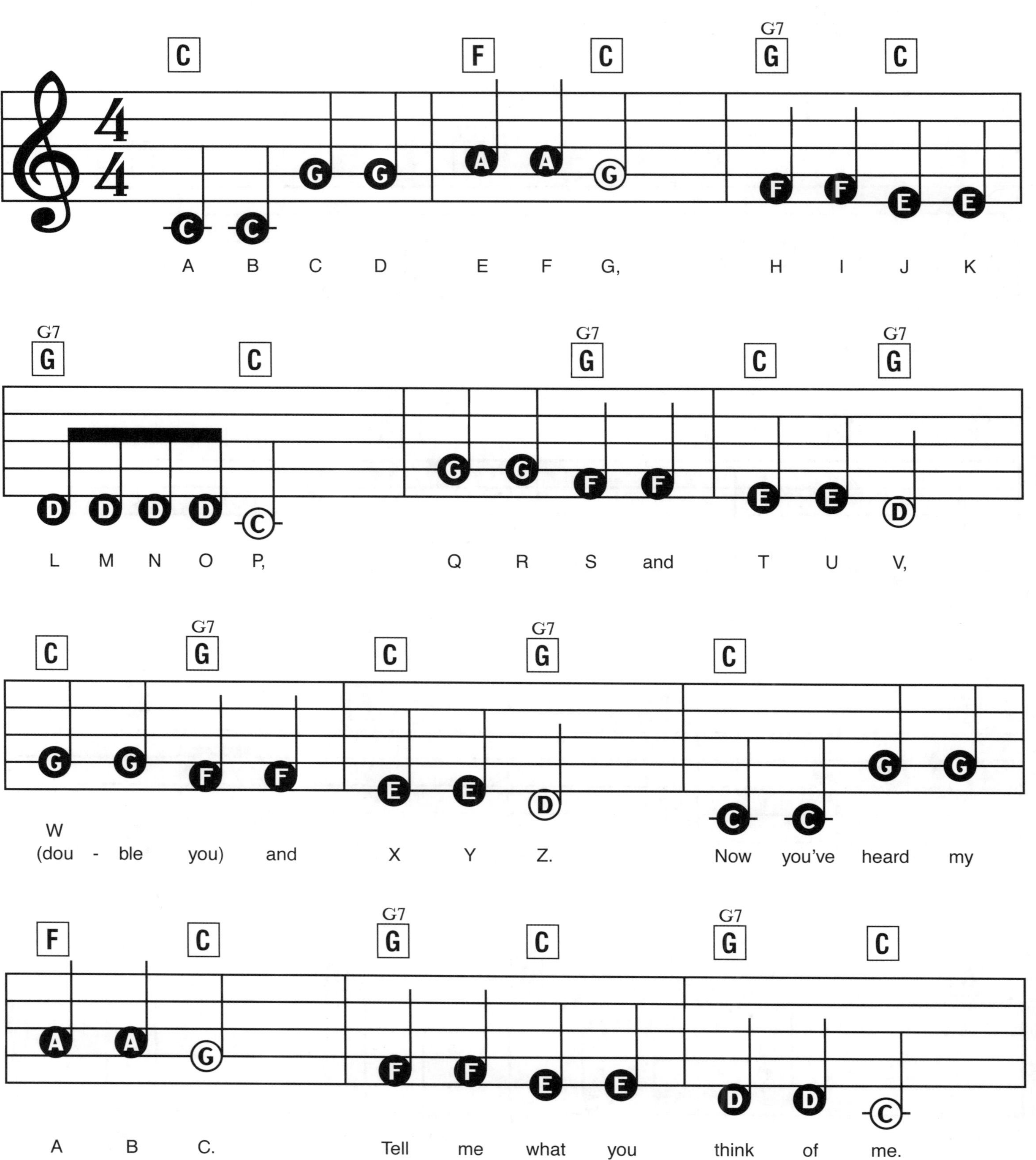

Copyright © 2003 by HAL LEONARD CORPORATION
International Copyright Secured All Rights Reserved

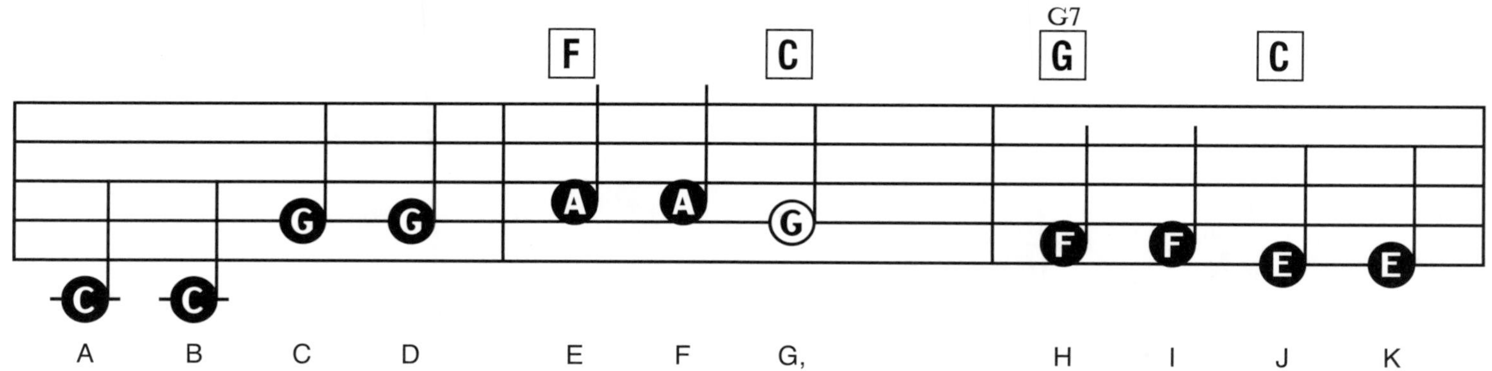
F C G7 G C
C C G G A A G F F E E
A B C D E F G, H I J K

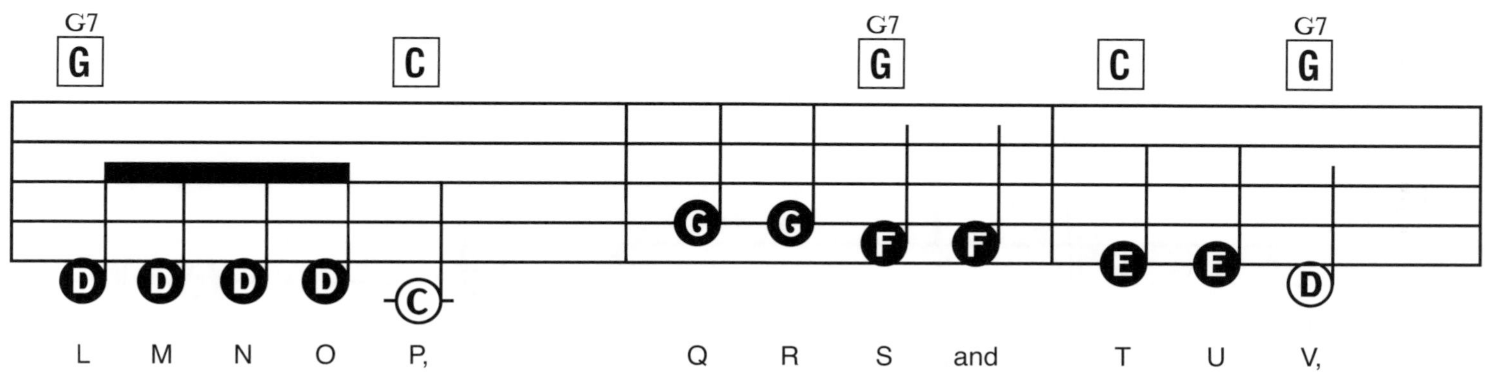
G7 G C G7 G C G7 G
D D D D C G G F F E E D
L M N O P, Q R S and T U V,

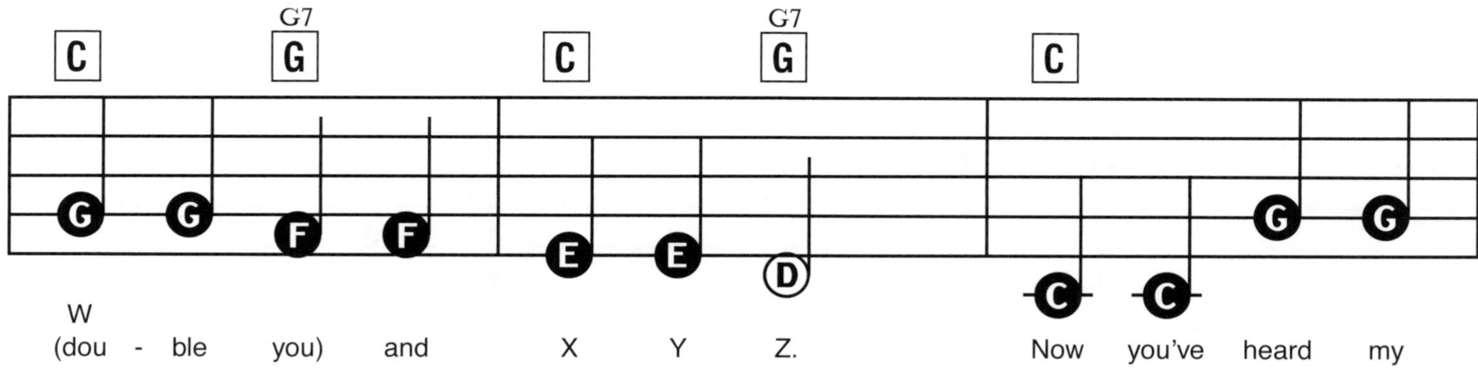
C G7 G C G7 G C
G G F F E E D C C G G
W (dou - ble you) and X Y Z. Now you've heard my

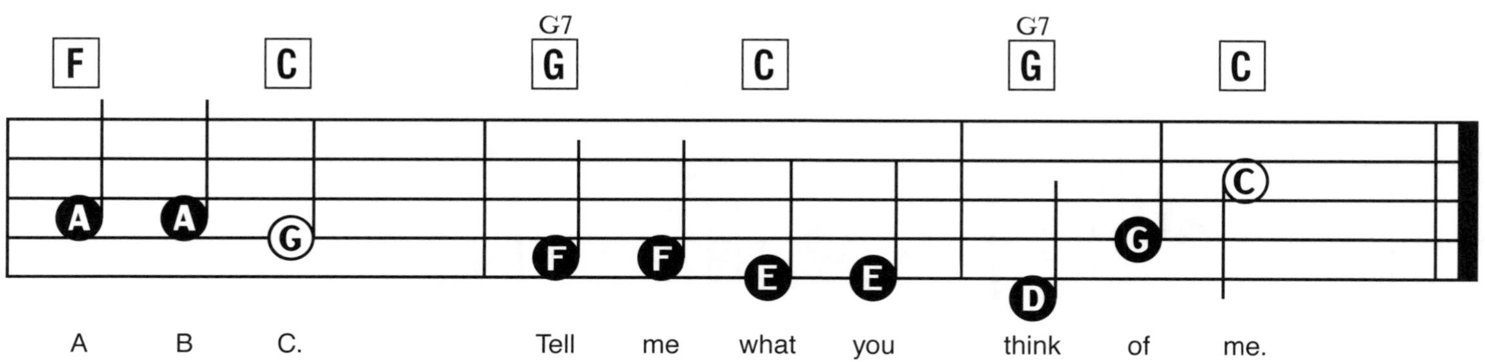
F C G7 G C G7 G C
A A G F F E E D G C
A B C. Tell me what you think of me.

Amazing Grace

Registration 6
Rhythm: Waltz

Words by John Newton
Traditional American Melody
From Carrell and Clayton's *Virginia Harmony*

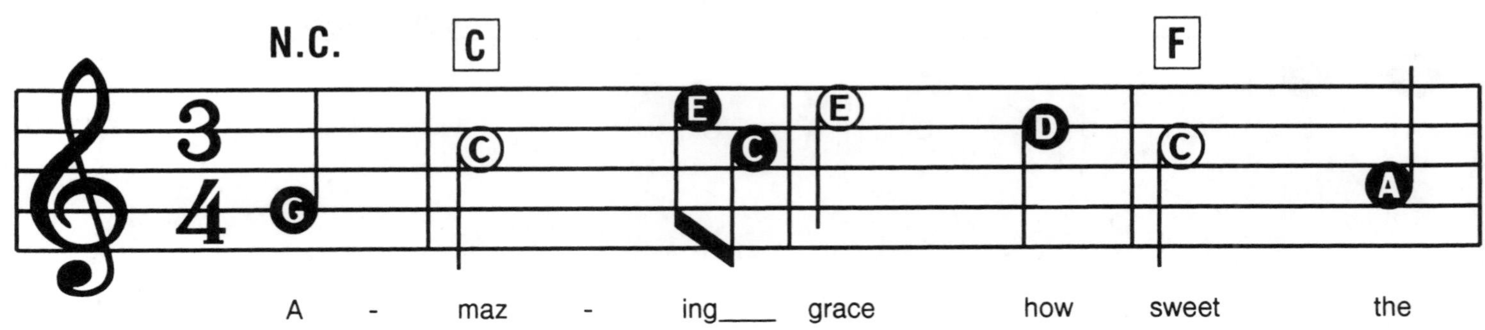

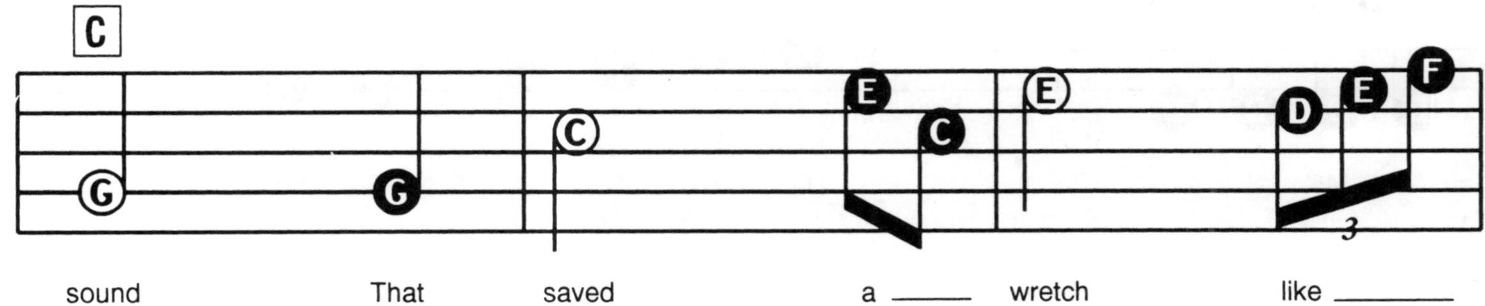

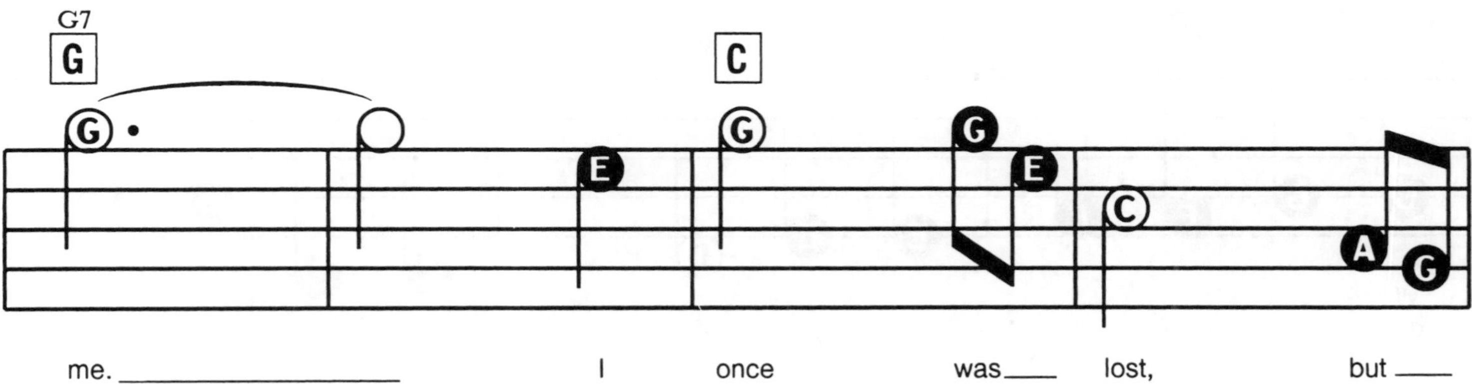

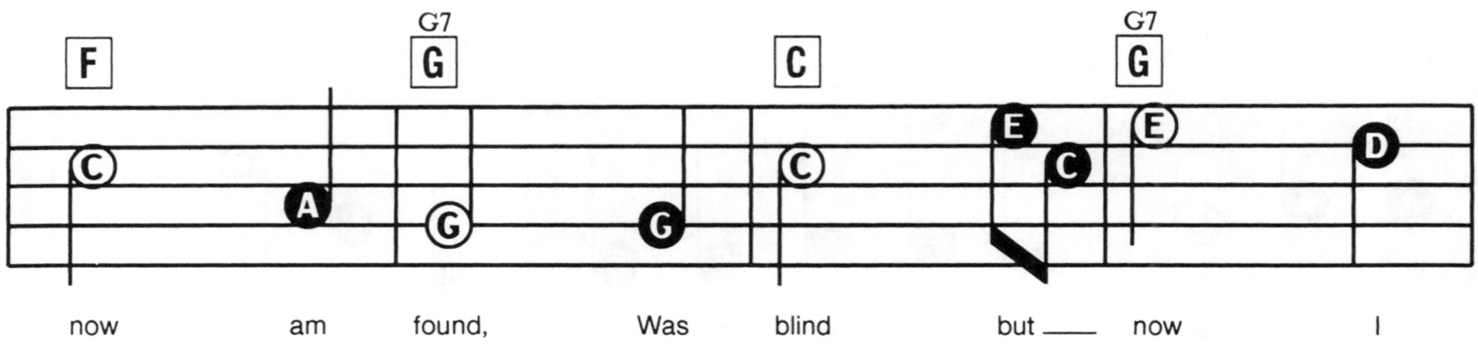

Copyright © 1993 by HAL LEONARD CORPORATION
International Copyright Secured All Rights Reserved

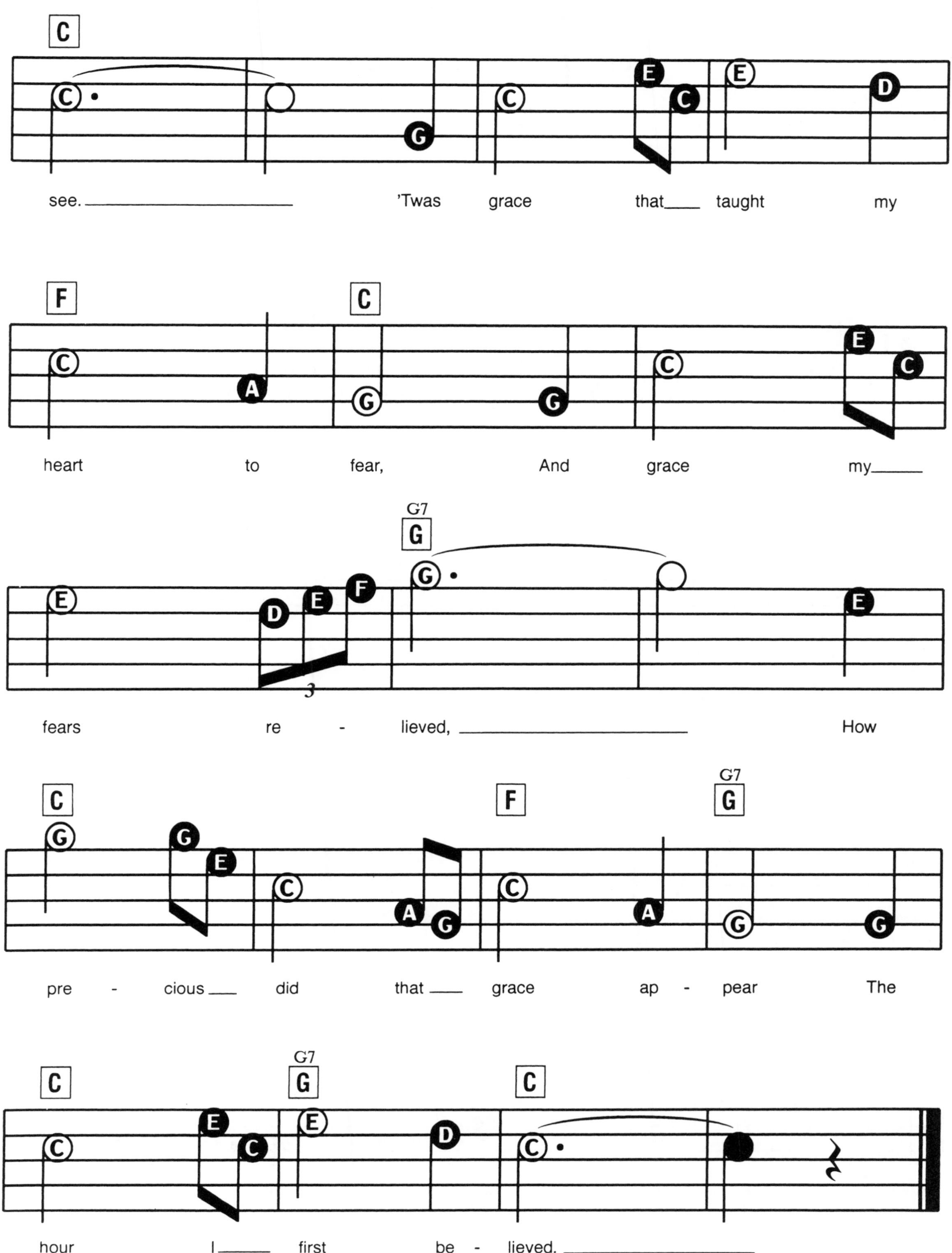
C
see. 'Twas grace that taught my
F C
heart to fear, And grace my
G7 G
fears re - lieved, How
C F G7 G
pre - cious did that grace ap - pear The
C G7 G C
hour I first be - lieved.

Baby Mine

from Walt Disney's DUMBO

Registration 1
Rhythm: Ballad or Fox Trot

Words by Ned Washington
Music by Frank Churchill

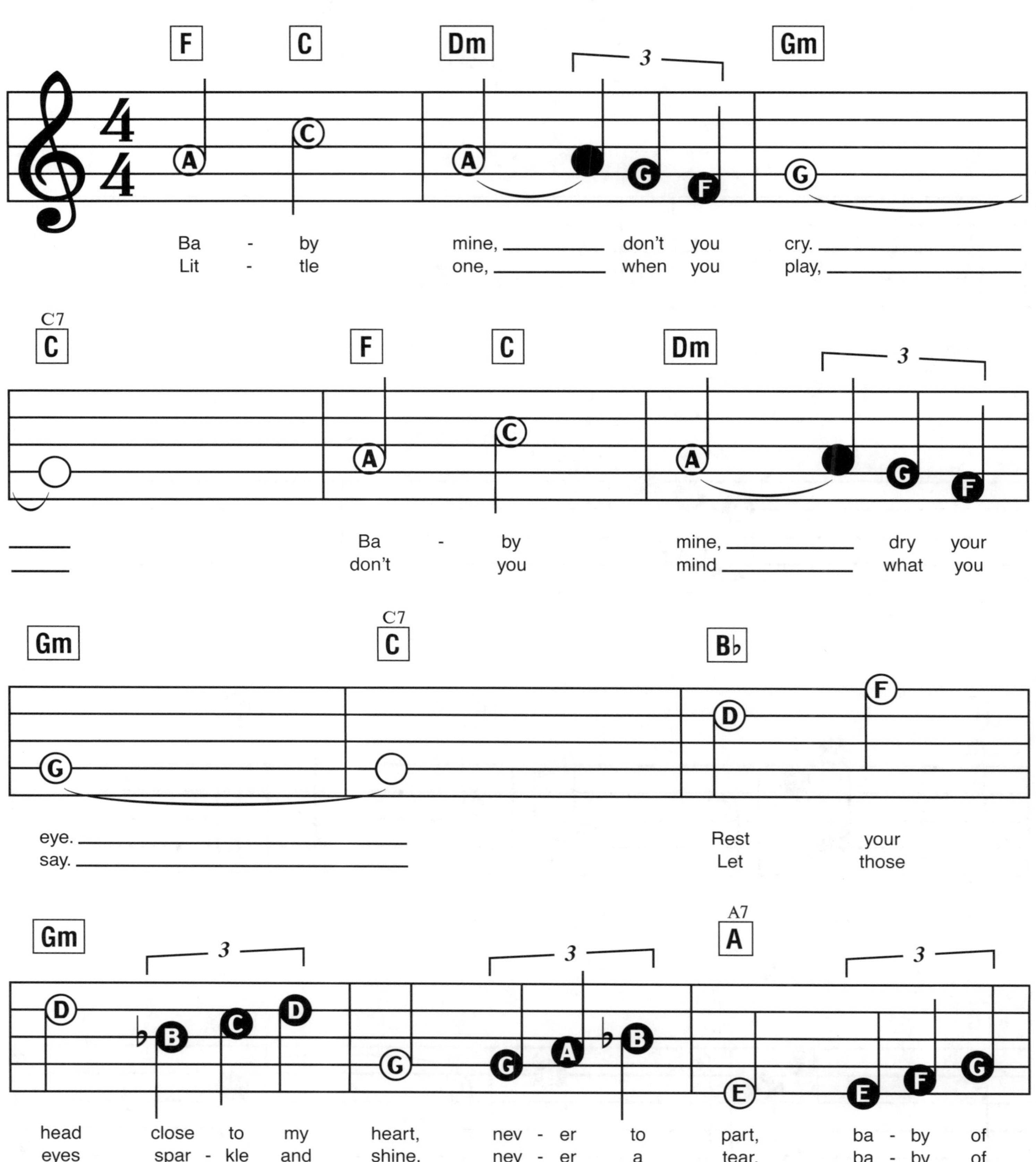

Copyright © 1941 by Walt Disney Productions
Copyright Renewed
World Rights Controlled by Bourne Co. (ASCAP)
International Copyright Secured All Rights Reserved

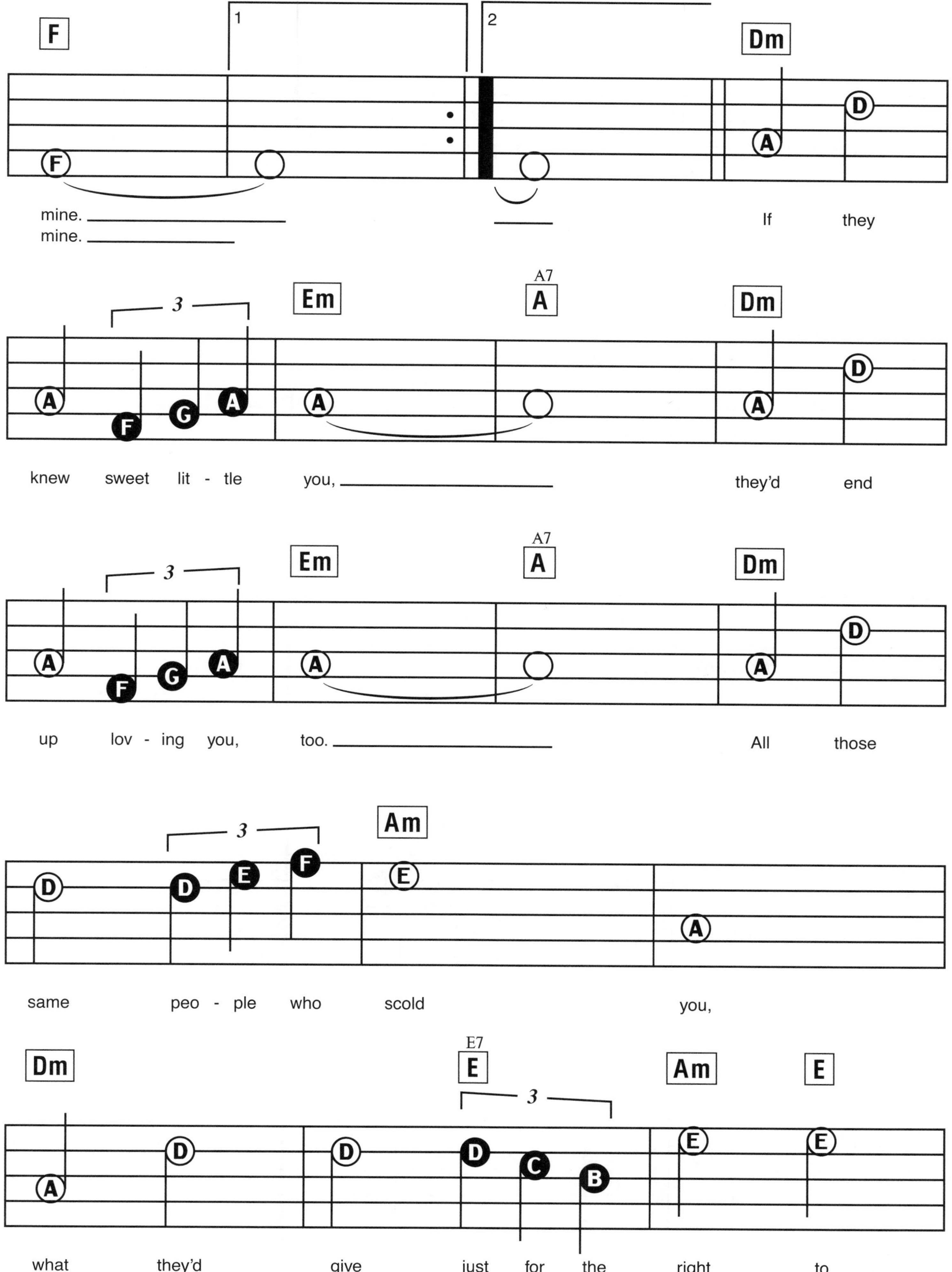
F
1
2
Dm
mine.
mine.
If they
Em
A7
A
Dm
knew sweet lit - tle you,
they'd end
Em
A7
A
Dm
up lov - ing you, too.
All those
Am
same peo - ple who scold
you,
Dm
E7
E
Am
E
what they'd give just for the right to

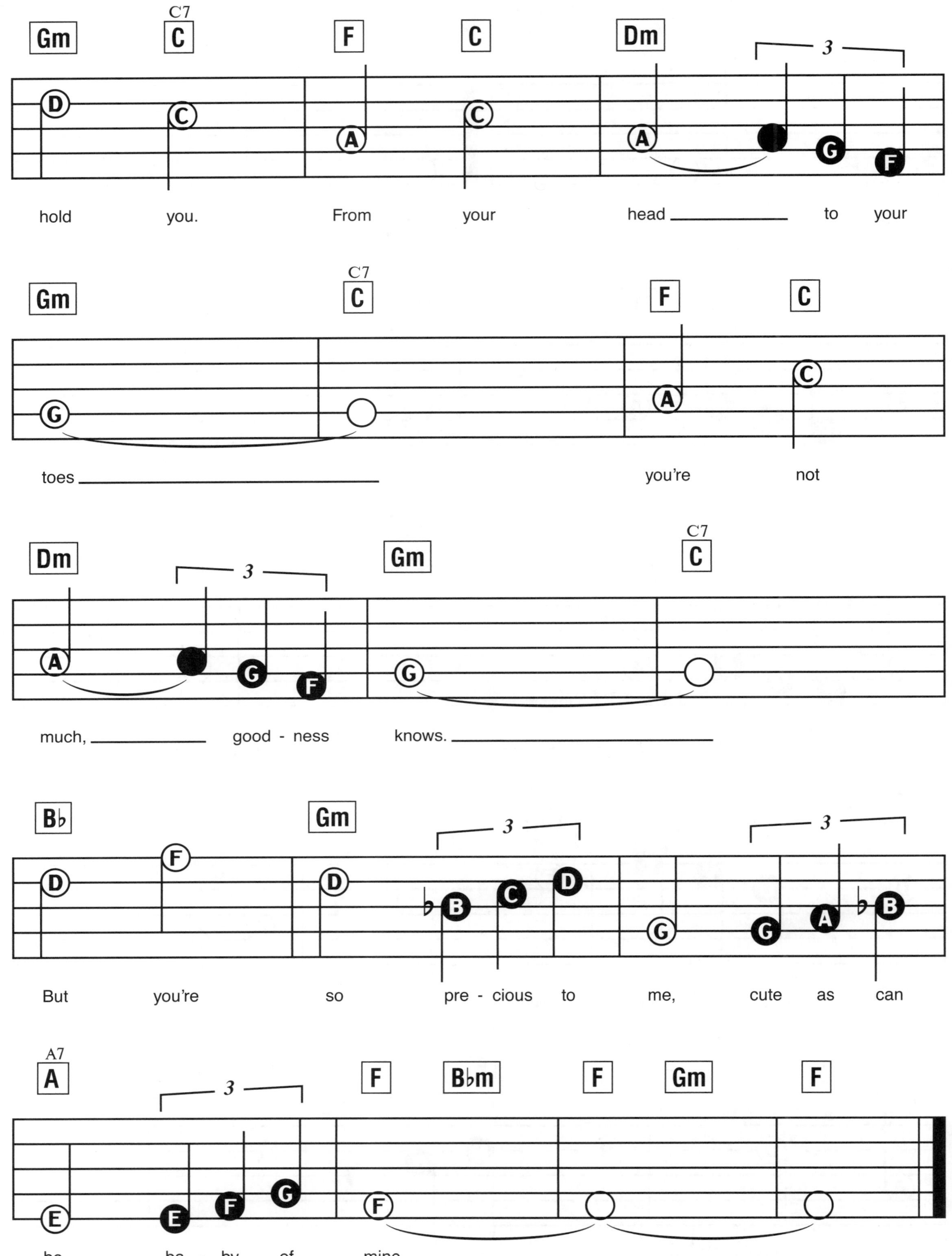
Gm C7 C F C Dm
3
hold you. From your head to your
Gm C7 C F C
toes you're not
Dm Gm C7 C
3
much, good - ness knows.
B♭ Gm
3 3
But you're so pre - cious to me, cute as can
A7 A F B♭m F Gm F
3
be, ba - by of mine.

Be Kind to Your Parents

from FANNY

Registration 5
Rhythm: Polka or March

Words and Music by
Harold Rome

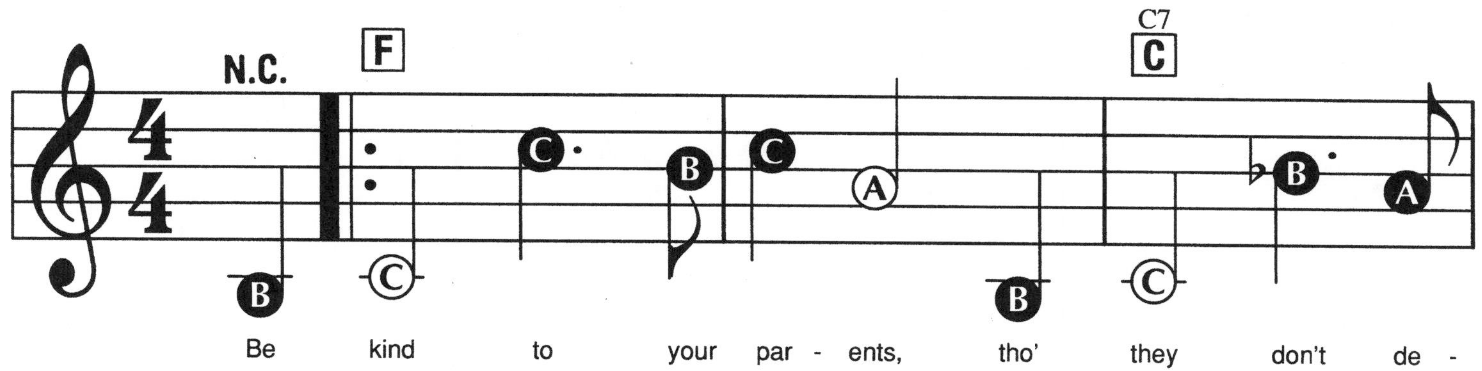

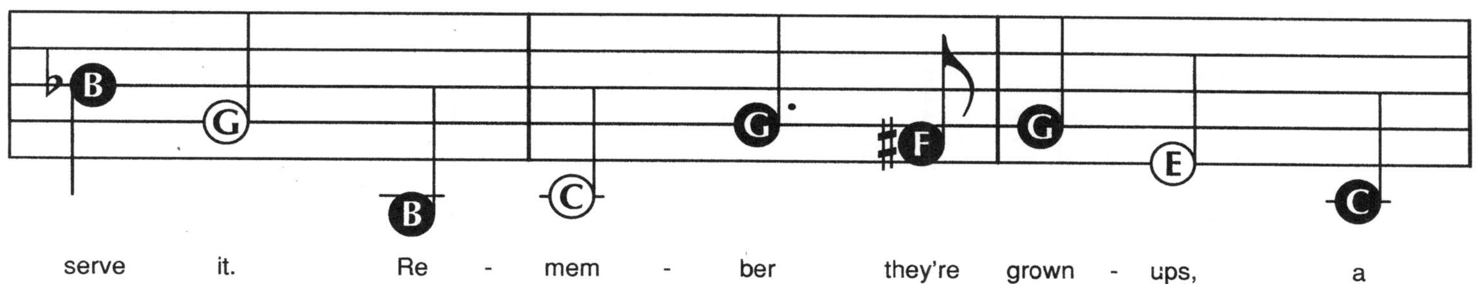

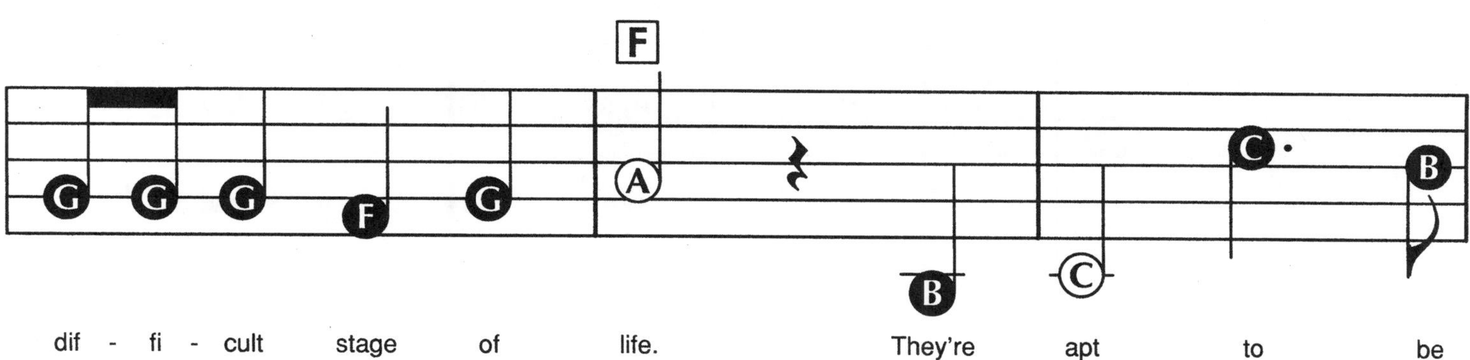

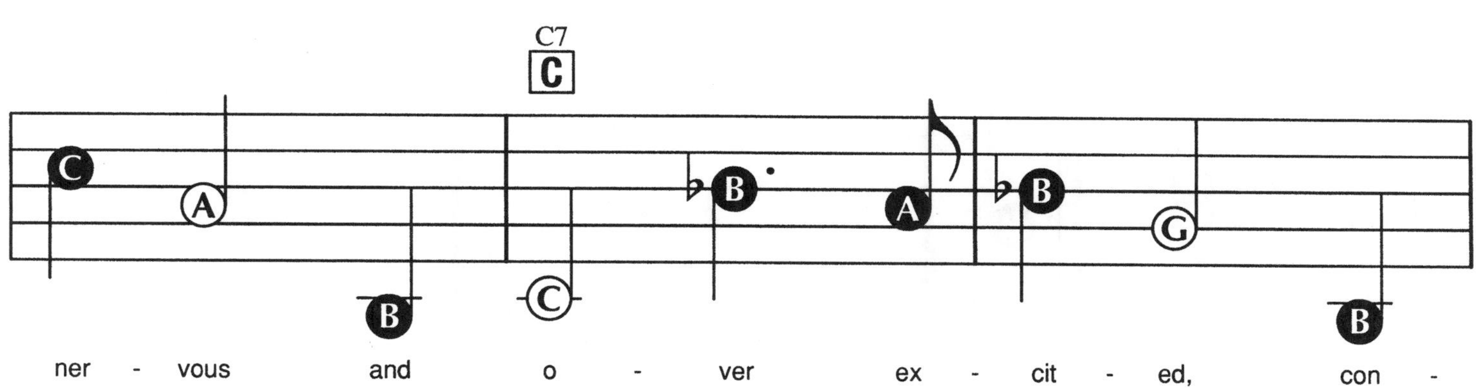

© 1954 (Renewed) CHAPPELL & CO., INC.
All Rights Reserved Used by Permission

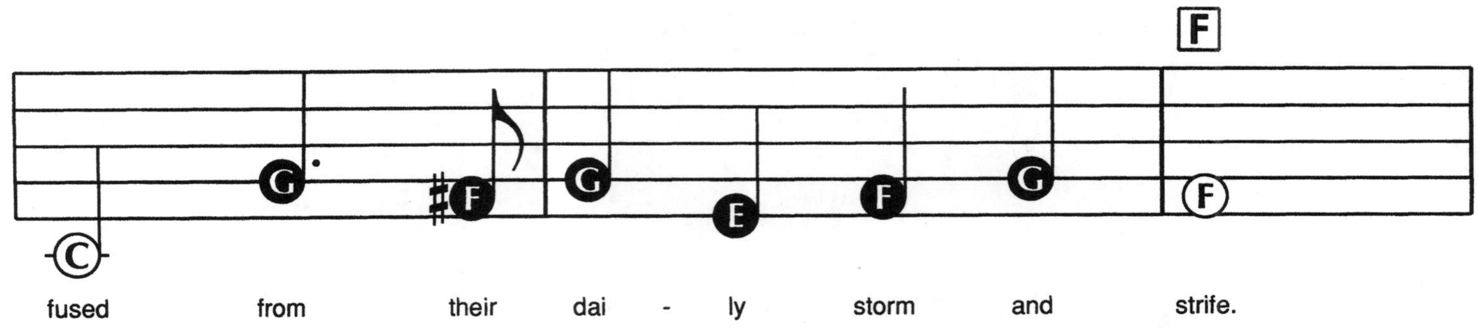
F
C
G
♯F
G
E
F
G
F
fused from their dai - ly storm and strife.

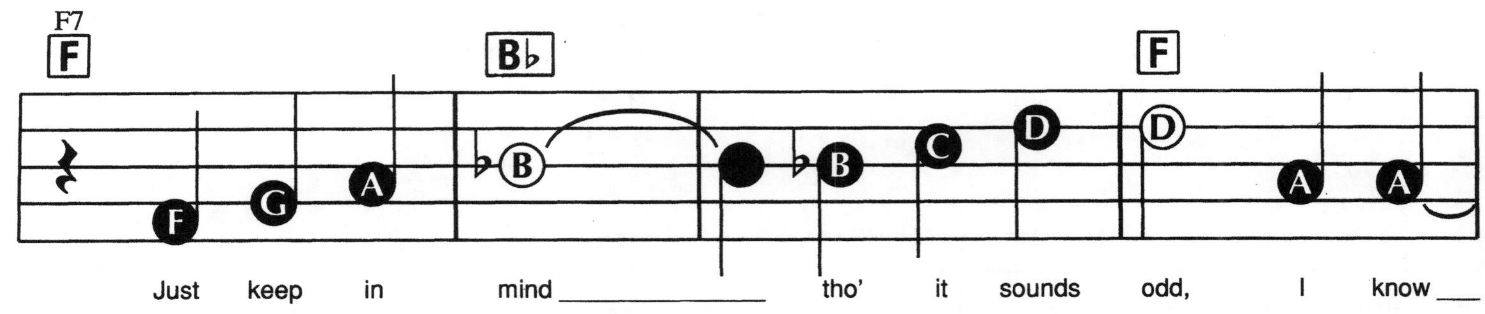
F7
F
B♭
F
F
G
A
♭B
♭B
C
D
D
A
A
Just keep in mind ______ tho' it sounds odd, I know ___

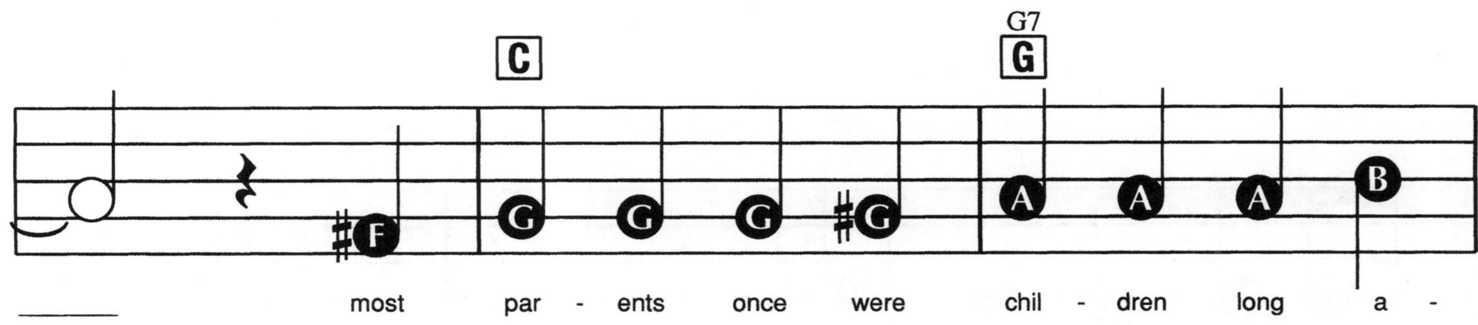
C
G7
G
♯F
G
G
G
♯G
A
A
A
B
______ most par - ents once were chil - dren long a -

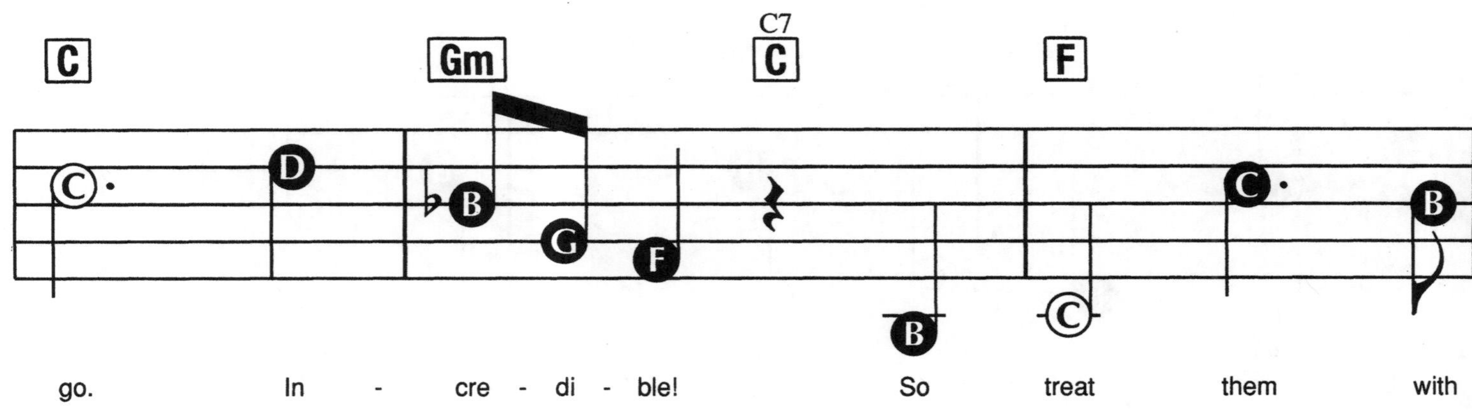
C
Gm
C7
C
F
C
D
♭B
G
F
B
C
C
B
go. In - cre - di - ble! So treat them with

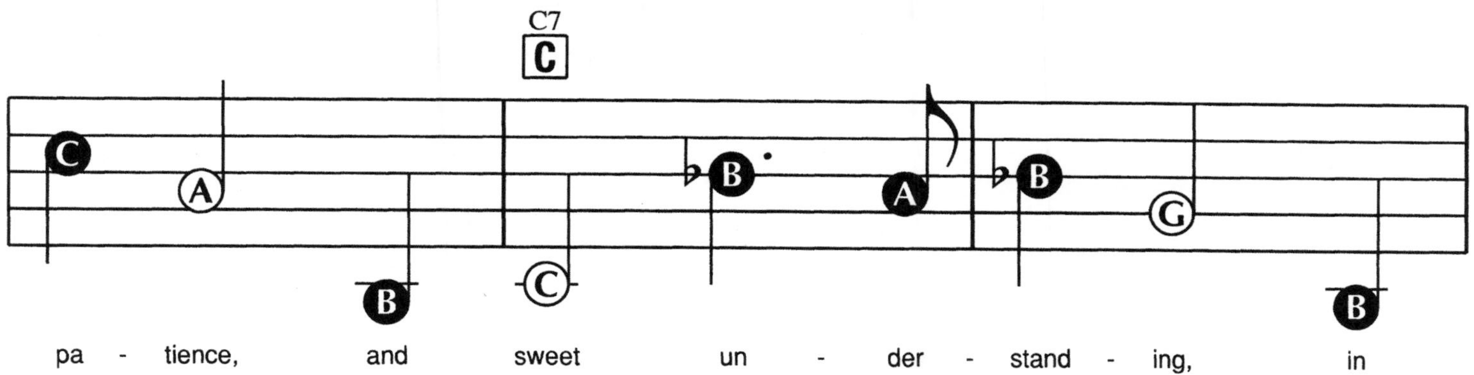
C7
C
pa - tience, and sweet un - der - stand - ing, in

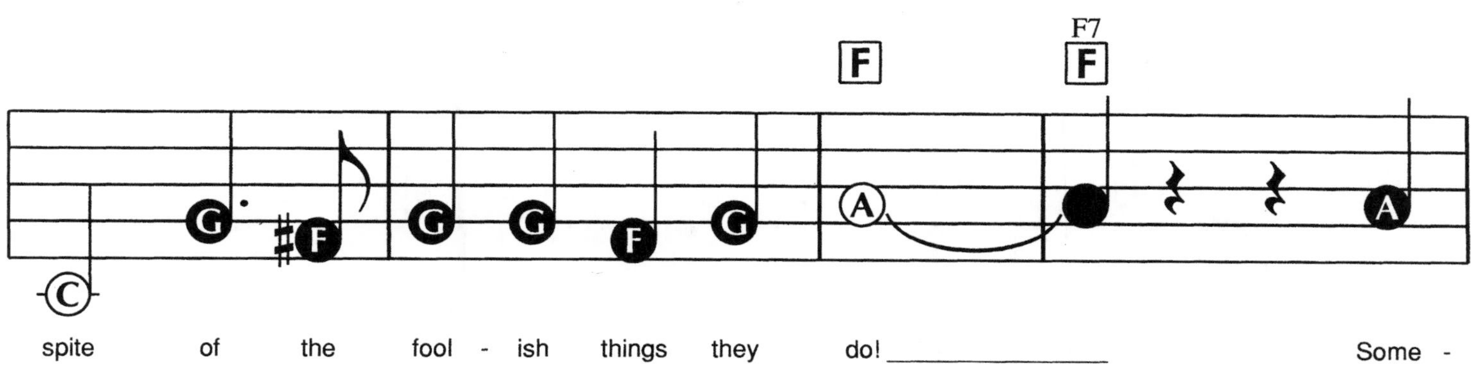
F
F7
F
spite of the fool - ish things they do!
Some -

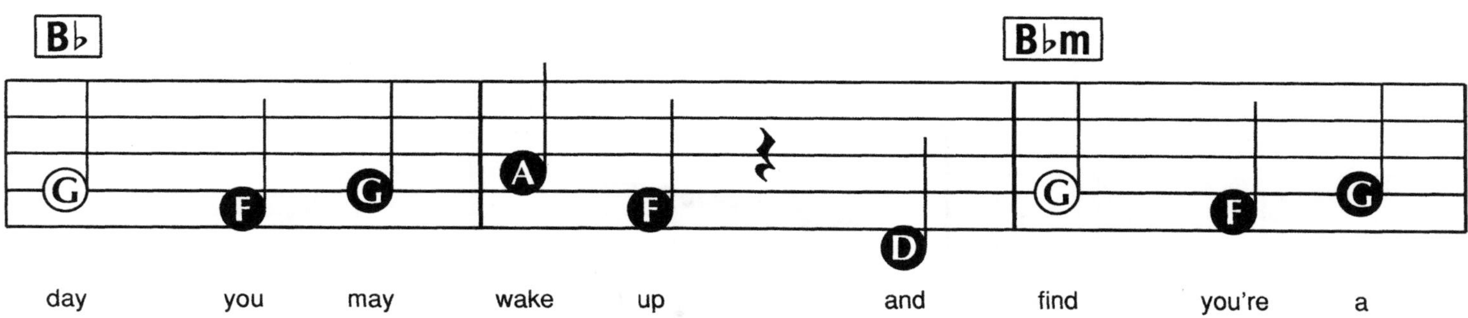
B♭
B♭m
day you may wake up and find you're a

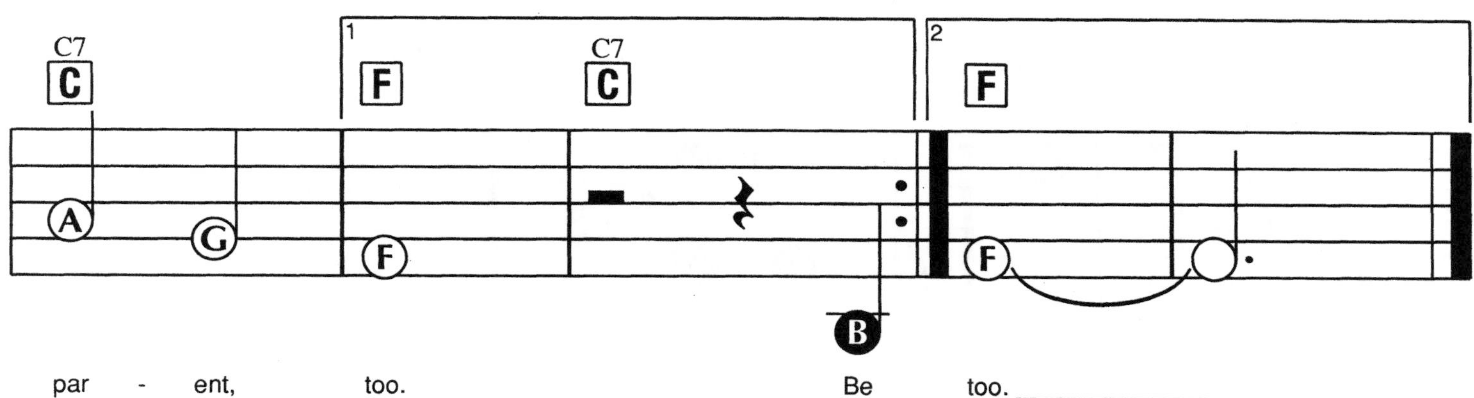
C7
C
1
F
C7
C
2
F
par - ent, too.
Be too.

The Ballad of Davy Crockett

from Walt Disney's DAVY CROCKETT

Registration 2
Rhythm: Fox Trot or Swing

Words by Tom Blackburn
Music by George Bruns

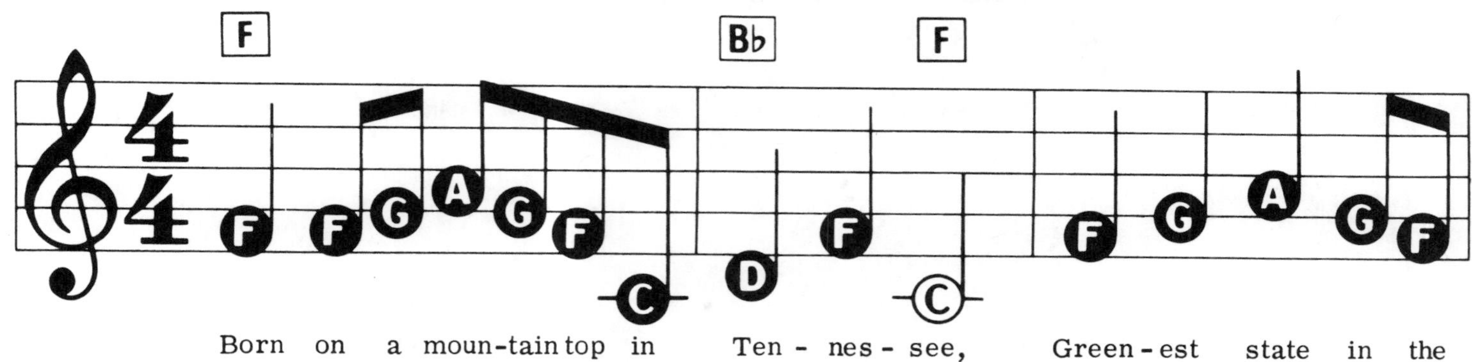

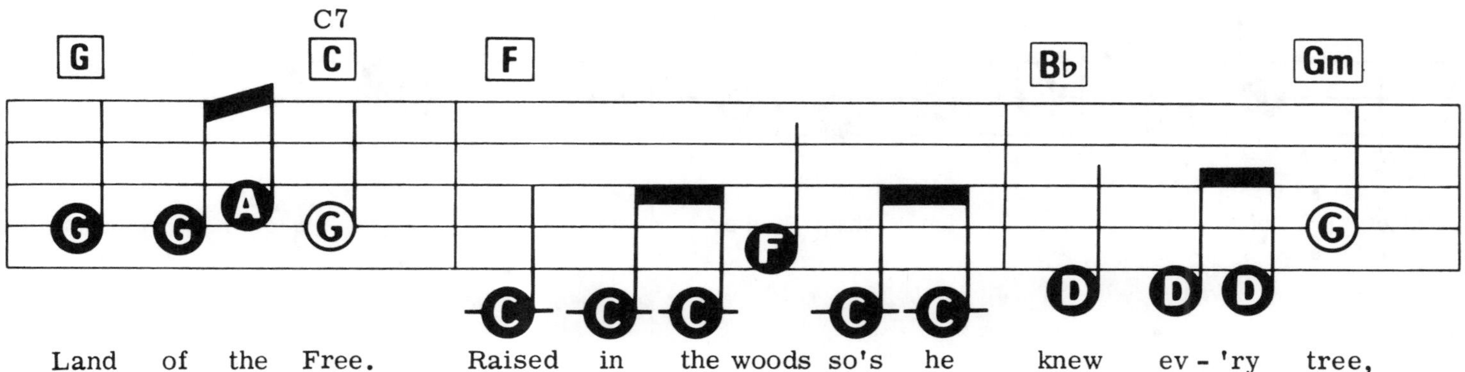

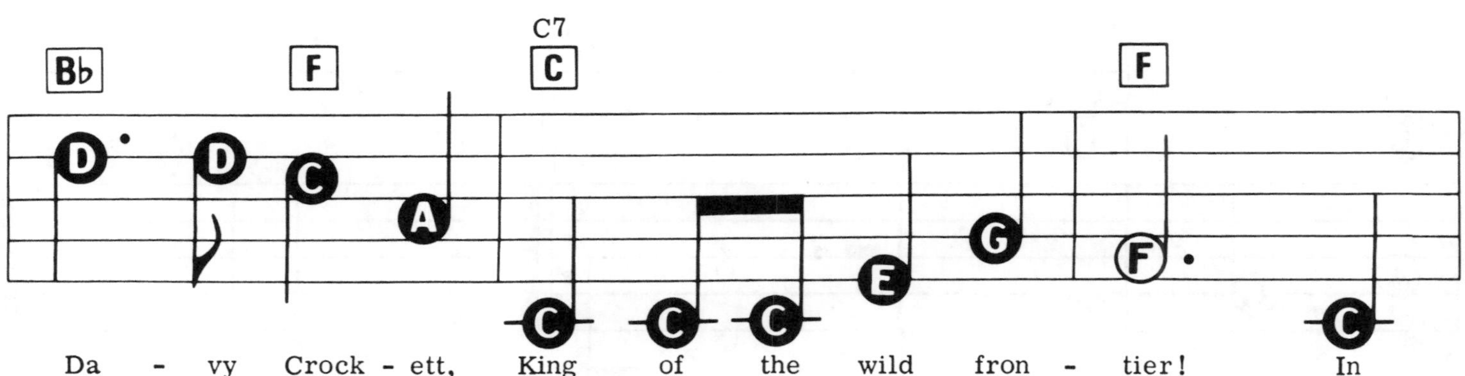

© 1954 Wonderland Music Company, Inc.
Copyright Renewed
All Rights Reserved. Used by Permission.

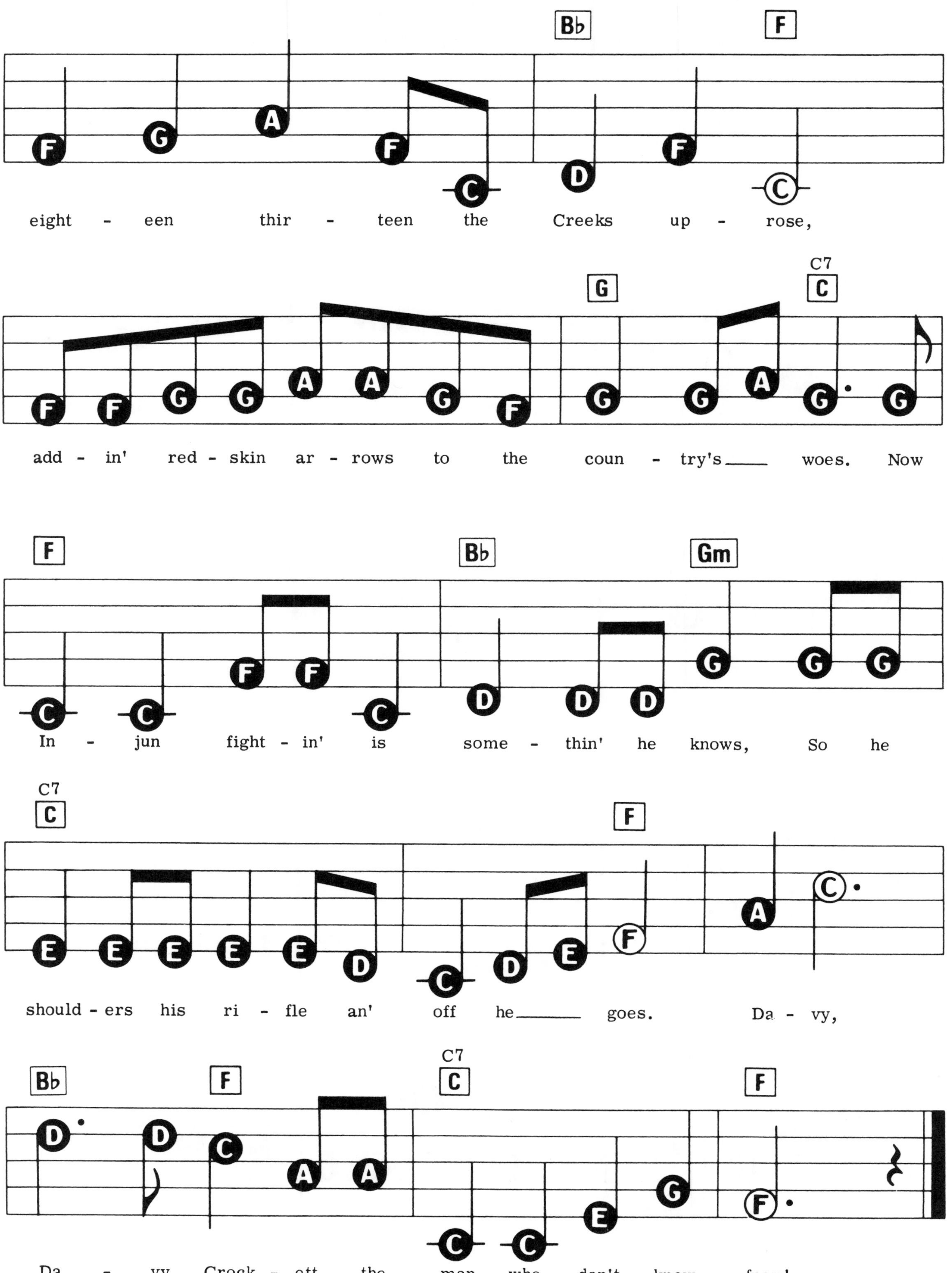
Bb F
eight - een thir - teen the Creeks up - rose,
G C7 C
add - in' red - skin ar - rows to the coun - try's woes. Now
F Bb Gm
In - jun fight - in' is some - thin' he knows, So he
C7 C F
should - ers his ri - fle an' off he goes. Da - vy,
Bb F C7 C F
Da - vy Crock - ett, the man who don't know fear!

The Bare Necessities
from Walt Disney's THE JUNGLE BOOK

Registration 4
Rhythm: Fox Trot or Swing

Words and Music by
Terry Gilkyson

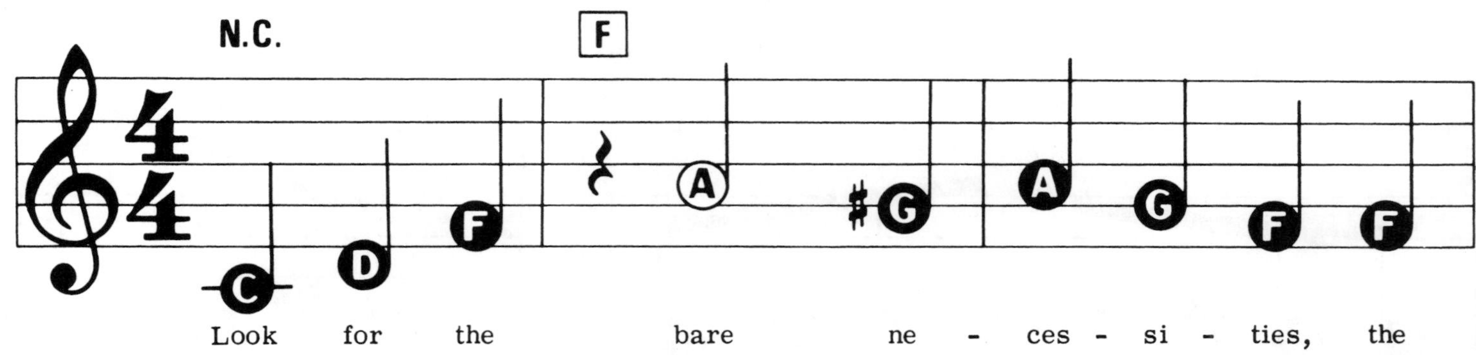

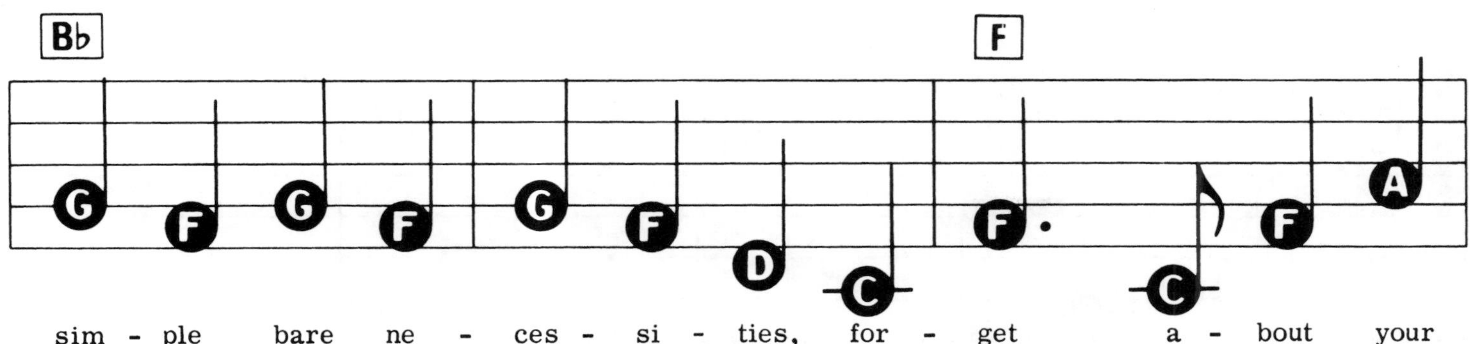

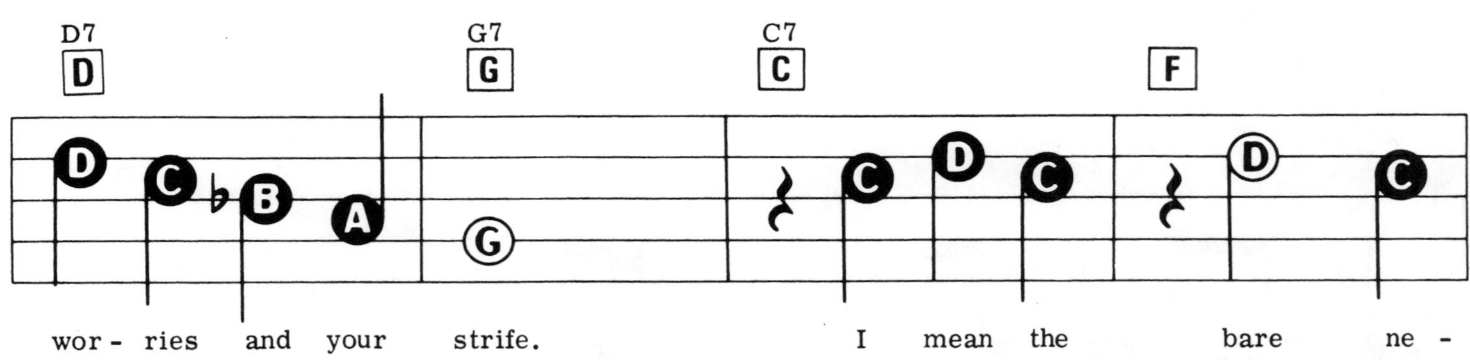

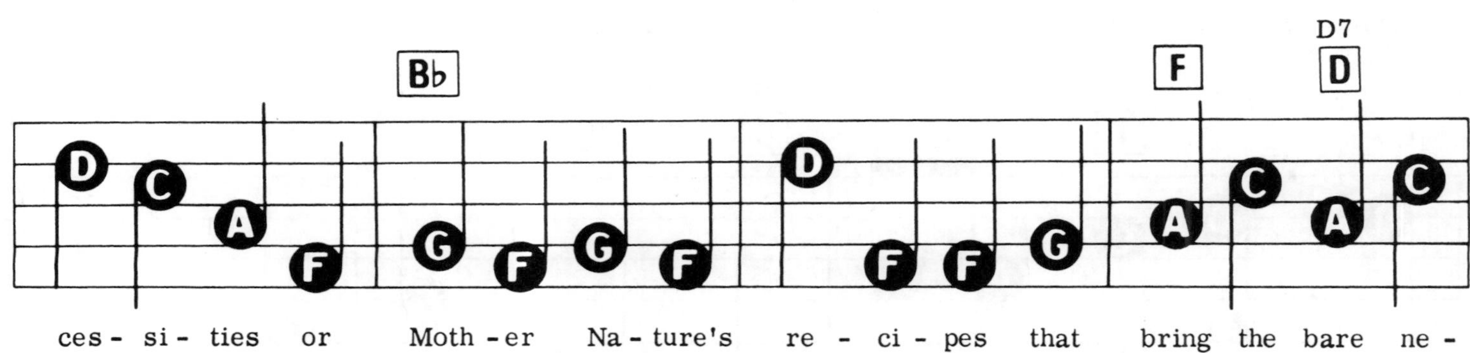

© 1964 Wonderland Music Company, Inc.
Copyright Renewed
All Rights Reserved. Used by Permission.

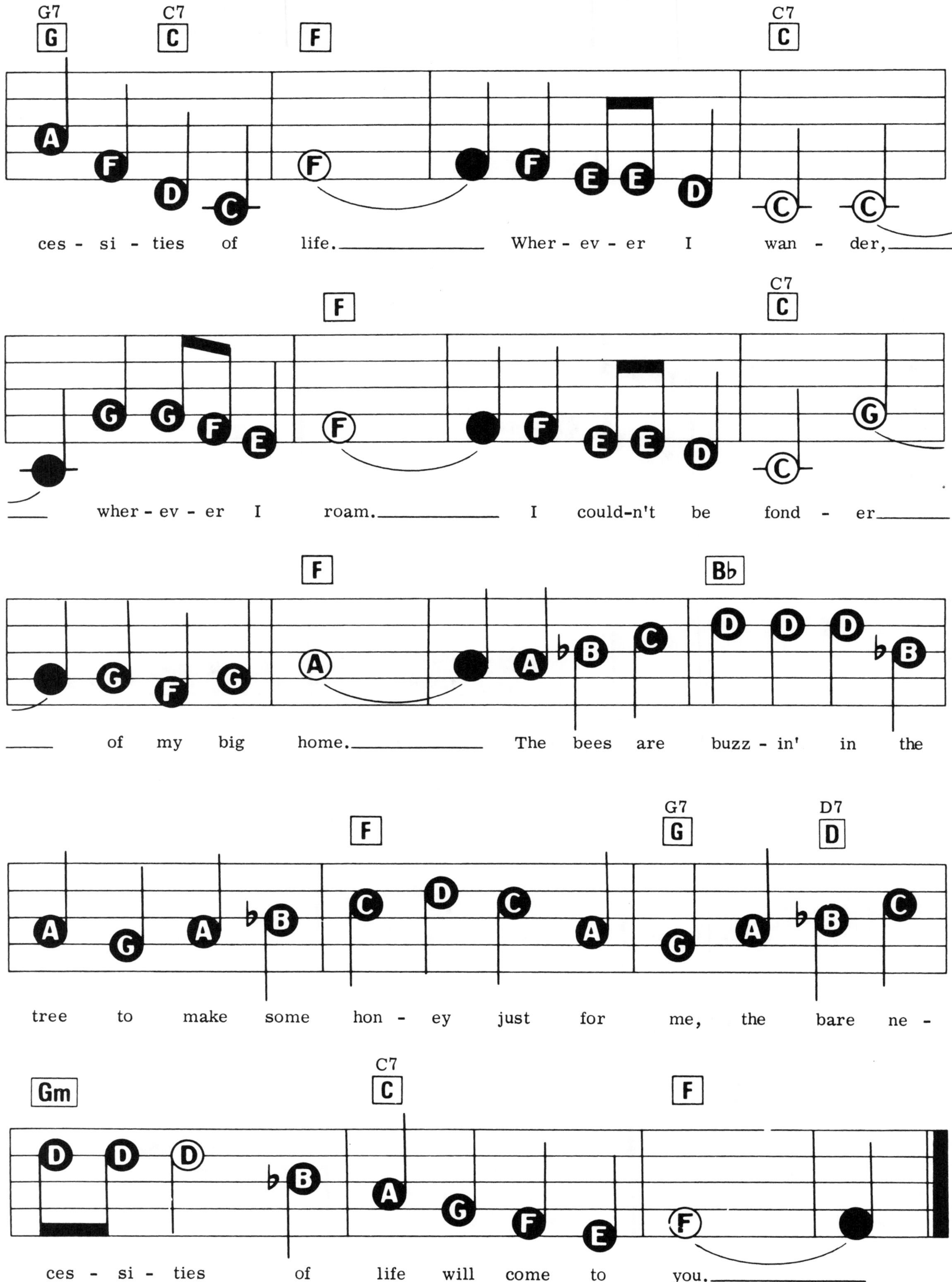
G7 C7 F C7
ces - si - ties of life. Wher - ev - er I wan - der,
F C7
wher - ev - er I roam. I could-n't be fond - er
F B♭
of my big home. The bees are buzz - in' in the
F G7 D7
tree to make some hon - ey just for me, the bare ne -
Gm C7 F
ces - si - ties of life will come to you.

Beauty and the Beast
from Walt Disney's BEAUTY AND THE BEAST

Registration 1
Rhythm: Pops or 8-Beat

Music by Alan Menken
Lyrics by Howard Ashman

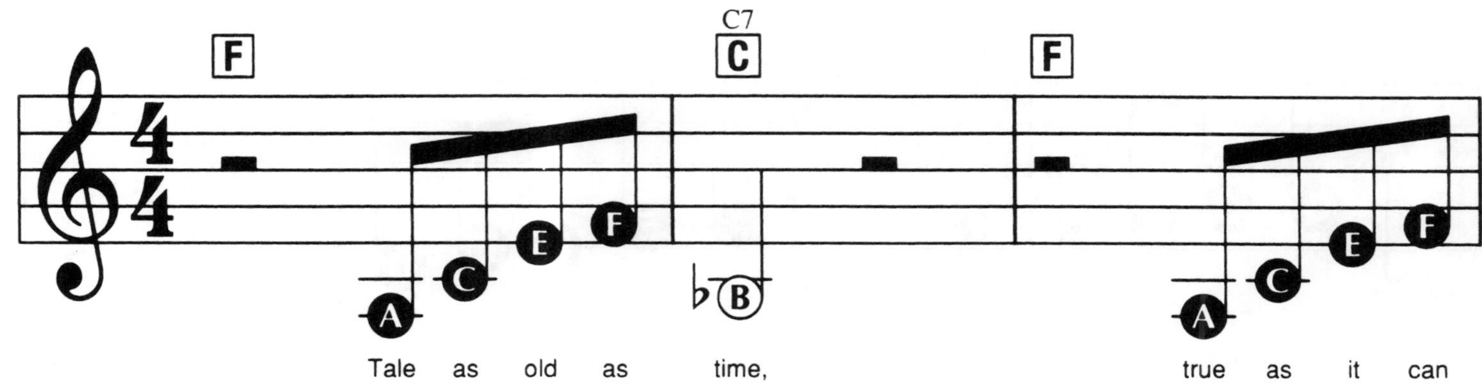

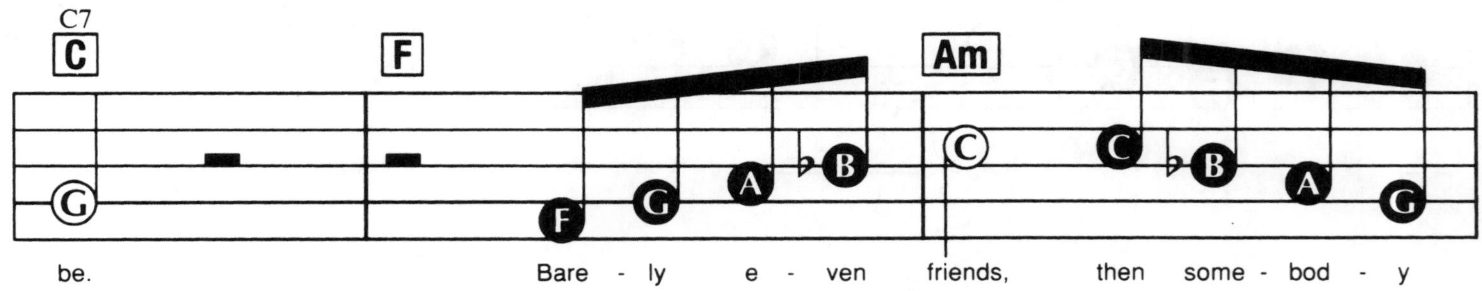

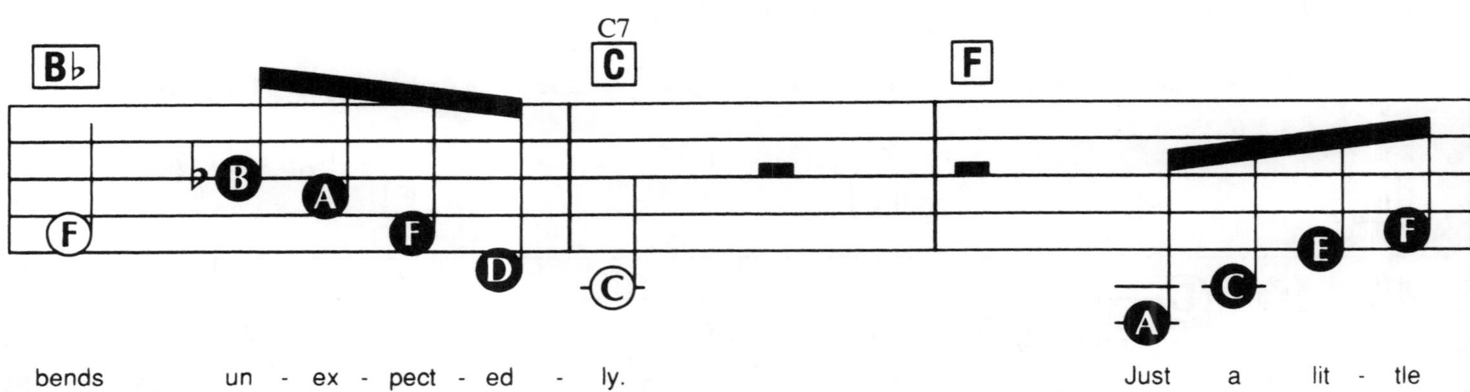

© 1991 Walt Disney Music Company and Wonderland Music Company, Inc.
All Rights Reserved. Used by Permission.

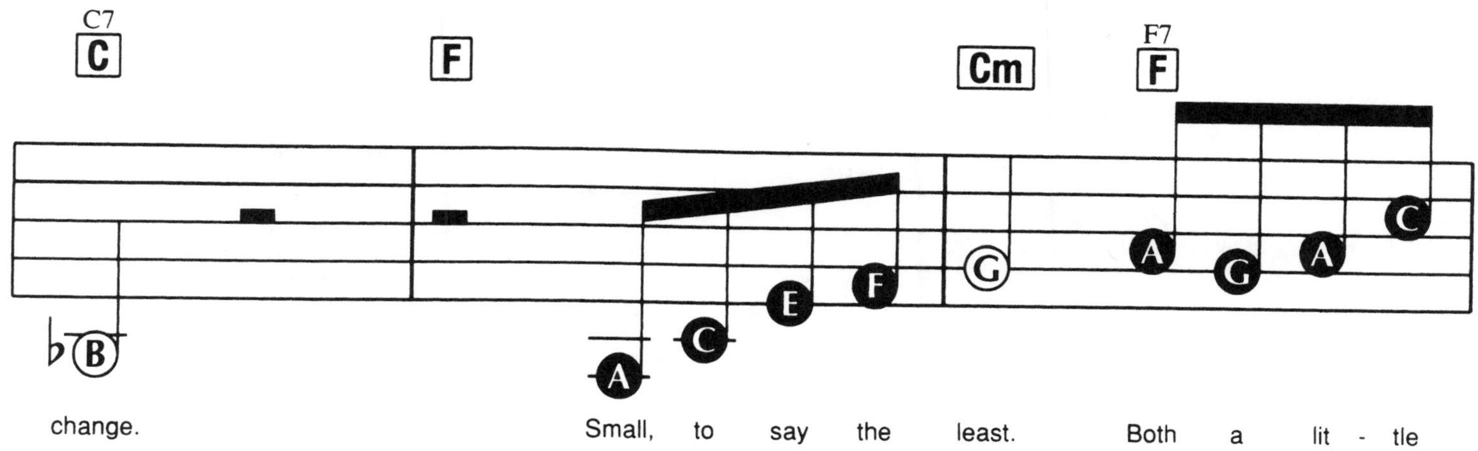
C7
C
F
Cm
F7
F
B
A
C
E
F
G
A
G
A
C
change.
Small, to say the least.
Both a lit - tle

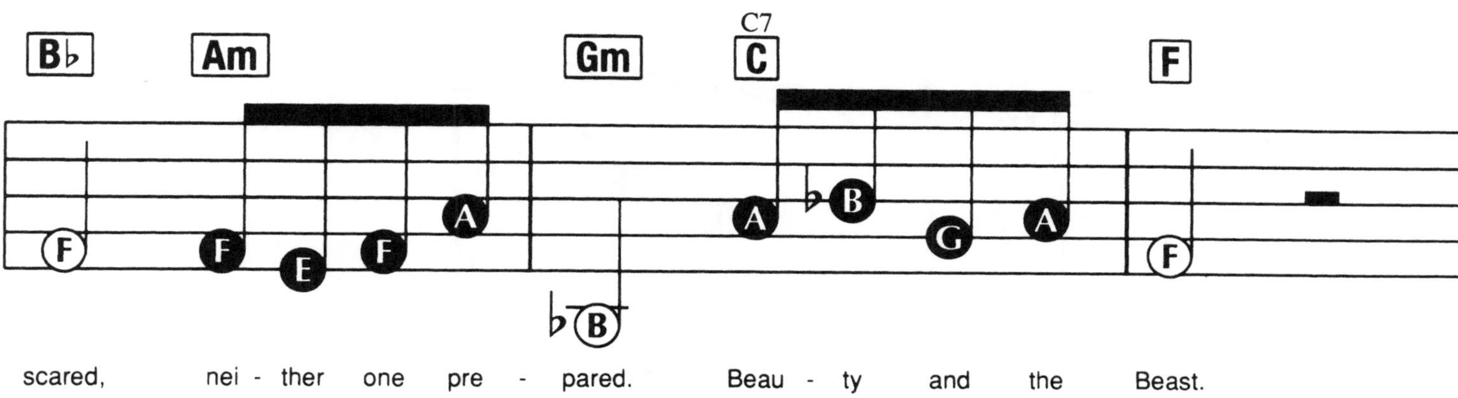
B♭
Am
Gm
C7
C
F
F
F
E
F
A
B
A
B
G
A
F
scared, nei - ther one pre - pared.
Beau - ty and the Beast.

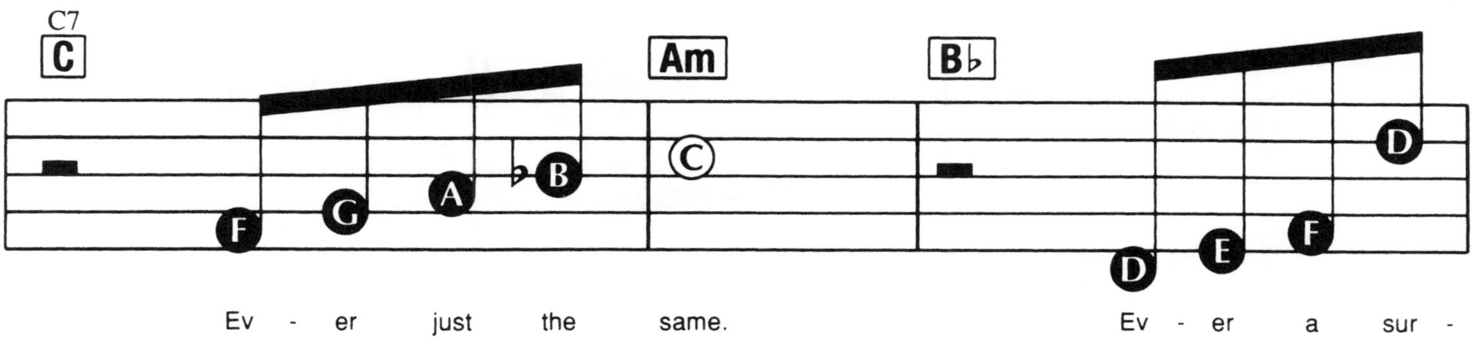
C7
C
Am
B♭
F
G
A
B
C
D
E
F
D
Ev - er just the same.
Ev - er a sur -

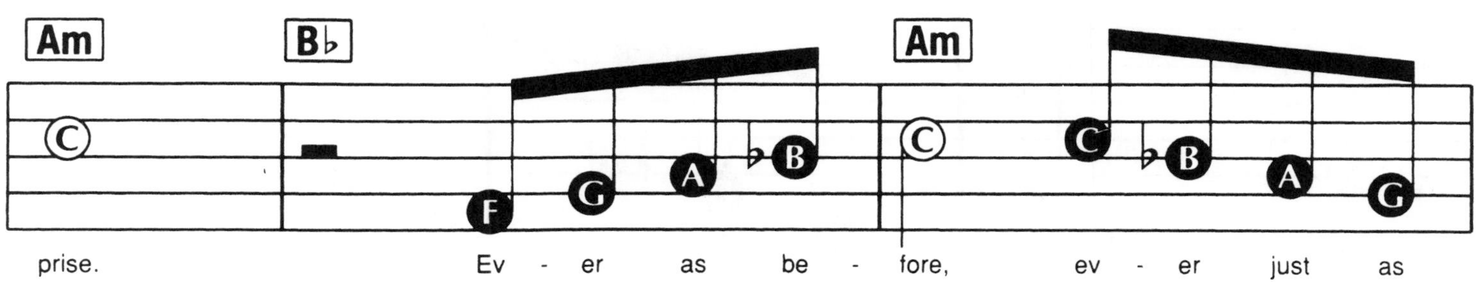
Am
B♭
Am
C
F
G
A
B
C
C
B
A
G
prise.
Ev - er as be - fore,
ev - er just as

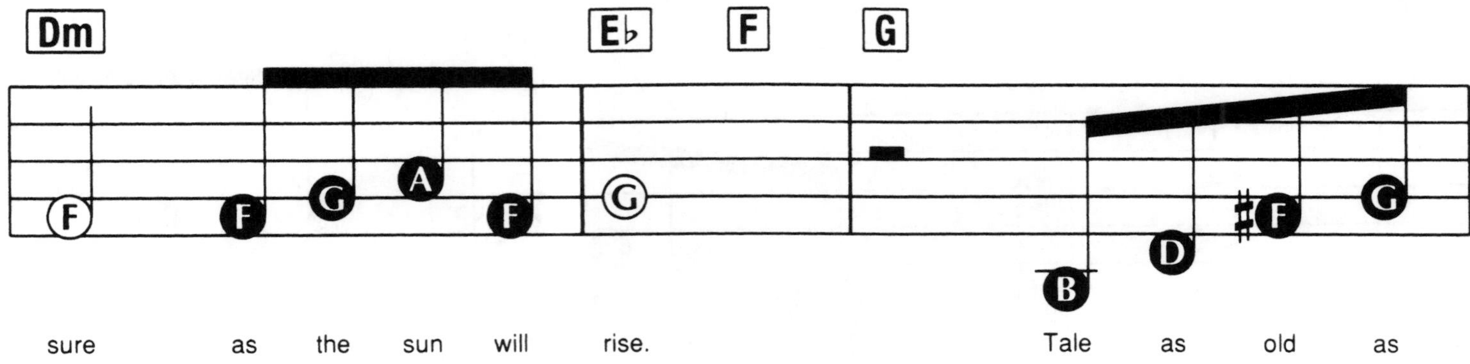
Dm
E♭
F
G
F
F
G
A
F
G
B
D
♯F
G
sure as the sun will rise. Tale as old as

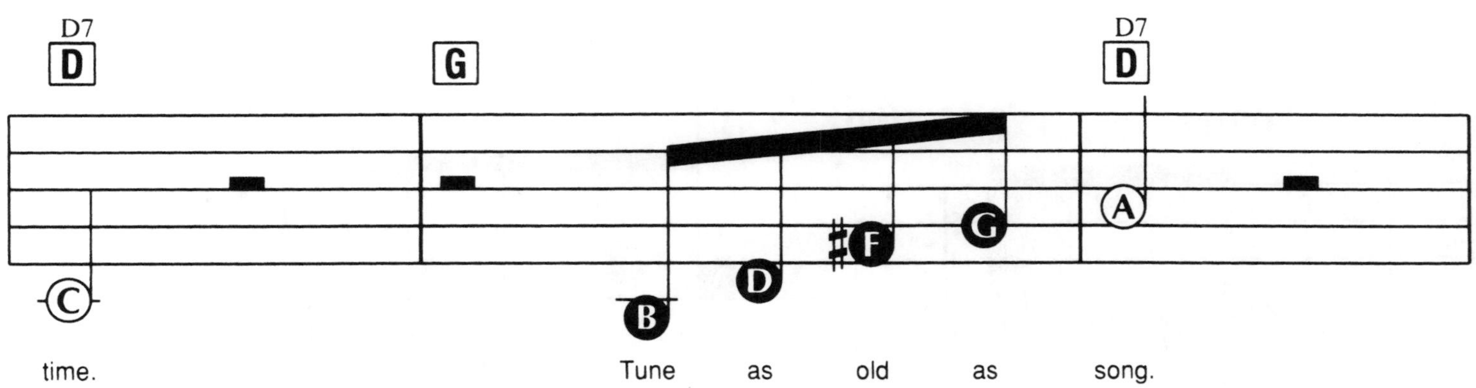
D7
D
G
D7
D
C
B
D
♯F
G
A
time. Tune as old as song.

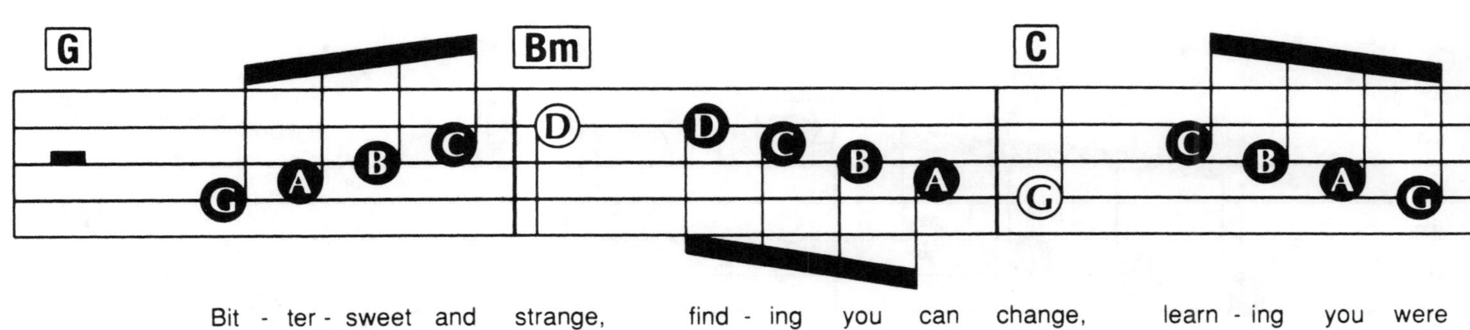
G
Bm
C
G
A
B
C
D
D
C
B
A
G
C
B
A
G
Bit - ter - sweet and strange, find - ing you can change, learn - ing you were

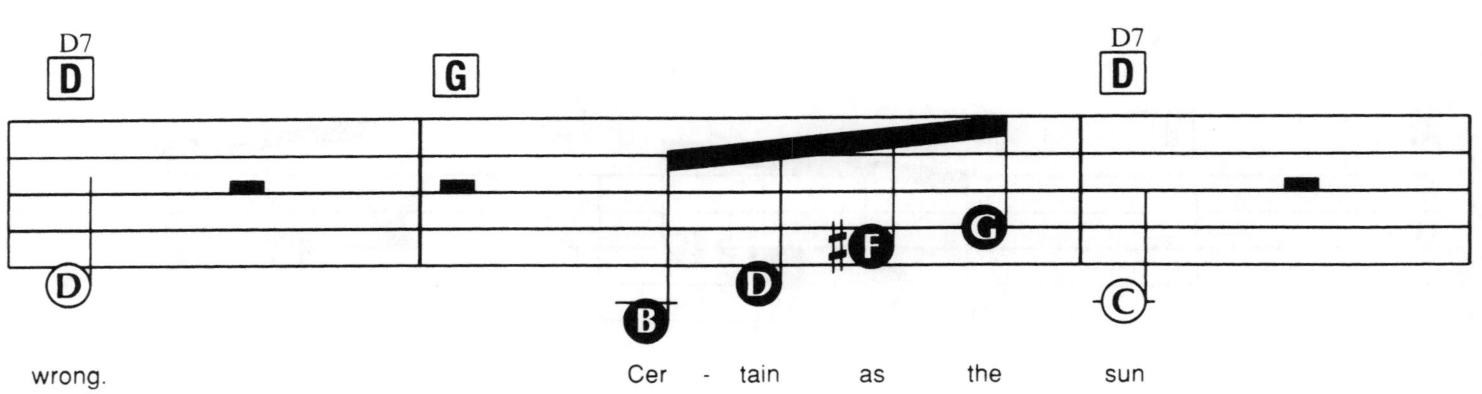
D7
D
G
D7
D
D
B
D
♯F
G
C
wrong. Cer - tain as the sun

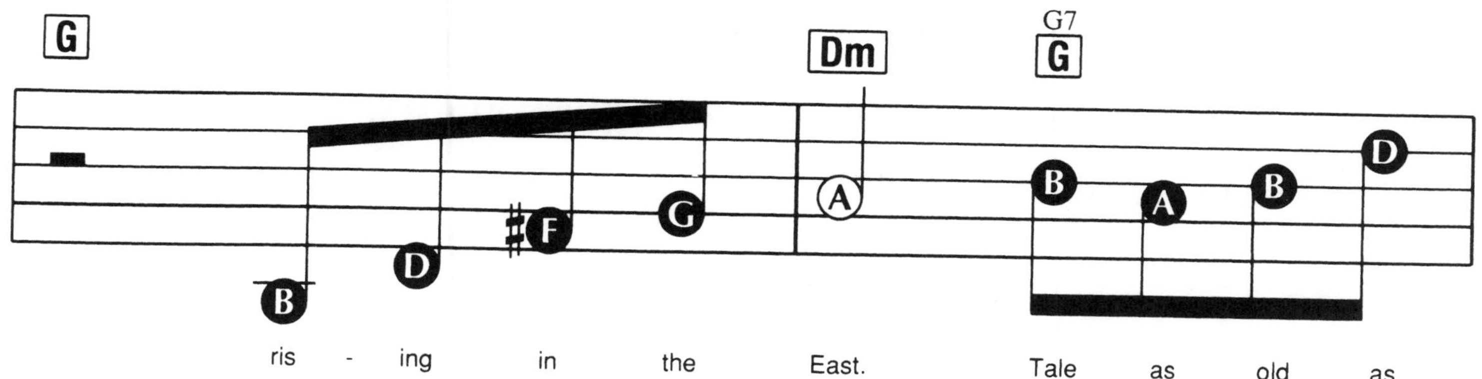
G
Dm
G7
G
B D F G A B A B D
ris - ing in the East. Tale as old as

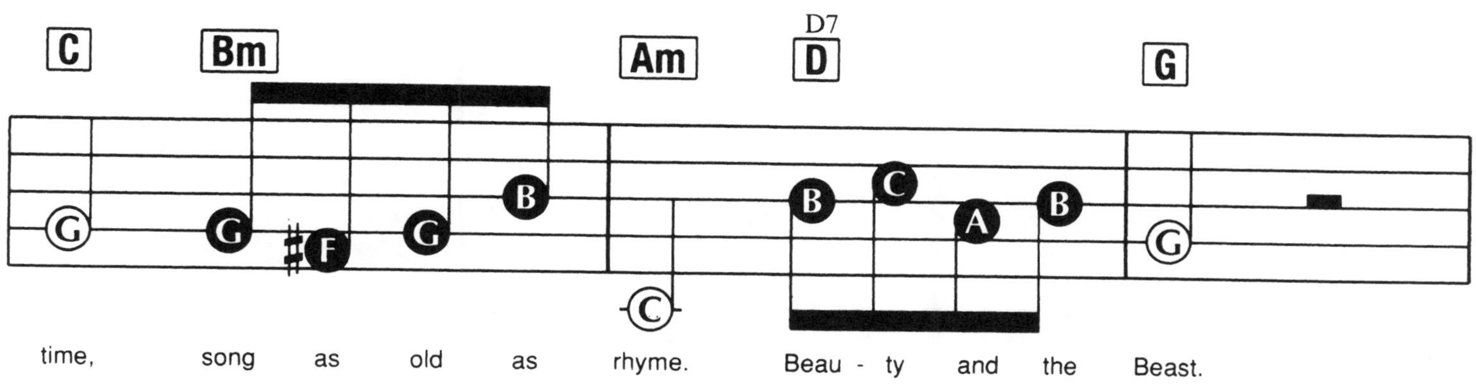
C
Bm
Am
D7
D
G
G G F G B C B C A B G
time, song as old as rhyme. Beau - ty and the Beast.

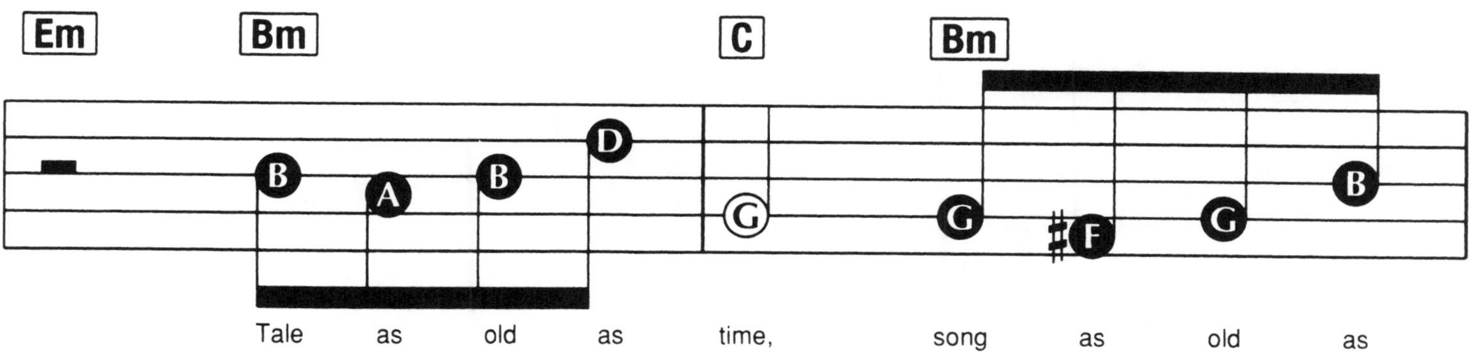
Em
Bm
C
Bm
B A B D G G F G B
Tale as old as time, song as old as

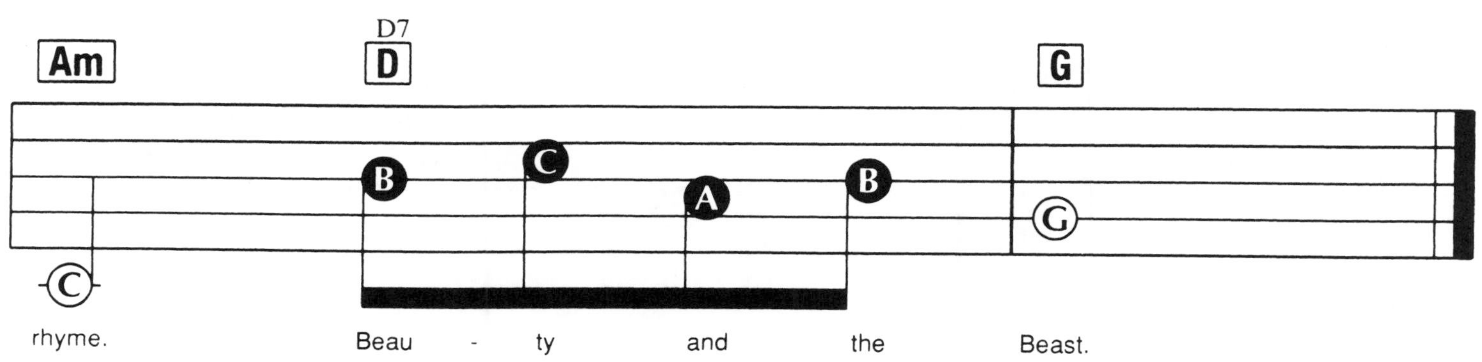
Am
D7
D
G
C B C A B G
rhyme. Beau - ty and the Beast.

Bibbibdi-Bobbidi-Boo

(The Magic Song)

from Walt Disney's CINDERELLA

Registration 8
Rhythm: Swing

Words by Jerry Livingston
Music by Mack David and Al Hoffman

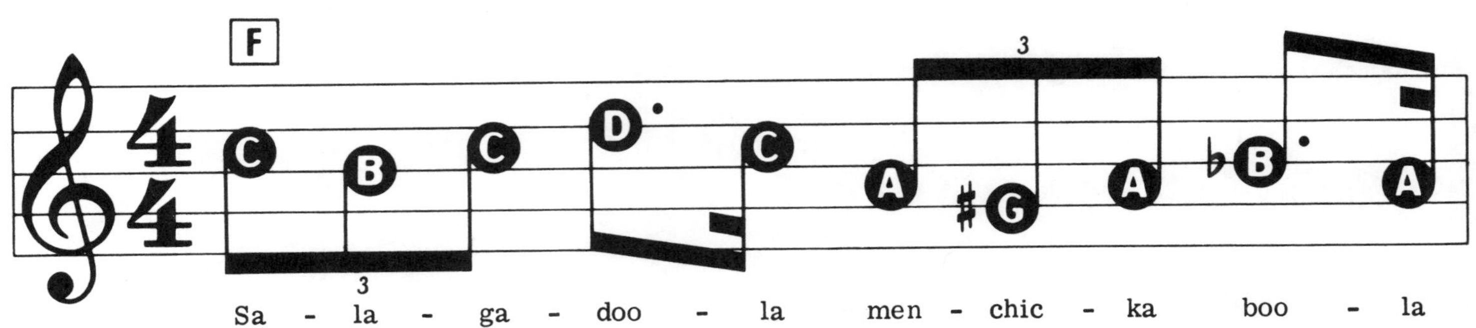

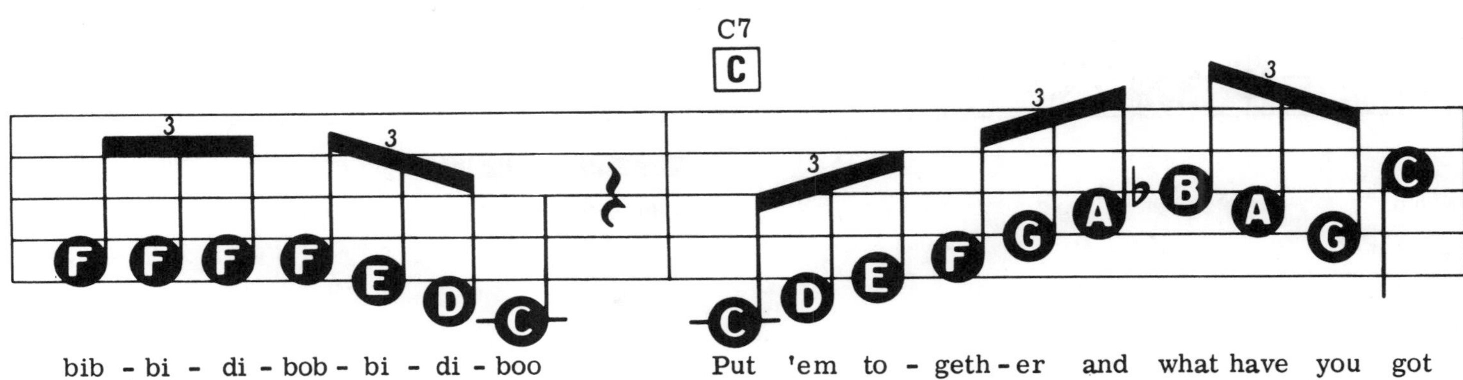

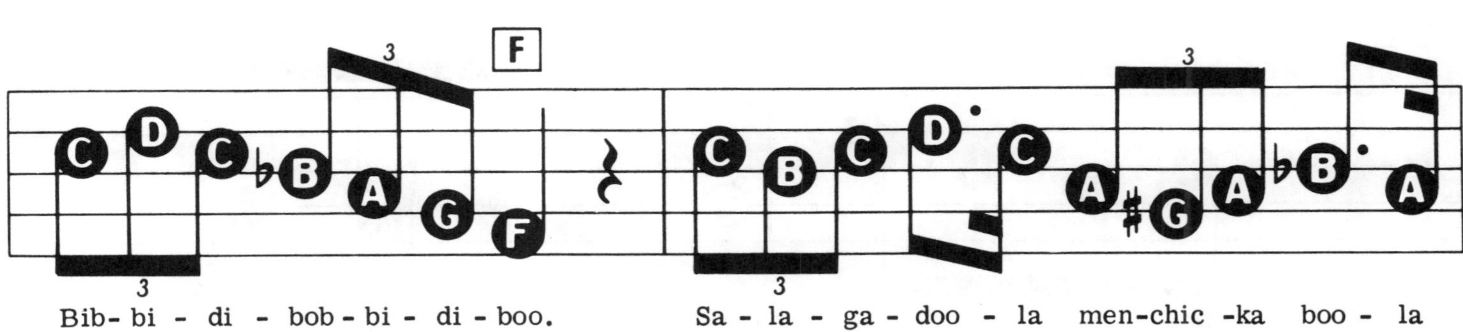

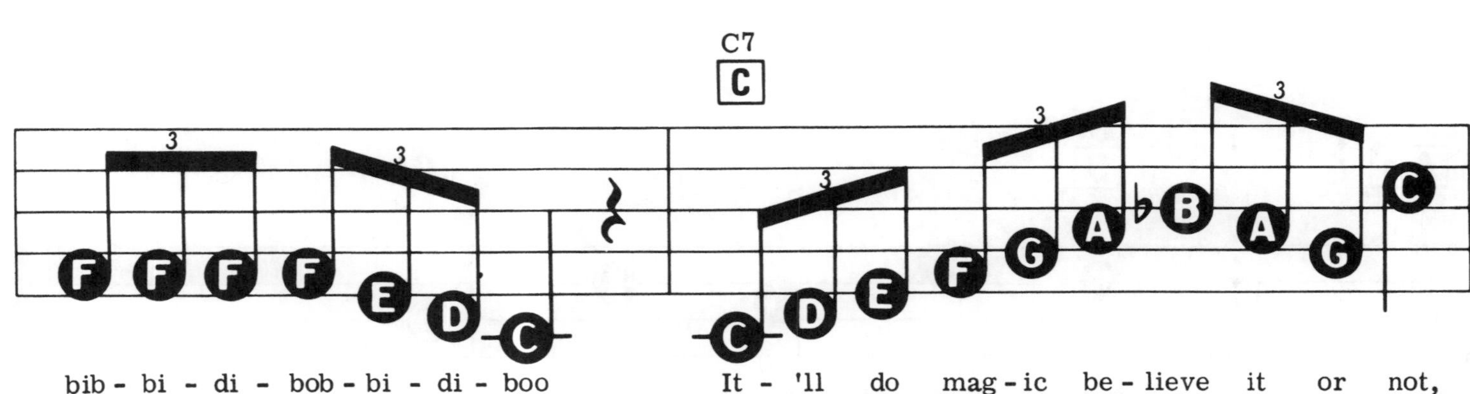

© 1948 Walt Disney Music Company
Copyright Renewed
All Rights Reserved. Used by Permission.

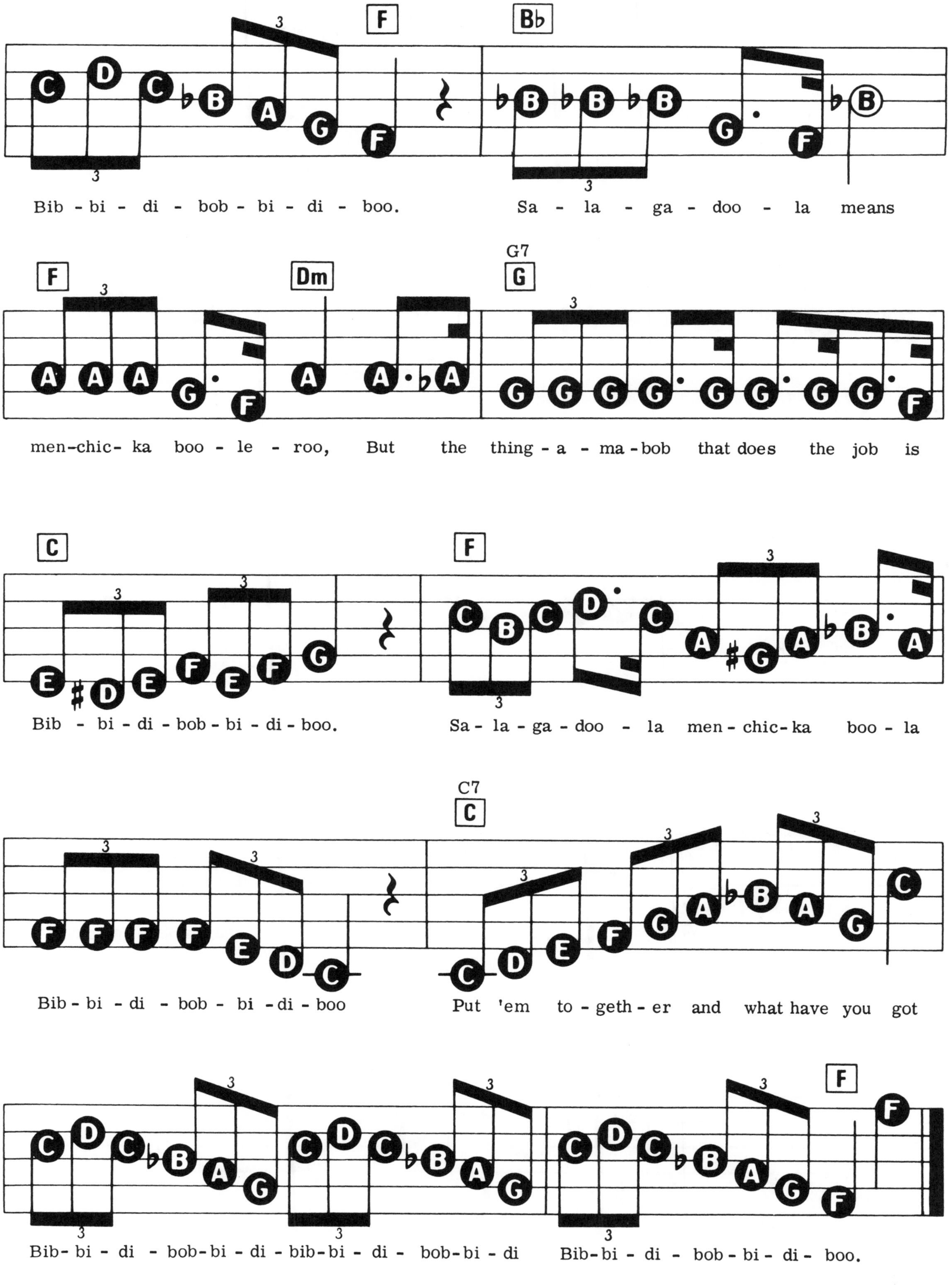

F Bb

Bib - bi - di - bob - bi - di - boo. Sa - la - ga - doo - la means

F Dm G7 G

men–chic- ka boo - le - roo, But the thing - a - ma - bob that does the job is

C F

Bib - bi - di - bob - bi - di - boo. Sa - la - ga - doo - la men - chic - ka boo - la

C7 C

Bib - bi - di - bob - bi - di - boo Put 'em to - geth - er and what have you got

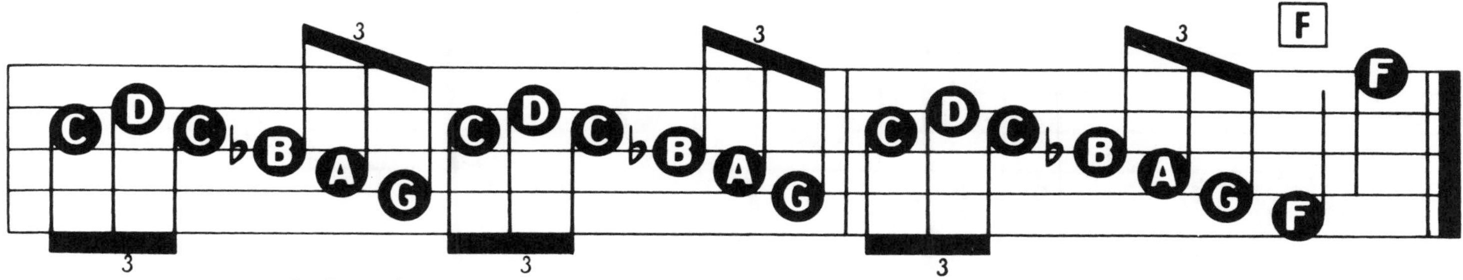

The Bible Tells Me So

Registration 8
Rhythm: Fox Trot

Words and Music by
Dale Evans

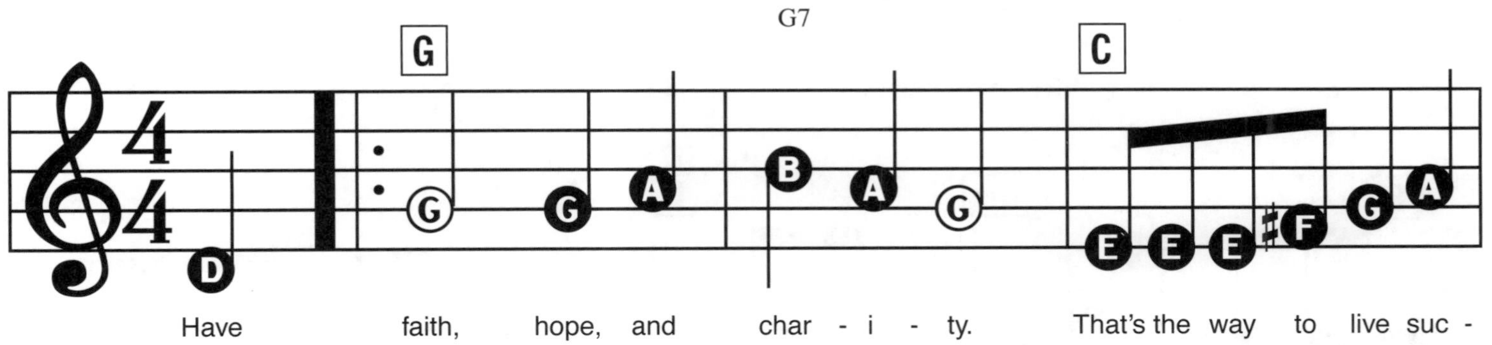

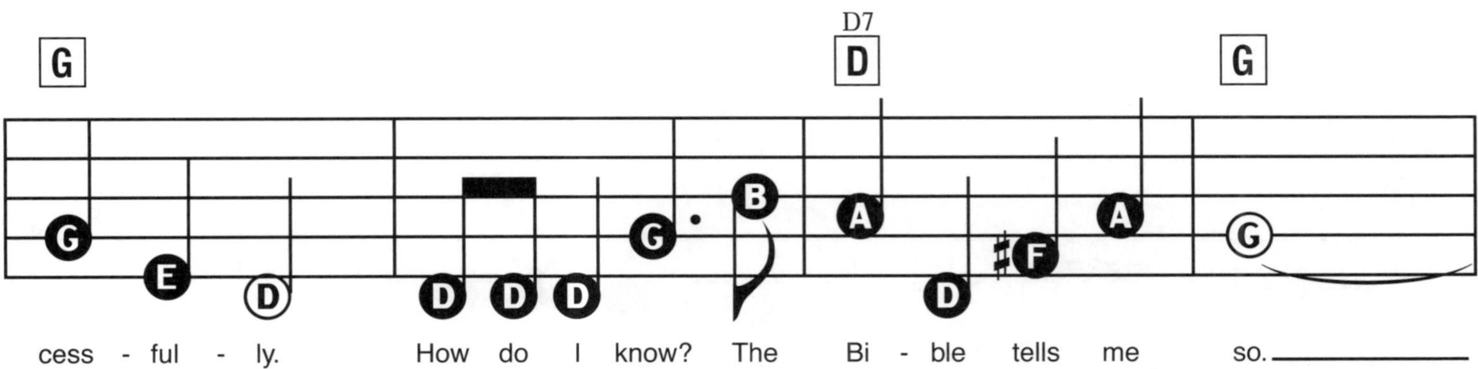

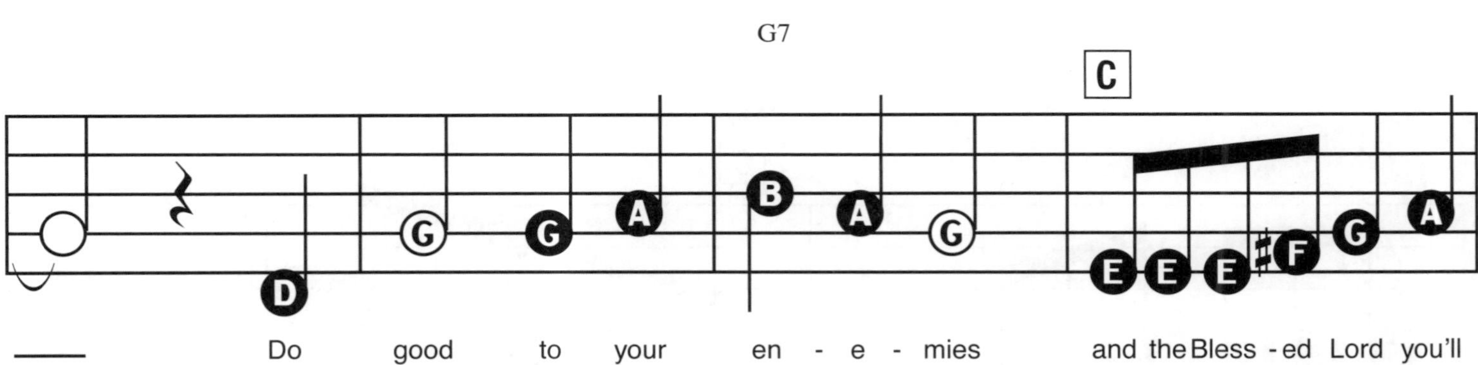

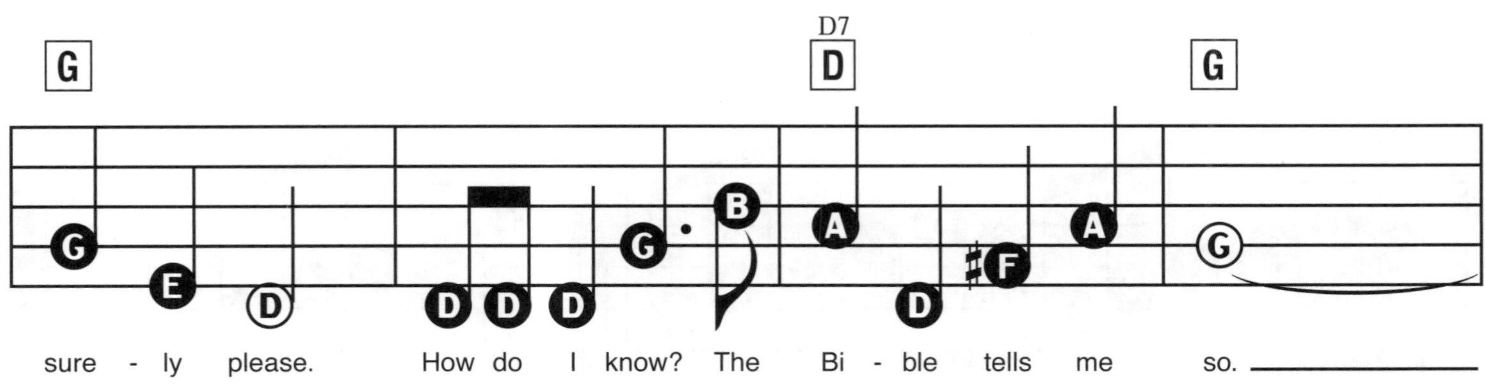

Copyright © 1955 Roy Rogers Music
Copyright Renewed
All Rights Administered by Sony/ATV Music Publishing LLC, 424 Church Street, Suite 1200, Nashville, TN 37219
International Copyright Secured All Rights Reserved

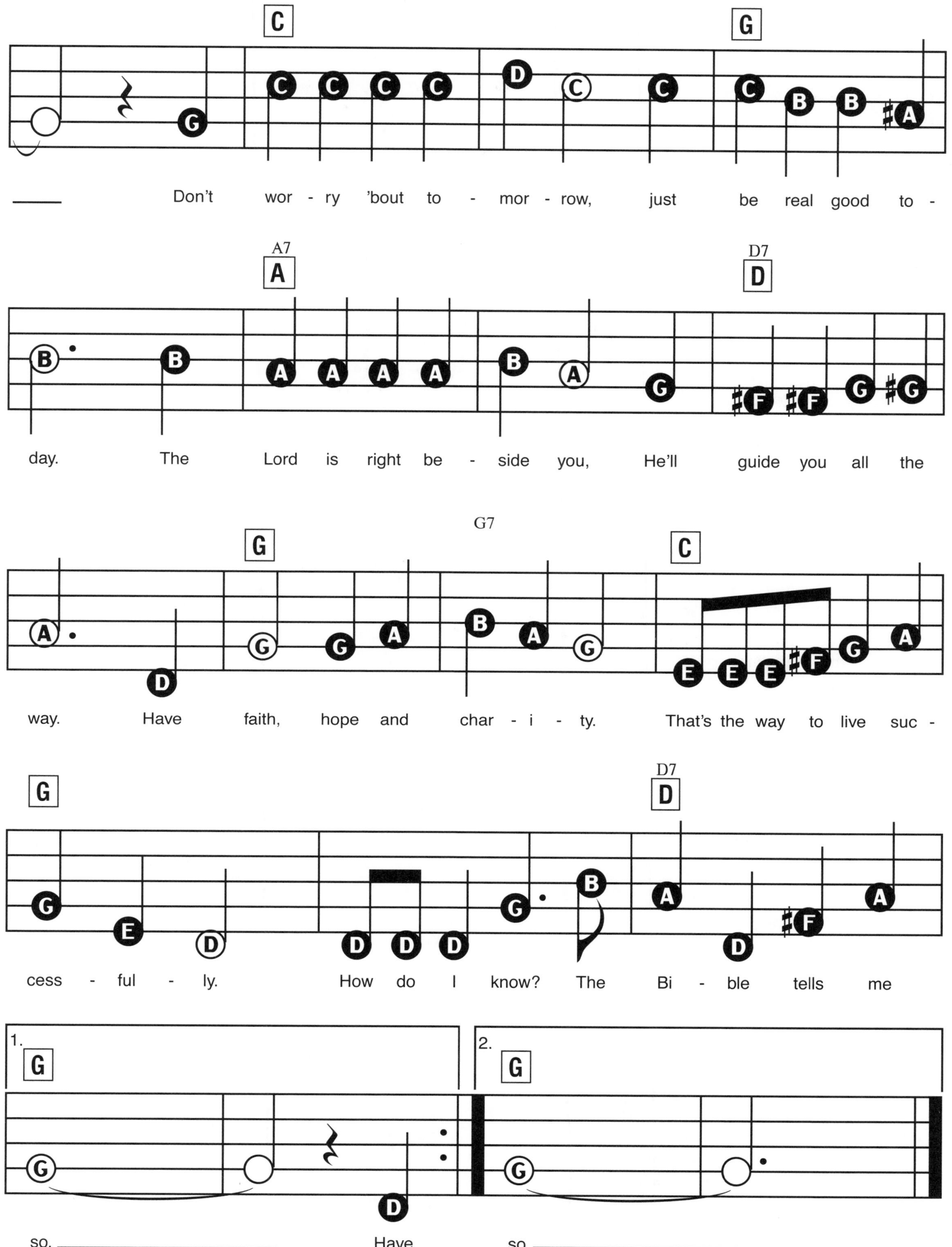
C
G
C C C C D C C C B B A
Don't wor - ry 'bout to - mor - row, just be real good to -
A7
A
D7
D
B B A A A A B A G F F G G
day. The Lord is right be - side you, He'll guide you all the
G
G7
C
A D G G A B A G E E E F G A
way. Have faith, hope and char - i - ty. That's the way to live suc -
G
D7
D
G E D D D D G B A D F A
cess - ful - ly. How do I know? The Bi - ble tells me
1.
G
G D
so. Have
2.
G
G
so.

The Blue Tail Fly
(Jimmy Crack Corn)

Registration 4
Rhythm: Fox Trot

Words and Music by Daniel Decatur Emmett

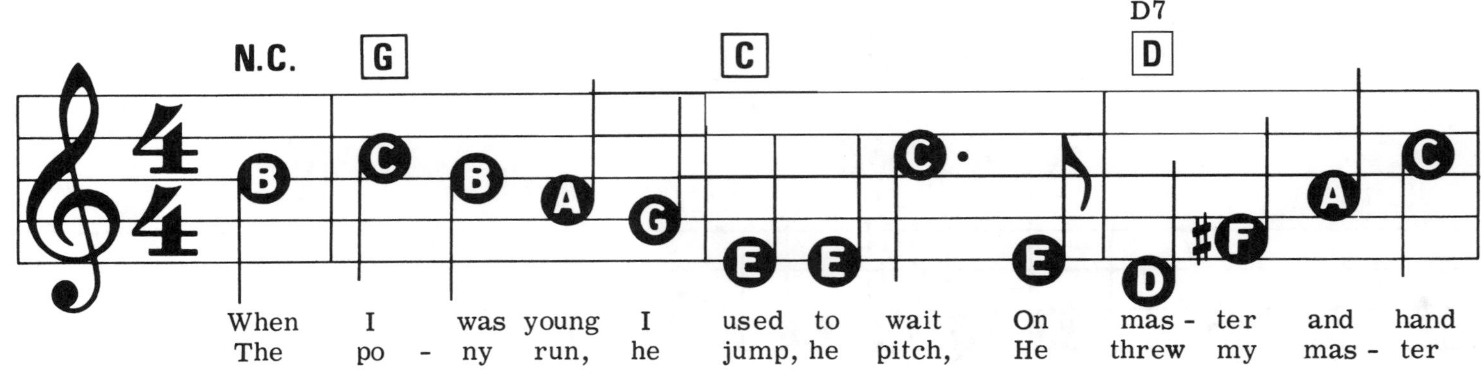

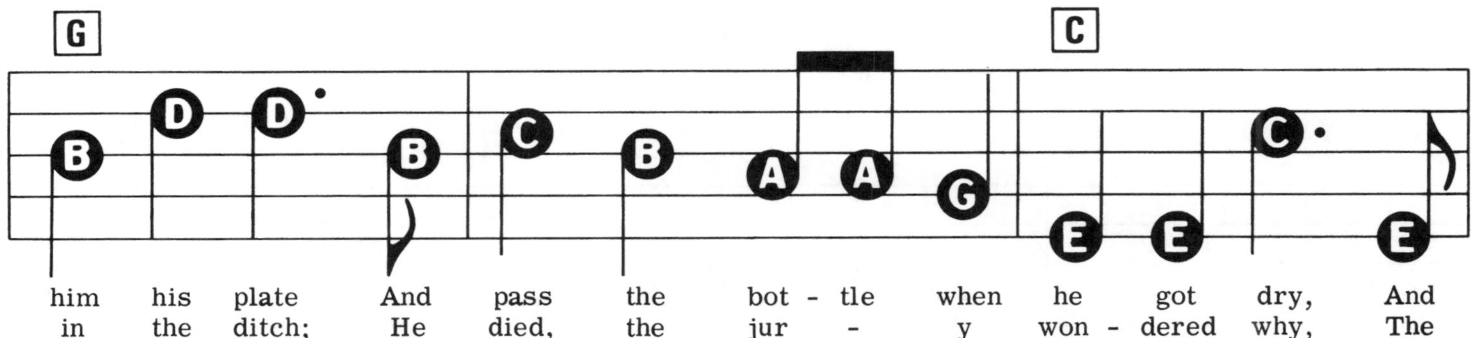

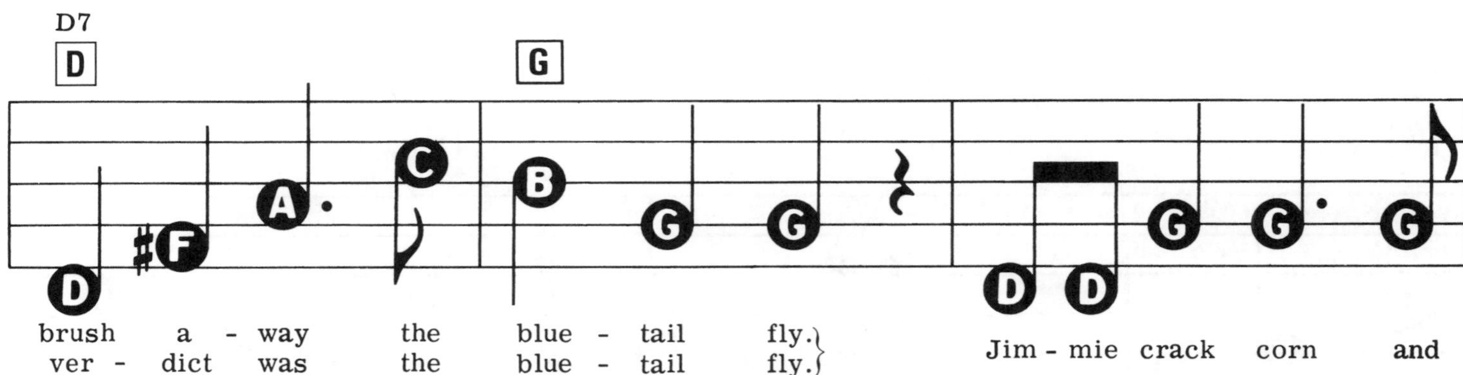

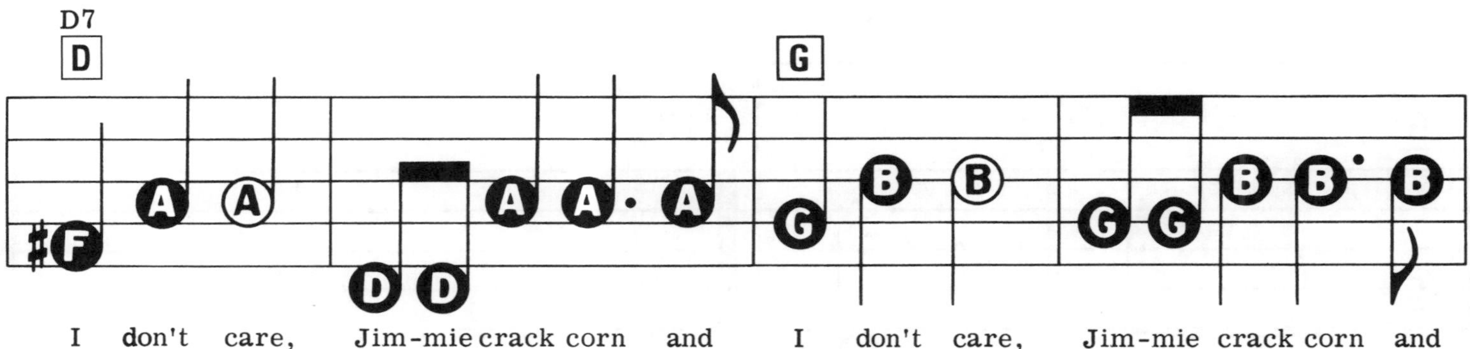

Copyright © 1975 by HAL LEONARD CORPORATION
International Copyright Secured All Rights Reserved

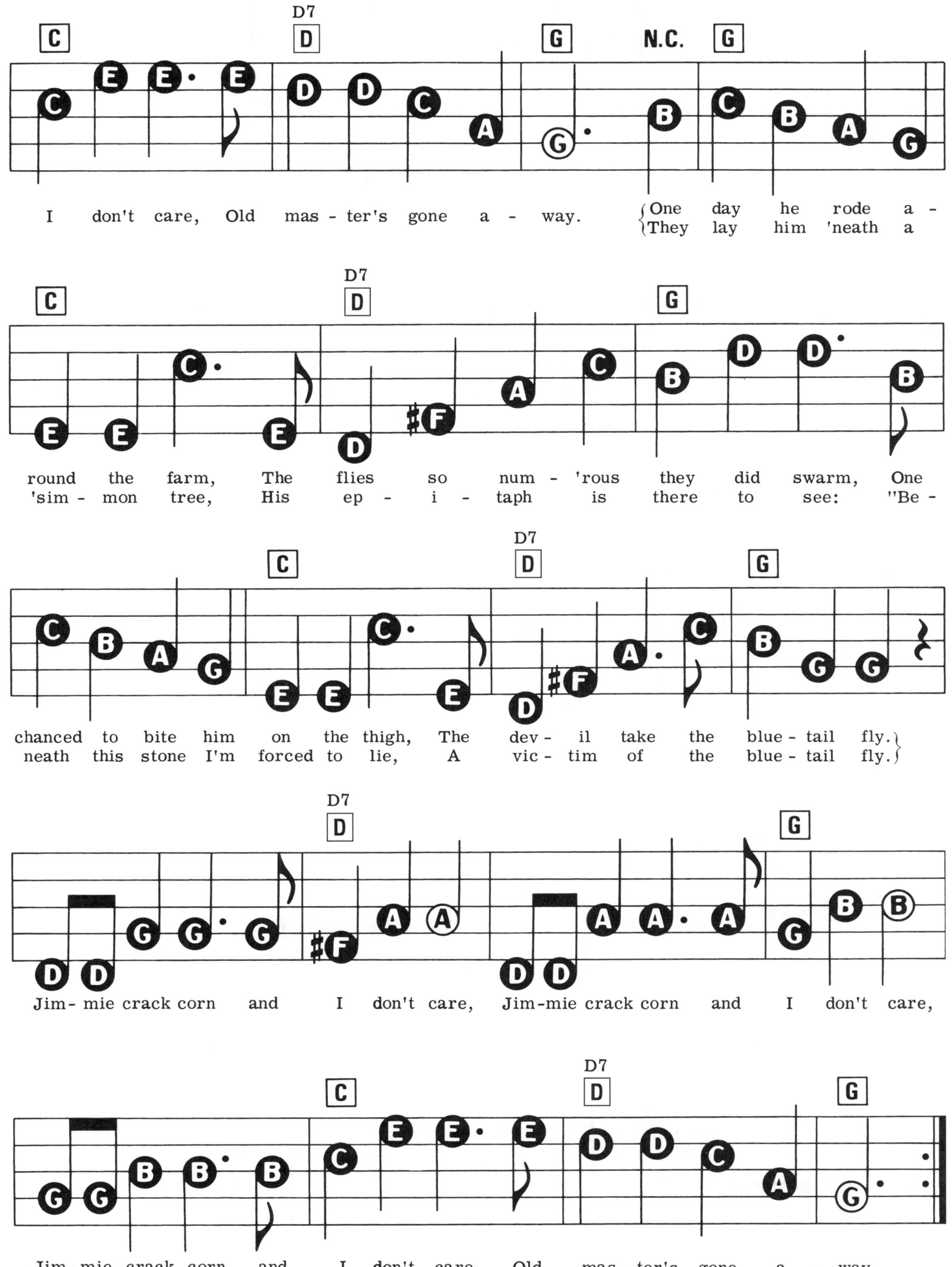
C D7 D G N.C. G
I don't care, Old mas - ter's gone a - way.
{One day he rode a -
{They lay him 'neath a
C D7 D G
round the farm, The flies so num - 'rous they did swarm, One
'sim - mon tree, His ep - i - taph is there to see: "Be -
C D7 D G
chanced to bite him on the thigh, The dev - il take the blue - tail fly.}
neath this stone I'm forced to lie, A vic - tim of the blue - tail fly.}
D7 D G
Jim- mie crack corn and I don't care, Jim-mie crack corn and I don't care,
C D7 D G
Jim - mie crack corn and I don't care, Old mas - ter's gone a - way.

"C" is for Cookie

from the Television Series SESAME STREET

Registration 9
Rhythm: Fox Trot

Words and Music by
Joe Raposo

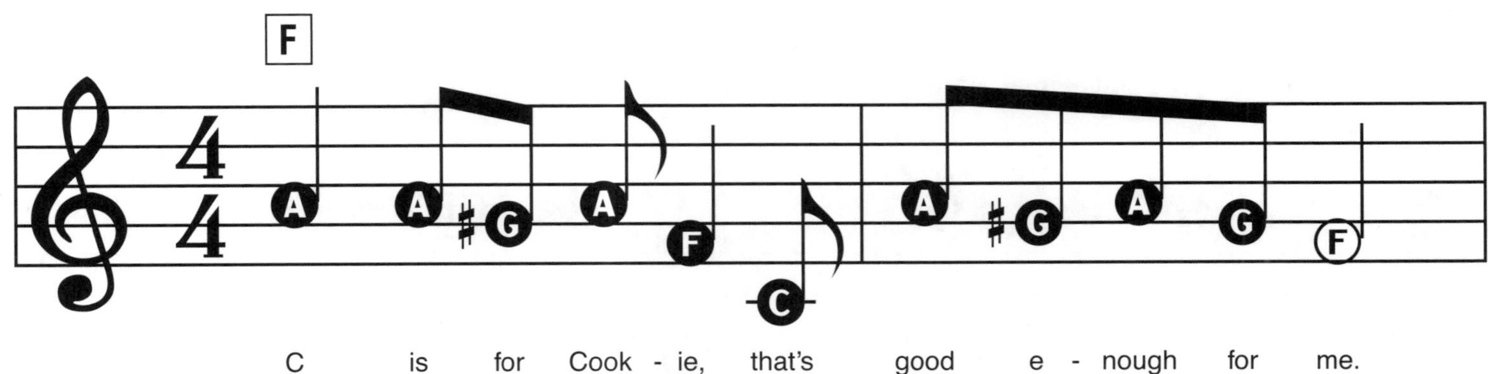

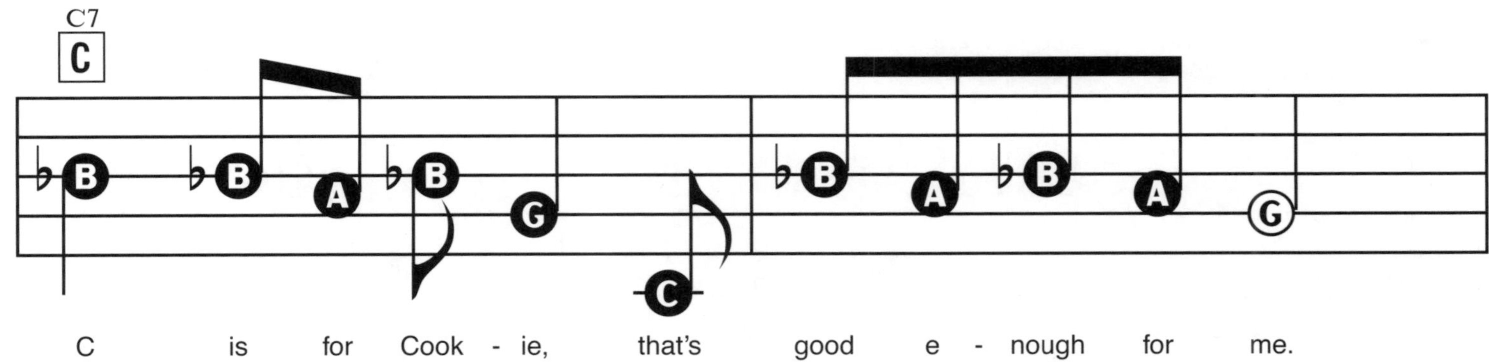

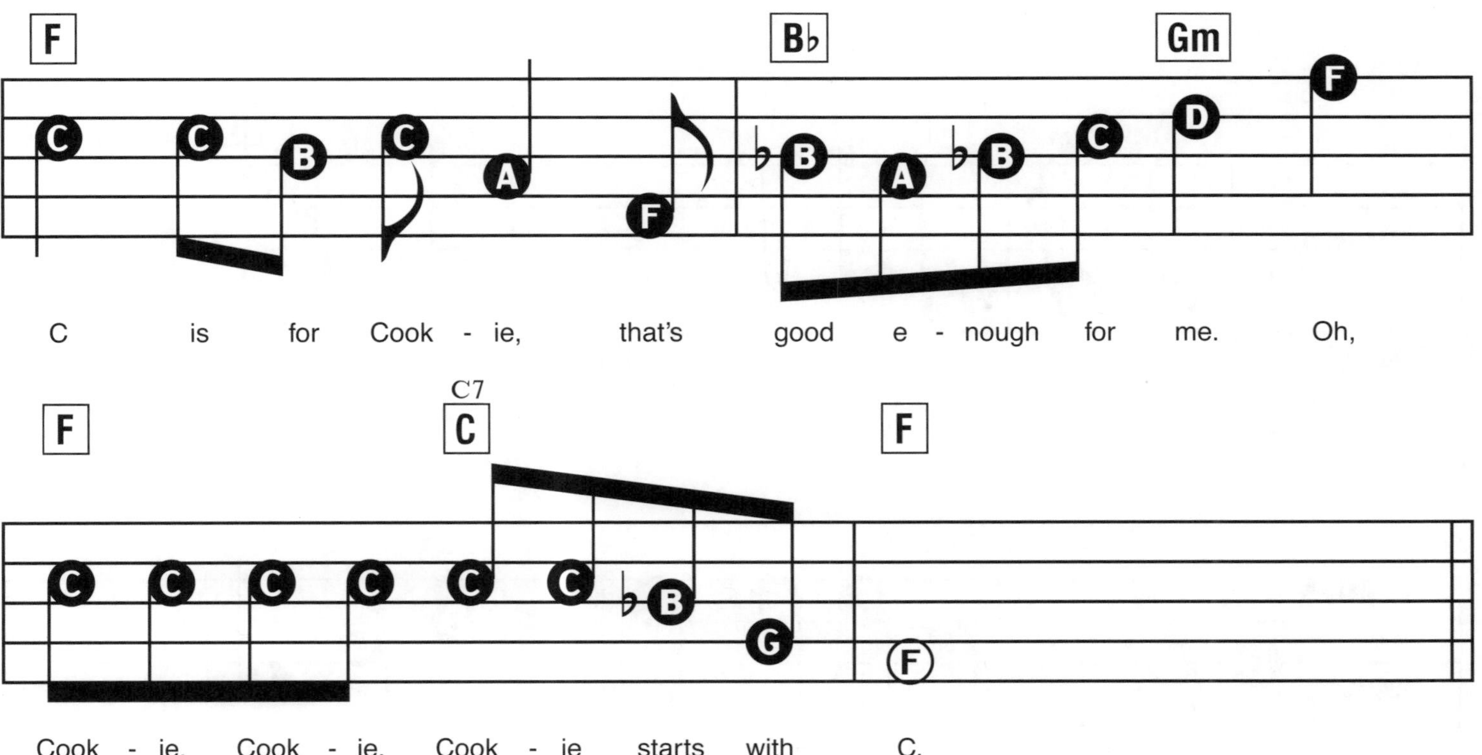

Copyright © 1973 by Jonico Music, Inc.
Copyright Renewed
International Copyright Secured All Rights Reserved

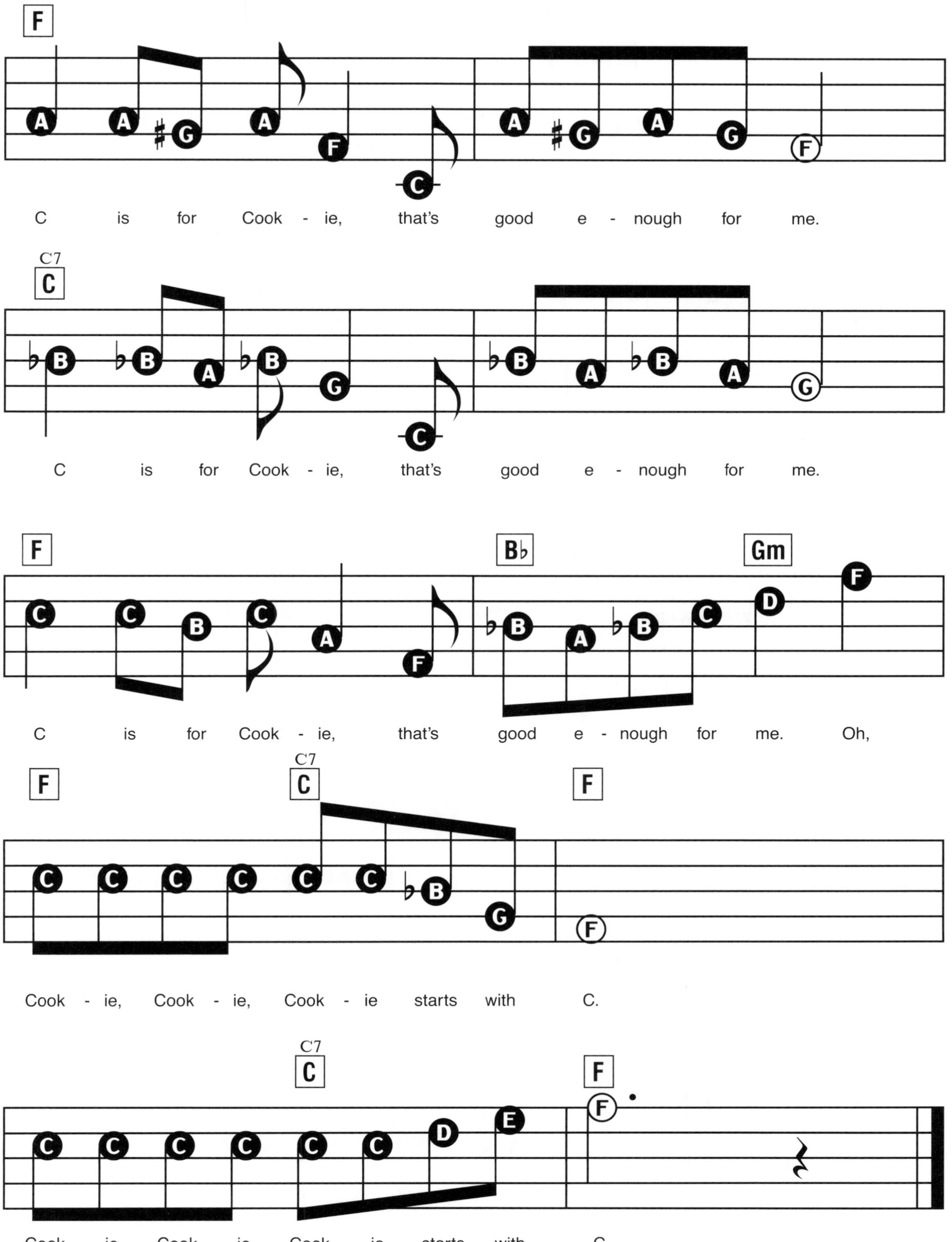
F
C is for Cook - ie, that's good e - nough for me.
C7
C
C is for Cook - ie, that's good e - nough for me.
F
Bb
Gm
C is for Cook - ie, that's good e - nough for me. Oh,
F
C7
C
F
Cook - ie, Cook - ie, Cook - ie starts with C.
C7
C
F
Cook - ie, Cook - ie, Cook - ie starts with C.

The Candy Man

from WILLY WONKA AND THE CHOCOLATE FACTORY

Registration 5
Rhythm: Swing or Jazz

Words and Music by Leslie Bricusse
and Anthony Newley

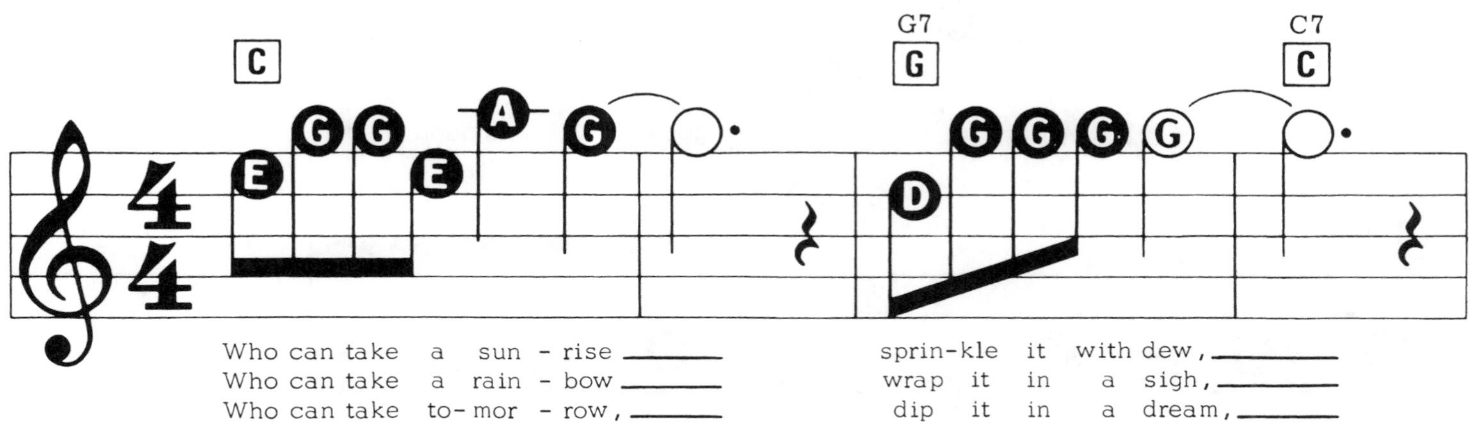

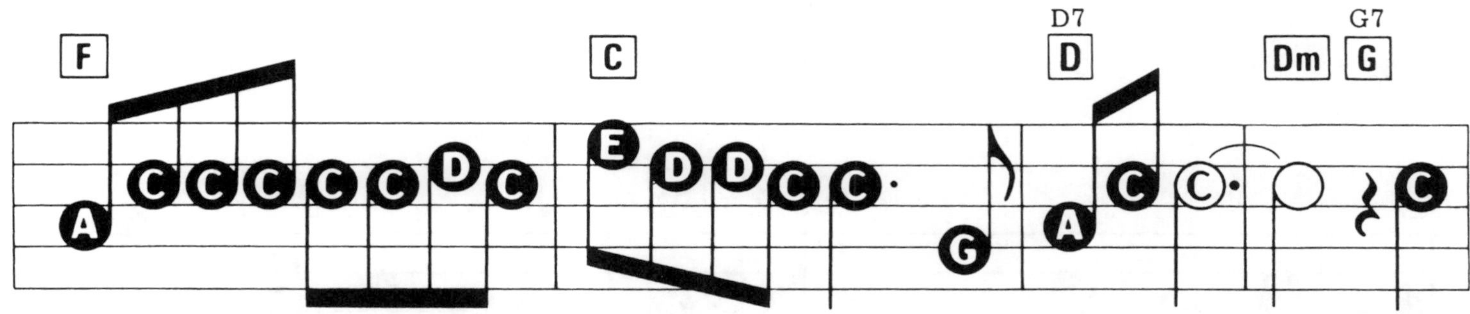

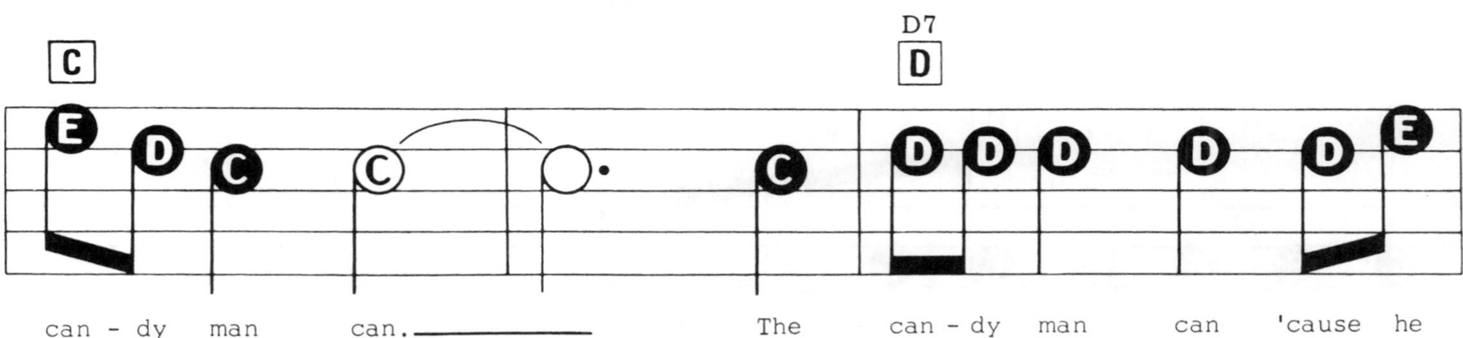

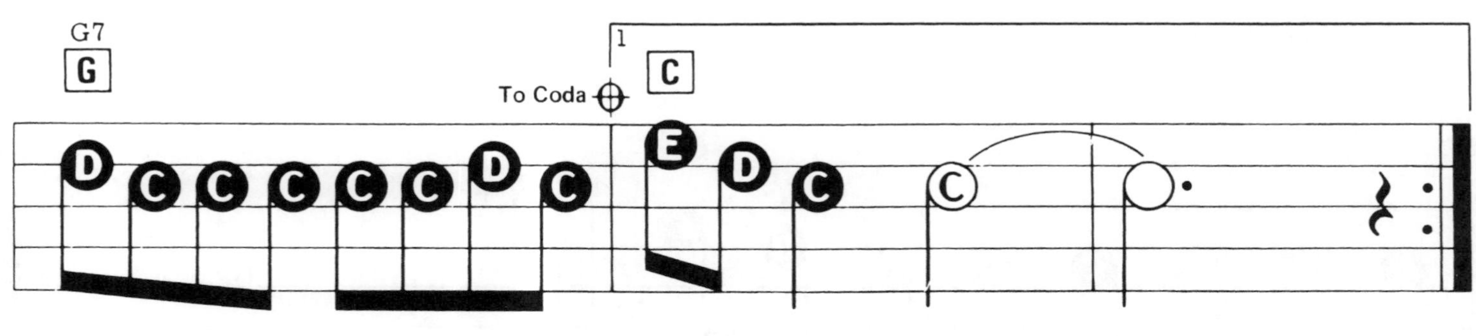

Copyright © 1970, 1971 by Taradam Music, Inc.
Copyright Renewed
International Copyright Secured All Rights Reserved

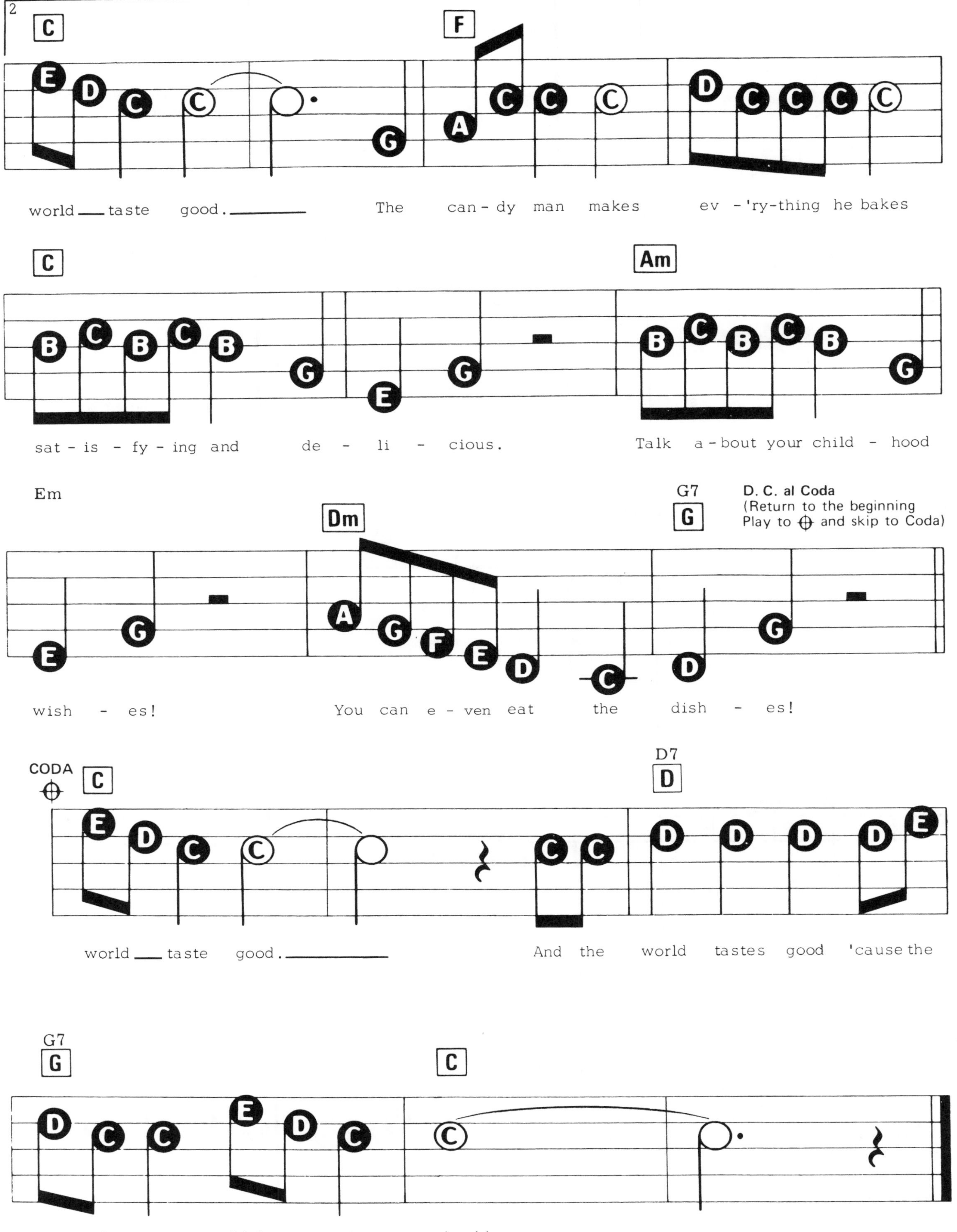
2
C
F
world — taste good. —
The can - dy man makes ev - 'ry-thing he bakes
C
Am
sat - is - fy - ing and de - li - cious.
Talk a - bout your child - hood
Em
Dm
G7
G
D. C. al Coda
(Return to the beginning
Play to ⊕ and skip to Coda)
wish - es!
You can e - ven eat the dish - es!
CODA
C
D7
D
world — taste good. —
And the world tastes good 'cause the
G7
G
C
can - dy man thinks — it should. —

Castle on a Cloud

from LES MISÉRABLES

Registration 2
Rhythm: Ballad

Music by Claude-Michel Schonberg
Lyrics by Alain Boublil, Jean-Marc Natel and Herbert Kretzmer

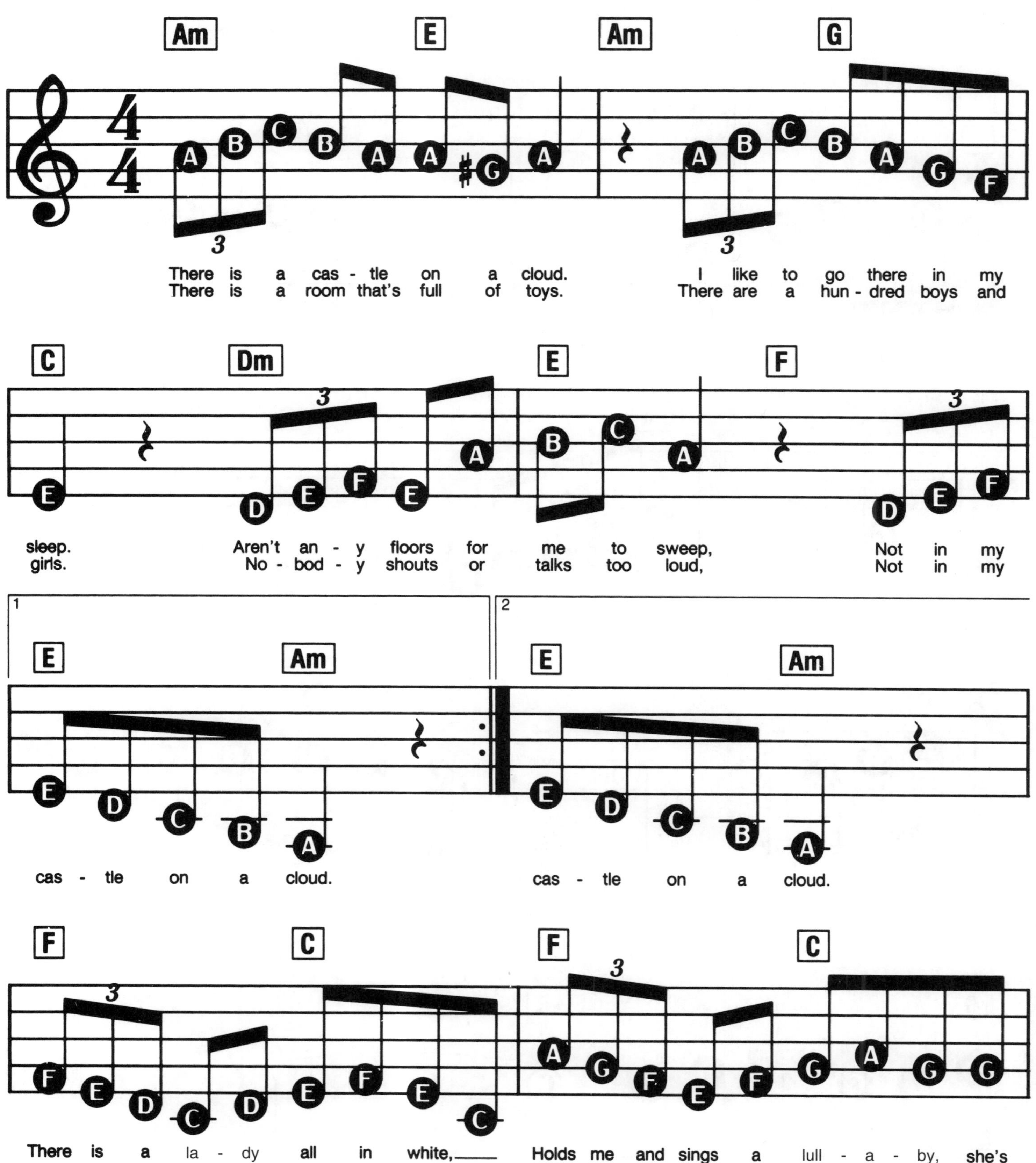

Music and Lyrics Copyright © 1980 by Editions Musicales Alain Boublil
English Lyrics Copyright © 1986 by Alain Boublil Music Ltd. (ASCAP)
Mechanical and Publication Rights for the U.S.A. Administered by Alain Boublil Music Ltd. (ASCAP) c/o Joel Faden & Co., Inc., MLM 250 West 57th St., 26th Floor, New York, NY 10107, Tel. (212) 246-7203, Fax (212) 246-7217, jfaden@joelfaden.com
International Copyright Secured. All Rights Reserved. This music is copyright. Photocopying is illegal.
All Performance Rights Restricted.

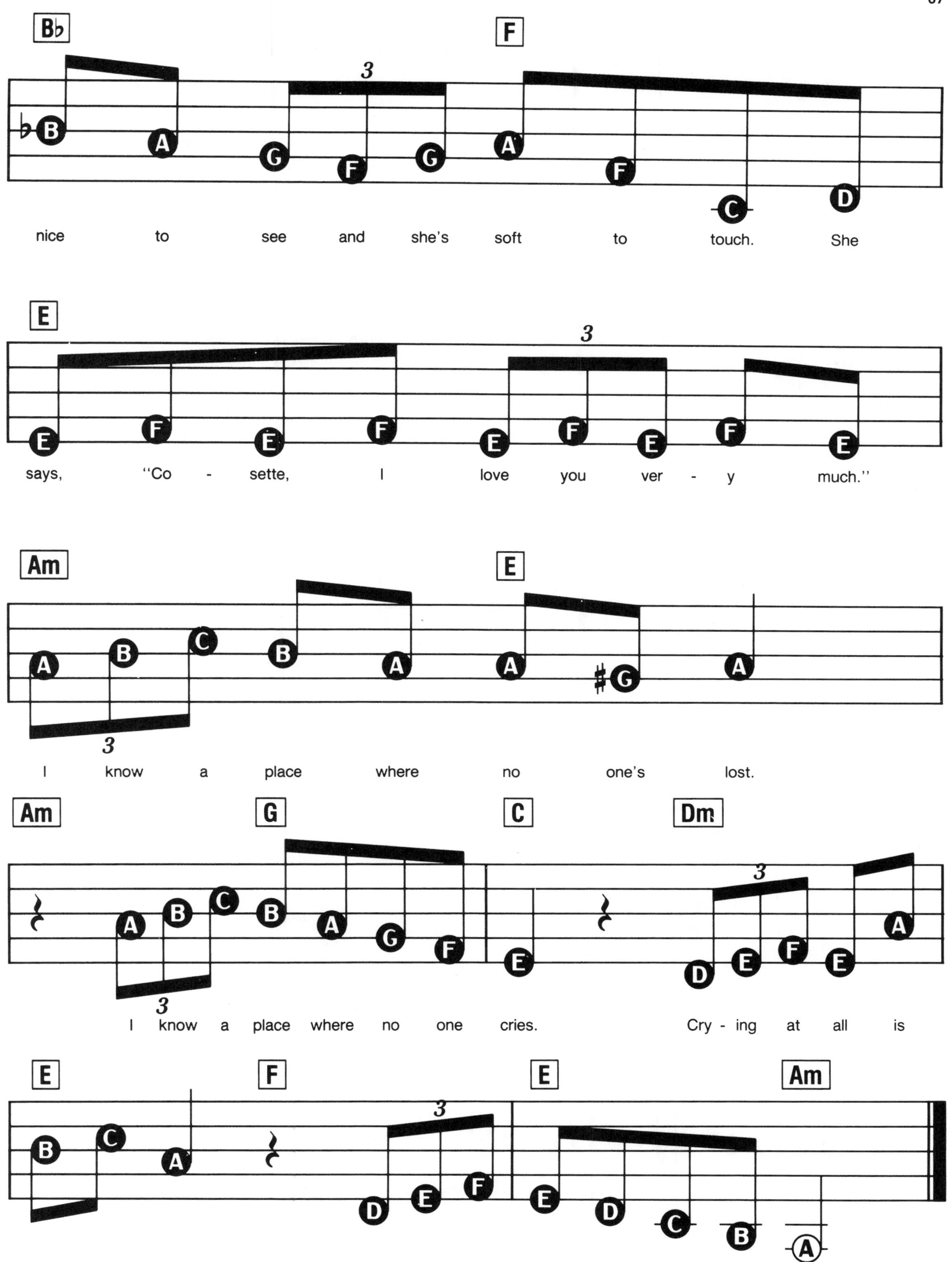
B♭
F
3
B
A
G
F
G
A
F
C
D
nice to see and she's soft to touch. She
E
3
E
F
E
F
E
F
E
F
E
says, "Co - sette, I love you ver - y much."
Am
E
A
B
C
B
A
A
♯G
A
3
I know a place where no one's lost.
Am
G
C
Dm
A
B
C
B
A
G
F
E
3
D
E
F
E
A
3
I know a place where no one cries. Cry - ing at all is
E
F
E
Am
B
C
A
3
D
E
F
E
D
C
B
A
not al - lowed, Not in my cas - tle on a cloud.

Chim Chim Cher-ee
from Walt Disney's MARY POPPINS

Registration 3
Rhythm: Waltz

Words and Music by Richard M. Sherman
and Robert B. Sherman

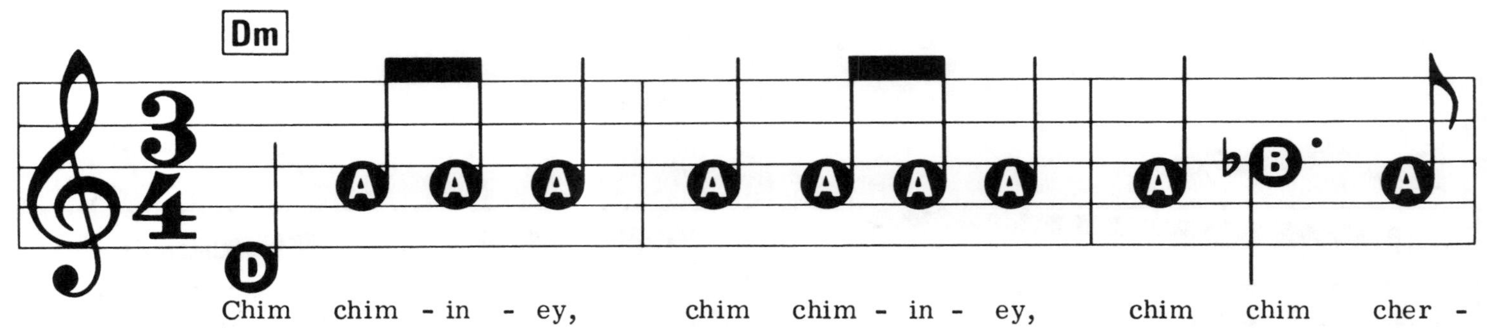

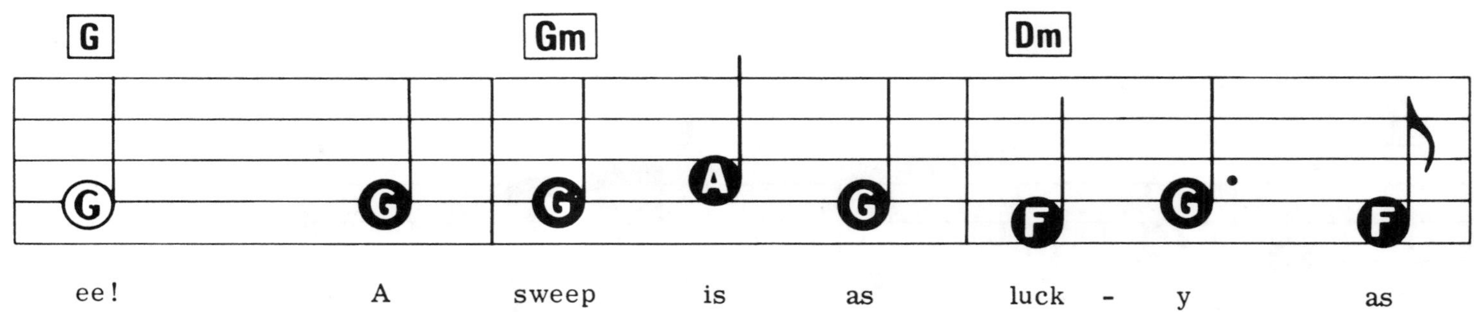

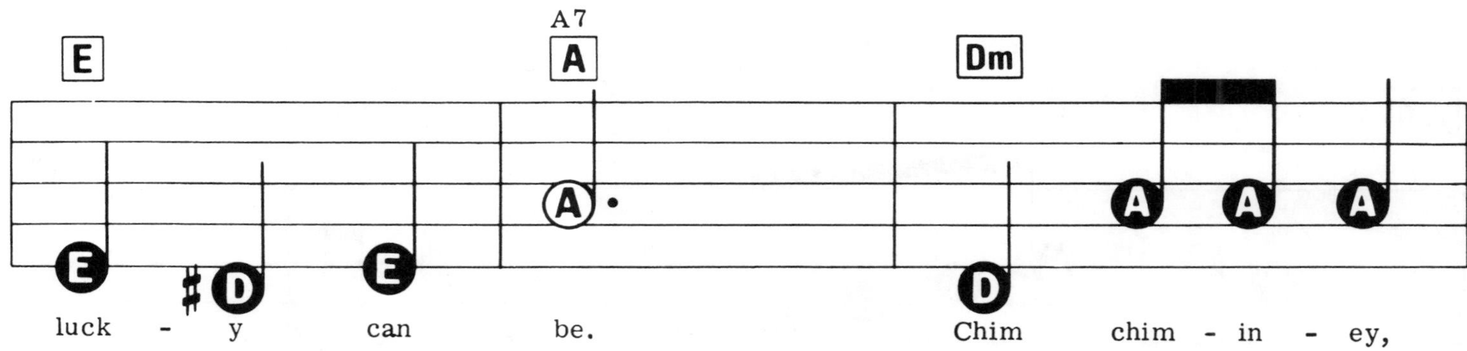

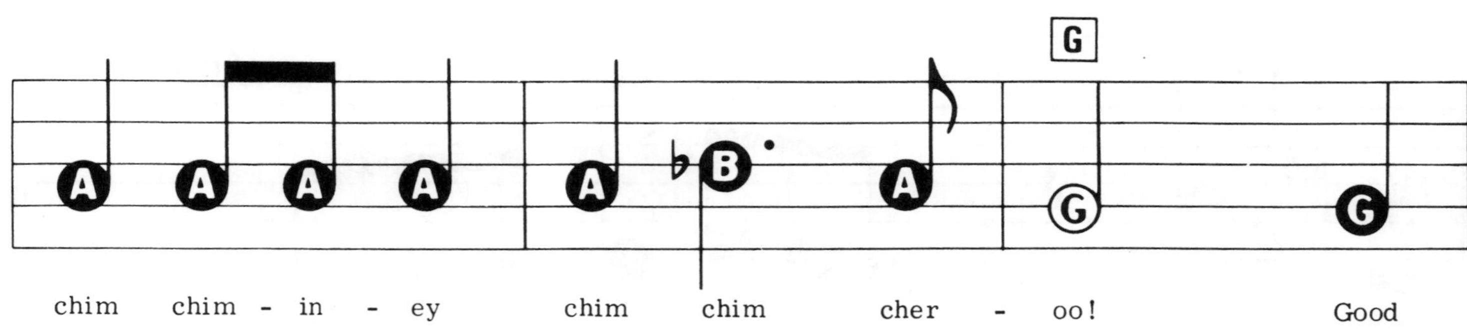

© 1963 Wonderland Music Company, Inc.
Copyright Renewed
All Rights Reserved. Used by Permission.

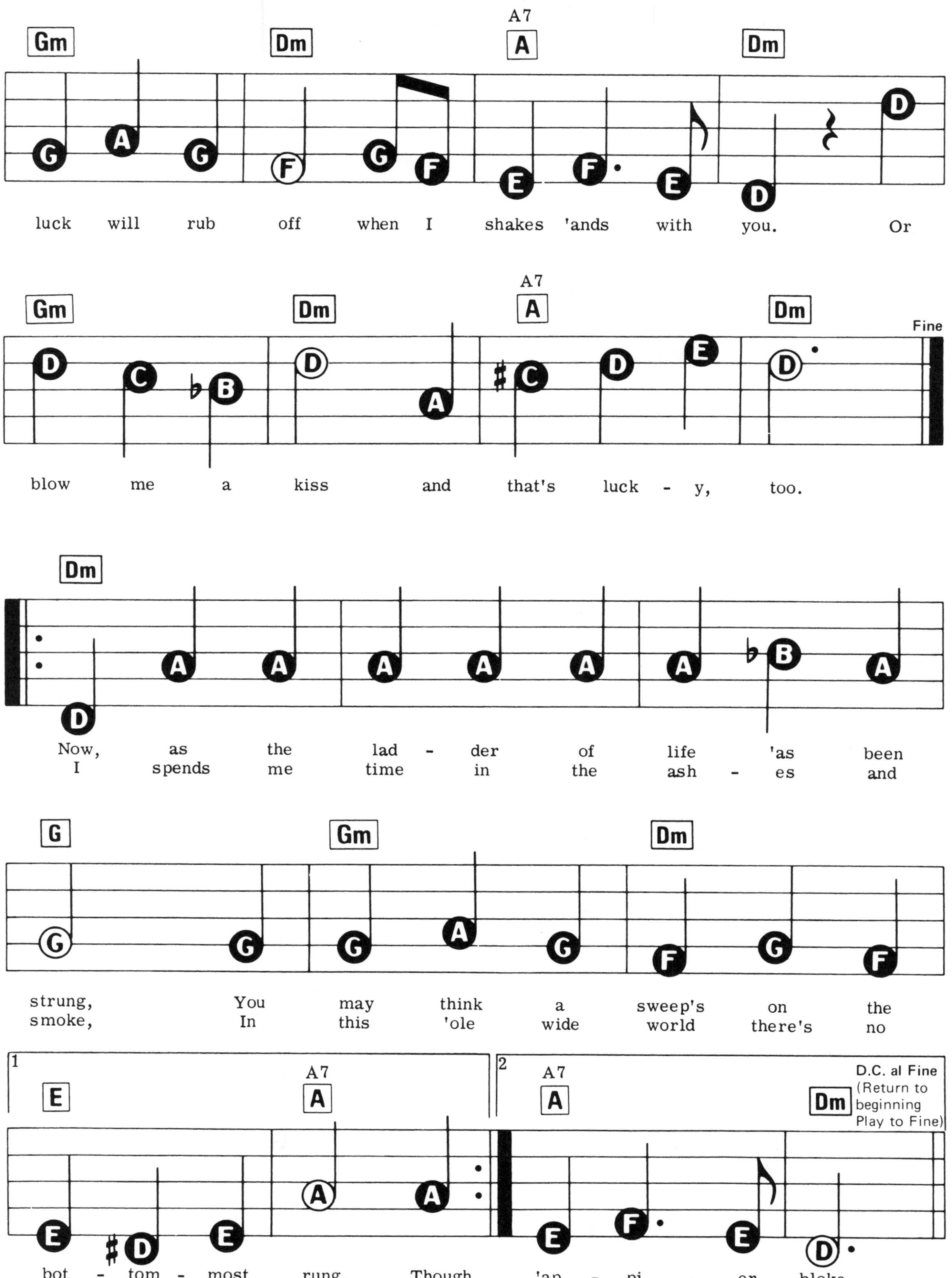
Gm Dm A7 A Dm
luck will rub off when I shakes 'ands with you. Or
Gm Dm A7 A Dm
Fine
blow me a kiss and that's luck - y, too.
Dm
Now, as the lad - der of life 'as been
I spends me time in the ash - es and
G Gm Dm
strung, You may think a sweep's on the
smoke, In this 'ole wide world there's no
1 E A7 A
bot - tom - most rung. Though
2 A7 A Dm
D.C. al Fine
(Return to beginning Play to Fine)
'ap - pi - er bloke.

Chitty Chitty Bang Bang

Registration 9
Rhythm: Fox Trot

Words and Music by Richard M. Sherman
and Robert B. Sherman

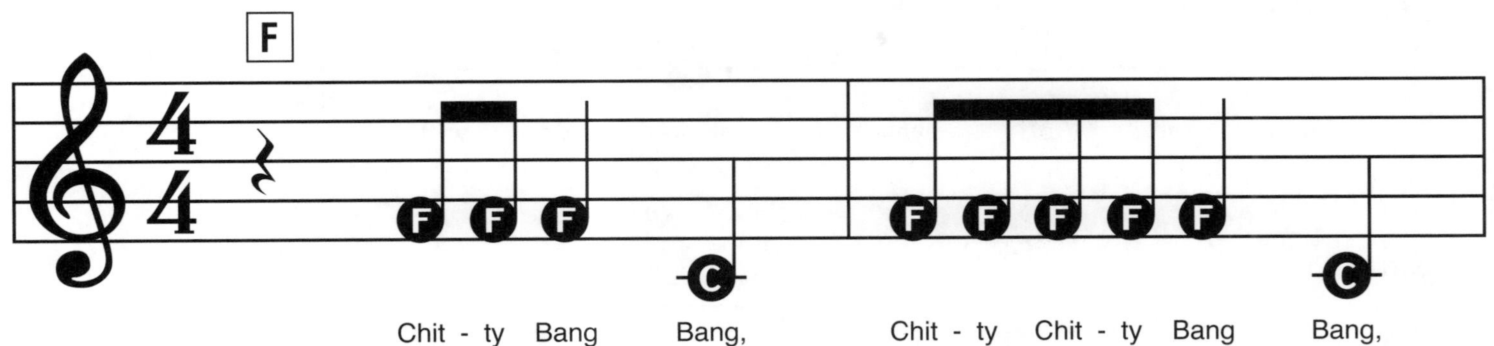

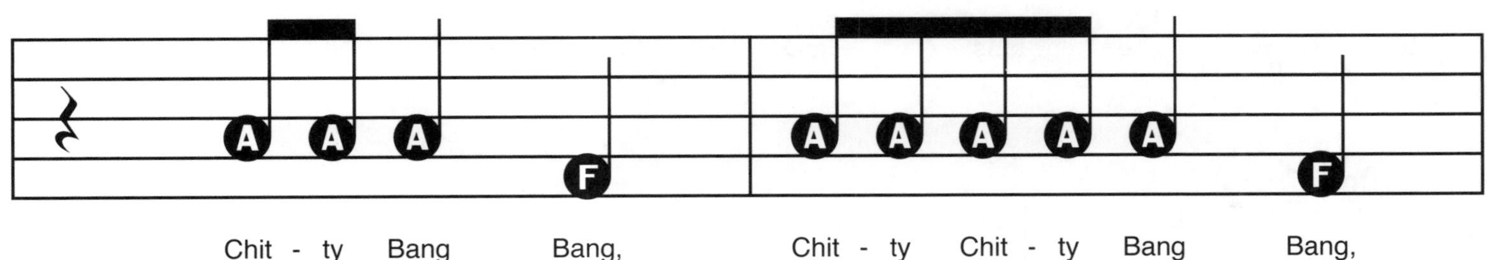

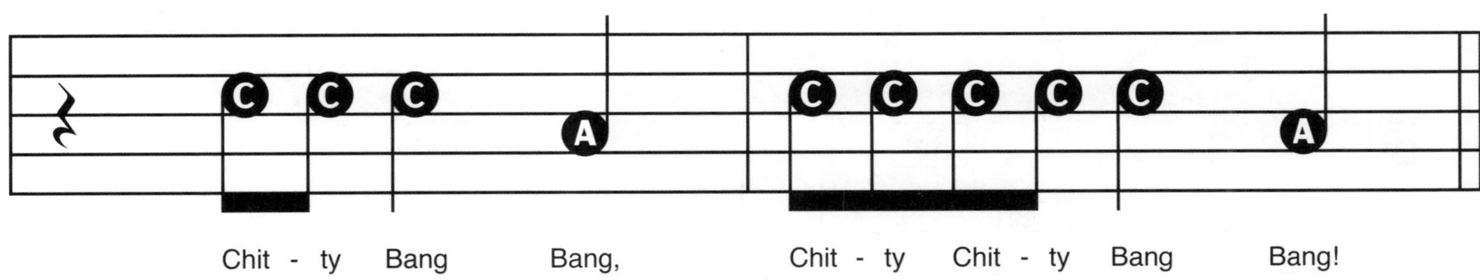

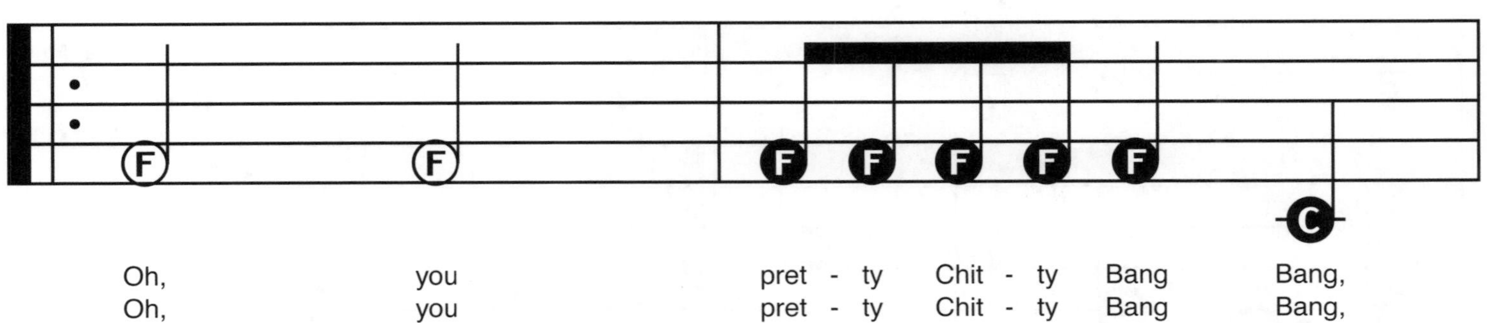

© 1968 (Renewed) EMI UNART CATALOG INC.
All Rights Administered by EMI UNART CATALOG INC. (Publishing) and ALFRED MUSIC (Print)
All Rights Reserved Used by Permission

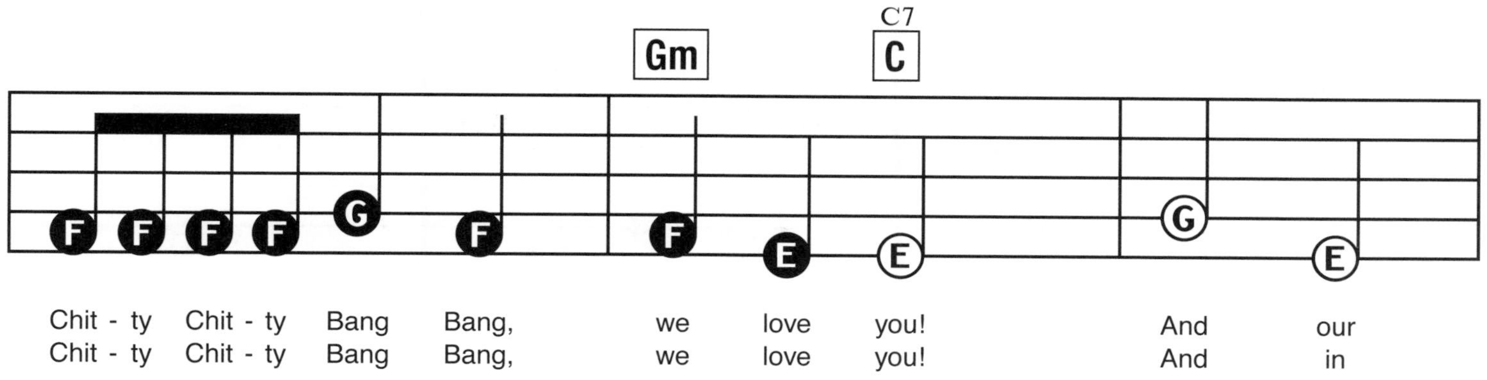

C7
Gm
C
F F F F G F F E E G E
Chit - ty Chit - ty Bang Bang, we love you! And our
Chit - ty Chit - ty Bang Bang, we love you! And in

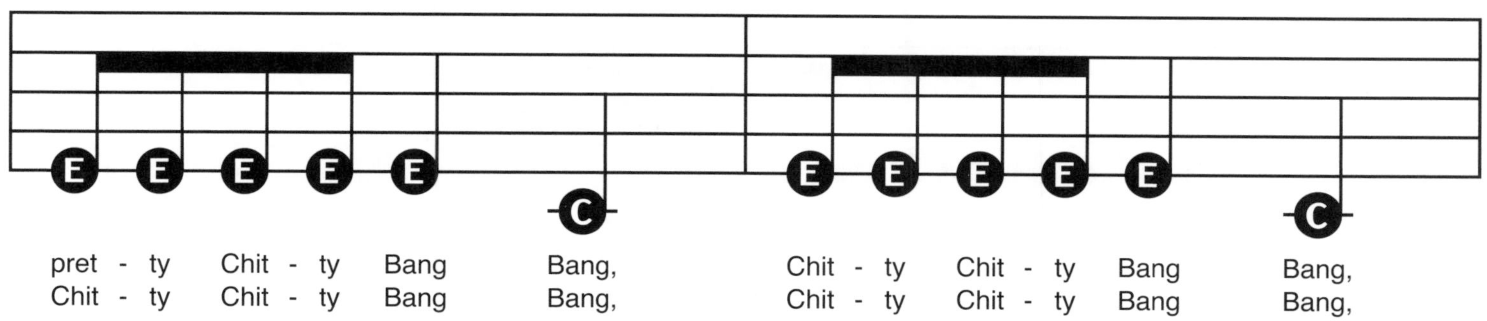

E E E E E C E E E E E C
pret - ty Chit - ty Bang Bang, Chit - ty Chit - ty Bang Bang,
Chit - ty Chit - ty Bang Bang, Chit - ty Chit - ty Bang Bang,

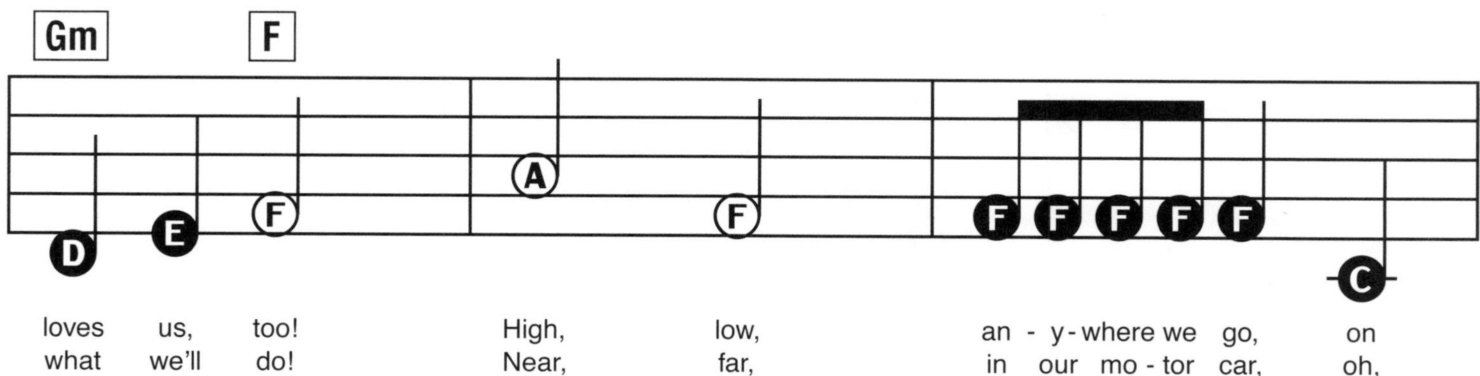

Gm
F
D E F A F F F F F F C
loves us, too! High, low, an - y - where we go, on
what we'll do! Near, far, in our mo - tor car, oh,

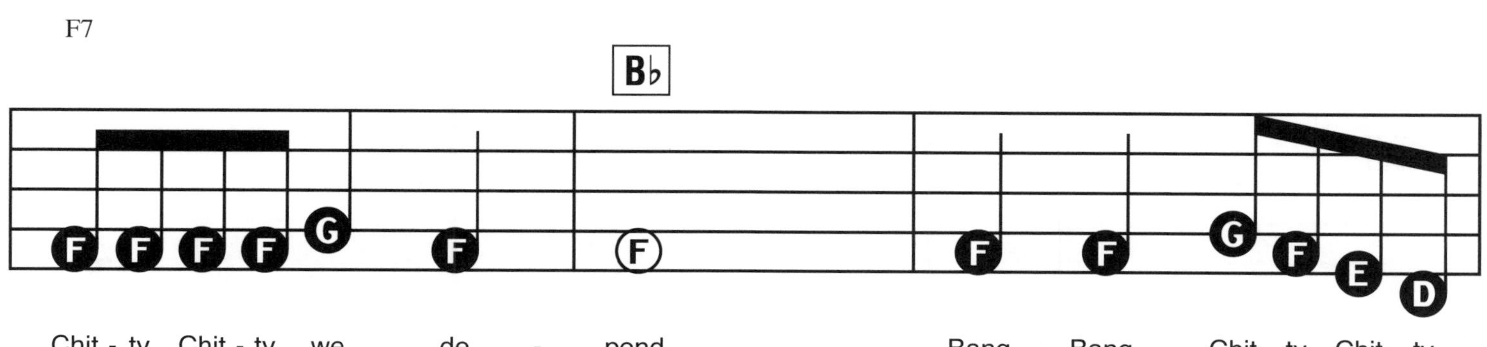

F7
B♭
F F F F G F F F F G F E D
Chit - ty Chit - ty we de - pend. Bang Bang, Chit - ty Chit - ty
what a hap - py time we'll spend. Bang Bang, Chit - ty Chit - ty

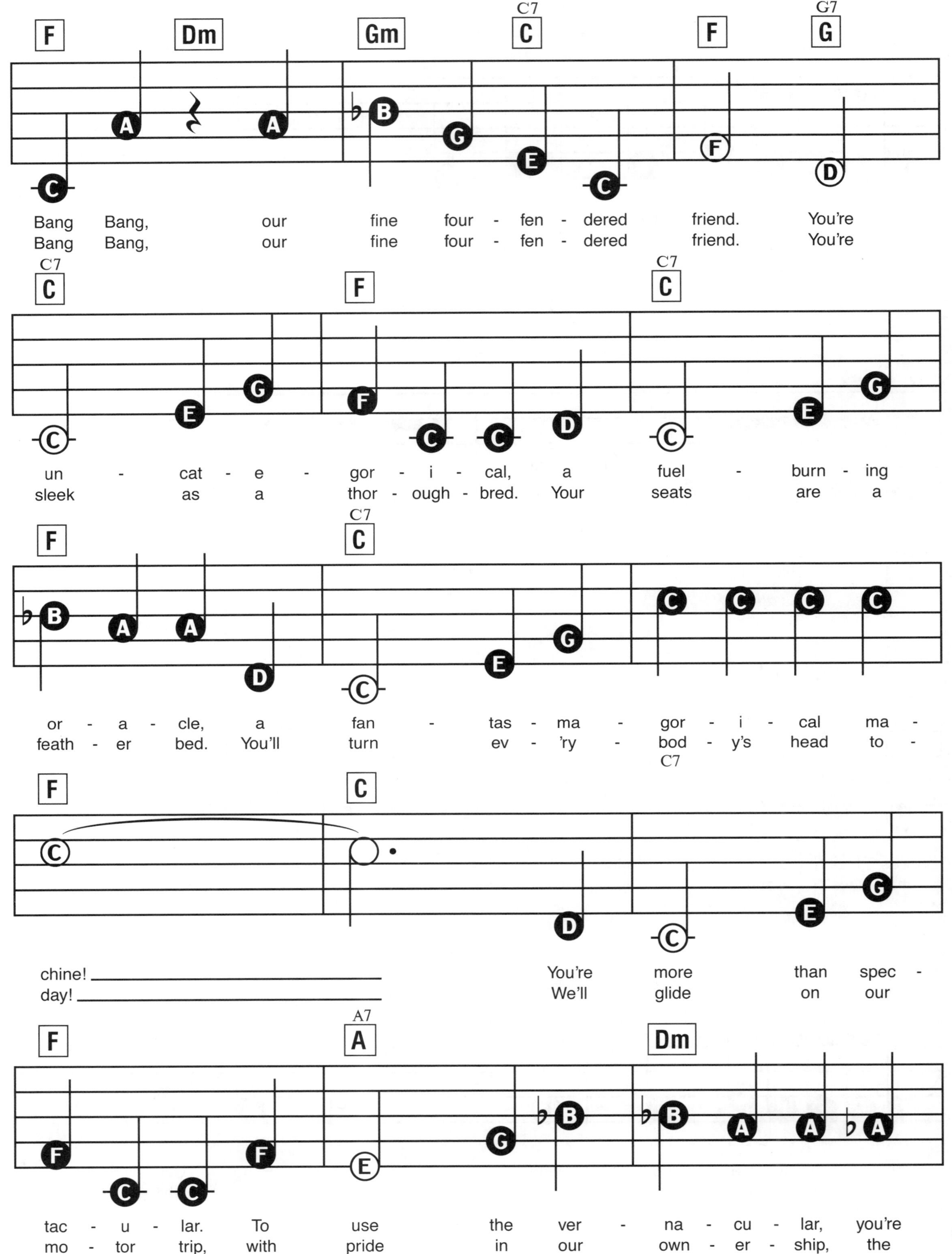
F Dm Gm C7 C F G7 G
Bang Bang, our fine four - fen - dered friend. You're
Bang Bang, our fine four - fen - dered friend. You're
C7 C F C7 C
un - cat - e - gor - i - cal, a fuel - burn - ing
sleek as a thor - ough - bred. Your seats are a
F C7 C
or - a - cle, a fan - tas - ma - gor - i - cal ma -
feath - er bed. You'll turn ev - 'ry - bod - y's head to -
F C C7
chine!
day!
You're more than spec -
We'll glide on our
F A7 A Dm
tac - u - lar. To use the ver - na - cu - lar, you're
mo - tor trip, with pride in our own - er - ship, the

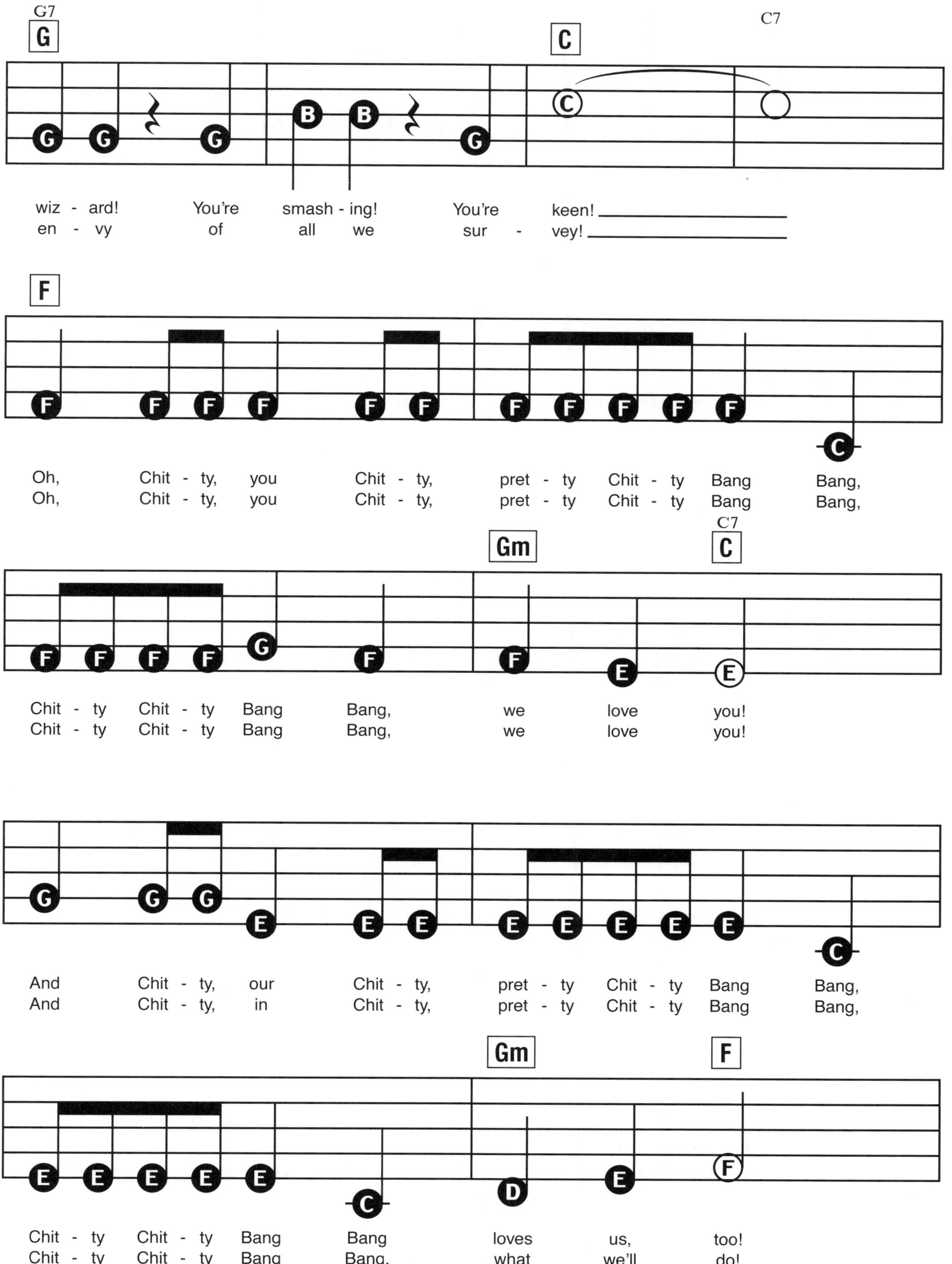
G7
G
C
C7
G
G
G
B
B
G
C
wiz - ard! You're smash - ing! You're keen!
en - vy of all we sur - vey!
F
F F F F F F F F F F F C
Oh, Chit - ty, you Chit - ty, pret - ty Chit - ty Bang Bang,
Oh, Chit - ty, you Chit - ty, pret - ty Chit - ty Bang Bang,
Gm
C7
C
F F F F G F F E E
Chit - ty Chit - ty Bang Bang, we love you!
Chit - ty Chit - ty Bang Bang, we love you!
G G G E E E E E E E E C
And Chit - ty, our Chit - ty, pret - ty Chit - ty Bang Bang,
And Chit - ty, in Chit - ty, pret - ty Chit - ty Bang Bang,
Gm
F
E E E E E C D E F
Chit - ty Chit - ty Bang Bang loves us, too!
Chit - ty Chit - ty Bang Bang, what we'll do!

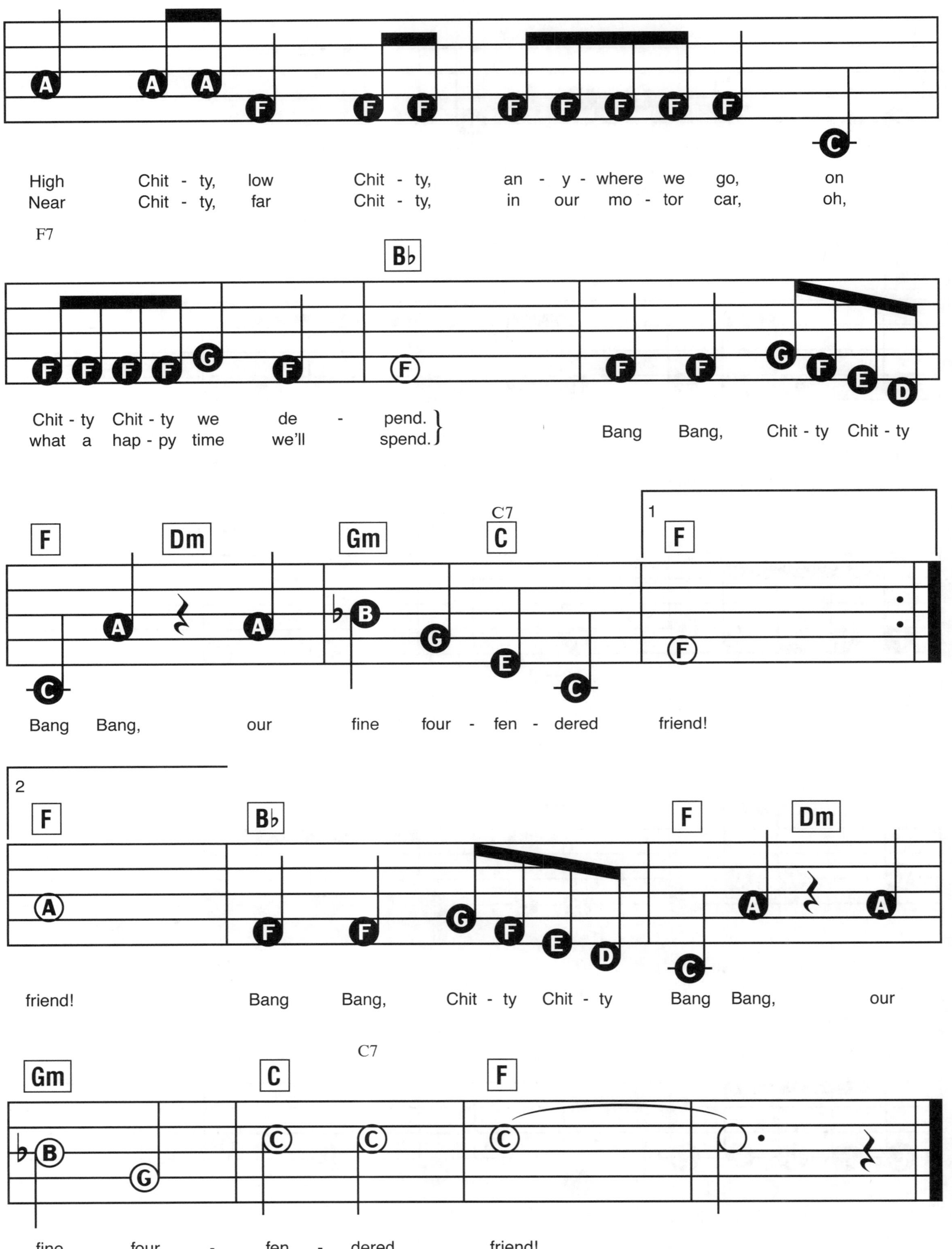
High Chit - ty, low Chit - ty, an - y - where we go, on
Near Chit - ty, far Chit - ty, in our mo - tor car, oh,
F7
B♭
Chit - ty Chit - ty we de - pend.
what a hap - py time we'll spend.
Bang Bang, Chit - ty Chit - ty
F
Dm
Gm
C7
C
1
F
Bang Bang, our fine four - fen - dered friend!
2
F
B♭
F
Dm
friend! Bang Bang, Chit - ty Chit - ty Bang Bang, our
Gm
C7
C
F
fine four - fen - dered friend!

Chopsticks

Registration 8
Rhythm: Waltz

By Arthur de Lulli

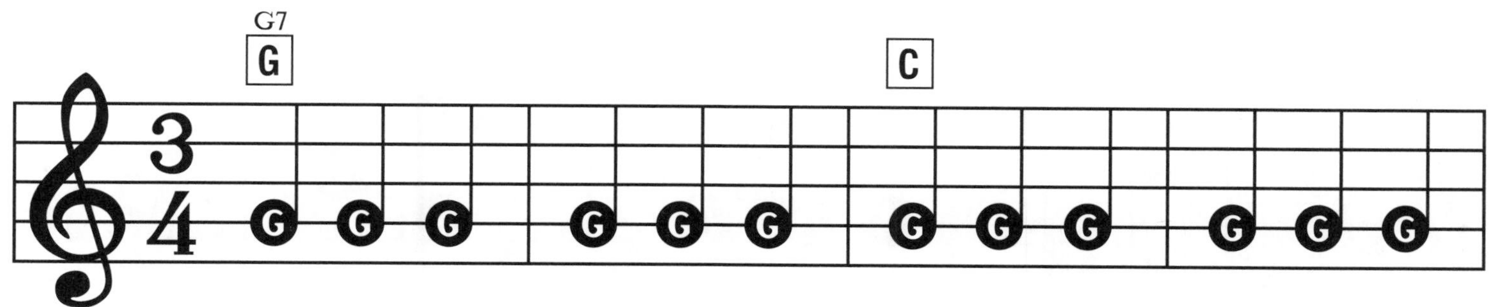

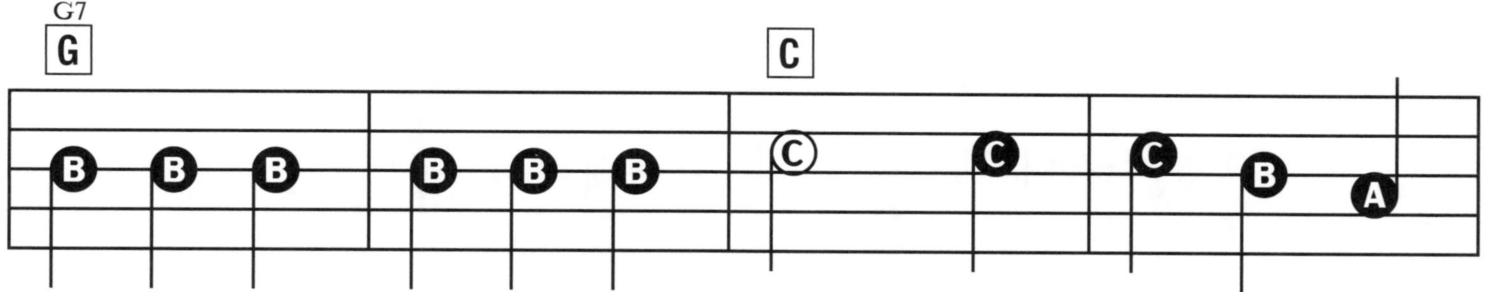

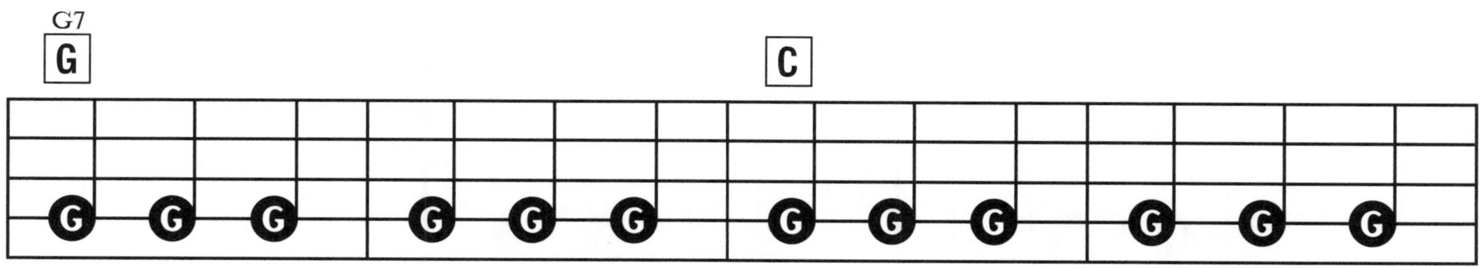

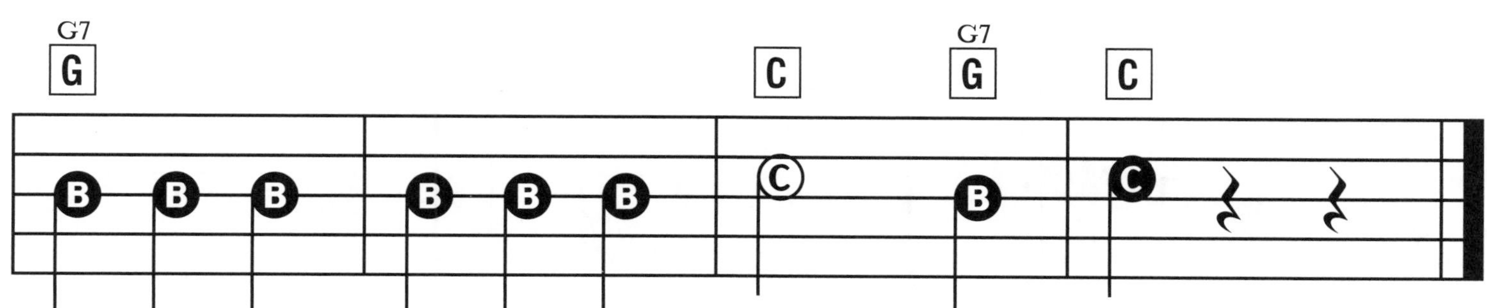

Copyright © 2016 by HAL LEONARD CORPORATION
International Copyright Secured All Rights Reserved

(Oh, My Darling) Clementine

Registration 4
Rhythm: Waltz

Words and Music by
Percy Montrose

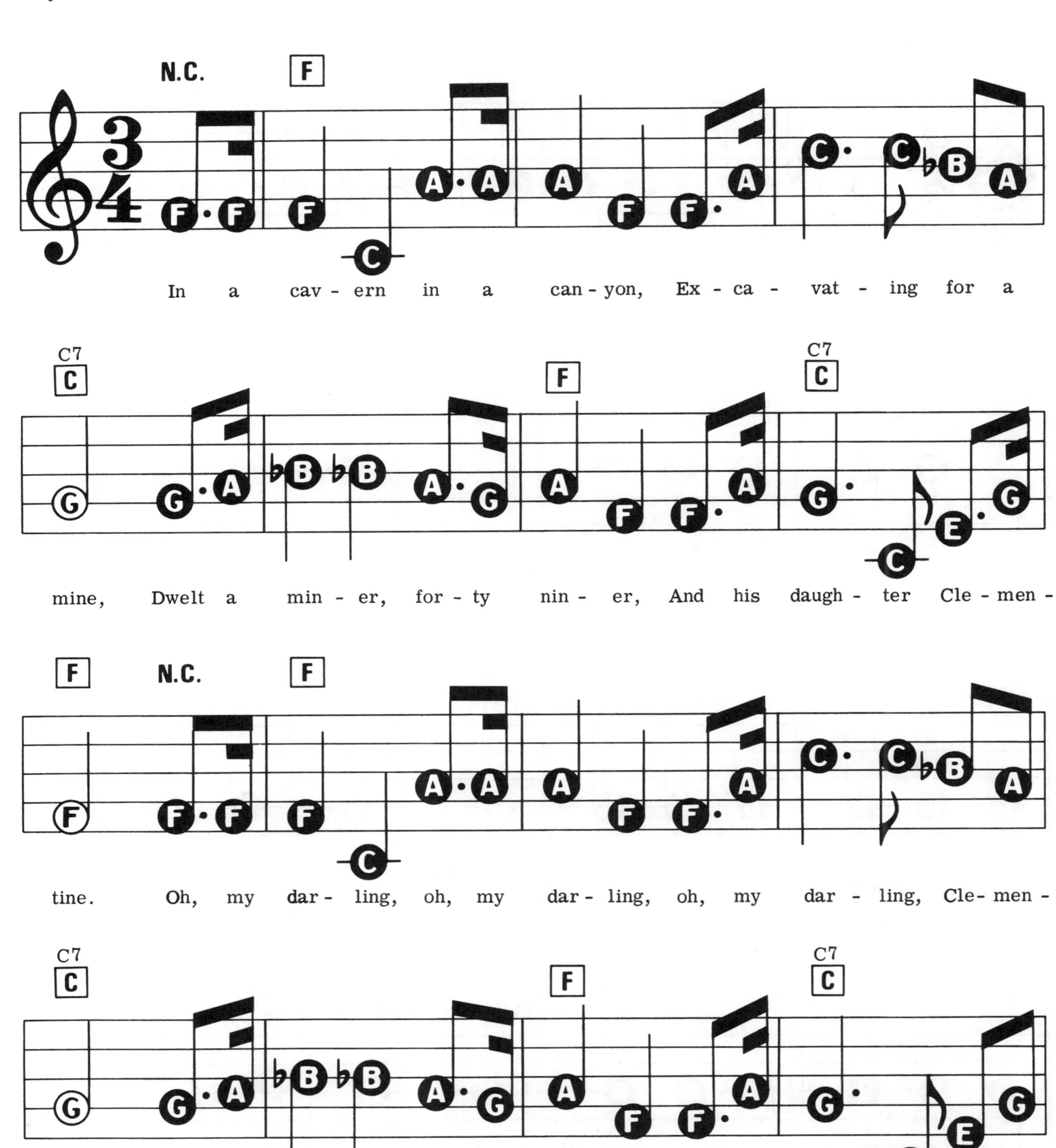

Copyright © 1975 by HAL LEONARD CORPORATION
International Copyright Secured All Rights Reserved

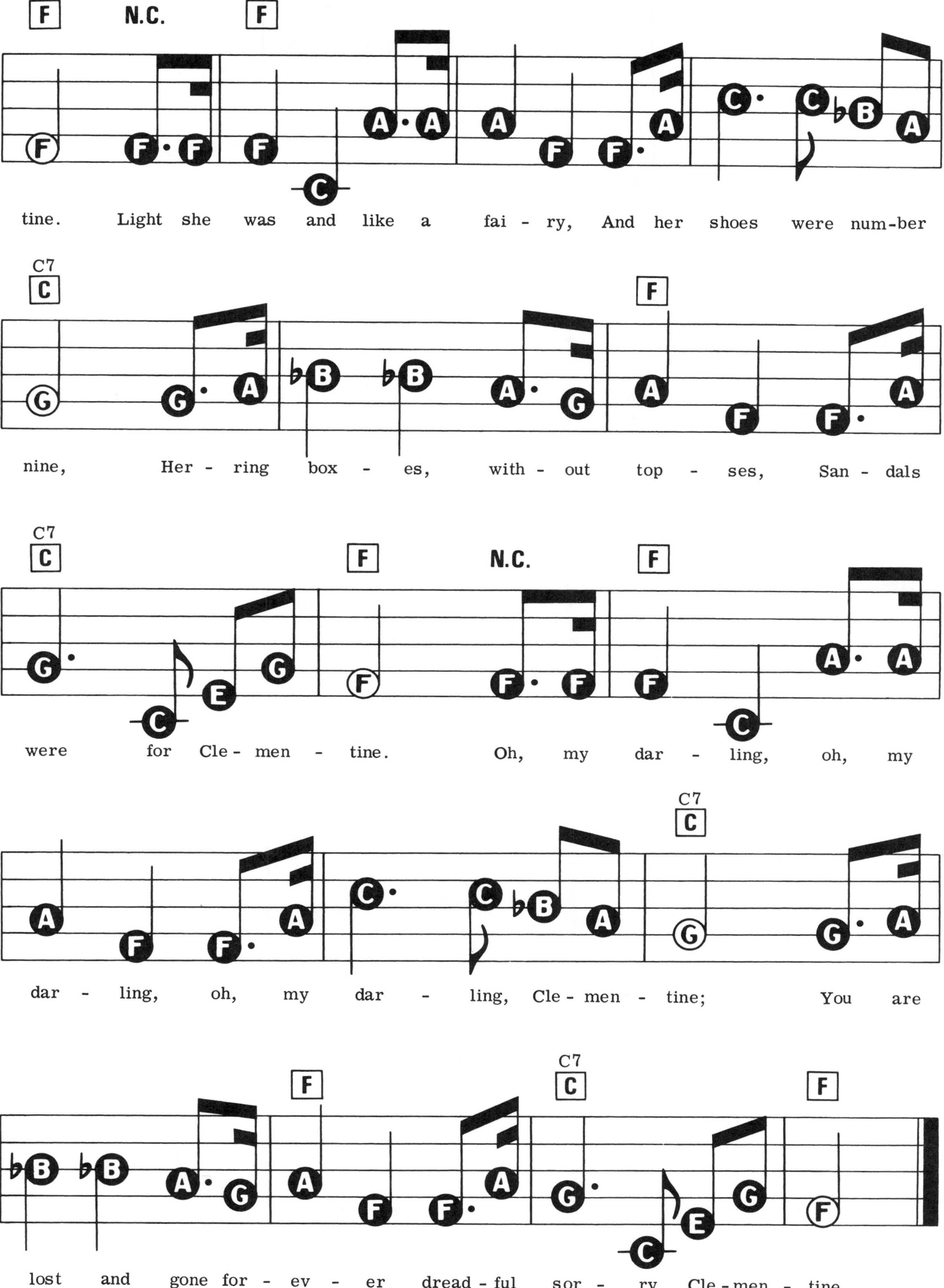
F N.C. F
tine. Light she was and like a fai - ry, And her shoes were num-ber
C7 C F
nine, Her - ring box - es, with - out top - ses, San - dals
C7 C F N.C. F
were for Cle - men - tine. Oh, my dar - ling, oh, my
C7 C
dar - ling, oh, my dar - ling, Cle - men - tine; You are
F C7 C F
lost and gone for - ev - er dread - ful sor - ry Cle - men - tine.

Consider Yourself

from the Broadway Musical OLIVER!

Registration 2
Rhythm: 6/8 March

Words and Music by
Lionel Bart

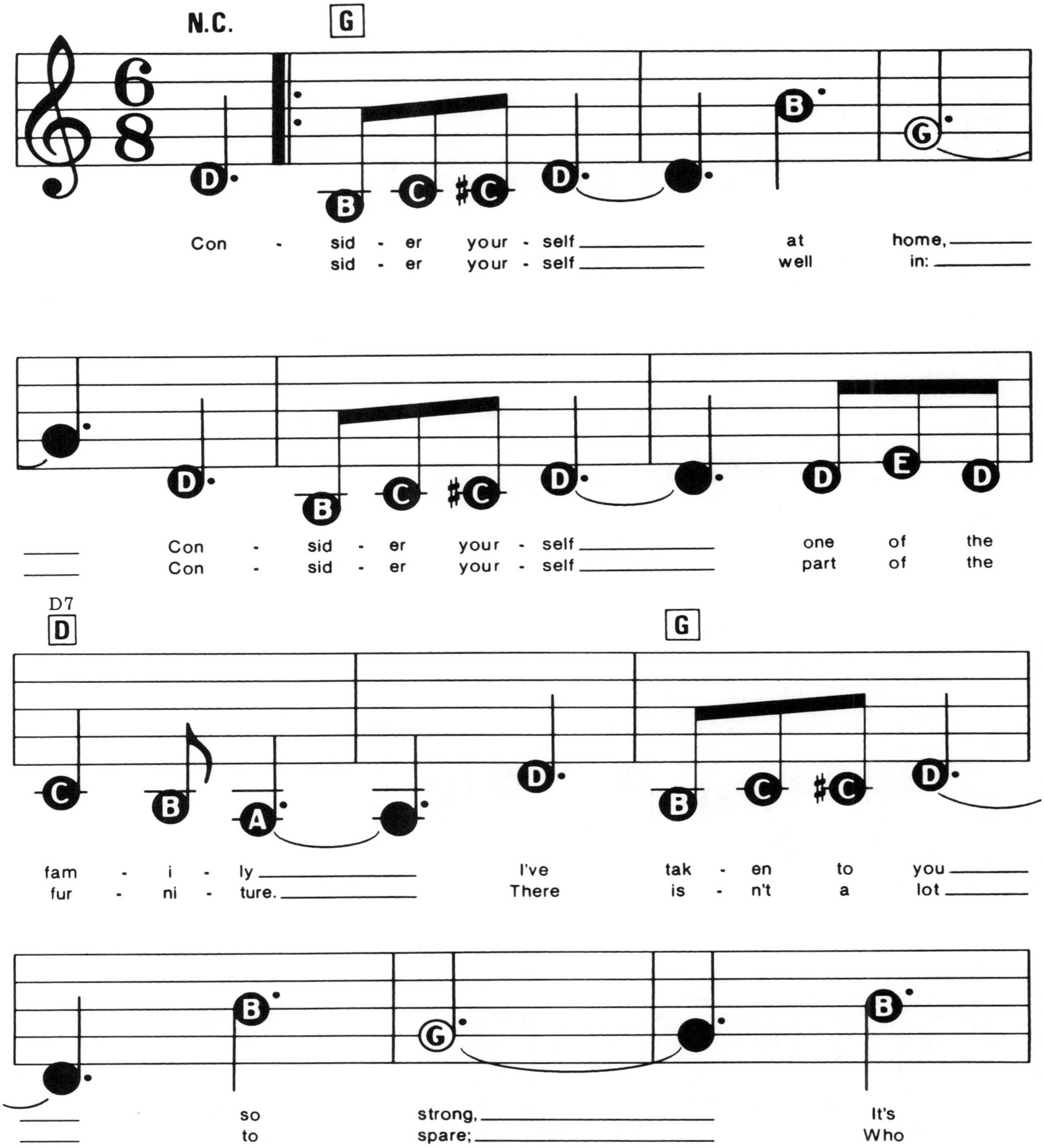

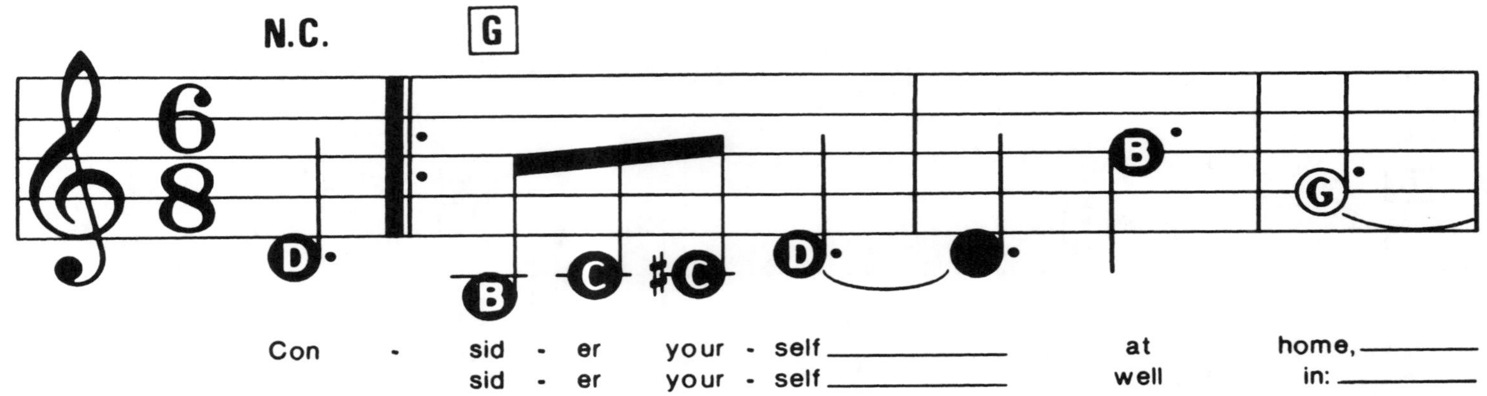

D B C ♯C D D E D

Con - sid - er your - self one of the
Con - sid - er your - self part of the

D7
D
G
C B A D B C ♯C D

fam - i - ly I've tak - en to you
fur - ni - ture. There is - n't a lot

B G B

so strong, It's
to spare; Who

© Copyright 1960 (Renewed) Lakeview Music Co. Ltd., London, England
TRO - Hollis Music, Inc., New York, controls all publication rights for the U.S.A. and Canada
International Copyright Secured
All Rights Reserved Including Public Performance For Profit
Used by Permission

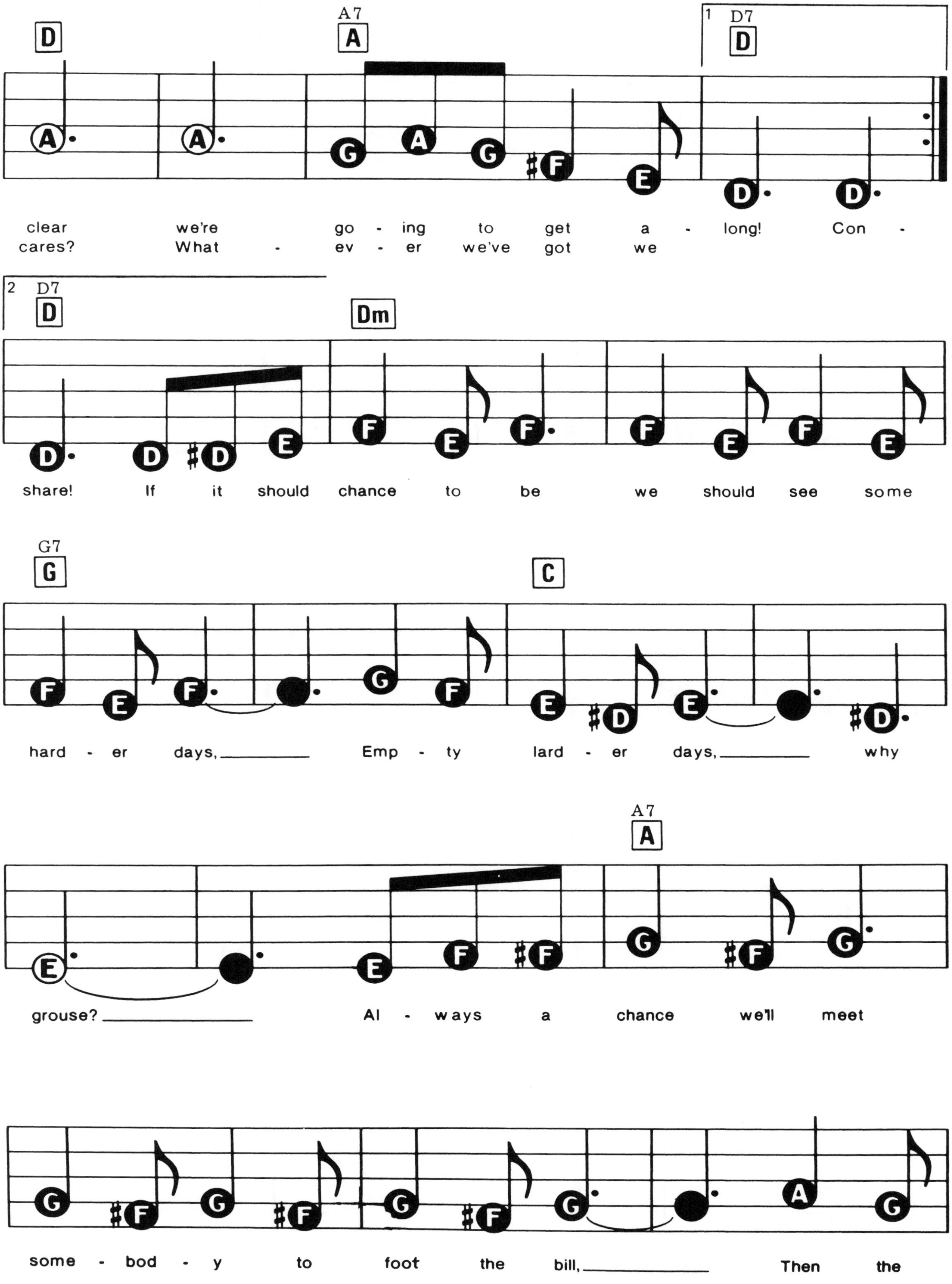

D A7 A 1 D7 D

clear we're go - ing to get a - long! Con -
cares? What - ev - er we've got we

2 D7 D Dm

share! If it should chance to be we should see some

G7 G C

hard - er days, ____ Emp - ty lard - er days, ____ why

A7 A

grouse? ____ Al - ways a chance we'll meet

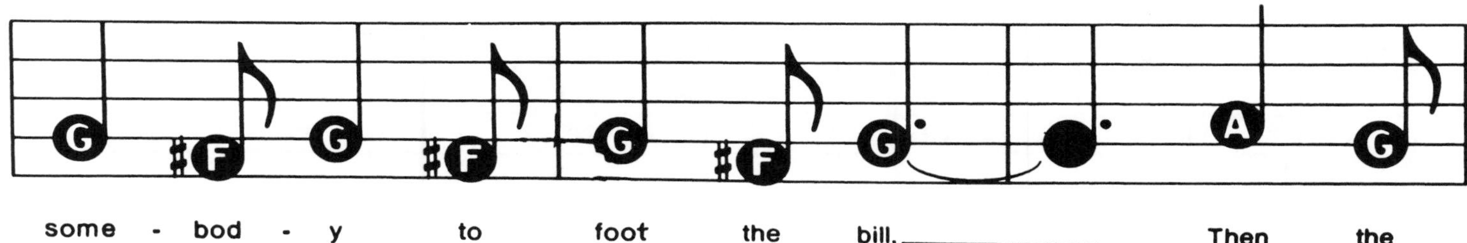

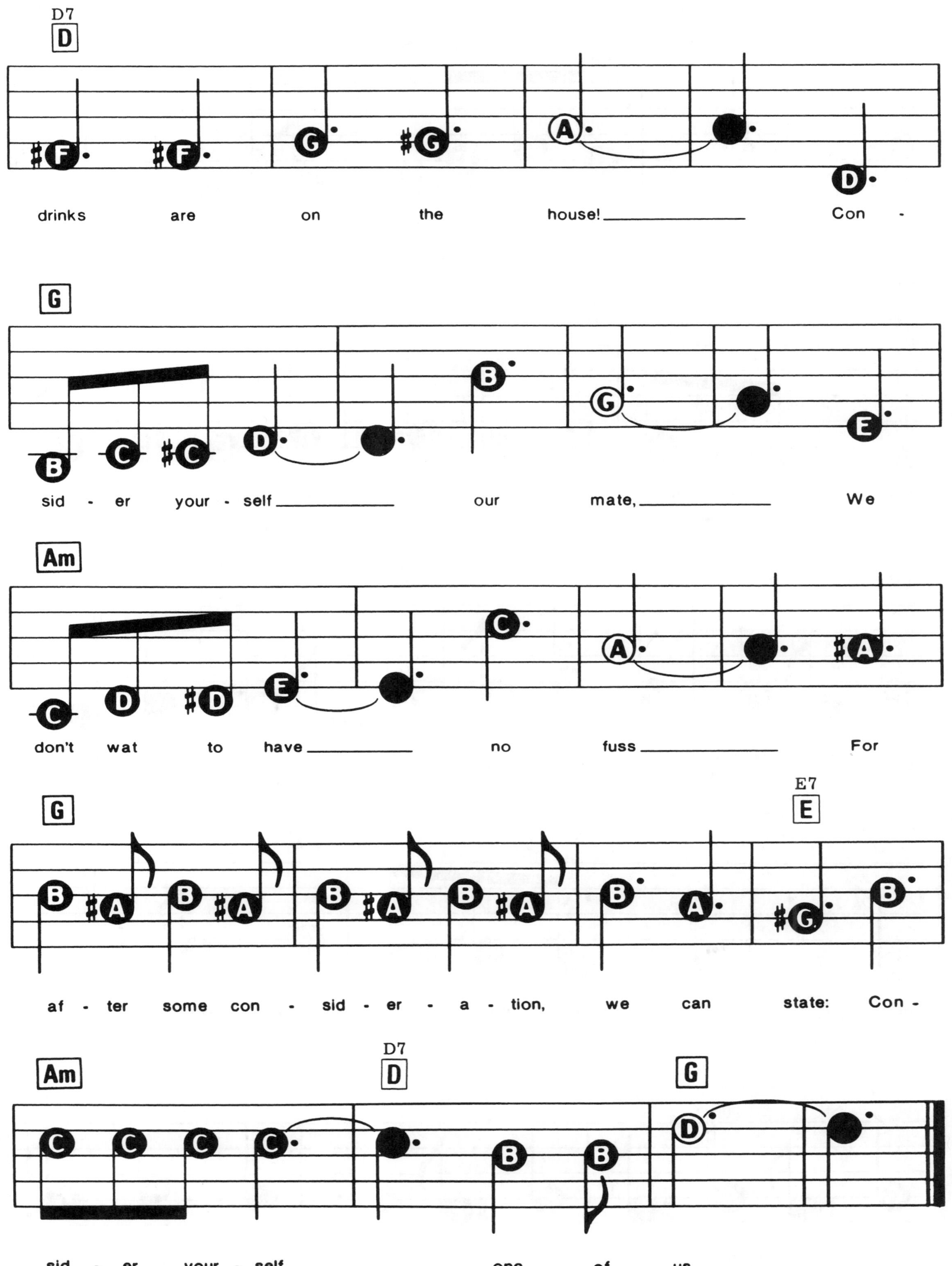
D7
D
drinks are on the house! Con -
G
sid - er your - self our mate, We
Am
don't wat to have no fuss For
G
E7
E
af - ter some con - sid - er - a - tion, we can state: Con -
Am
D7
D
G
sid - er your - self one of us.

Dites-Moi
(Tell Me Why)
from SOUTH PACIFIC

Registration 1
Rhythm: Fox Trot

Lyrics by Oscar Hammerstein II
Music by Richard Rodgers

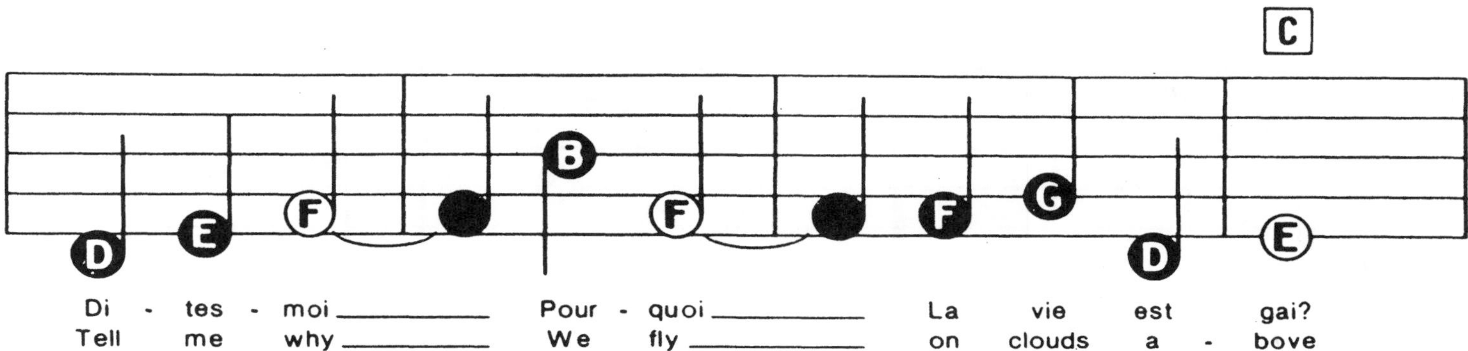

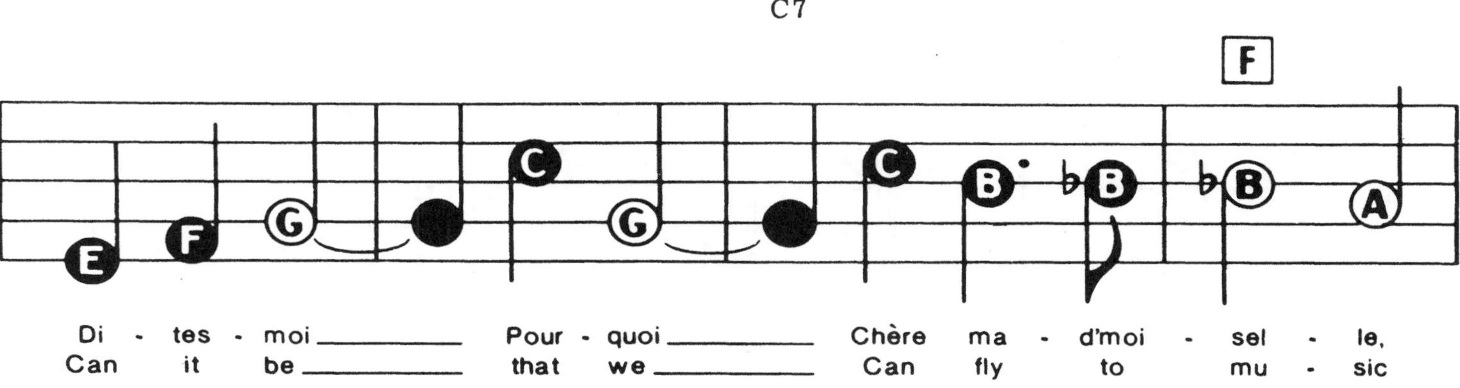

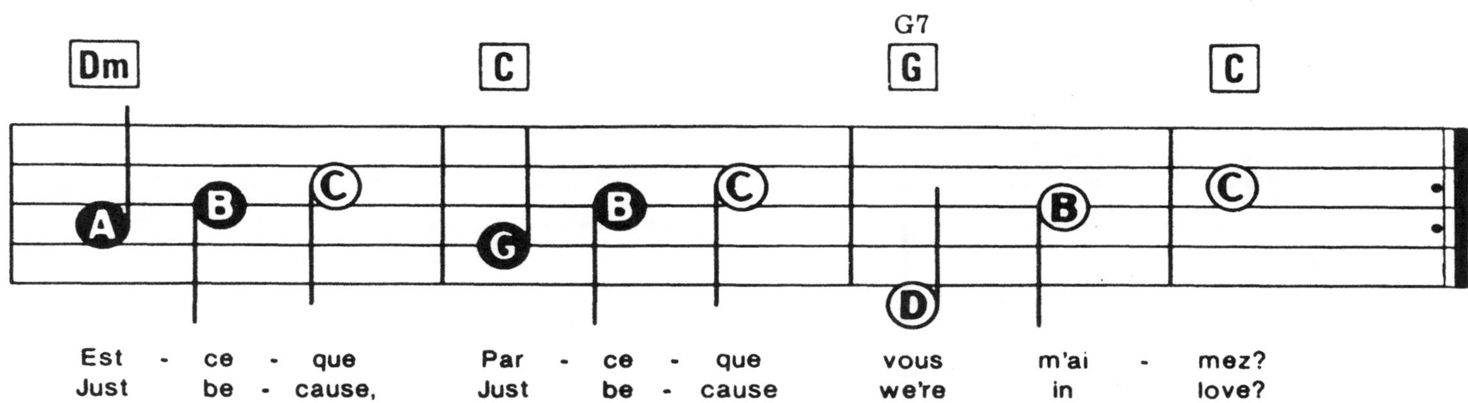

Copyright © 1949 by Richard Rodgers and Oscar Hammerstein II
Copyright Renewed
Williamson Music, a Division of Rodgers & Hammerstein: an Imagem Company, owner of publication and allied rights throughout the world
International Copyright Secured All Rights Reserved

Cruella De Vil

from Walt Disney's 101 DALMATIANS

Registration 9
Rhythm: Swing

Words and Music by
Mel Leven

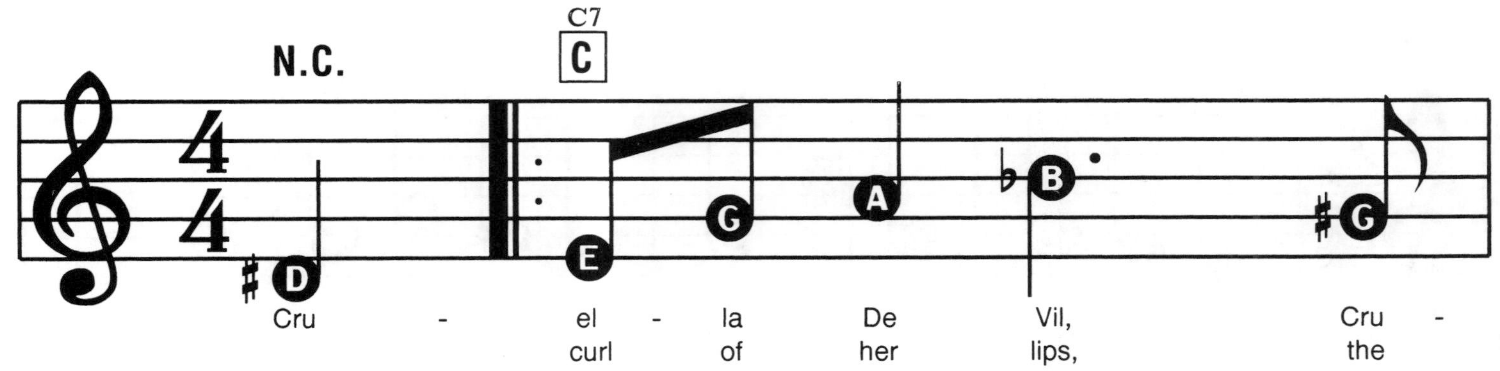

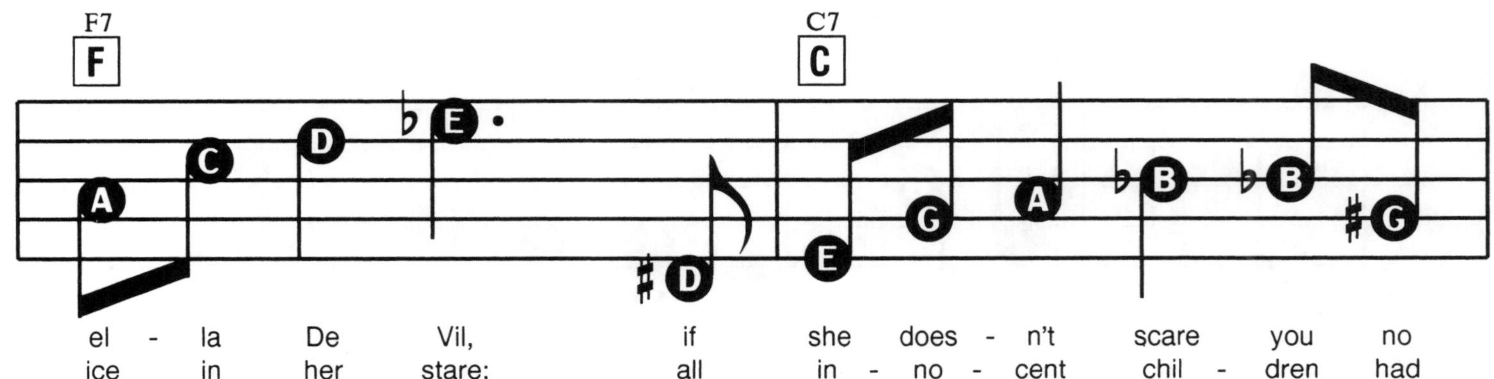

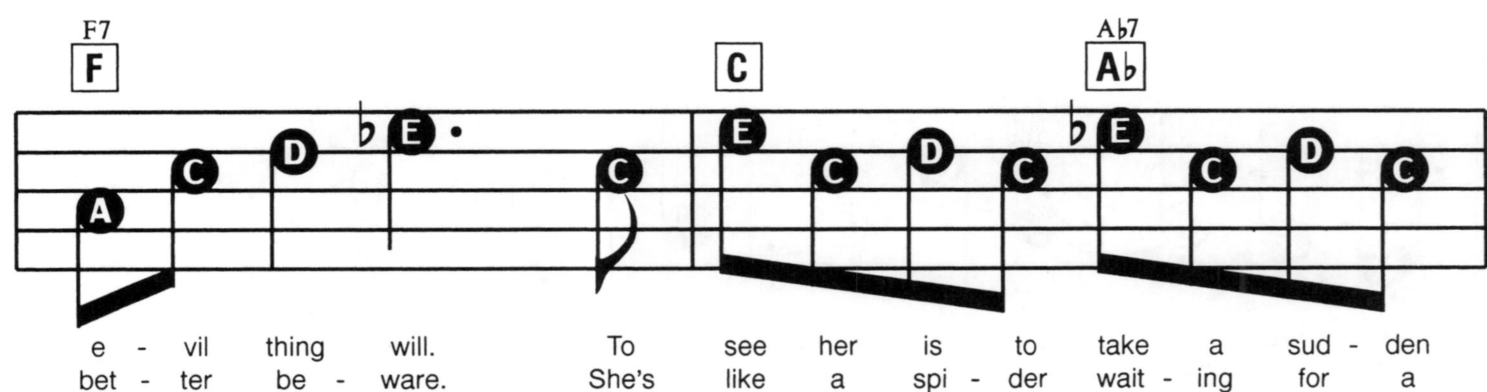

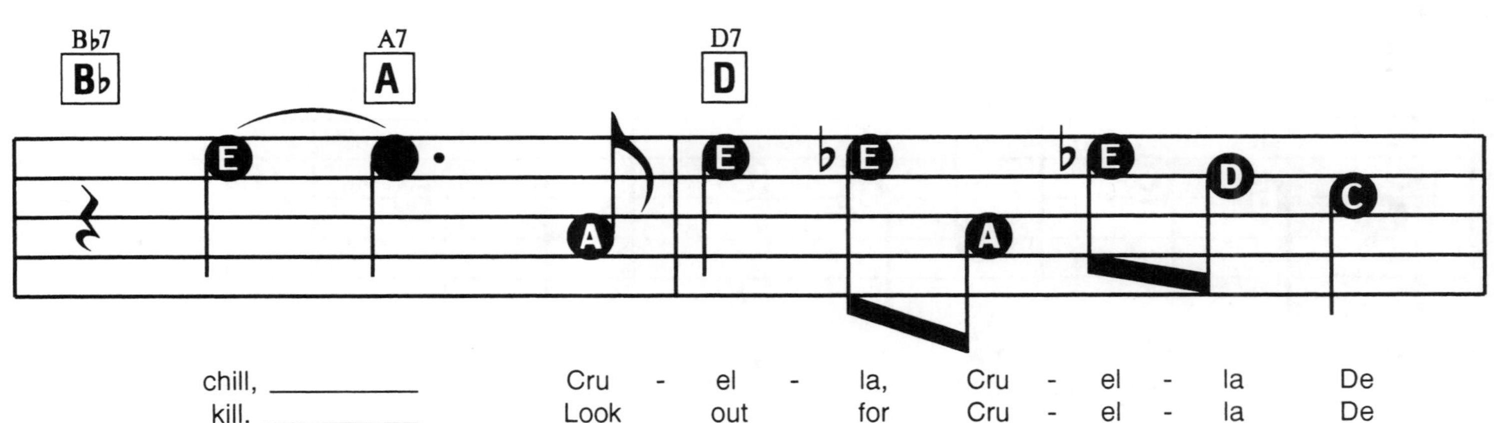

© 1959 Walt Disney Music Company
Copyright Renewed
All Rights Reserved. Used by Permission.

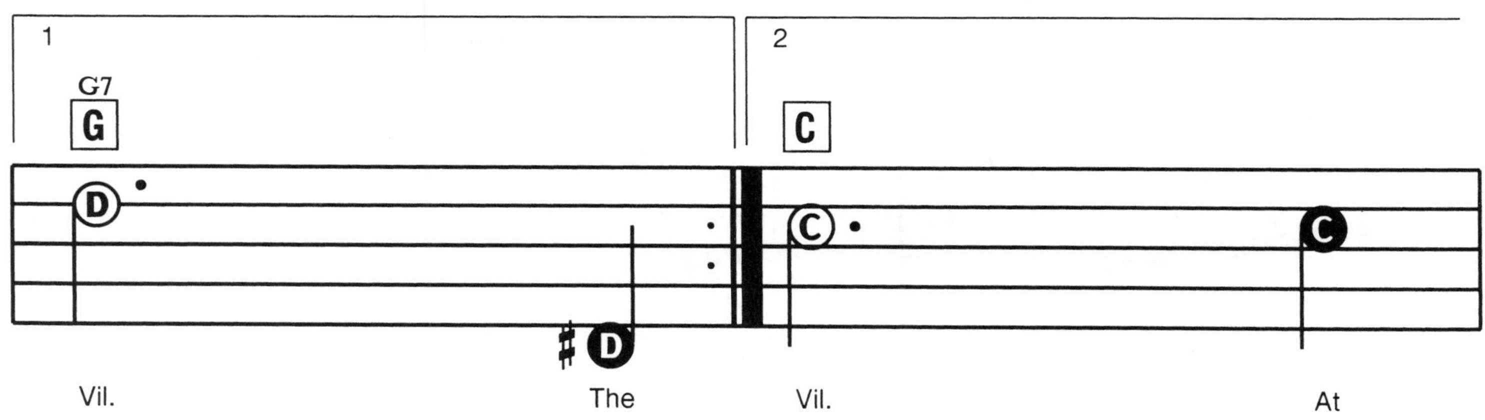
1
G7
G
D
D
Vil.
The
2
C
C
C
Vil.
At

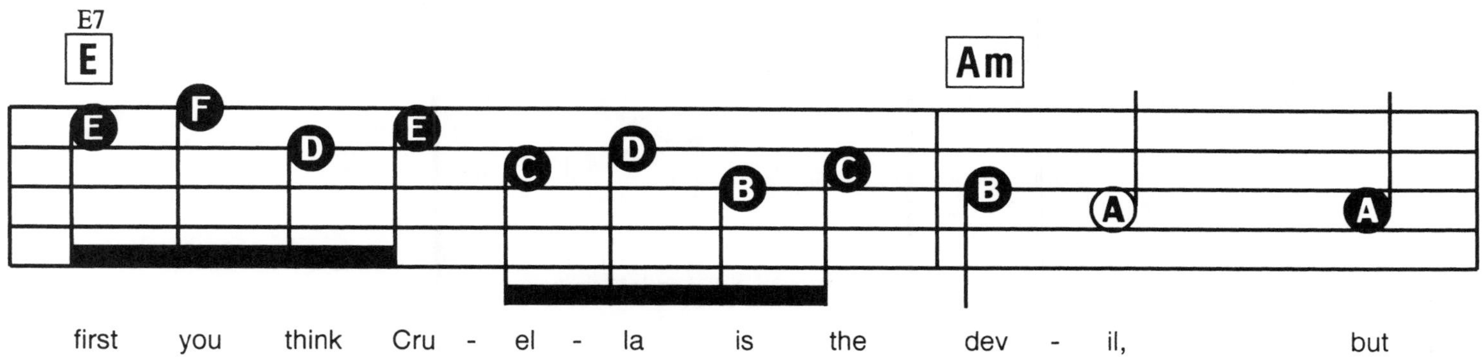
E7
E
Am
E F D E C D B C B A A
first you think Cru - el - la is the dev - il, but

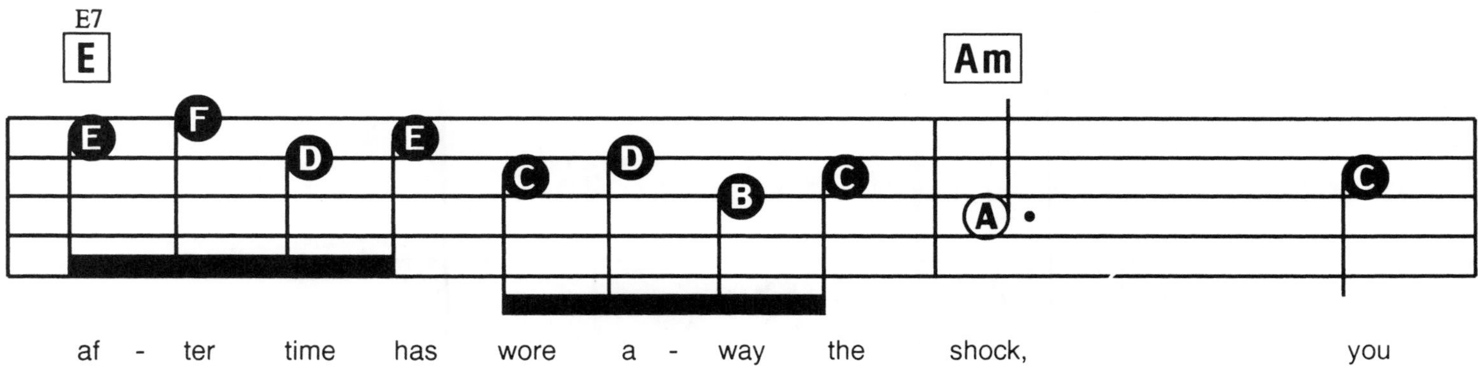
E7
E
Am
E F D E C D B C A C
af - ter time has wore a - way the shock, you

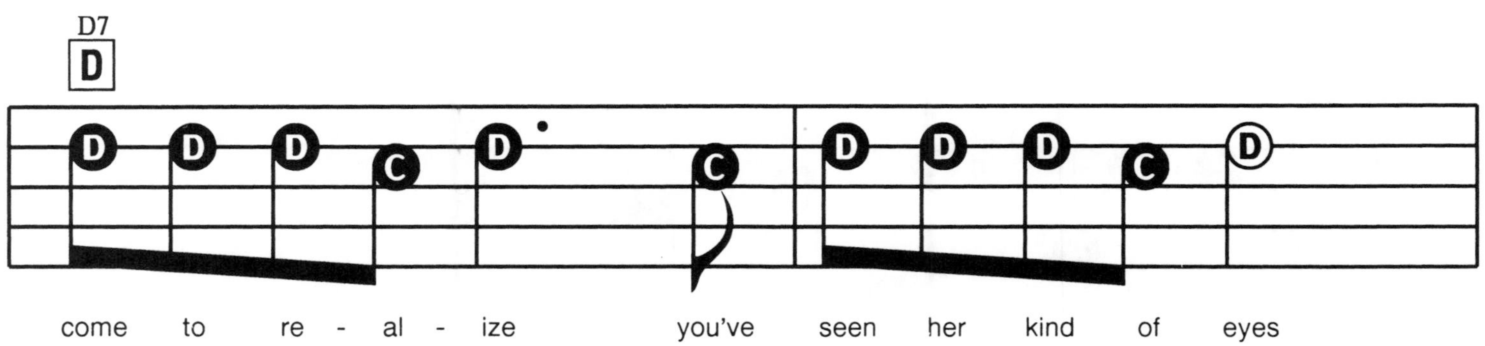
D7
D
D D D C D C D D D C D
come to re - al - ize you've seen her kind of eyes

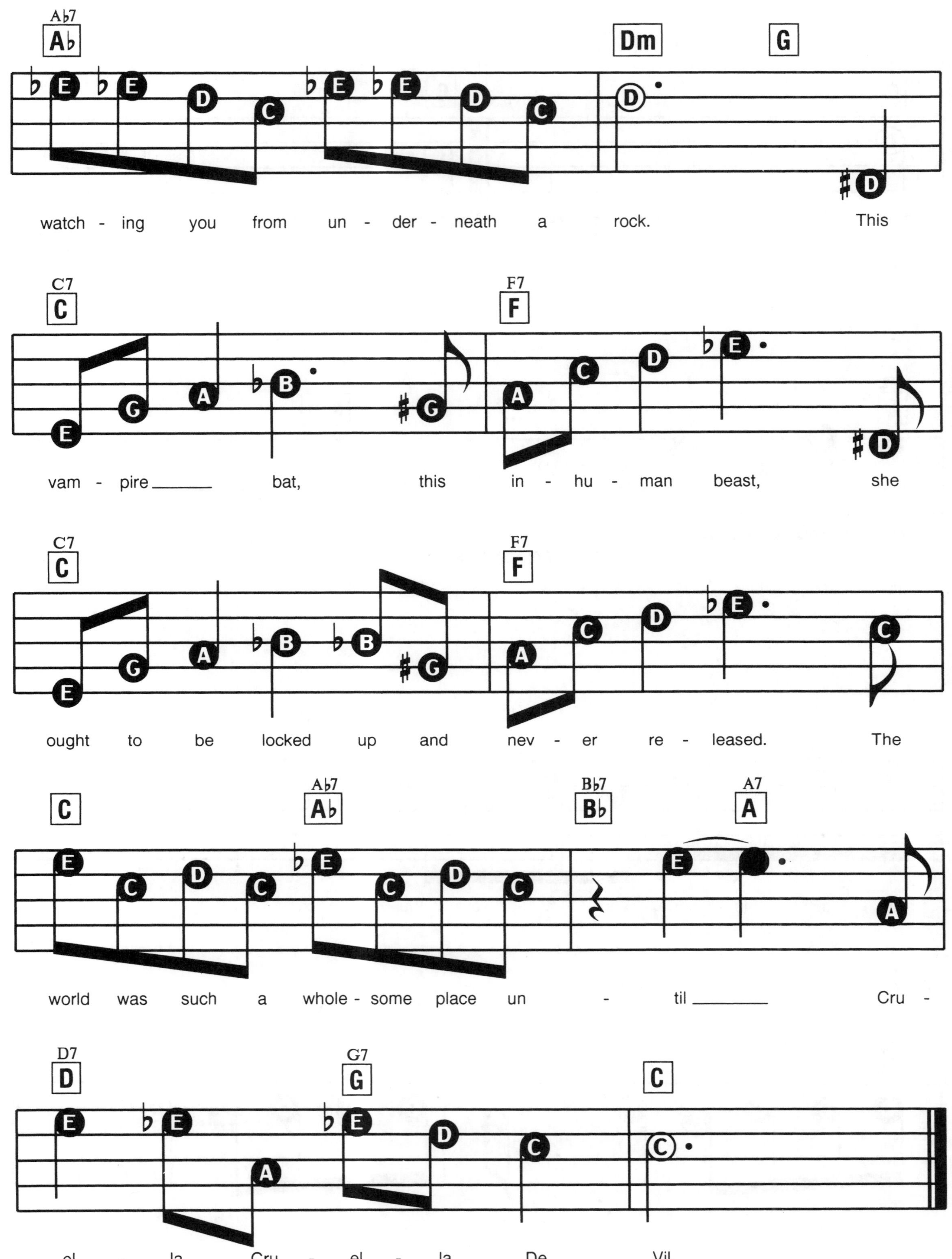
A♭7
A♭
Dm
G
E
E
D
C
E
E
D
C
D
D
watch - ing you from un - der - neath a rock. This
C7
C
F7
F
E
G
A
B
G
A
C
D
E
D
vam - pire bat, this in - hu - man beast, she
C7
C
F7
F
E
G
A
B
B
G
A
C
D
E
C
ought to be locked up and nev - er re - leased. The
C
A♭7
A♭
B♭7
B♭
A7
A
E
C
D
C
E
C
D
C
E
A
world was such a whole - some place un - til Cru -
D7
D
G7
G
C
E
E
A
E
D
C
C
el - la, Cru - el - la De Vil.

Down by the Station

Registration 2
Rhythm: March or Polka

Traditional

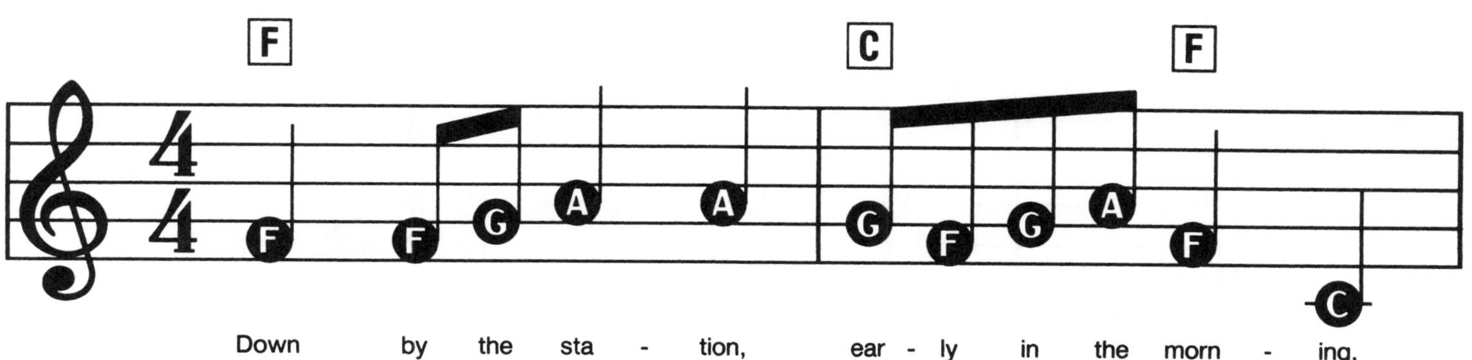

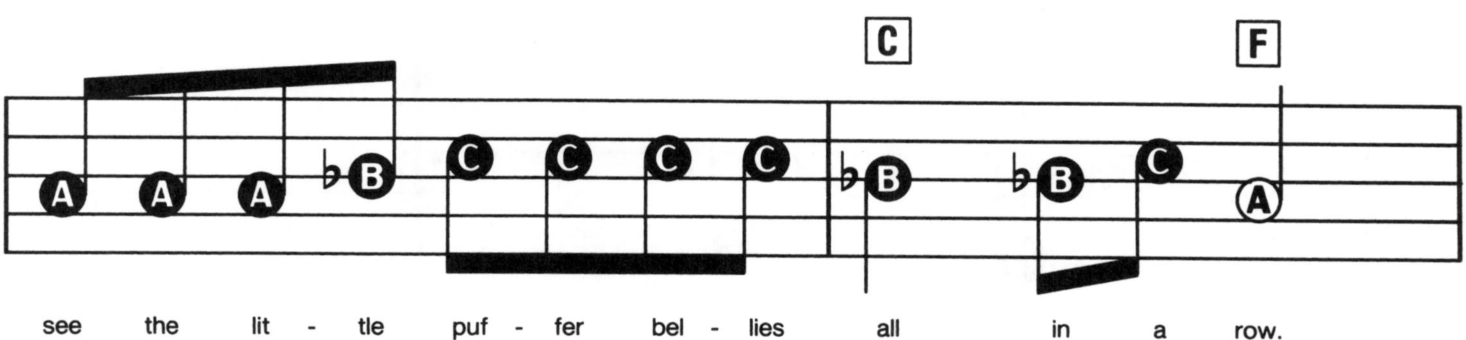

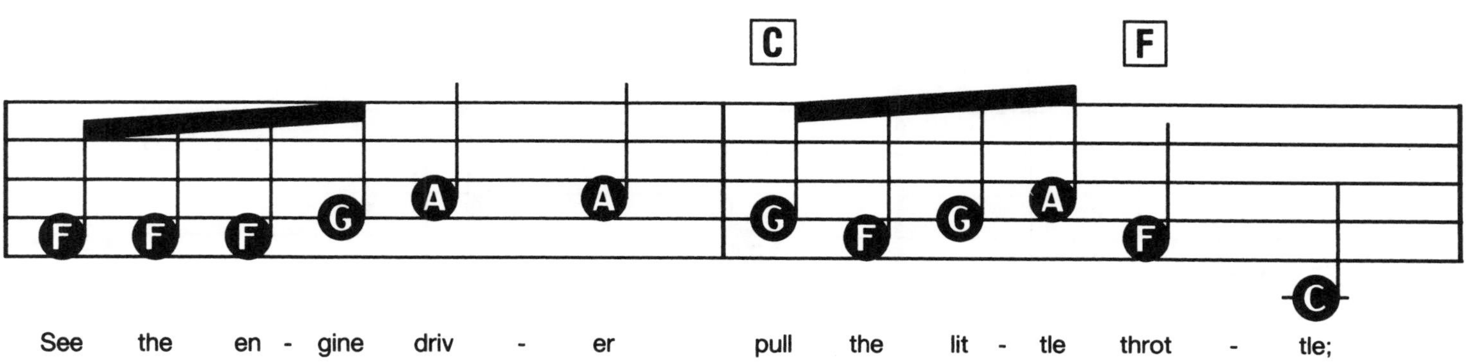

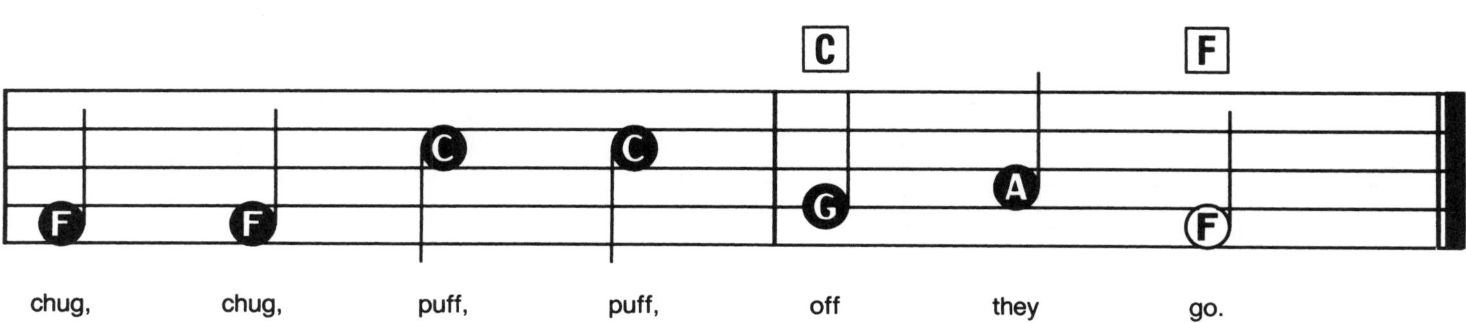

Copyright © 1989 by HAL LEONARD CORPORATION
International Copyright Secured All Rights Reserved

Do-Re-Mi
from THE SOUND OF MUSIC

Registration 4
Rhythm: Fox Trot or March

Lyrics by Oscar Hammerstein II
Music by Richard Rodgers

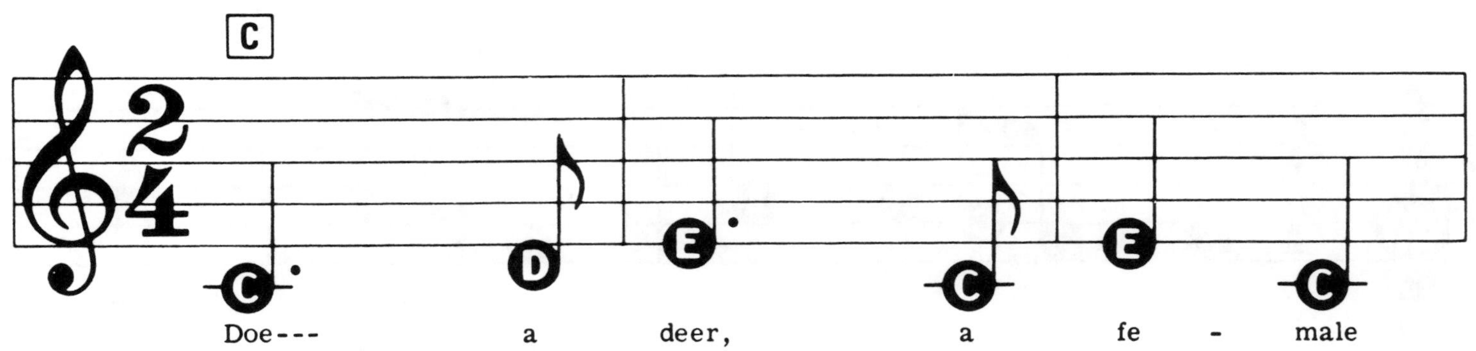

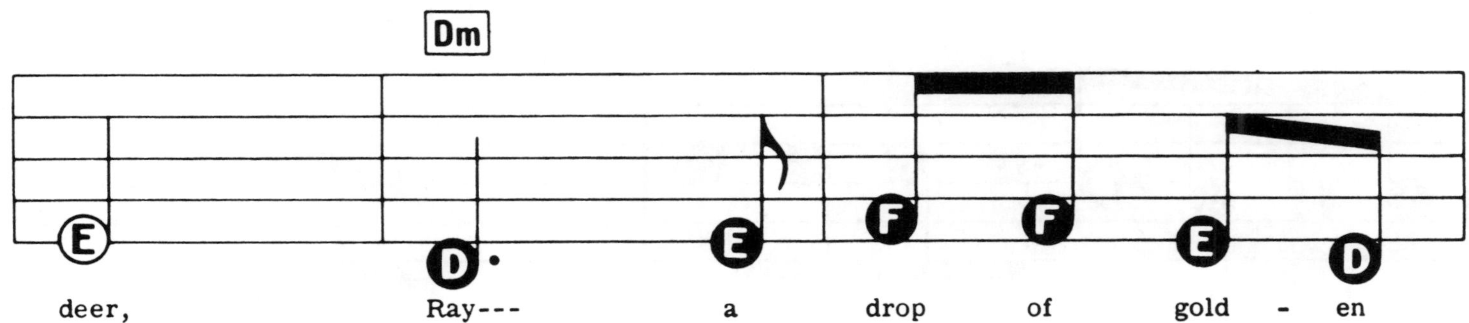

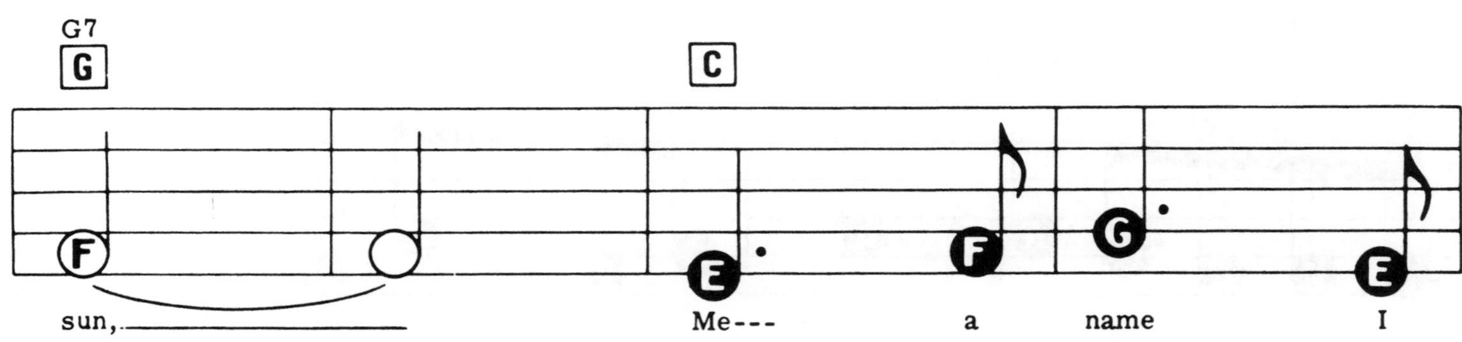

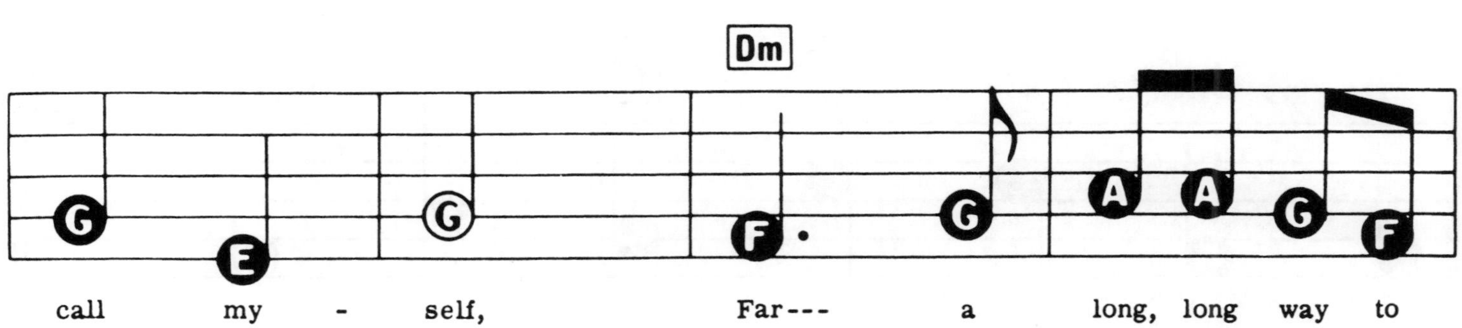

Copyright © 1959 by Richard Rodgers and Oscar Hammerstein II
Copyright Renewed
Williamson Music, a Division of Rodgers & Hammerstein: an Imagem Company, owner of publication and allied rights throughout the world
International Copyright Secured All Rights Reserved

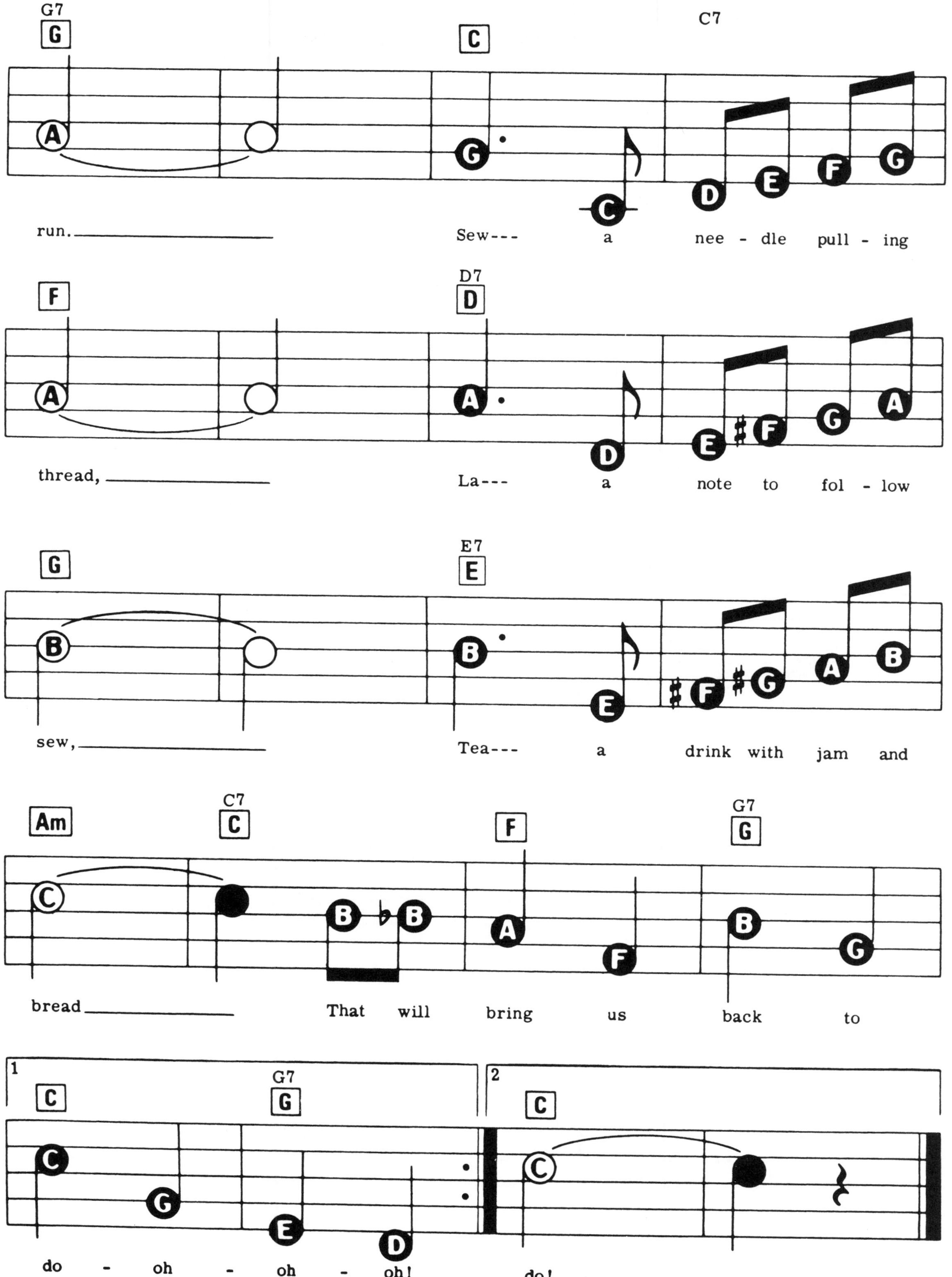
G7
G
C
C7
A
G
C
D
E
F
G
run.
Sew---
a
nee - dle
pull - ing
F
D7
D
A
A
D
E
♯F
G
A
thread,
La---
a
note
to
fol - low
G
E7
E
B
B
E
♯F
♯G
A
B
sew,
Tea---
a
drink
with
jam
and
Am
C7
C
F
G7
G
C
B
♭B
A
F
B
G
bread
That
will
bring
us
back
to
1
C
G7
G
C
G
E
D
2
C
C
do
-
oh
-
oh
-
oh!
do!

A Dream Is a Wish Your Heart Makes

from Walt Disney's CINDERELLA

Registration 3
Rhythm: Waltz

Words and Music by Mack David,
Al Hoffman and Jerry Livingston

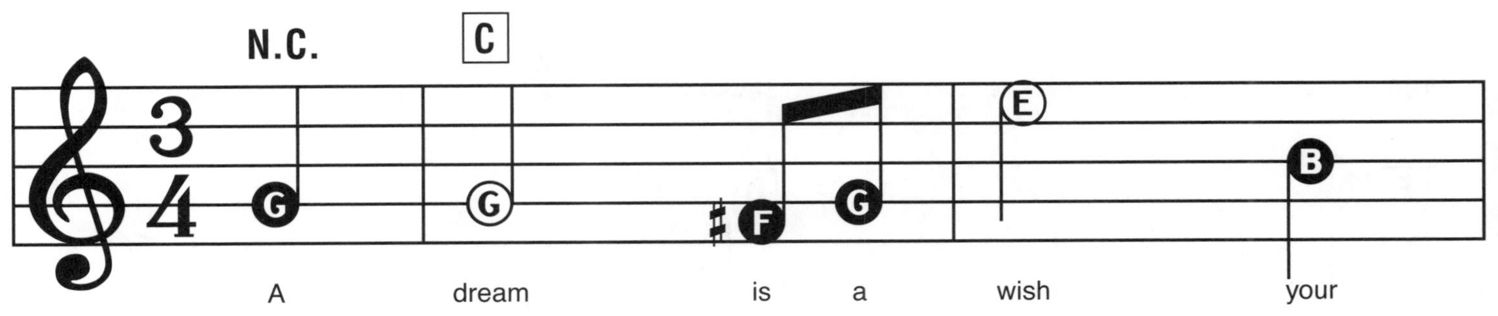

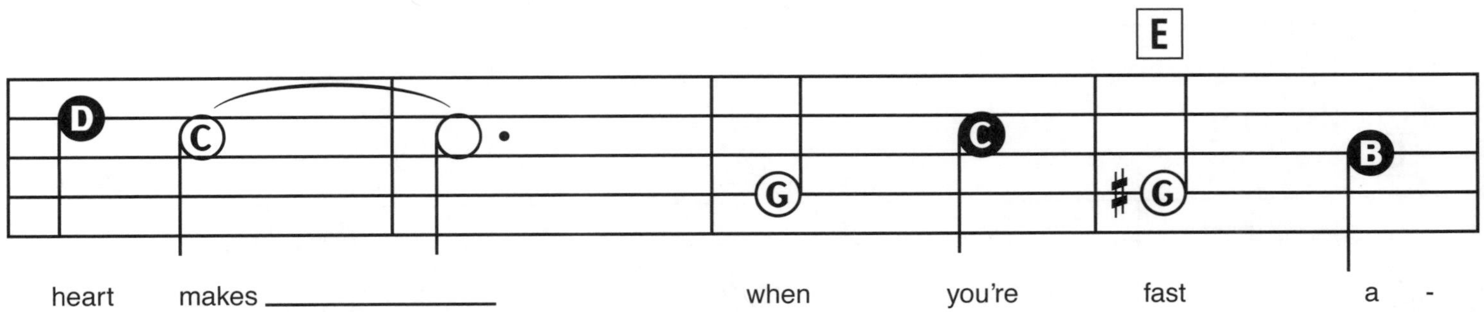

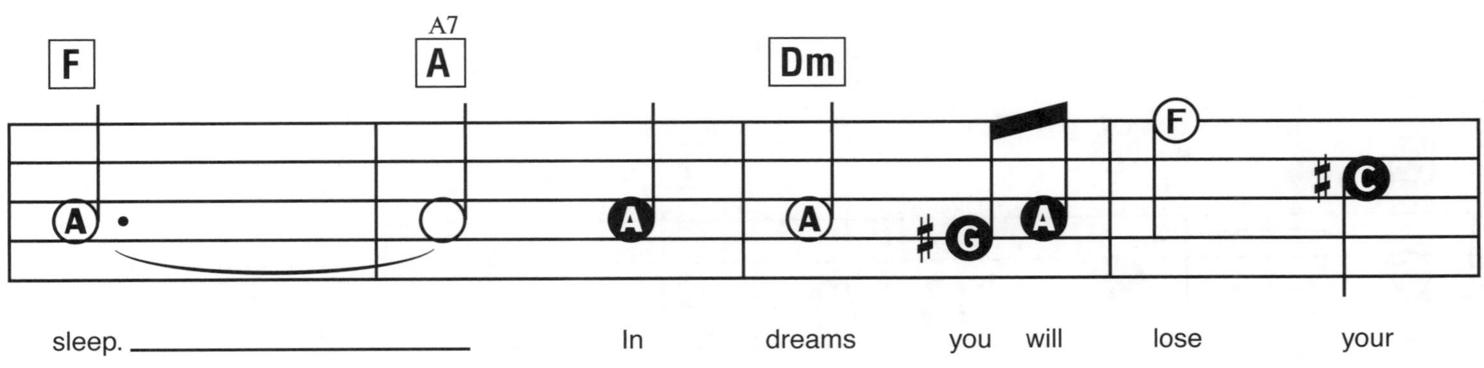

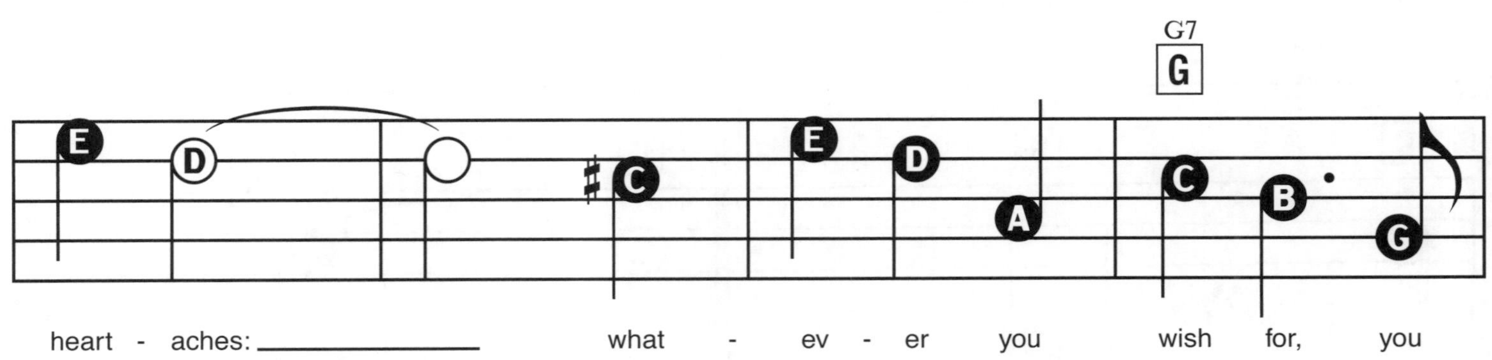

© 1948 Walt Disney Music Company
Copyright Renewed
All Rights Reserved. Used by Permission.

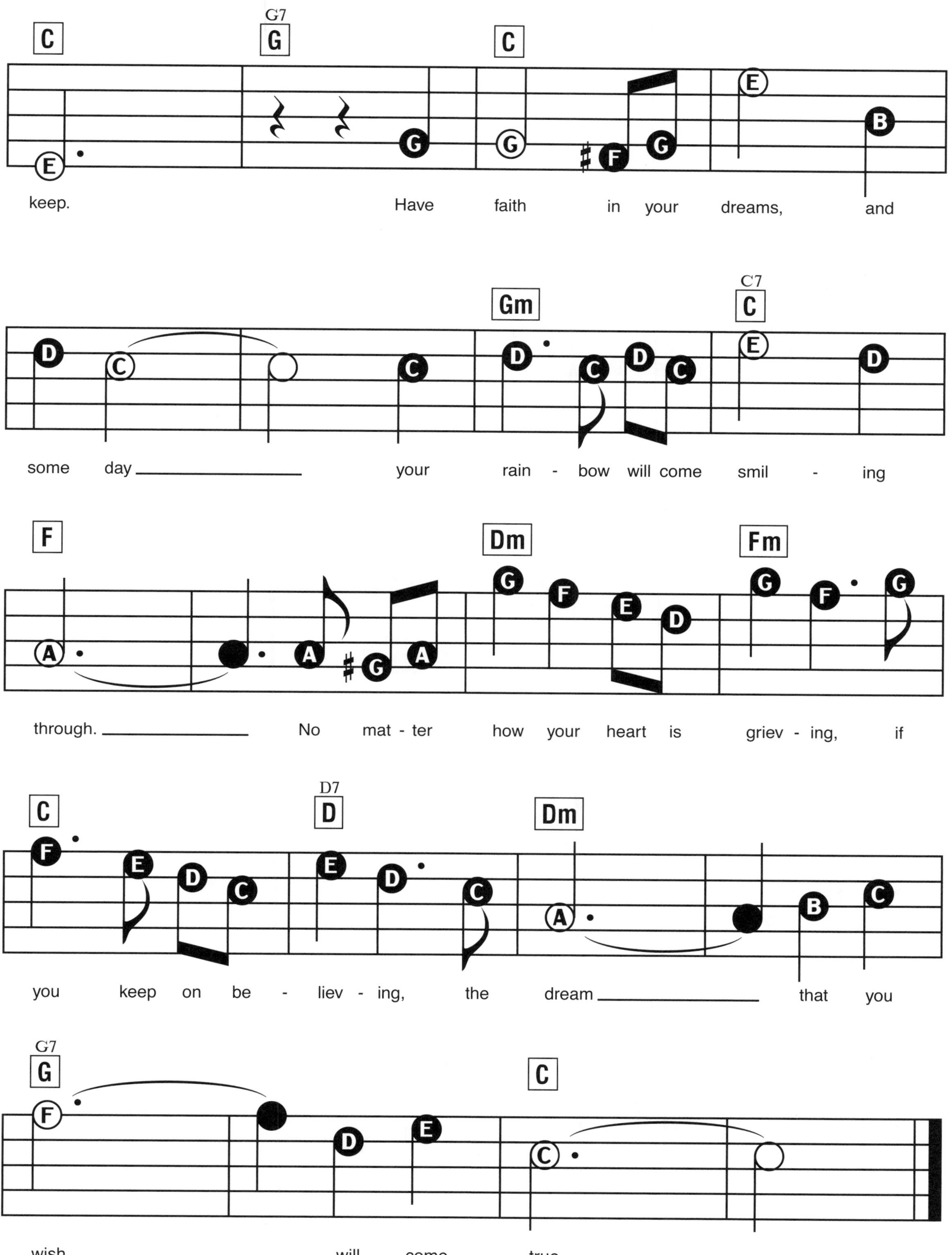
C G7 G C
keep. Have faith in your dreams, and
Gm C7 C
some day ___ your rain - bow will come smil - ing
F Dm Fm
through. ___ No mat - ter how your heart is griev - ing, if
C D7 D Dm
you keep on be - liev - ing, the dream ___ that you
G7 G C
wish ___ will come true. ___

Ev'rybody Wants to Be a Cat

from Walt Disney's THE ARISTOCATS

Registration 10
Rhythm: Fox Trot

Words by Floyd Huddleston
Music by Al Rinker

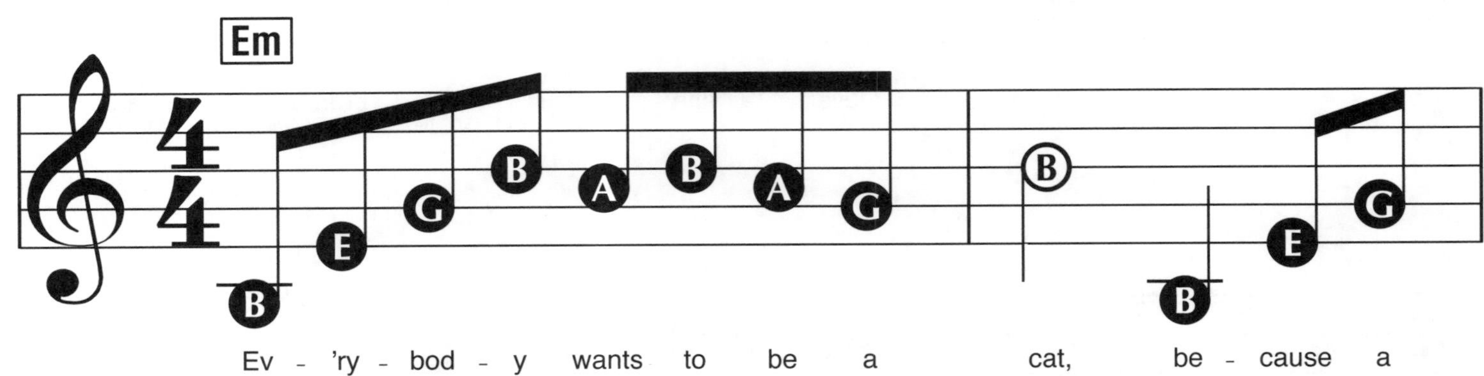

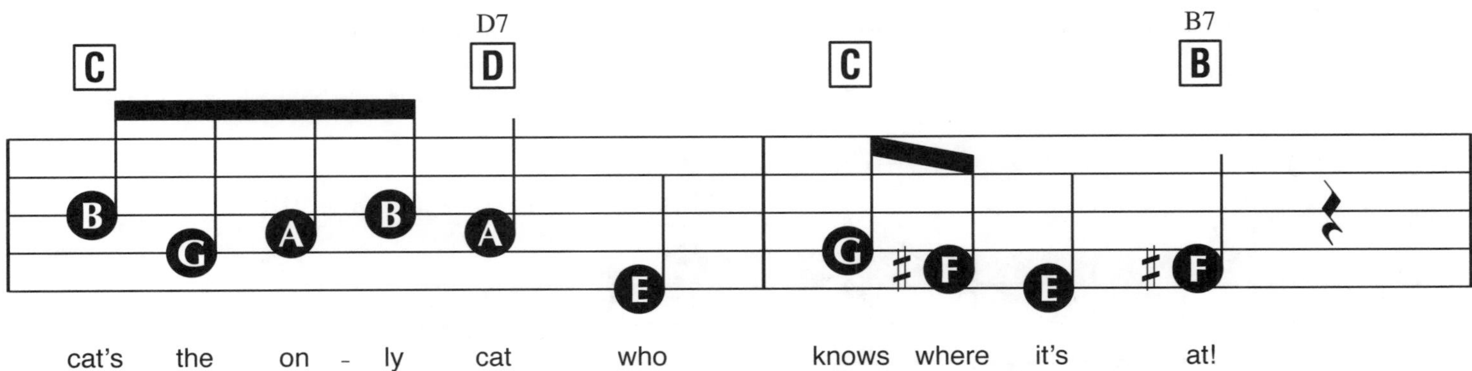

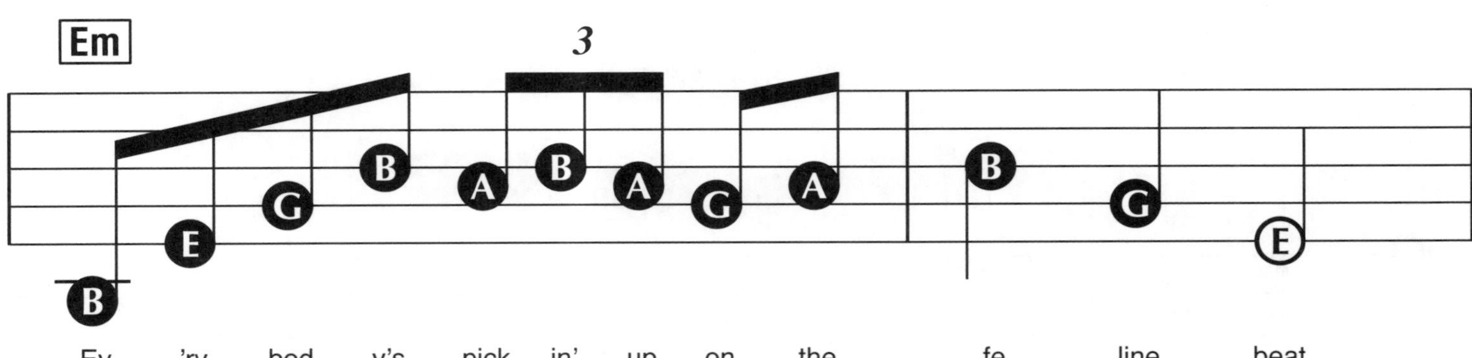

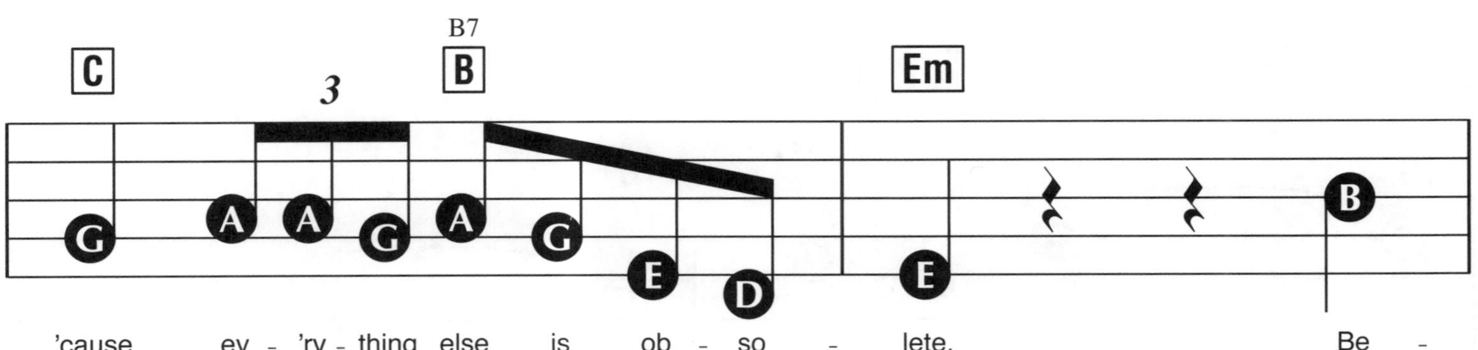

© 1968 Walt Disney Music Company
Copyright Renewed
All Rights Reserved Used by Permission

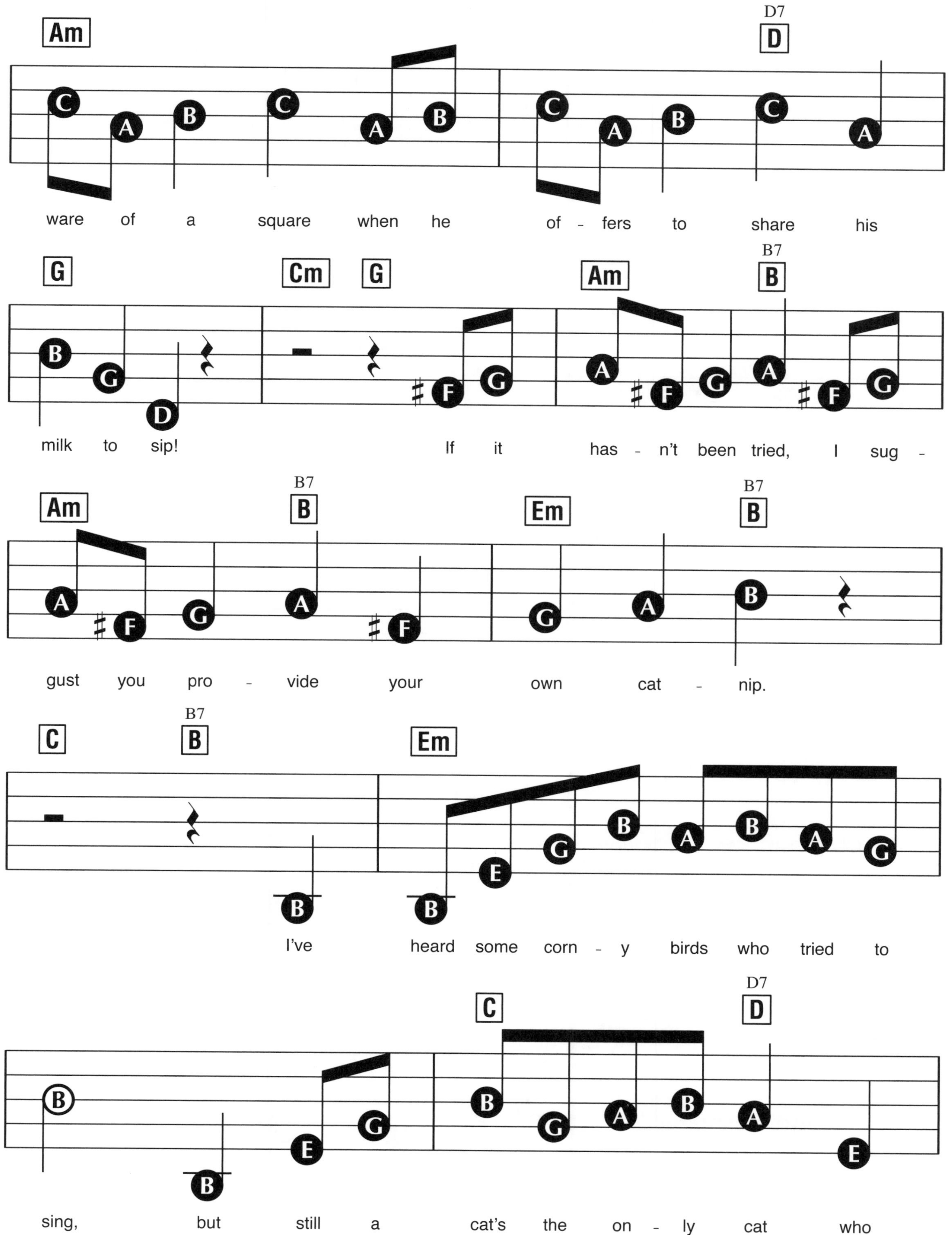
Am
C A B C A B
D7 D
C A B C A
ware of a square when he of - fers to share his
G
B G D
Cm G
F G
Am
A F G
B7 B
A F G
milk to sip! If it has - n't been tried, I sug -
Am
A F G
B7 B
A F
Em
G A
B7 B
B
gust you pro - vide your own cat - nip.
C
B7 B
B
Em
B E G B A B A G
I've heard some corn - y birds who tried to
B B E G
C
B G A B
D7 D
A E
sing, but still a cat's the on - ly cat who

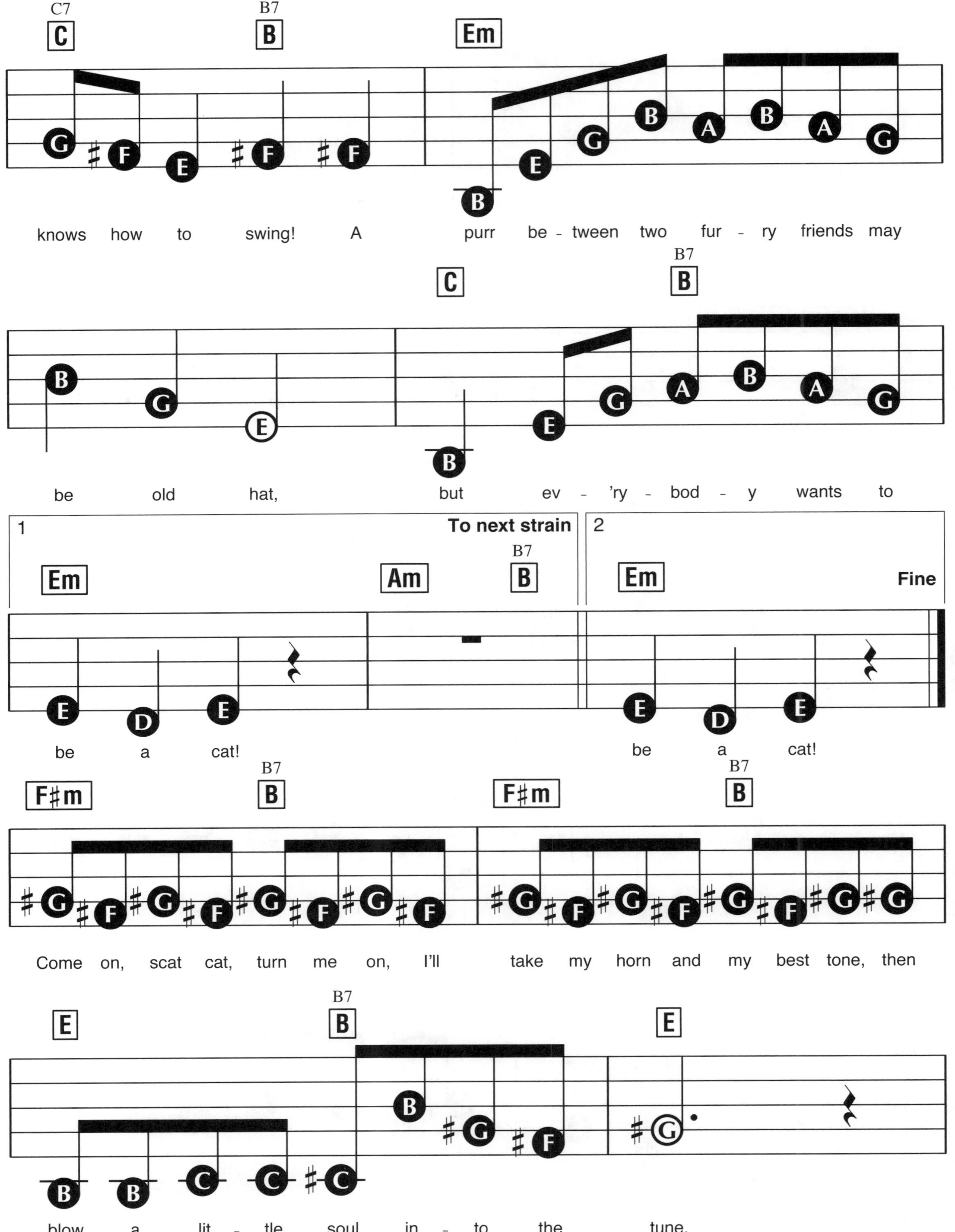
C7 C
B7 B
Em
knows how to swing! A purr be - tween two fur - ry friends may
C
B7 B
be old hat, but ev - 'ry - bod - y wants to
1
To next strain
Em
Am
B7 B
2
Em
Fine
be a cat!
be a cat!
F♯m
B7 B
F♯m
B7 B
Come on, scat cat, turn me on, I'll take my horn and my best tone, then
E
B7 B
E
blow a lit - tle soul in - to the tune.

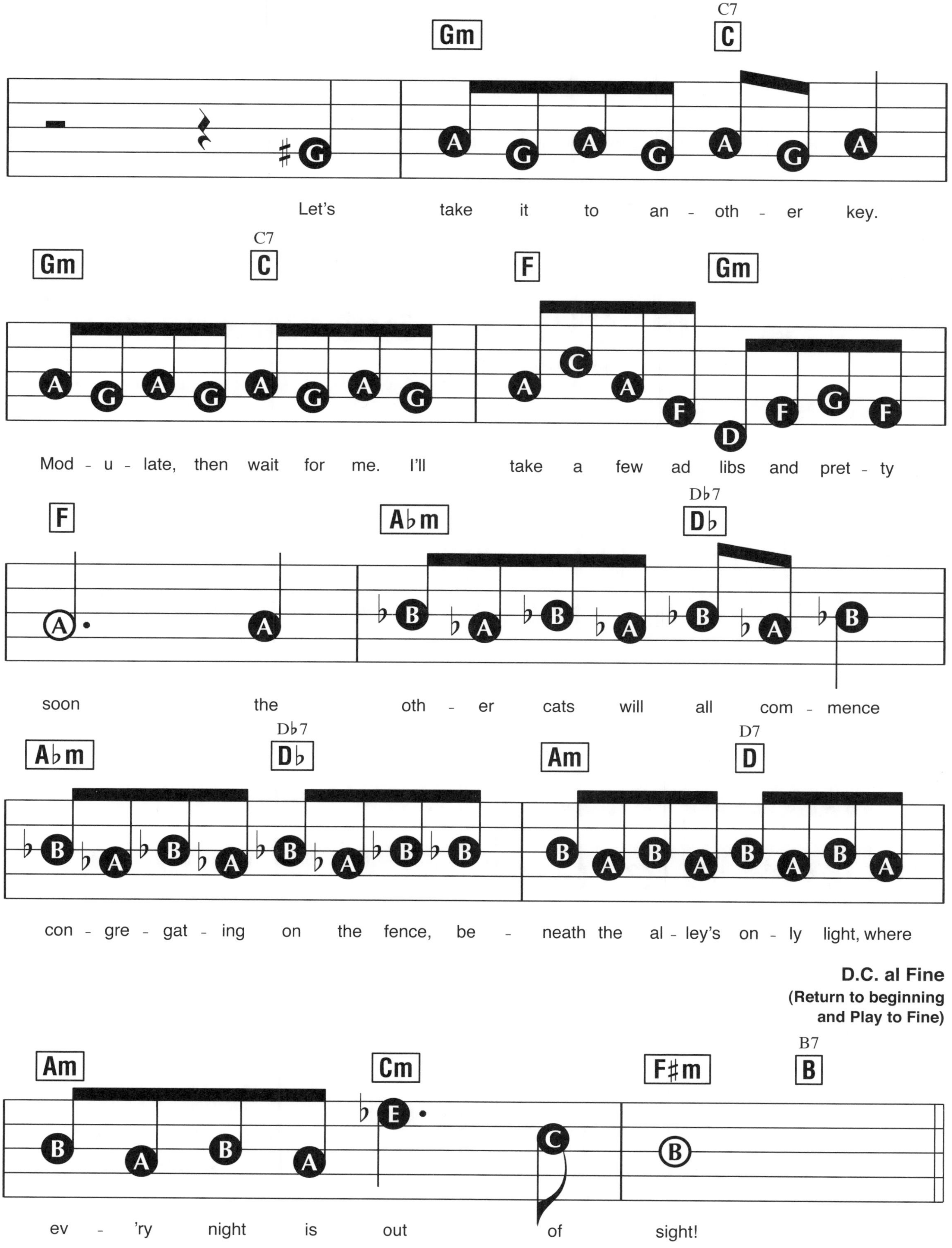

Gm C7 C

Let's take it to an - oth - er key.

Gm C7 C F Gm

Mod - u - late, then wait for me. I'll take a few ad libs and pret - ty

F A♭m D♭7 D♭

soon the oth - er cats will all com - mence

A♭m D♭7 D♭ Am D7 D

con - gre - gat - ing on the fence, be - neath the al - ley's on - ly light, where

D.C. al Fine
(Return to beginning and Play to Fine)

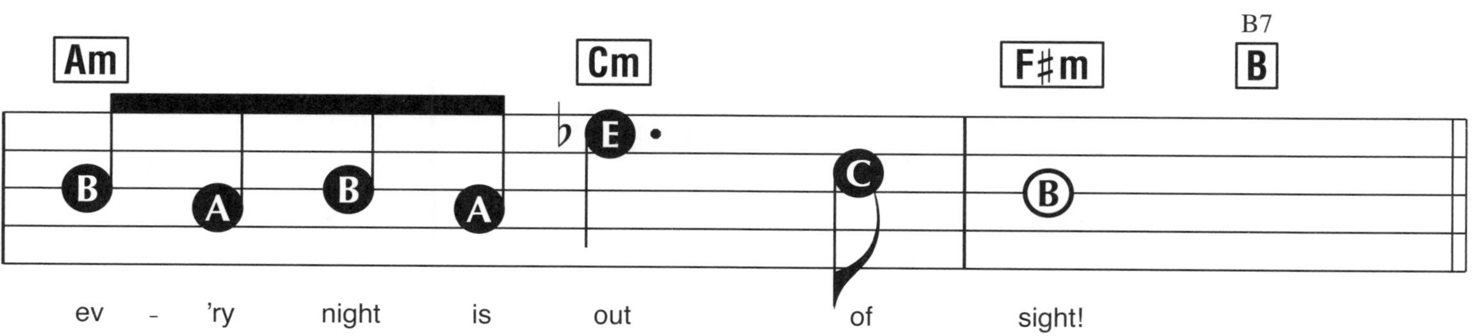

Food, Glorious Food

Registration 4
Rhythm: March

Words and Music by
Lionel Bart

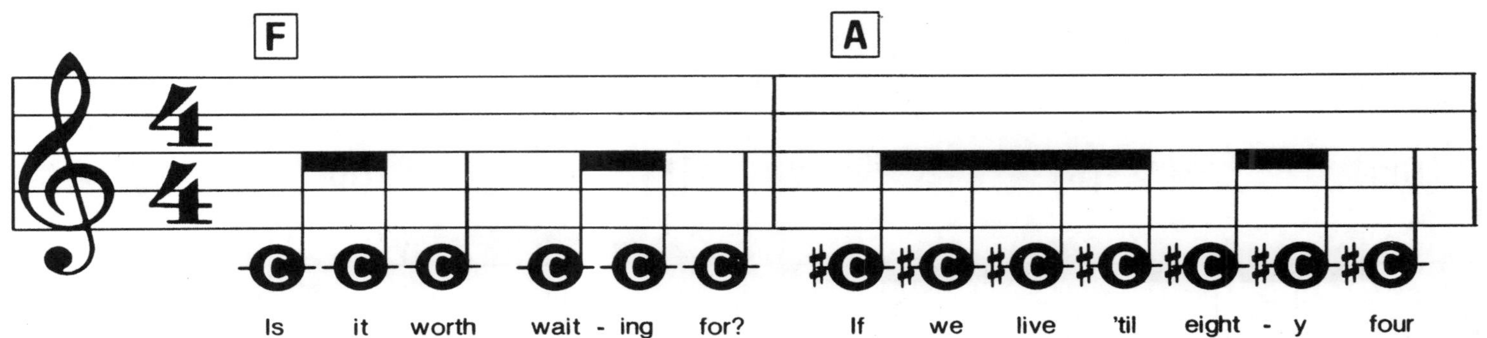

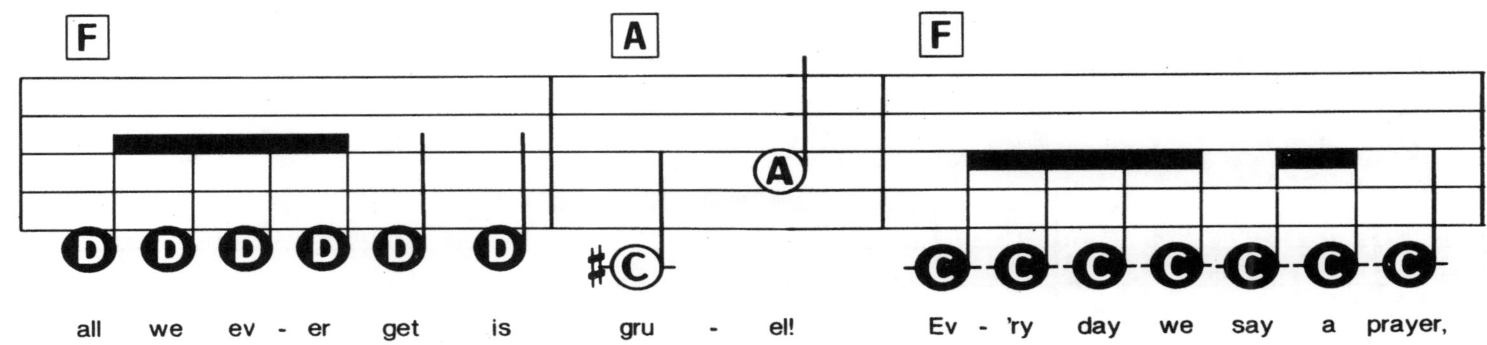

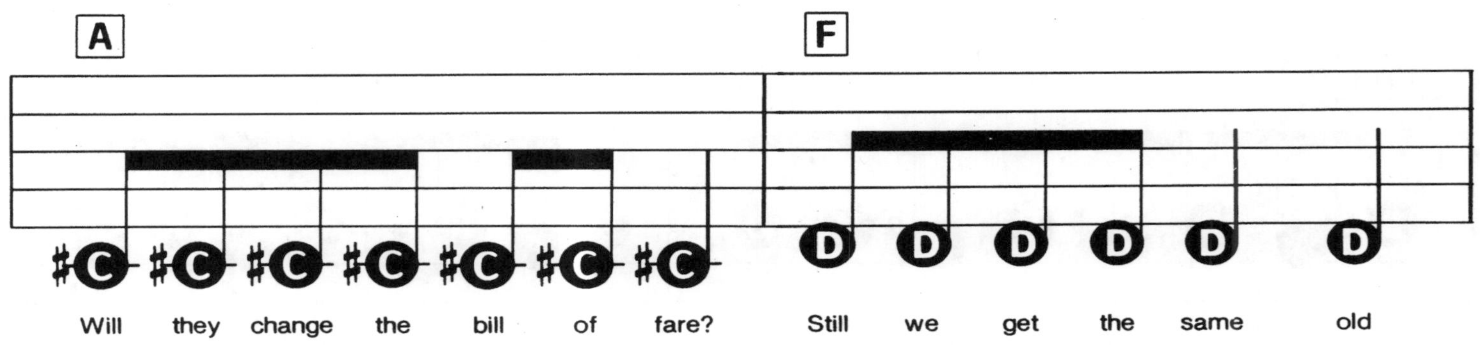

© Copyright 1960 (Renewed) Lakeview Music Co. Ltd., London, England
TRO - Hollis Music, Inc., New York, controls all publication rights for the U.S.A. and Canada
International Copyright Secured
All Rights Reserved Including Public Performance For Profit
Used by Permission

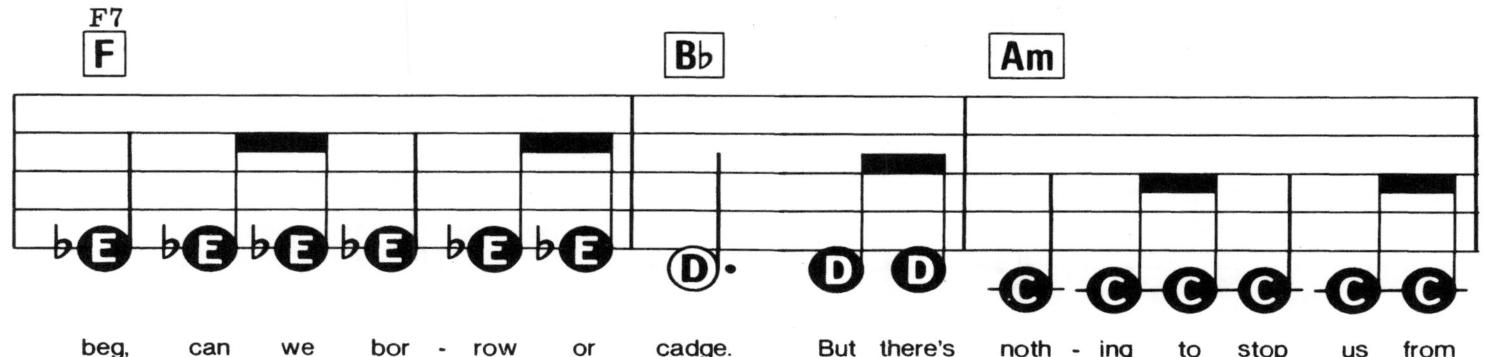
F7
F
B♭
Am
E E E E E E
D D D
C C C C C C
beg, can we bor - row or cadge. But there's noth - ing to stop us from

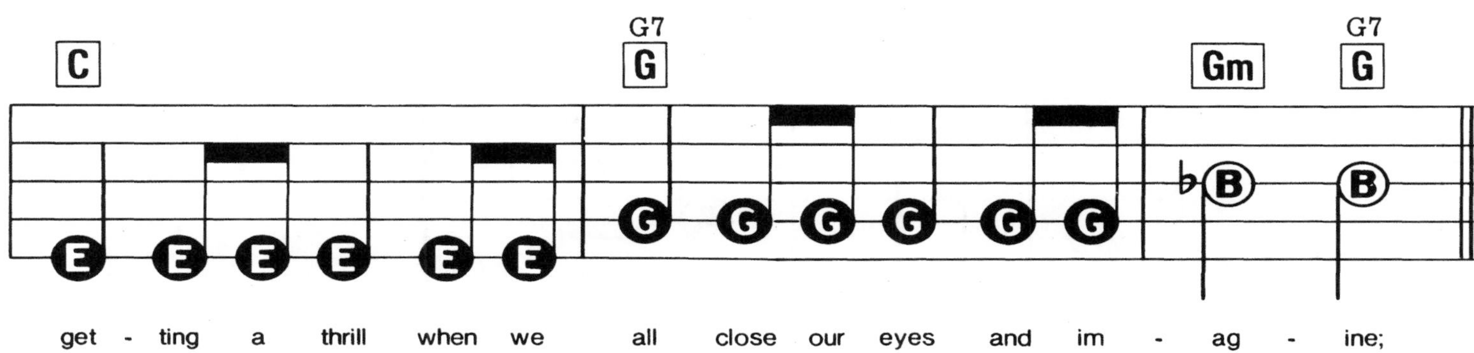
C
G7
G
Gm
G7
G
E E E E E E
G G G G G G
B B
get - ting a thrill when we all close our eyes and im - ag - ine;

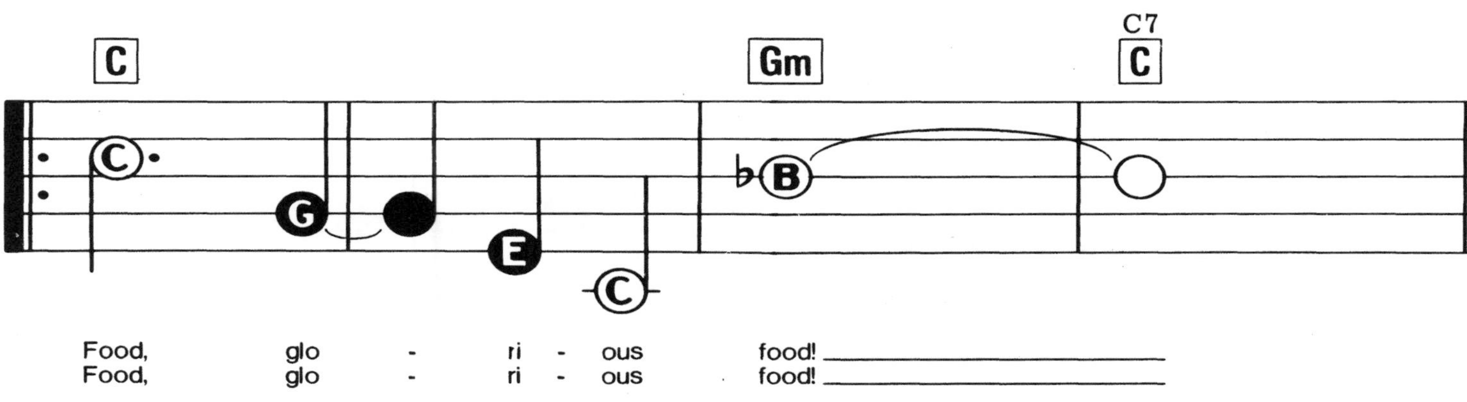
C
Gm
C7
C
C G E C B
Food, glo - ri - ous food!
Food, glo - ri - ous food!

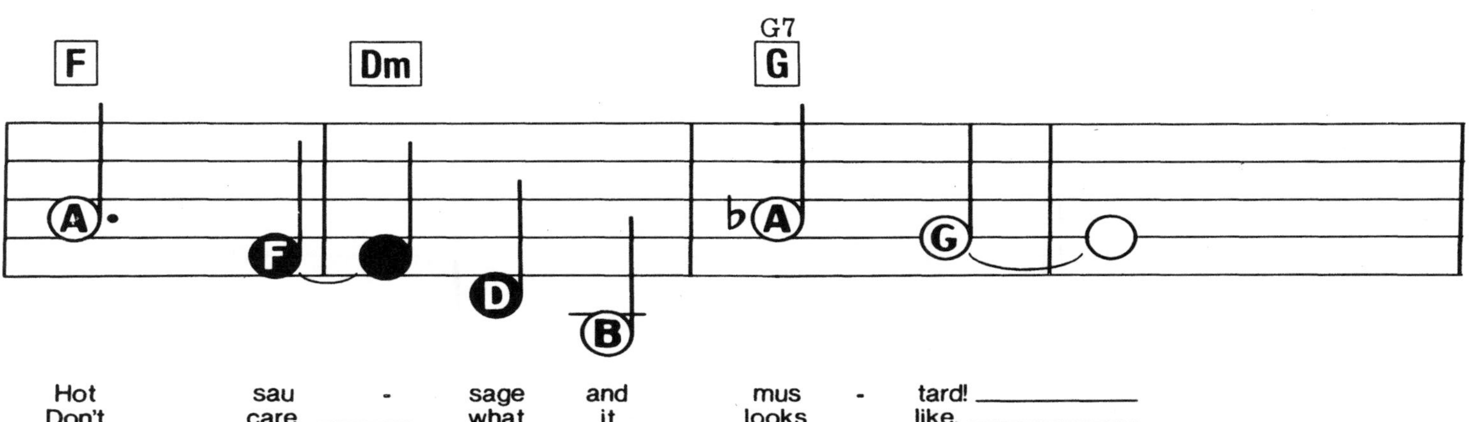
F
Dm
G7
G
A F D B A G
Hot sau - sage and mus - tard!
Don't care what it looks like,

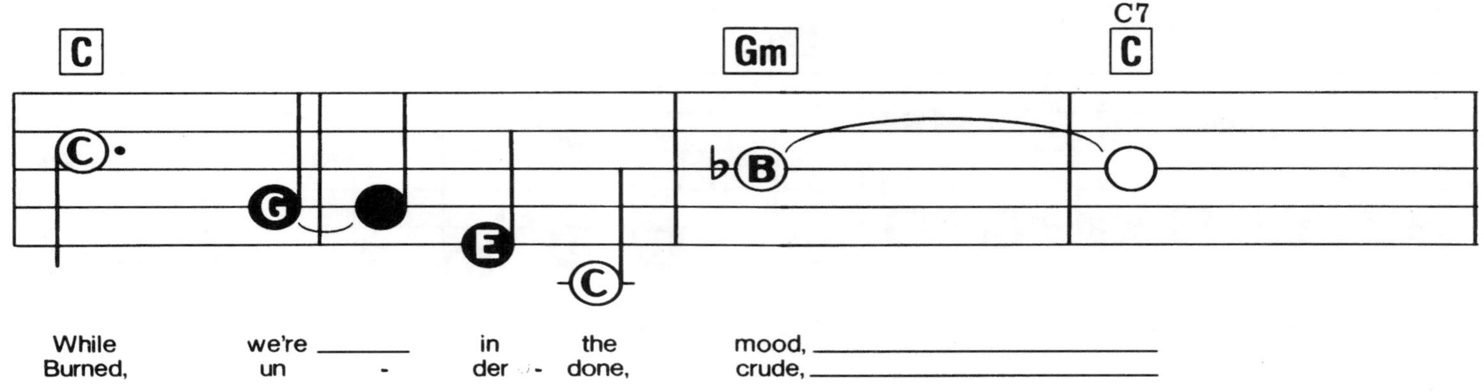
C
Gm
C7
C
C
G
E
C
B
While we're in the mood,
Burned, un - der - done, crude,

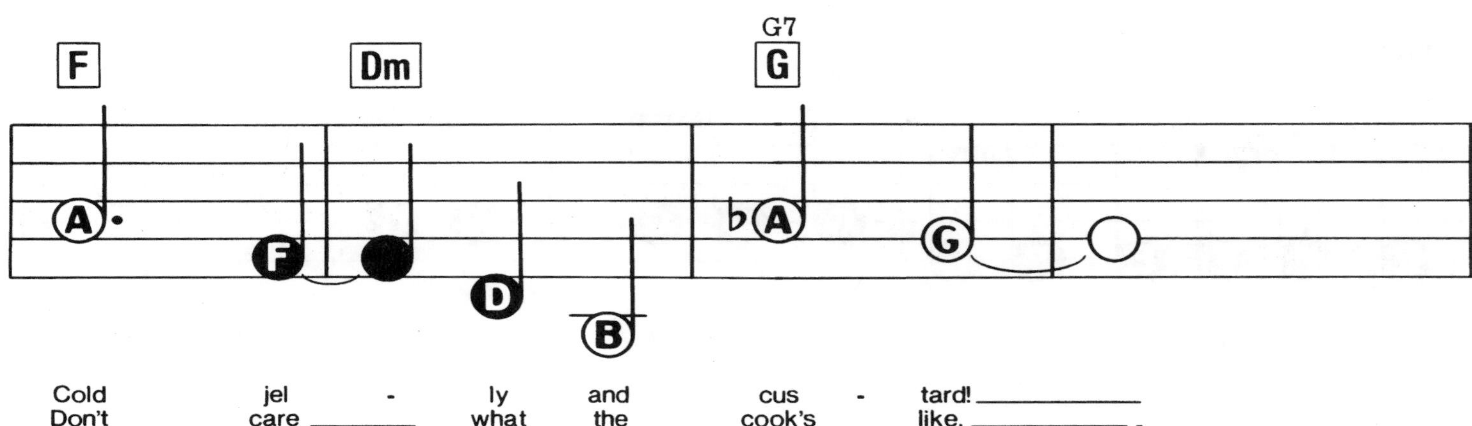
F
Dm
G7
G
A
F
D
B
A
G
Cold jel - ly and cus - tard!
Don't care what the cook's like.

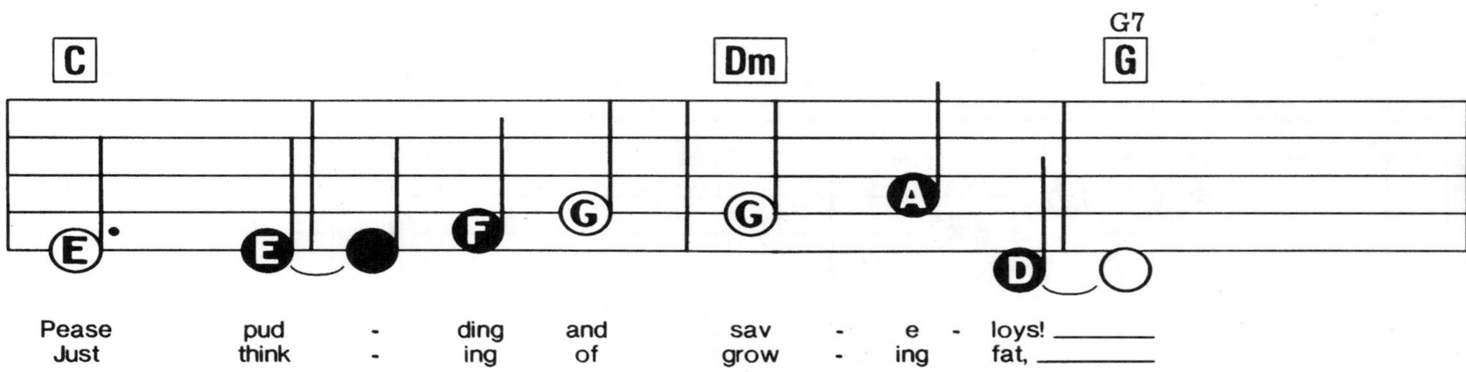
C
Dm
G7
G
E
E
F
G
G
A
D
Pease pud - ding and sav - e - loys!
Just think - ing of grow - ing fat,

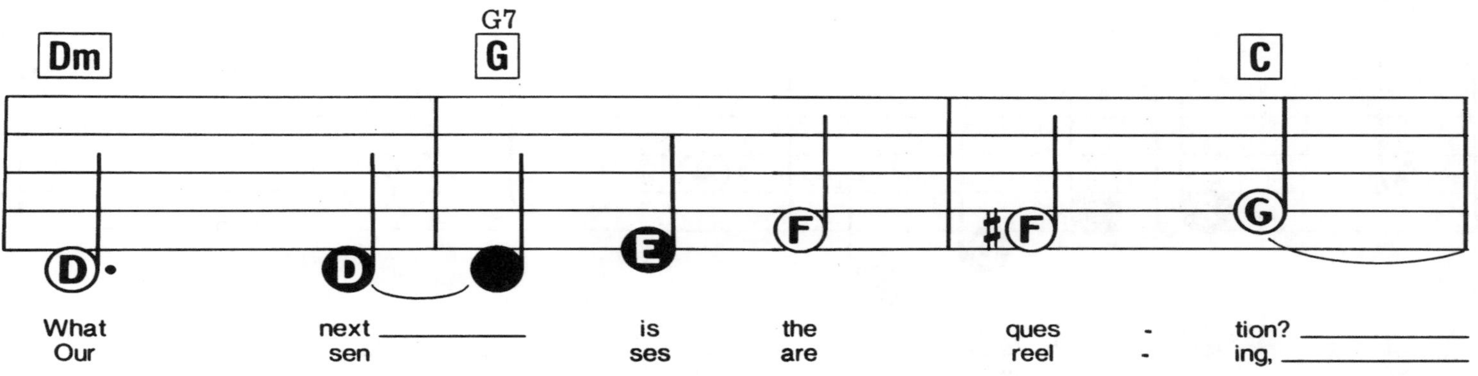
Dm
G7
G
C
D
D
E
F
F
G
What next is the ques - tion?
Our sen ses are reel - ing,

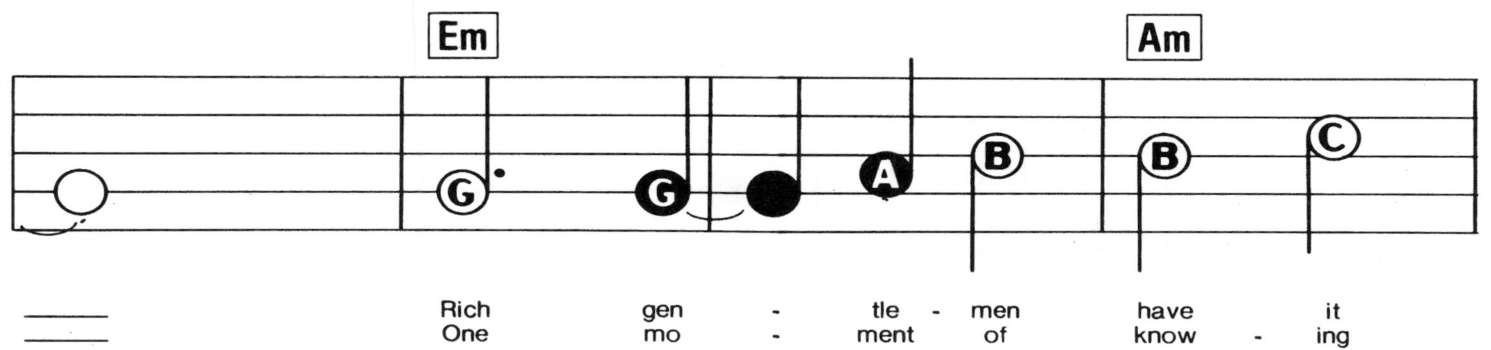
Em
Am
Rich gen - tle - men have it
One mo - ment of know - ing

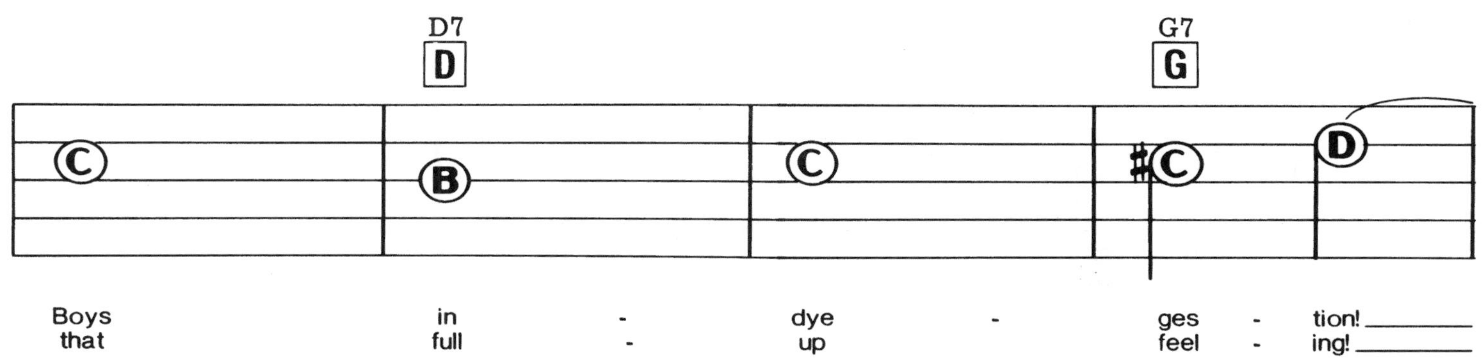
D7
D
G7
G
Boys in - dye - ges - tion!
that full - up feel - ing!

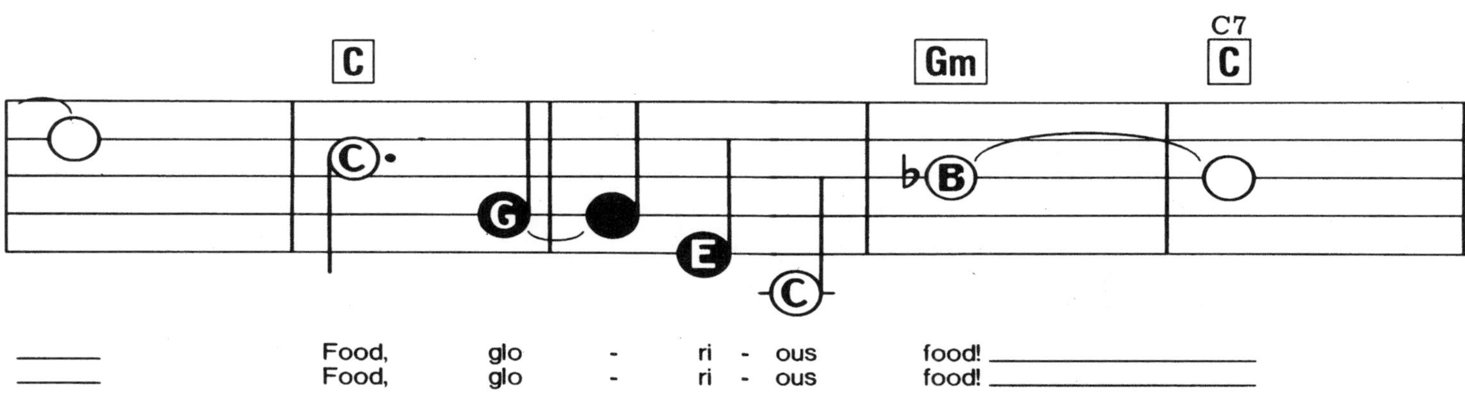
C
Gm
C7
C
Food, glo - ri - ous food!
Food, glo - ri - ous food!

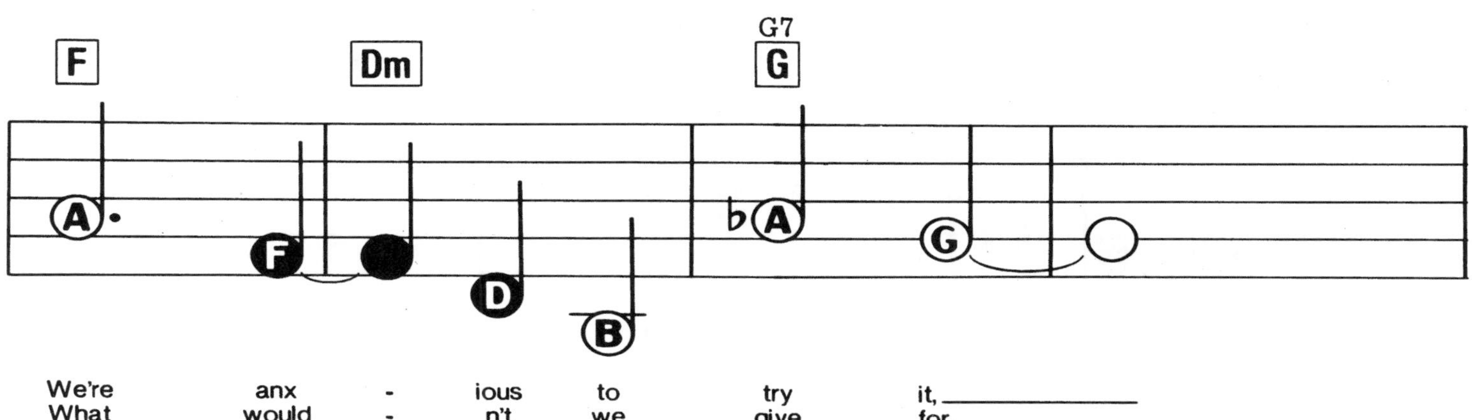
F
Dm
G7
G
We're anx - ious to try it,
What would - n't we give for,

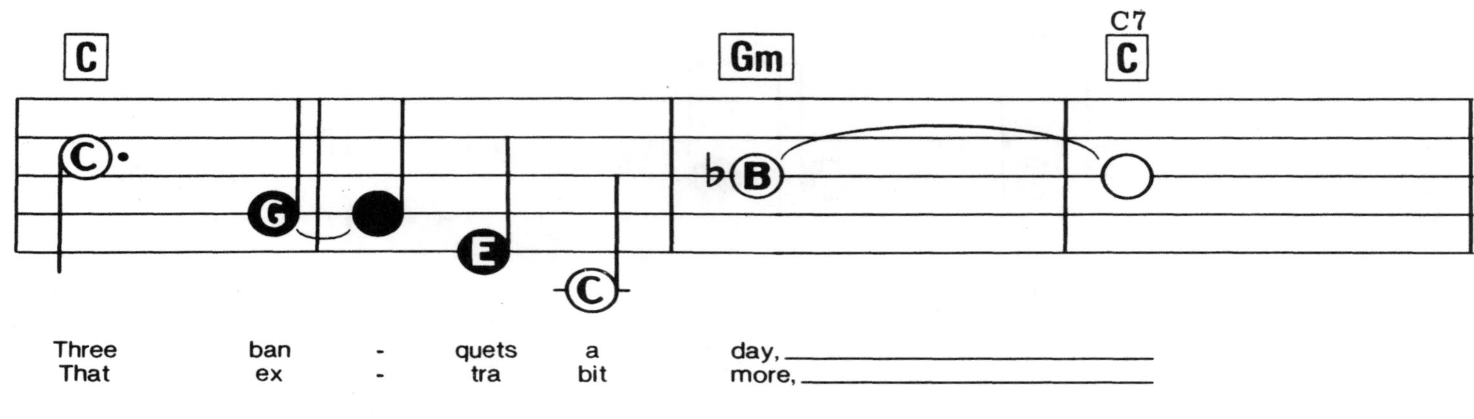
C
Gm
C7
C
C
G
E
C
B
Three ban - quets a day,
That ex - tra bit more,

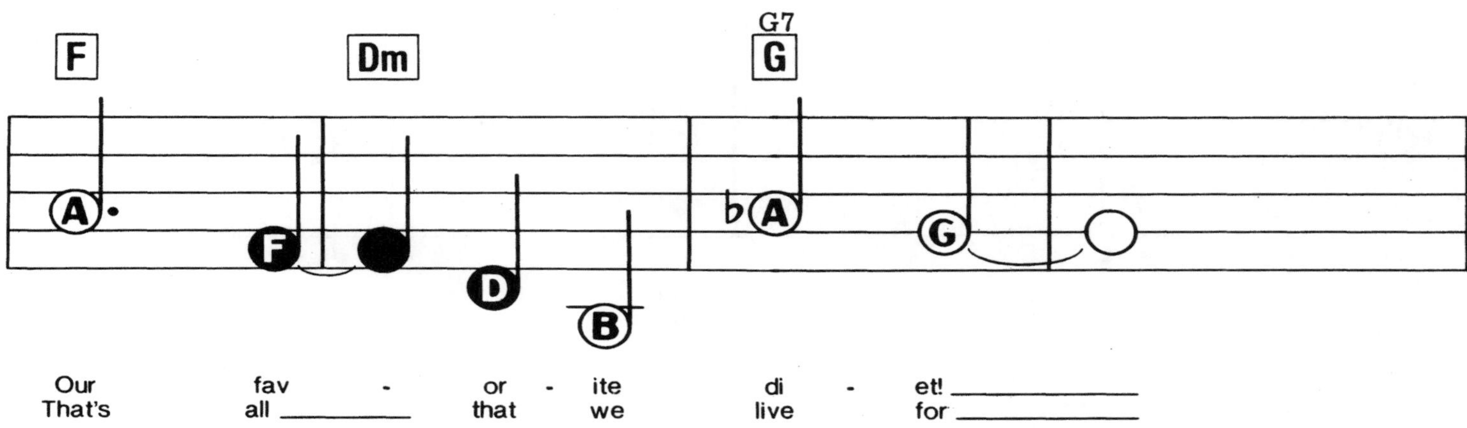
F
Dm
G7
G
A
F
D
B
A
G
Our fav - or - ite di - et!
That's all that we live for

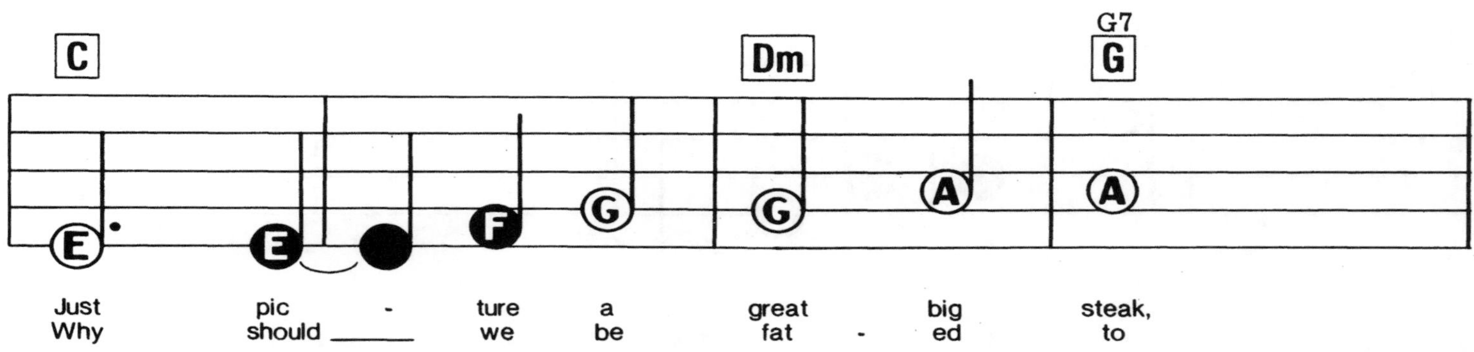
C
Dm
G7
G
E
E
F
G
G
A
A
Just pic - ture a great big steak,
Why should we be fat - ed to

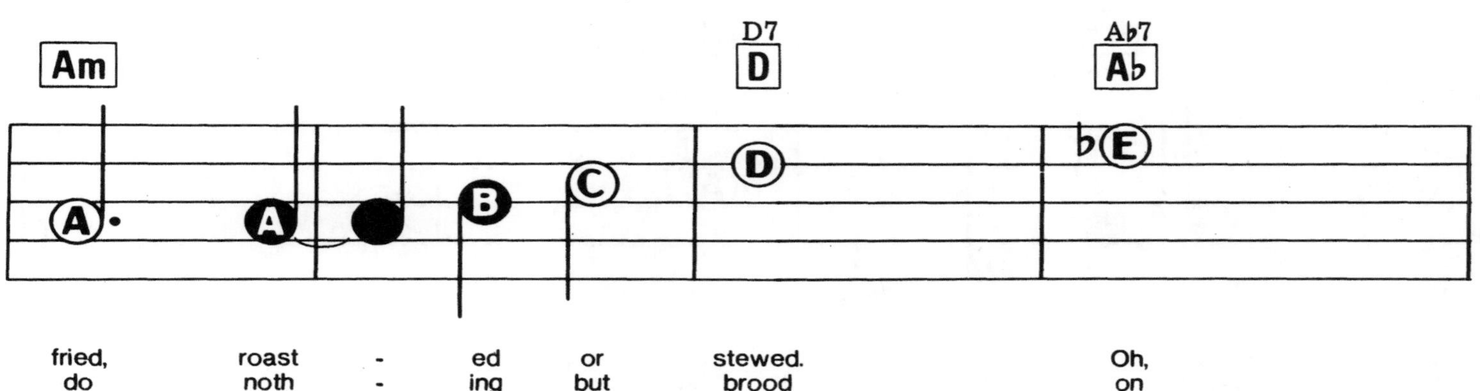
Am
D7
D
Ab7
Ab
A
A
B
C
D
E
fried, roast - ed or stewed. Oh,
do noth - ing but brood on

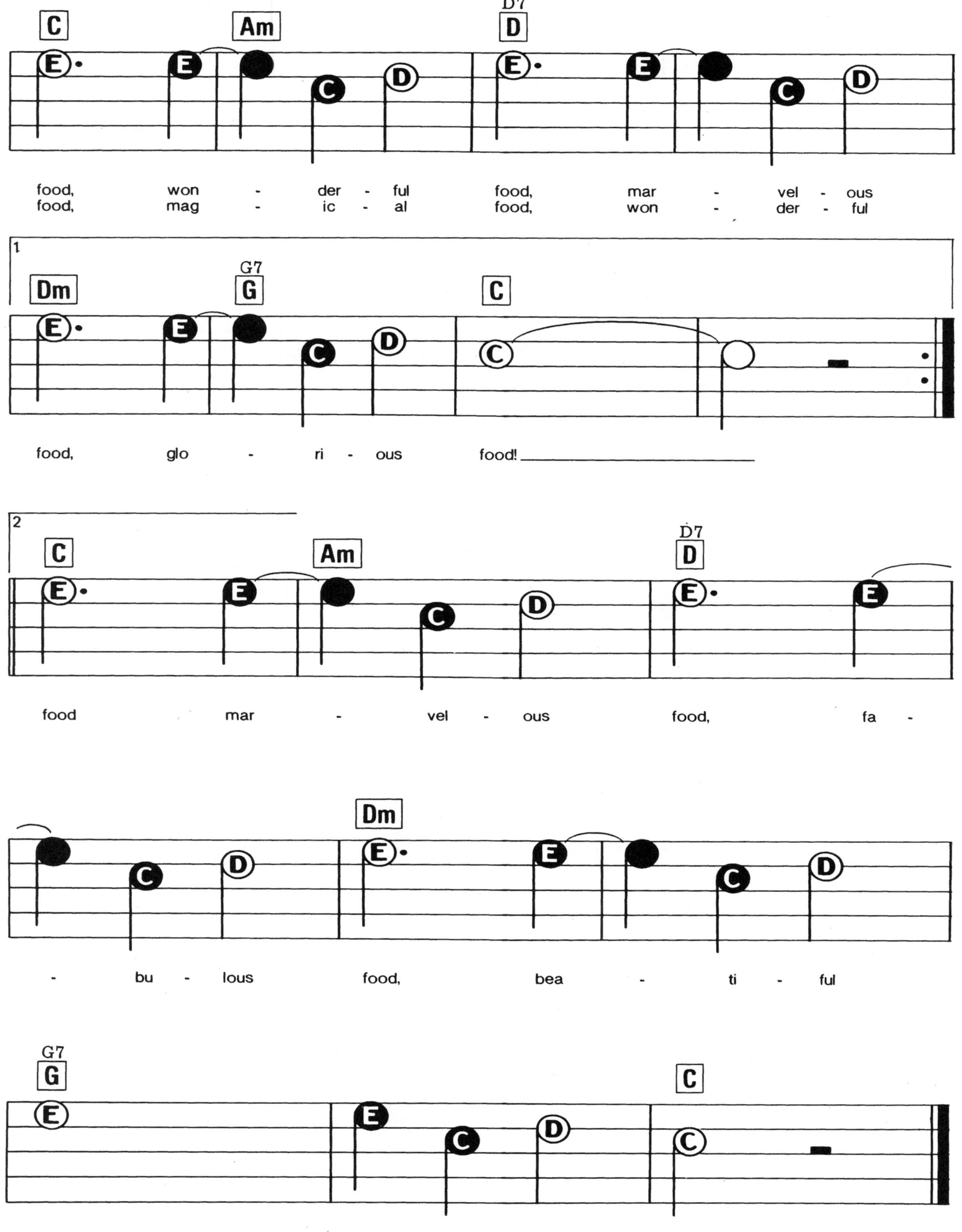
C
Am
D7
D
E E E C D E E E C D
food, won - der - ful food, mar - vel - ous
food, mag - ic - al food, won - der - ful
1
Dm
G7
G
C
E E E C D C
food, glo - ri - ous food!
2
C
Am
D7
D
E E E C D E E
food mar - vel - ous food, fa -
Dm
E C D E E E C D
- bu - lous food, bea - ti - ful
G7
G
C
E E C D C
food, glo - ri - ous food!

Frère Jacques
(Are You Sleeping?)

Registration 8
Rhythm: Fox Trot

Traditional

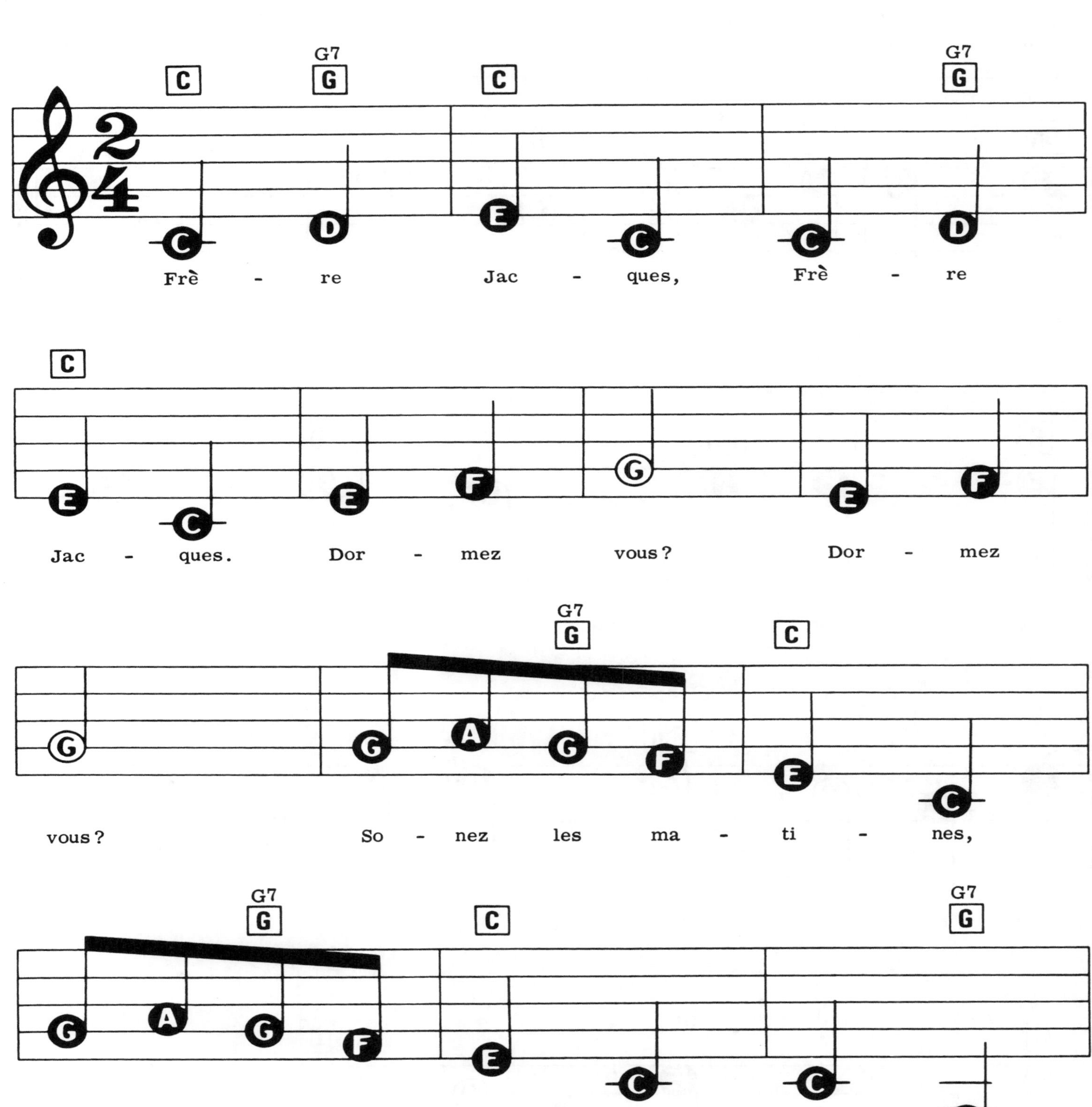

Copyright © 1976 by HAL LEONARD CORPORATION
International Copyright Secured All Rights Reserved

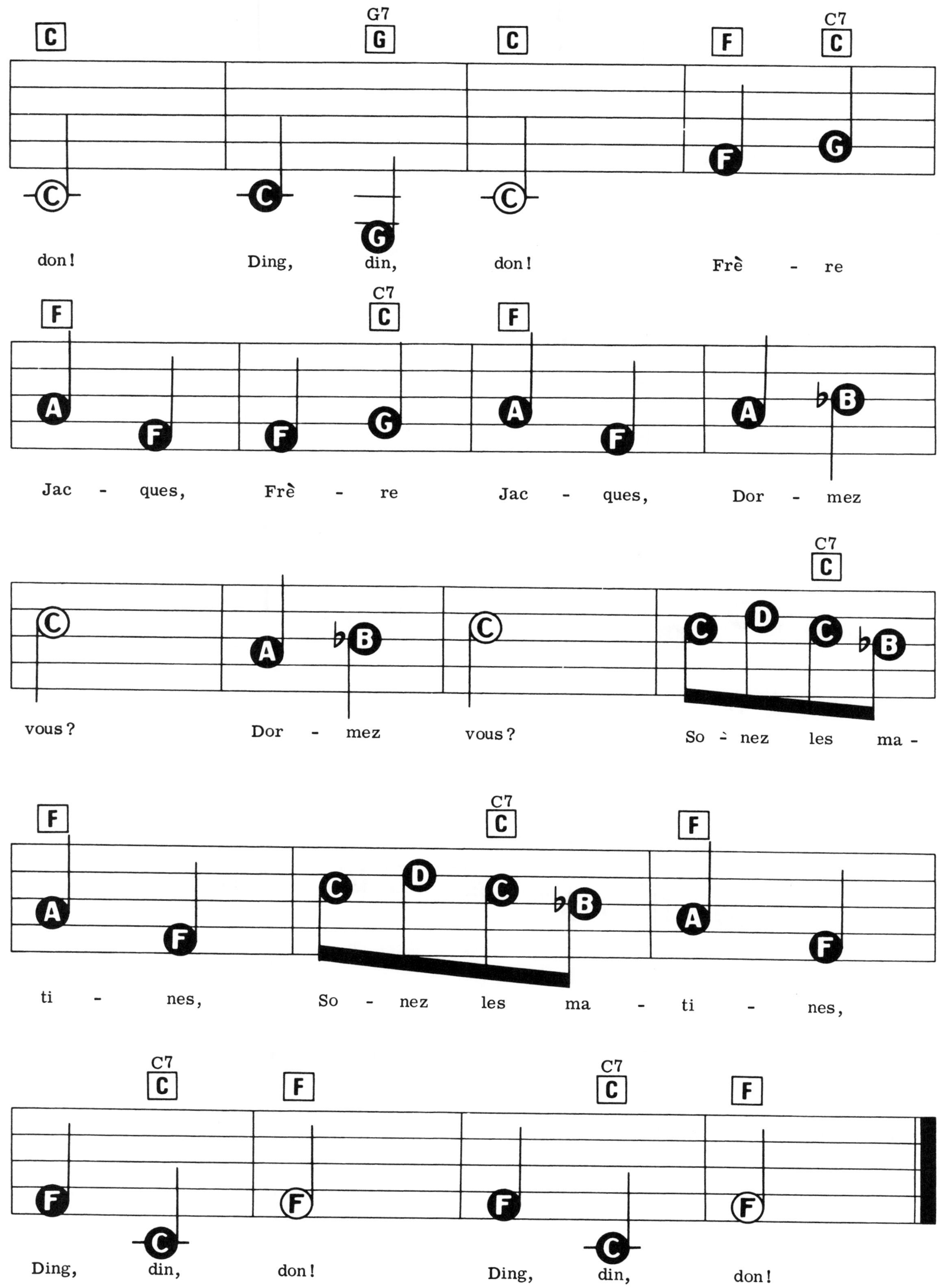
C
G7
G
C
F
C7
C
don!
Ding,
din,
don!
Frè - re
F
C7
C
F
Jac - ques,
Frè - re
Jac - ques,
Dor - mez
C7
C
vous?
Dor - mez
vous?
So - nez les ma -
F
C7
C
F
ti - nes,
So - nez les ma - ti - nes,
C7
C
F
C7
C
F
Ding,
din,
don!
Ding,
din,
don!

Friend Like Me

from Walt Disney's ALADDIN

Registration 1
Rhythm: Polka or March

Music by Alan Menken
Lyrics by Howard Ashman

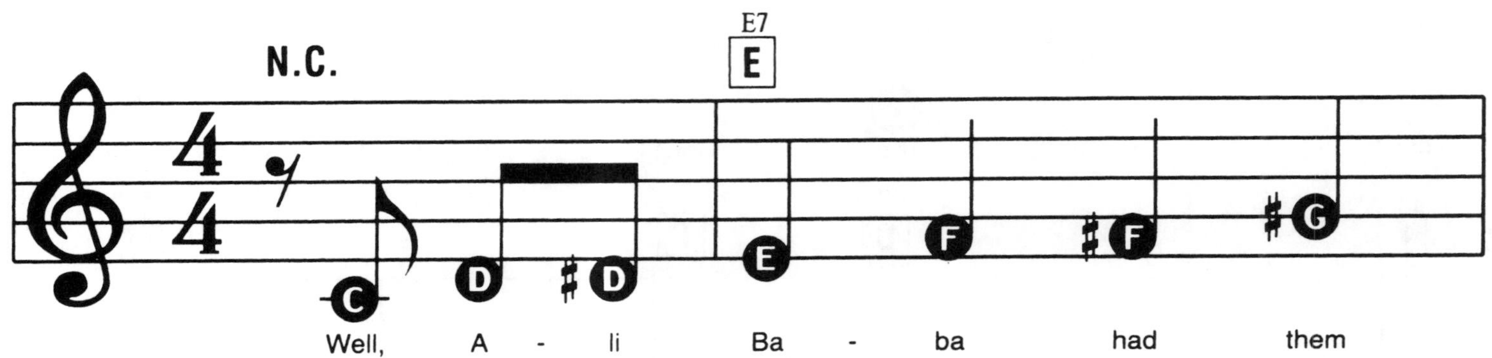

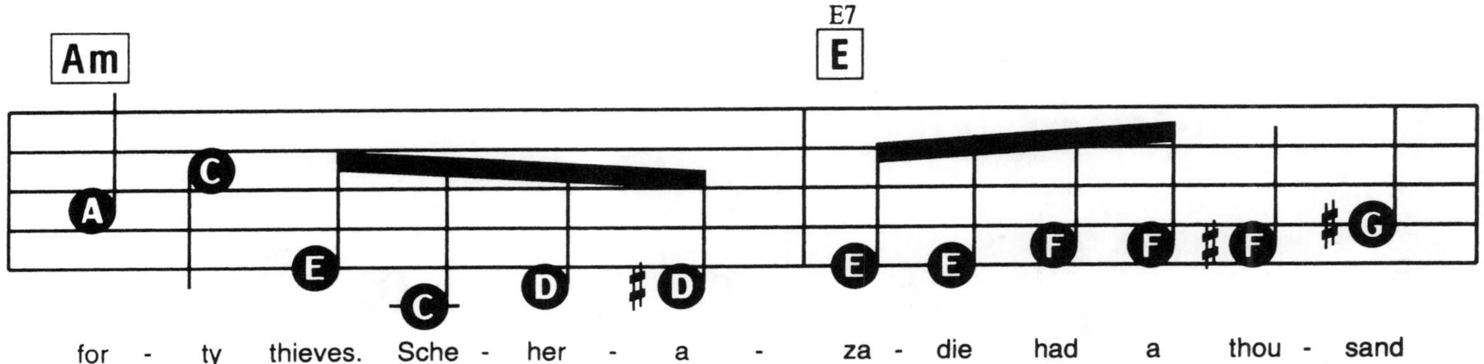

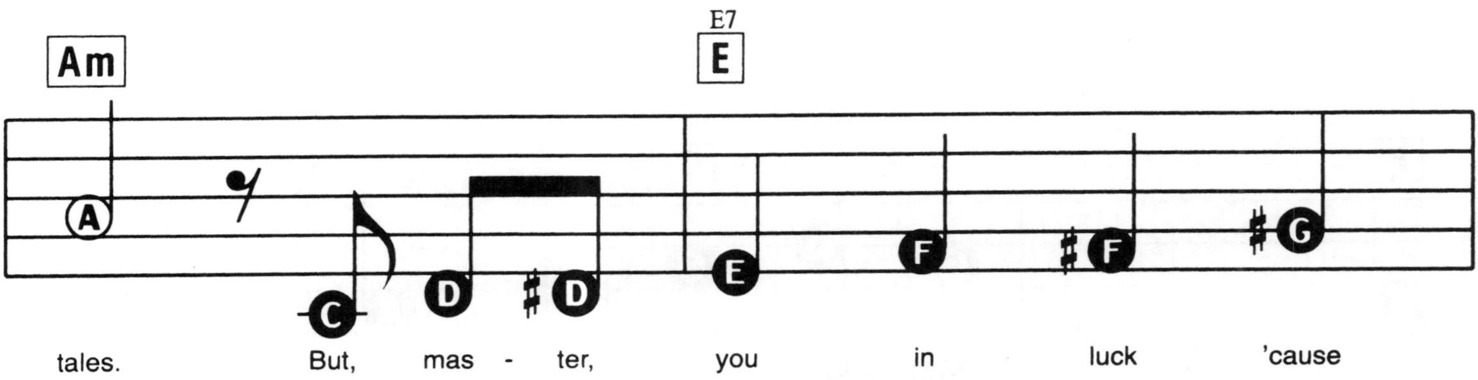

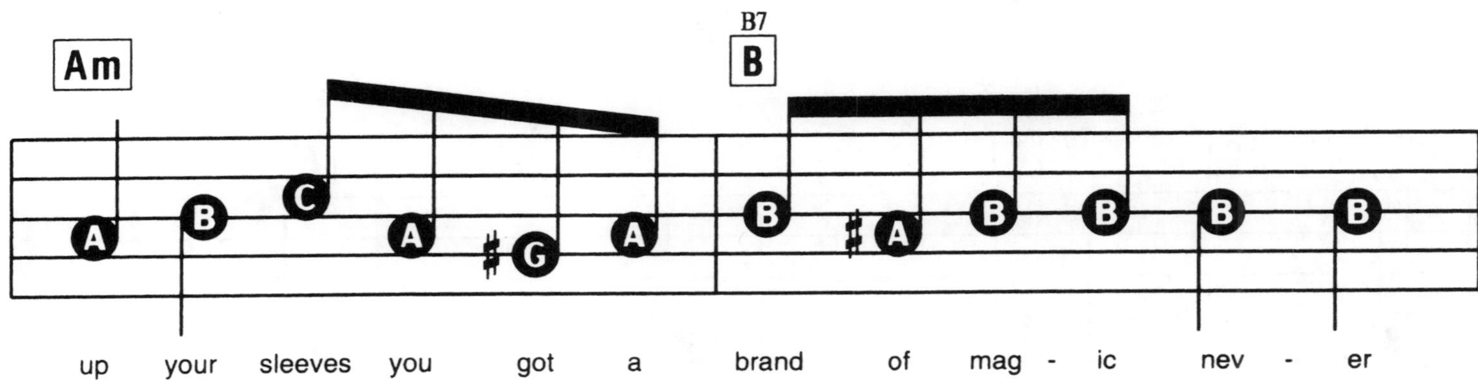

© 1992 Walt Disney Music Company and Wonderland Music Company, Inc.
All Rights Reserved. Used by Permission.

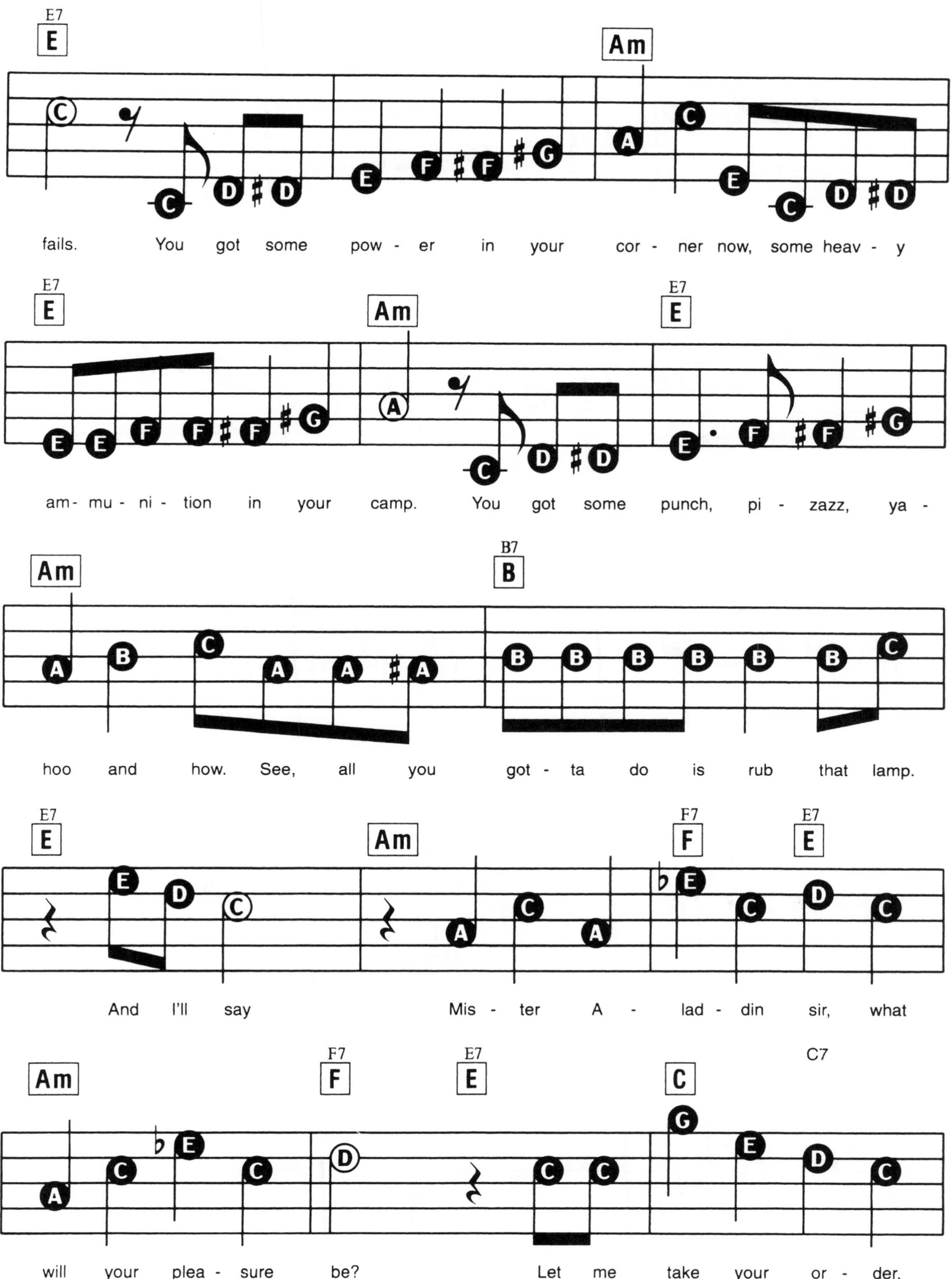
E7 E Am
fails. You got some pow - er in your cor - ner now, some heav - y
E7 E Am E7 E
am- mu - ni - tion in your camp. You got some punch, pi - zazz, ya -
Am B7 B
hoo and how. See, all you got - ta do is rub that lamp.
E7 E Am F7 F E7 E
And I'll say Mis - ter A - lad - din sir, what
Am F7 F E7 E C C7
will your plea - sure be? Let me take your or - der,

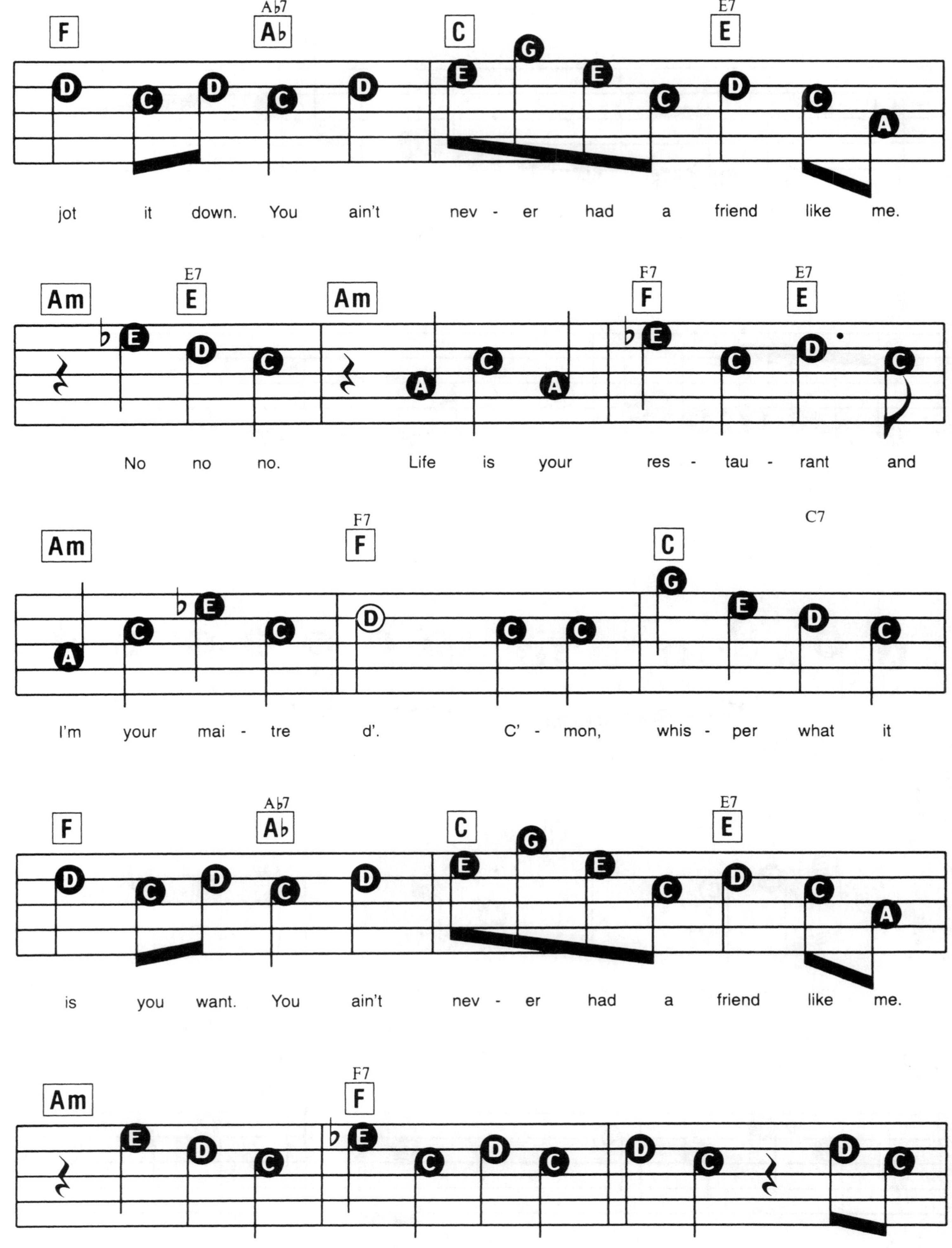
F
A♭7
A♭
C
E7
E
D C D C D E G E C D C A
jot it down. You ain't nev - er had a friend like me.
Am
E7
E
Am
F7
F
E7
E
E D C A C A E C D C
No no no. Life is your res - tau - rant and
Am
F7
F
C
C7
A C E C D C C G E D C
I'm your mai - tre d'. C' - mon, whis - per what it
F
A♭7
A♭
C
E7
E
D C D C D E G E C D C A
is you want. You ain't nev - er had a friend like me.
Am
F7
F
E D C E C D C D C D C
Yes sir, we pride our - selves on ser - vice. You're the

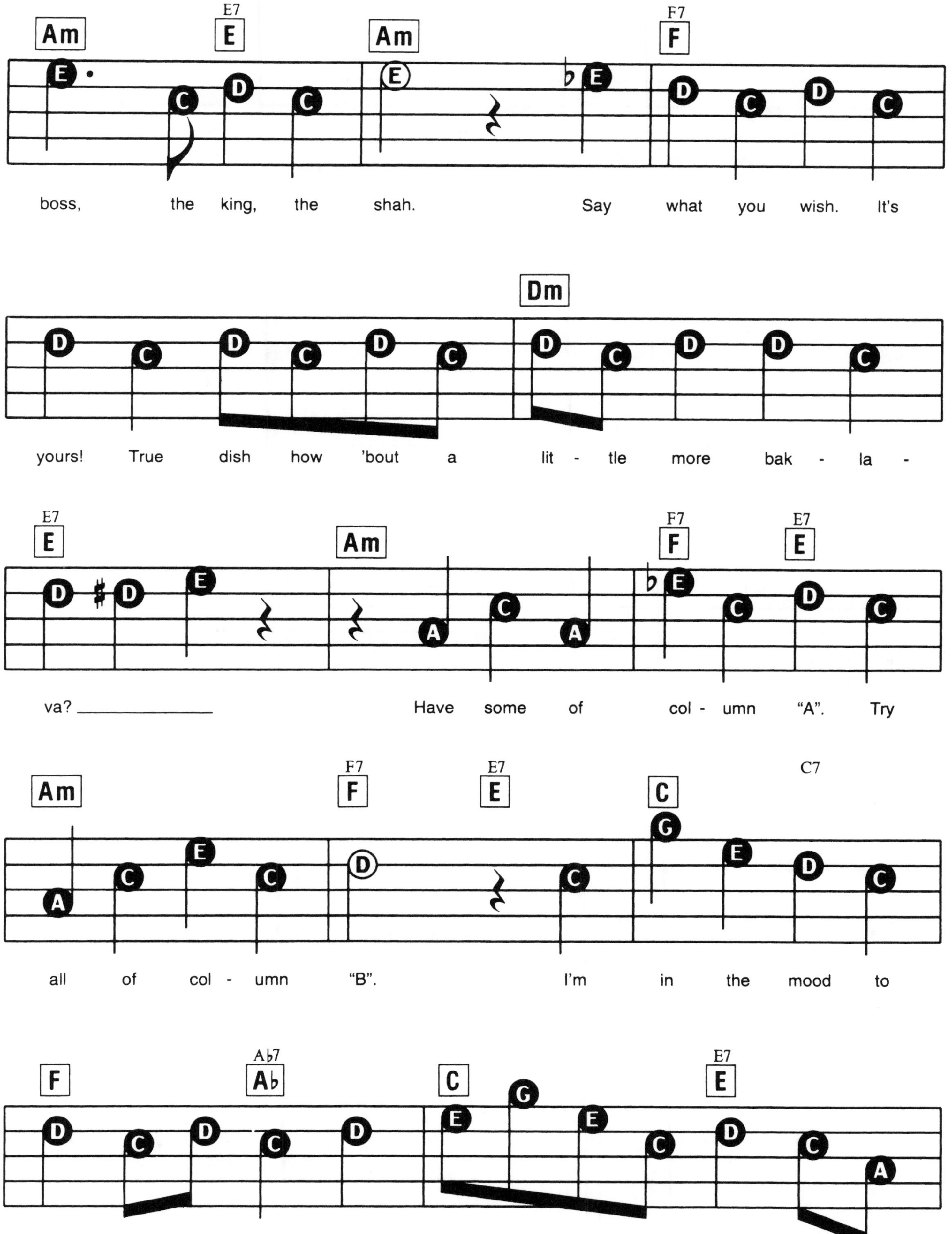
Am E7 E Am F7 F
boss, the king, the shah. Say what you wish. It's
Dm
yours! True dish how 'bout a lit - tle more bak - la -
E7 E Am F7 F E7 E
va? Have some of col - umn "A". Try
Am F7 F E7 E C C7
all of col - umn "B". I'm in the mood to
F A♭7 A♭ C E7 E
help you, dude, you ain't nev - er had a friend like me.

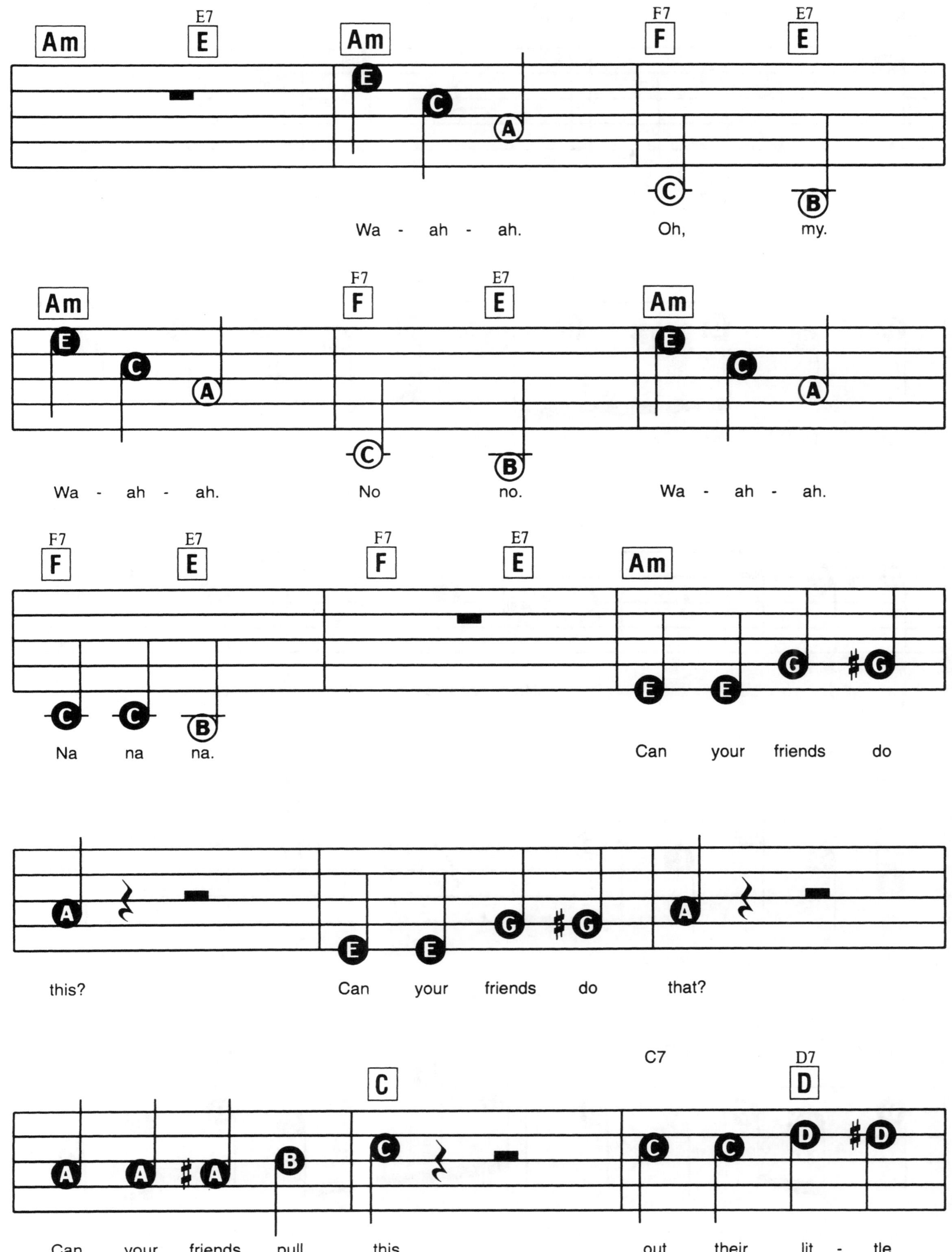
Am
E7 E
Am
F7 F
E7 E
Wa - ah - ah.
Oh,
my.
Am
F7 F
E7 E
Am
Wa - ah - ah.
No
no.
Wa - ah - ah.
F7 F
E7 E
F7 F
E7 E
Am
Na
na
na.
Can
your
friends
do
this?
Can
your
friends
do
that?
C
C7
D7 D
Can
your
friends
pull
this
out
their
lit - tle

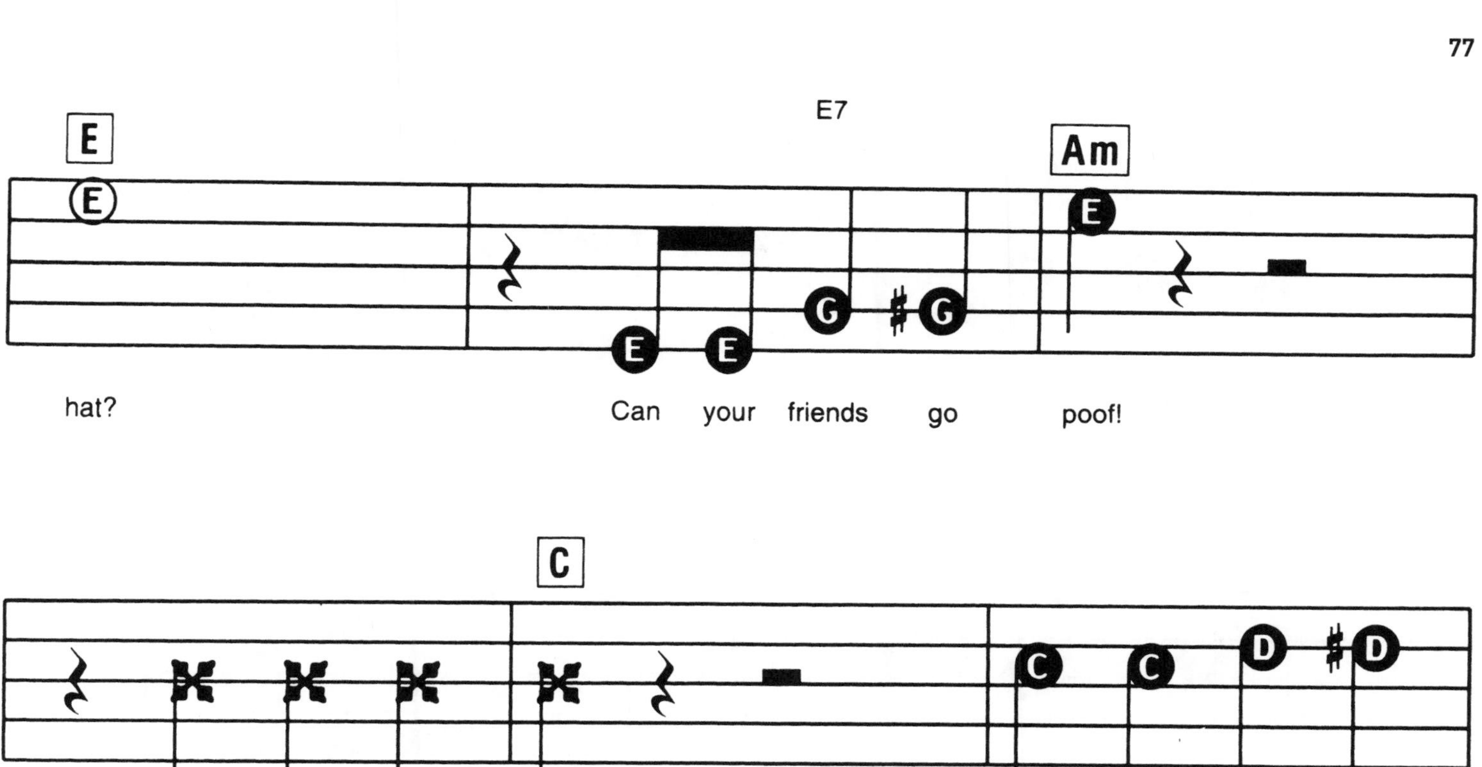
E
E7
Am
E
E E G ♯G E
hat?
Can your friends go poof!
C
Well, look - y here.
C C D ♯D
Can your friends go

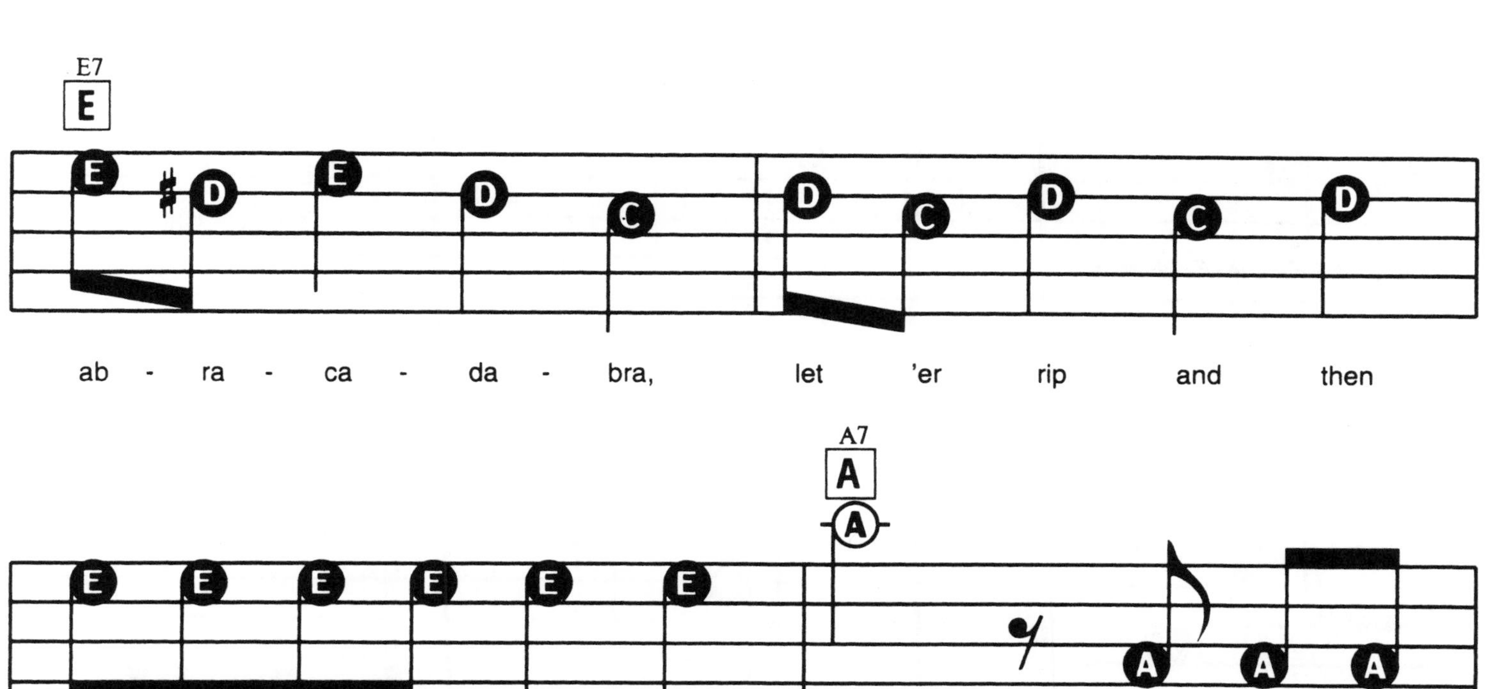
E7
E
E ♯D E D C D C D C D
ab - ra - ca - da - bra, let 'er rip and then
A7
A
E E E E E E A A A A
make the suck - er dis - ap - pear? So don - cha

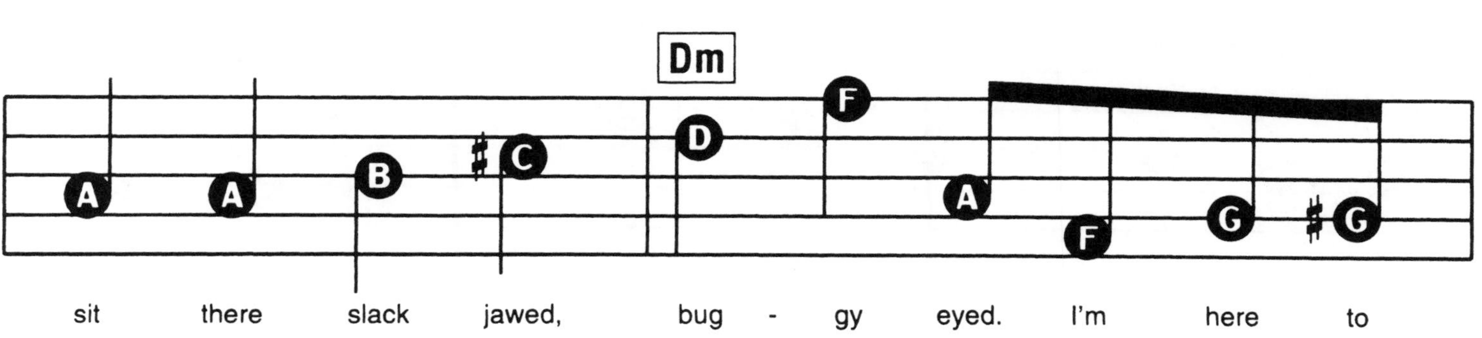
Dm
A A B ♯C D F A F G ♯G
sit there slack jawed, bug - gy eyed. I'm here to

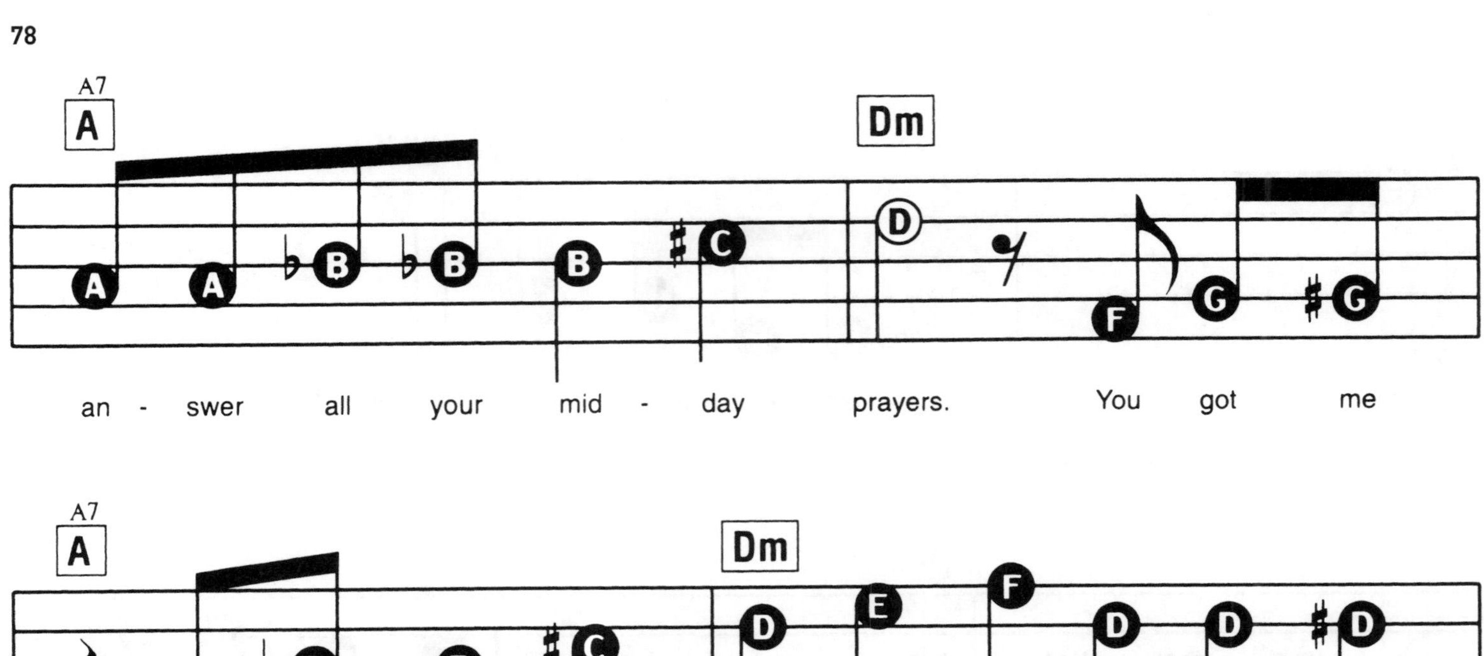
A7
A
Dm
an - swer all your mid - day prayers. You got me

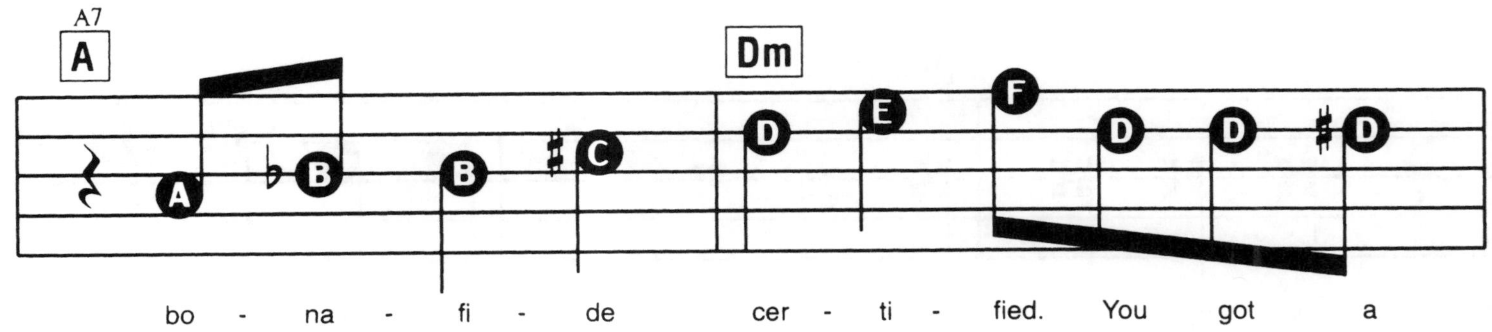
A7
A
Dm
bo - na - fi - de cer - ti - fied. You got a

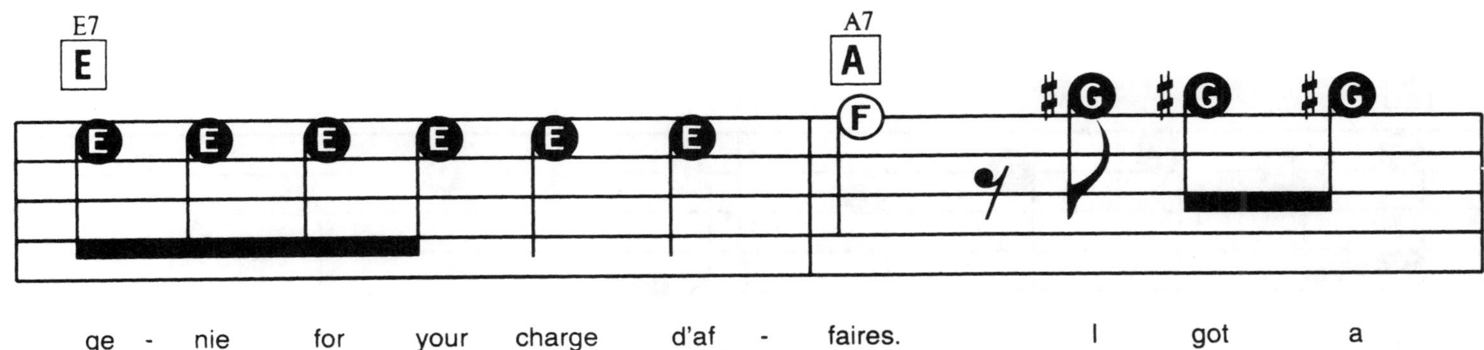
E7
E
A7
A
ge - nie for your charge d'af - faires. I got a

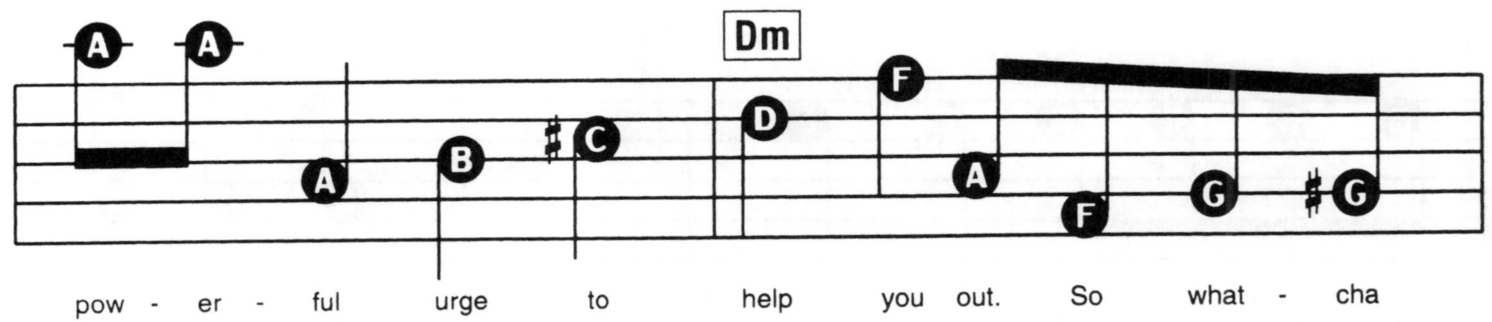
Dm
pow - er - ful urge to help you out. So what - cha

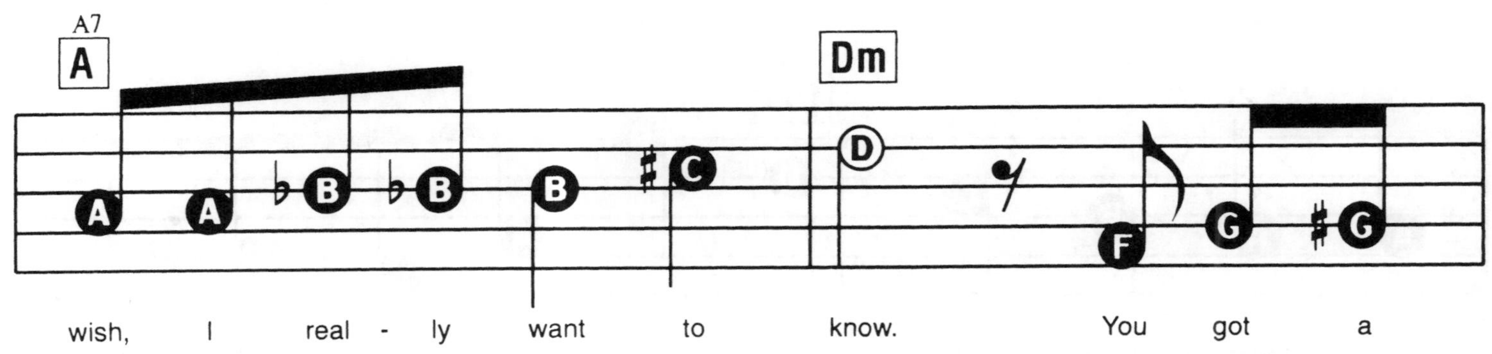
A7
A
Dm
wish, I real - ly want to know. You got a

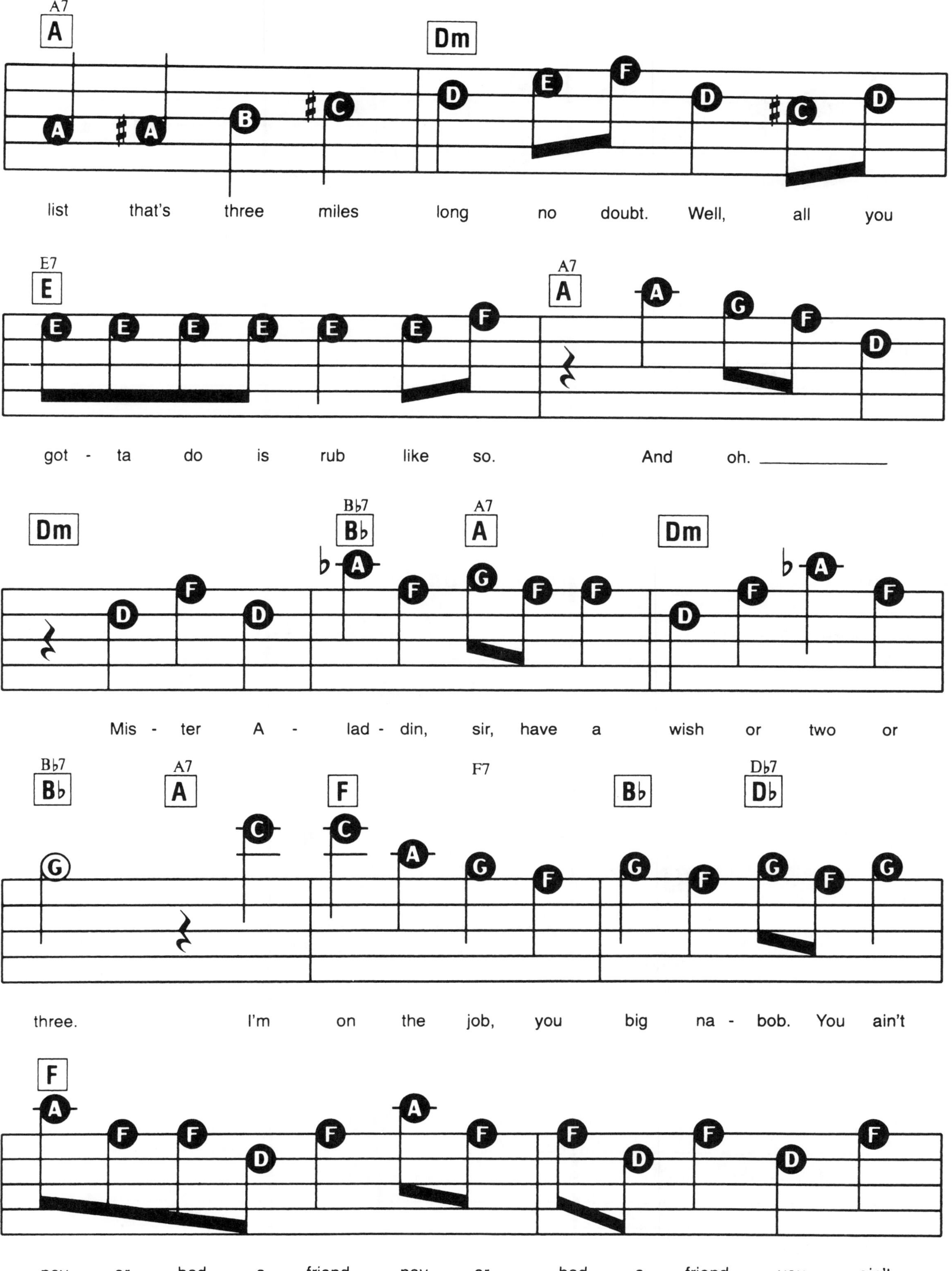
A7 A Dm
list that's three miles long no doubt. Well, all you
E7 E A7 A
got - ta do is rub like so. And oh.
Dm B♭7 B♭ A7 A Dm
Mis - ter A - lad - din, sir, have a wish or two or
B♭7 B♭ A7 A F F7 B♭ D♭7 D♭
three. I'm on the job, you big na - bob. You ain't
F
nev - er had a friend, nev - er had a friend, you ain't

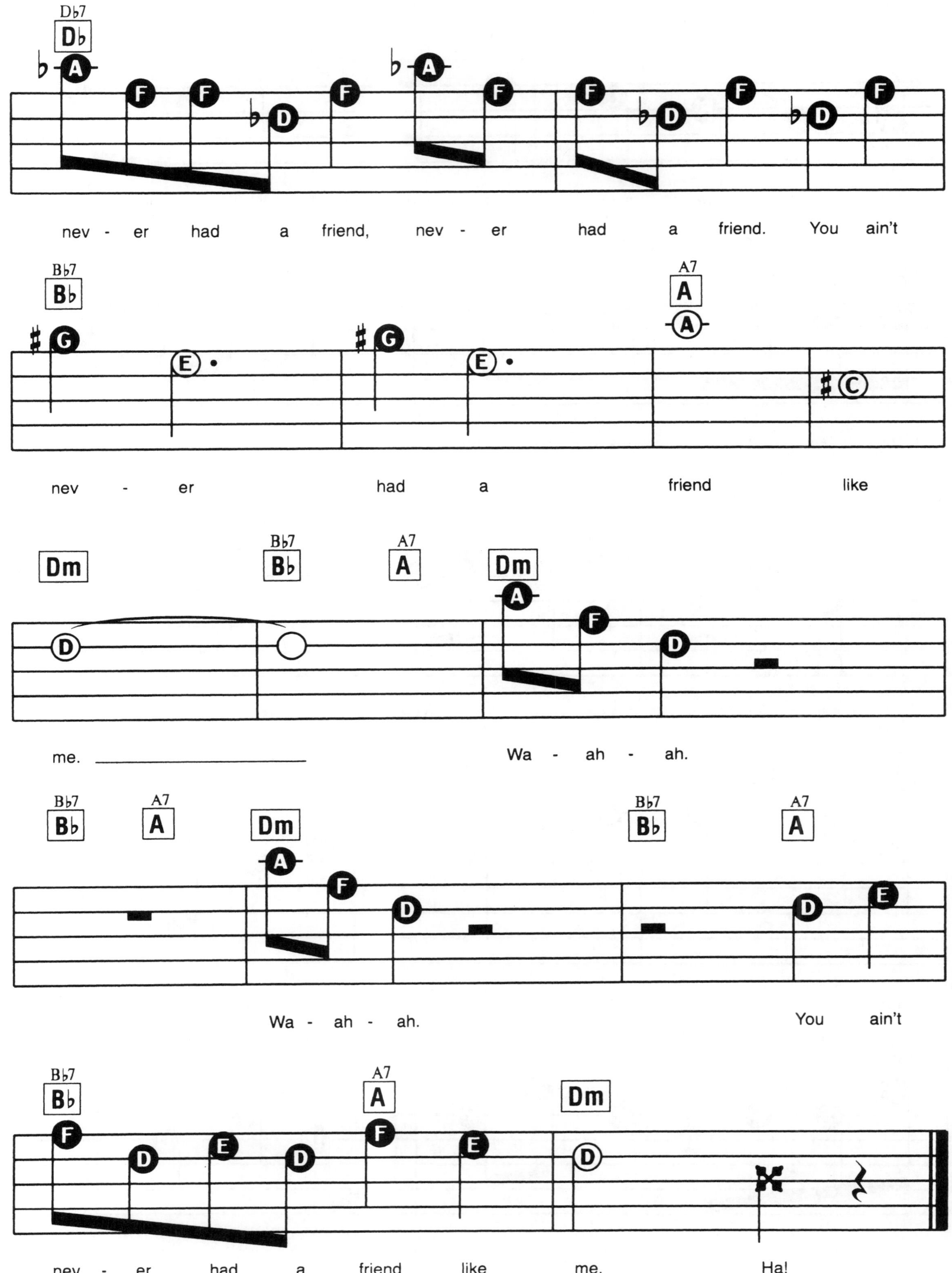

D♭7
D♭
A F F D F A F F D F D F
nev - er had a friend, nev - er had a friend. You ain't
B♭7
B♭
A7
A
G E G E A C
nev - er had a friend like
Dm
B♭7
B♭
A7
A
Dm
D A F D
me. Wa - ah - ah.
B♭7
B♭
A7
A
Dm
B♭7
B♭
A7
A
A F D D E
Wa - ah - ah. You ain't
B♭7
B♭
A7
A
Dm
F D E D F E D
nev - er had a friend like me. Ha!

Hakuna Matata

from Walt Disney Pictures' THE LION KING

Registration 5
Rhythm: Swing

Music by Elton John
Lyrics by Tim Rice

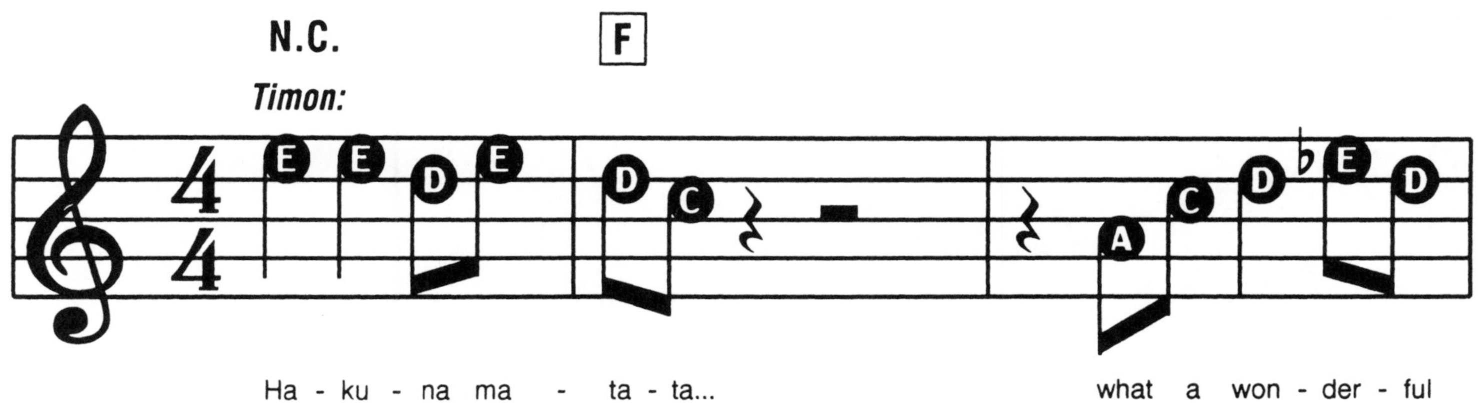

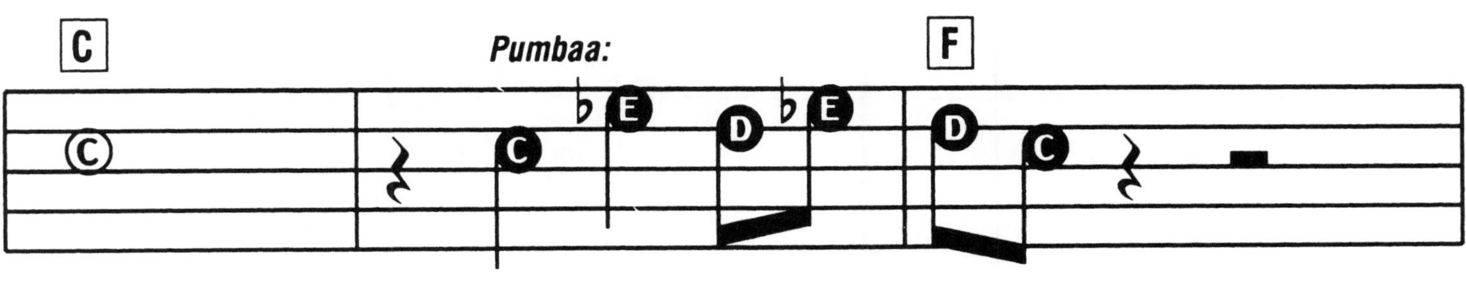

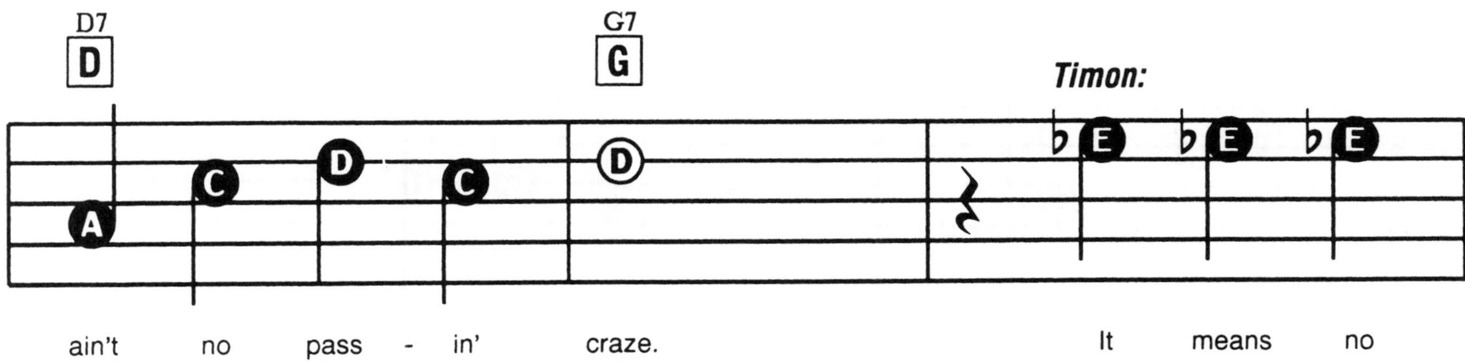

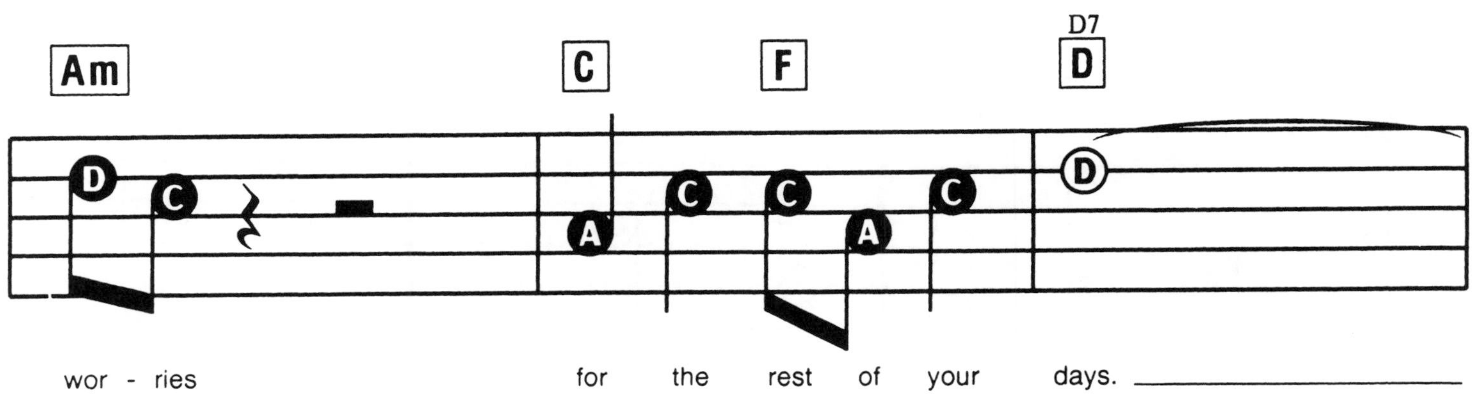

© 1994 Wonderland Music Company, Inc.
All Rights Reserved. Used by Permission.

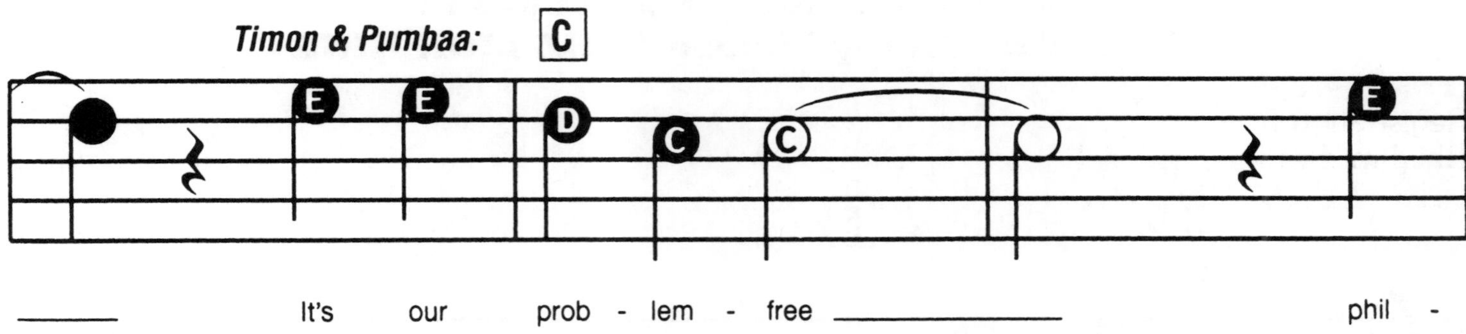
Timon & Pumbaa:
C
E E D C C E
It's our prob - lem - free phil -

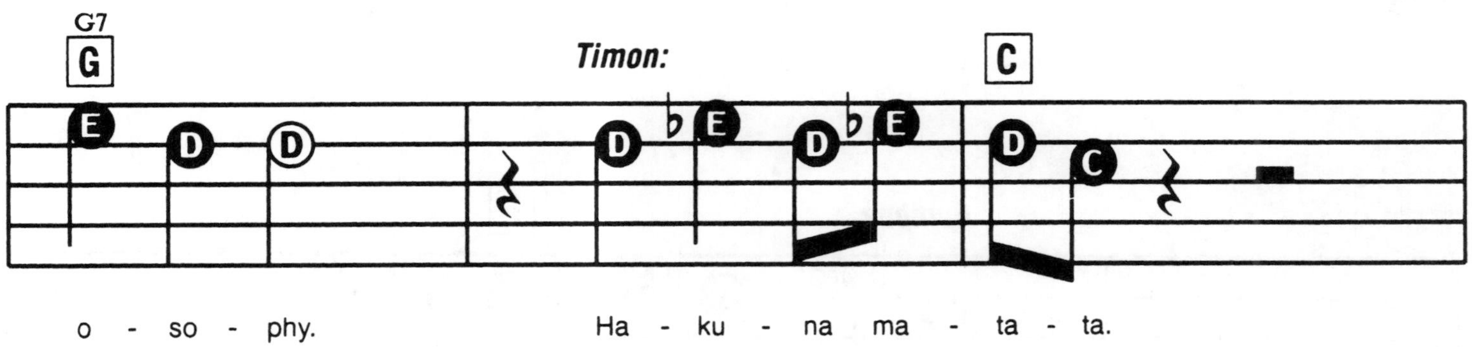
G7
G
Timon:
C
E D D D E D E D C
o - so - phy. Ha - ku - na ma - ta - ta.

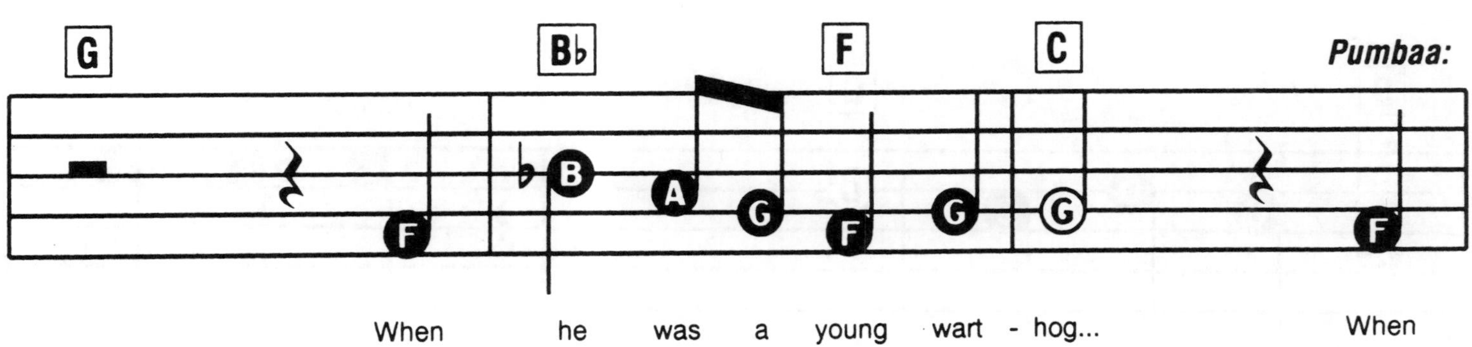
G
B♭
F
C
Pumbaa:
F B A G F G G F
When he was a young wart - hog... When

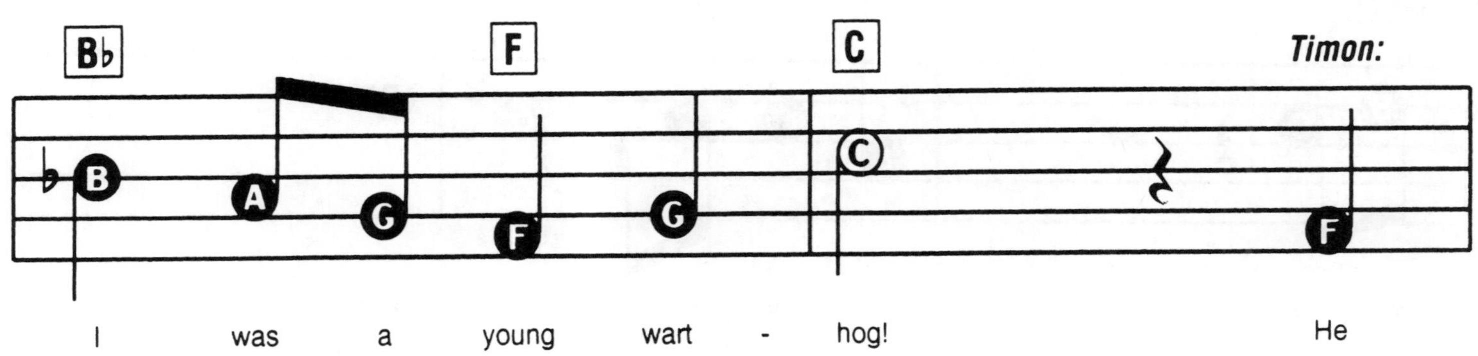
B♭
F
C
Timon:
B A G F G C F
I was a young wart - hog! He

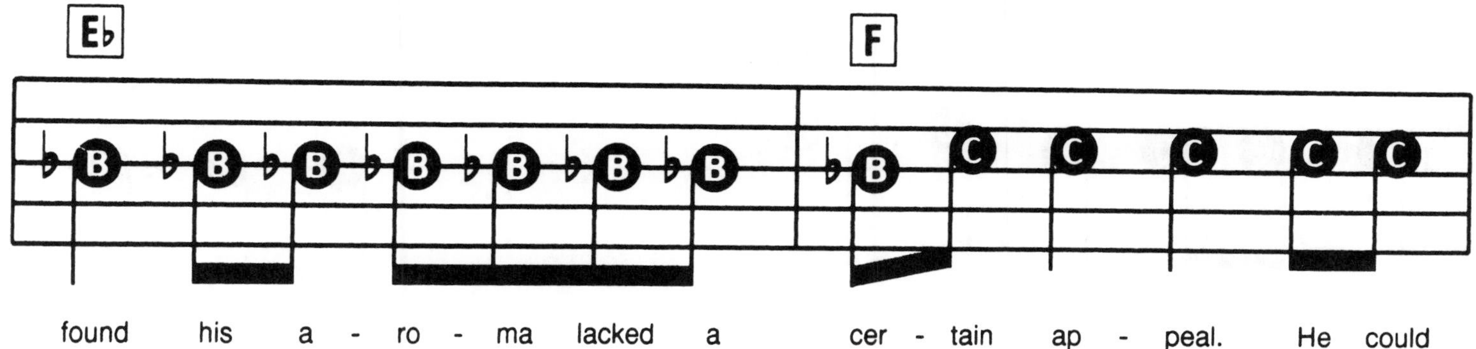
E♭
F
B B B B B B B
B C C C C C
found his a - ro - ma lacked a
cer - tain ap - peal. He could

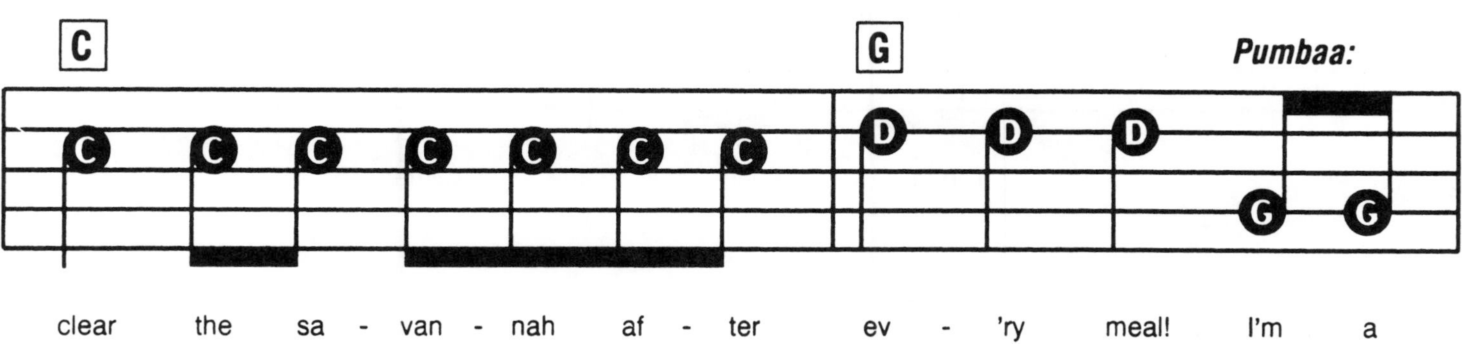
C
G
Pumbaa:
C C C C C C C
D D D G G
clear the sa - van - nah af - ter
ev - 'ry meal! I'm a

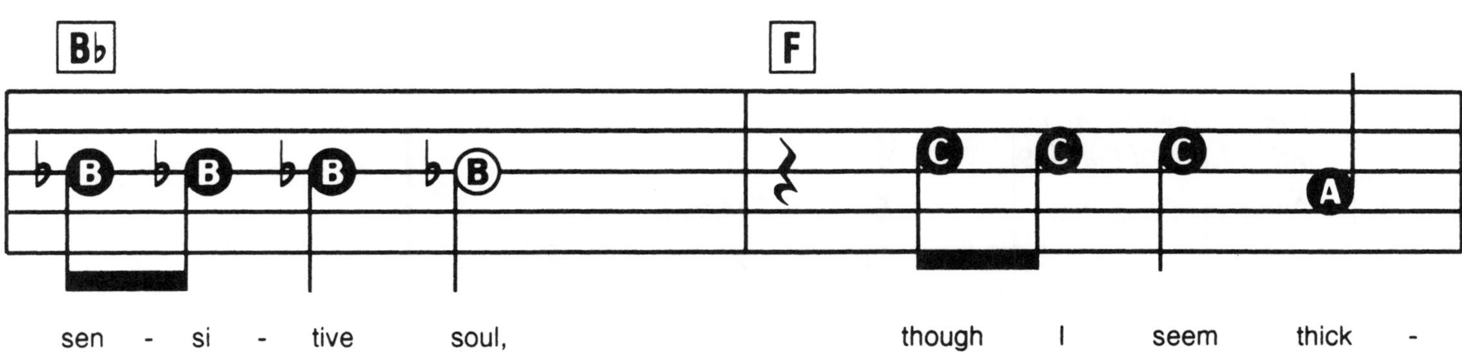
B♭
F
B B B B
C C C A
sen - si - tive soul,
though I seem thick -

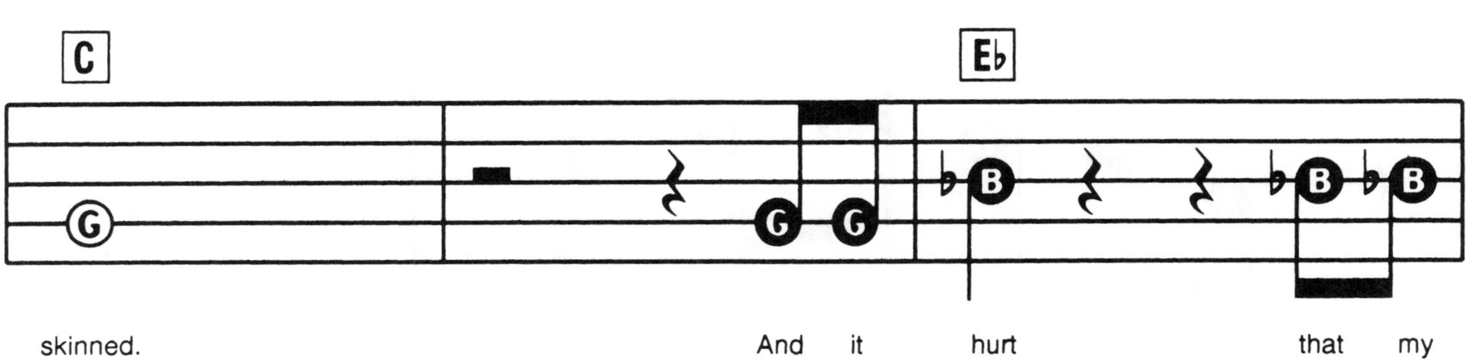
C
E♭
G
G G
B B B
skinned.
And it
hurt that my

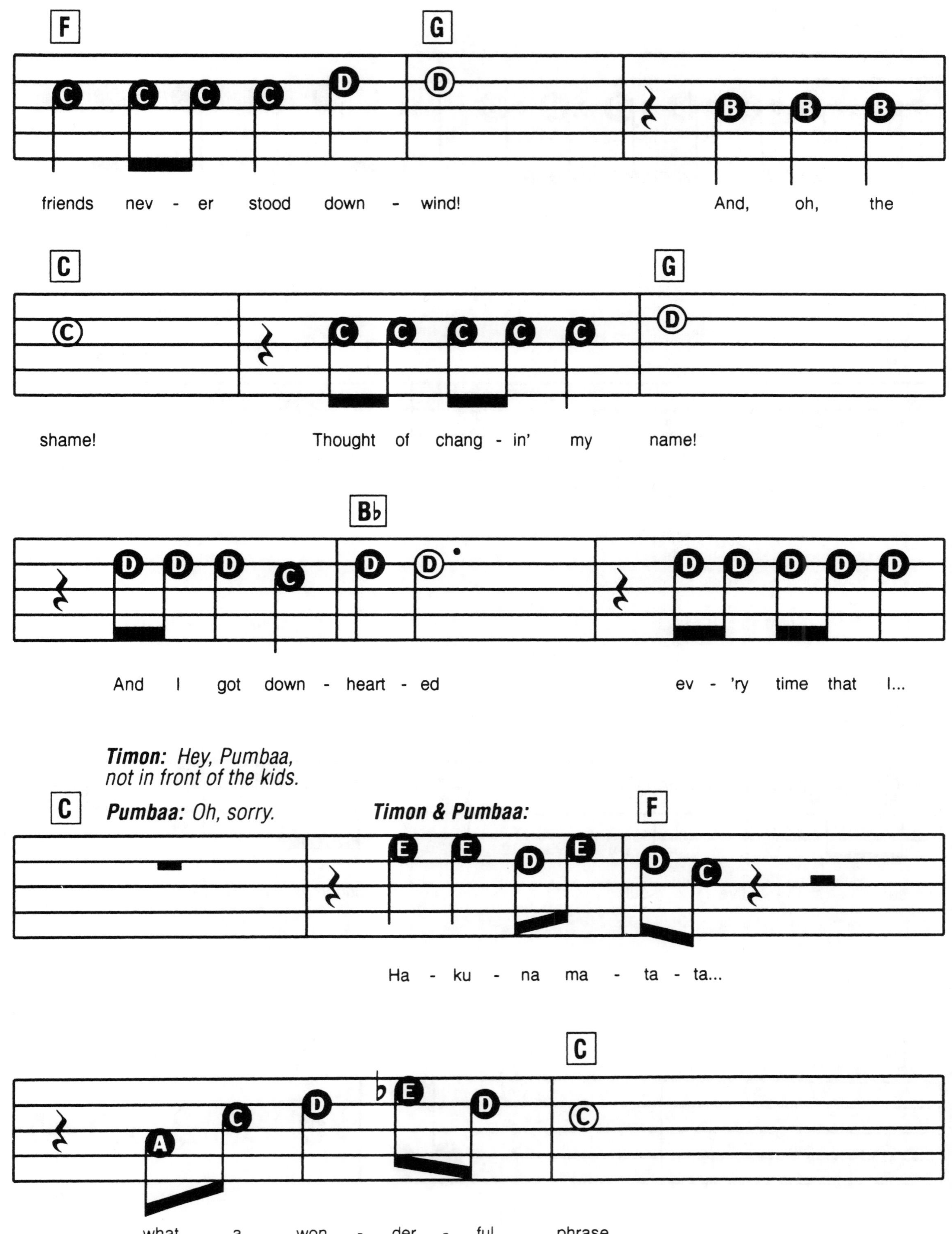
F
G
friends nev - er stood down - wind! And, oh, the
C
G
shame! Thought of chang - in' my name!
B♭
And I got down - heart - ed ev - 'ry time that I...
Timon: Hey, Pumbaa, not in front of the kids.
C
Pumbaa: Oh, sorry.
Timon & Pumbaa:
F
Ha - ku - na ma - ta - ta...
C
what a won - der - ful phrase.

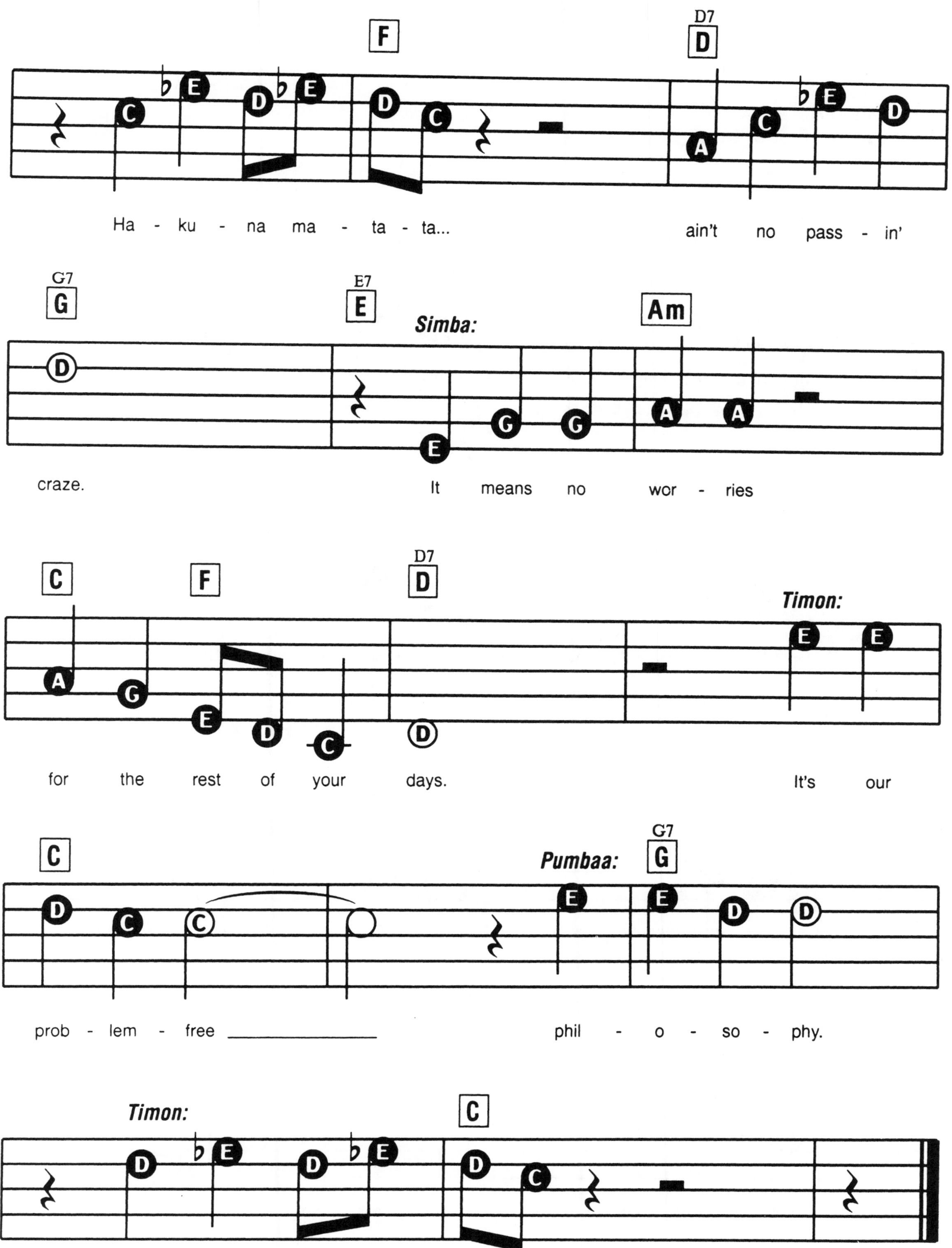
F
D7
D
Ha - ku - na ma - ta - ta...
ain't no pass - in'
G7
G
E7
E
Simba:
Am
craze.
It means no wor - ries
C
F
D7
D
Timon:
for the rest of your days.
It's our
C
Pumbaa:
G7
G
prob - lem - free
phil - o - so - phy.
Timon:
C
Ha - ku - na ma - ta - ta.

Getting to Know You
from THE KING AND I

Registration 8
Rhythm: Fox Trot or Swing

Lyrics by Oscar Hammerstein II
Music by Richard Rodgers

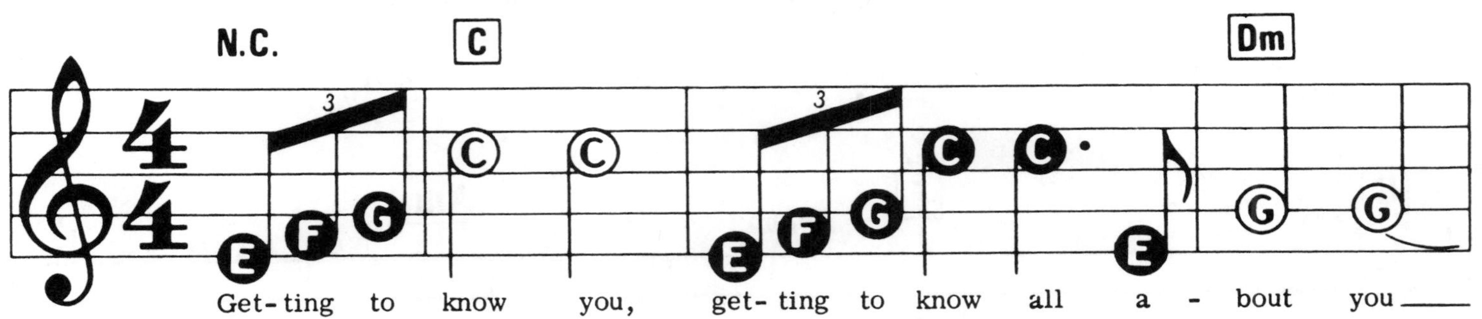

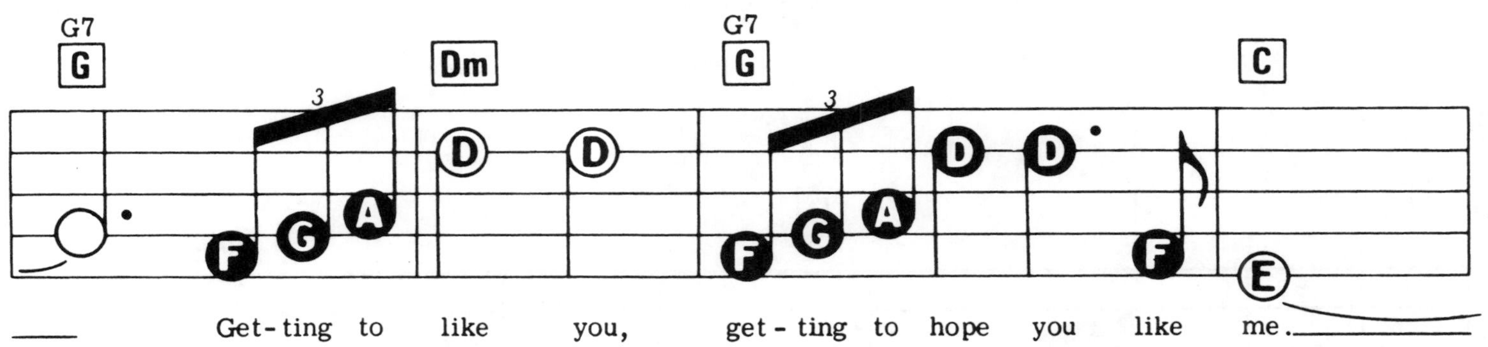

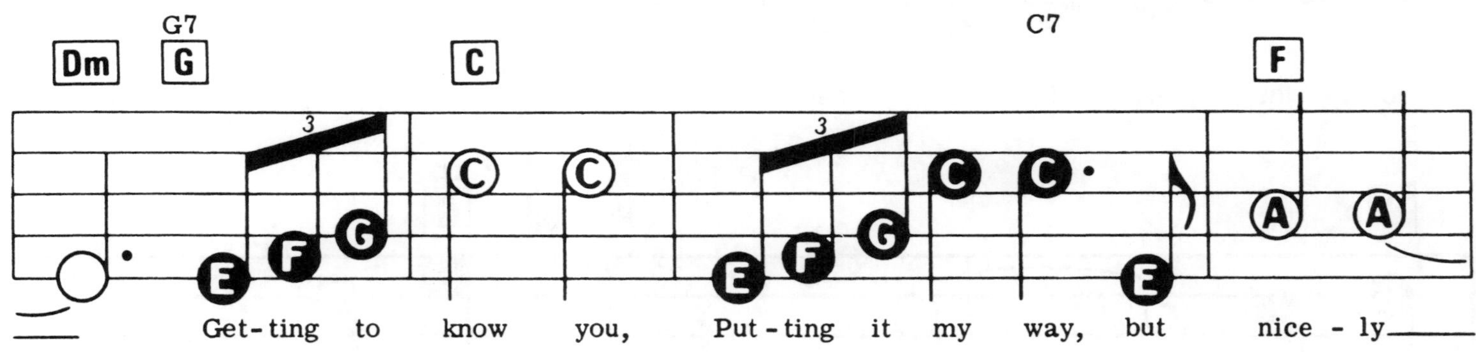

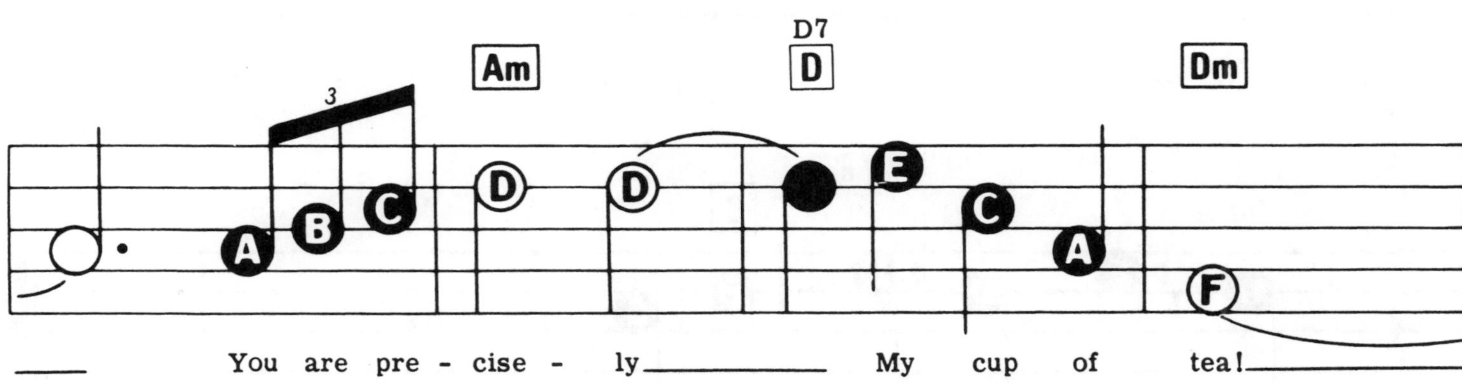

Copyright © 1951 by Richard Rodgers and Oscar Hammerstein II
Copyright Renewed
Williamson Music, a Division of Rodgers & Hammerstein: an Imagem Company, owner of publication and allied rights throughout the world
International Copyright Secured All Rights Reserved

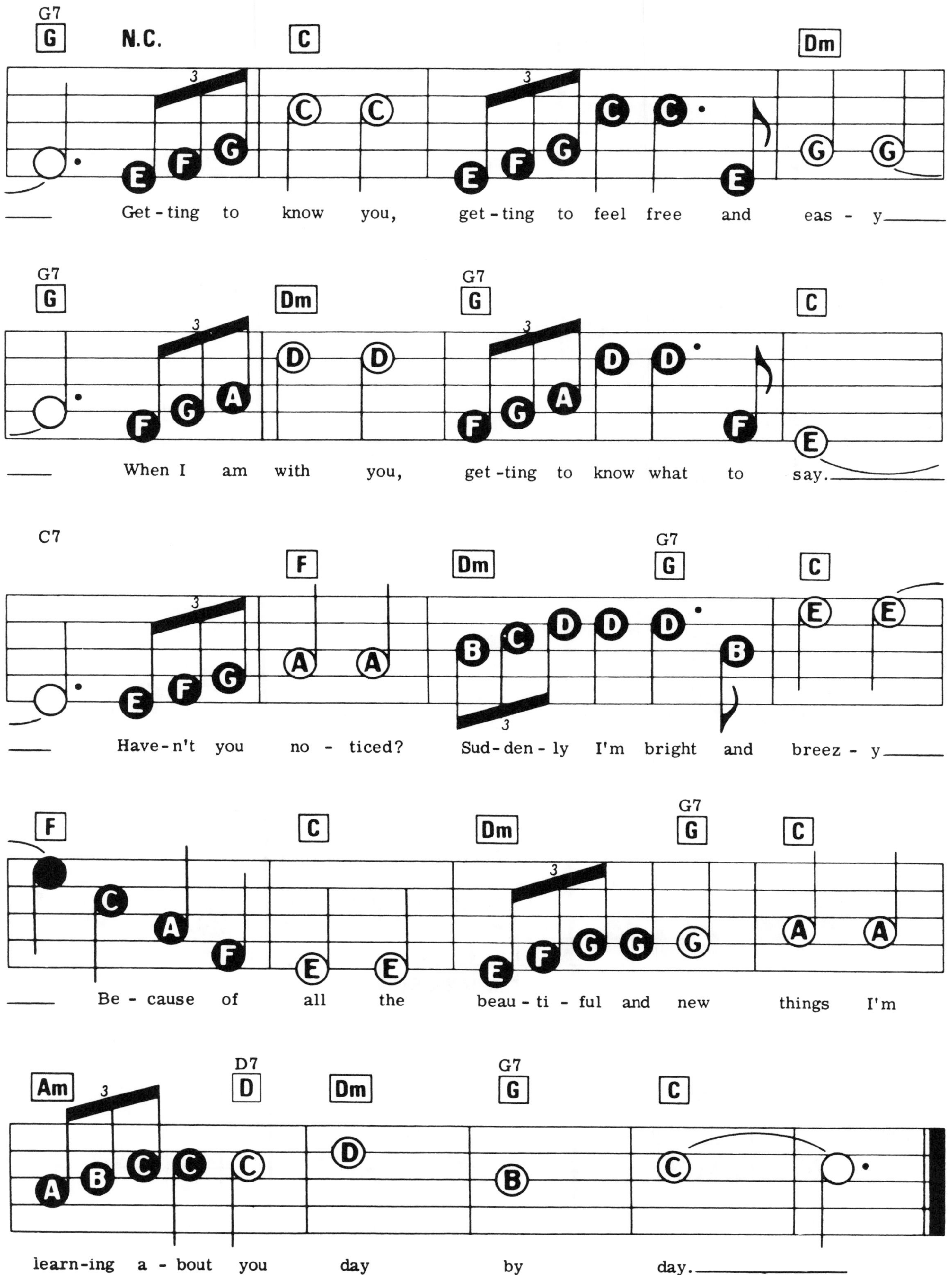
G7 G N.C. C Dm
Get-ting to know you, get-ting to feel free and eas-y
G7 G Dm G7 G C
When I am with you, get-ting to know what to say.
C7 F Dm G7 G C
Have-n't you no-ticed? Sud-den-ly I'm bright and breez-y
F C Dm G7 G C
Be-cause of all the beau-ti-ful and new things I'm
Am D7 D Dm G7 G C
learn-ing a-bout you day by day.

Give a Little Whistle

from Walt Disney's PINOCCHIO

Registration 9
Rhythm: Fox Trot or Swing

Words by Ned Washington
Music by Leigh Harline

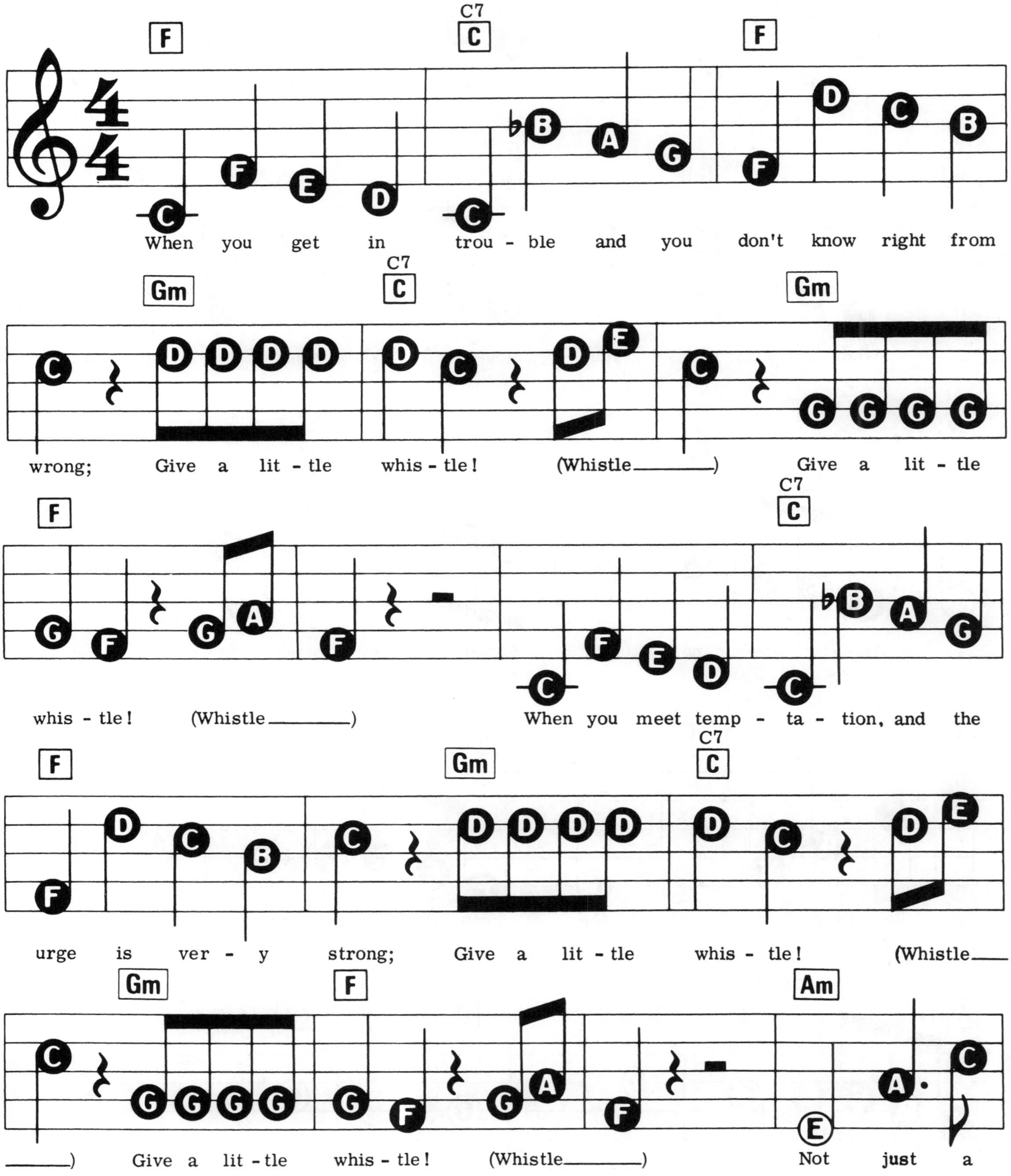

When you get in trou - ble and you don't know right from

wrong; Give a lit - tle whis - tle! (Whistle______) Give a lit - tle

whis - tle! (Whistle______) When you meet temp - ta - tion, and the

urge is ver - y strong; Give a lit - tle whis - tle! (Whistle____

______) Give a lit - tle whis - tle! (Whistle______) Not just a

Copyright © 1940 by Bourne Co. (ASCAP)
Copyright Renewed
International Copyright Secured All Rights Reserved

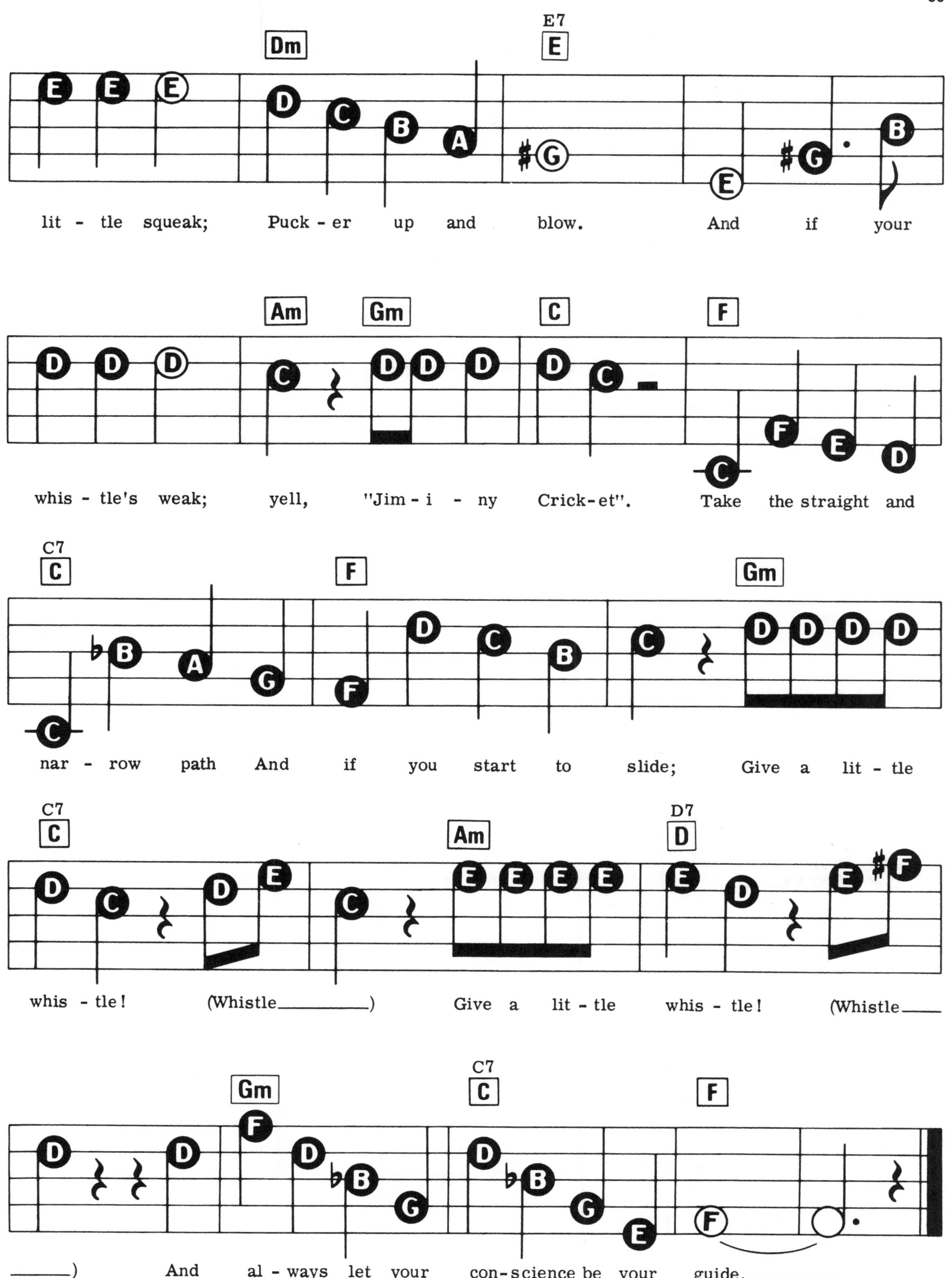
Dm
E7
E
lit - tle squeak; Puck - er up and blow. And if your
Am
Gm
C
F
whis - tle's weak; yell, "Jim - i - ny Crick - et". Take the straight and
C7
C
F
Gm
nar - row path And if you start to slide; Give a lit - tle
C7
C
Am
D7
D
whis - tle! (Whistle________) Give a lit - tle whis - tle! (Whistle____
Gm
C7
C
F
______) And al - ways let your con - science be your guide.________

Golden Slumbers

Registration 4
Rhythm: Ballad

Words and Music by John Lennon
and Paul McCartney

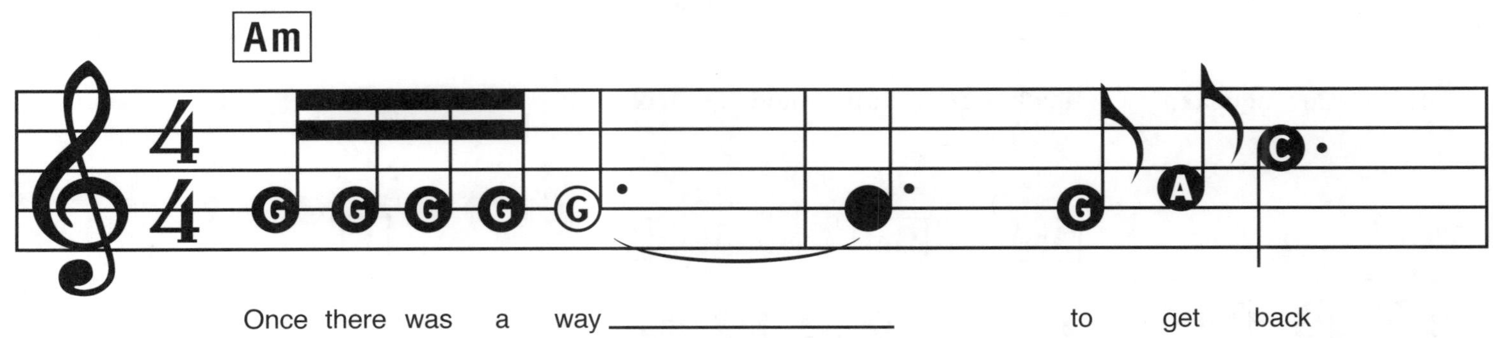

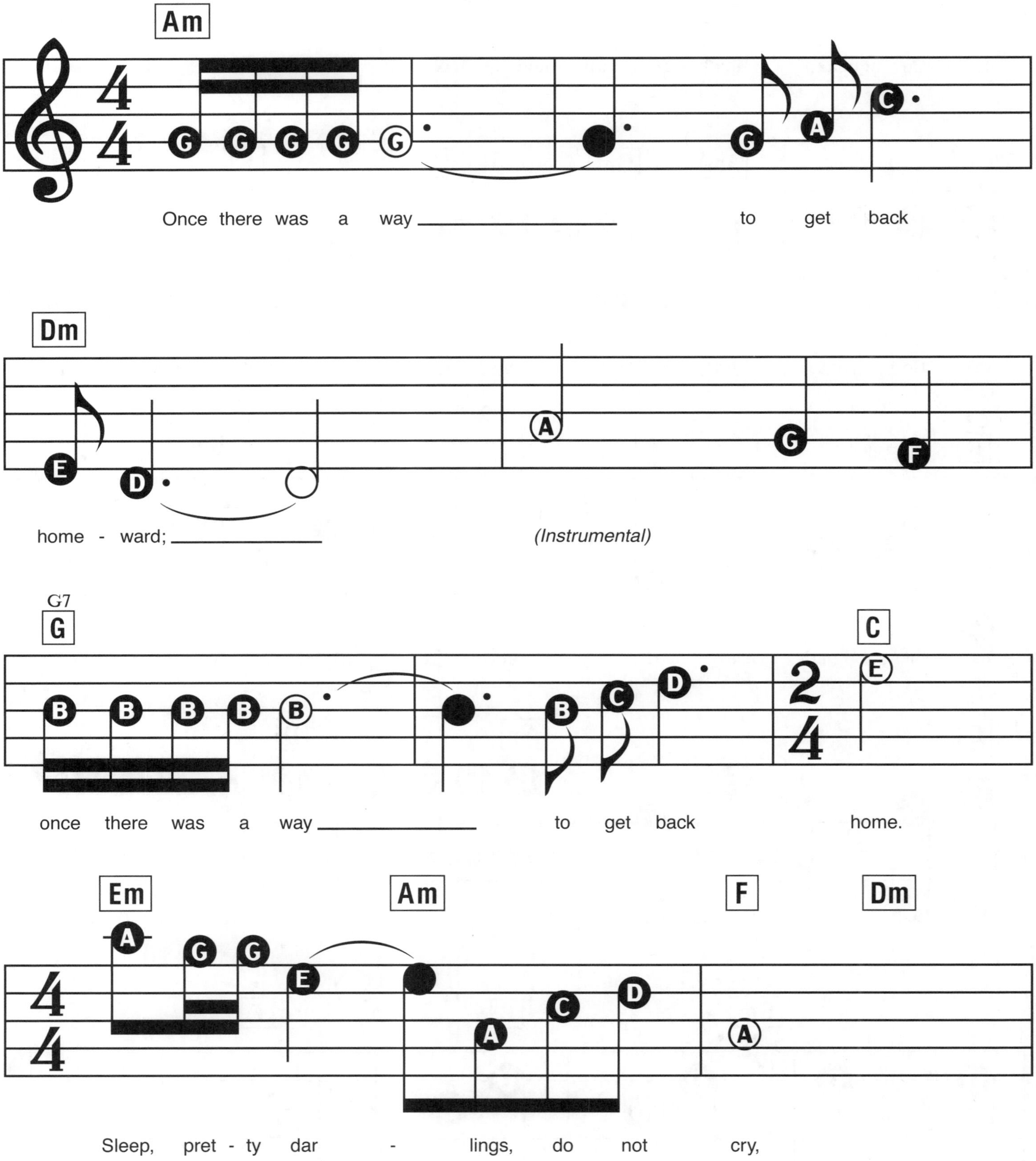

Dm

E D A G F

home - ward; (Instrumental)

G7
G

B B B B B B B C D

C

E

once there was a way to get back home.

Em Am F Dm

A G G E A C D A

Sleep, pret - ty dar - lings, do not cry,

Copyright © 1969 Sony/ATV Music Publishing LLC
Copyright Renewed
All Rights Administered by Sony/ATV Music Publishing LLC, 424 Church Street, Suite 1200, Nashville, TN 37210
International Copyright Secured All Rights Reserved

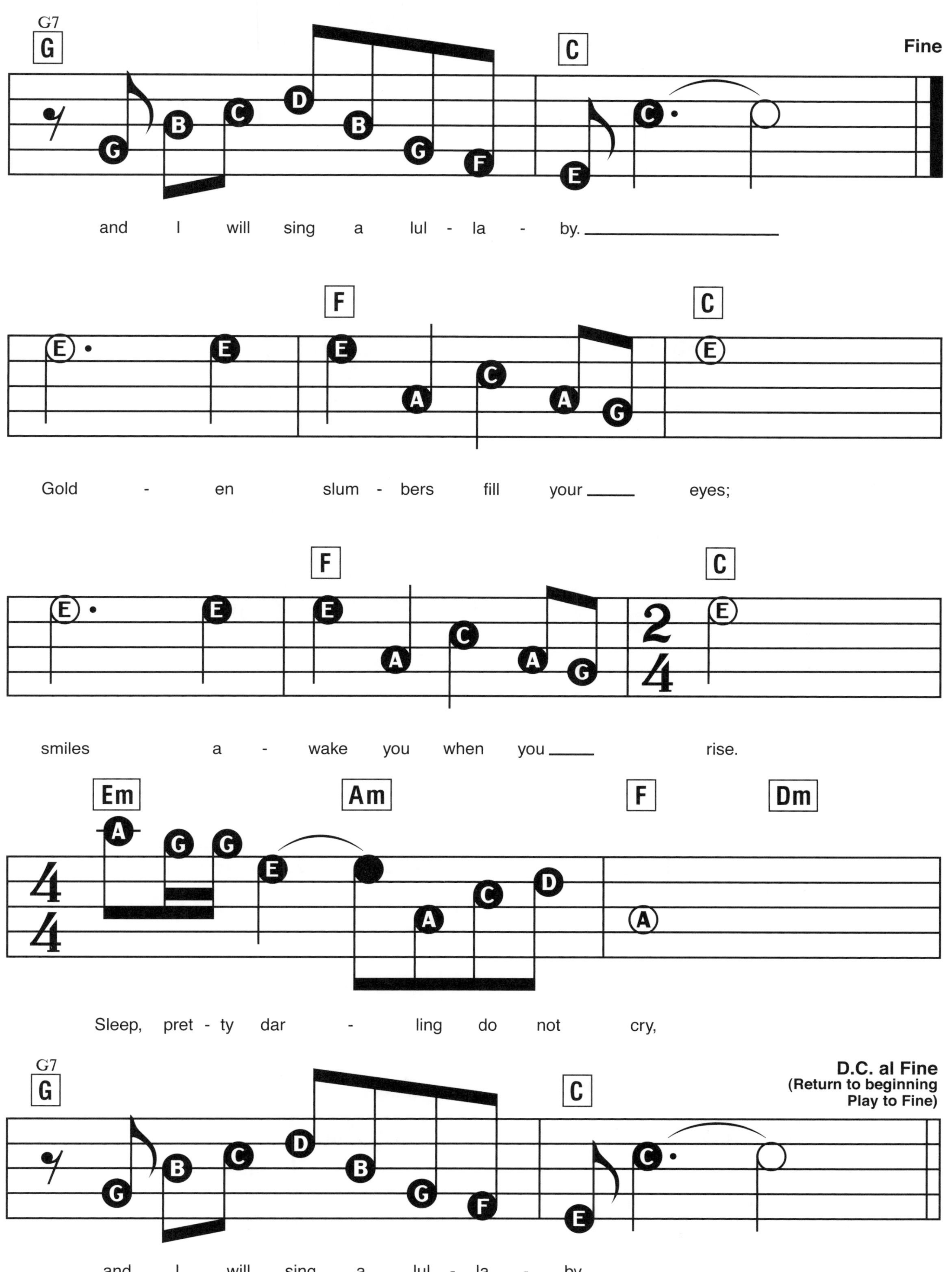
G7
G
C
Fine
and I will sing a lul - la - by.
F
C
Gold - en slum - bers fill your eyes;
F
C
smiles a - wake you when you rise.
Em
Am
F
Dm
Sleep, pret - ty dar - ling do not cry,
G7
G
C
D.C. al Fine
(Return to beginning
Play to Fine)
and I will sing a lul - la - by.

Good Night

Registration 3
Rhythm: Ballad

Words and Music by John Lennon
and Paul McCartney

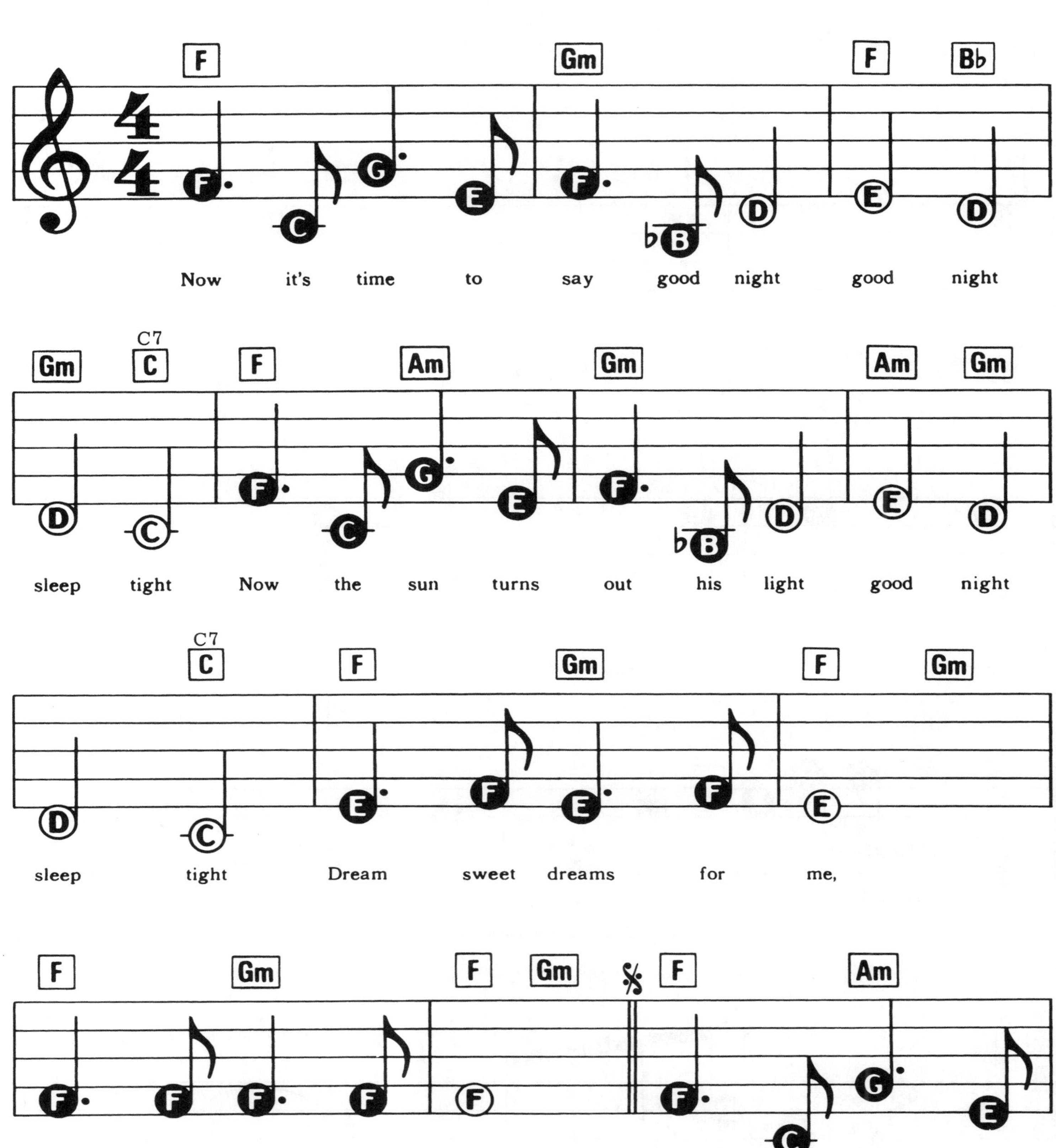

Copyright © 1968 Sony/ATV Music Publishing LLC
Copyright Renewed
All Rights Administered by Sony/ATV Music Publishing LLC, 424 Church Street, Suite 1200, Nashville, TN 37219
International Copyright Secured All Rights Reserved

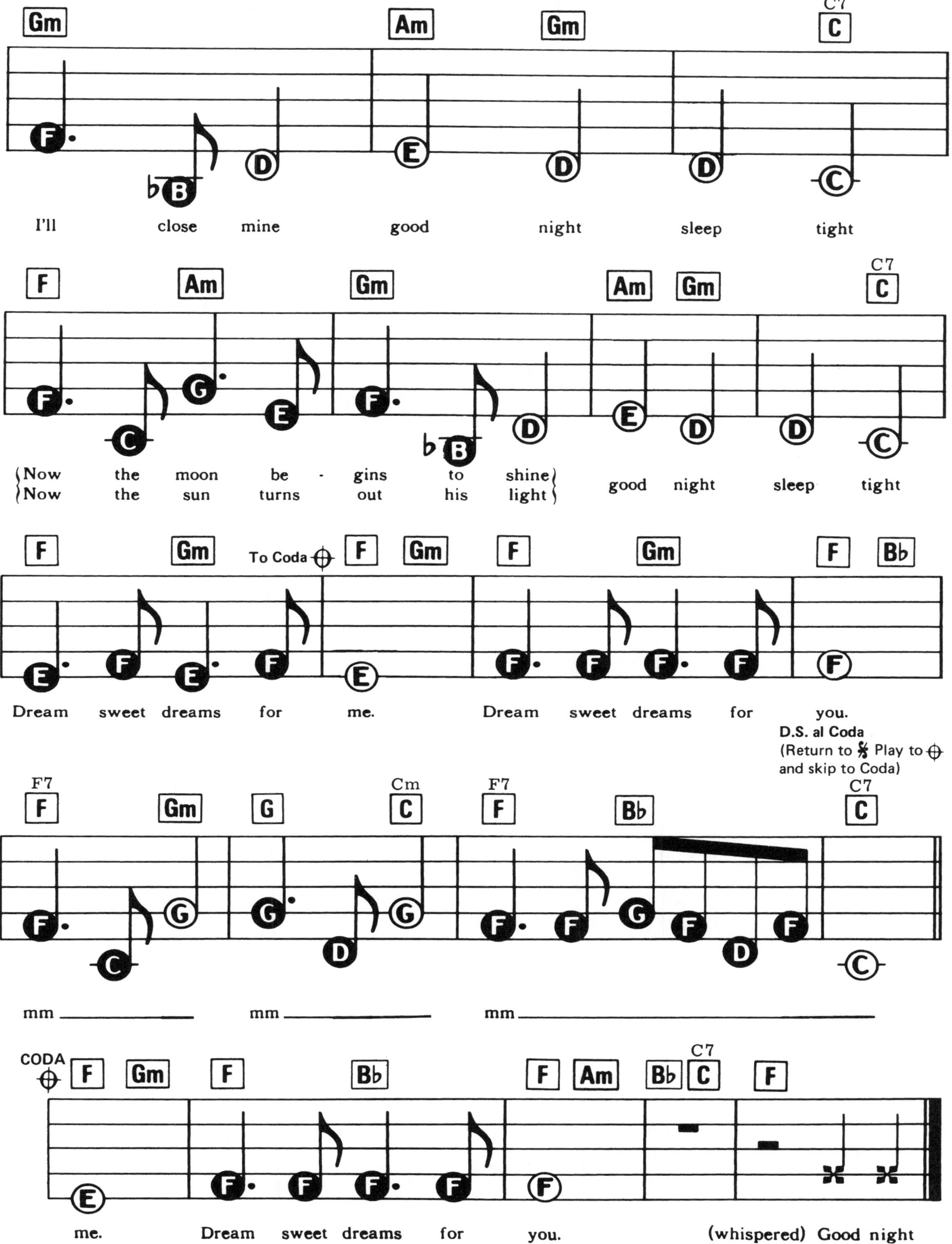
Gm
Am
Gm
C7
C
F
B♭
D
E
D
D
C
I'll
close
mine
good
night
sleep
tight
F
Am
Gm
Am
Gm
C7
C
Now the moon be - gins to shine
Now the sun turns out his light
good
night
sleep
tight
F
Gm
To Coda
F
Gm
F
Gm
F
B♭
Dream sweet dreams for me.
Dream sweet dreams for you.
D.S. al Coda
(Return to 𝄋 Play to ⊕
and skip to Coda)
F7
F
Gm
G
Cm
C
F7
F
B♭
C7
C
mm
mm
mm
CODA
F
Gm
F
B♭
F
Am
B♭
C7
C
F
me.
Dream sweet dreams for you.
(whispered) Good night

Happy Birthday to You

Registration 8
Rhythm: Waltz or None

Words and Music by Mildred J. Hill
and Patty S. Hill

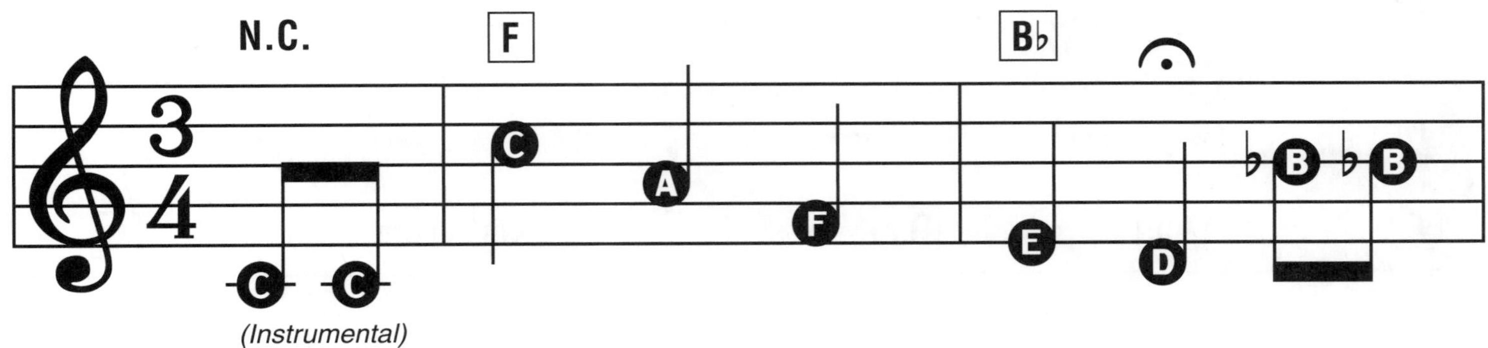

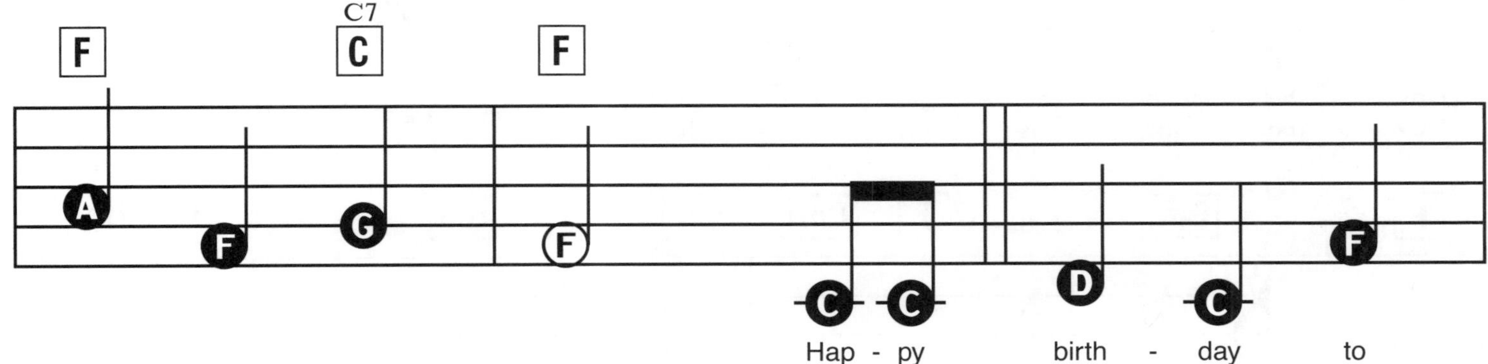

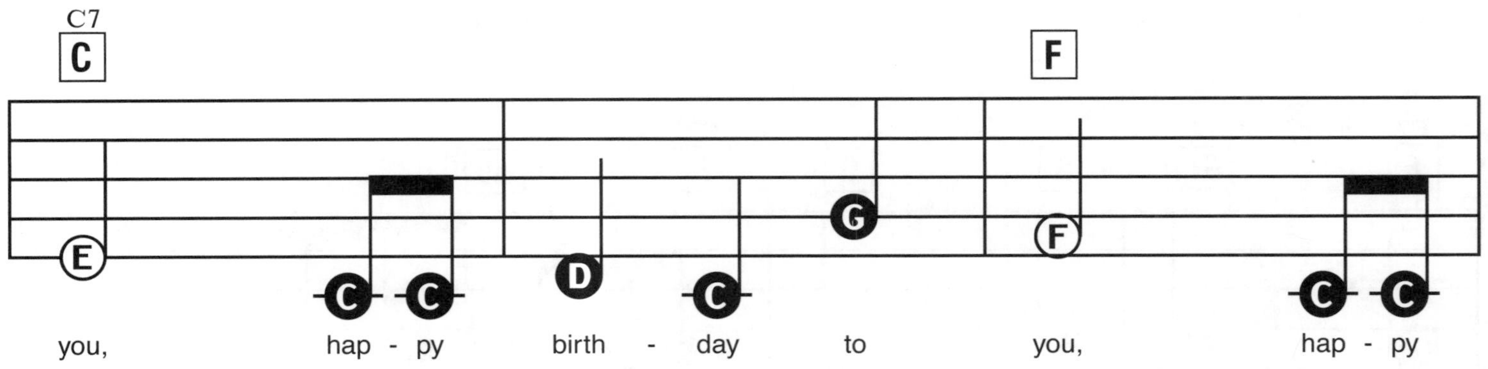

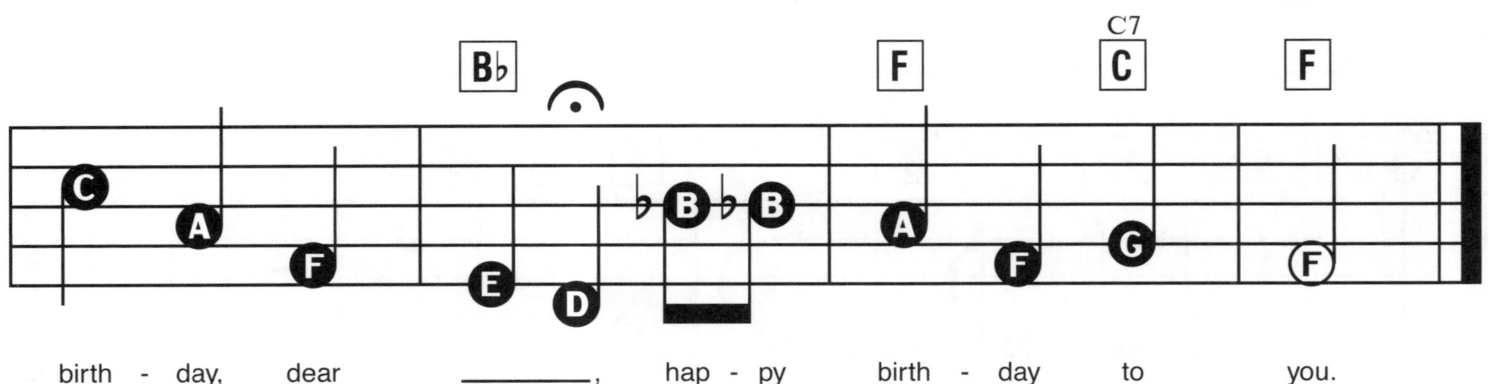

Copyright © 2016 by HAL LEONARD CORPORATION
International Copyright Secured All Rights Reserved

Happy Trails

from the Television Series THE ROY ROGERS SHOW

Registration 5
Rhythm: Swing or Pops

Words and Music by
Dale Evans

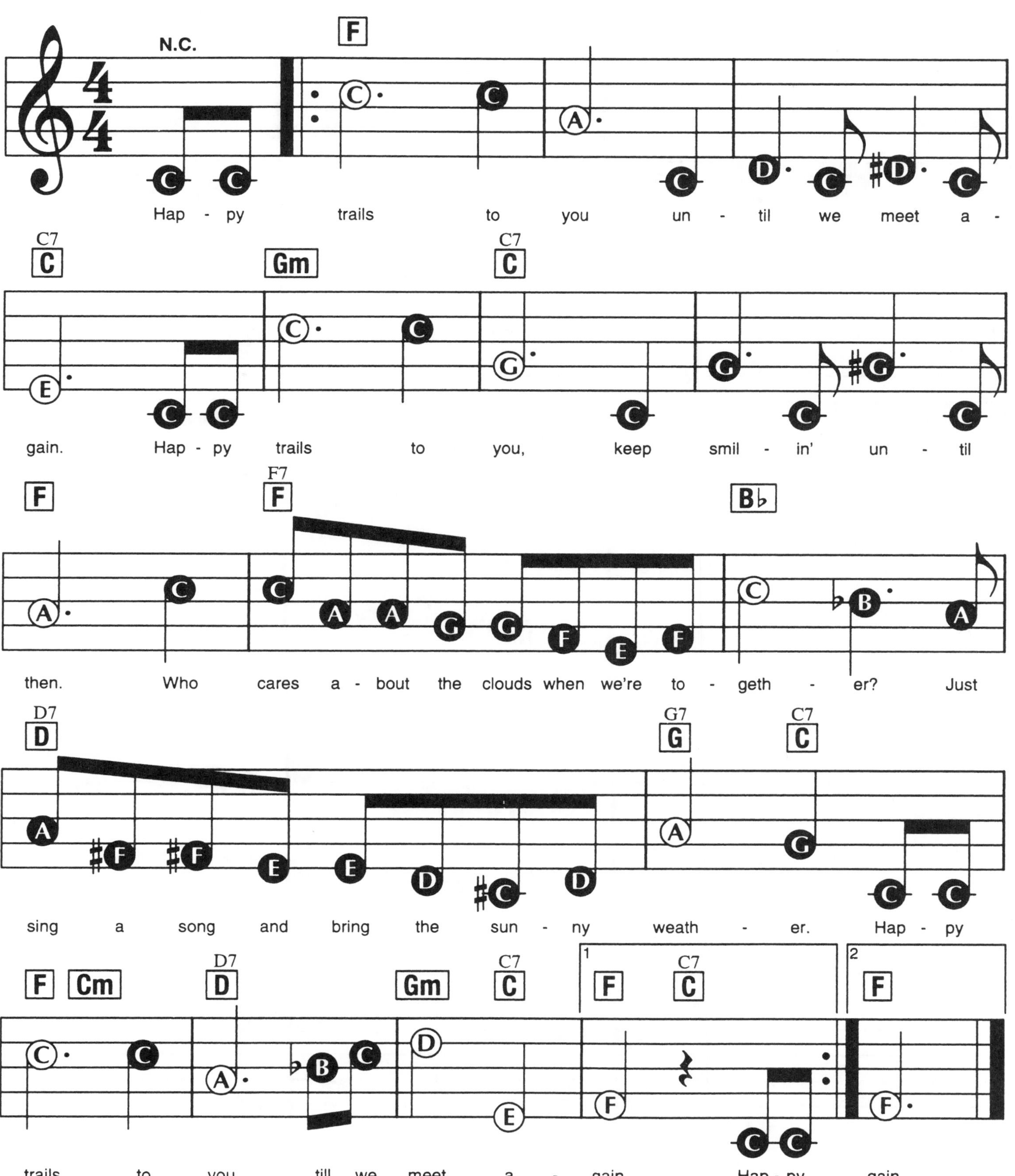

Copyright © 1952 Roy Rogers Music
Copyright Renewed
All Rights Administered by Sony/ATV Music Publishing LLC, 424 Church Street, Suite 1200, Nashville, TN 37219
International Copyright Secured All Rights Reserved

Heart and Soul

from the Paramount Short Subject A SONG IS BORN

Registration 8
Rhythm: Swing

Words by Frank Loesser
Music by Hoagy Carmichael

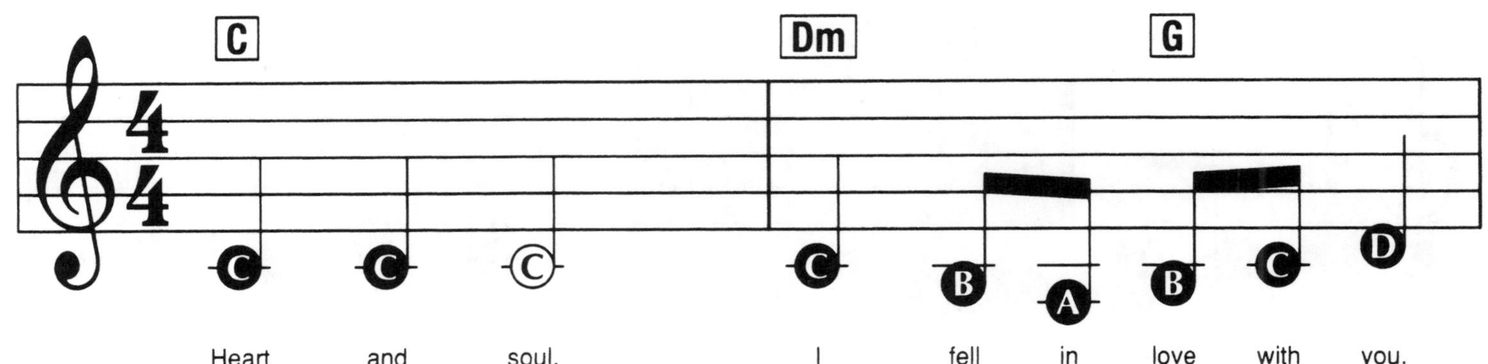

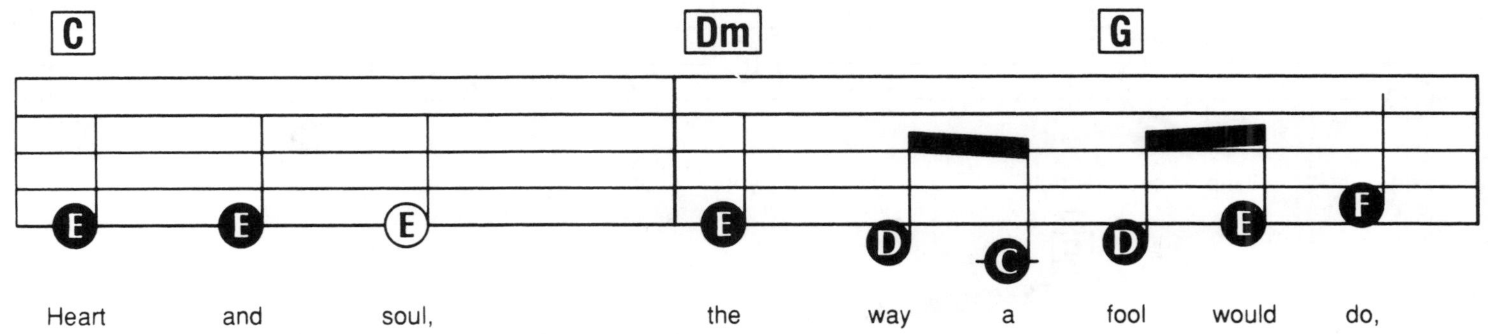

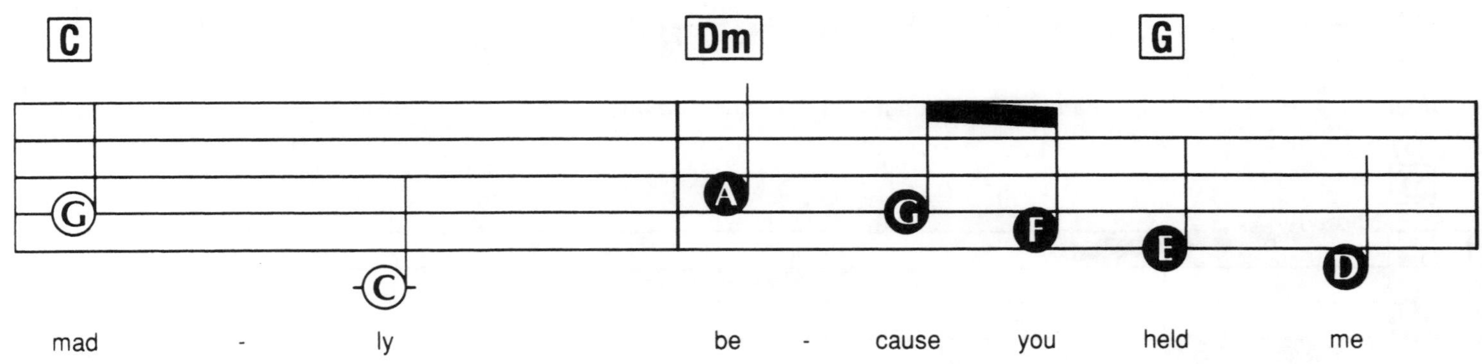

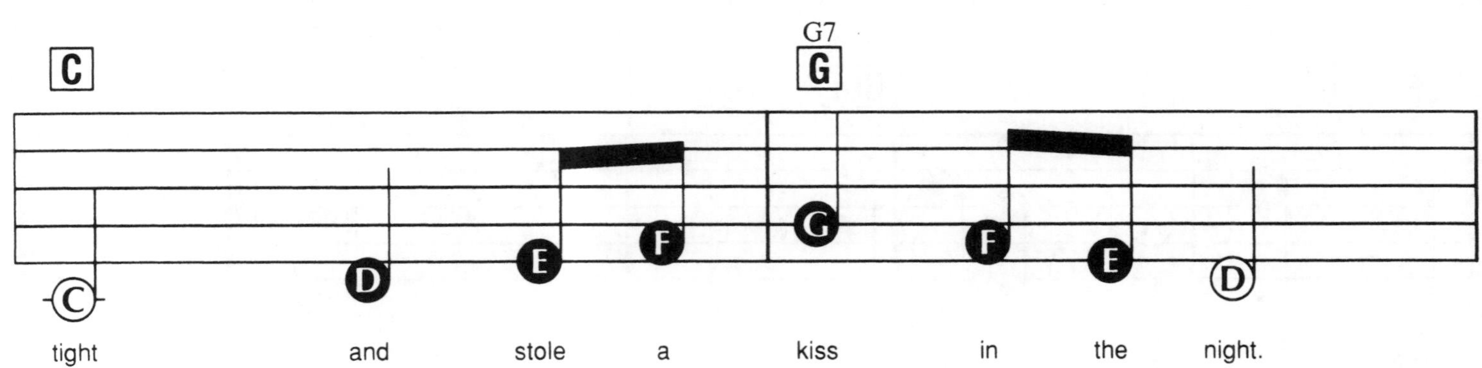

Copyright © 1938 Sony/ATV Music Publishing LLC
Copyright Renewed
All Rights Administered by Sony/ATV Music Publishing LLC, 424 Church Street, Suite 1200, Nashville, TN 37219
International Copyright Secured All Rights Reserved

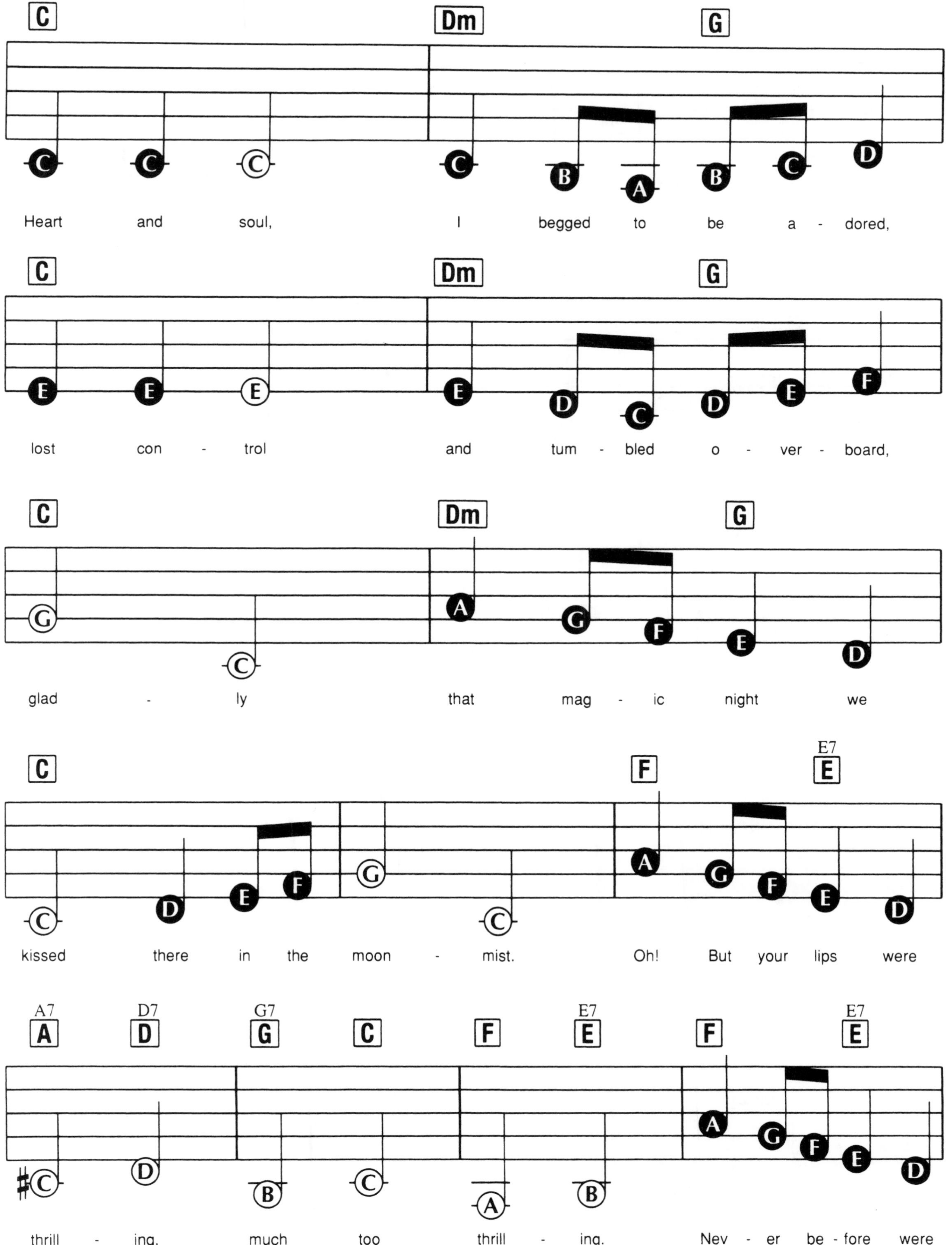
C Dm G
C C C C B A B C D
Heart and soul, I begged to be a - dored,
C Dm G
E E E E D C D E F
lost con - trol and tum - bled o - ver - board,
C Dm G
G C A G F E D
glad - ly that mag - ic night we
C F E7 E
C D E F G C A G F E D
kissed there in the moon - mist. Oh! But your lips were
A7 A D7 D G7 G C F E7 E F E7 E
♯C D B C A B A G F E D
thrill - ing, much too thrill - ing. Nev - er be - fore were

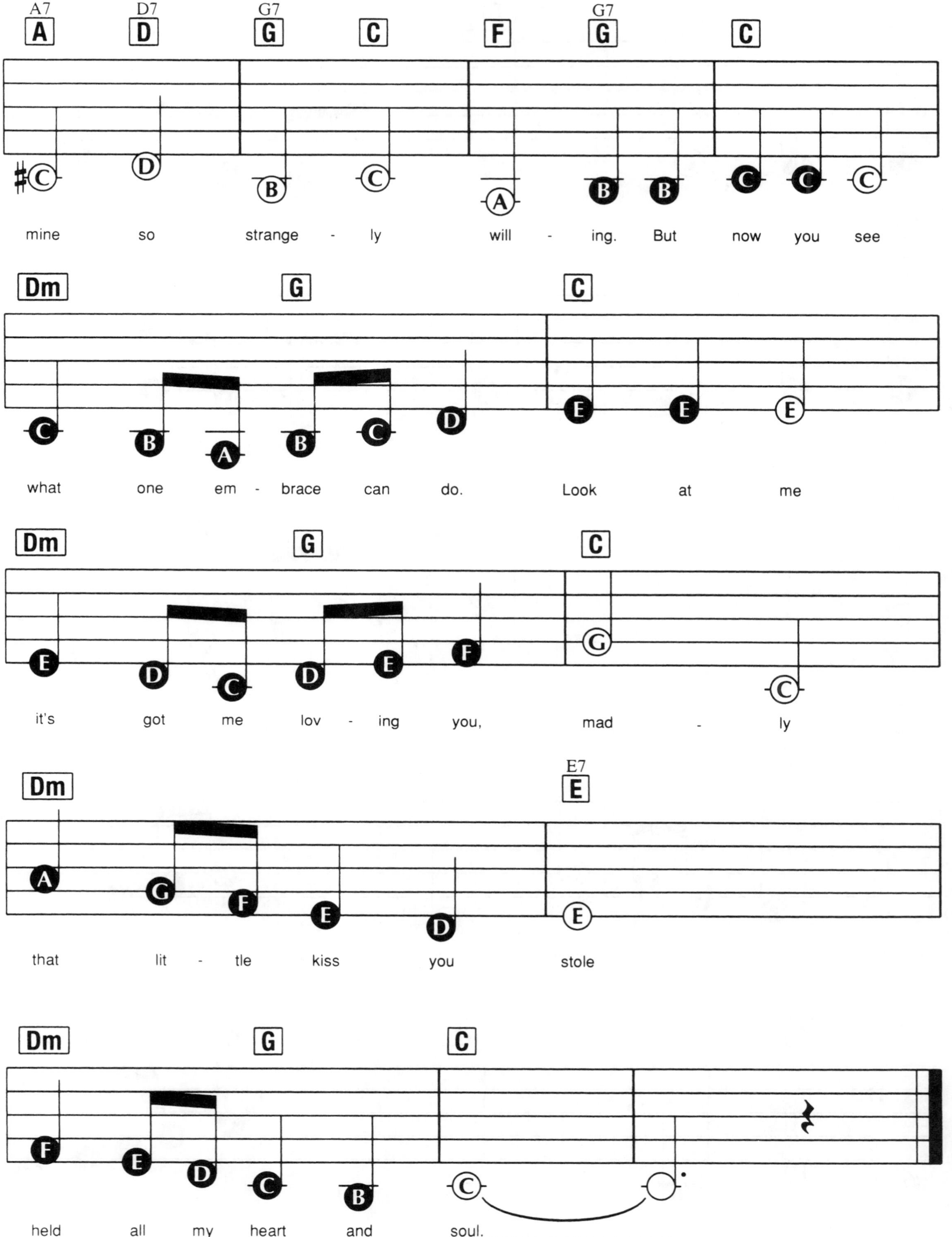
A7 D7 G7 G7
A D G C F G C
mine so strange - ly will - ing. But now you see
Dm G C
what one em - brace can do. Look at me
Dm G C
it's got me lov - ing you, mad - ly
Dm E7 E
that lit - tle kiss you stole
Dm G C
held all my heart and soul.

How Much Is That Doggie in the Window

Registration 2
Rhythm: Waltz

Words and Music by
Bob Merrill

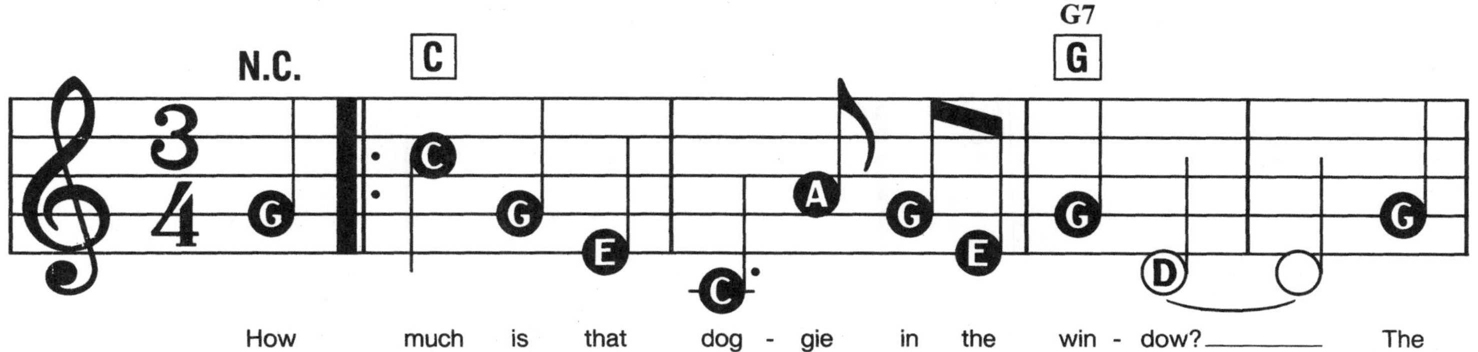

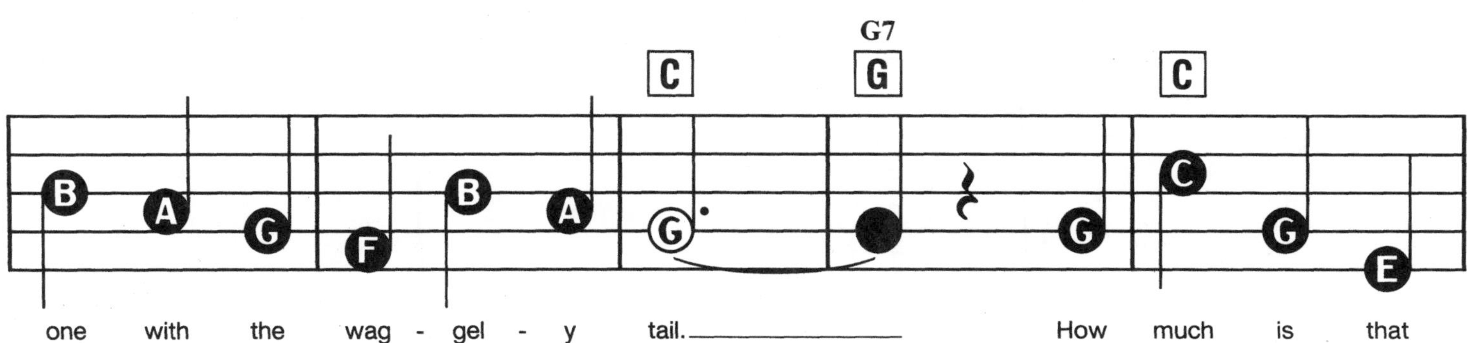

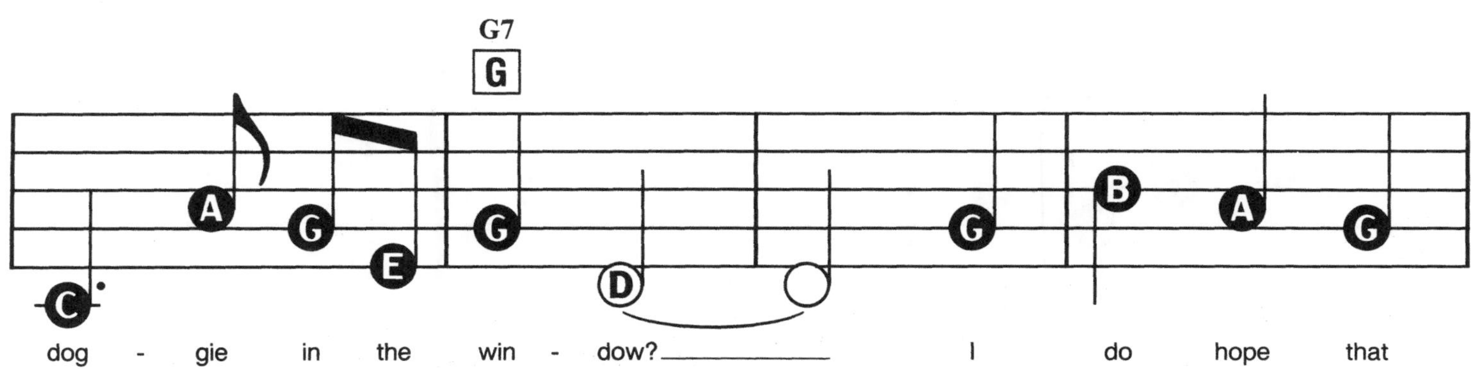

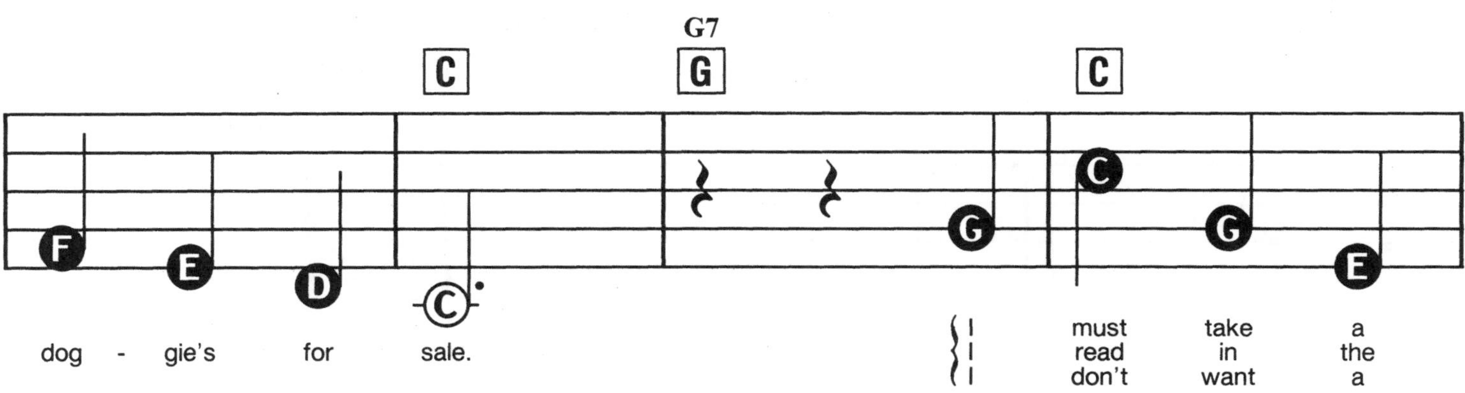

Copyright © 1952 Golden Bell Songs
Copyright Renewed 1980
Administered by Music & Media International, Inc.
International Copyright Secured All Rights Reserved

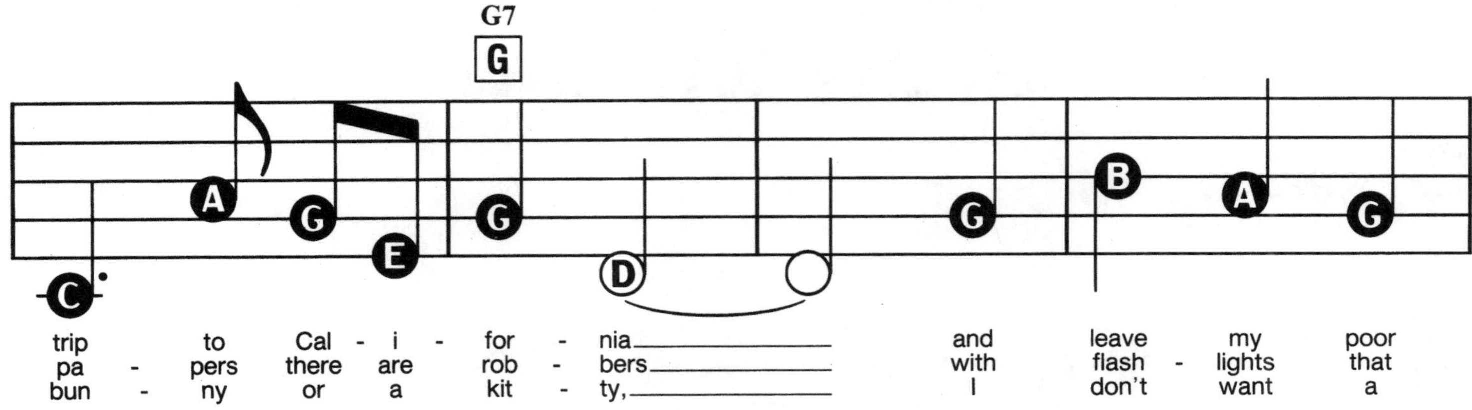
G7
G
C A G E G D G B A G
trip to Cal - i - for - nia. and leave my poor
pa - pers there are rob - bers with flash - lights that
bun - ny or a kit - ty, I don't want a

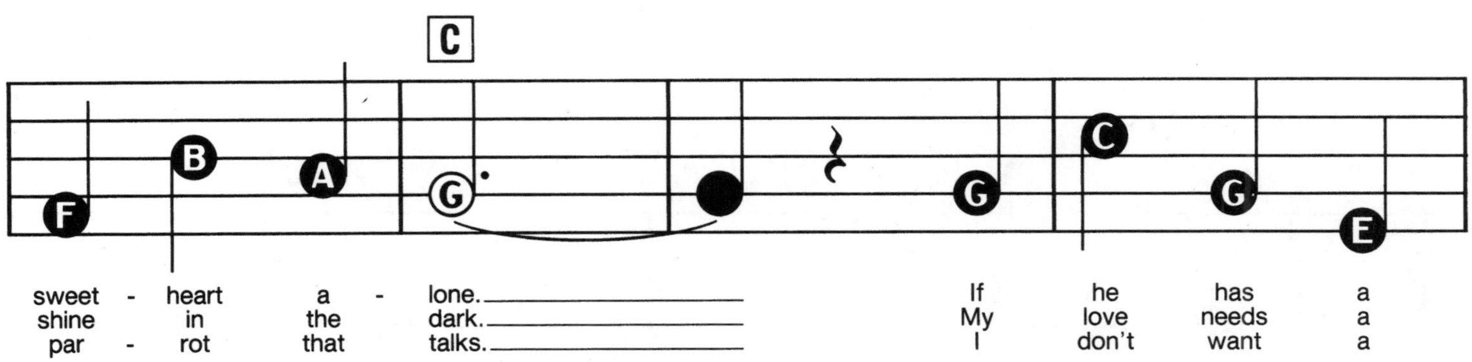
C
F B A G G C G E
sweet - heart a - lone. If he has a
shine in the dark. My love needs a
par - rot that talks. I don't want a

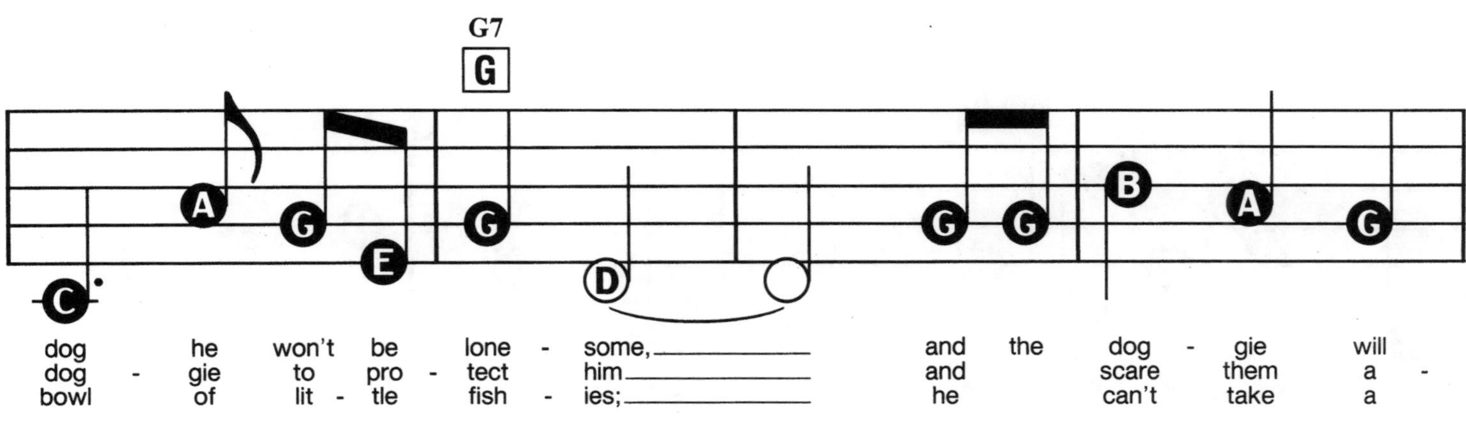
G7
G
C A G E G D G G B A G
dog he won't be lone - some, and the dog - gie will
dog - gie to pro - tect him and scare them a -
bowl of lit - tle fish - ies; he can't take a

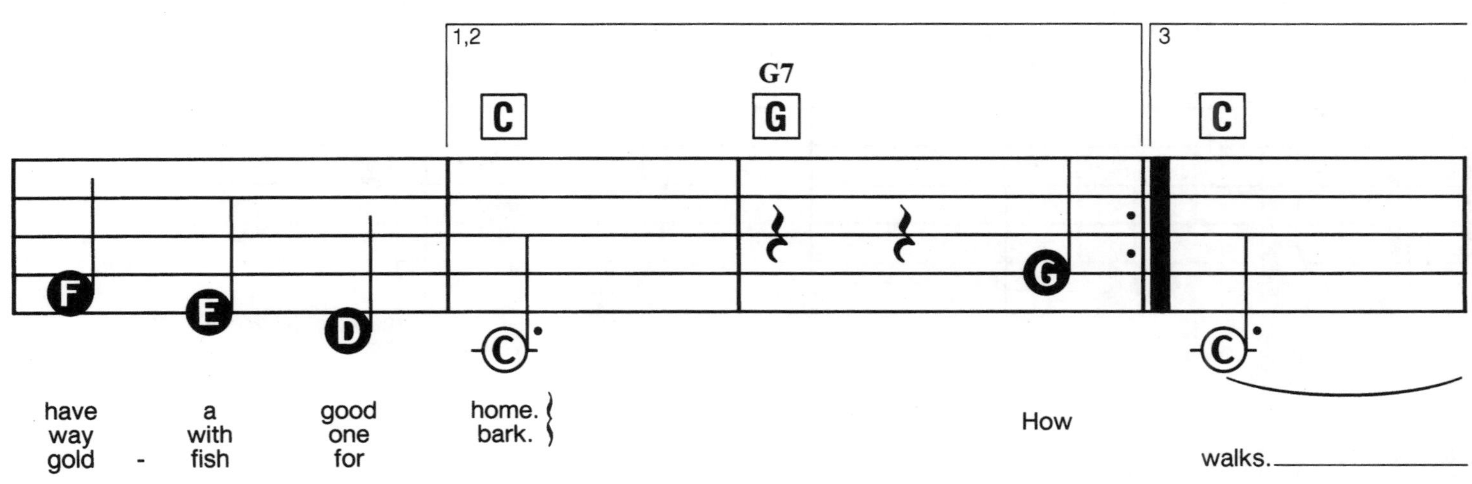
1,2
3
C
G7
G
C
F E D C G C
have a good home.
way with one bark.
gold - fish for
How
walks.

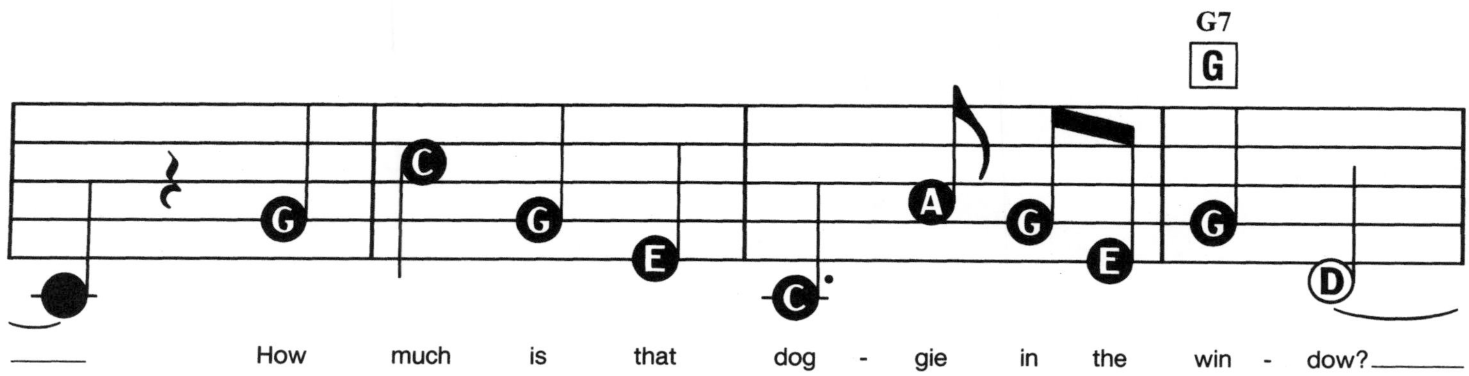
G7
G
C G G C G E C A G E G D
How much is that dog - gie in the win - dow?

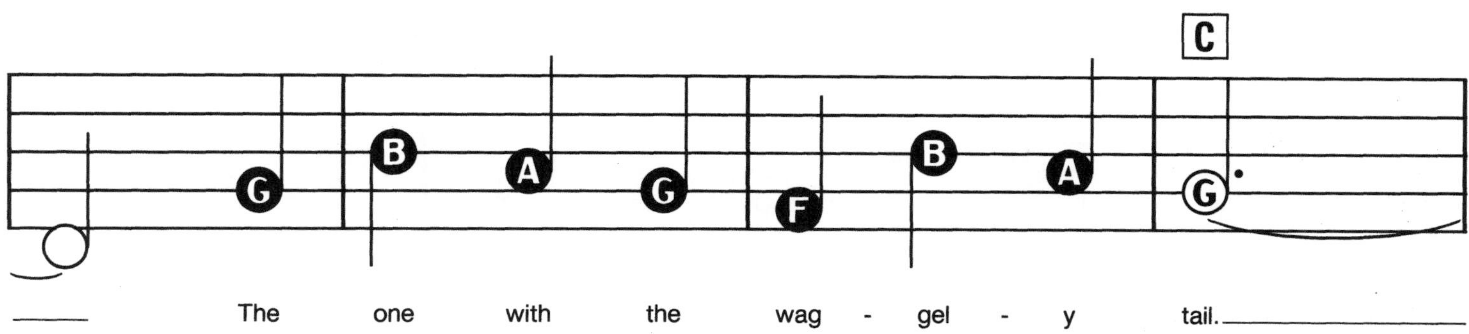
C
G B A G F B A G
The one with the wag - gel - y tail.

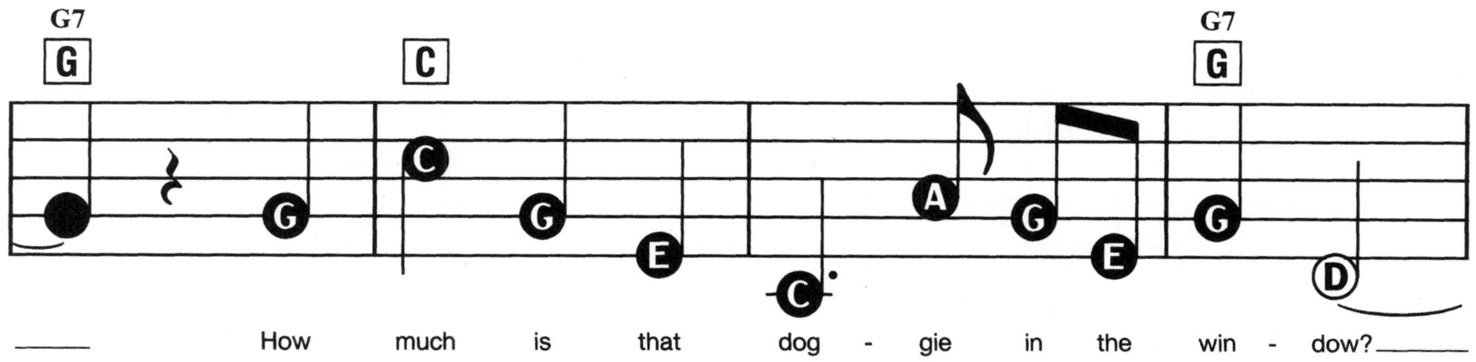
G7
G
C
G7
G
G C G E C A G E G D
How much is that dog - gie in the win - dow?

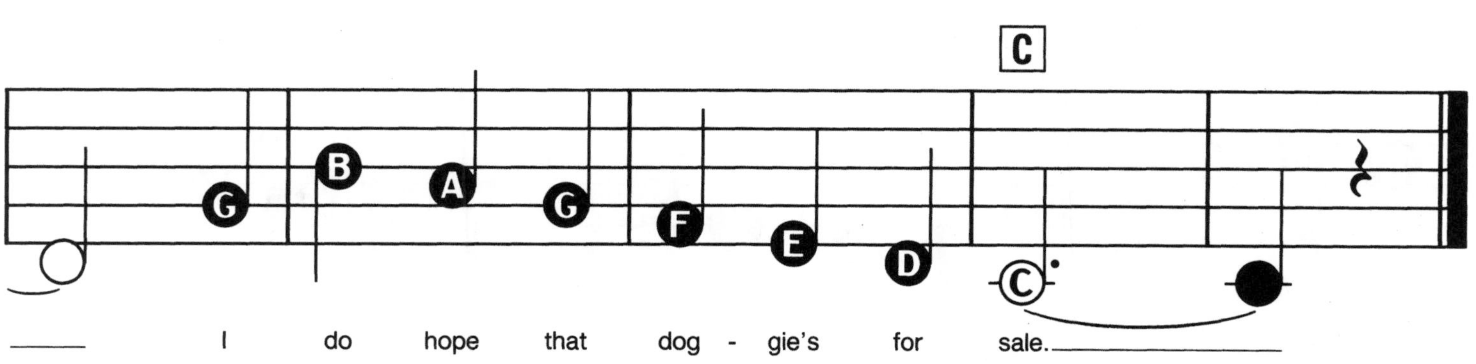
C
G B A G F E D C
I do hope that dog - gie's for sale.

Heigh-Ho

The Dwarfs' Marching Song from Walt Disney's SNOW WHITE AND THE SEVEN DWARFS

Registration 4
Rhythm: March

Words by Larry Morey
Music by Frank Churchill

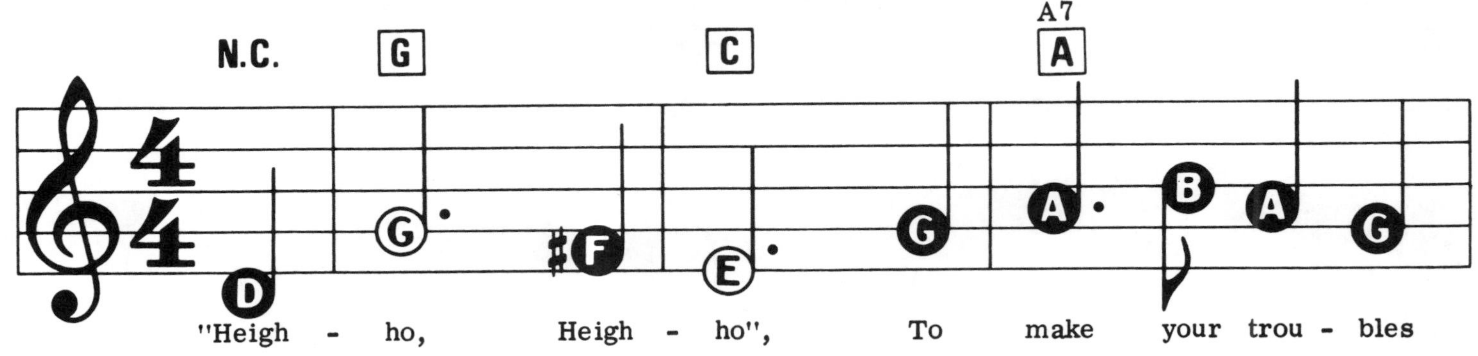

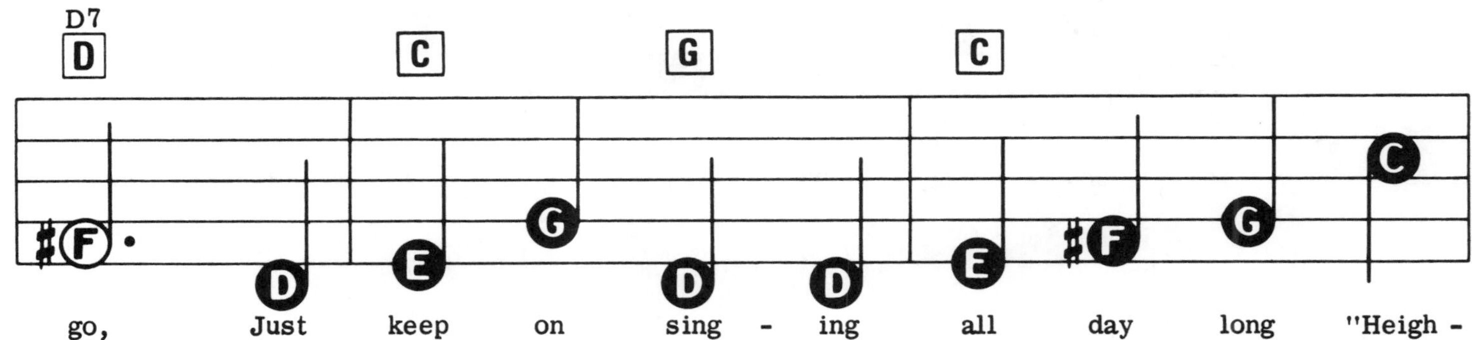

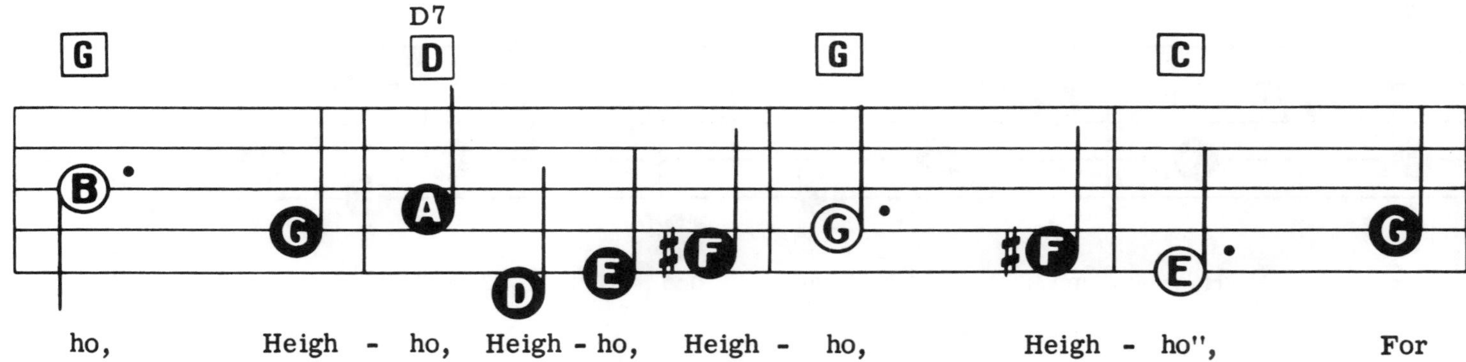

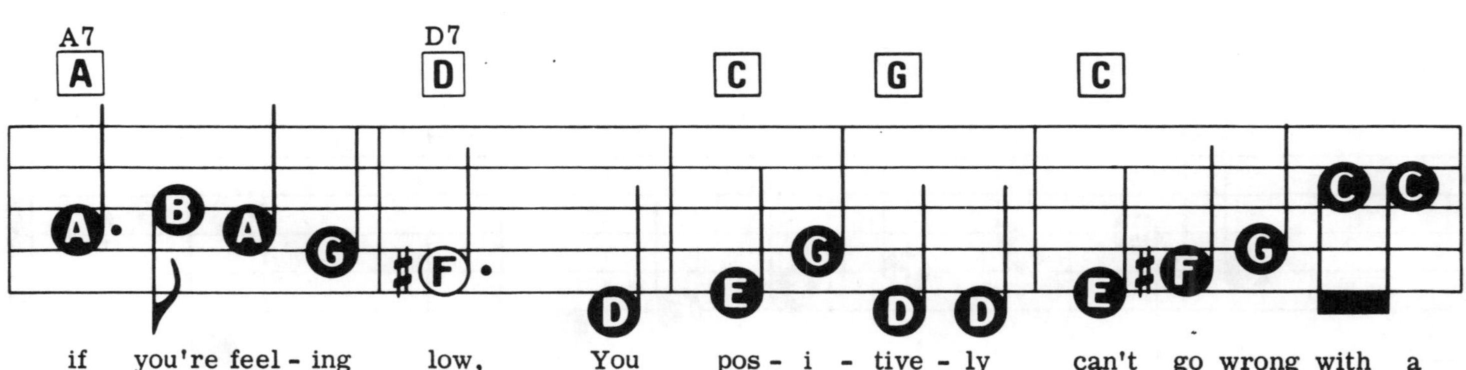

Copyright © 1937 by Bourne Co. (ASCAP)
Copyright Renewed
International Copyright Secured All Rights Reserved

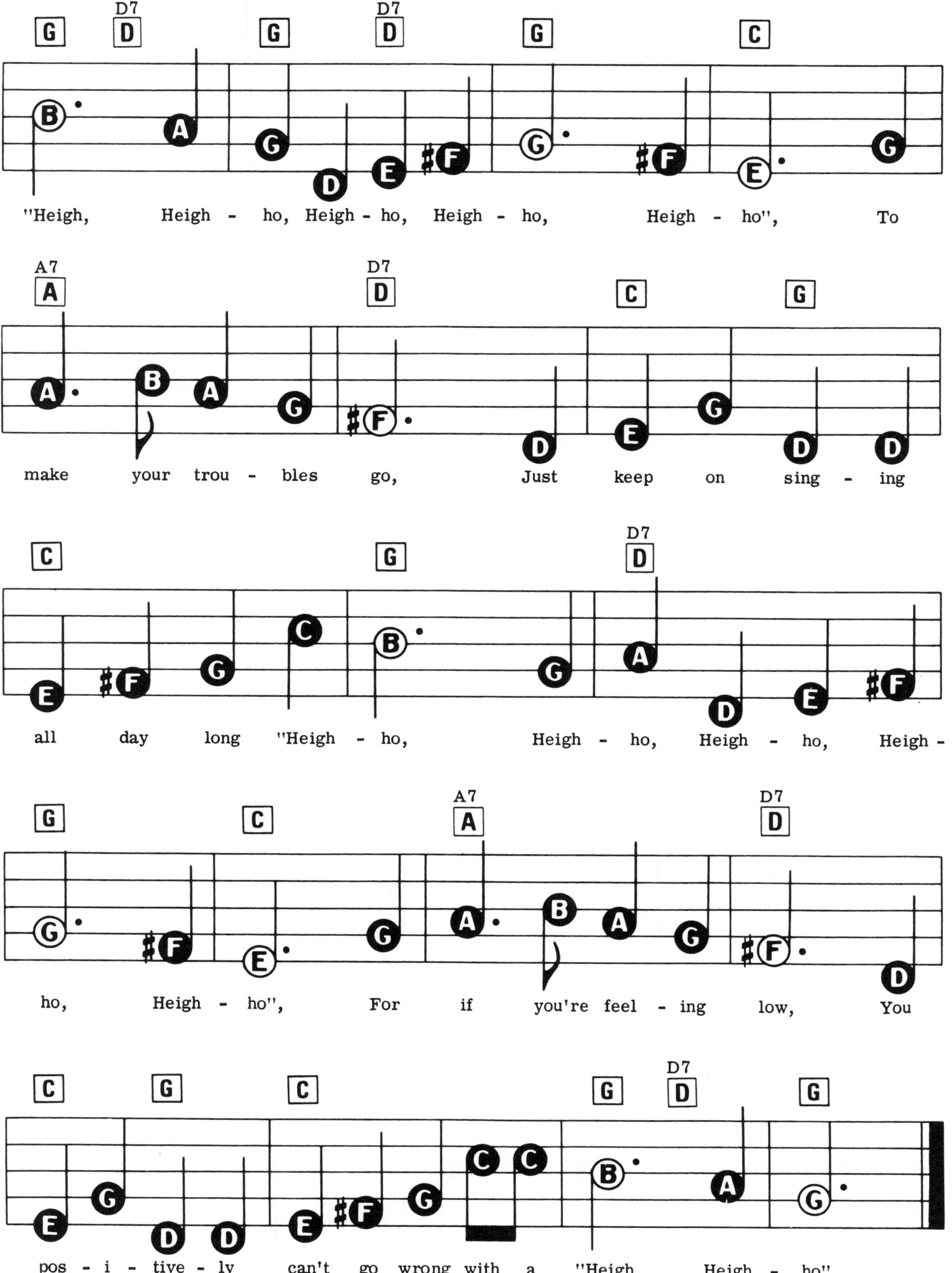
G D7 D G D7 D G C
"Heigh, Heigh - ho, Heigh - ho, Heigh - ho, Heigh - ho", To
A7 A D7 D C G
make your trou - bles go, Just keep on sing - ing
C G D7 D
all day long "Heigh - ho, Heigh - ho, Heigh - ho, Heigh -
G C A7 A D7 D
ho, Heigh - ho", For if you're feel - ing low, You
C G C G D7 D G
pos - i - tive - ly can't go wrong with a "Heigh Heigh - ho".

The Hokey Pokey

Registration 5
Rhythm: Fox Trot or Swing

Words and Music by Charles P. Macak, Tafft Baker and Larry LaPrise

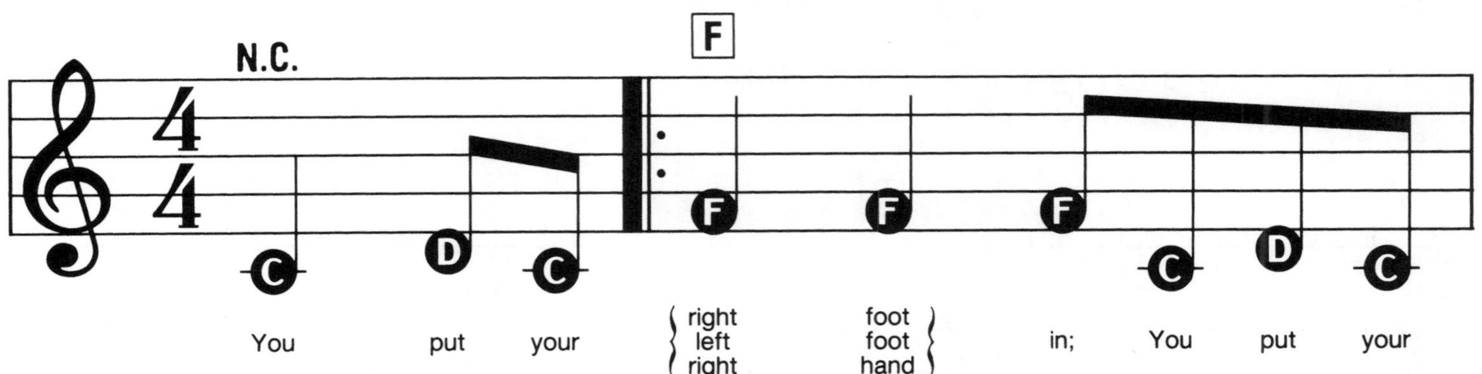

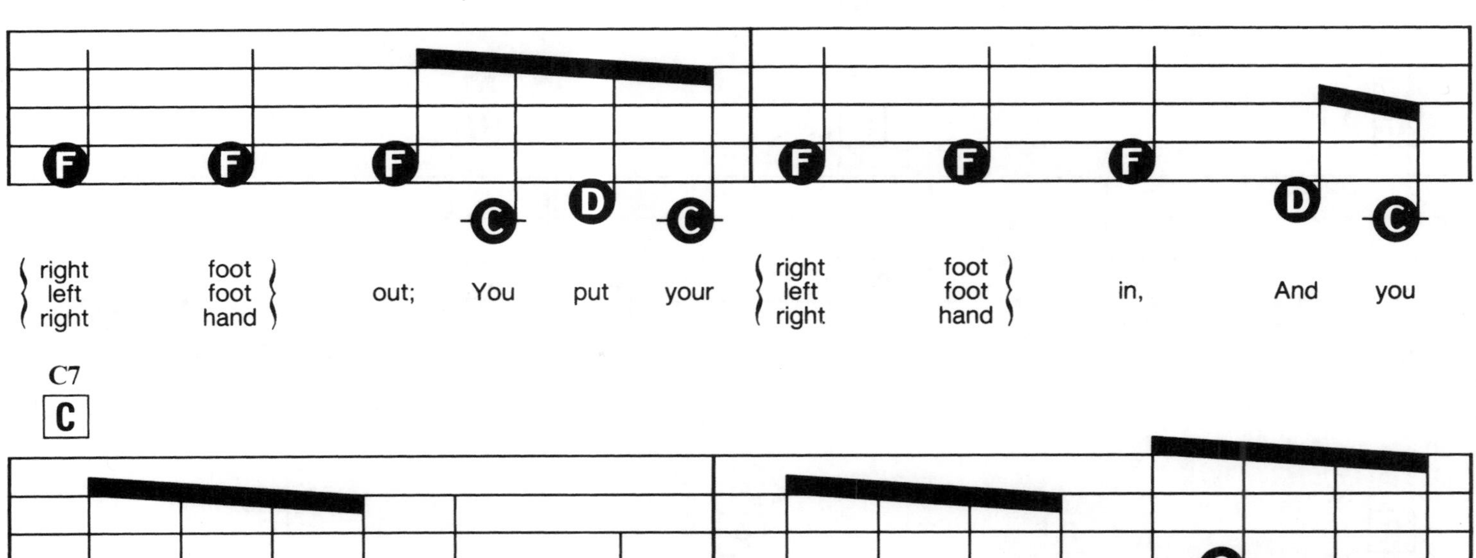

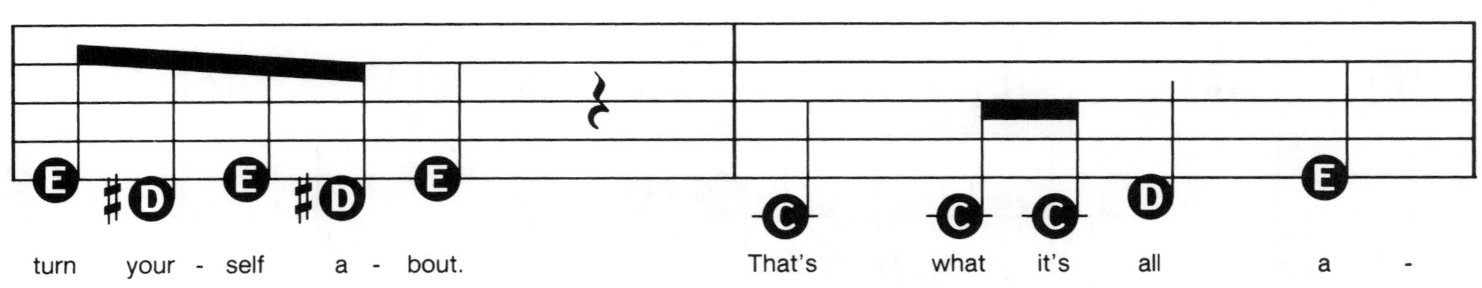

Copyright © 1950 Sony/ATV Music Publishing LLC
Copyright Renewed
All Rights Administered by Sony/ATV Music Publishing LLC, 424 Church Street, Suite 1200, Nashville, TN 37219
International Copyright Secured All Rights Reserved

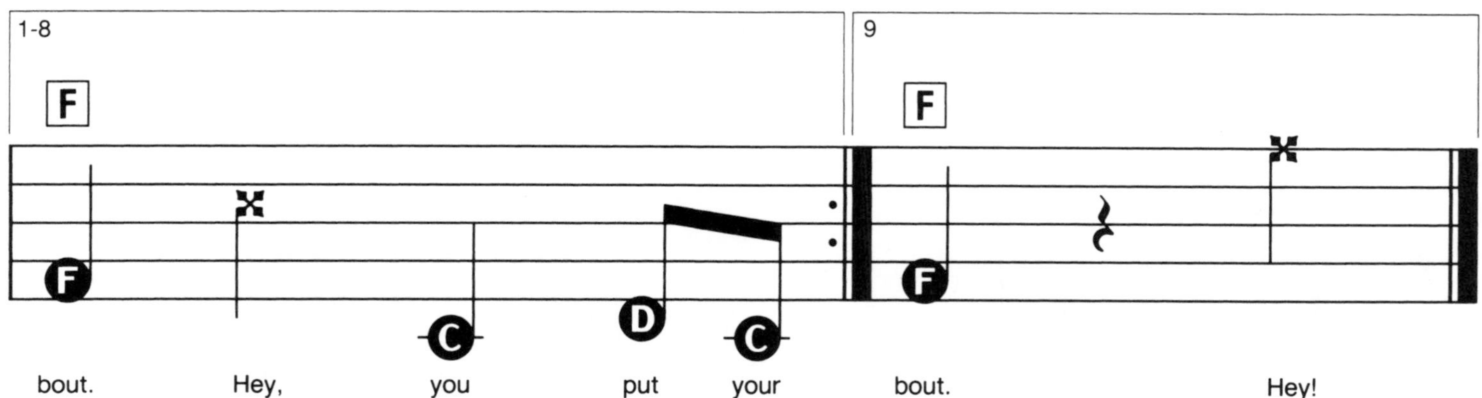

Additional Lyrics

4. Hey, you put your left hand in;
   You put your left hand out;
   You put your left hand in,
   And you shake it all about.
   You do the Hokey-Pokey,
   And you turn yourself about.
   That's what it's all about.

5. Hey, you put your right shoulder in;
   You put your right shoulder out;
   Etc.

6. Hey, you put your left shoulder in;
   You put your left shoulder out;
   Etc.

7. Hey, you put your right hip in;
   You put your right hip out;
   Etc.

8. Hey, you put your left hip in;
   You put your left hip out;
   Etc.

9. Hey, you put your whole self in;
   You put your whole self out;
   Etc.

I Whistle a Happy Tune

from THE KING AND I

Registration 1
Rhythm: Fox Trot or Swing

Lyrics by Oscar Hammerstein II
Music by Richard Rodgers

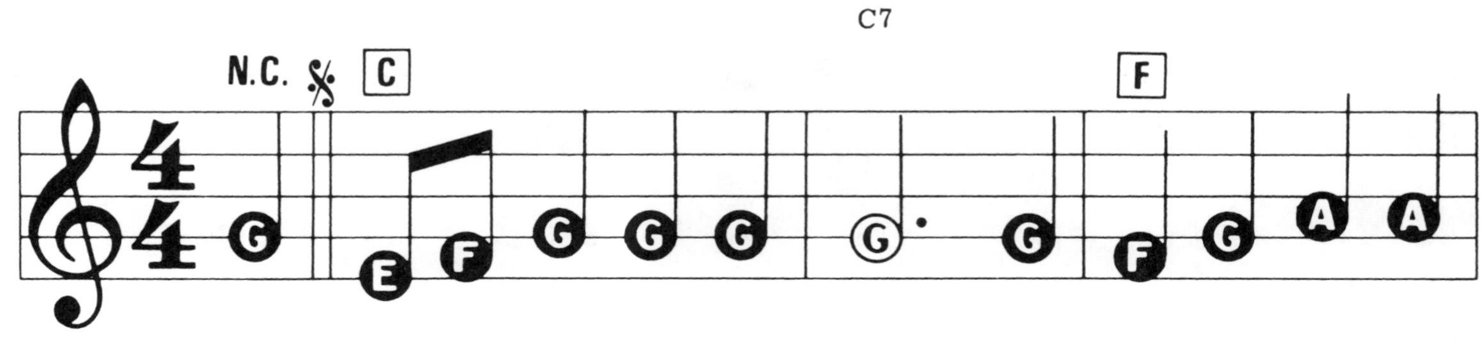

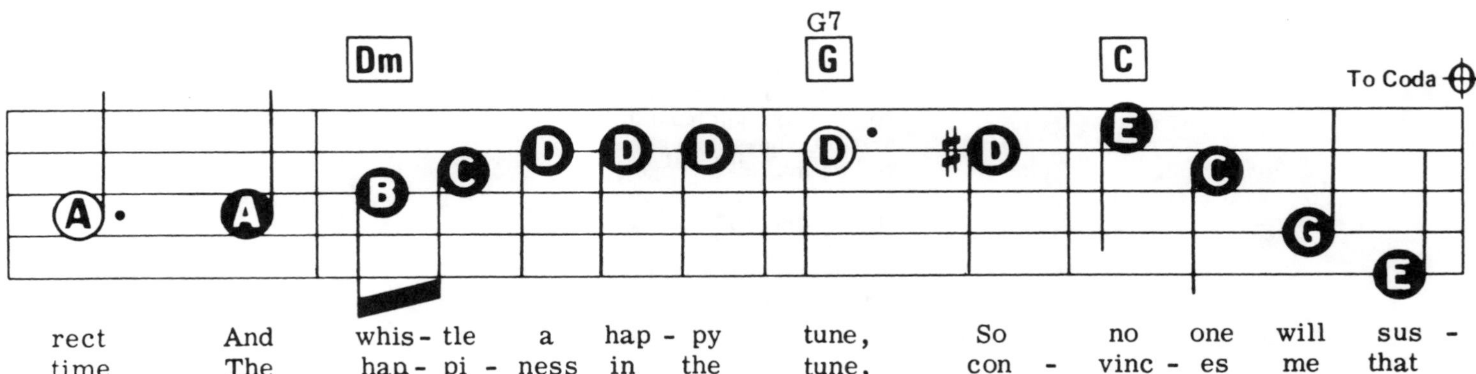

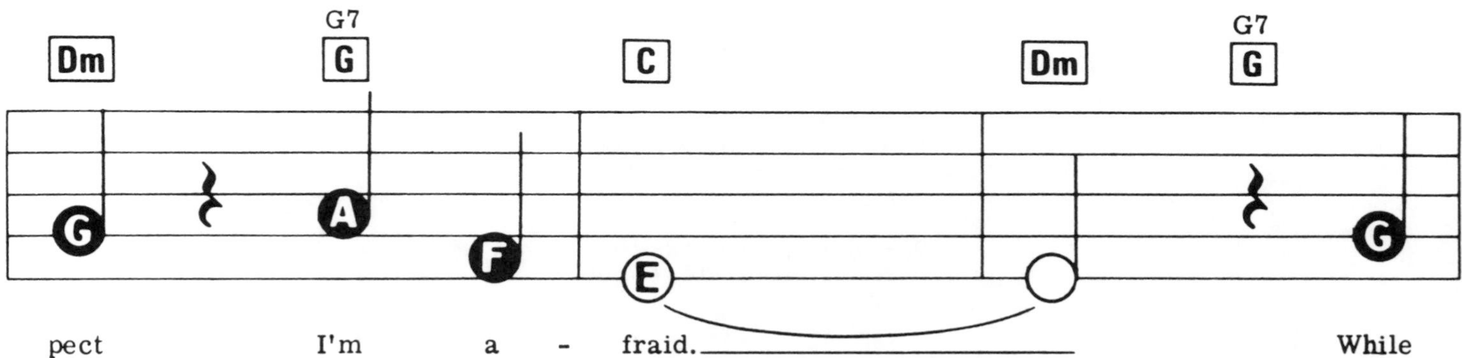

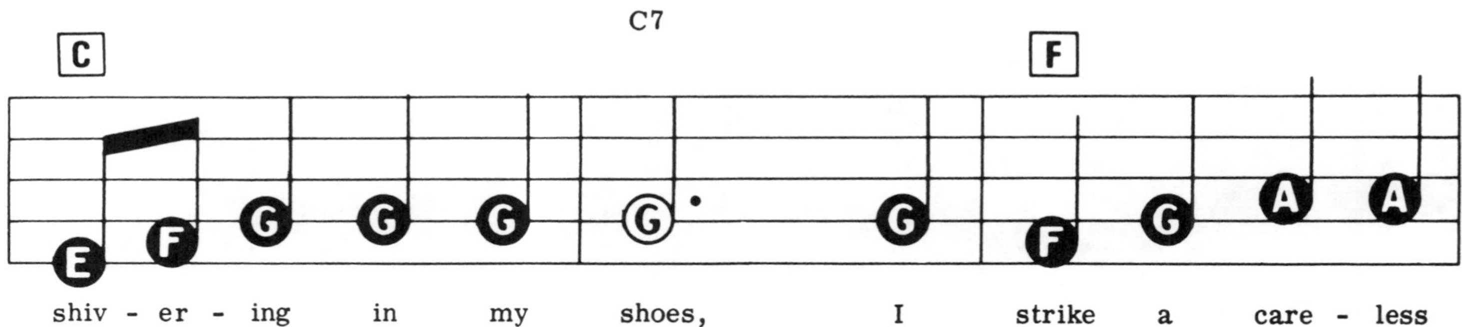

Copyright © 1951 by Richard Rodgers and Oscar Hammerstein II
Copyright Renewed
Williamson Music, a Division of Rodgers & Hammerstein: an Imagem Company, owner of publication and allied rights throughout the world
International Copyright Secured All Rights Reserved

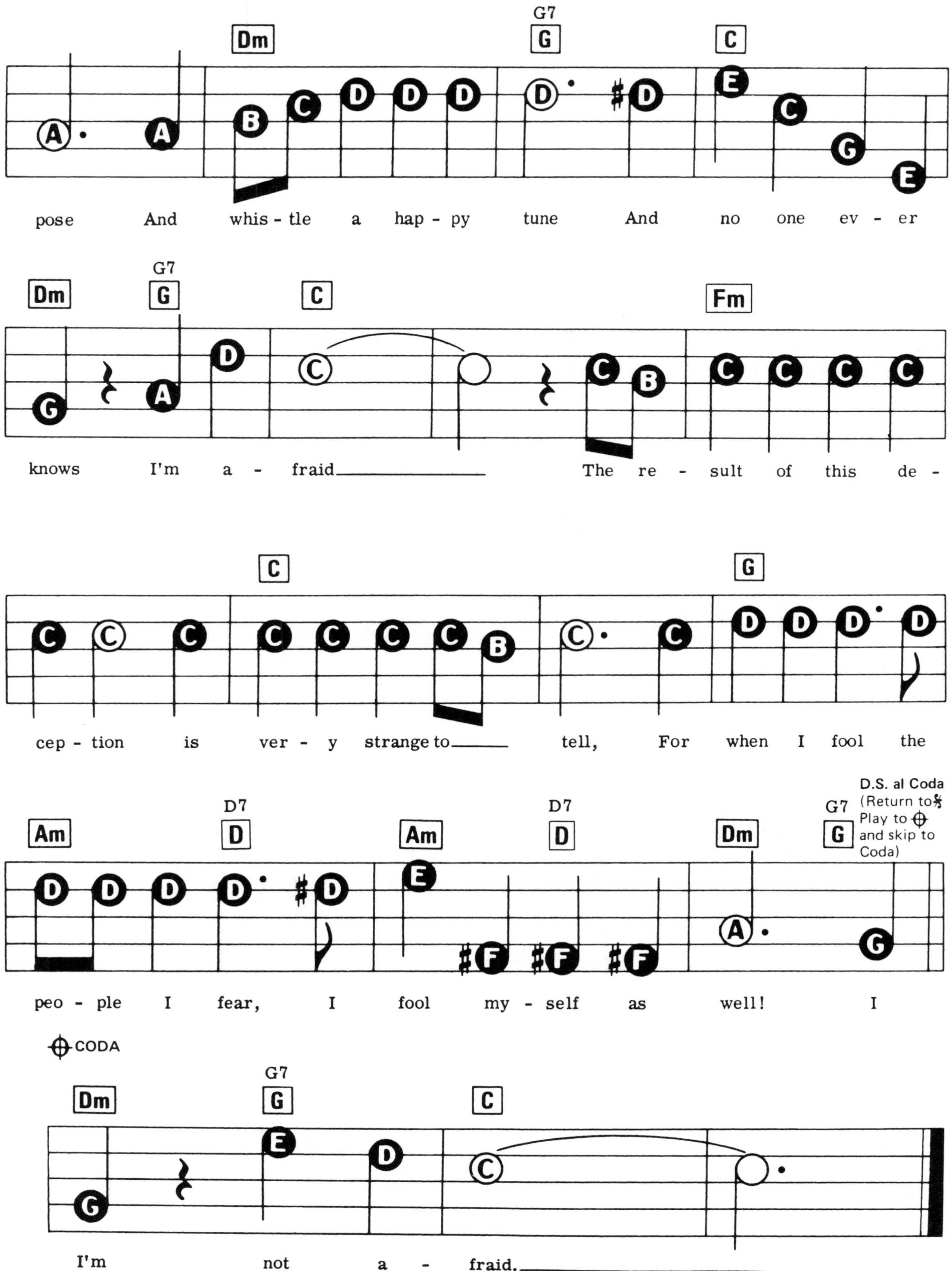
Dm
G7
G
C
pose And whis - tle a hap - py tune And no one ev - er
Dm
G7
G
C
Fm
knows I'm a - fraid
The re - sult of this de -
C
G
cep - tion is ver - y strange to tell, For when I fool the
Am
D7
D
Am
D7
D
Dm
G7
G
D.S. al Coda
(Return to 𝄋
Play to ⊕
and skip to
Coda)
peo - ple I fear, I fool my - self as well! I
⊕ CODA
Dm
G7
G
C
I'm not a - fraid.

I'm Late

from Walt Disney's ALICE IN WONDERLAND

Registration 1
Rhythm: Fox Trot or Swing

Words by Bob Hilliard
Music by Sammy Fain

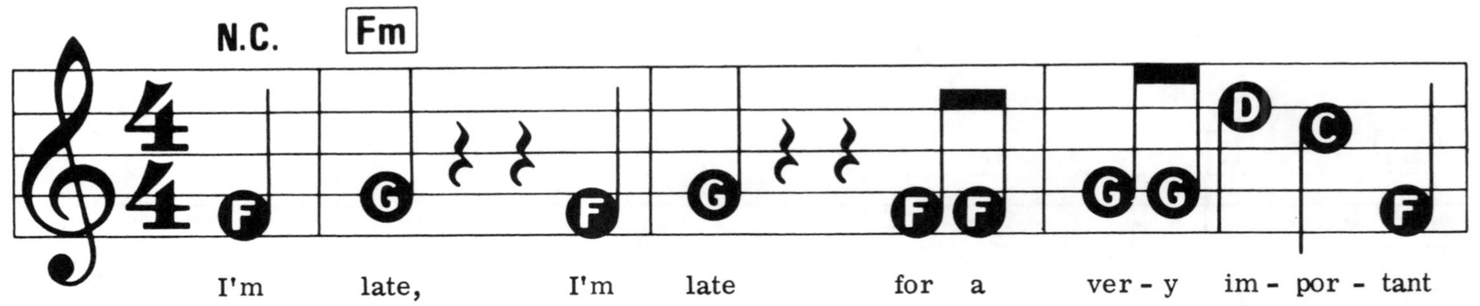

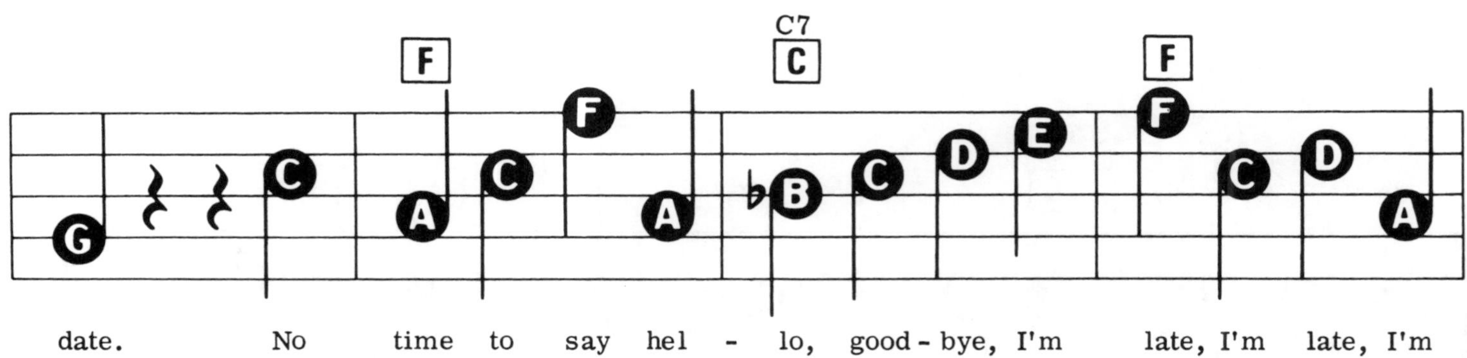

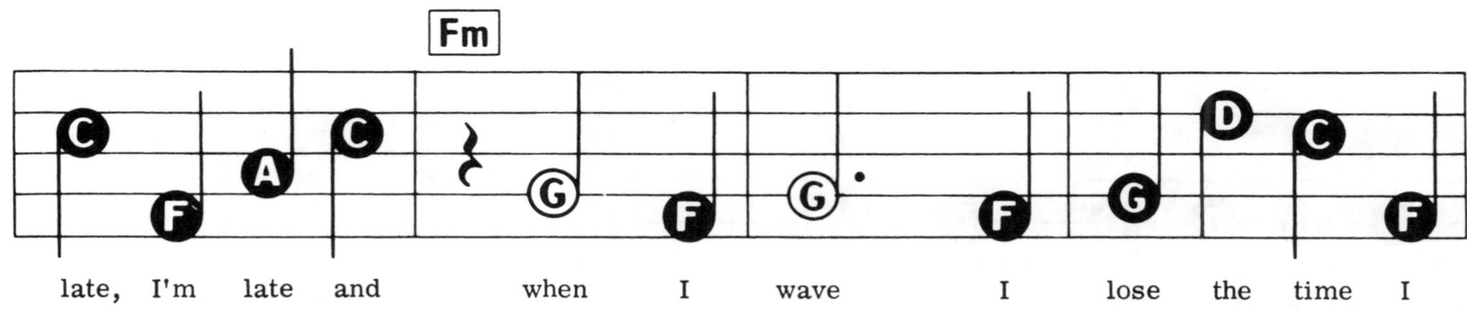

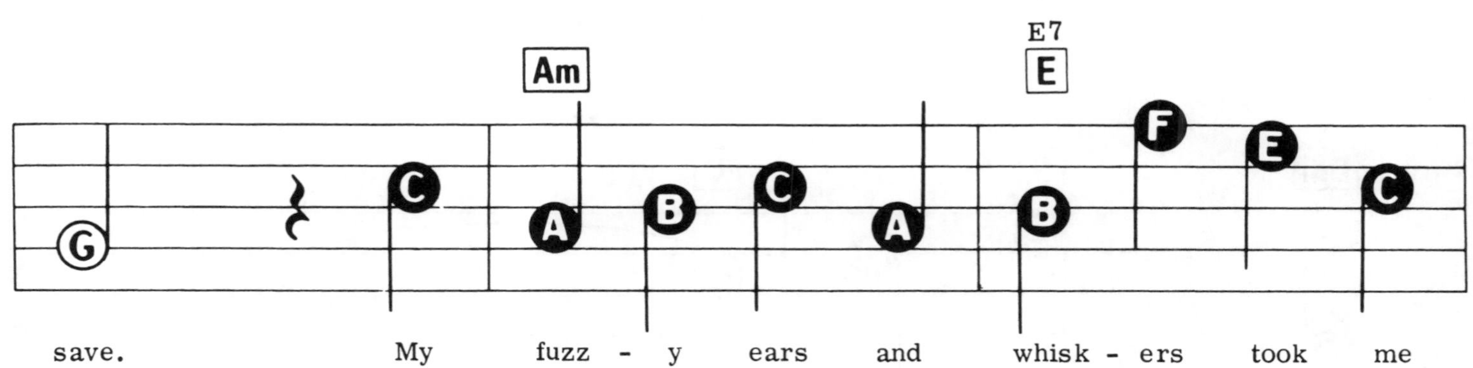

© 1949 Walt Disney Music Company
Copyright Renewed
All Rights Reserved. Used by Permission.

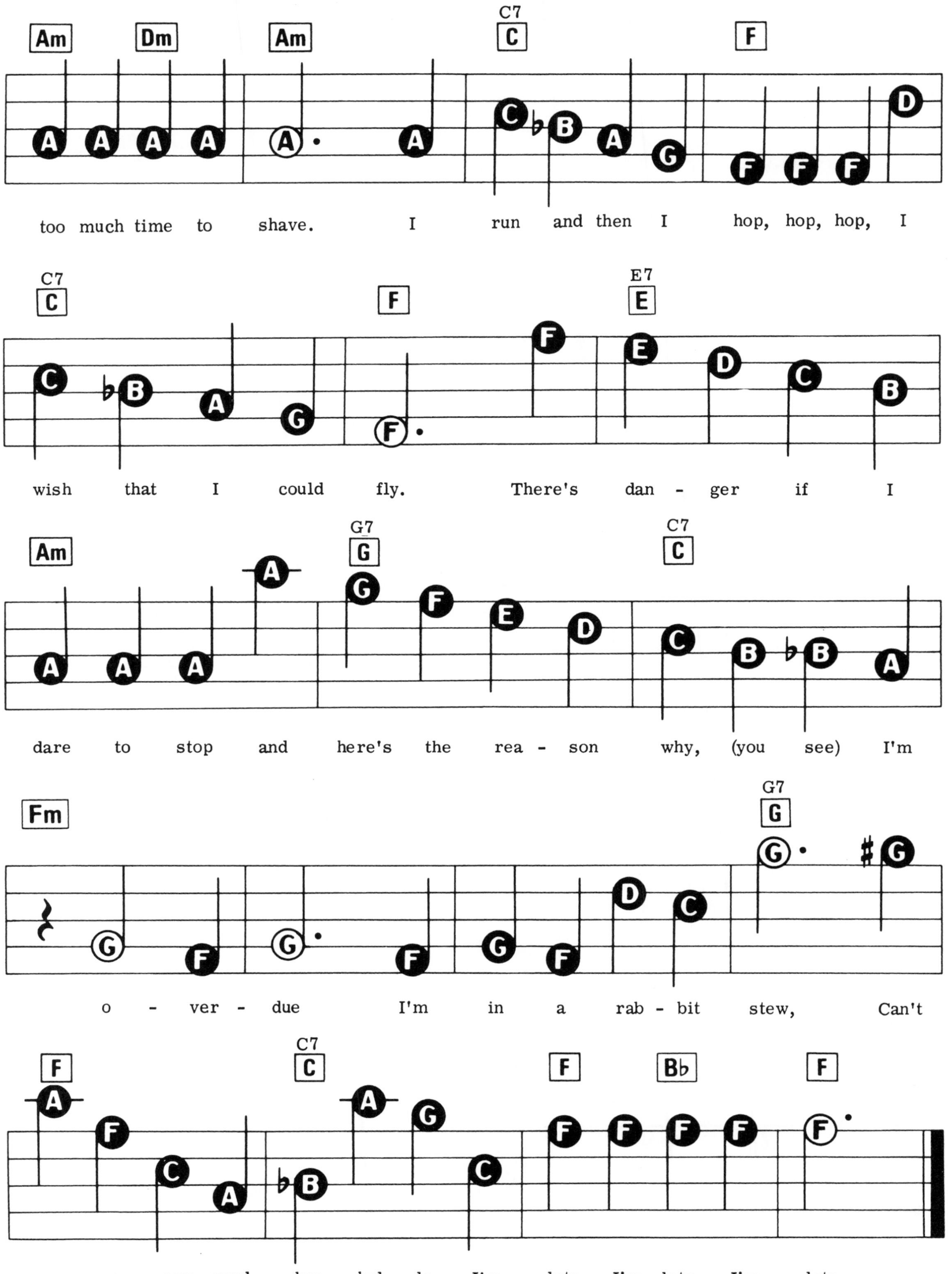
Am Dm Am C7 C F
too much time to shave. I run and then I hop, hop, hop, I
C7 C F E7 E
wish that I could fly. There's dan - ger if I
Am G7 G C7 C
dare to stop and here's the rea - son why, (you see) I'm
Fm G7 G
o - ver - due I'm in a rab - bit stew, Can't
F C7 C F B♭ F
e - ven say good - bye, hel - lo, I'm late, I'm late, I'm late.

I'm Popeye the Sailor Man

Theme from the Paramount Cartoon POPEYE THE SAILOR

Registration 9
Rhythm: Waltz

Words and Music by
Sammy Lerner

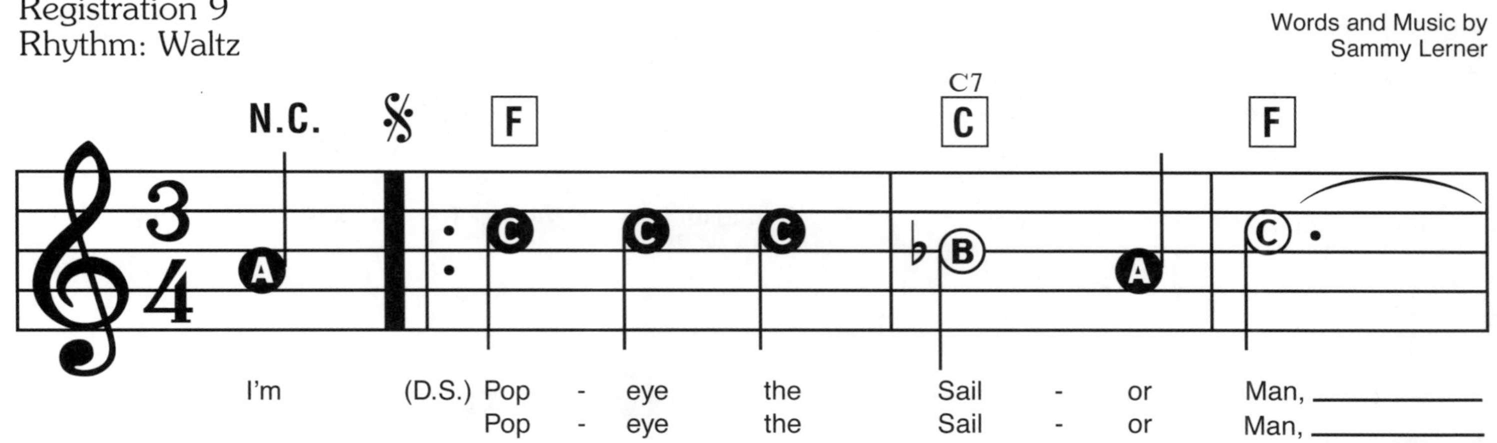

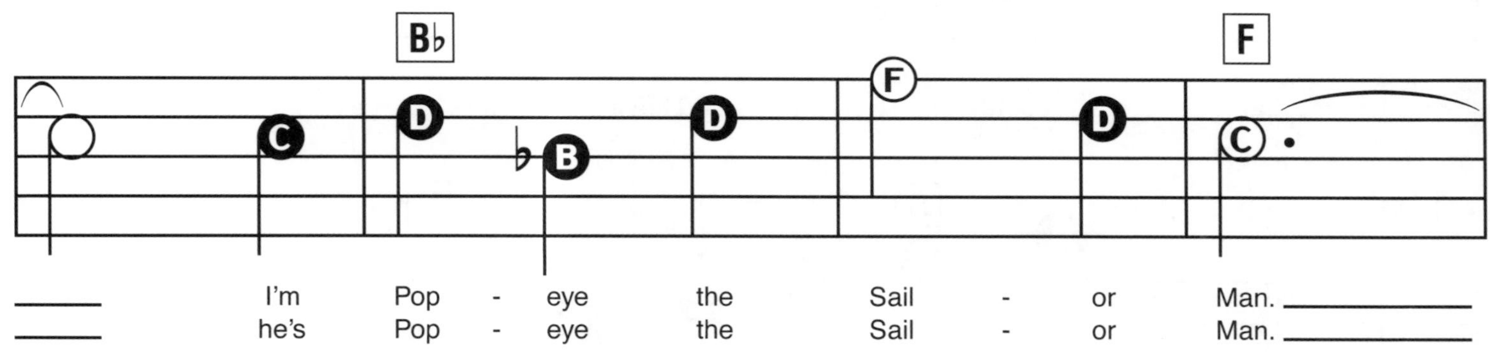

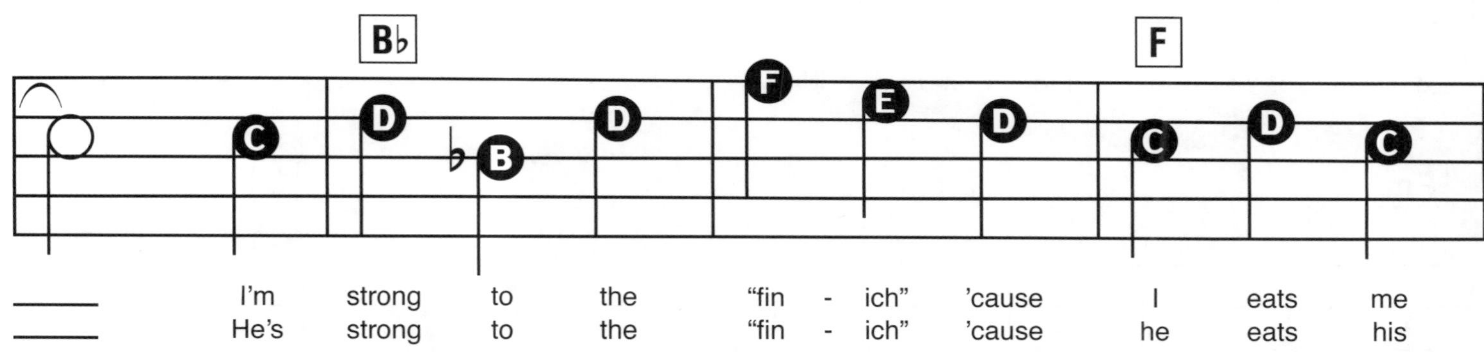

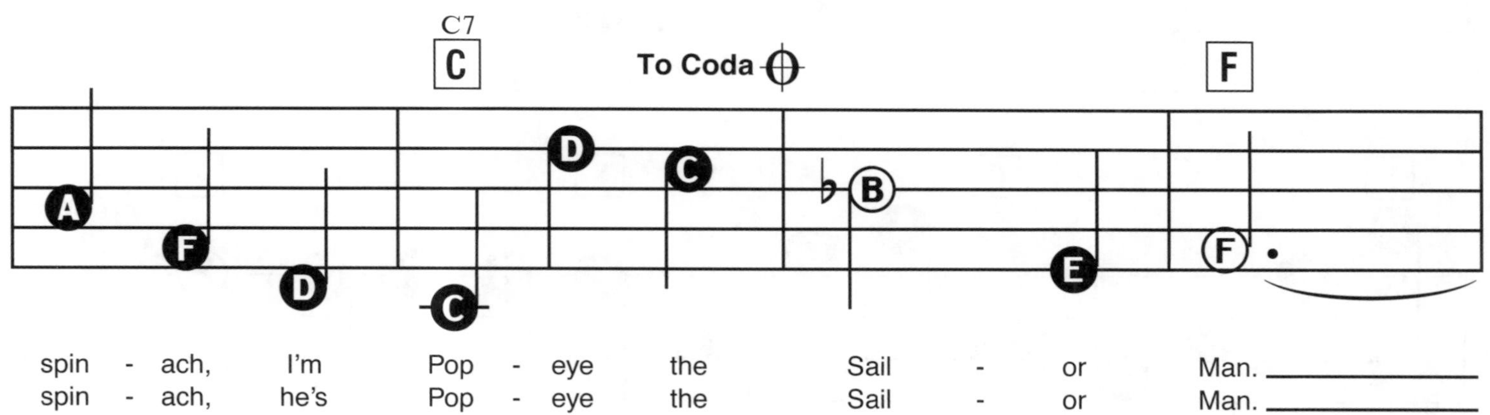

Copyright (c) 1934 Sony/ATV Music Publishing LLC
Copyright Renewed
All Rights Administered by Sony/ATV Music Publishing LLC, 424 Church Street, Suite 1200, Nashville, TN 37219
International Copyright Secured All Rights Reserved

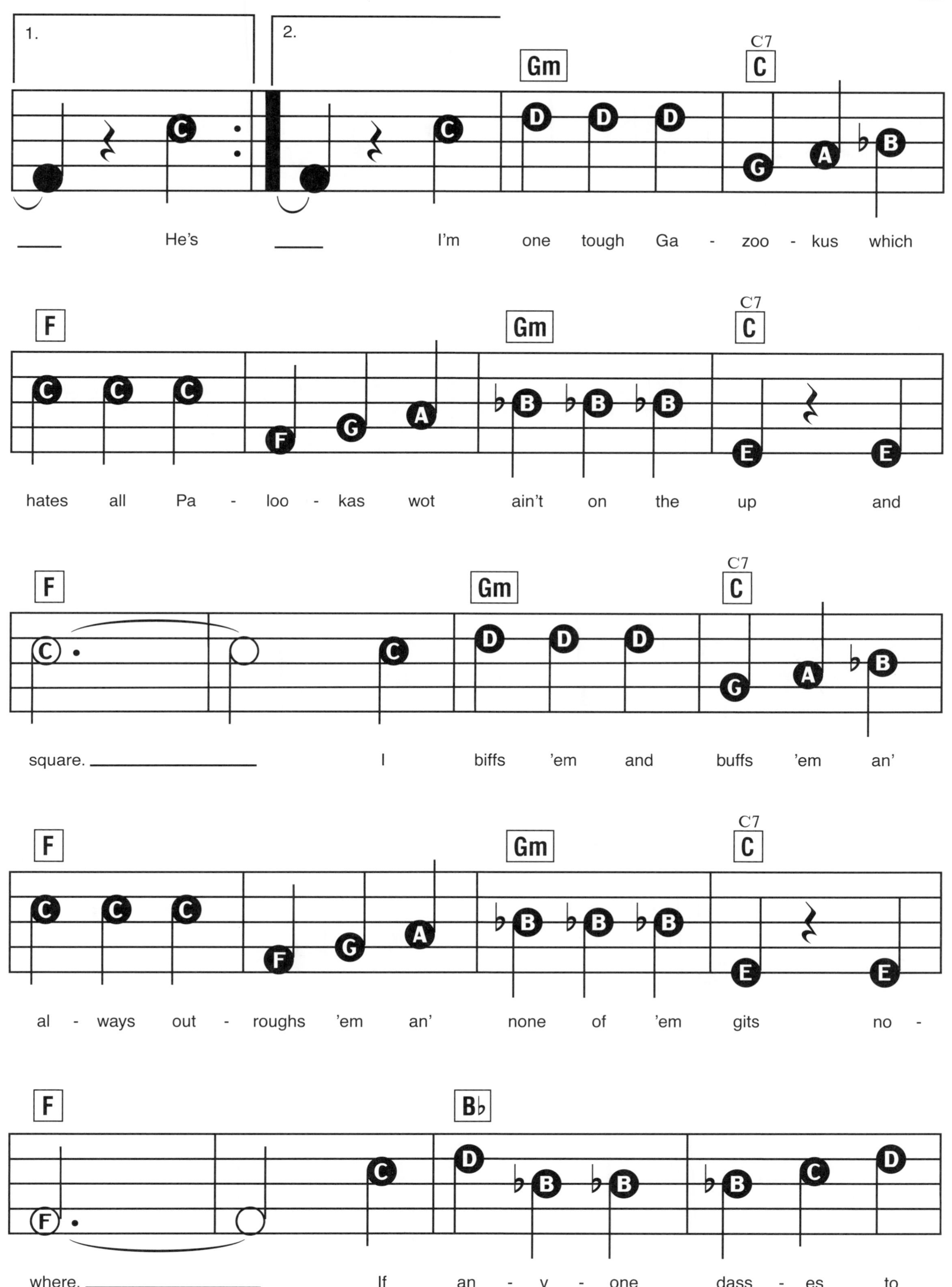
1.
2.
Gm
C7
C
He's
I'm
one tough Ga - zoo - kus which
F
Gm
C7
C
hates all Pa - loo - kas wot ain't on the up and
F
Gm
C7
C
square.
I biffs 'em and buffs 'em an'
F
Gm
C7
C
al - ways out - roughs 'em an' none of 'em gits no -
F
B♭
where.
If an - y - one dass - es to

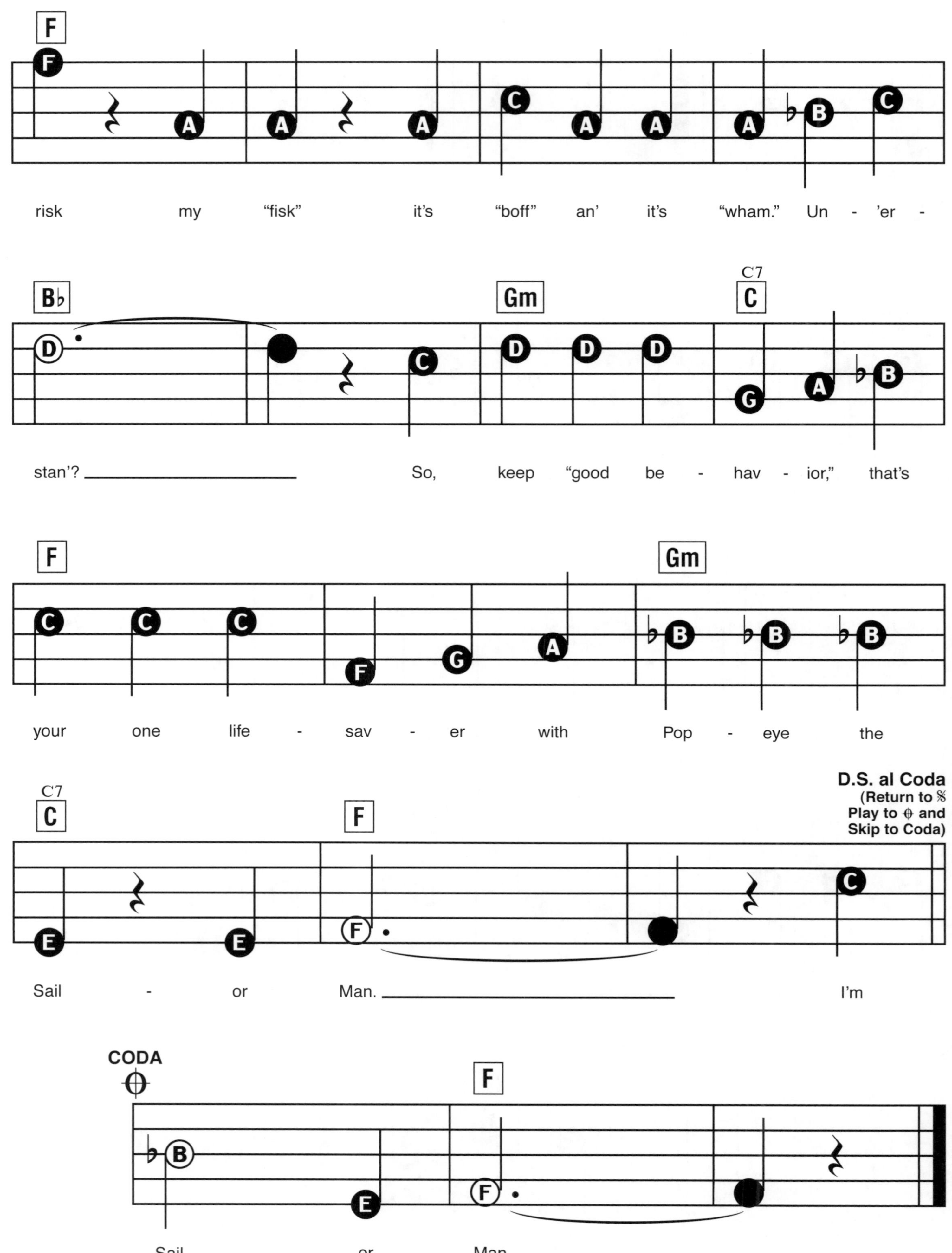
F
F
A
A
A
C
A
A
A
B
C
risk my "fisk" it's "boff" an' it's "wham." Un - 'er -
B♭
Gm
C7
C
D
C
D
D
D
G
A
B
stan'? So, keep "good be - hav - ior," that's
F
Gm
C
C
C
F
G
A
B
B
B
your one life - sav - er with Pop - eye the
D.S. al Coda
(Return to 𝄋
Play to ⊕ and
Skip to Coda)
C7
C
F
E
E
F
C
Sail - or Man. I'm
CODA
F
B
E
F
Sail - or Man.

If I Only Had a Brain

from THE WIZARD OF OZ

Registration 2
Rhythm: Swing

Lyric by E.Y. "Yip" Harburg
Music by Harold Arlen

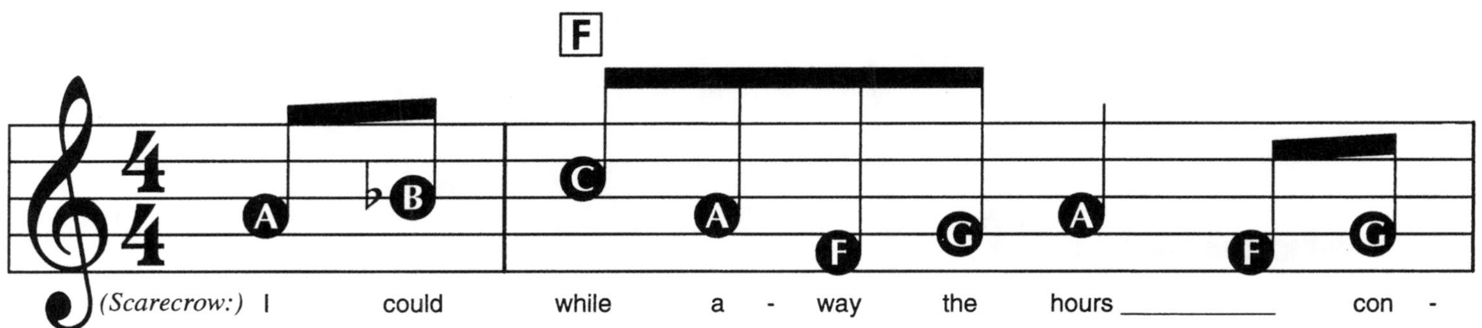

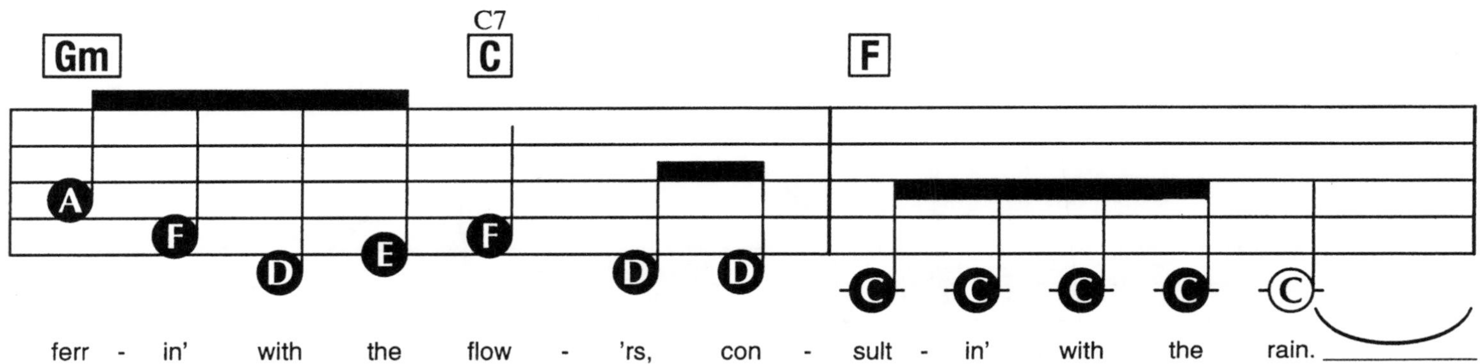

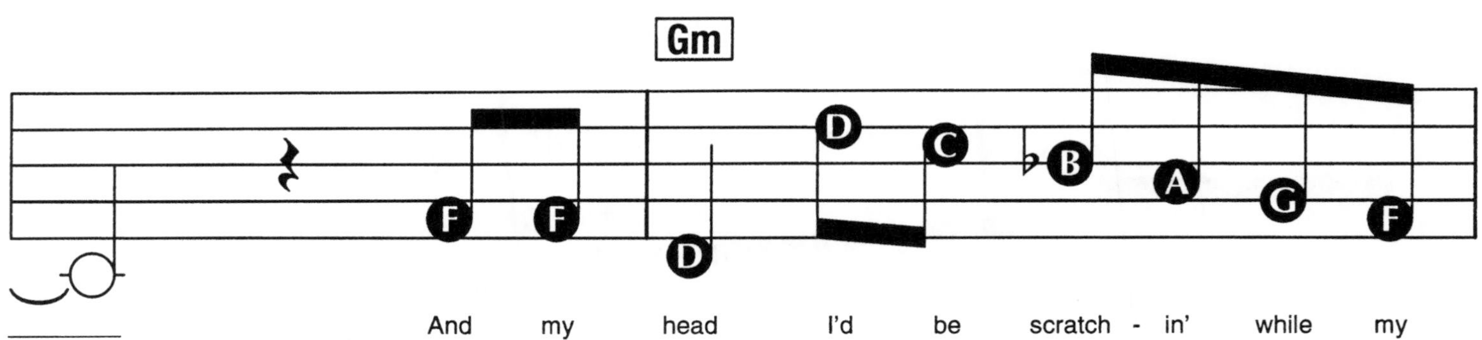

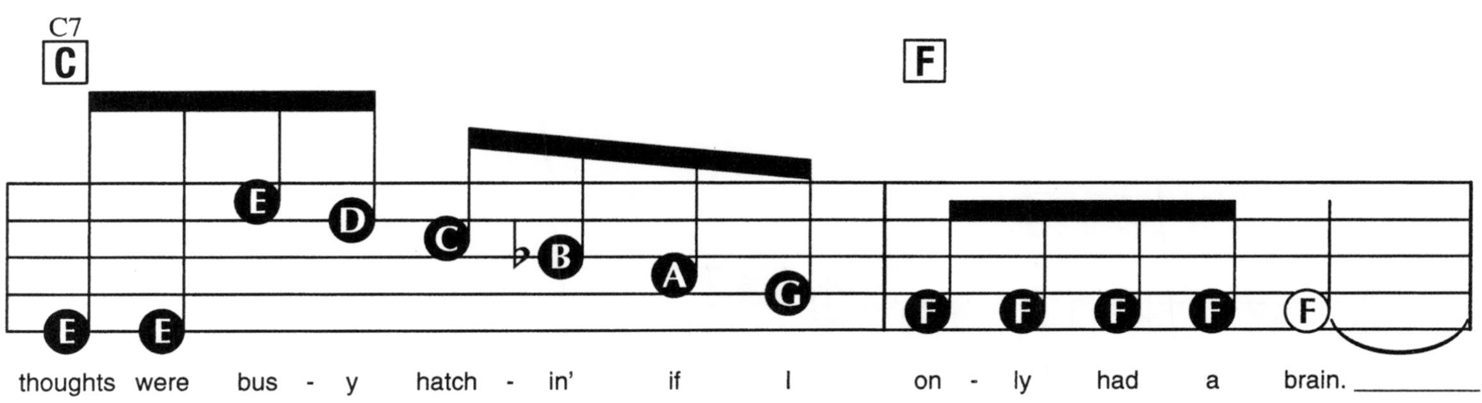

© 1938 (Renewed) METRO-GOLDWYN-MAYER INC.
© 1939 (Renewed) EMI FEIST CATALOG INC.
All Rights Administered by EMI FEIST CATALOG INC. (Publishing) and ALFRED MUSIC (Print)
All Rights Reserved Used by Permission

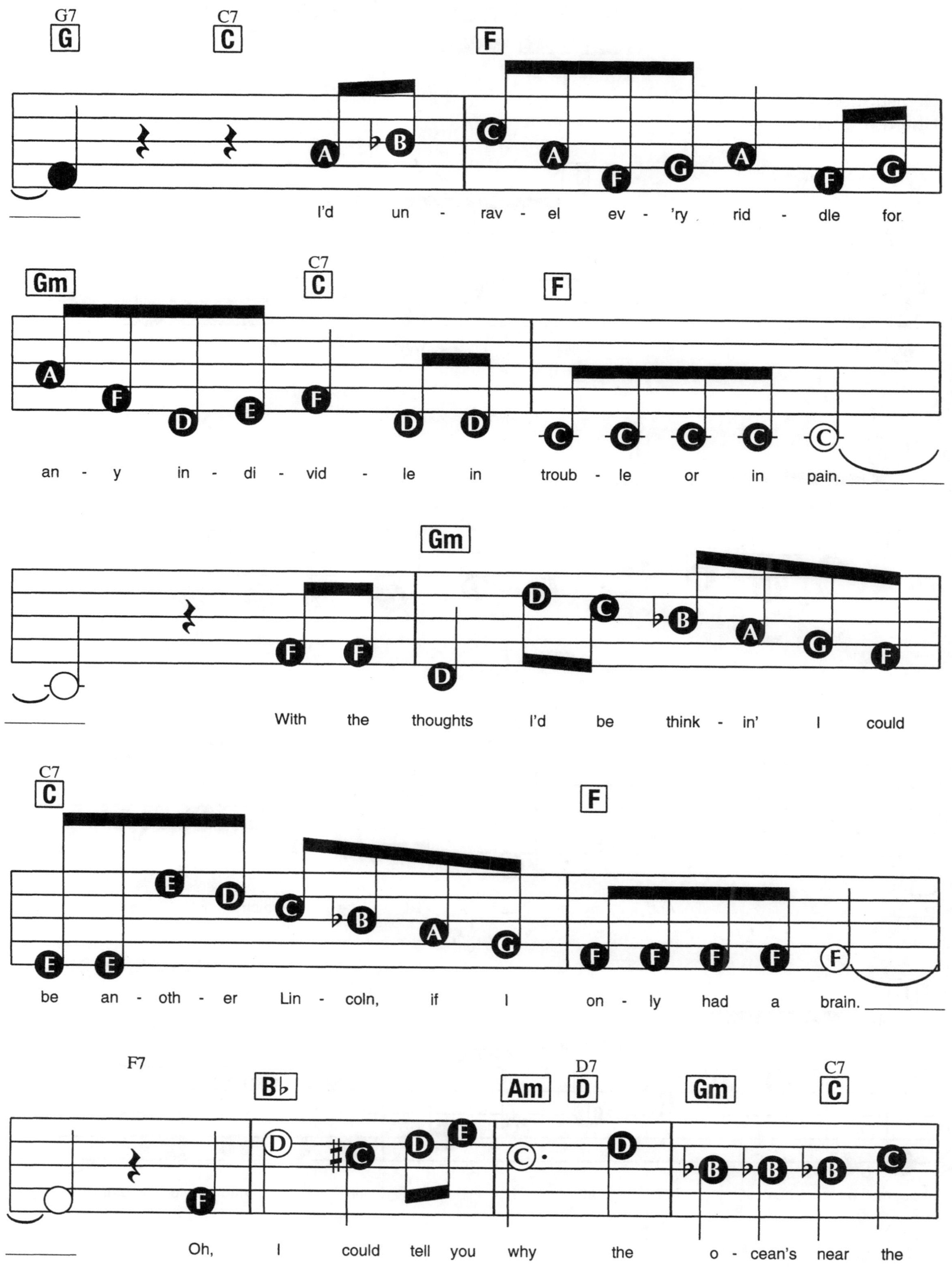
G7 G C7 C F
I'd un - rav - el ev - 'ry rid - dle for
Gm C7 C F
an - y in - di - vid - le in troub - le or in pain.
Gm
With the thoughts I'd be think - in' I could
C7 C F
be an - oth - er Lin - coln, if I on - ly had a brain.
F7 B♭ Am D7 D Gm C7 C
Oh, I could tell you why the o - cean's near the

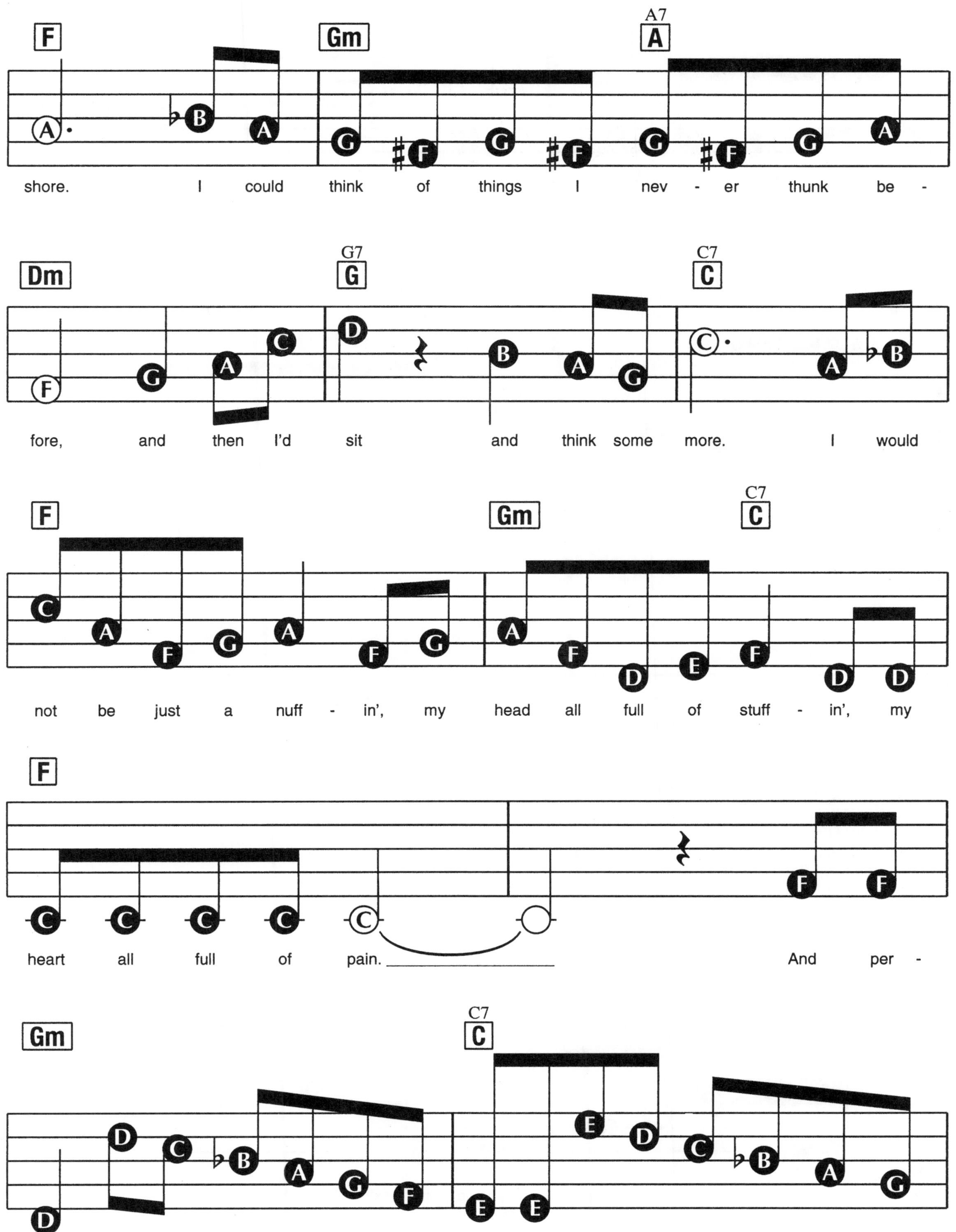
F
Gm
A7
A
A B A G F G F G F G A
shore. I could think of things I nev - er thunk be -
Dm
G7
G
C7
C
F G A C D B A G C A B
fore, and then I'd sit and think some more. I would
F
Gm
C7
C
C A F G A F G A F D E F D D
not be just a nuff - in', my head all full of stuff - in', my
F
C C C C C F F
heart all full of pain. And per -
Gm
C7
C
D D C B A G F E E E D C B A G
haps I'd de - serve you and be e - ven wor - thy erv you if I

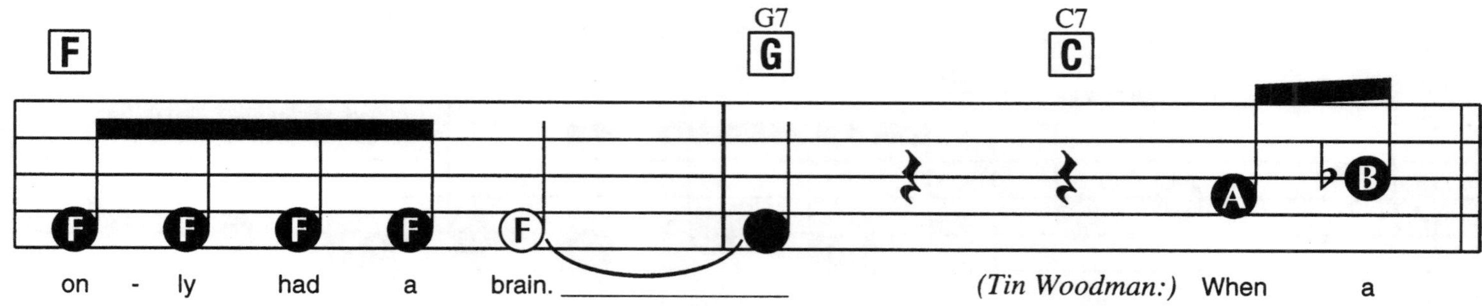
F
G7
G
C7
C
F F F F F
A B
on - ly had a brain.
(Tin Woodman:) When a

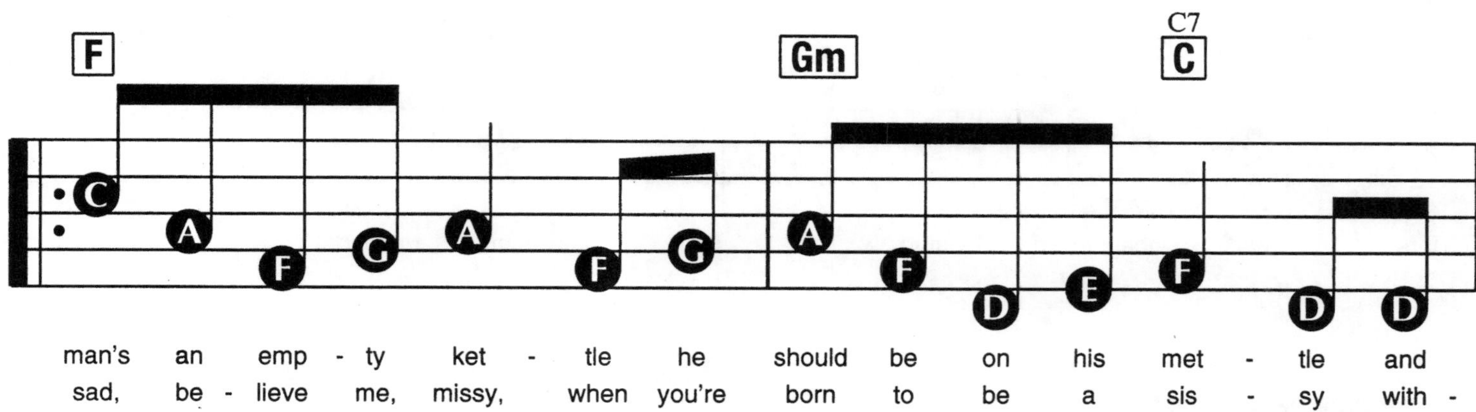
F
Gm
C7
C
C A F G A F G A F D E F D D
man's an emp - ty ket - tle he should be on his met - tle and
sad, be - lieve me, missy, when you're born to be a sis - sy with -

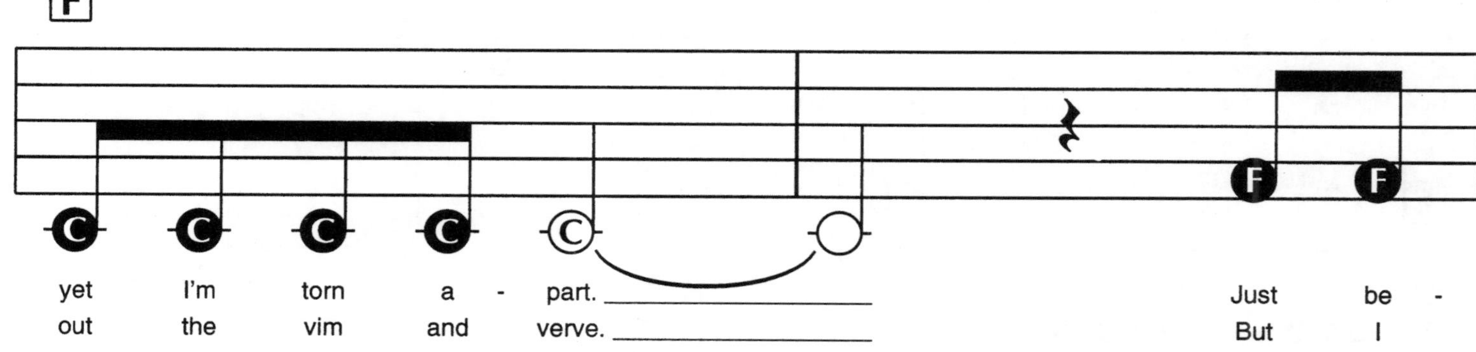
F
C C C C C
F F
yet I'm torn a - part.
out the vim and verve.
Just be -
But I

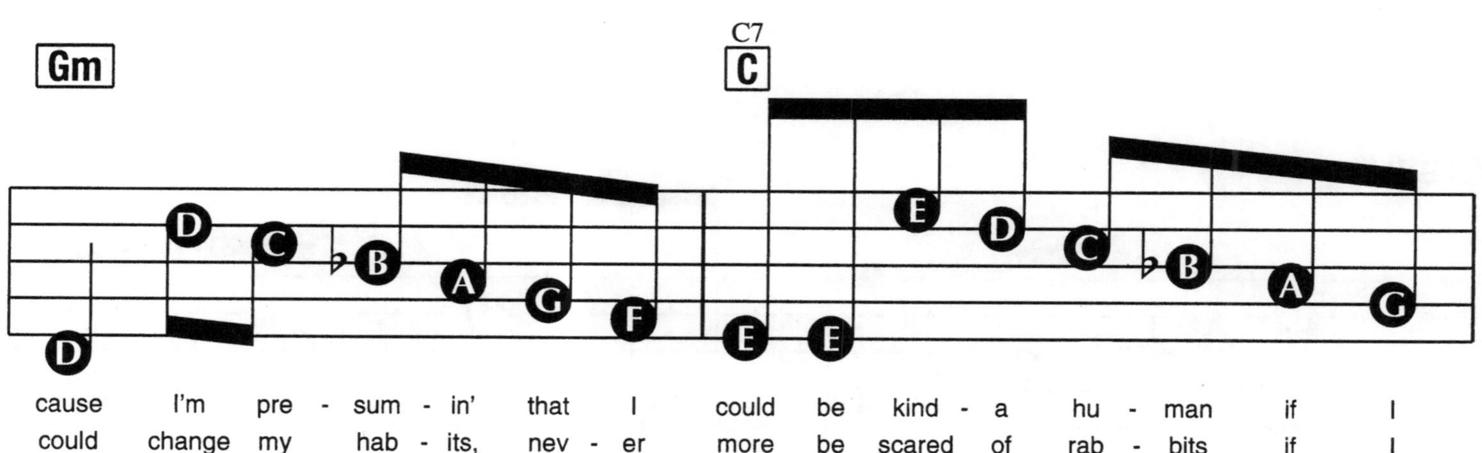
Gm
C7
C
D D C B A G F E E E D C B A G
cause I'm pre - sum - in' that I could be kind - a hu - man if I
could change my hab - its, nev - er more be scared of rab - bits if I

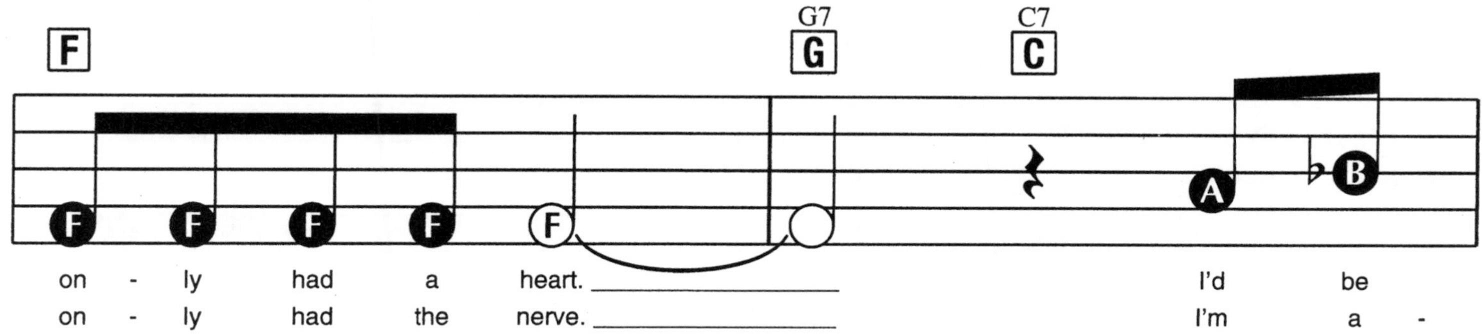
F
G7
G
C7
C
F F F F F
A B
on - ly had a heart.
I'd be
on - ly had the nerve.
I'm a -

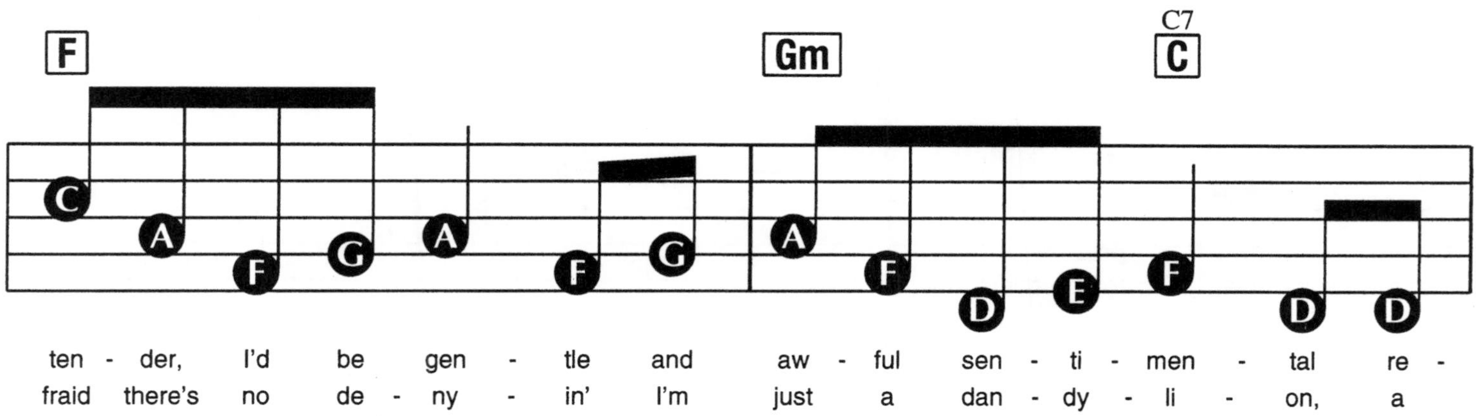
F
Gm
C7
C
C A F G A F G A F D E F D D
ten - der, I'd be gen - tle and aw - ful sen - ti - men - tal re -
fraid there's no de - ny - in' I'm just a dan - dy - li - on, a

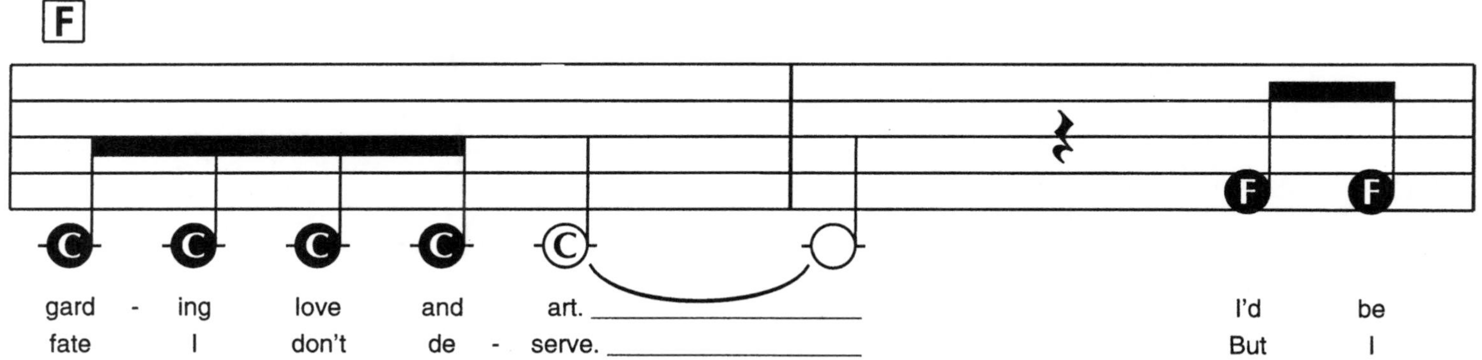
F
C C C C C
F F
gard - ing love and art.
I'd be
fate I don't de - serve.
But I

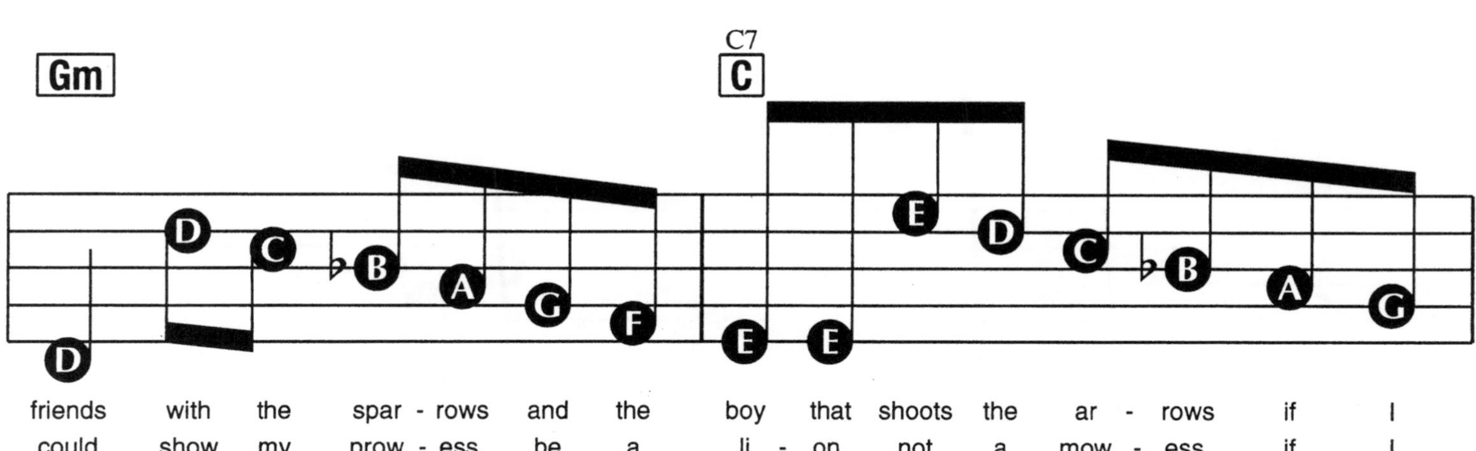
Gm
C7
C
D D C B A G F E E E D C B A G
friends with the spar - rows and the boy that shoots the ar - rows if I
could show my prow - ess, be a li - on, not a mow - ess, if I

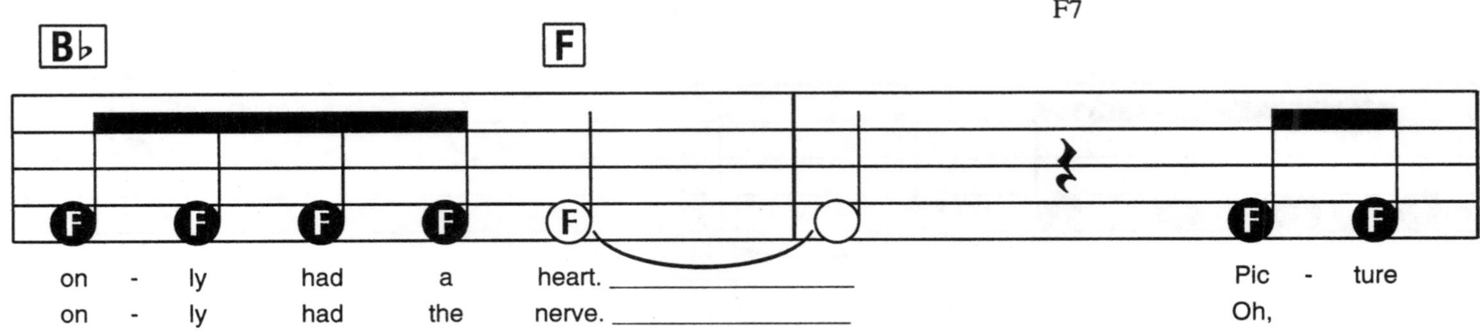
B♭
F
F7
on - ly had a heart. Pic - ture
on - ly had the nerve. Oh,

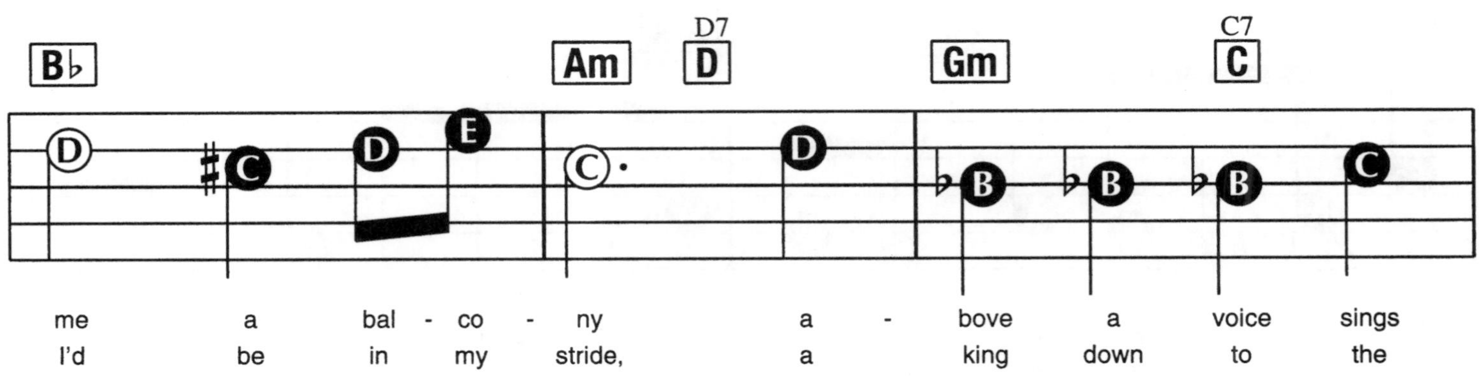
B♭
Am
D7
D
Gm
C7
C
me a bal - co - ny a - bove a voice sings
I'd be in my stride, a king down to the

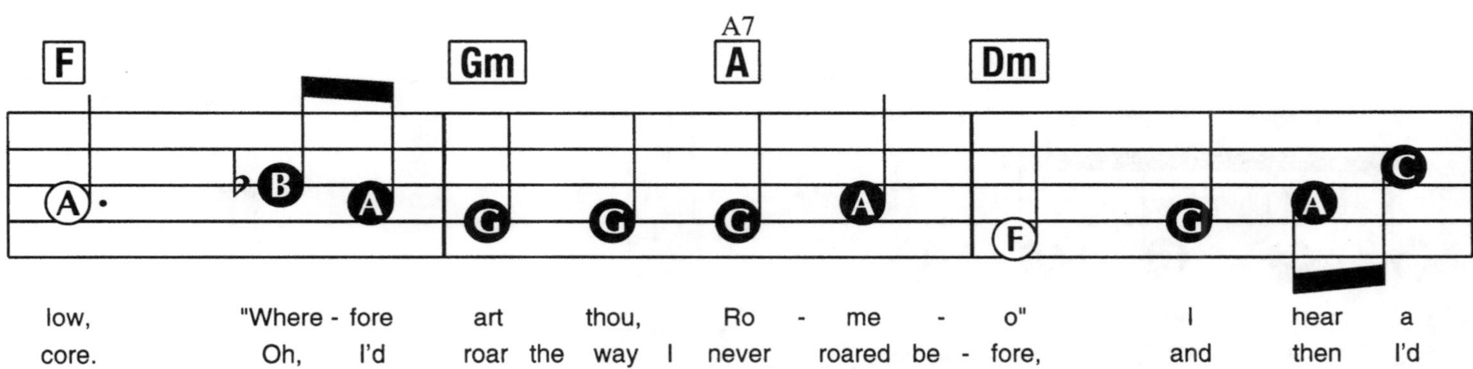
F
Gm
A7
A
Dm
low, "Where - fore art thou, Ro - me - o" I hear a
core. Oh, I'd roar the way I never roared be - fore, and then I'd

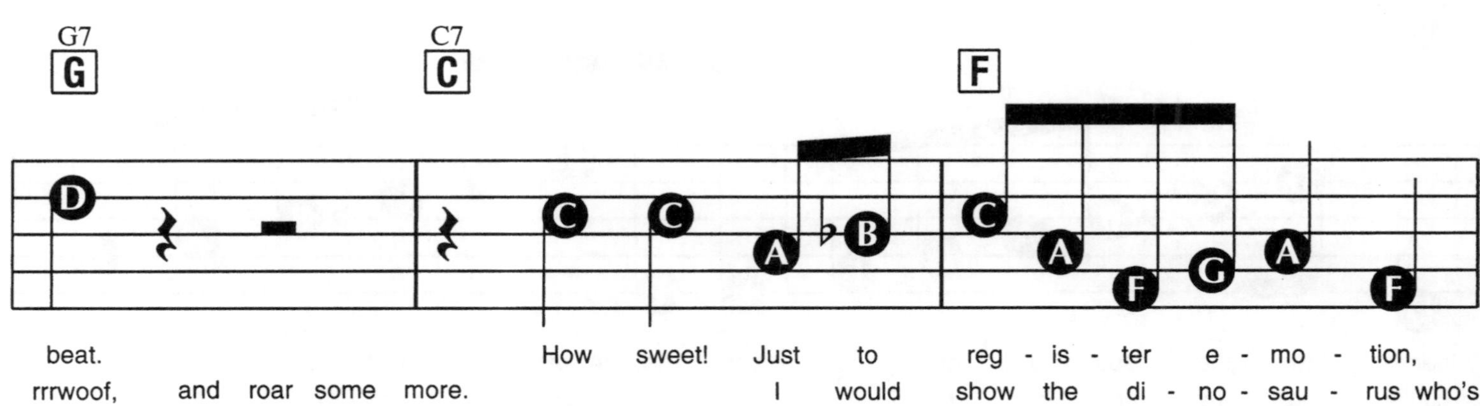
G7
G
C7
C
F
beat. How sweet! Just to reg - is - ter e - mo - tion,
rrrwoof, and roar some more. I would show the di - no - sau - rus who's

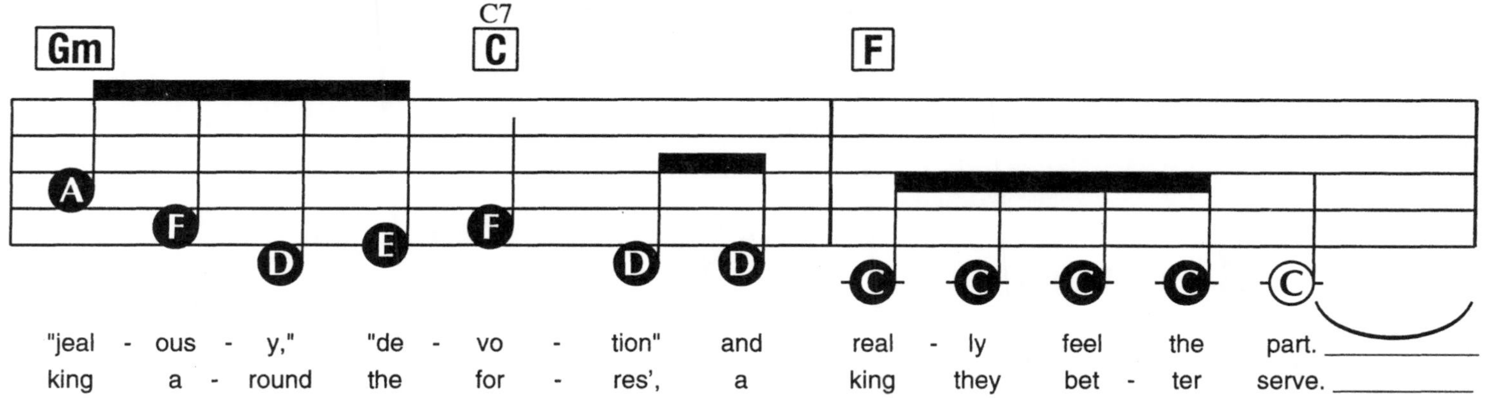
Gm
C7
C
F
A F D E F D D C C C C C
"jeal - ous - y," "de - vo - tion" and real - ly feel the part.
king a - round the for - res', a king they bet - ter serve.

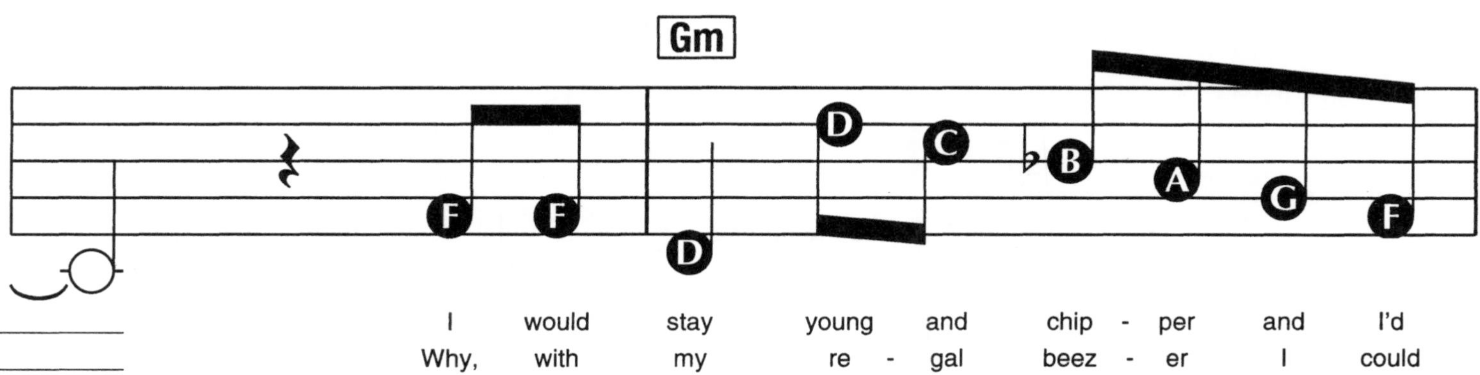
Gm
F F D D C B A G F
I would stay young and chip - per and I'd
Why, with my re - gal beez - er I could

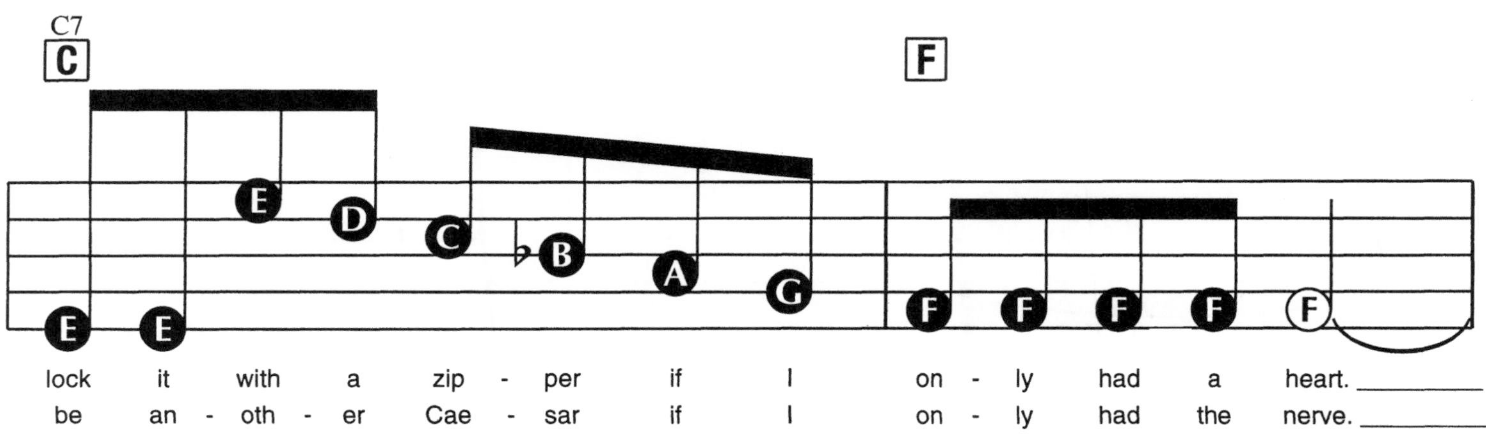
C7
C
F
E E E D C B A G F F F F F
lock it with a zip - per if I on - ly had a heart.
be an - oth - er Cae - sar if I on - ly had the nerve.

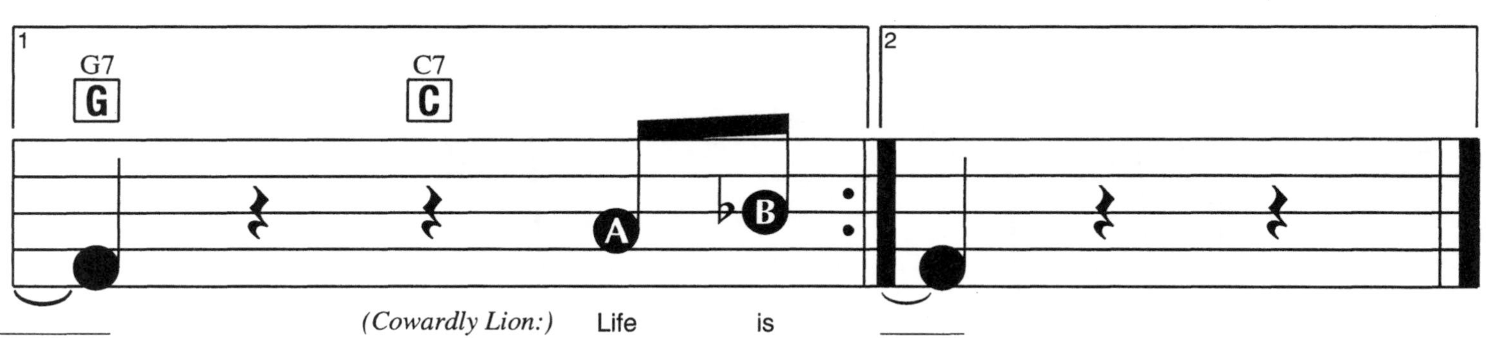
1
G7
G
C7
C
A B
2
(Cowardly Lion:) Life is

I've Been Working on the Railroad

Registration 2
Rhythm: 6/8 March

American Folksong

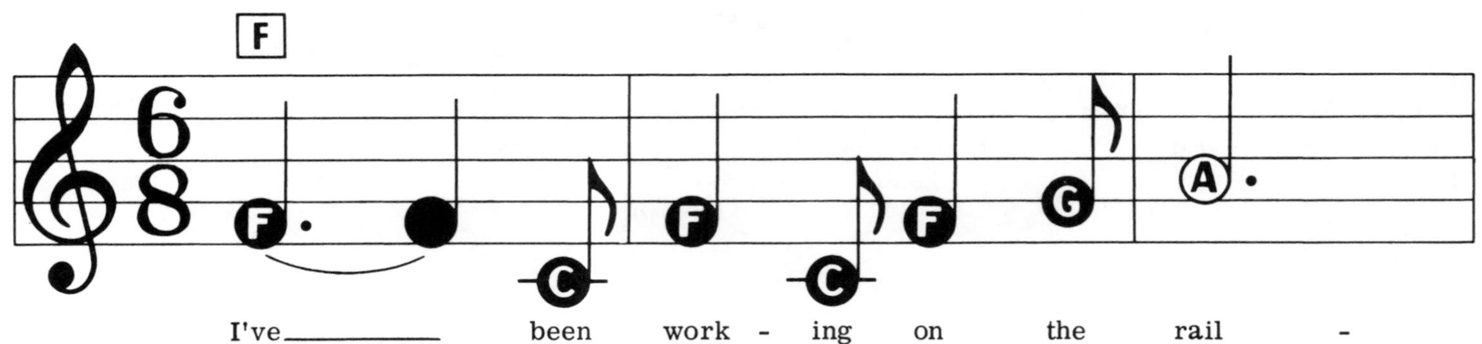

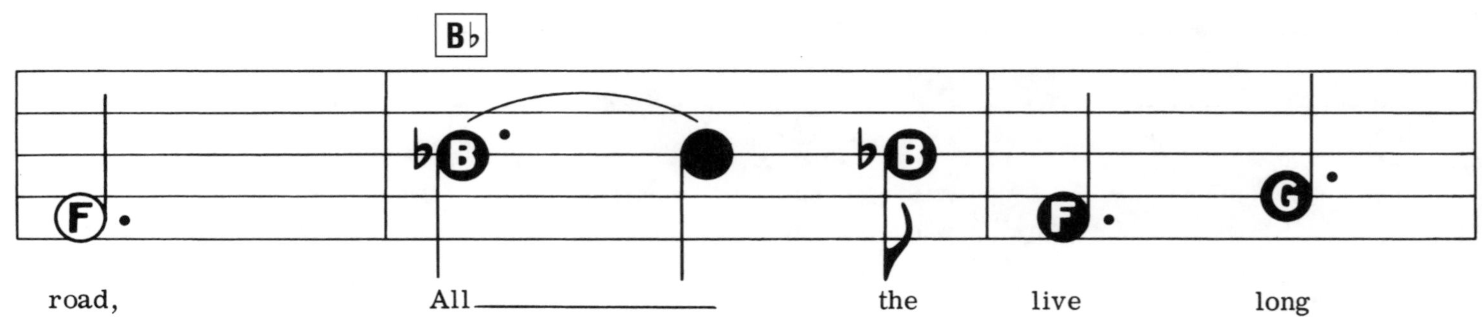

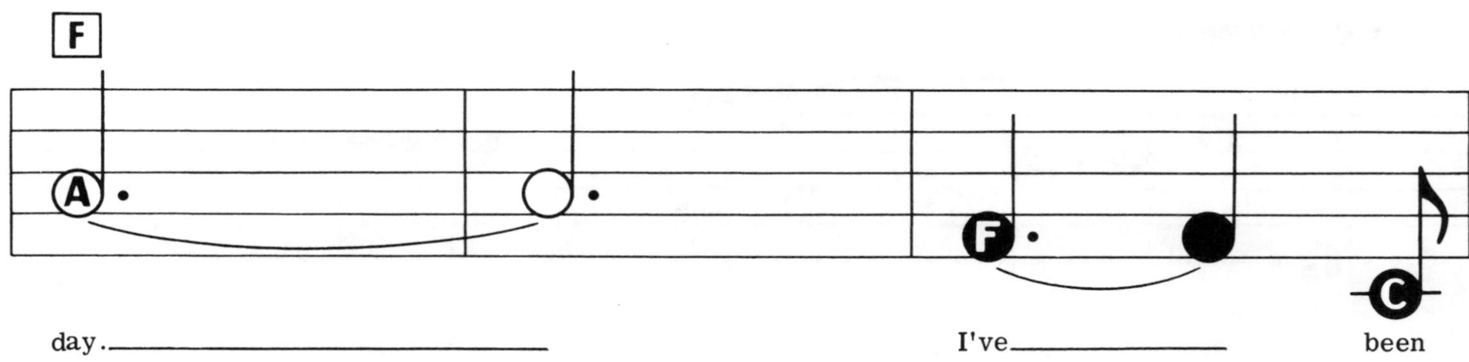

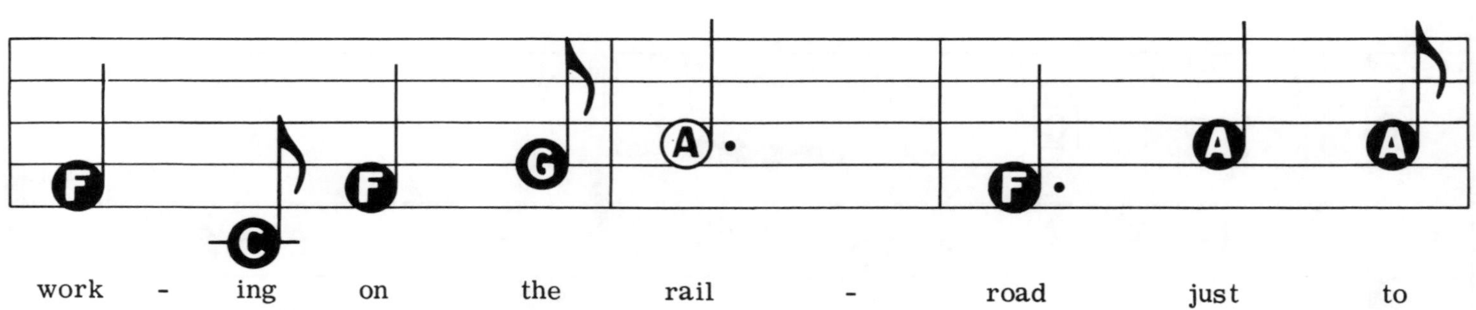

Copyright © 1975 by HAL LEONARD CORPORATION
International Copyright Secured All Rights Reserved

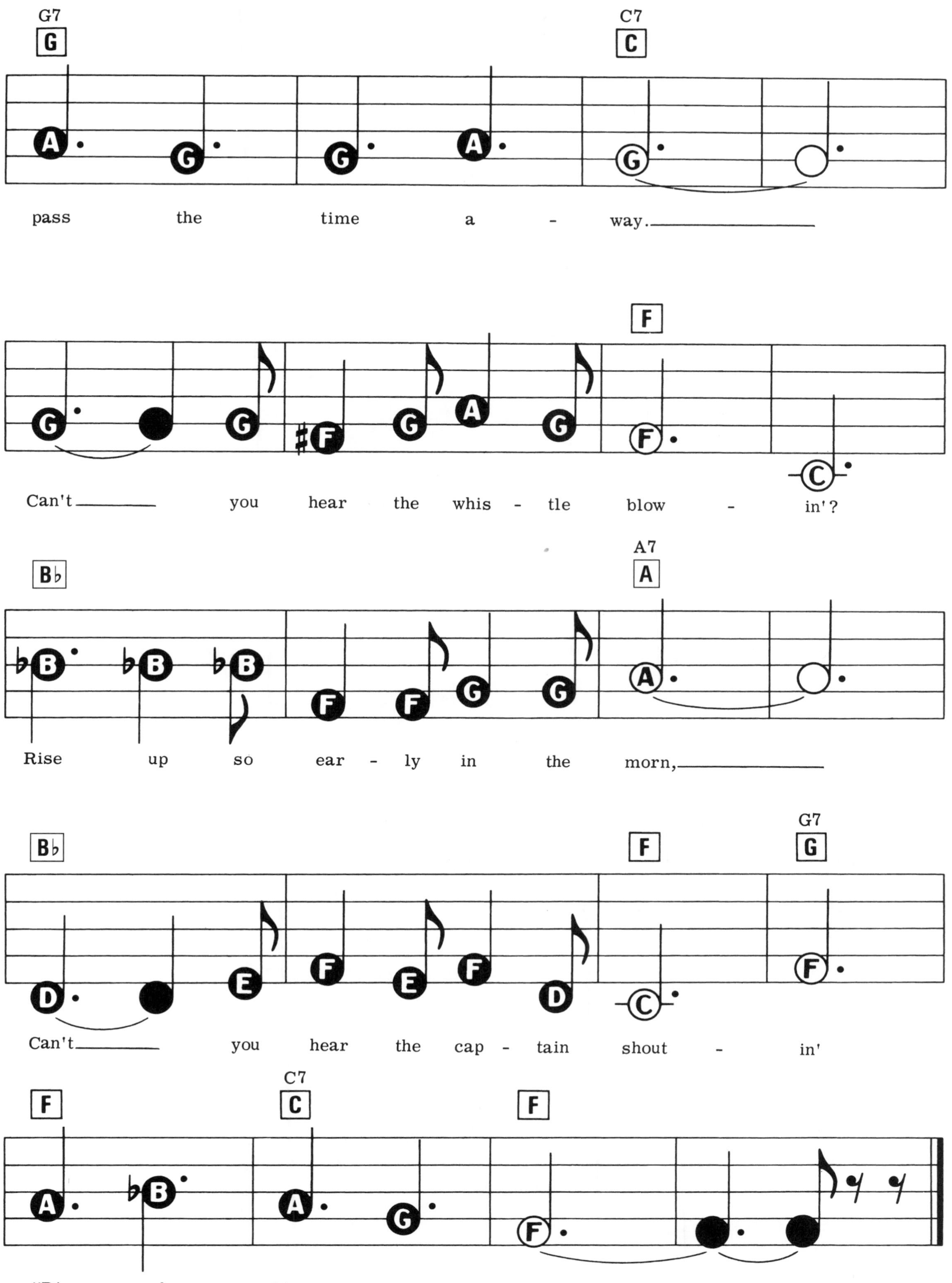
G7 G C7 C
pass the time a - way.
F
Can't you hear the whis - tle blow - in'?
B♭ A7 A
Rise up so ear - ly in the morn,
B♭ F G7 G
Can't you hear the cap - tain shout - in'
F C7 C F
"Di - nah blow your horn!"

I've Got No Strings

from Walt Disney's PINOCCHIO

Registration 2
Rhythm: Fox Trot or Swing

Words by Ned Washington
Music by Leigh Harline

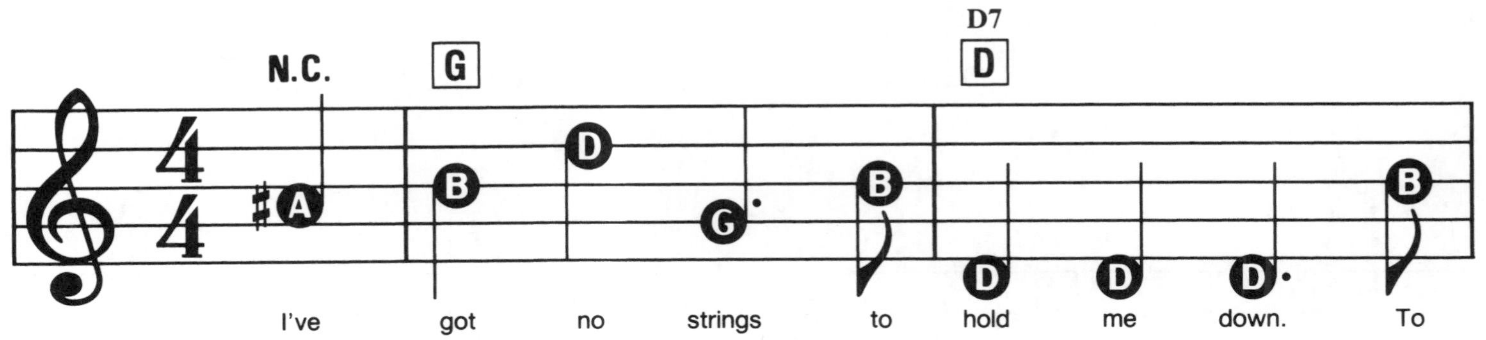

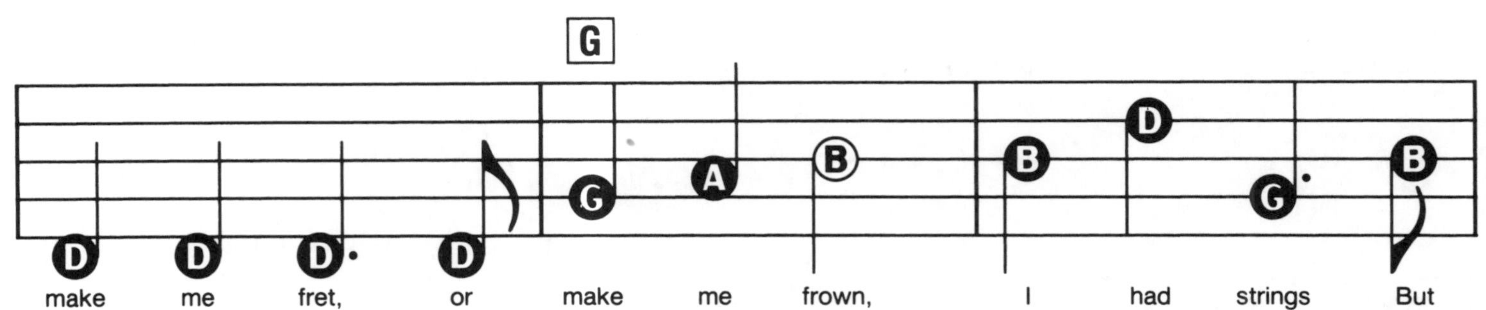

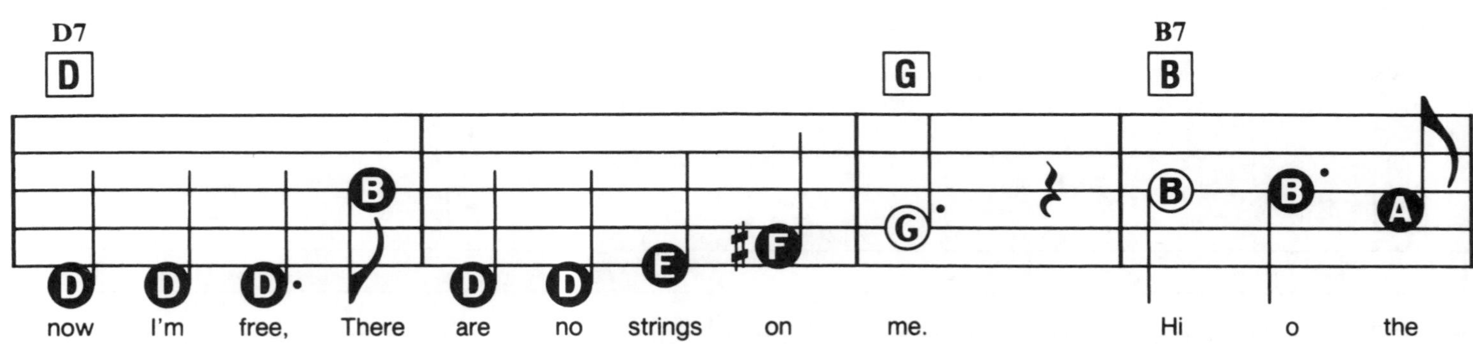

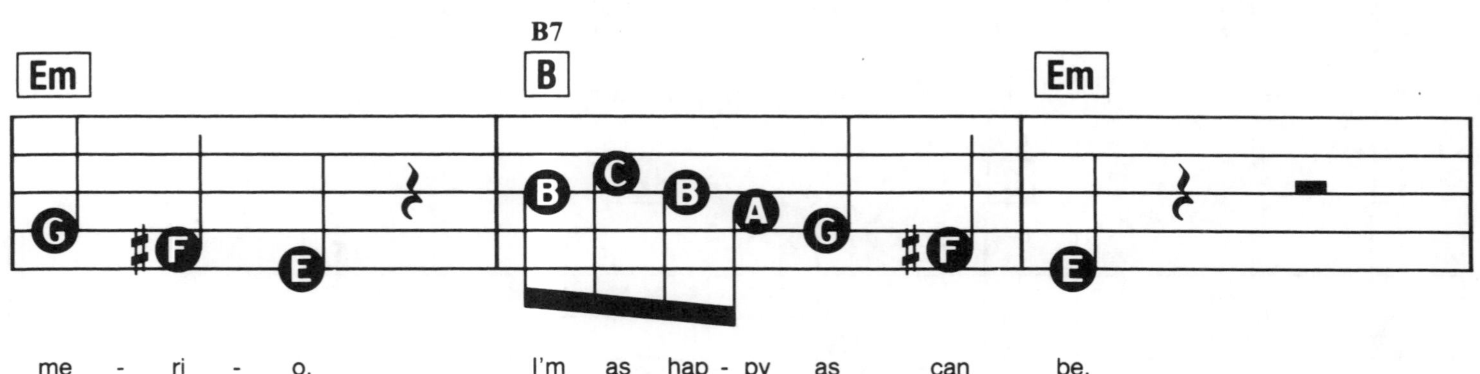

Copyright © 1940 by Bourne Co. (ASCAP)
Copyright Renewed
International Copyright Secured All Rights Reserved

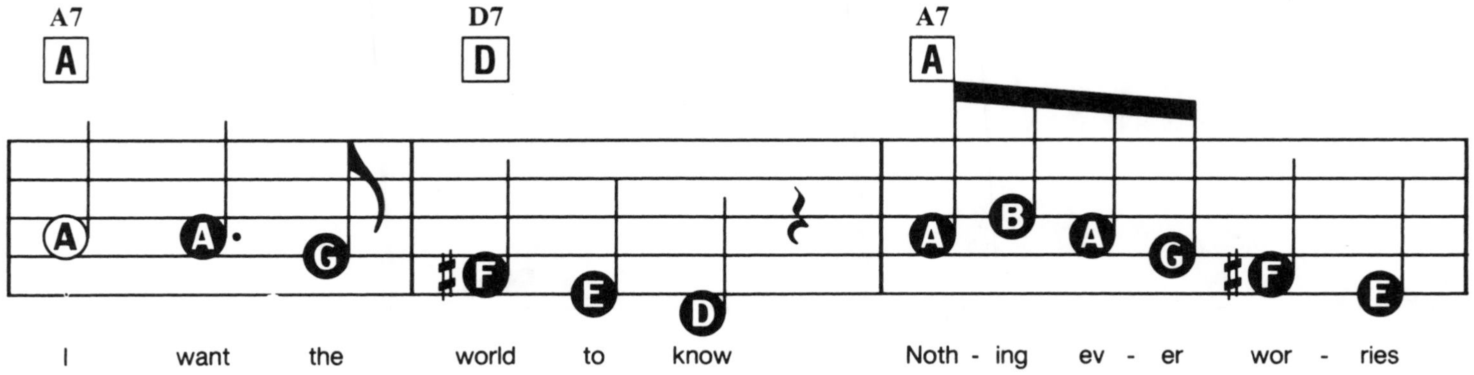
A7
A
D7
D
A7
A
I want the world to know
Noth - ing ev - er wor - ries

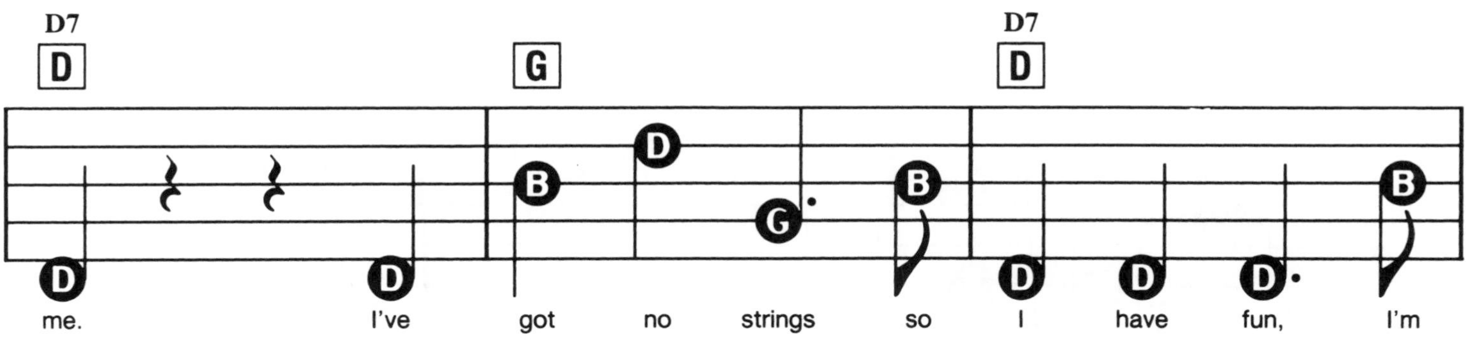
D7
D
G
D7
D
me. I've got no strings so I have fun, I'm

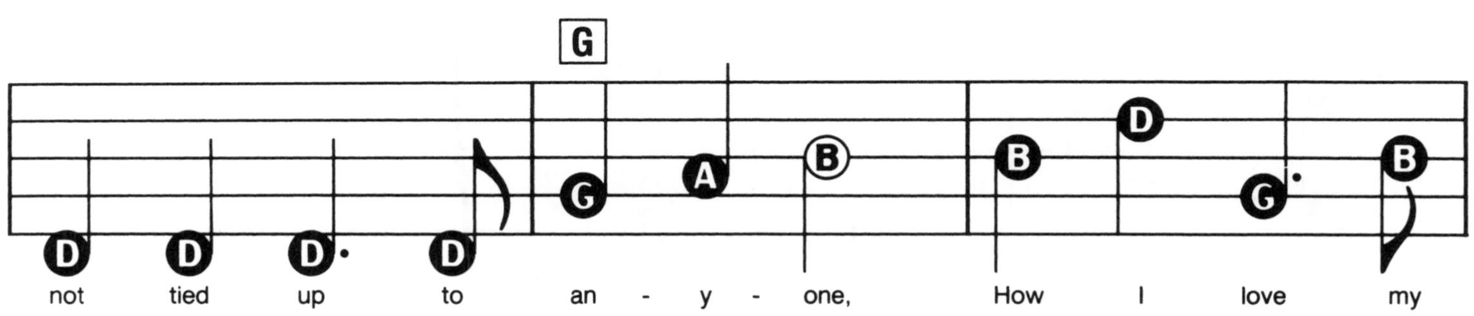
G
not tied up to an - y - one, How I love my

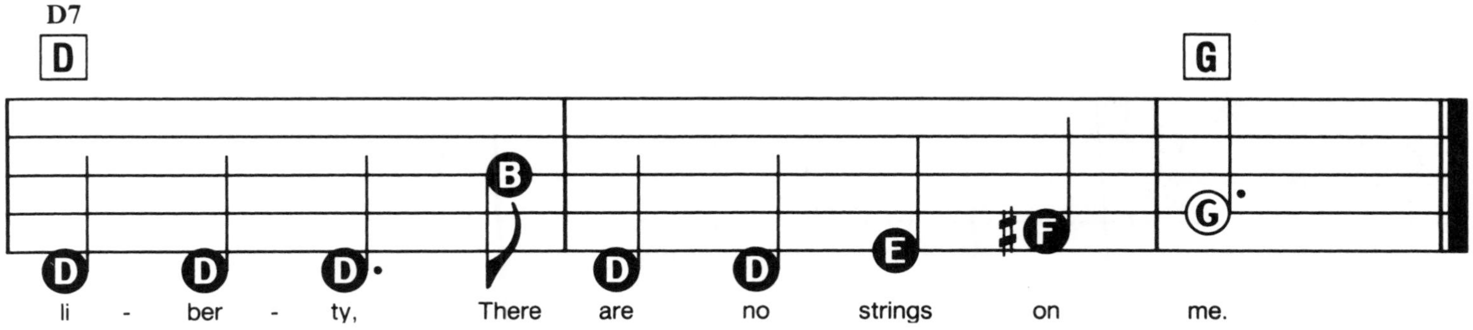
D7
D
G
li - ber - ty, There are no strings on me.

Imagine

Registration 8
Rhythm: 8-Beat or Rock

Words and Music by
John Lennon

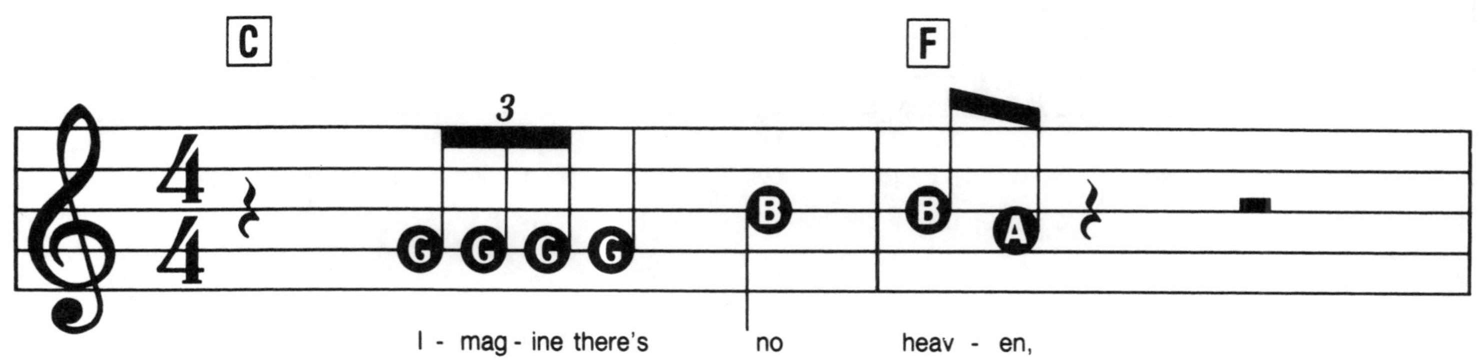

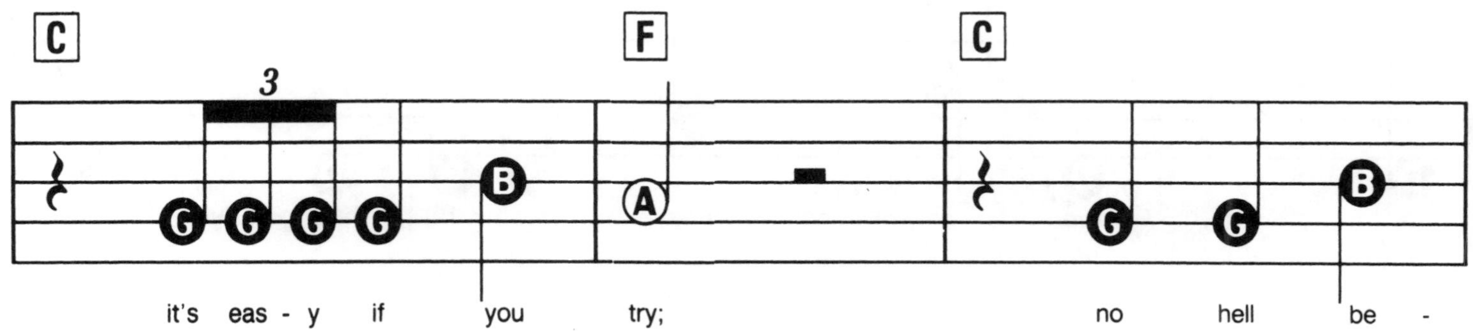

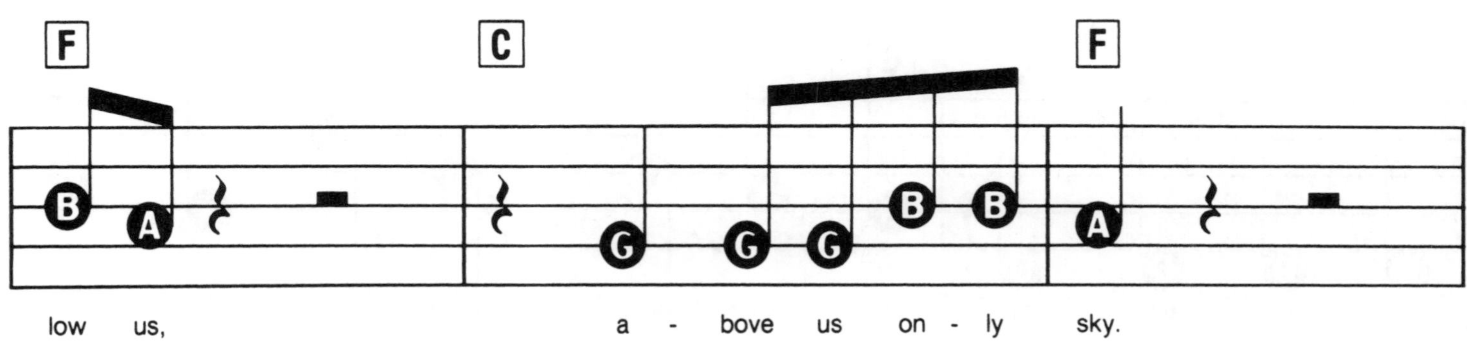

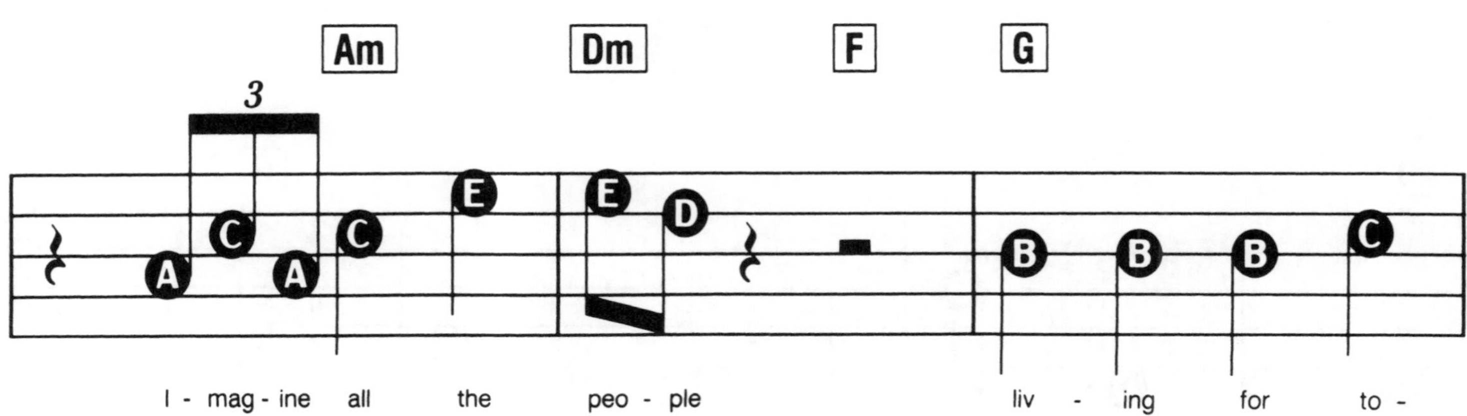

© 1971 (Renewed) LENONO MUSIC
All Rights Administered by DOWNTOWN DMP SONGS/DOWNTOWN MUSIC PUBLISHING LLC
All Rights Reserved Used by Permission

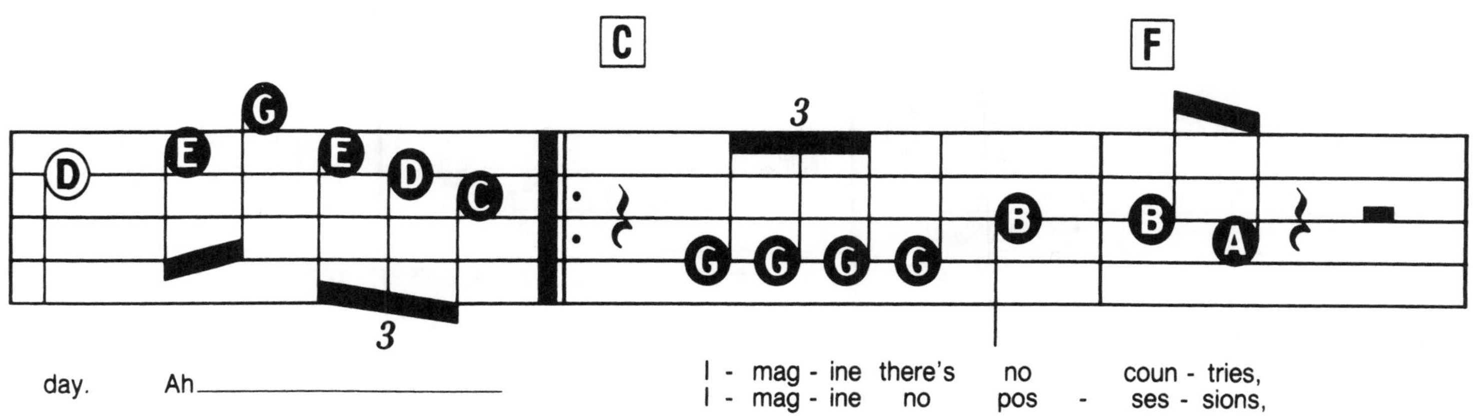
C
F
3
D
E
G
E
D
C
3
G
G
G
G
B
B
A
day. Ah
I - mag - ine there's no coun - tries,
I - mag - ine no pos - ses - sions,

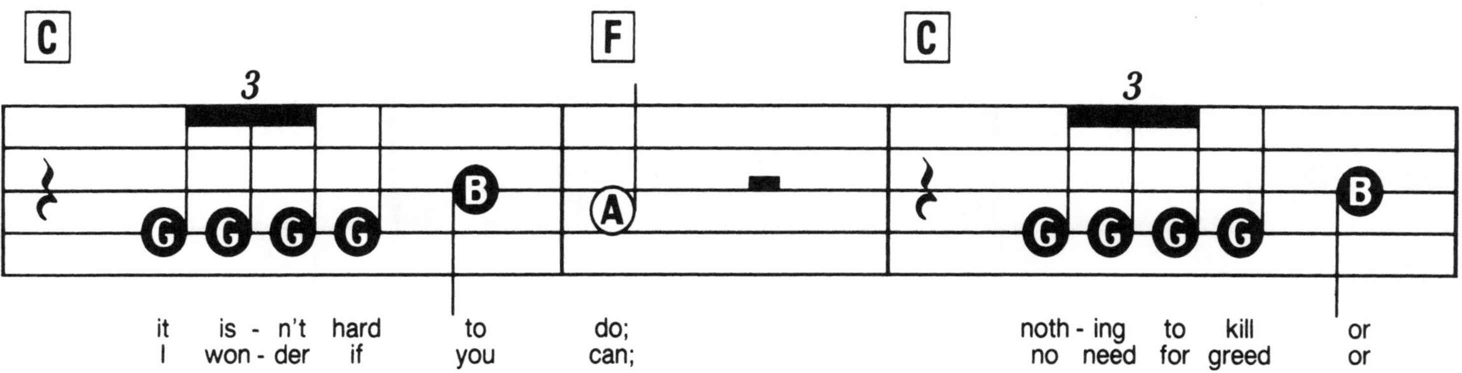
C
F
C
3
G
G
G
G
B
A
3
G
G
G
G
B
it is - n't hard to do;
I won - der if you can;
noth - ing to kill or
no need for greed or

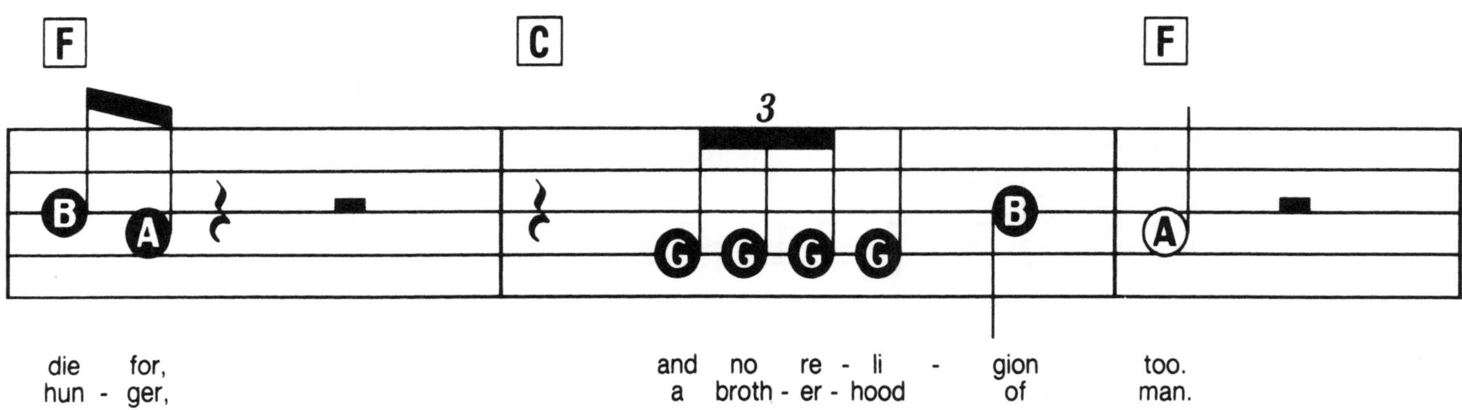
F
C
F
B
A
3
G
G
G
G
B
A
die for,
hun - ger,
and no re - li - gion too.
a broth - er - hood of man.

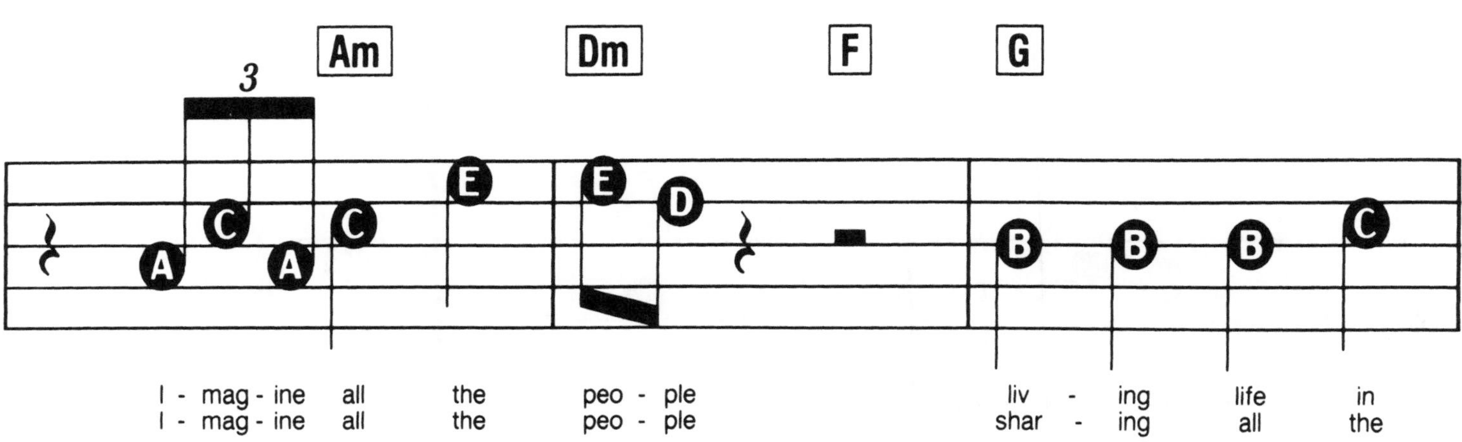
Am
Dm
F
G
3
A
C
A
C
E
E
D
B
B
B
C
I - mag - ine all the peo - ple
I - mag - ine all the peo - ple
liv - ing life in
shar - ing all the

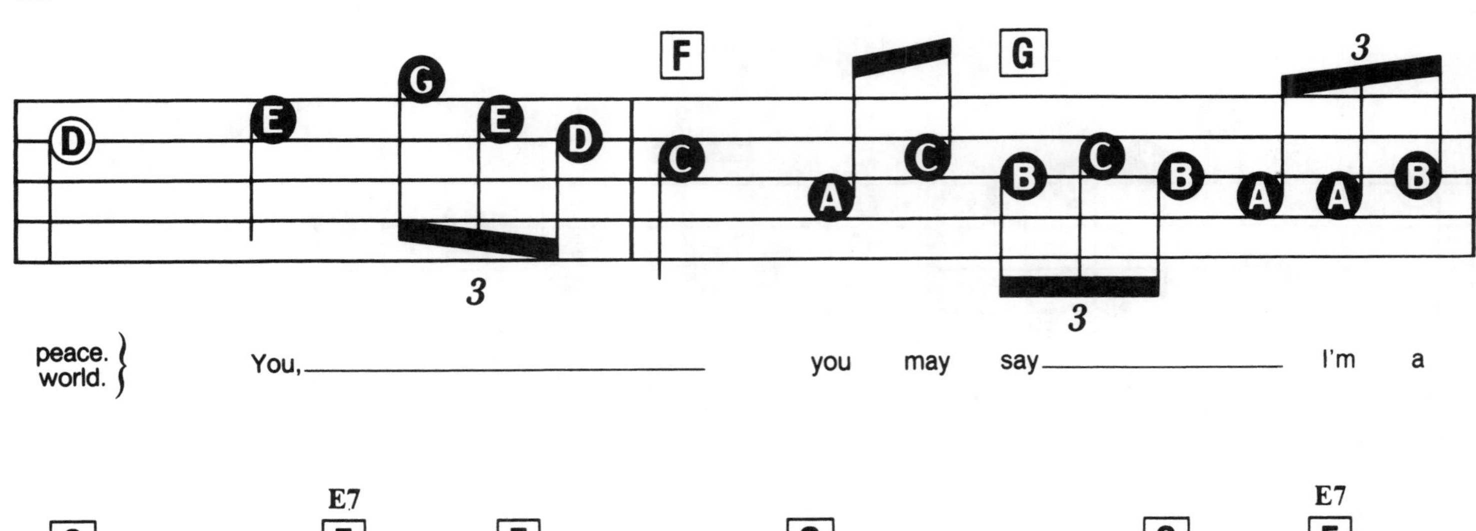
F
G
3
3
3
peace.
world.
You,
you may say
I'm a

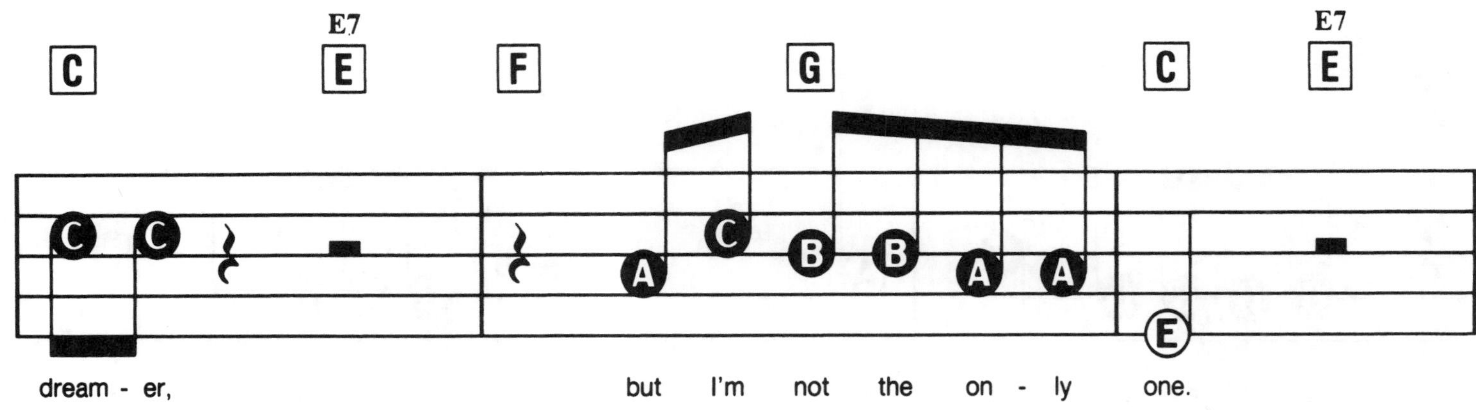
C
E7
E
F
G
C
E7
E
dream - er,
but I'm not the on - ly
one.

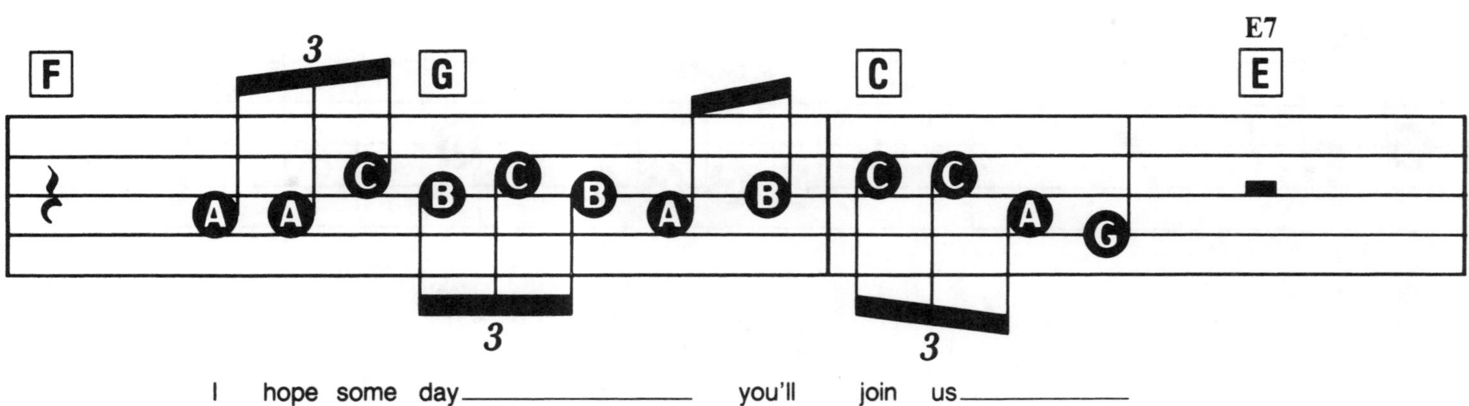
F
3
G
C
E7
E
3
3
I hope some day
you'll join us

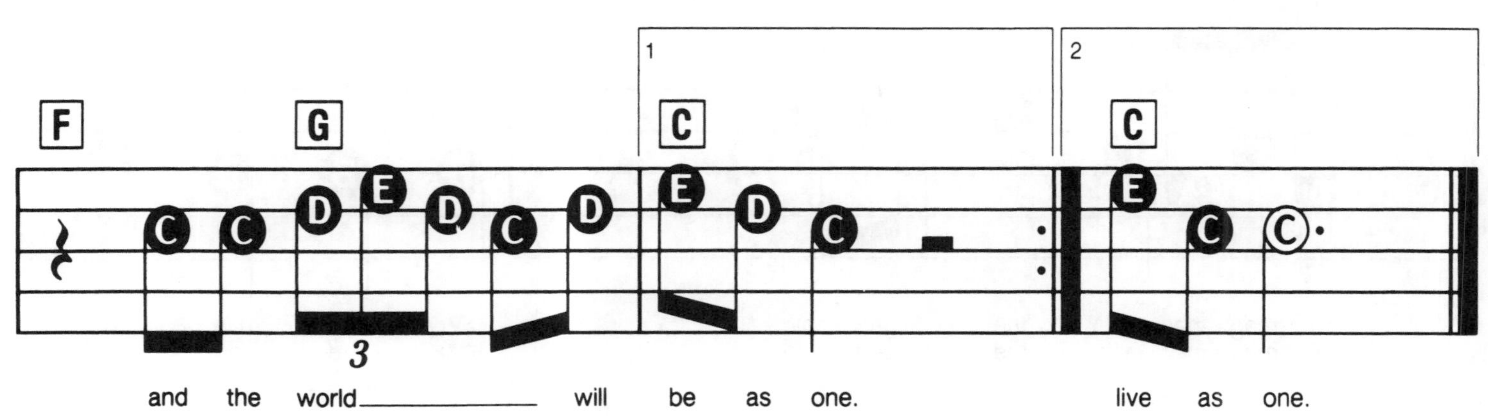
1
2
F
G
C
C
3
and the world
will be as one.
live as one.

John Jacob Jingleheimer Schmidt

Registration 2
Rhythm: Polka or March

Traditional

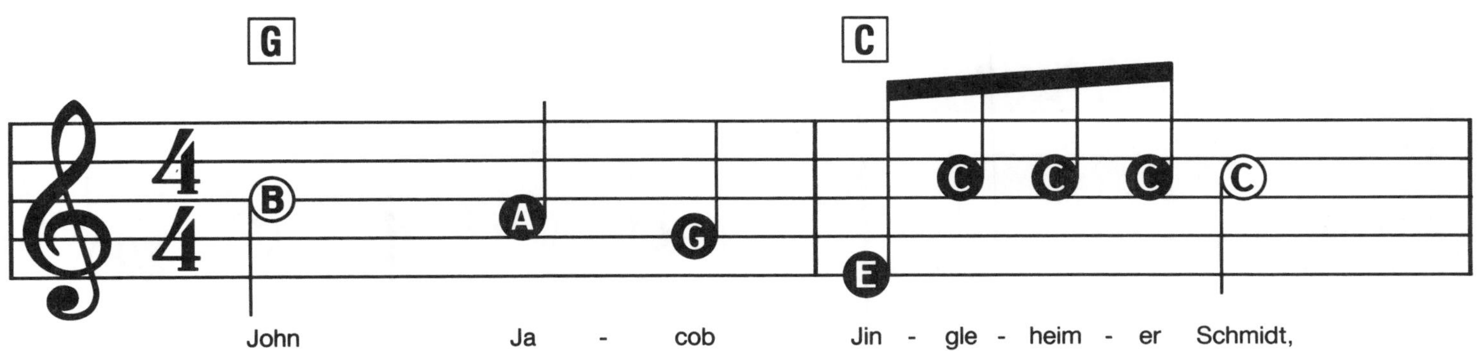

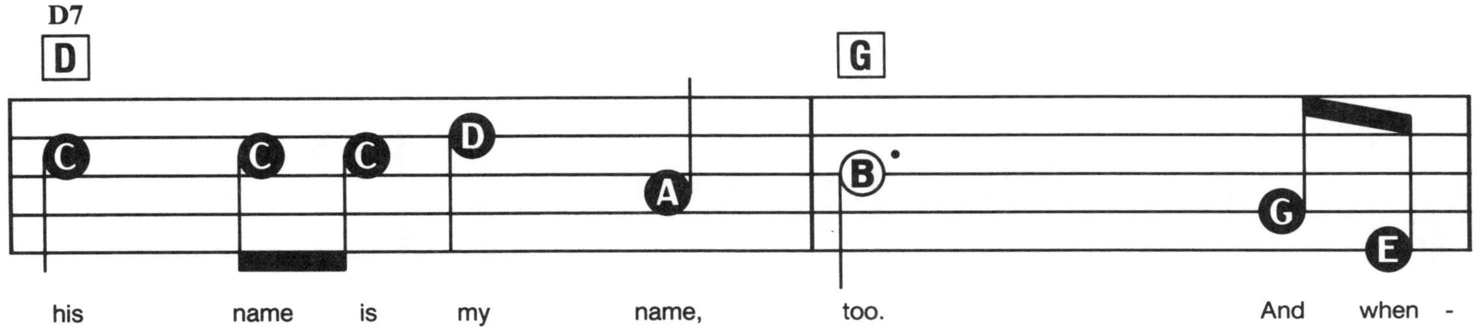

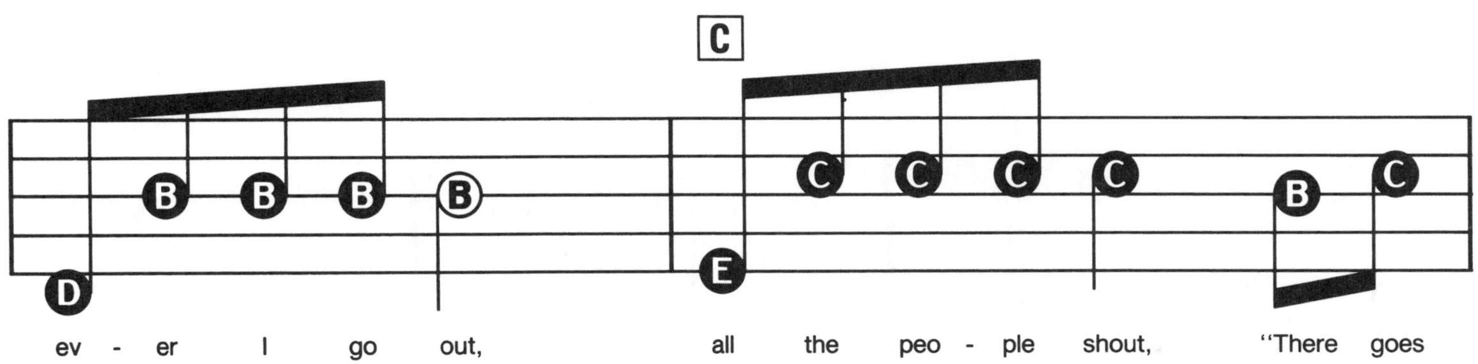

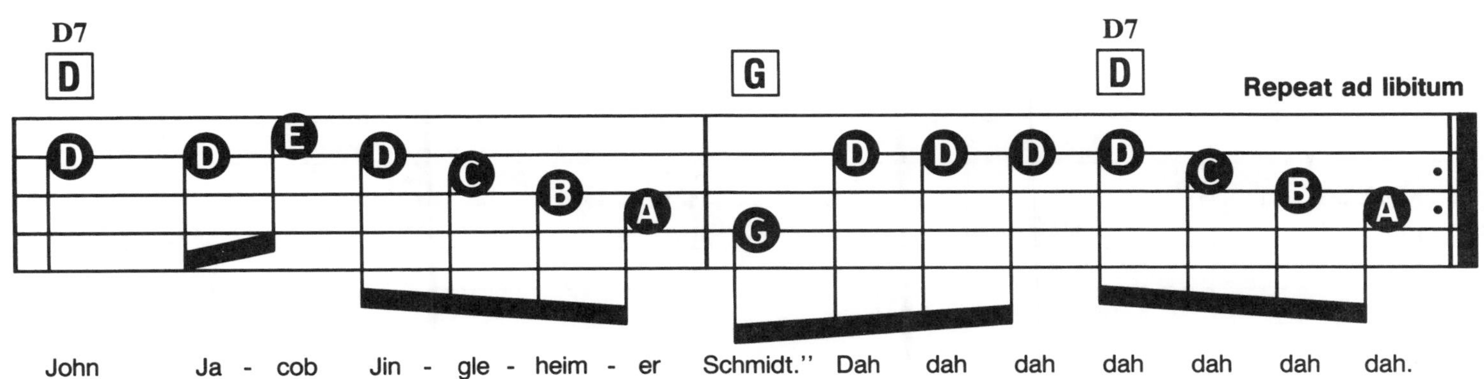

Copyright © 1989 by HAL LEONARD CORPORATION
International Copyright Secured All Rights Reserved

It's a Small World

from Disneyland Resort® and Magic Kingdom® Park

Registration 2
Rhythm: March

Words and Music by Richard M. Sherman
and Robert B. Sherman

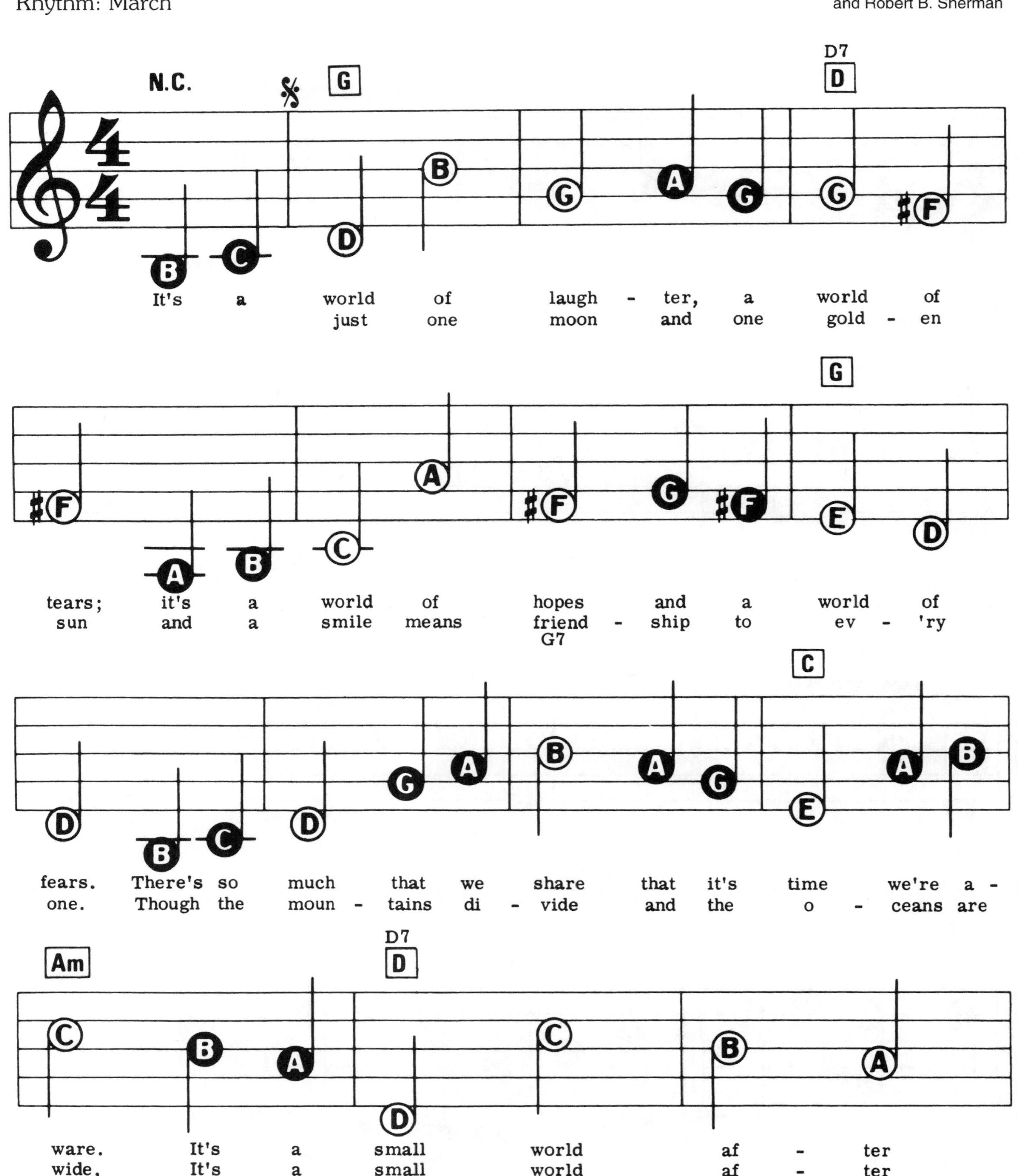

© 1963 Wonderland Music Company, Inc.
Copyright Renewed
All Rights Reserved Used by Permission

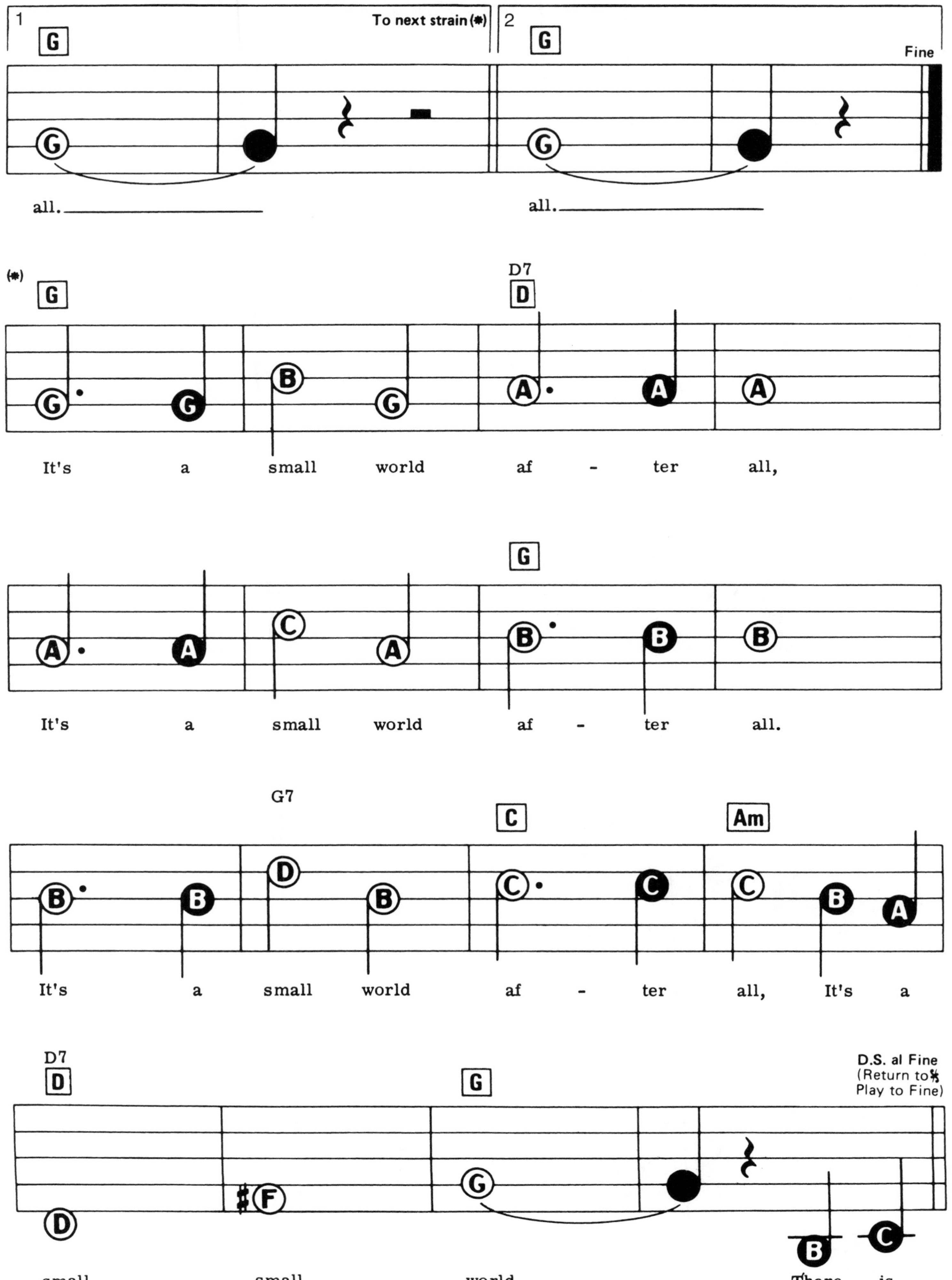
1
To next strain (✱)
G
G
all.
2
G
Fine
G
all.
(✱)
G
G G B G
It's a small world
D7
D
A A A
af - ter all,
A A C A
It's a small world
G
B B B
af - ter all.
G7
B B D B
It's a small world
C
C C
af - ter
Am
C B A
all, It's a
D7
D
D
small,
♯F
small
G
G
world.
D.S. al Fine
(Return to 𝄋
Play to Fine)
B C
There is

Kumbaya

Registration 4
Rhythm: Ballad or Fox Trot

Congo Folksong

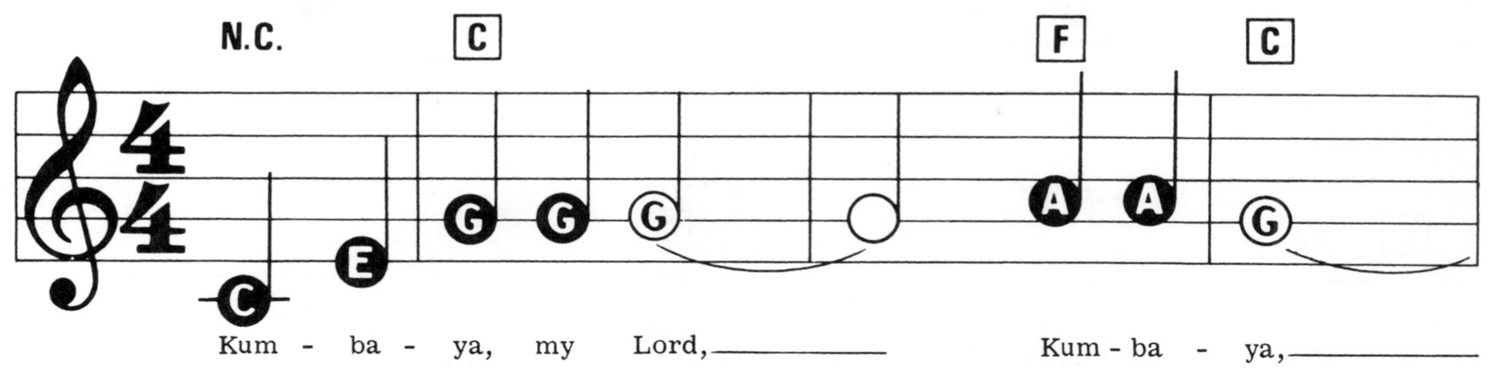

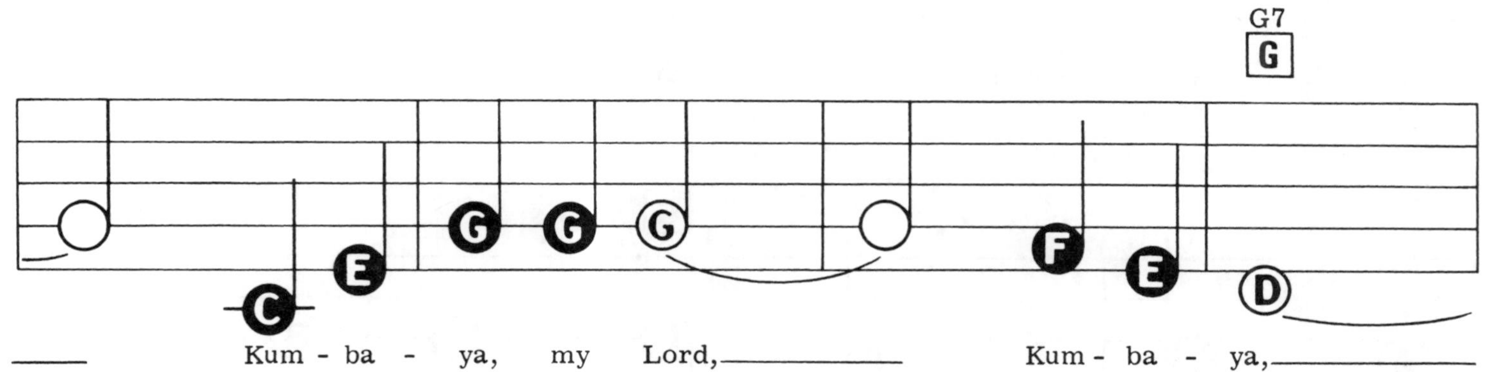

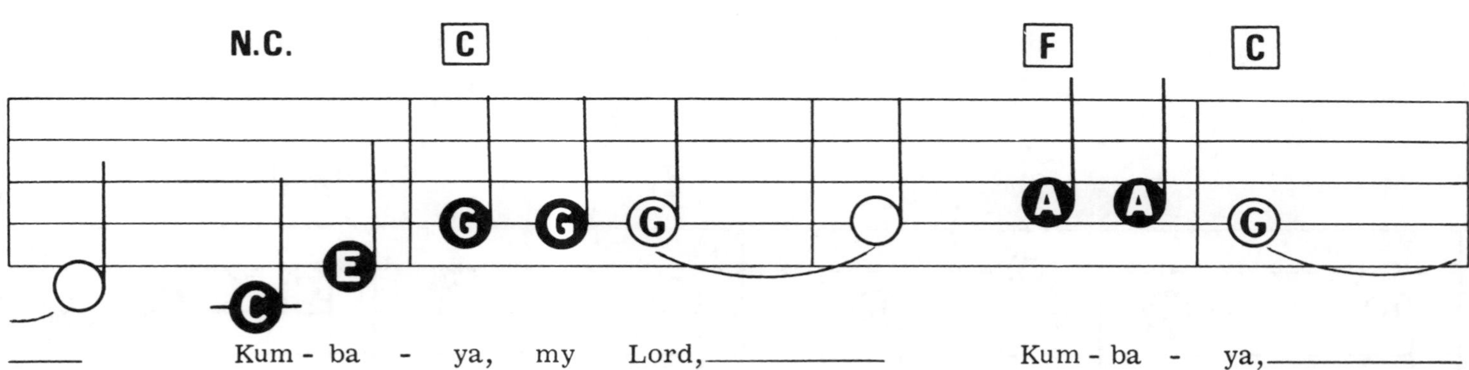

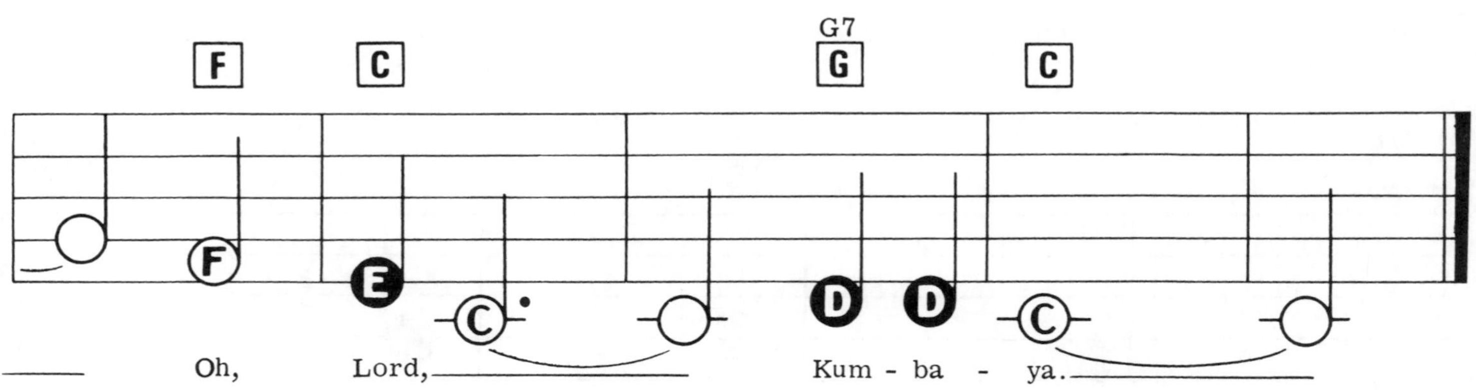

Copyright © 1975 by HAL LEONARD CORPORATION
International Copyright Secured All Rights Reserved

Let It Go

from Disney's Animated Feature FROZEN

Registration 8
Rhythm: Rock or Dance

Music and Lyrics by Kristen Anderson-Lopez
and Robert Lopez

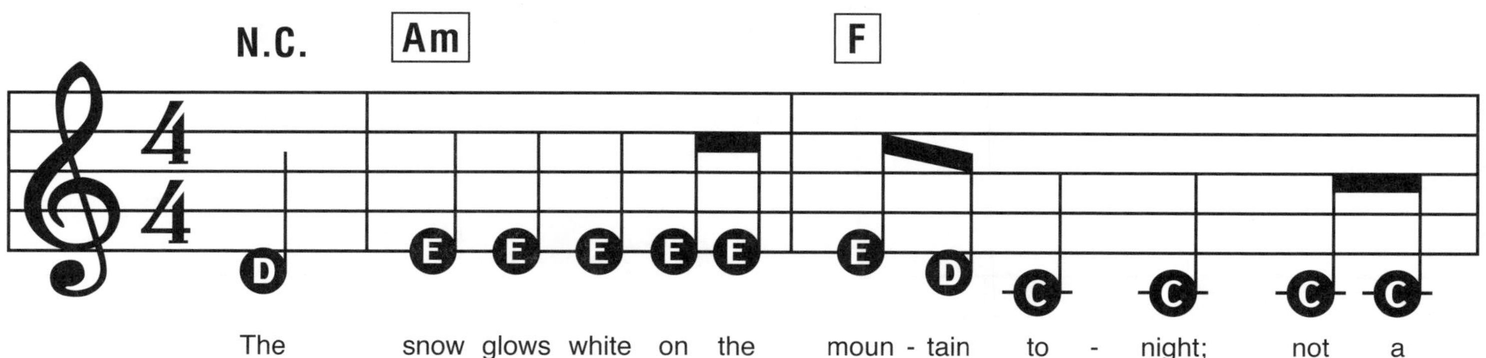

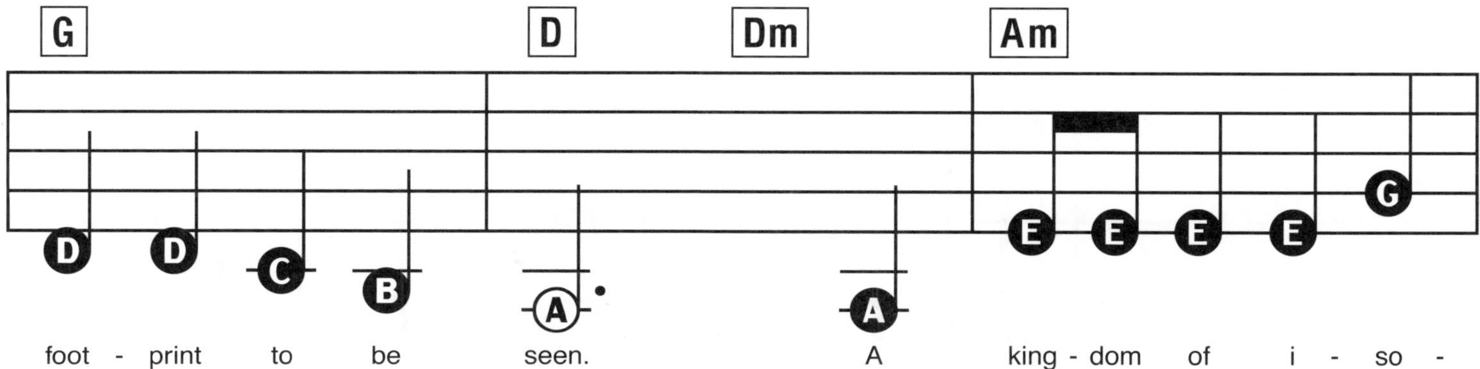

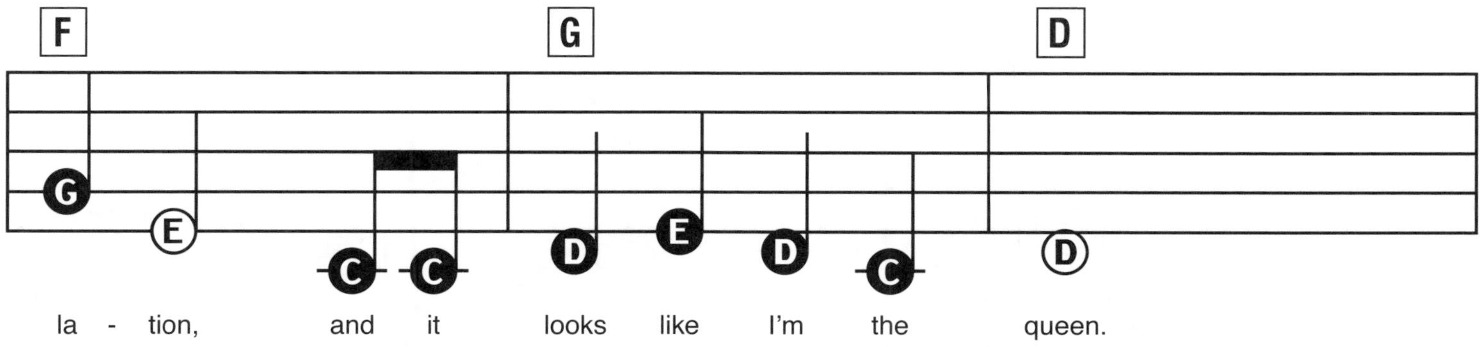

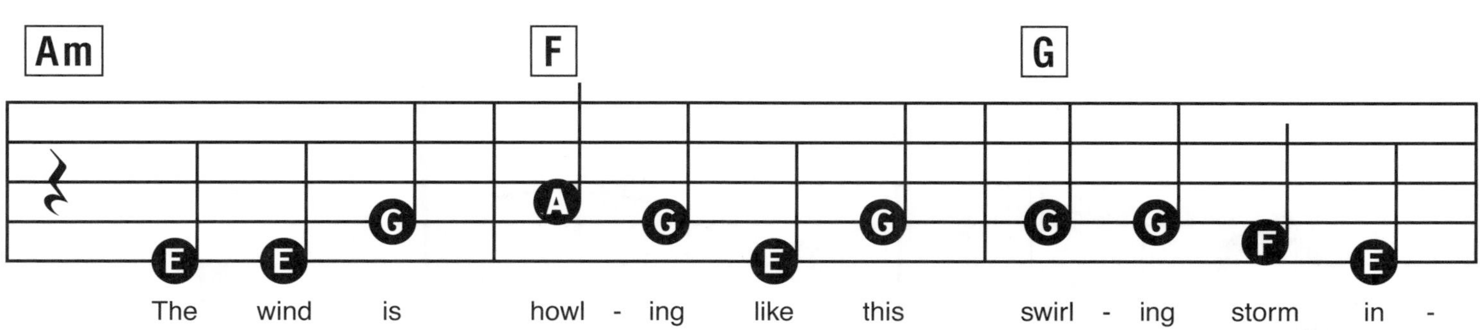

© 2013 Wonderland Music Company, Inc.
All Rights Reserved Used by Permission

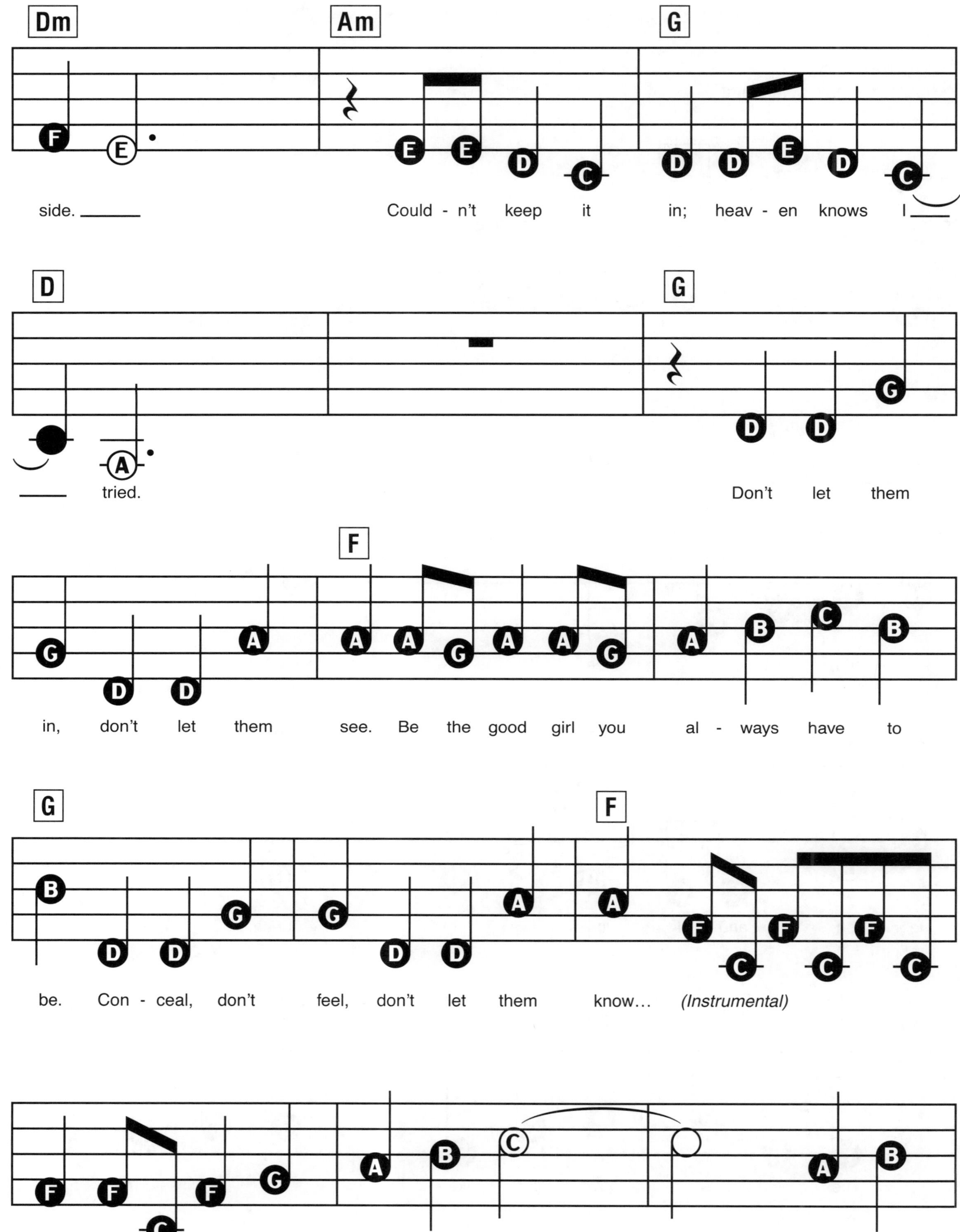
Dm
Am
G
F
E
E
E
D
C
D
D
E
D
C
side.
Could - n't keep it in; heav - en knows I
D
G
A
D
D
G
tried.
Don't let them
F
G
D
D
A
A
A
G
A
A
G
A
B
C
B
in, don't let them see. Be the good girl you al - ways have to
G
F
B
D
D
G
G
D
D
A
A
F
C
F
C
F
C
be. Con - ceal, don't feel, don't let them know... (Instrumental)
F
F
C
F
G
A
B
C
A
B
Well, now they know.
Let it

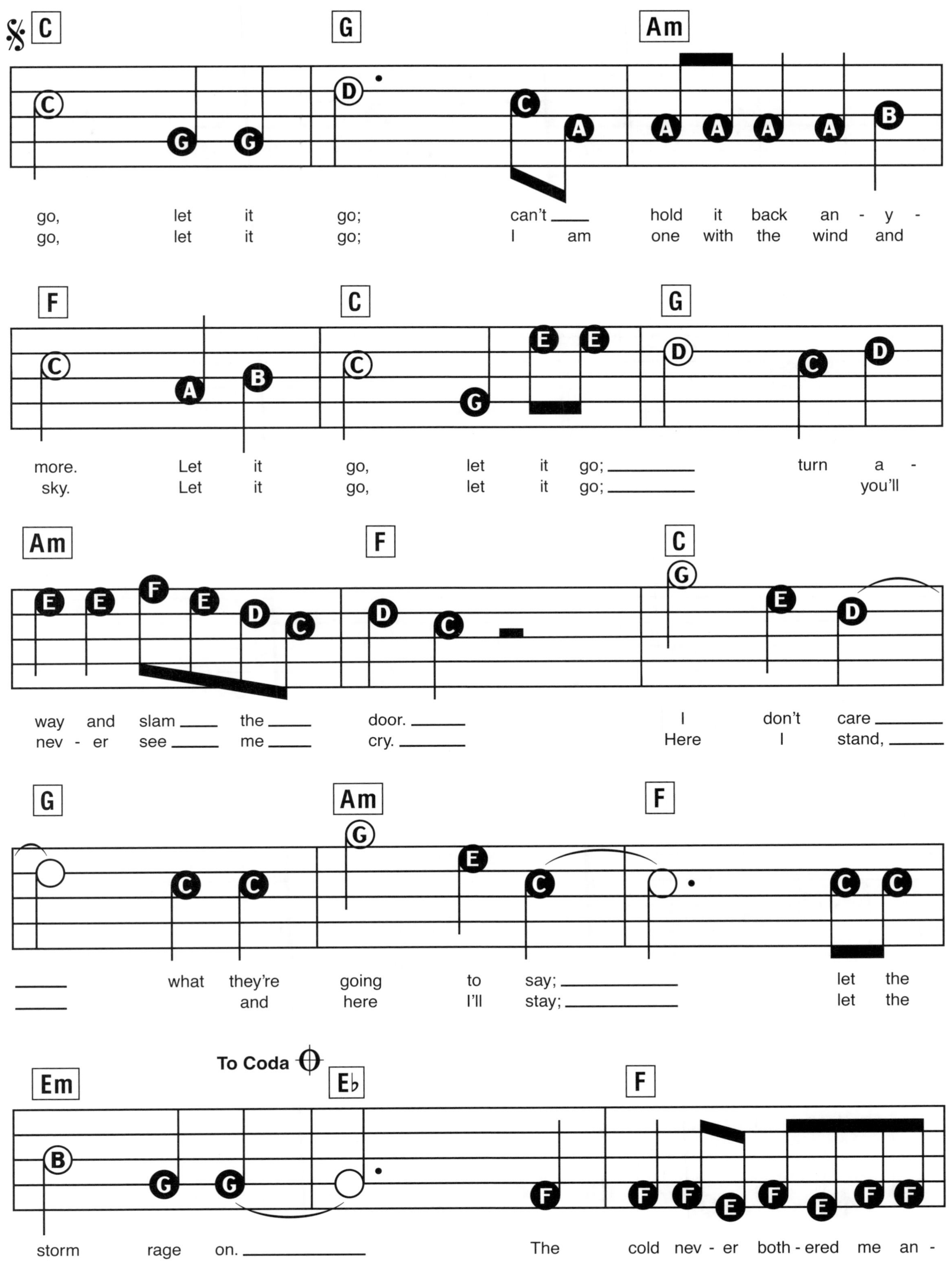
C G Am
go, let it go; can't ___ hold it back an - y -
go, let it go; I am one with the wind and
F C G
more. Let it go, let it go; ___ turn a -
sky. Let it go, let it go; ___ you'll
Am F C
way and slam ___ the ___ door. ___ I don't care ___
nev - er see ___ me ___ cry. ___ Here I stand, ___
G Am F
___ what they're going to say; ___ let the
___ and here I'll stay; ___ let the
To Coda
Em E♭ F
storm rage on. ___ The cold nev - er both - ered me an -
storm rage on. ___

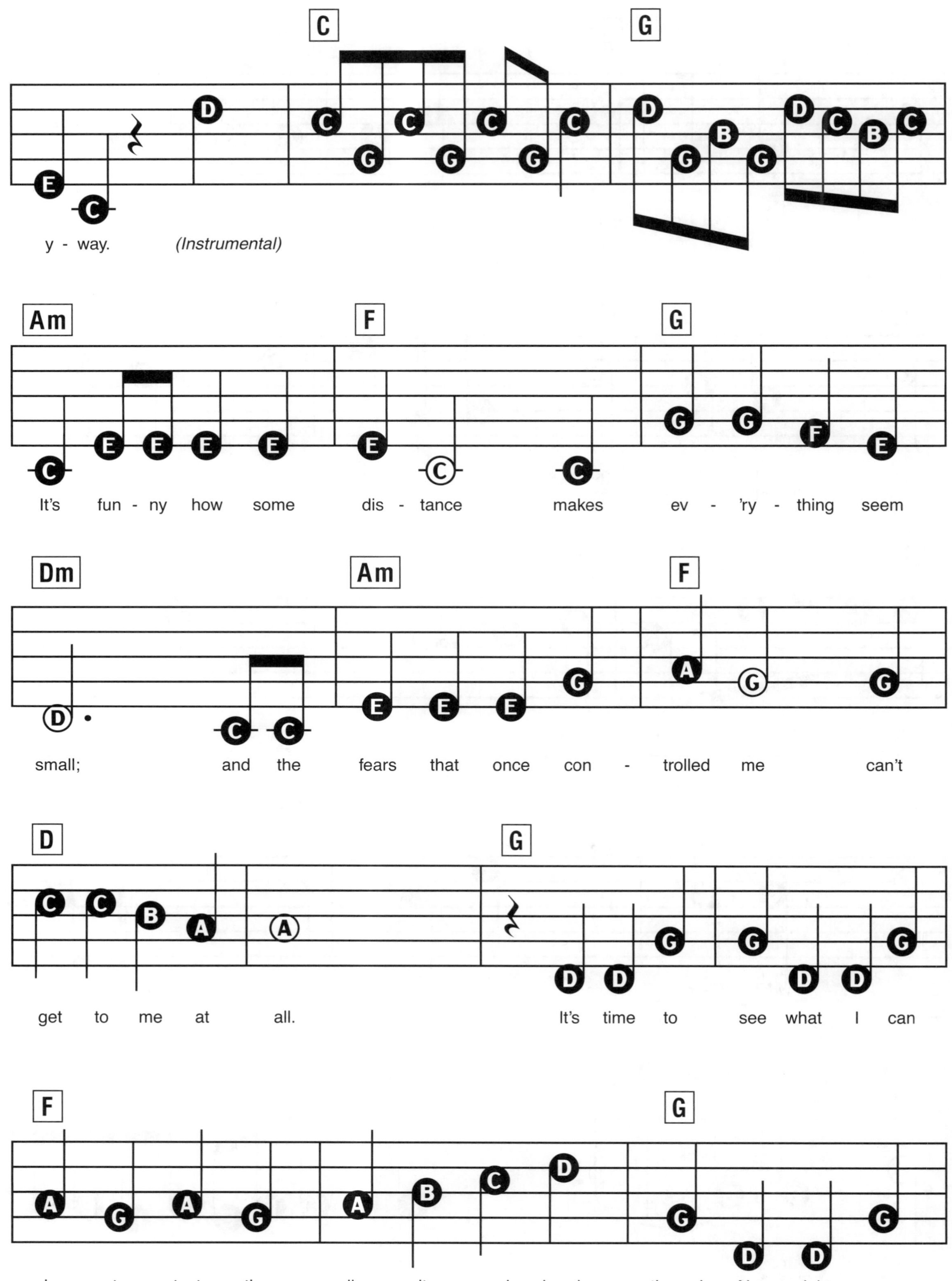
C G
y - way. (Instrumental)
Am F G
It's fun - ny how some dis - tance makes ev - 'ry - thing seem
Dm Am F
small; and the fears that once con - trolled me can't
D G
get to me at all. It's time to see what I can
F G
do, to test the lim - its and break through. No right, no

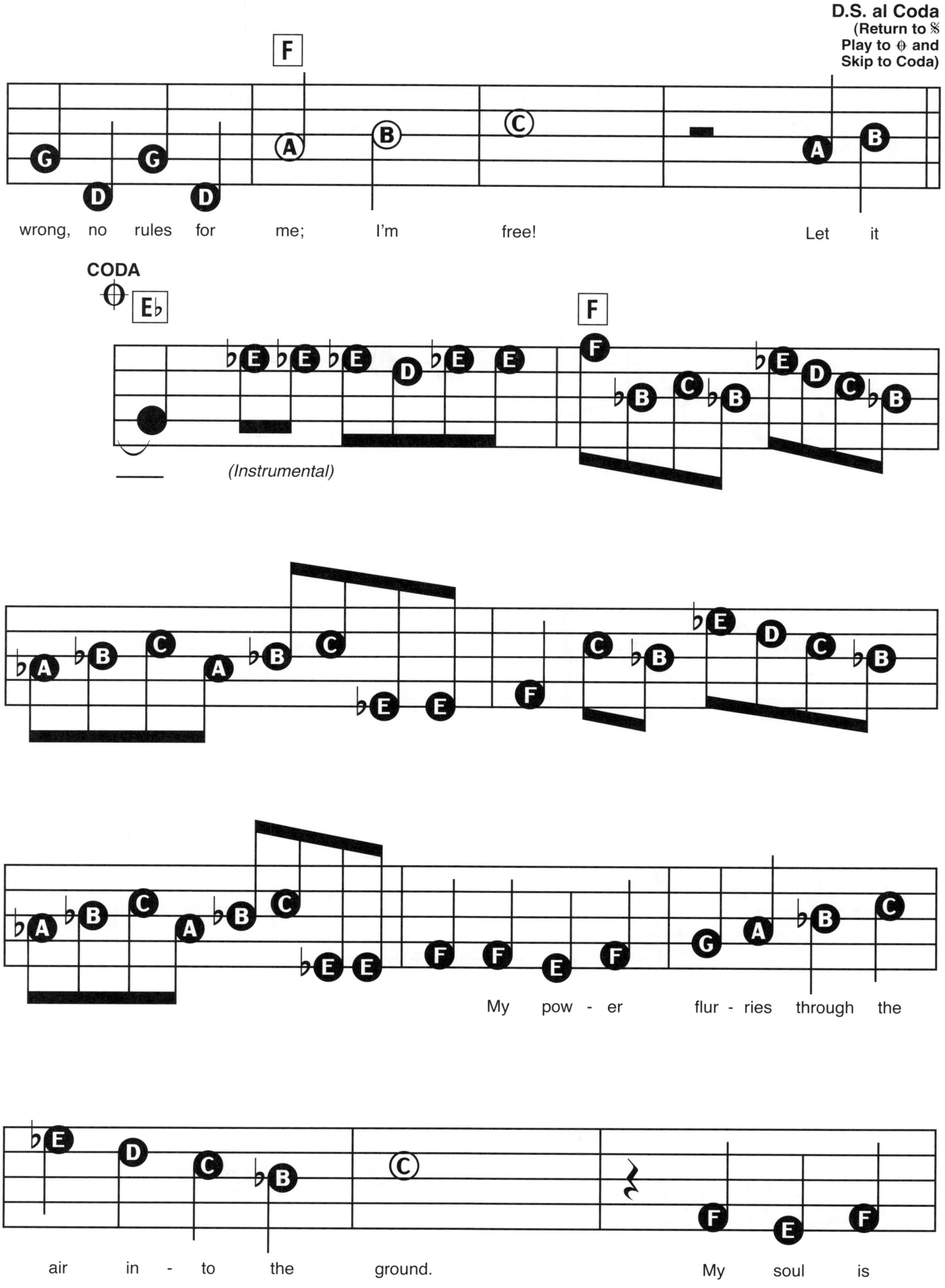

D.S. al Coda
(Return to 𝄋
Play to 𝄌 and
Skip to Coda)

F

wrong, no rules for me; I'm free! Let it

CODA

E♭

(Instrumental)

F

My pow - er flur - ries through the

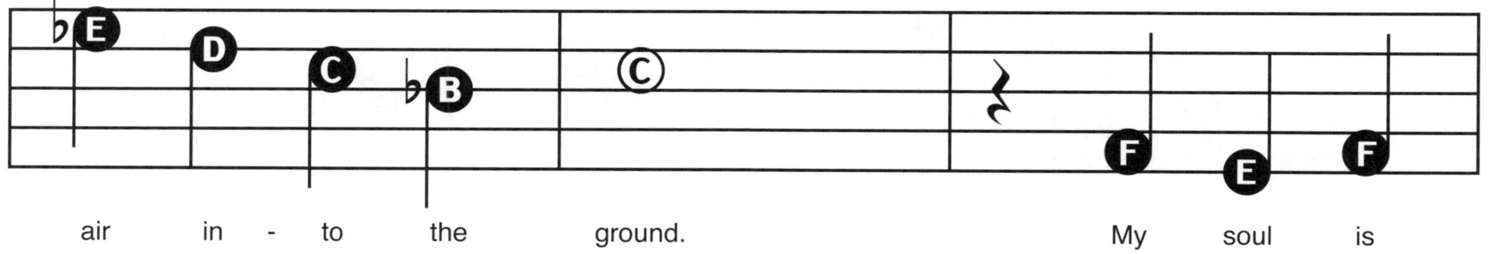

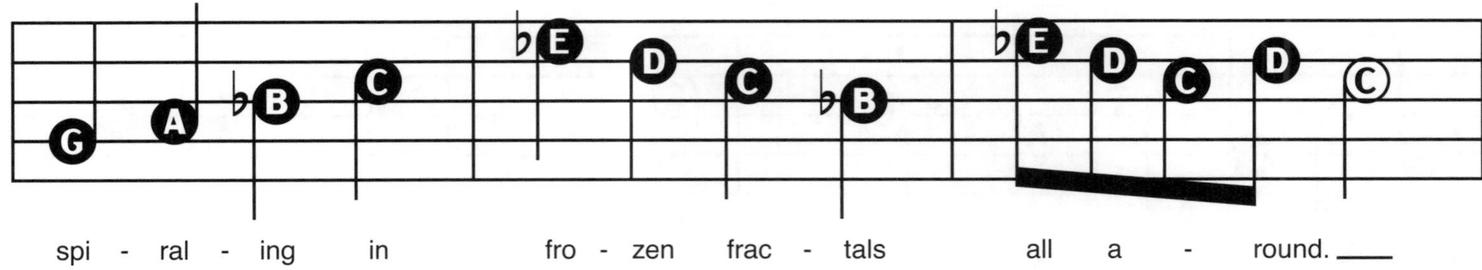
G
A
♭B
C
♭E
D
C
♭B
♭E
D
C
D
C
spi - ral - ing in fro - zen frac - tals all a - round.

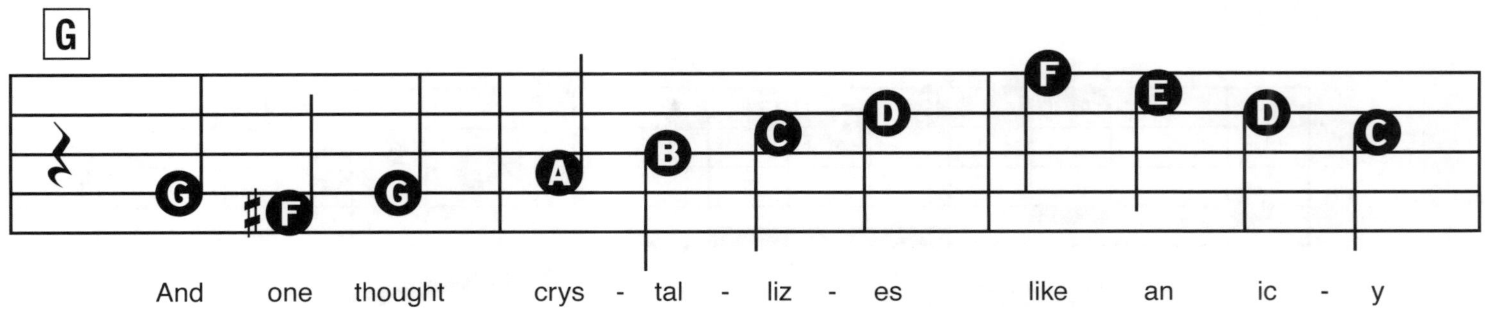
G
G
♯F
G
A
B
C
D
F
E
D
C
And one thought crys - tal - liz - es like an ic - y

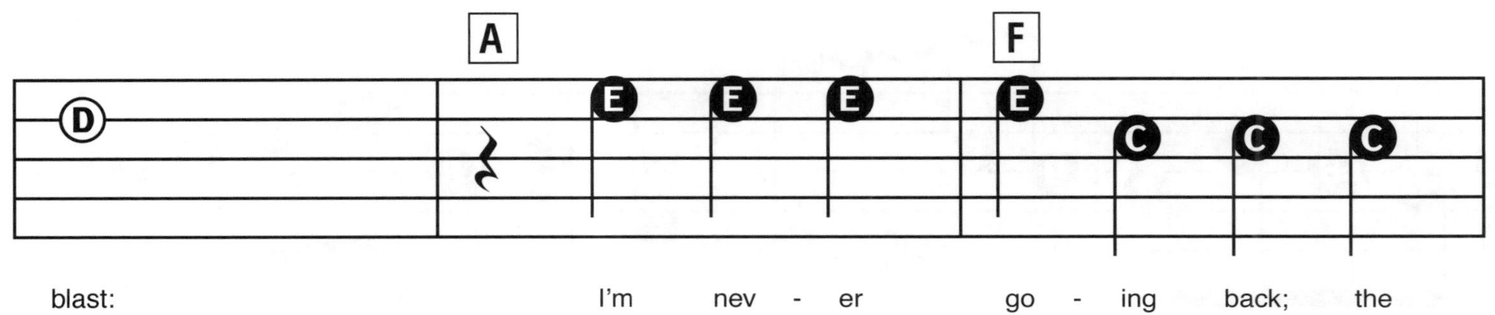
A
F
D
E
E
E
E
C
C
C
blast: I'm nev - er go - ing back; the

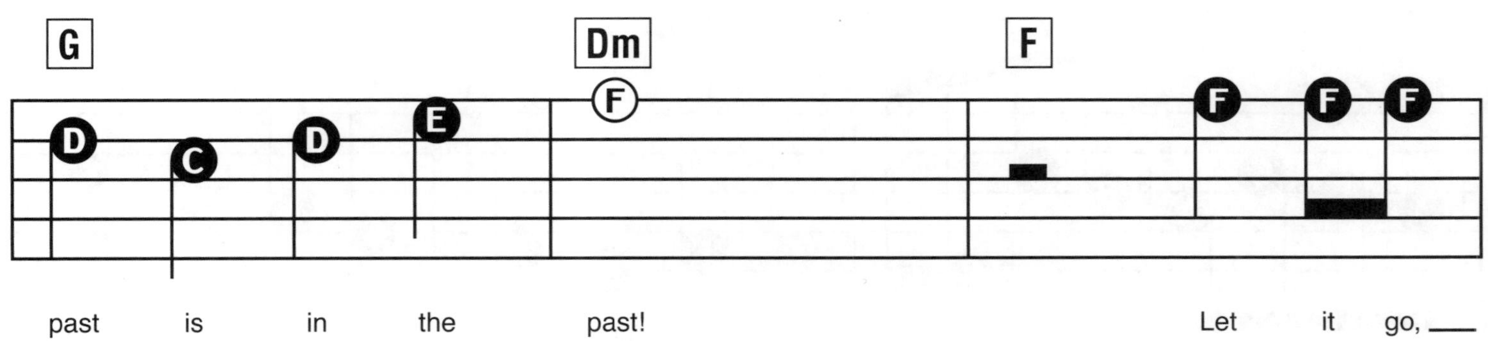
G
Dm
F
D
C
D
E
F
F
F
F
past is in the past! Let it go,

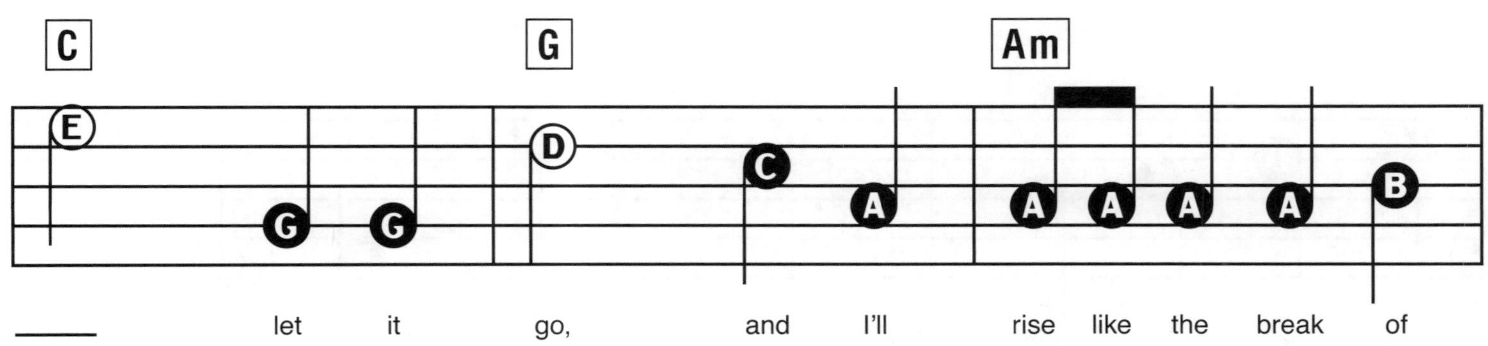
C
G
Am
E
G
G
D
C
A
A
A
A
A
B
let it go, and I'll rise like the break of

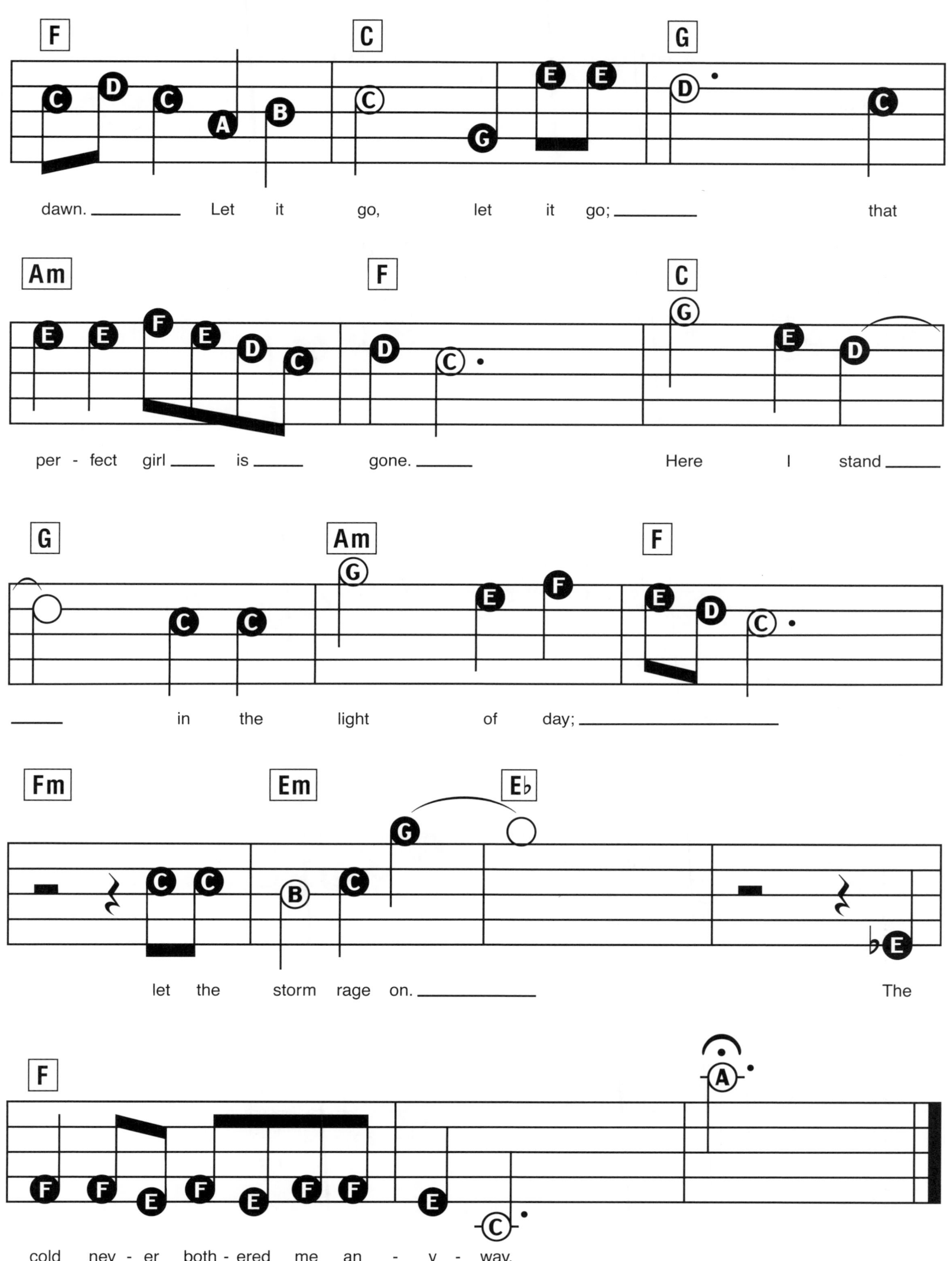
F
C
G
C D C A B C G E E D C
dawn. Let it go, let it go; that
Am
F
C
E E F E D C D C G E D
per - fect girl is gone. Here I stand
G
Am
F
C C G E F E D C
in the light of day;
Fm
Em
E♭
C C B C G
let the storm rage on.
E
The
F
F F E F E F F E C A
cold nev - er both - ered me an - y - way.

Lavender Blue
(Dilly Dilly)
from Walt Disney's SO DEAR TO MY HEART

Registration 2
Rhythm: Fox Trot or Swing

Words by Larry Morey
Music by Eliot Daniel

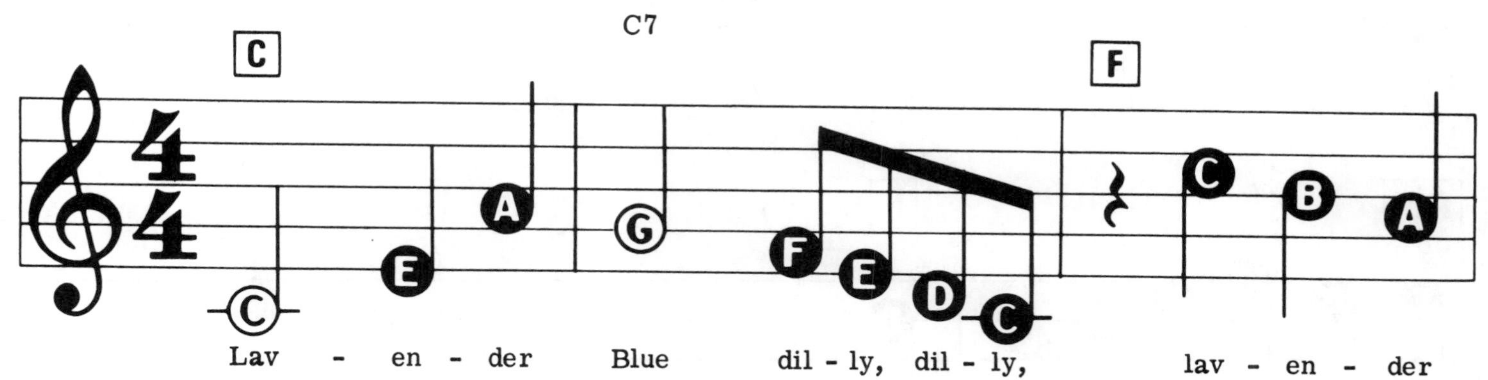

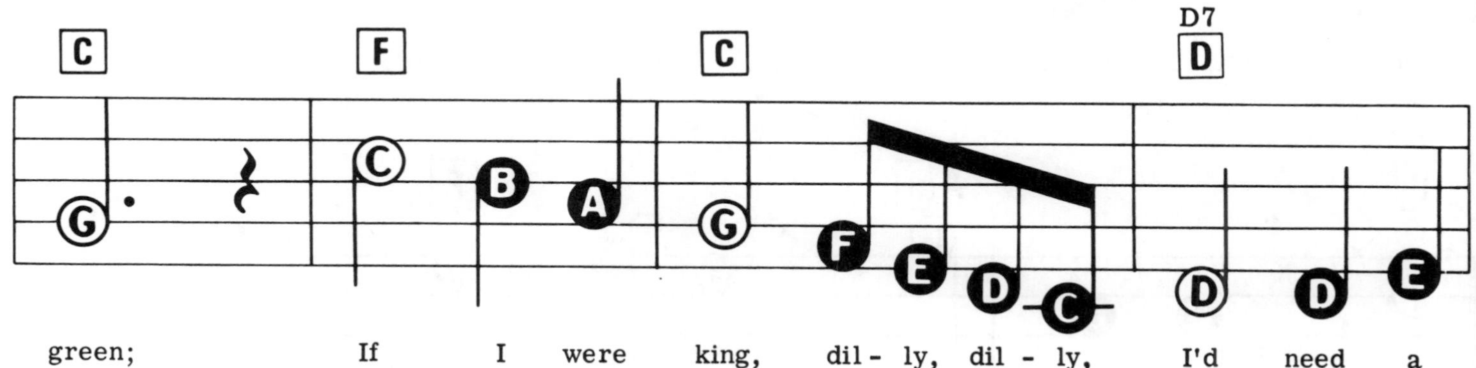

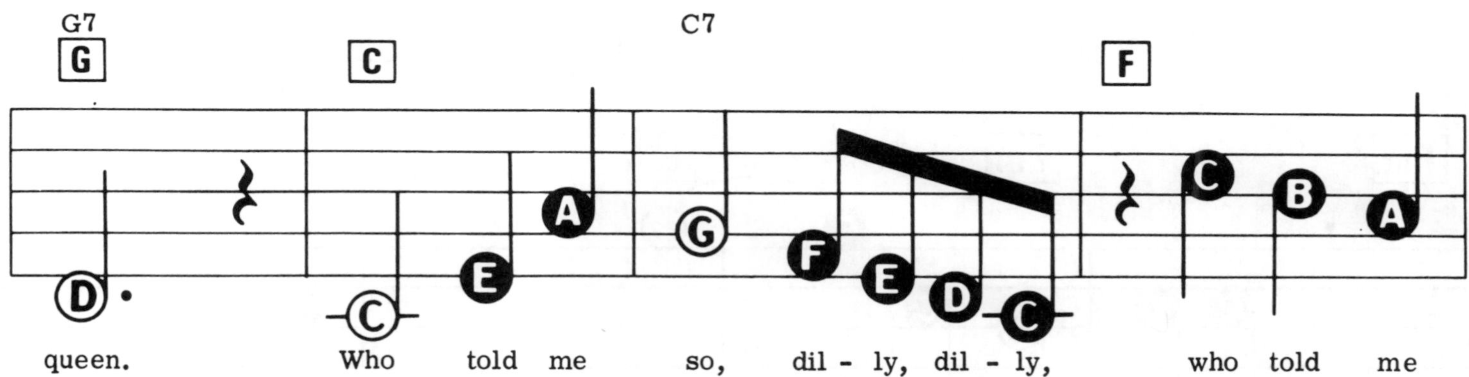

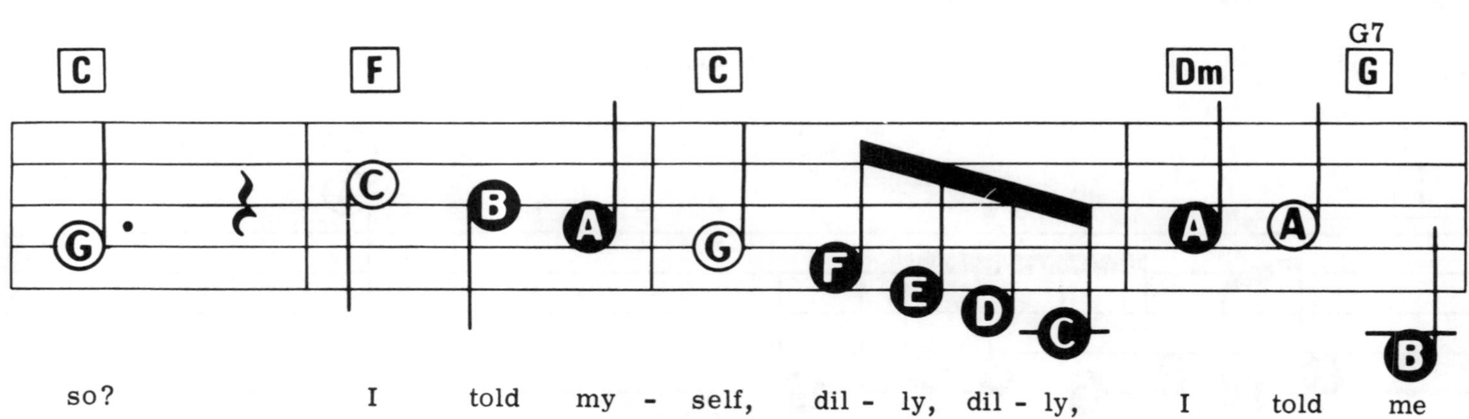

© 1948 Walt Disney Music Company
Copyright Renewed
All Rights Reserved. Used by Permission.

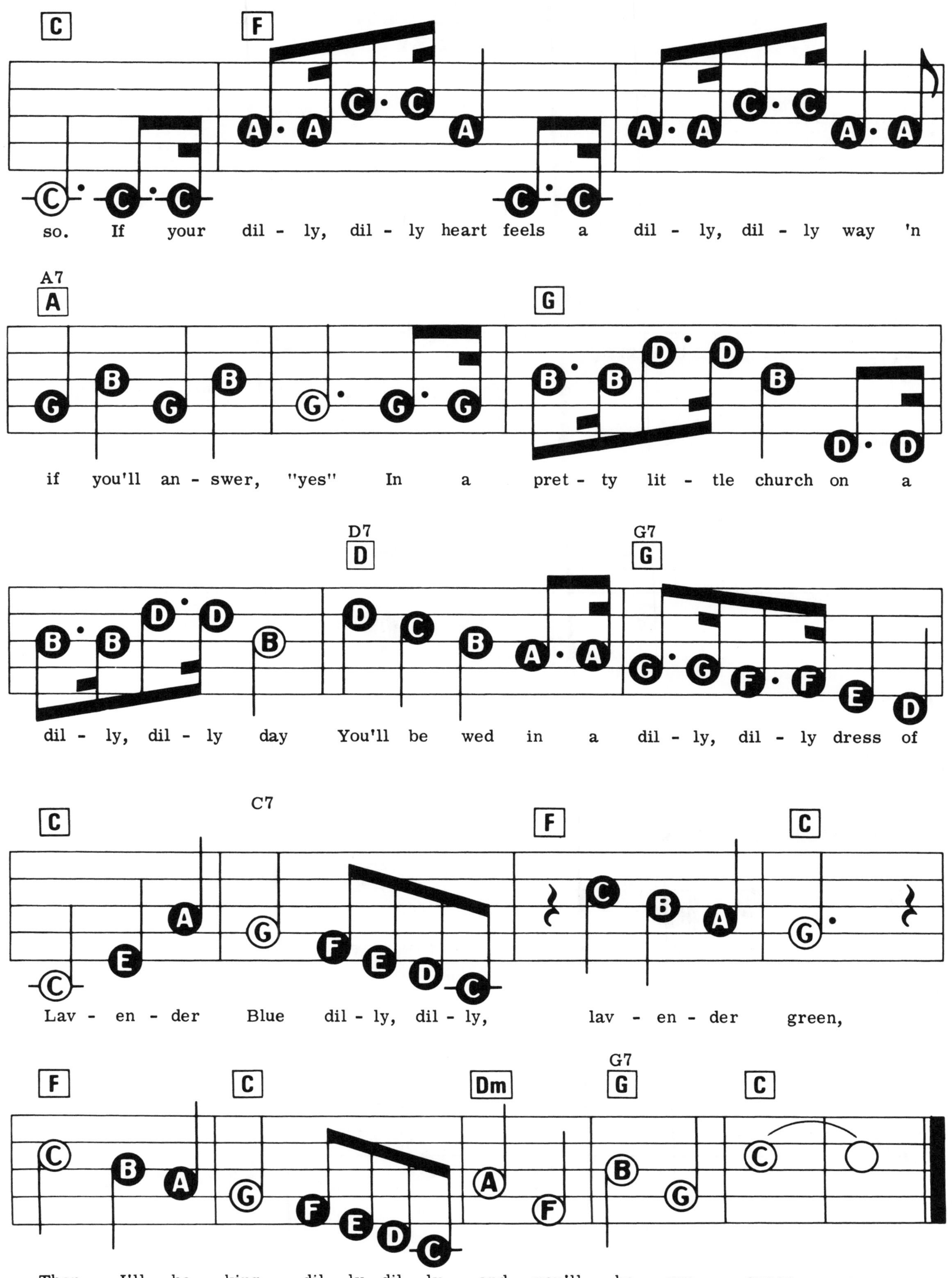
C F
so. If your dil - ly, dil - ly heart feels a dil - ly, dil - ly way 'n
A7 A G
if you'll an - swer, "yes" In a pret - ty lit - tle church on a
D7 D G7 G
dil - ly, dil - ly day You'll be wed in a dil - ly, dil - ly dress of
C C7 F C
Lav - en - der Blue dil - ly, dil - ly, lav - en - der green,
F C Dm G7 G C
Then I'll be king, dil - ly, dil - ly and you'll be my queen.

Let Me Entertain You

from GYPSY

Registration 9
Rhythm: Fox Trot or Polka

Lyrics by Stephen Sondheim
Music by Jule Styne

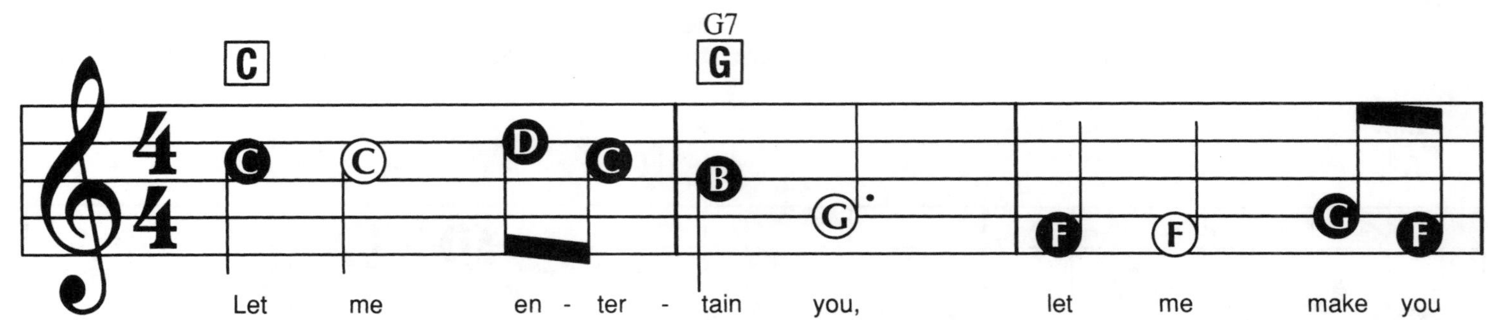

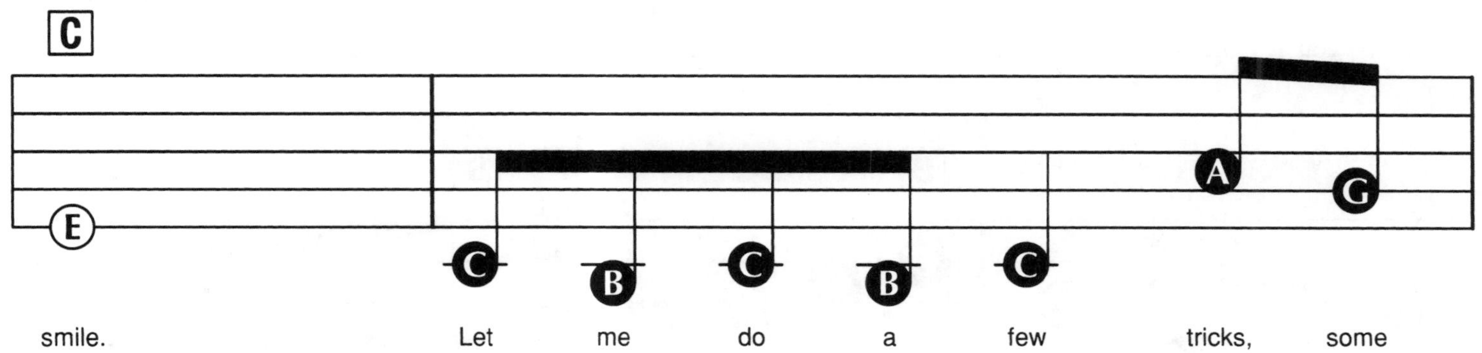

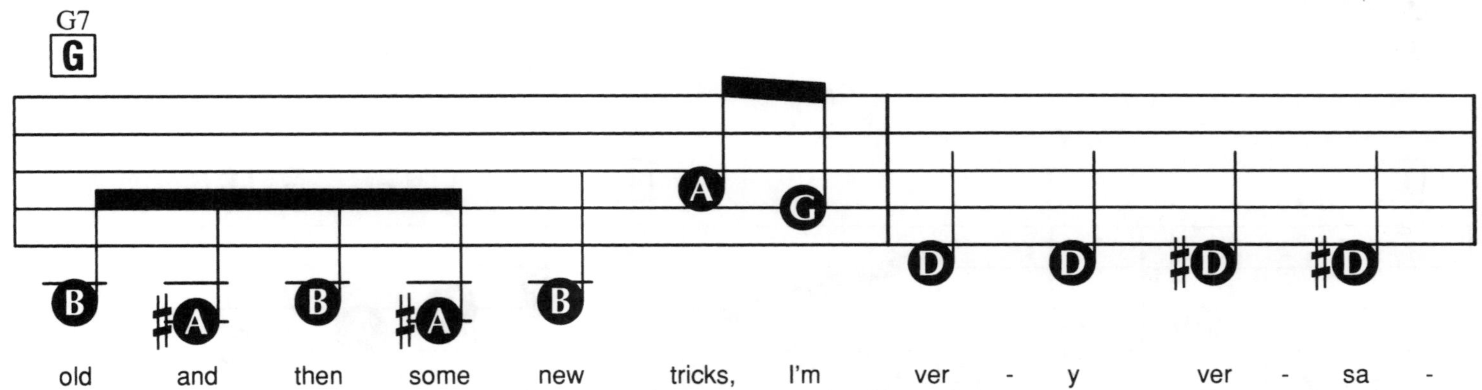

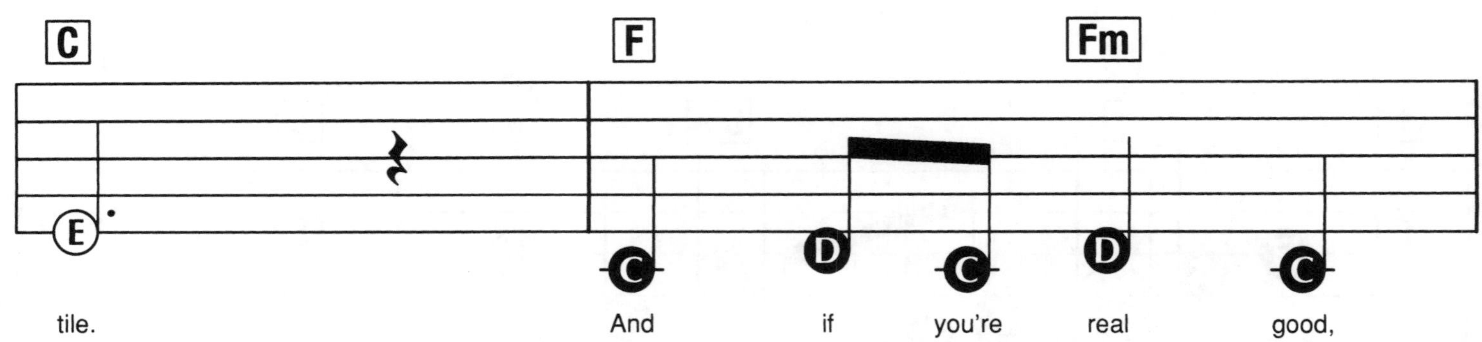

© 1959 (Renewed) STRATFORD MUSIC CORPORATION and WILLIAMSON MUSIC CO.
All Rights Administered by CHAPPELL & CO., INC.
All Rights Reserved Used by Permission

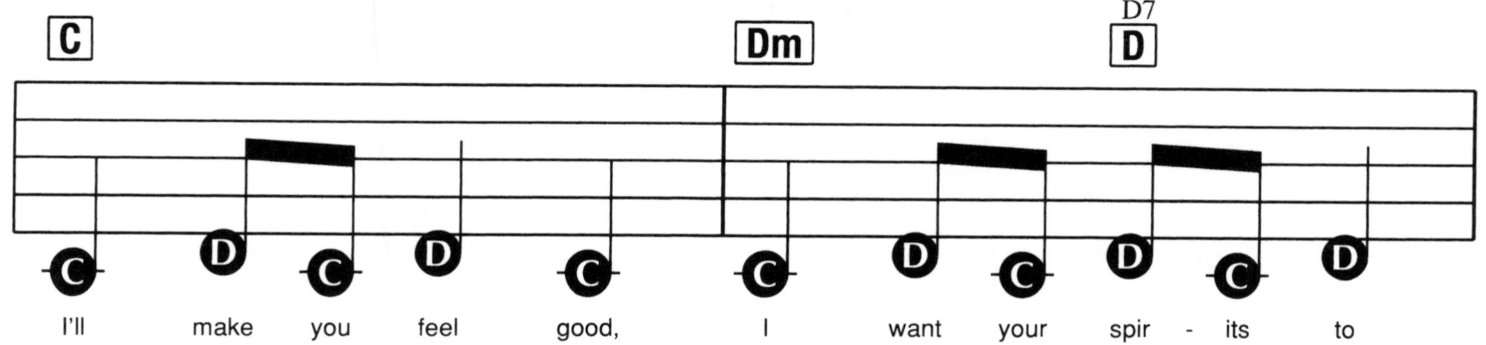
C
Dm
D7
D
I'll make you feel good, I want your spir - its to

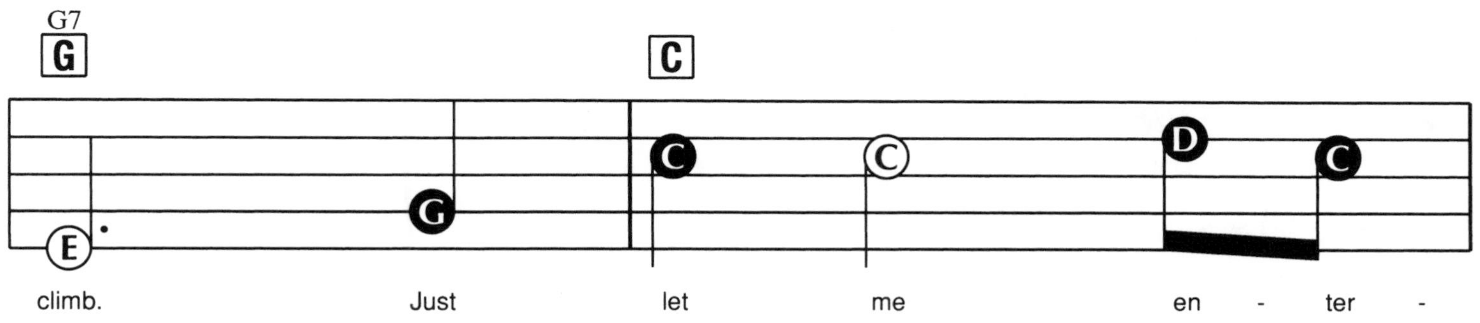
G7
G
C
climb. Just let me en - ter -

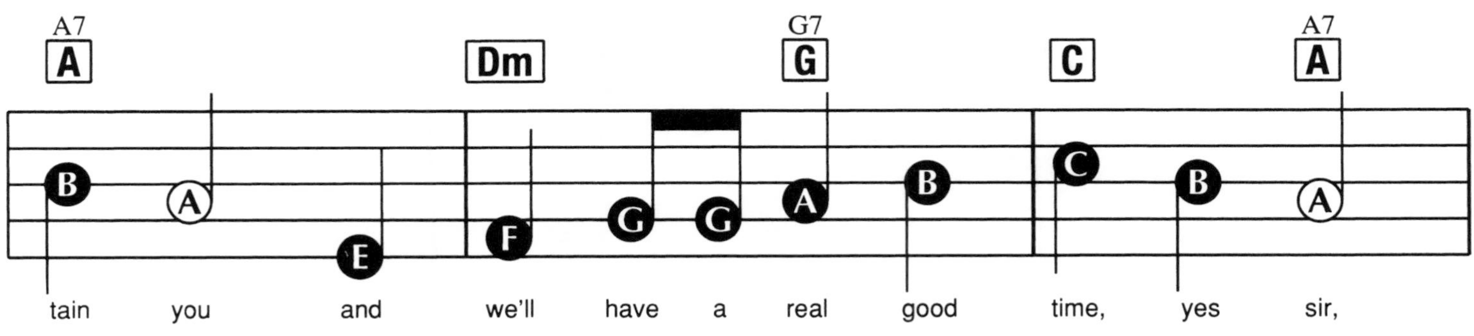
A7
A
Dm
G7
G
C
A7
A
tain you and we'll have a real good time, yes sir,

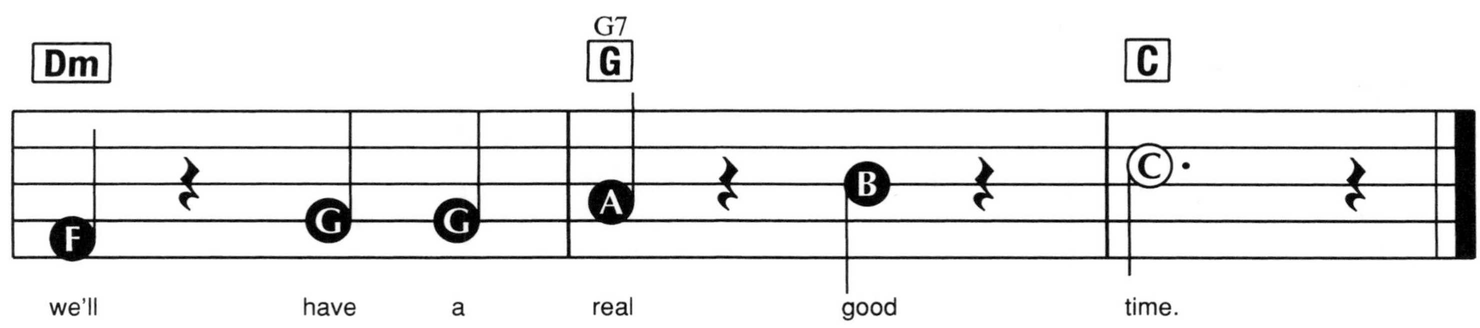
Dm
G7
G
C
we'll have a real good time.

Little April Shower

from Walt Disney's BAMBI

Registration 4
Rhythm: Fox Trot

Words by Larry Morey
Music by Frank Churchill

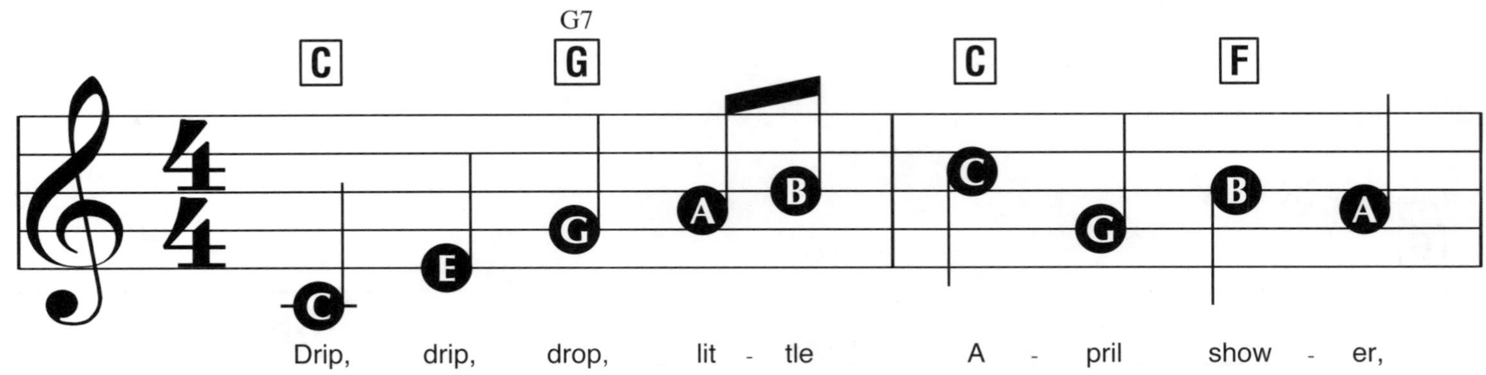

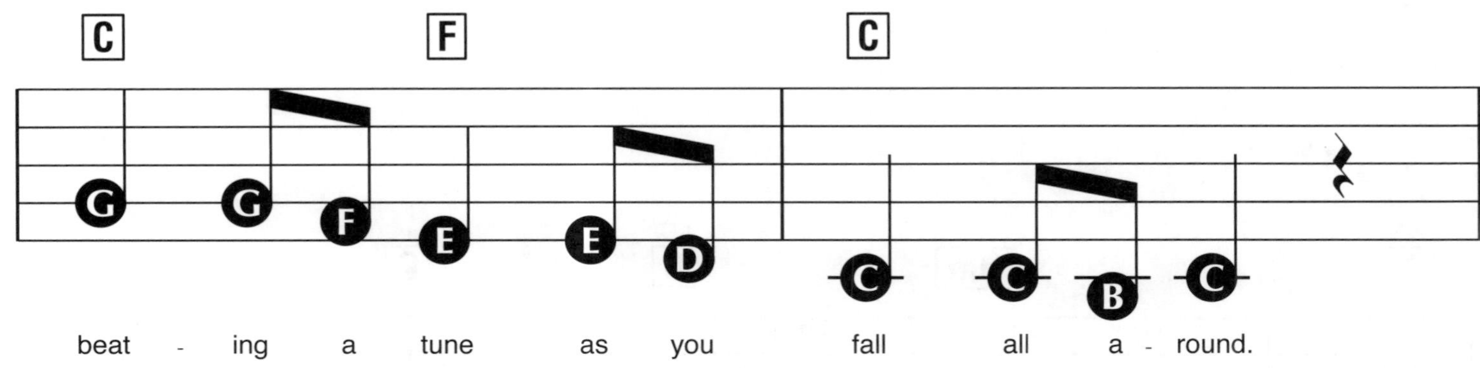

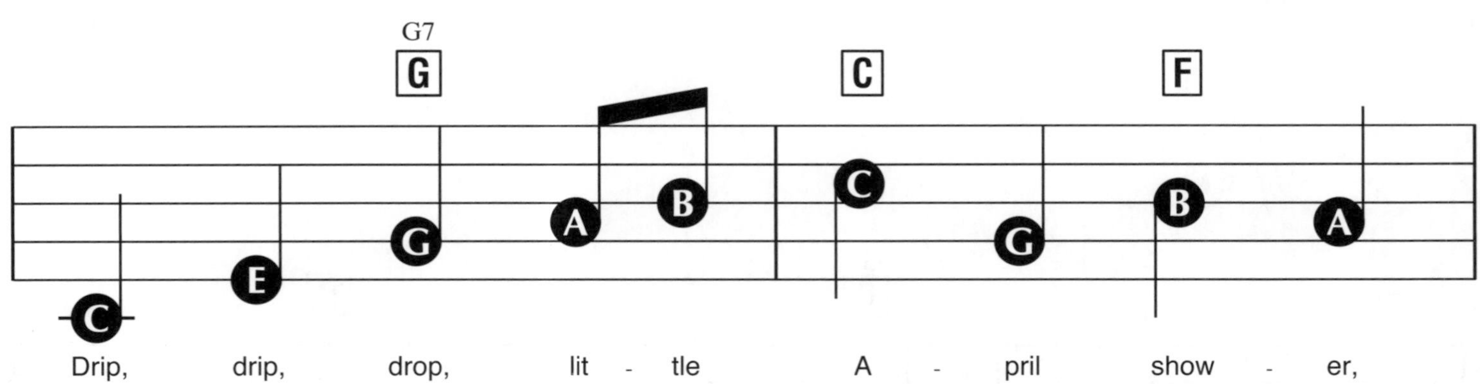

© 1942 Walt Disney Music Company and Wonderland Music Company, Inc.
Copyright Renewed
All Rights Reserved. Used by Permission.

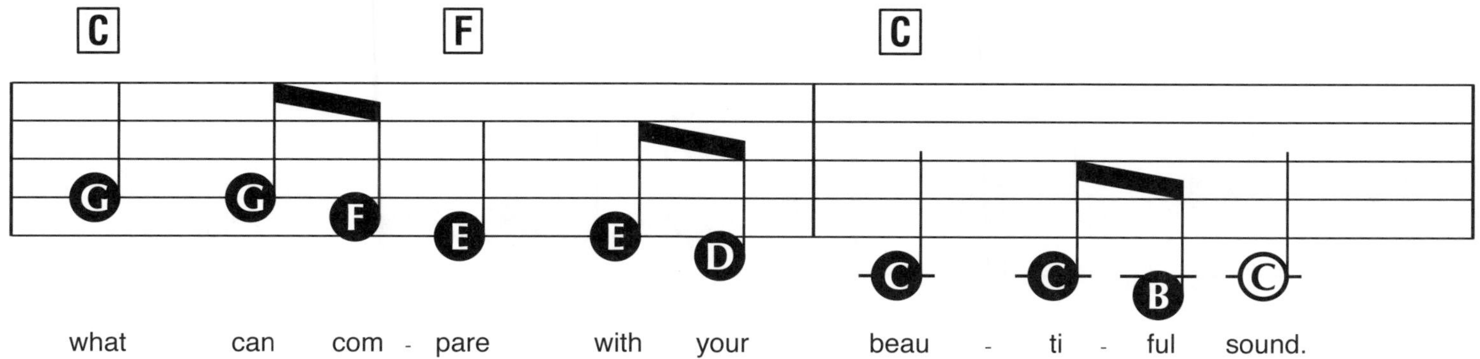
C
F
C
G G F E E D C C B C
what can com - pare with your beau - ti - ful sound.

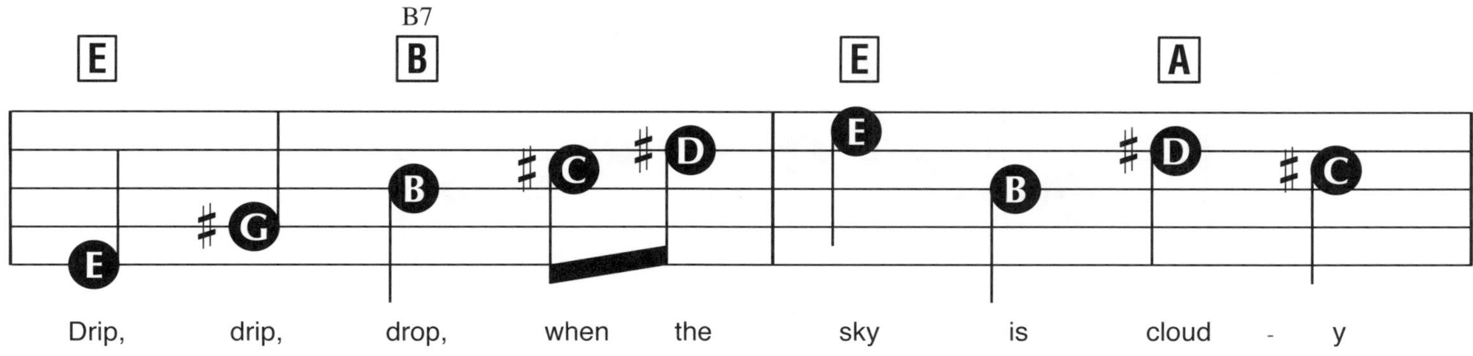
B7
E
B
E
A
E G B C D E B D C
Drip, drip, drop, when the sky is cloud - y

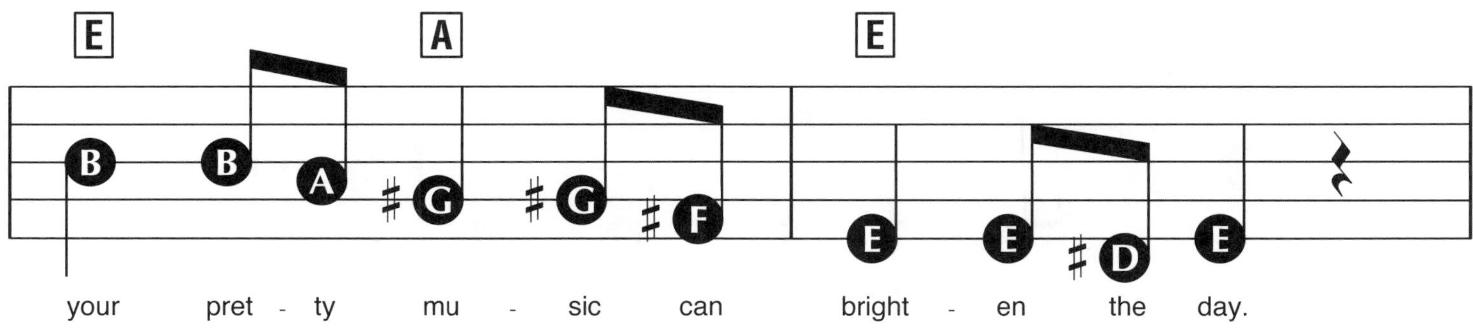
E
A
E
B B A G G F E E D E
your pret - ty mu - sic can bright - en the day.

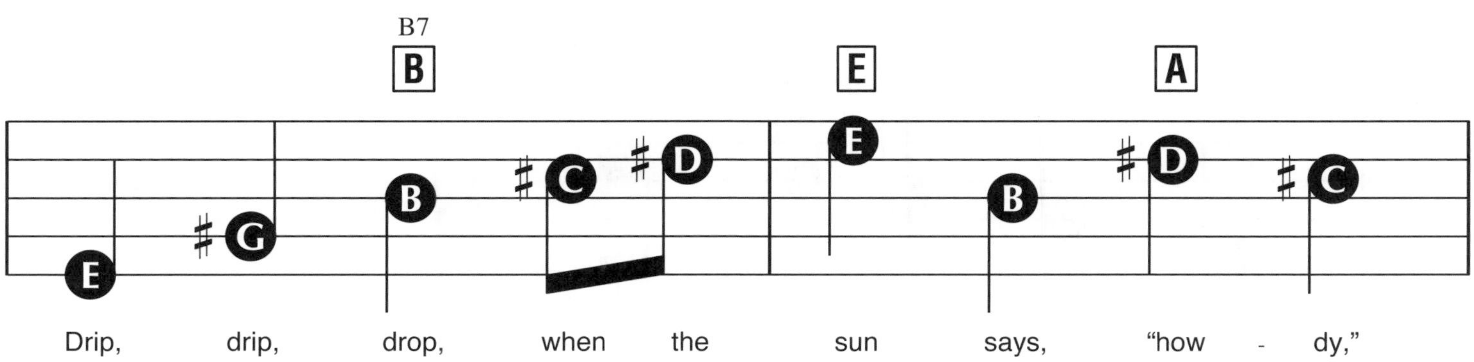
B7
B
E
A
E G B C D E B D C
Drip, drip, drop, when the sun says, "how - dy,"

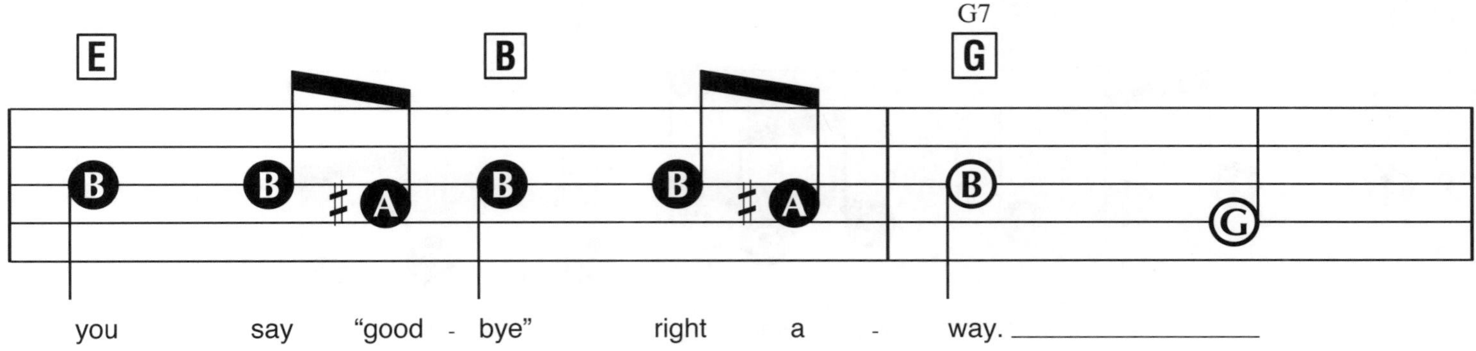
E
B
G7
G
you say "good - bye" right a - way.

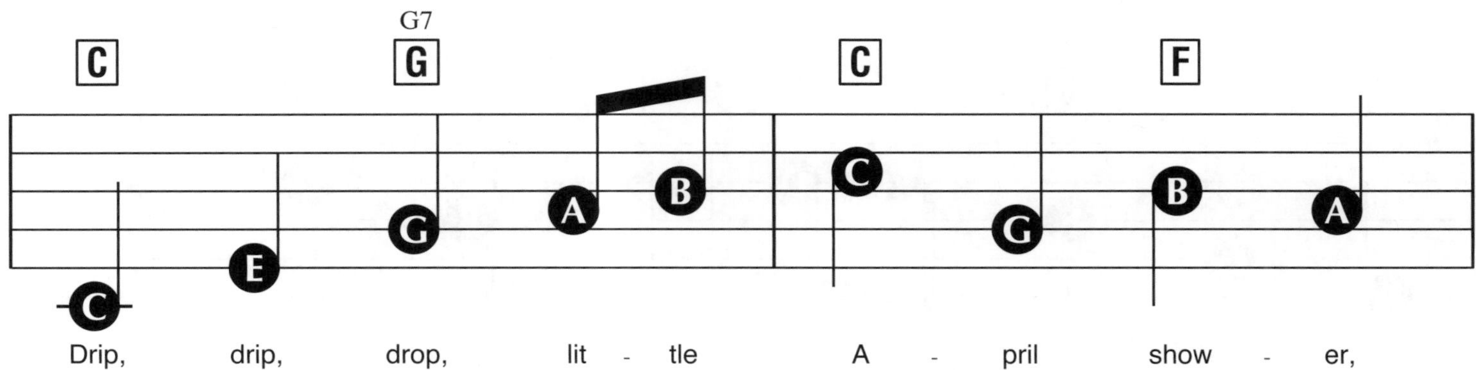
C
G7
G
C
F
Drip, drip, drop, lit - tle A - pril show - er,

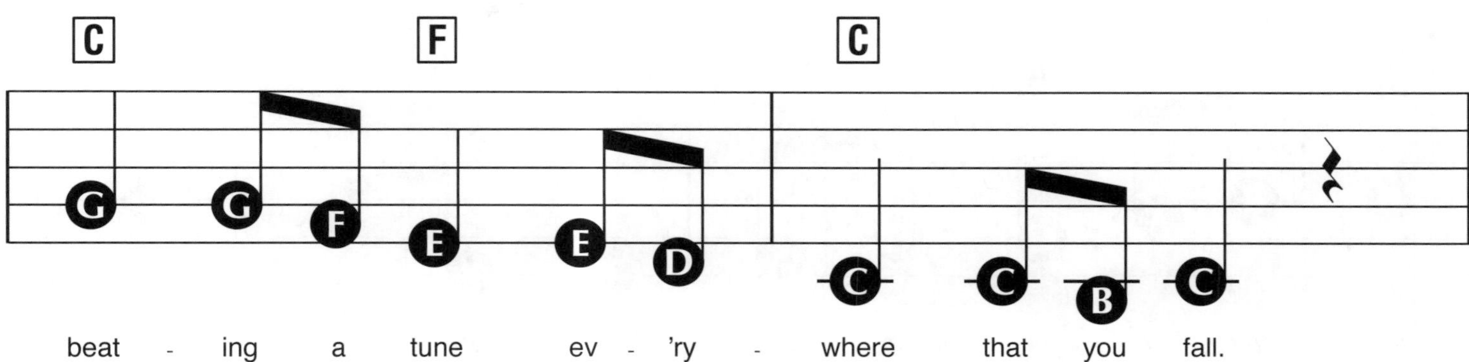
C
F
C
beat - ing a tune ev - 'ry - where that you fall.

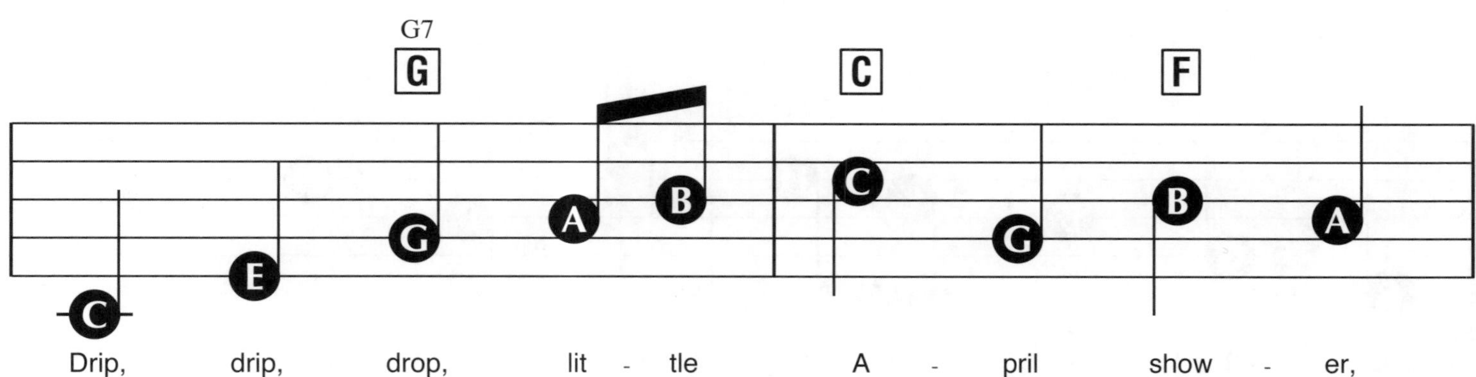
G7
G
C
F
Drip, drip, drop, lit - tle A - pril show - er,

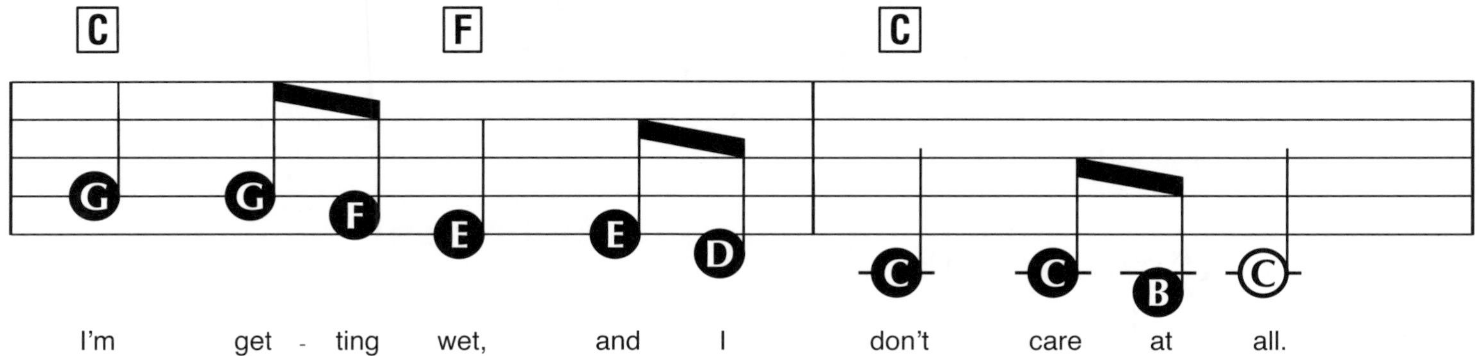
C
F
C
G
G
F
E
E
D
C
C
B
C
I'm get - ting wet, and I don't care at all.

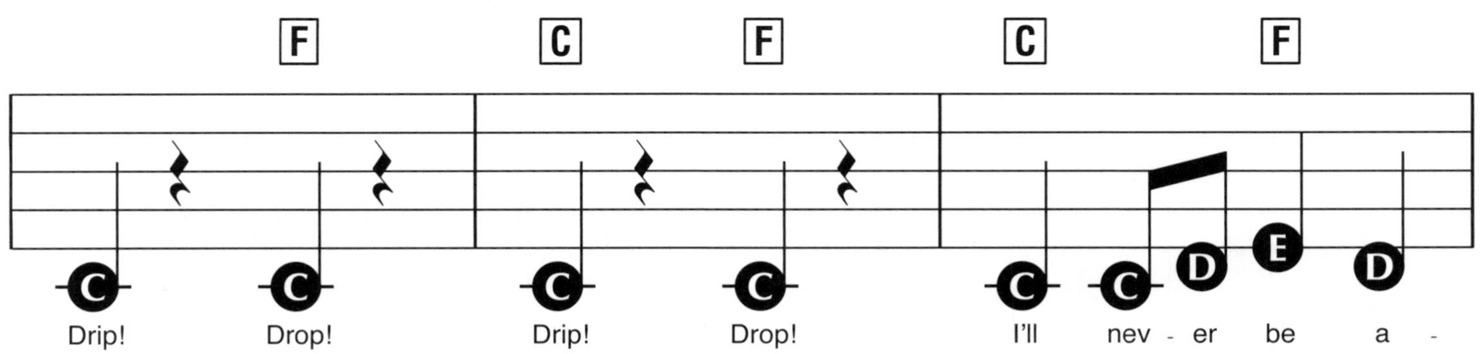
F
C
F
C
F
C
C
C
C
C
C
D
E
D
Drip! Drop! Drip! Drop! I'll nev - er be a -

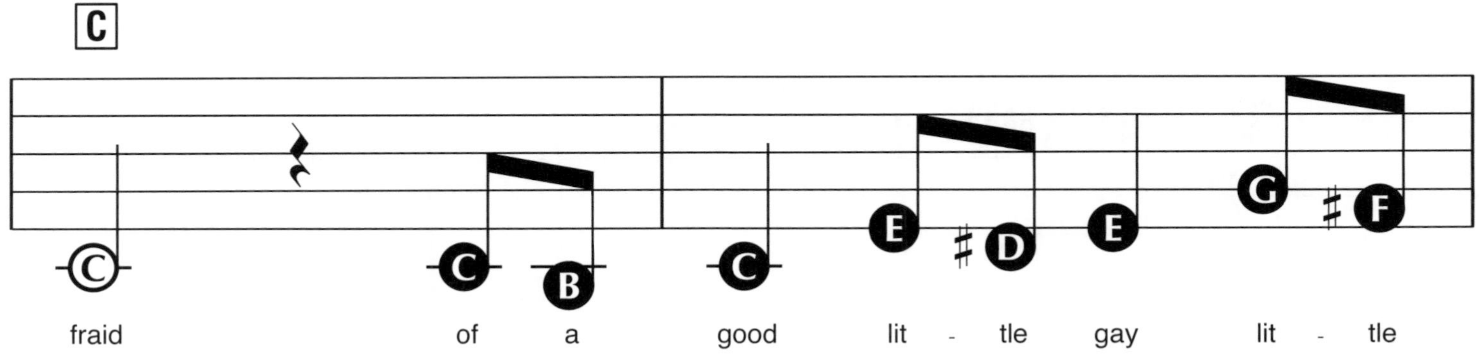
C
C
C
B
C
E
D
E
G
F
fraid of a good lit - tle gay lit - tle

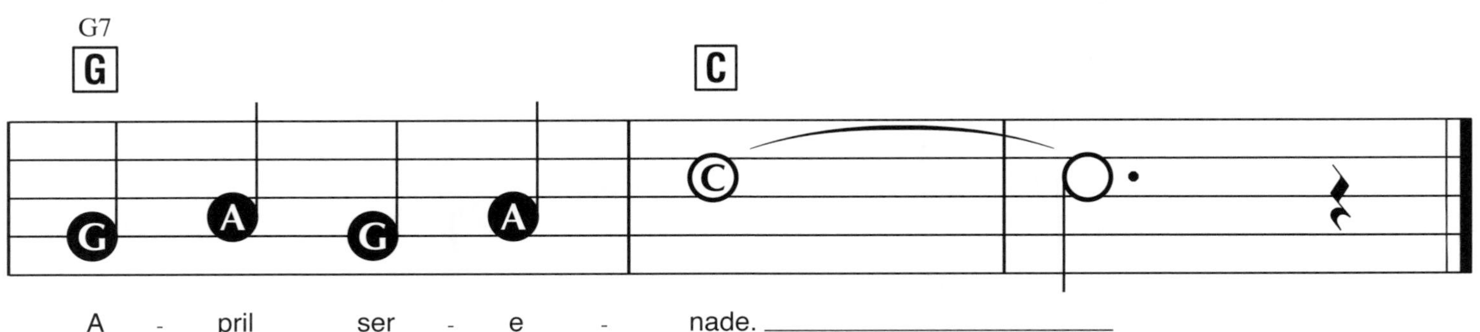
G7
G
C
G
A
G
A
C
A - pril ser - e - nade.

Little People

from LES MISÉRABLES

Registration 7
Rhythm: Swing or Shuffle

Music by Claude-Michel Schönberg
Lyrics by Alain Boublil, Jean-Marc Natel
and Herbert Kretzmer

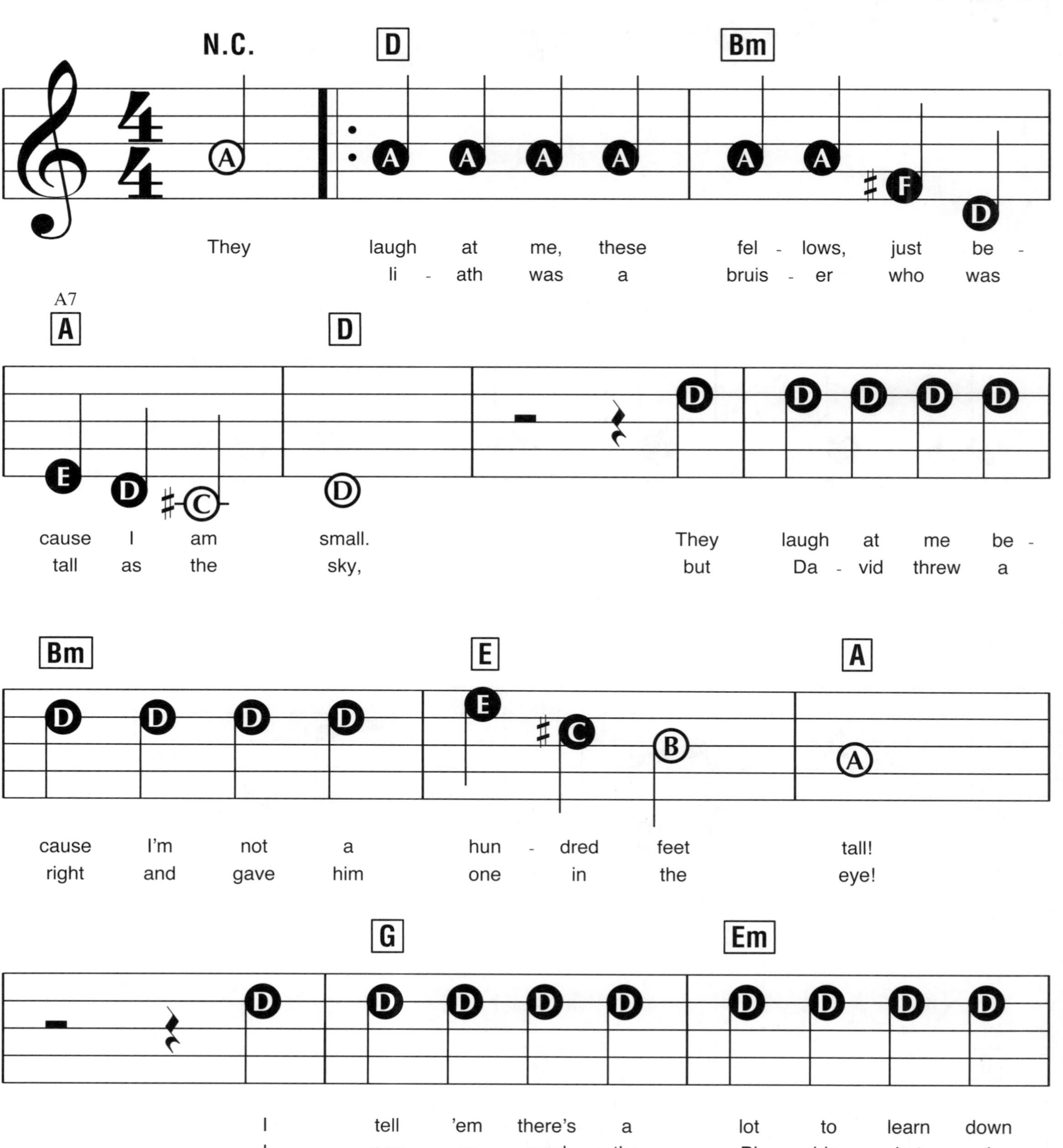

Music and Lyrics Copyright © 1980 by Editions Musicales Alain Boublil
English Lyrics Copyright © 1986 by Alain Boublil Music Ltd. (ASCAP)
Mechanical and Publication Rights for the U.S.A. Administered by
Alain Boublil Music Ltd. (ASCAP) c/o Joel Faden & Co., Inc.,
MLM 250 West 57th St., 26th Floor, New York, NY 10107,
Tel. (212) 246-7203, Fax (212) 246-7217, Email jfaden@joelfaden.com
International Copyright Secured. All Rights Reserved. This music is copyright.
Photocopying is illegal.
All Performance Rights Restricted.

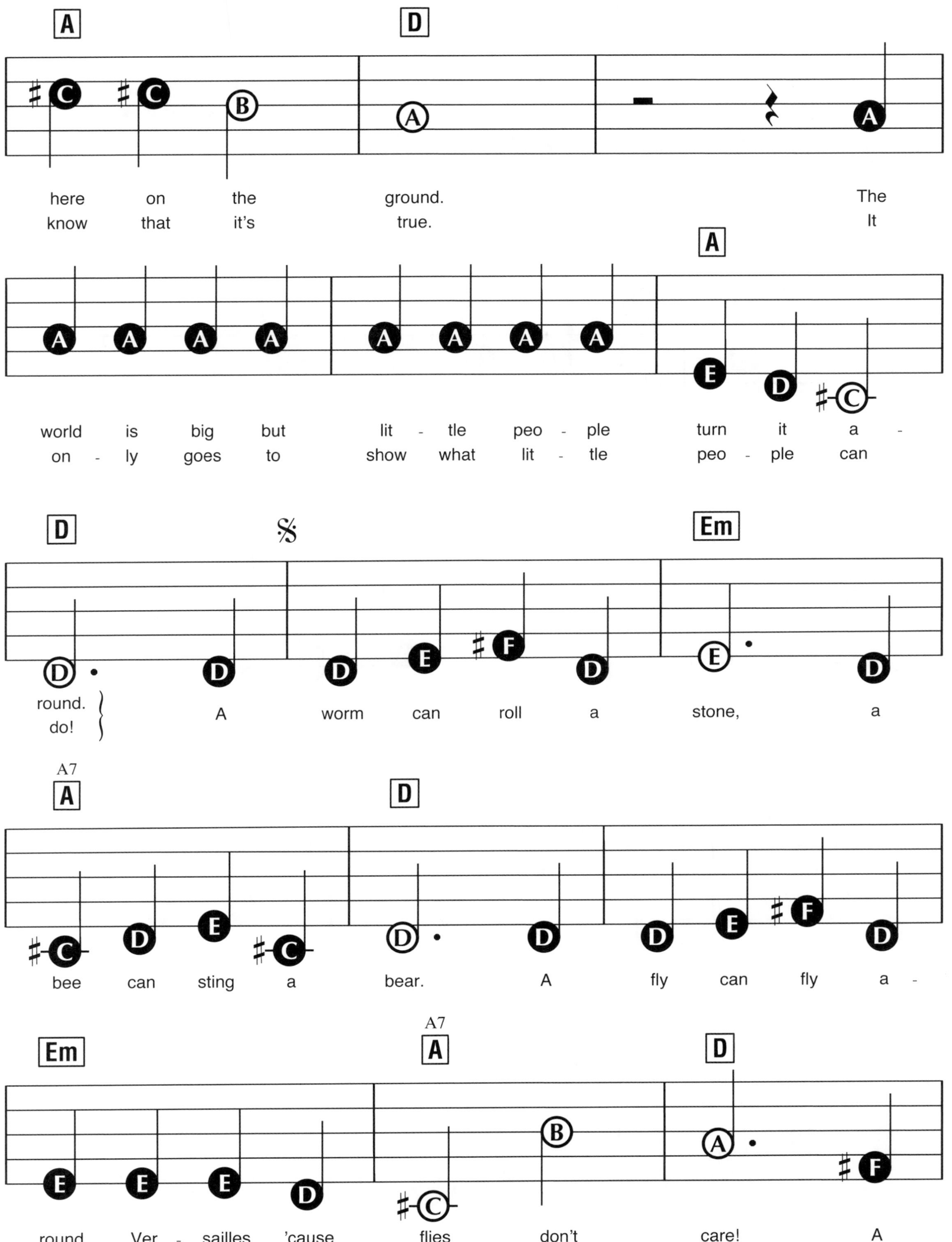
A
D
here on the ground.
know that it's true.
The
It
world is big but lit - tle peo - ple
on - ly goes to show what lit - tle
A
turn it a -
peo - ple can
D
Em
round.
do!
A worm can roll a stone, a
A7
A
D
bee can sting a bear. A fly can fly a -
Em
A7
A
D
round Ver - sailles 'cause flies don't care! A

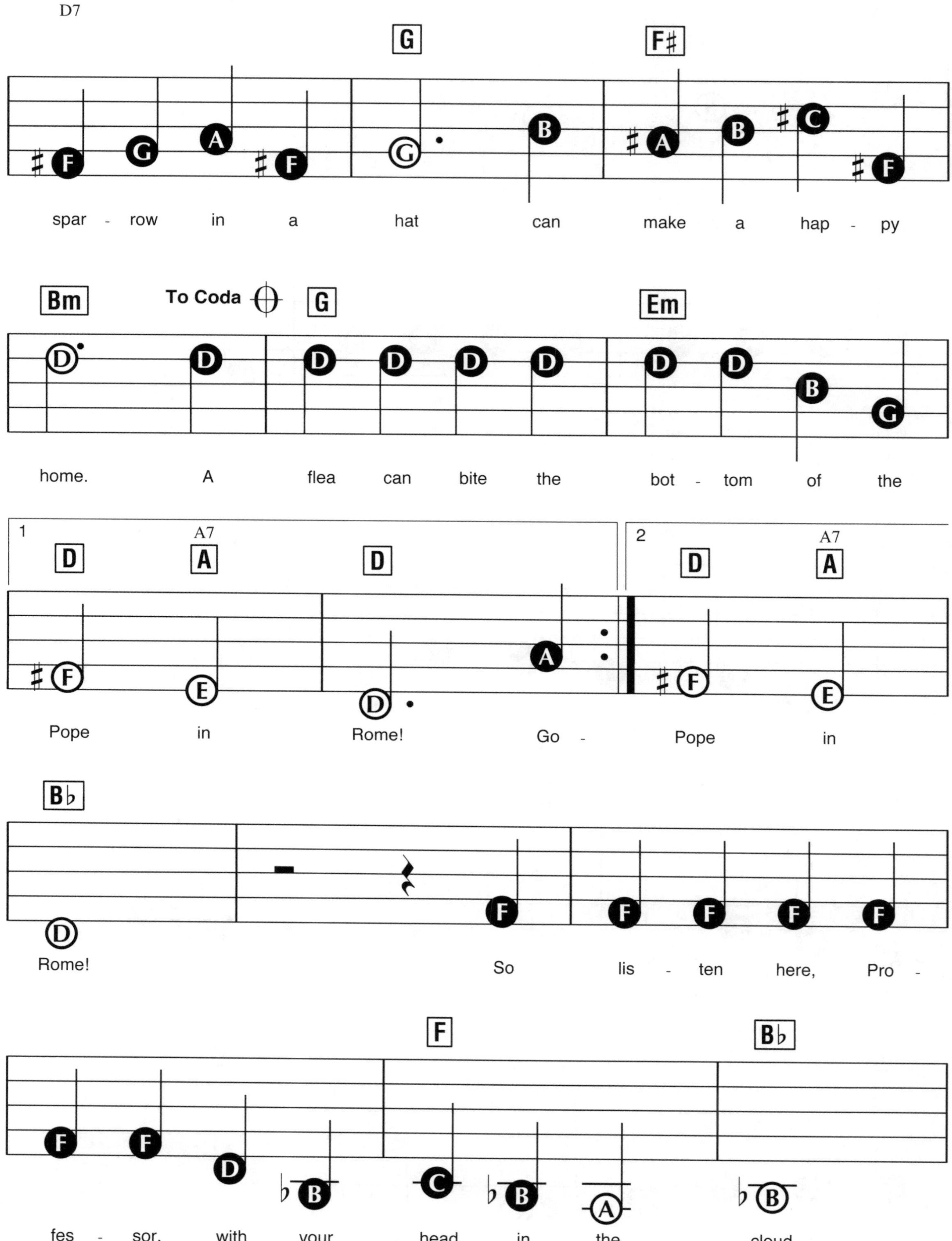
D7
G
F♯
spar - row in a hat can make a hap - py
Bm
To Coda
G
Em
home. A flea can bite the bot - tom of the
1
D
A7
A
D
Pope in Rome! Go -
2
D
A7
A
Pope in
B♭
Rome! So lis - ten here, Pro -
F
B♭
fes - sor, with your head in the cloud.

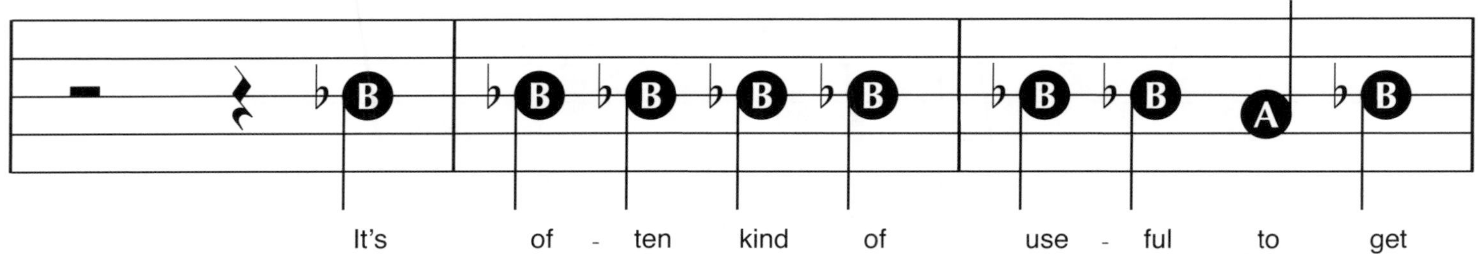
B
B B B B
B B A B
It's of - ten kind of use - ful to get

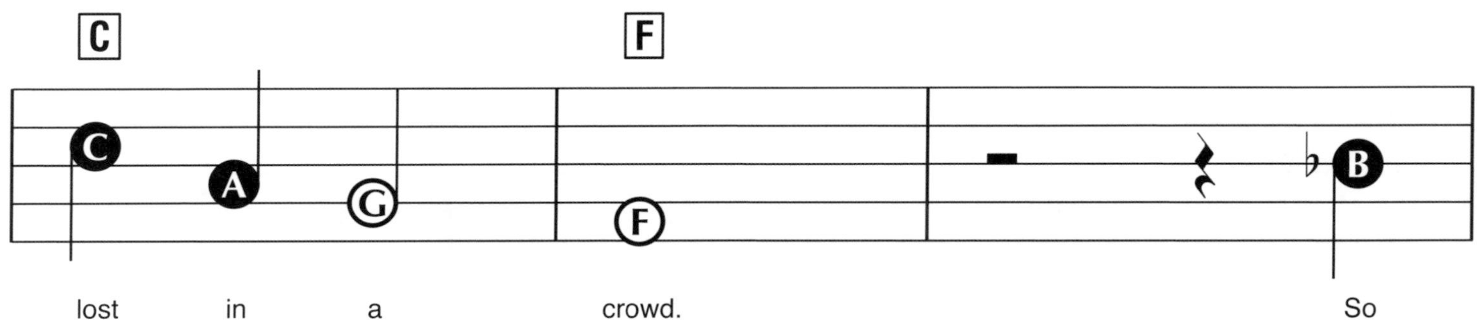
C
F
C A G
F
B
lost in a crowd. So

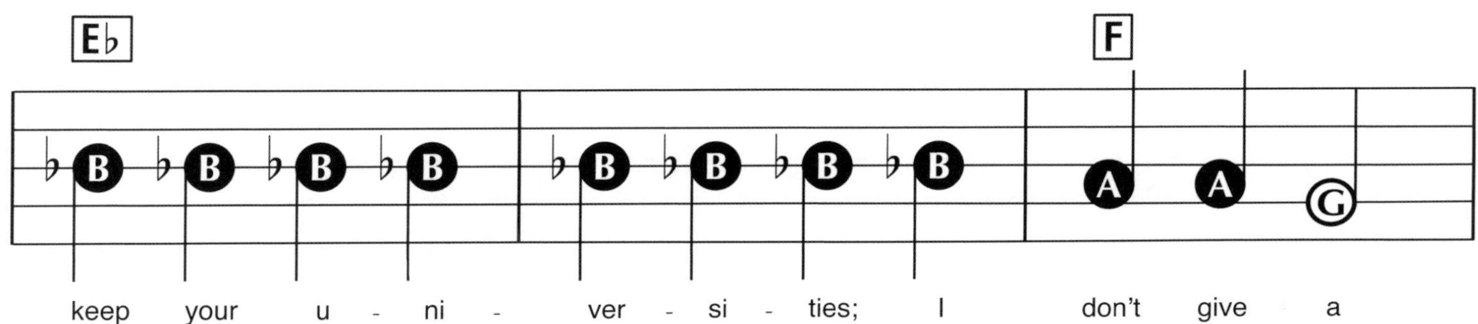
E♭
F
B B B B
B B B B
A A G
keep your u - ni - ver - si - ties; I don't give a

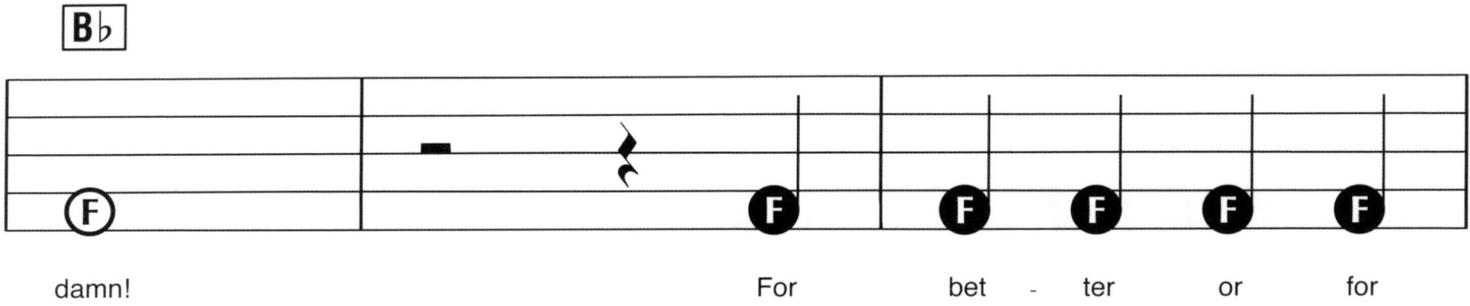
B♭
F
F
F F F F
damn! For bet - ter or for

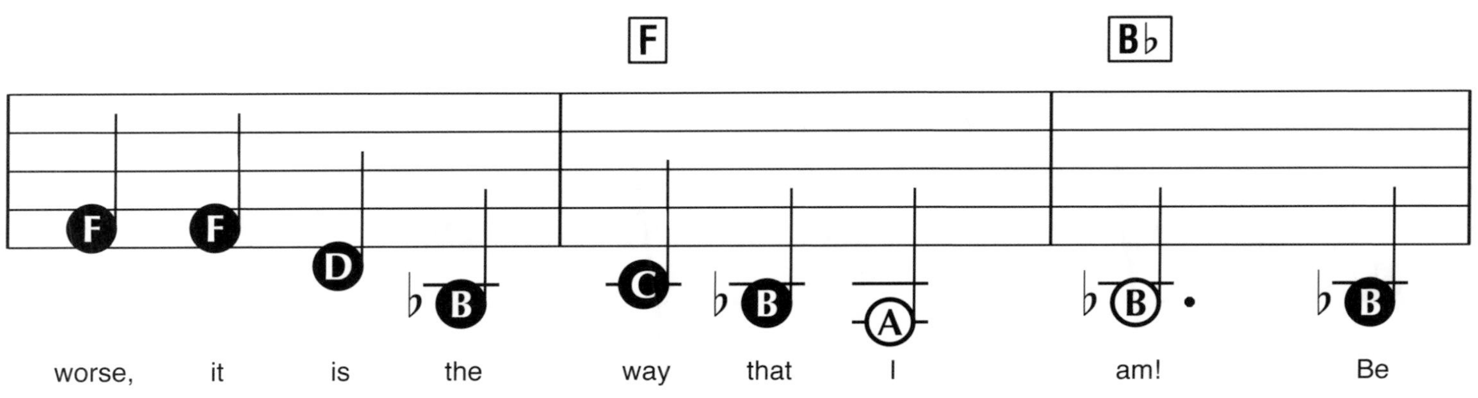
F
B♭
F F D B
C B A
B B
worse, it is the way that I am! Be

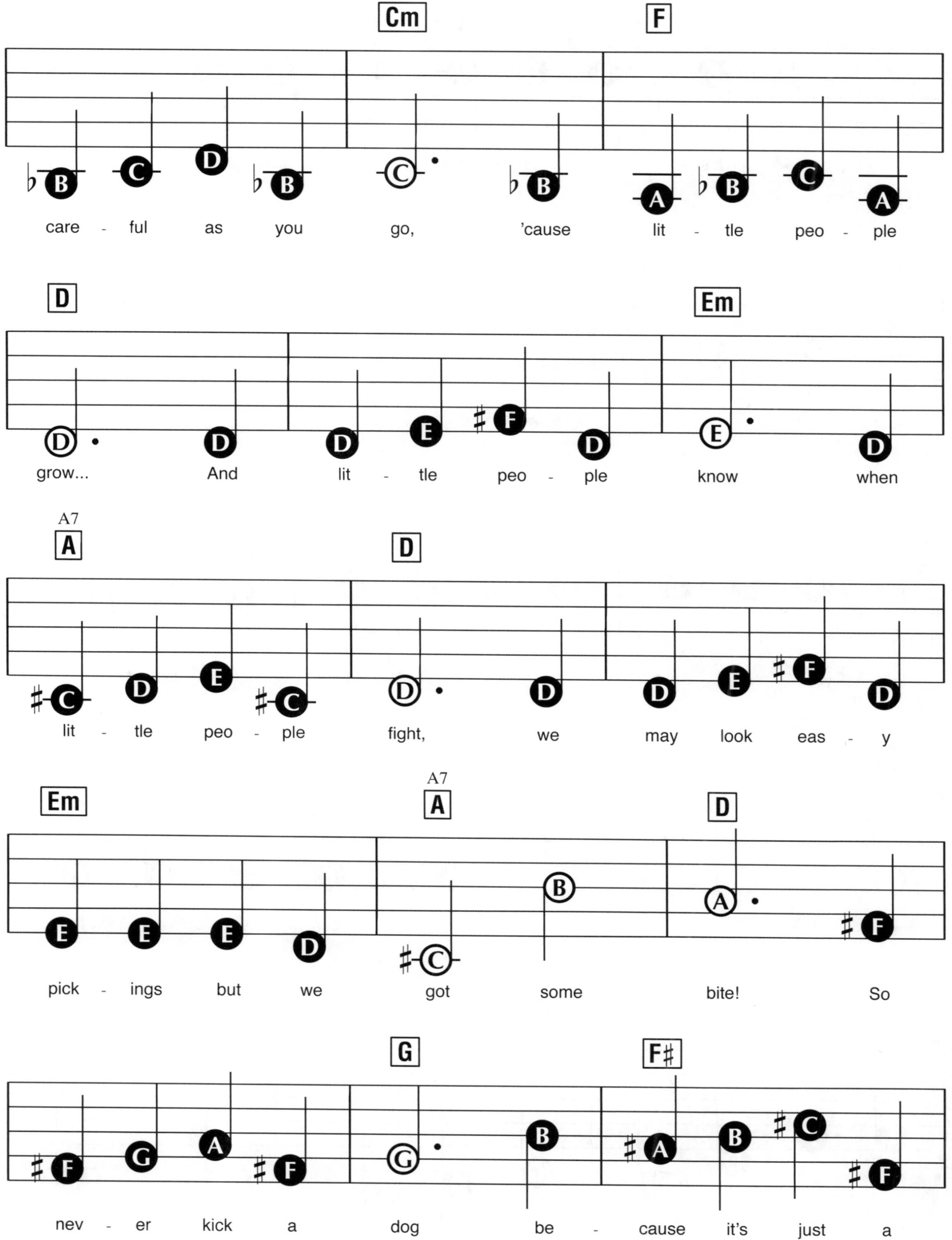
Cm
F
♭B
C
D
♭B
C
♭B
A
♭B
C
A
care - ful as you go, 'cause lit - tle peo - ple
D
Em
D
D
D
E
♯F
D
E
D
grow... And lit - tle peo - ple know when
A7
A
D
♯C
D
E
♯C
D
D
D
E
♯F
D
lit - tle peo - ple fight, we may look eas - y
Em
A7
A
D
E
E
E
D
♯C
B
A
♯F
pick - ings but we got some bite! So
G
F♯
♯F
G
A
♯F
G
B
♯A
B
♯C
♯F
nev - er kick a dog be - cause it's just a

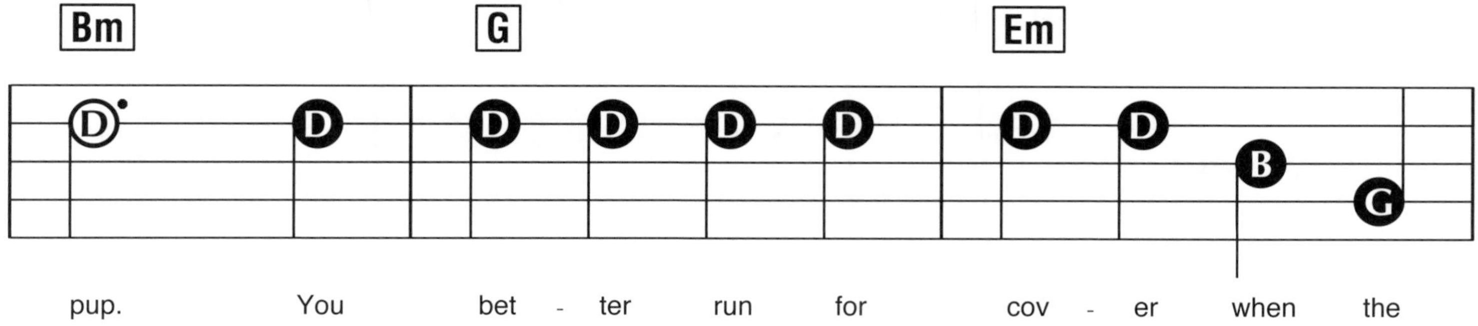

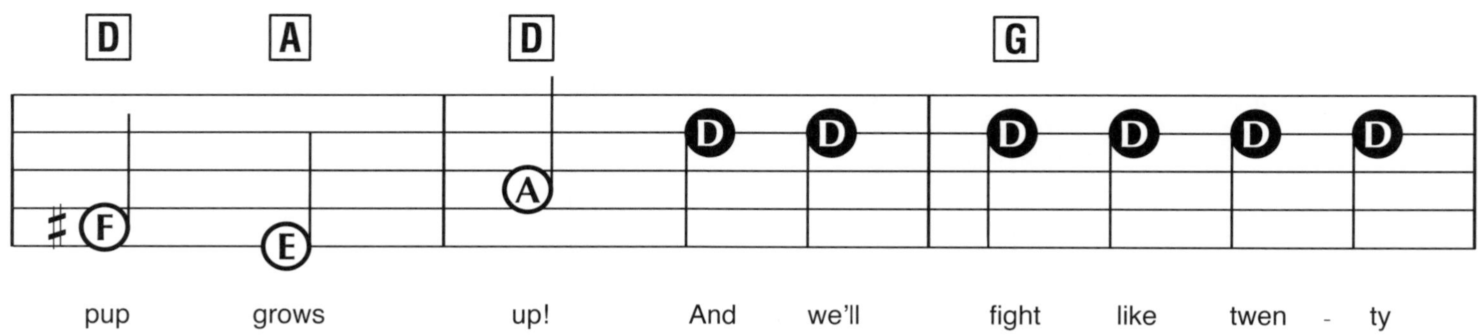

D.S. al Coda
(Return to 𝄋
Play to ⊕ and
Skip to Coda)

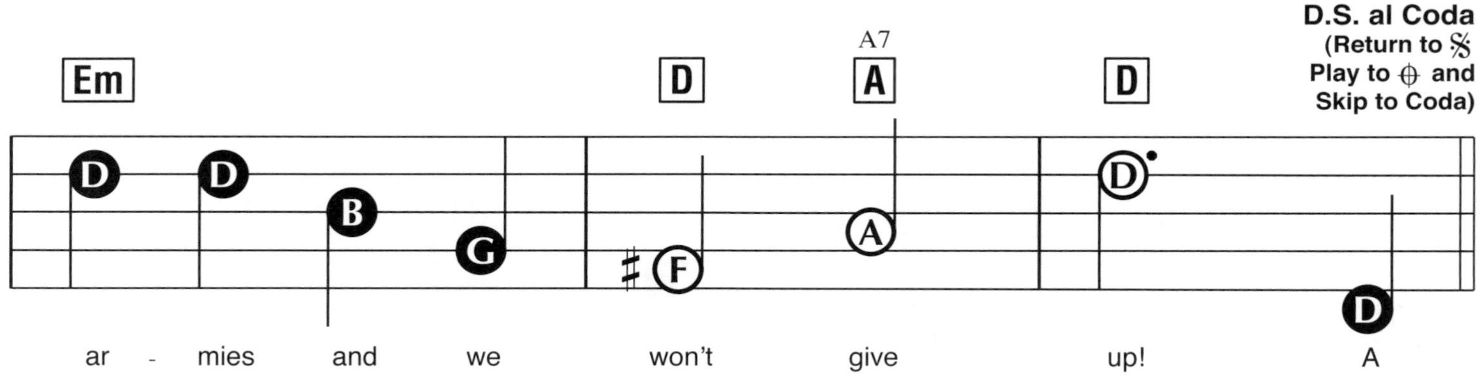

CODA

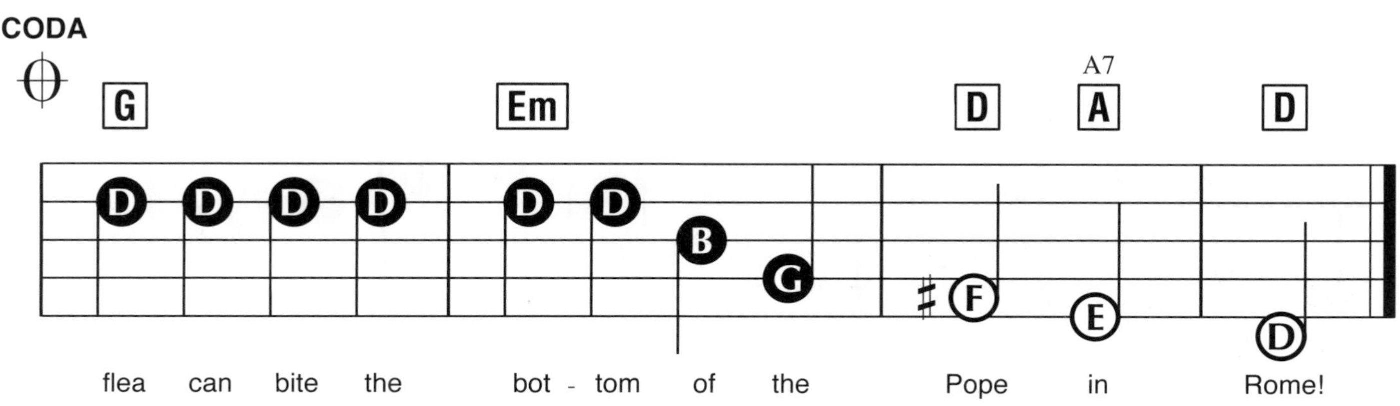

Mickey Mouse March

from Walt Disney's THE MICKEY MOUSE CLUB

Registration 5
Rhythm: 6/8 March

Words and Music by
Jimmie Dodd

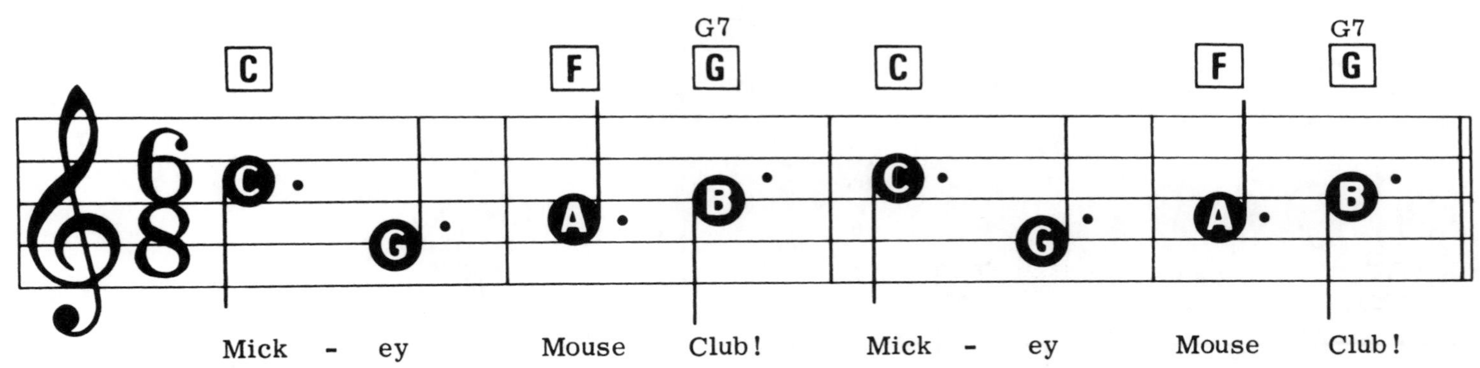

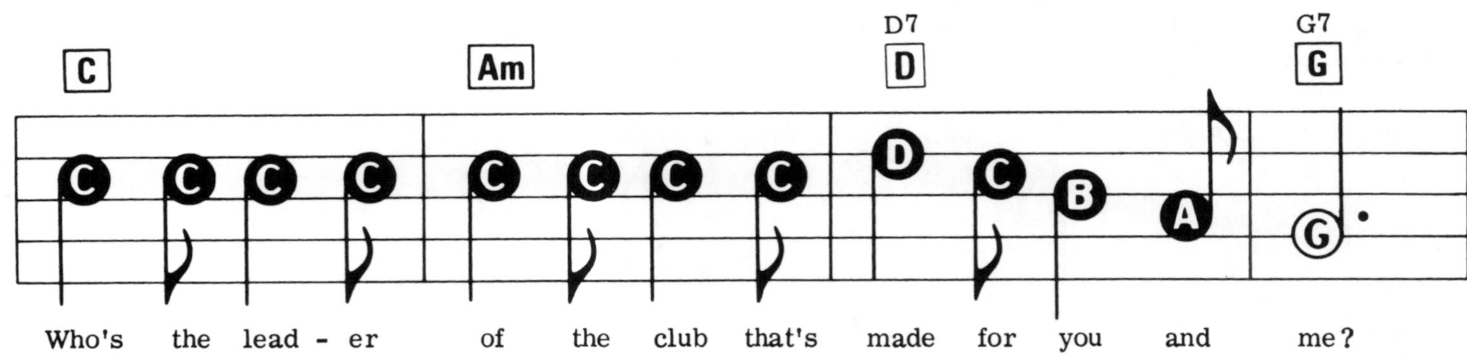

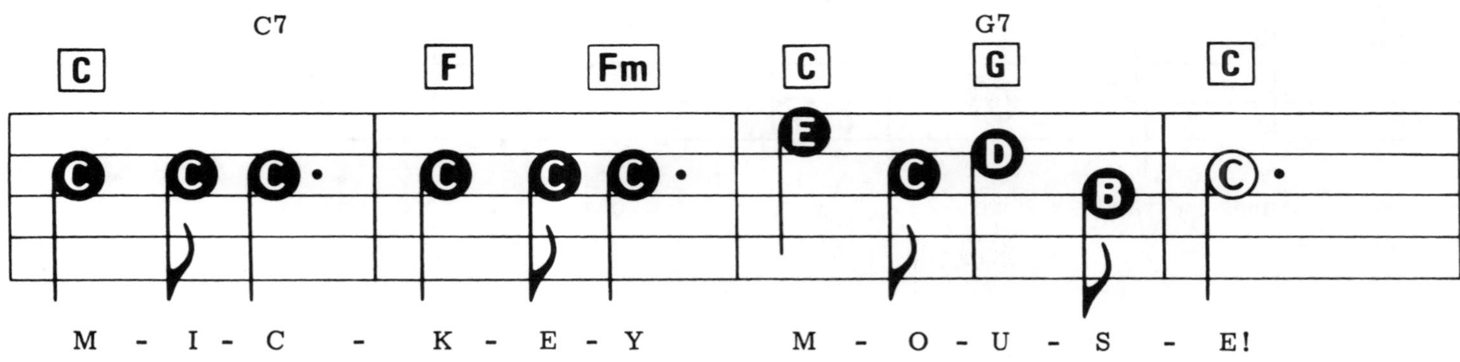

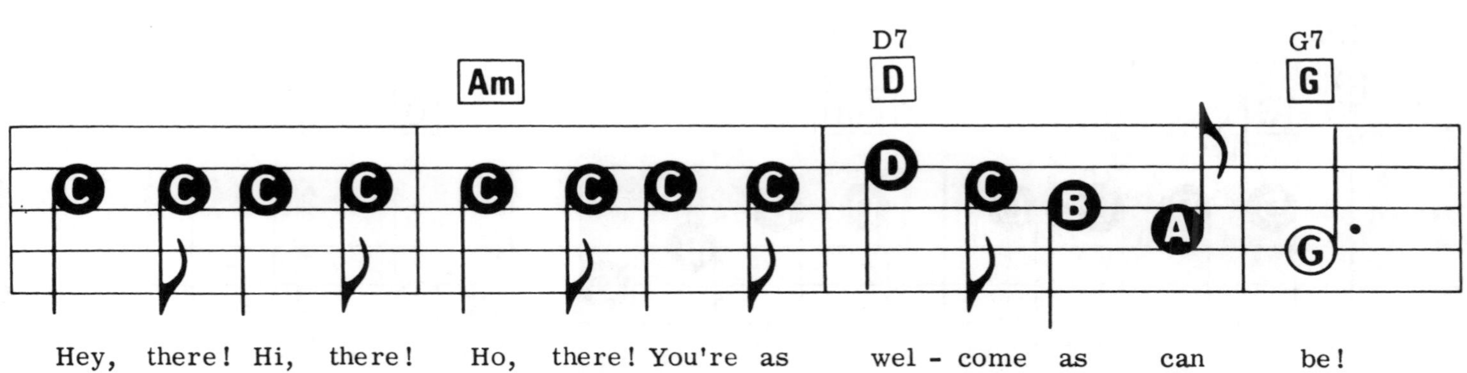

© 1955 Walt Disney Music Company
Copyright Renewed
All Rights Reserved. Used by Permission.

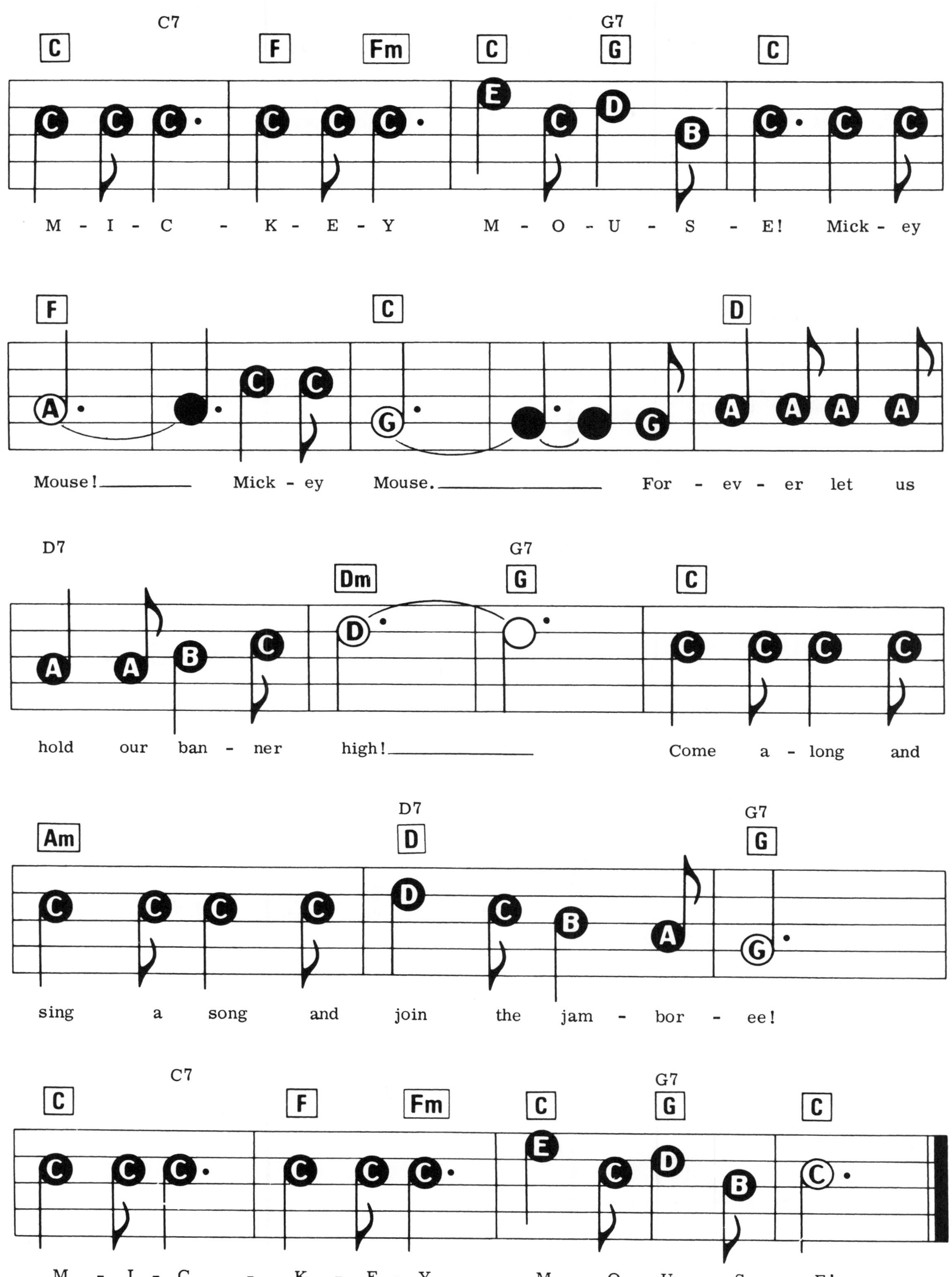
C C7 F Fm C G7 G C
M - I - C - K - E - Y M - O - U - S - E! Mick - ey
F C D
Mouse! Mick - ey Mouse. For - ev - er let us
D7 Dm G7 G C
hold our ban - ner high! Come a - long and
Am D7 D G7 G
sing a song and join the jam - bor - ee!
C C7 F Fm C G7 G C
M - I - C - K - E - Y M - O - U - S - E!

My Bonnie Lies Over the Ocean

Registration 3
Rhythm: Waltz

Traditional

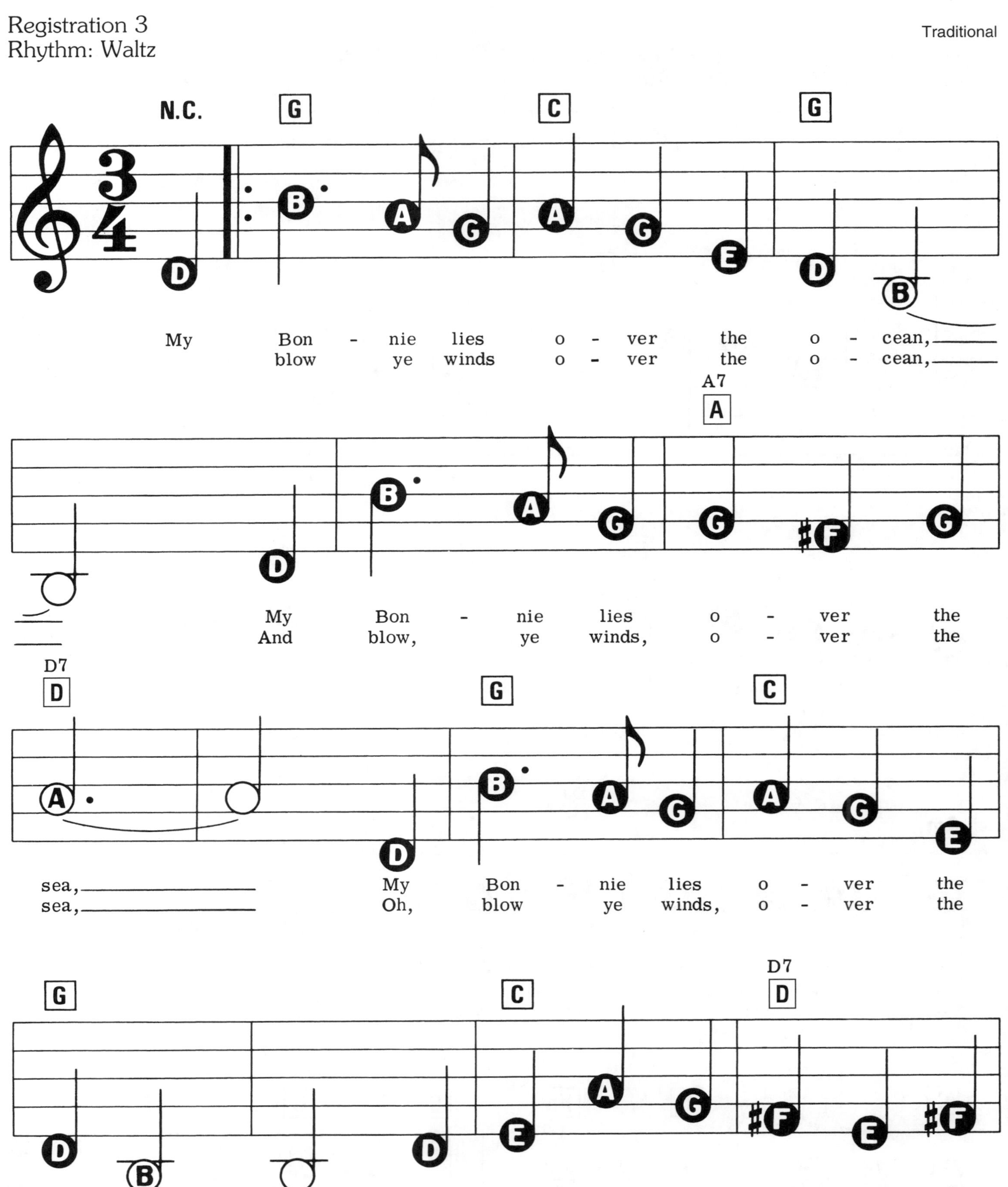

Copyright © 1975 by HAL LEONARD CORPORATION
International Copyright Secured All Rights Reserved

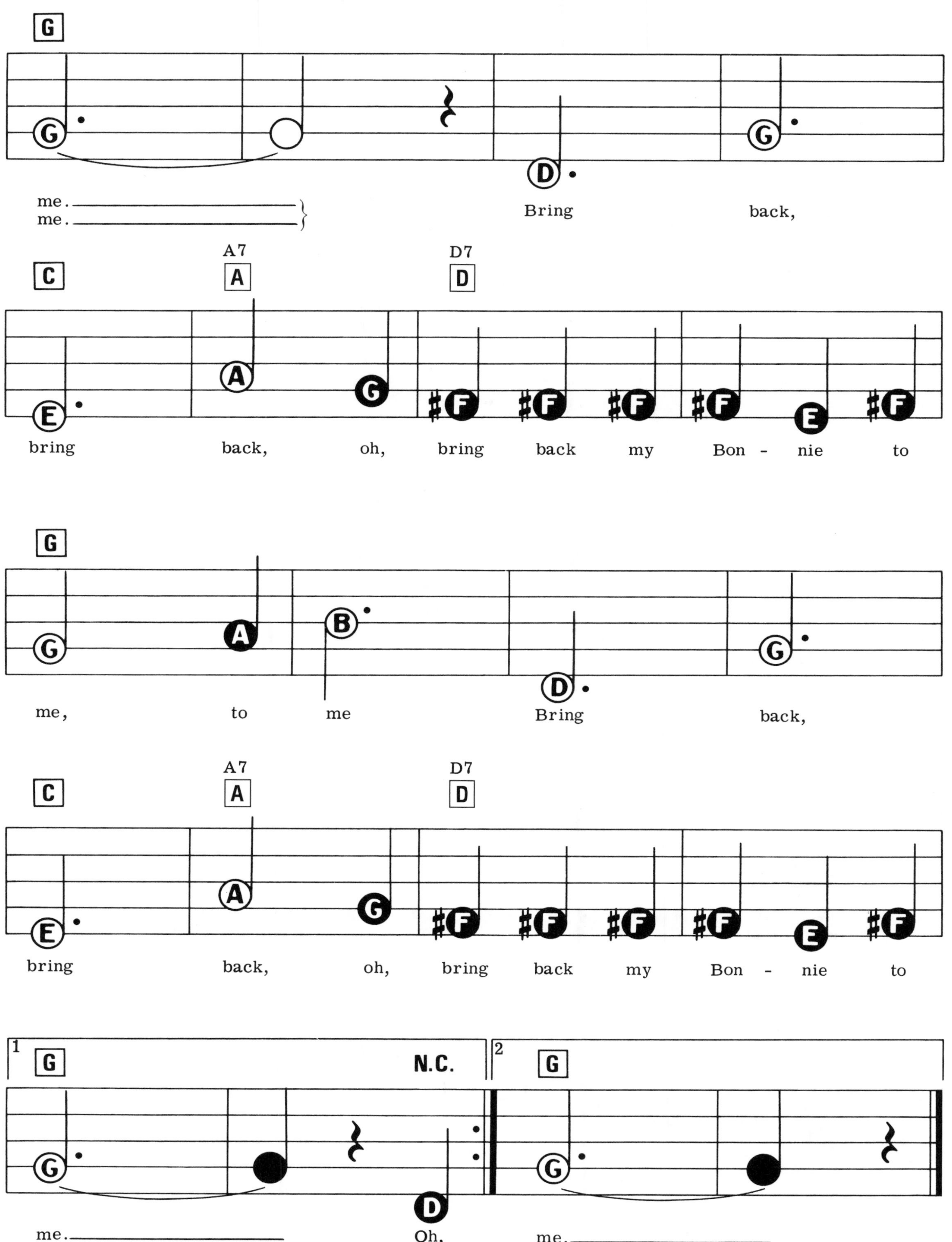
G
me.
me.
Bring
back,
C
A7
A
D7
D
bring
back,
oh,
bring
back
my
Bon - nie
to
G
me,
to
me
Bring
back,
C
A7
A
D7
D
bring
back,
oh,
bring
back
my
Bon - nie
to
1
G
N.C.
me.
Oh,
2
G
me.

My Favorite Things
from THE SOUND OF MUSIC

Registration 1
Rhythm: Waltz

Lyrics by Oscar Hammerstein II
Music by Richard Rodgers

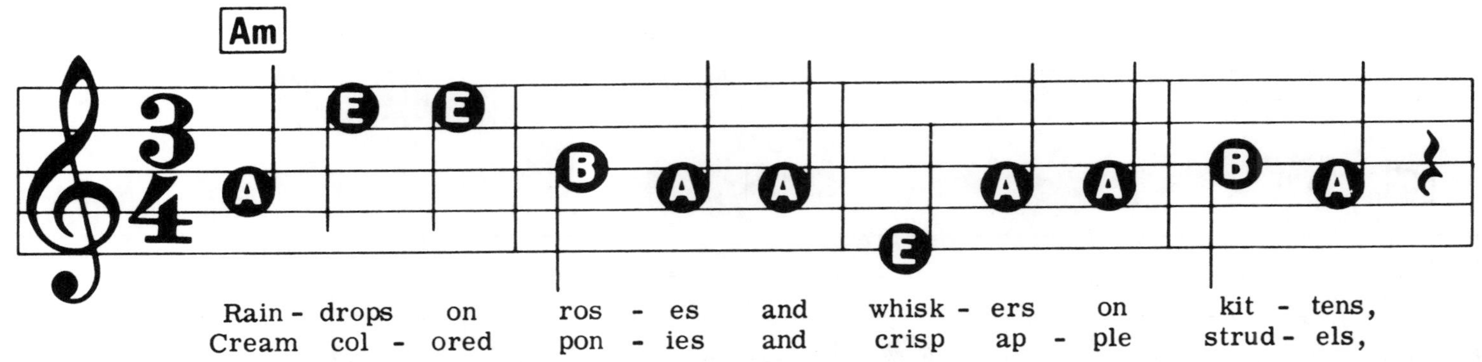

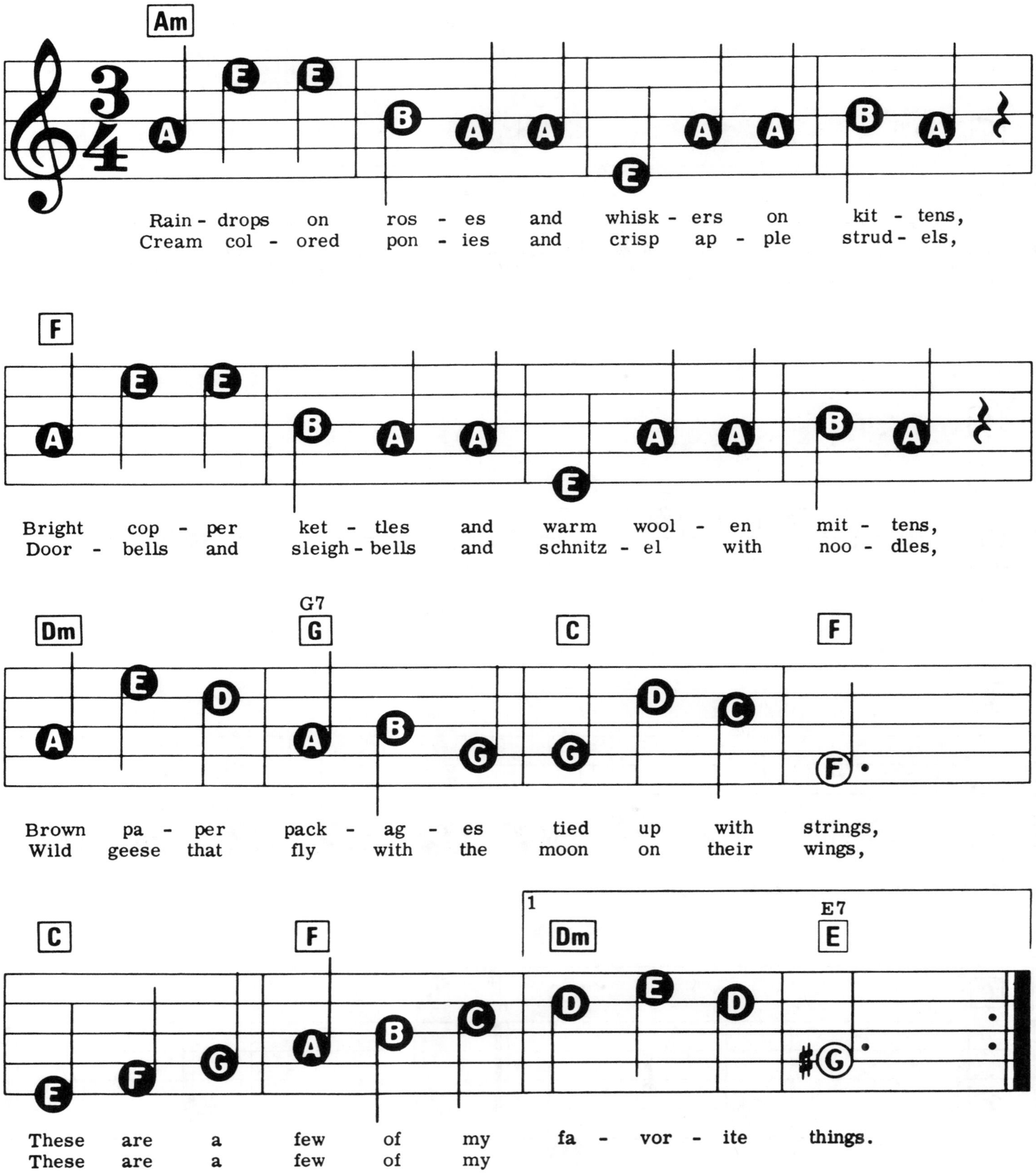

Am
Rain - drops on ros - es and whisk - ers on kit - tens,
Cream col - ored pon - ies and crisp ap - ple strud - els,
F
Bright cop - per ket - tles and warm wool - en mit - tens,
Door - bells and sleigh - bells and schnitz - el with noo - dles,
Dm
G7
G
C
F
Brown pa - per pack - ag - es tied up with strings,
Wild geese that fly with the moon on their wings,
C
F
1
Dm
E7
E
These are a few of my fa - vor - ite things.
These are a few of my

Copyright © 1959 by Richard Rodgers and Oscar Hammerstein II
Copyright Renewed
Williamson Music, a Division of Rodgers & Hammerstein: an Imagem Company, owner of publication and allied rights throughout the world
International Copyright Secured All Rights Reserved

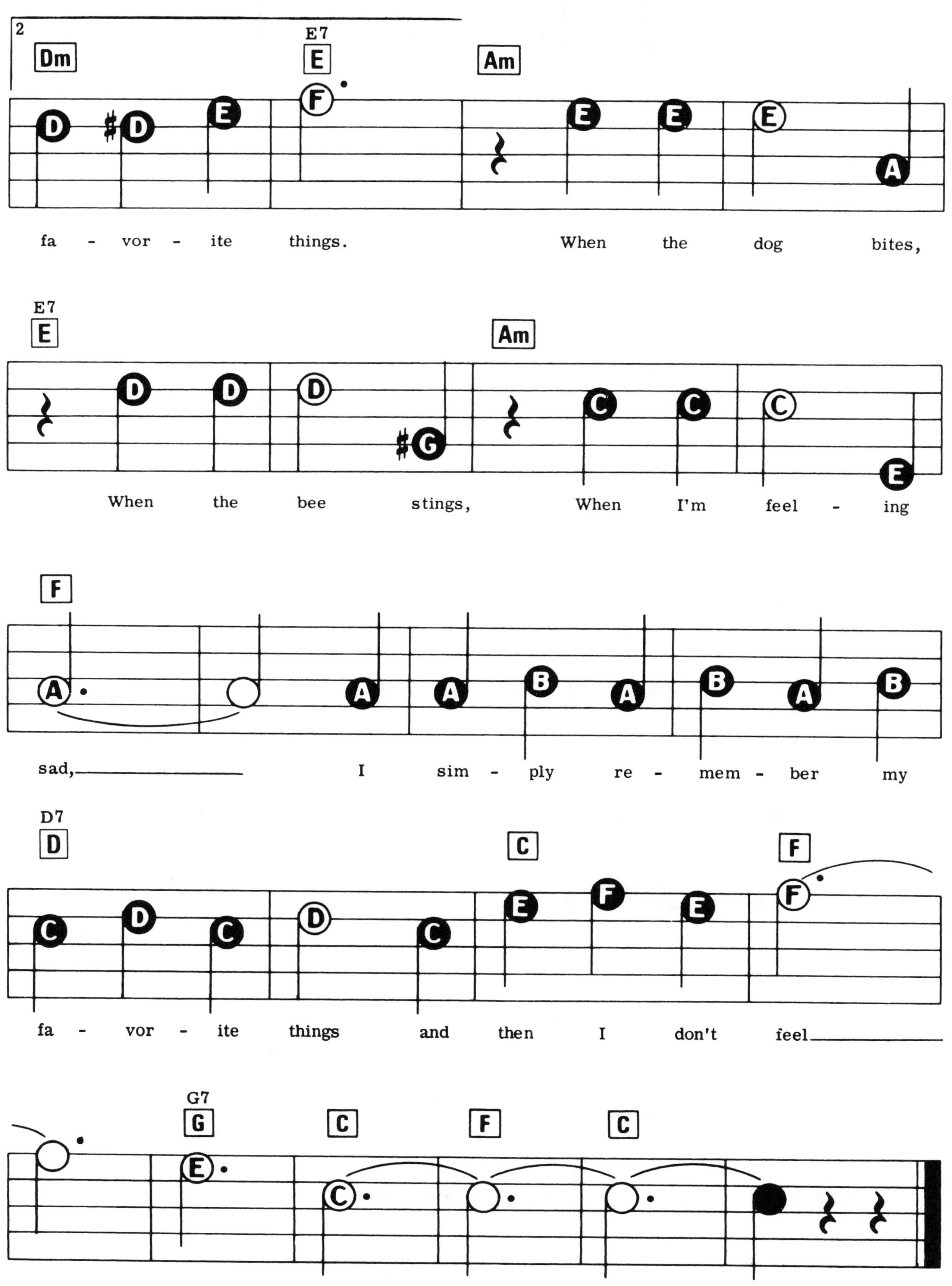
2
Dm E7 E Am
fa - vor - ite things. When the dog bites,
E7 E Am
When the bee stings, When I'm feel - ing
F
sad, I sim - ply re - mem - ber my
D7 D C F
fa - vor - ite things and then I don't feel
G7 G C F C
so bad.

Never Smile at a Crocodile

from Walt Disney's PETER PAN

Registration 4
Rhythm: Swing or Fox Trot

Words by Jack Lawrence
Music by Frank Churchill

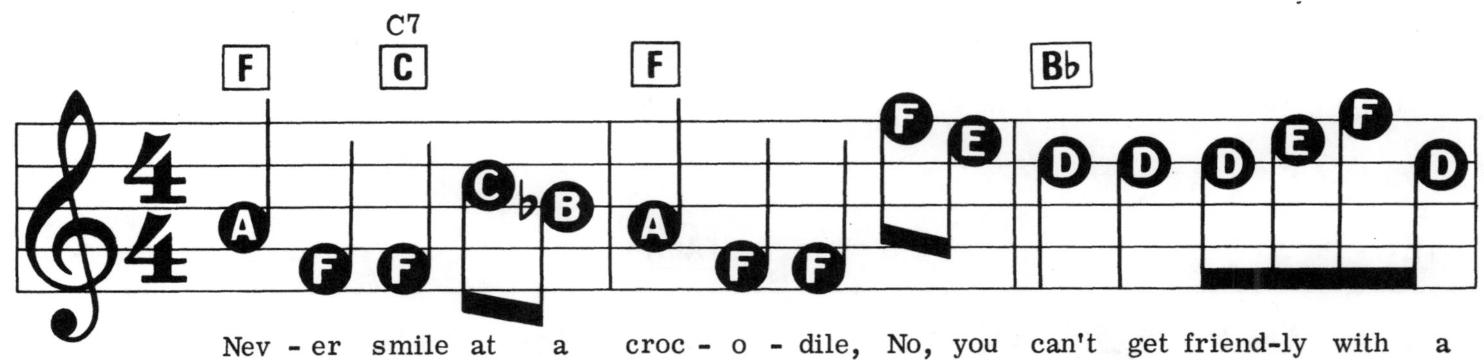

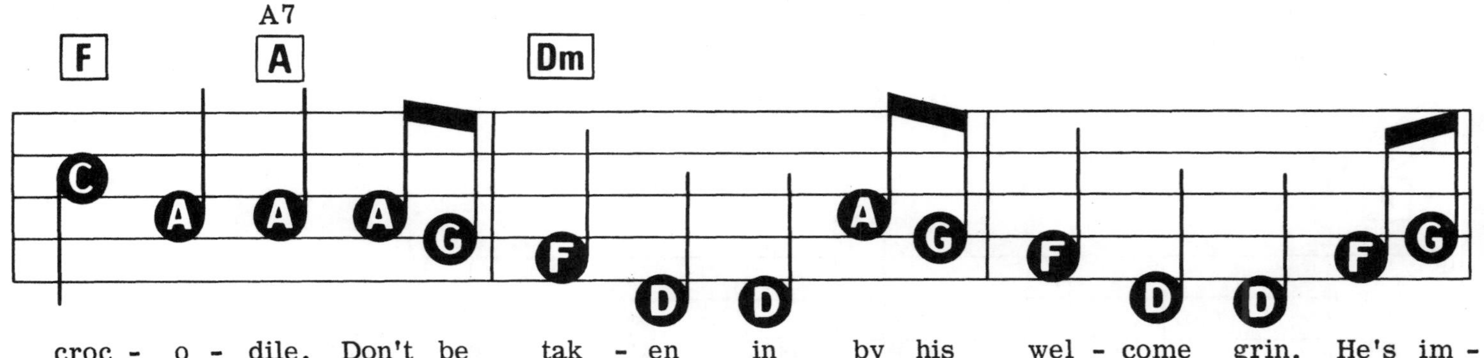

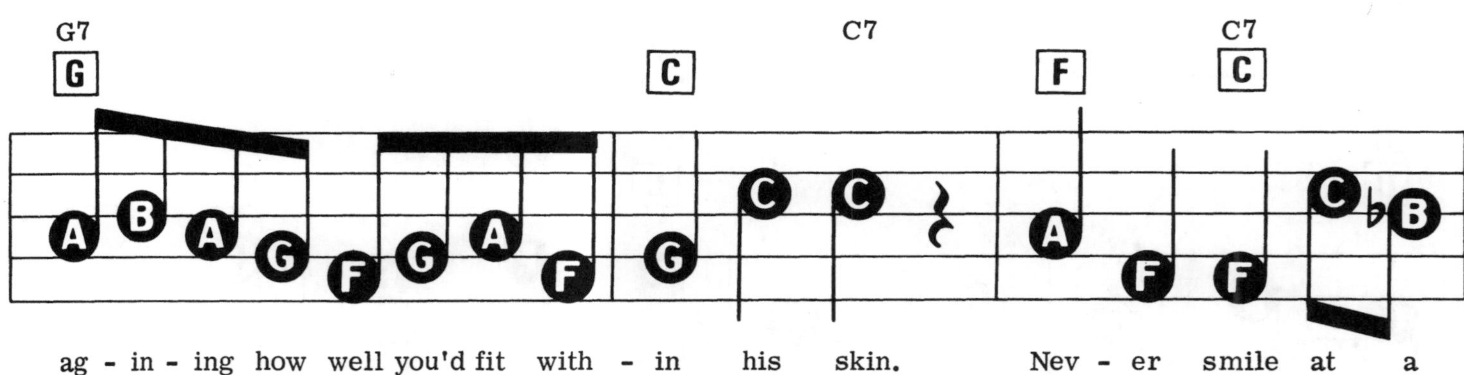

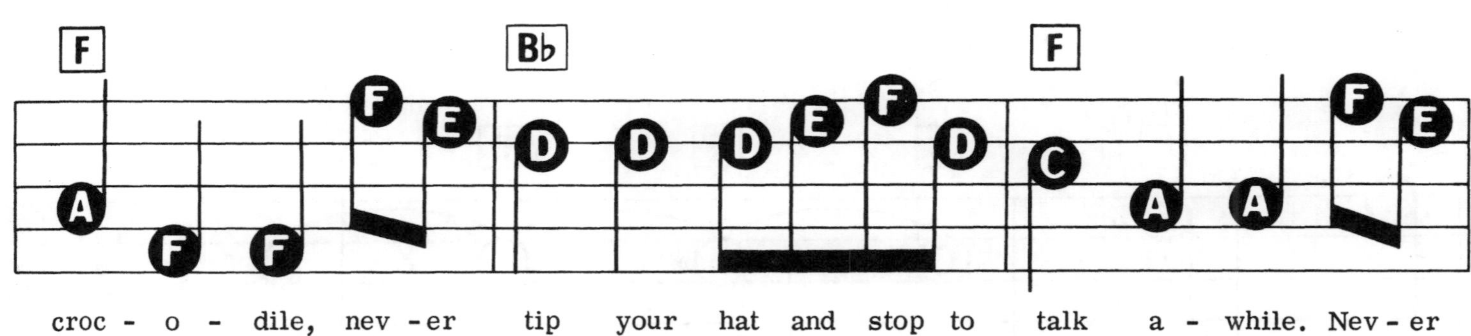

© 1952 Walt Disney Music Company
Copyright Renewed
All Rights Reserved. Used by Permission.

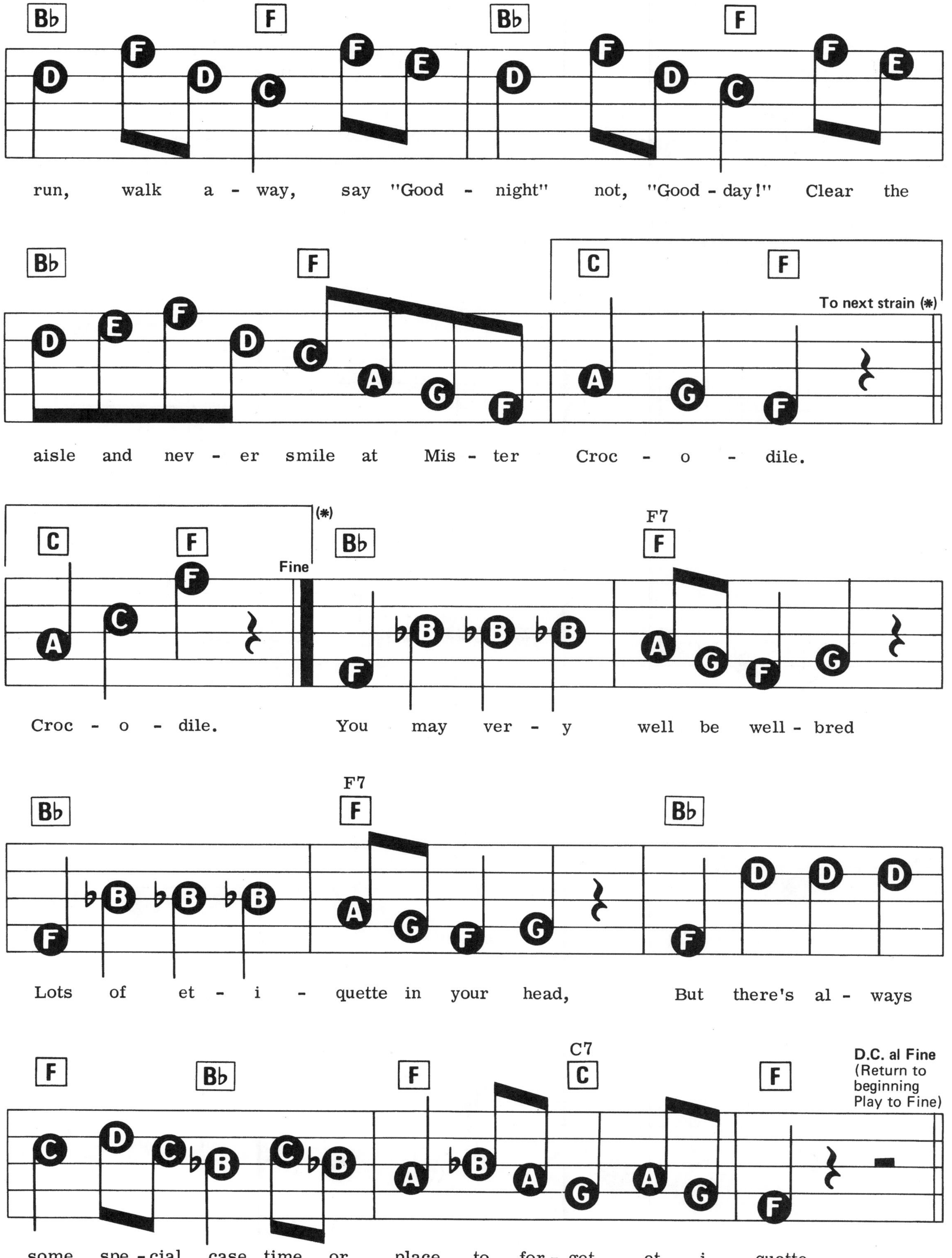
B♭
F
B♭
F
D F D C F E D F D C F E
run, walk a - way, say "Good - night" not, "Good - day!" Clear the
B♭
F
C
F
To next strain (✱)
D E F D C A G F A G F
aisle and nev - er smile at Mis - ter Croc - o - dile.
C
F
Fine
(✱)
B♭
F7
F
A C F F ♭B ♭B ♭B A G F G
Croc - o - dile. You may ver - y well be well - bred
B♭
F7
F
B♭
F ♭B ♭B ♭B A G F G F D D D
Lots of et - i - quette in your head, But there's al - ways
F
B♭
F
C7
C
F
D.C. al Fine
(Return to beginning Play to Fine)
C D C ♭B C ♭B A ♭B A G A G F
some spe - cial case, time or place to for - get et - i - quette.

Michael, Row the Boat Ashore

Registration 2
Rhythm: Swing

Traditional Folksong

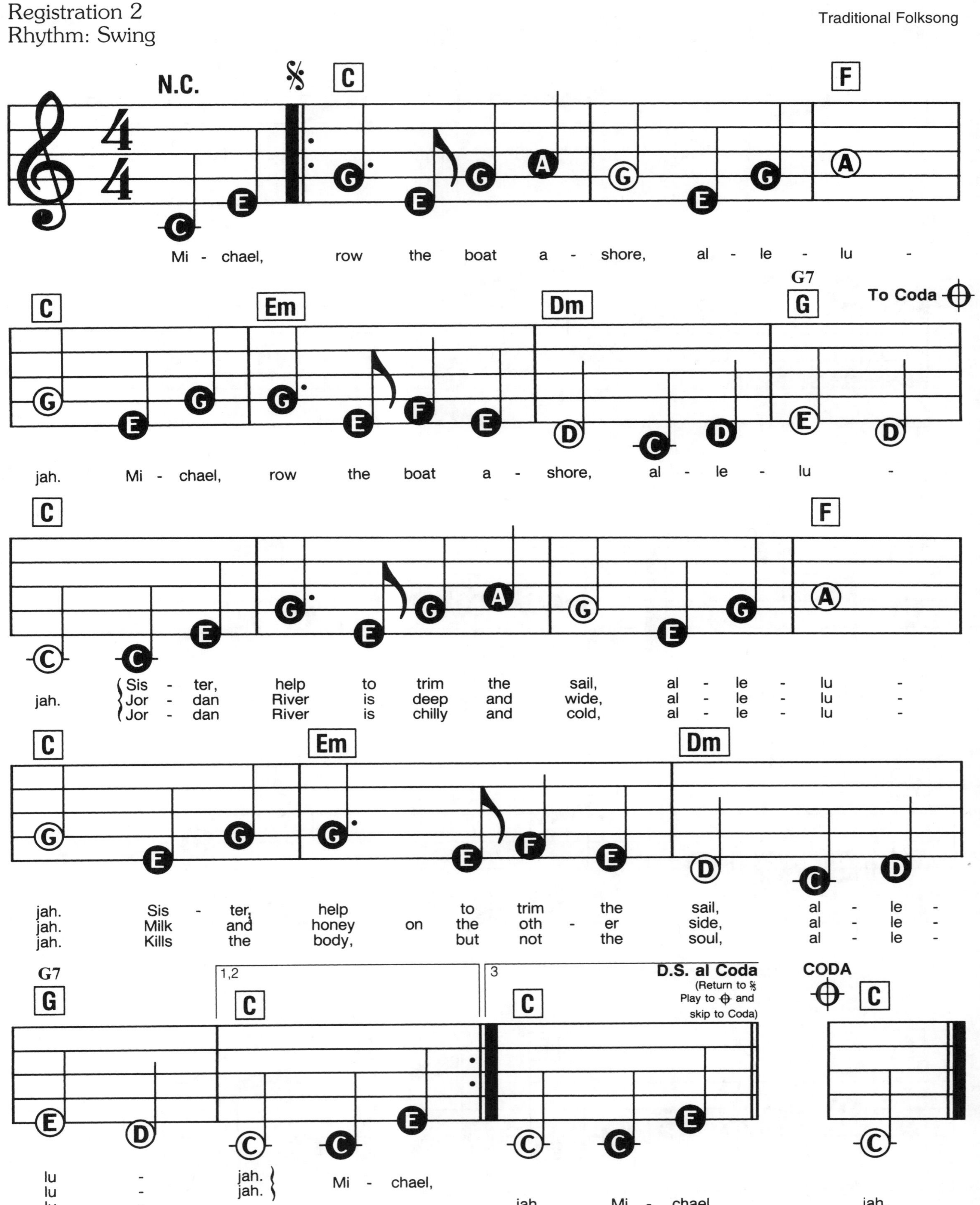

Copyright © 1989 by HAL LEONARD CORPORATION
International Copyright Secured All Rights Reserved

Octopus's Garden

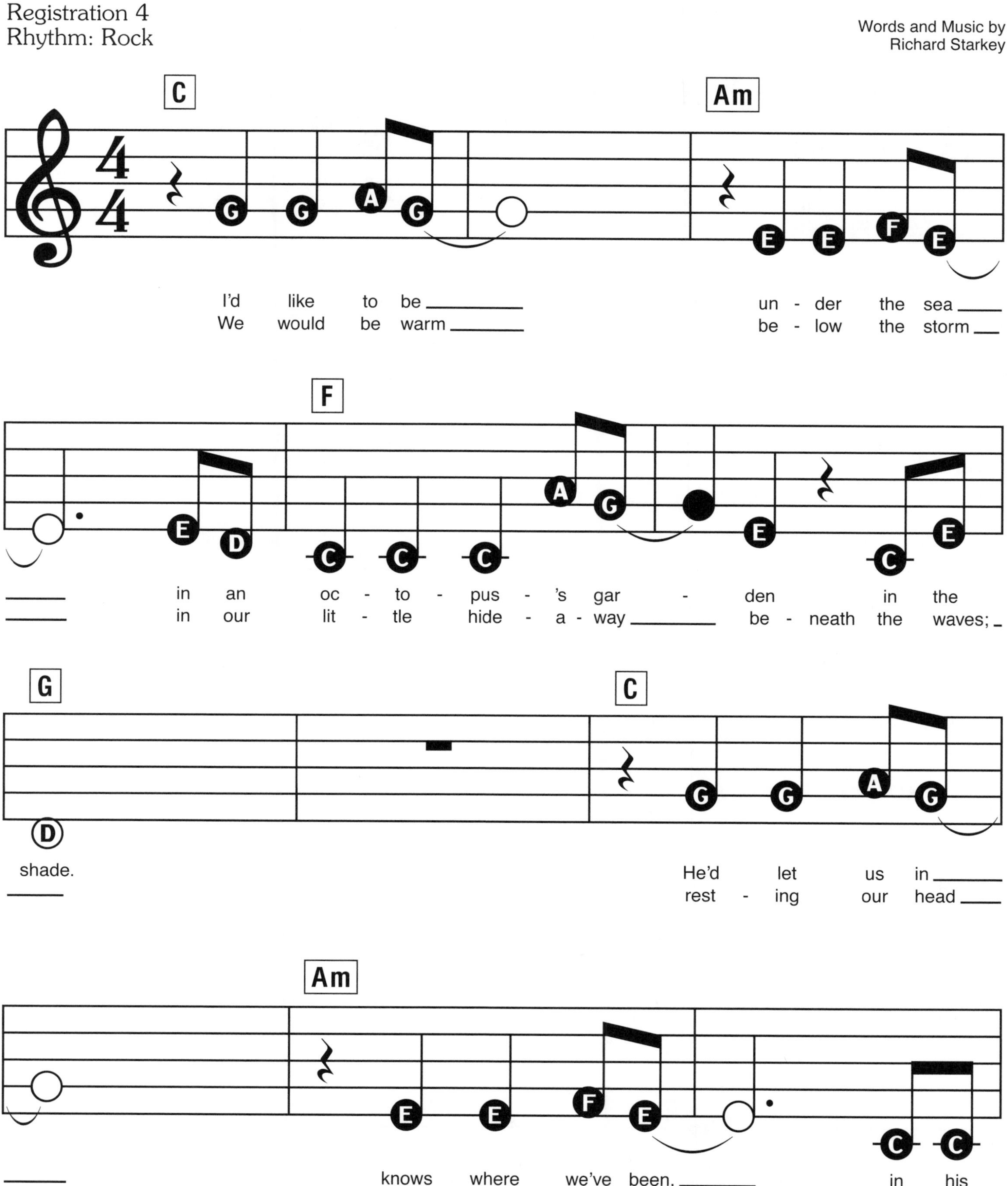

Copyright © 1969 STARTLING MUSIC LTD.
Copyright Renewed
All Rights Reserved

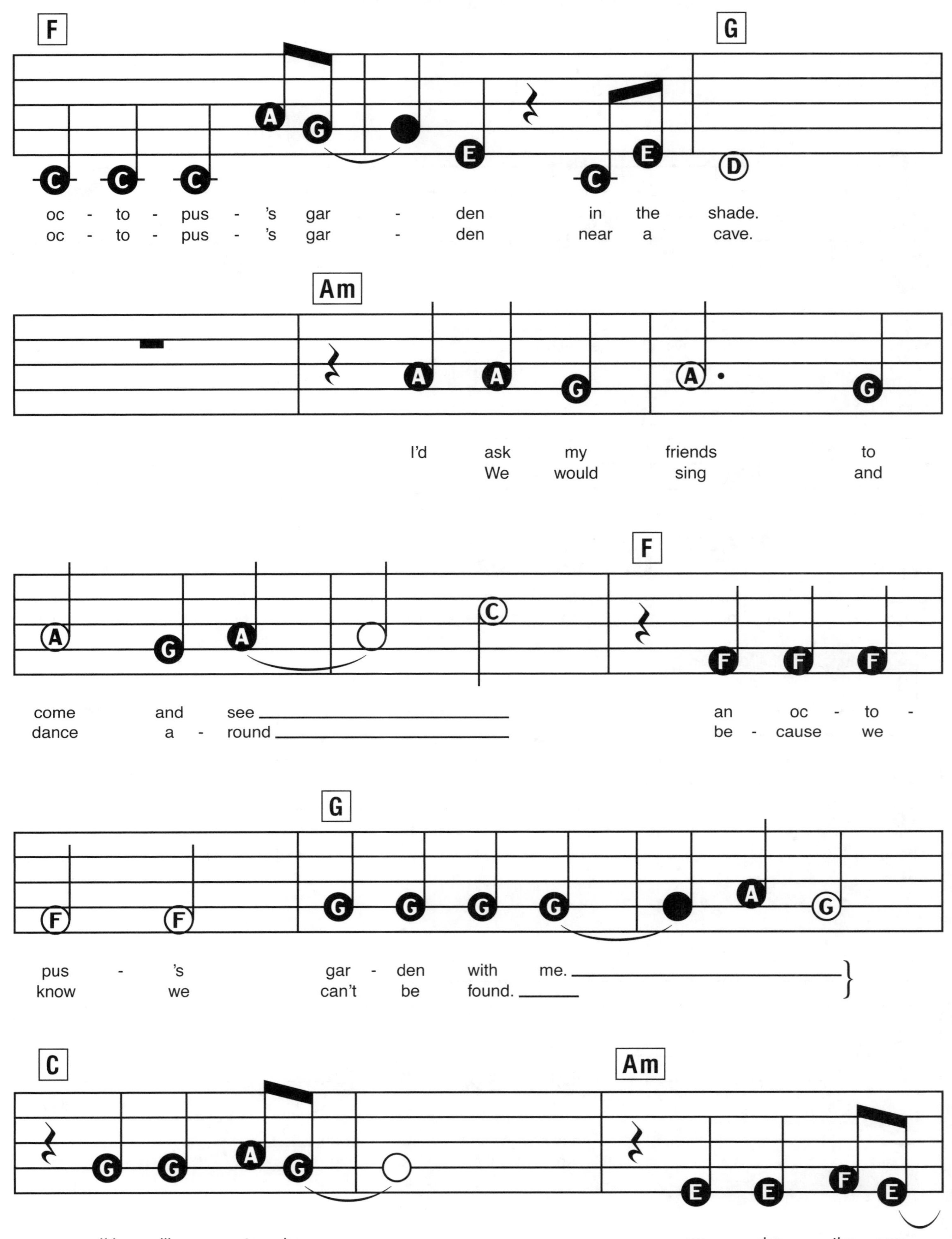
F
G
oc - to - pus - 's gar - den in the shade.
oc - to - pus - 's gar - den near a cave.
Am
I'd ask my friends to
We would sing and
F
come and see
dance a - round
an oc - to -
be - cause we
G
pus - 's gar - den with me.
know we can't be found.
C
Am
I'd like to be
un - der the sea

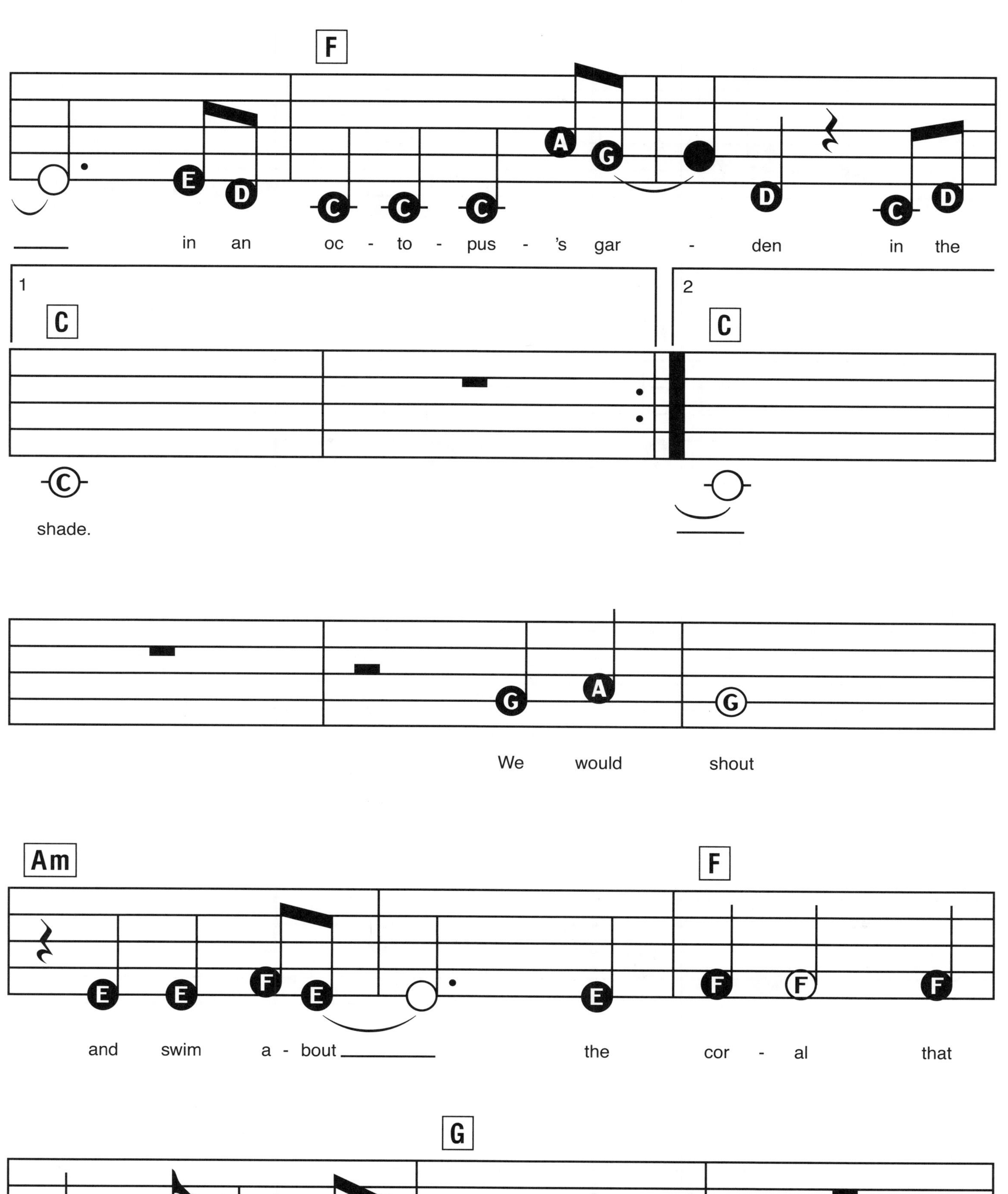
F
in an oc - to - pus - 's gar - den in the
1
C
shade.
2
C
We would shout
Am
and swim a - bout
F
the cor - al that
lies be - neath the waves.
G

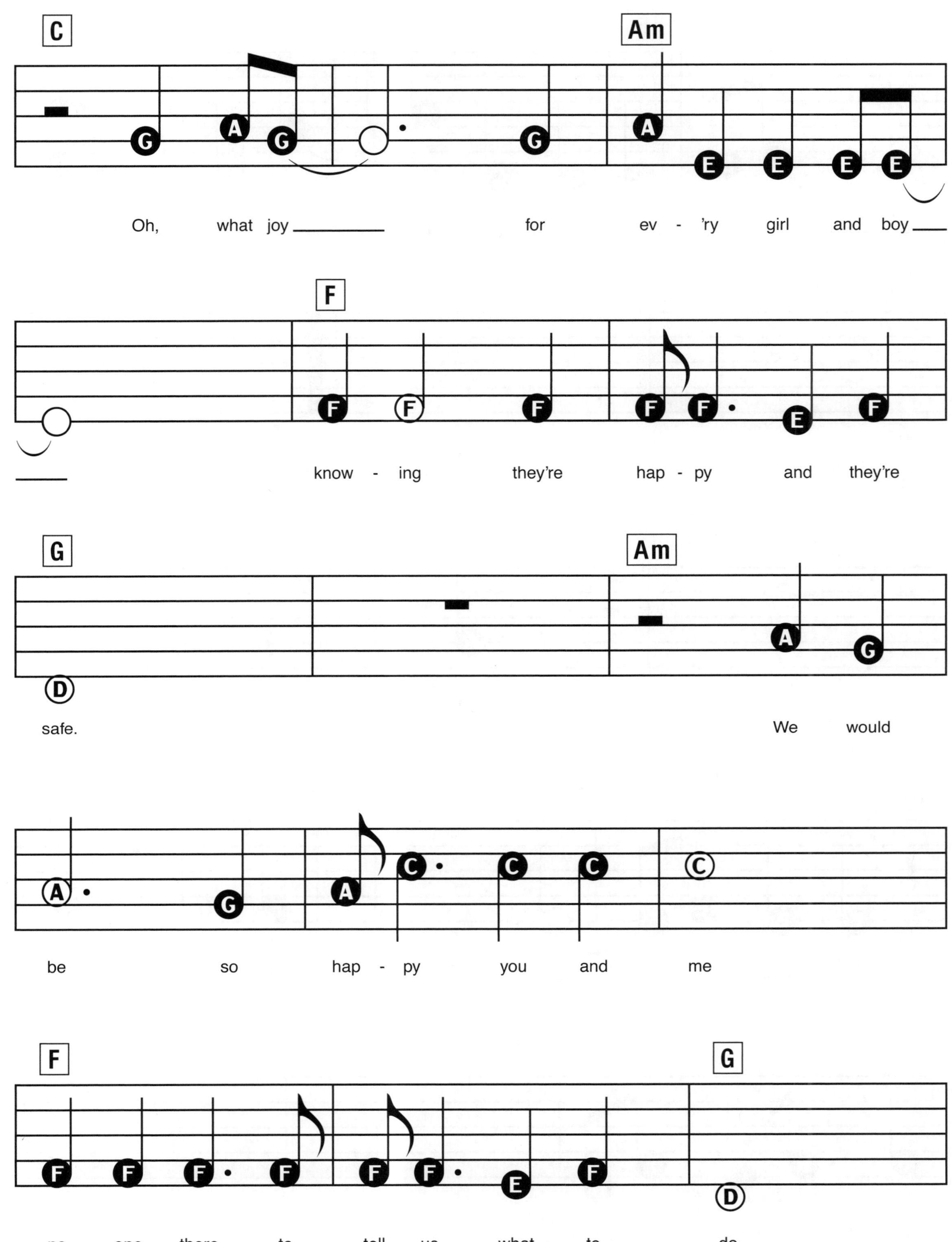
C
Am
Oh, what joy for ev - 'ry girl and boy
F
know - ing they're hap - py and they're
G
Am
safe. We would
be so hap - py you and me
F
G
no one there to tell us what to do.

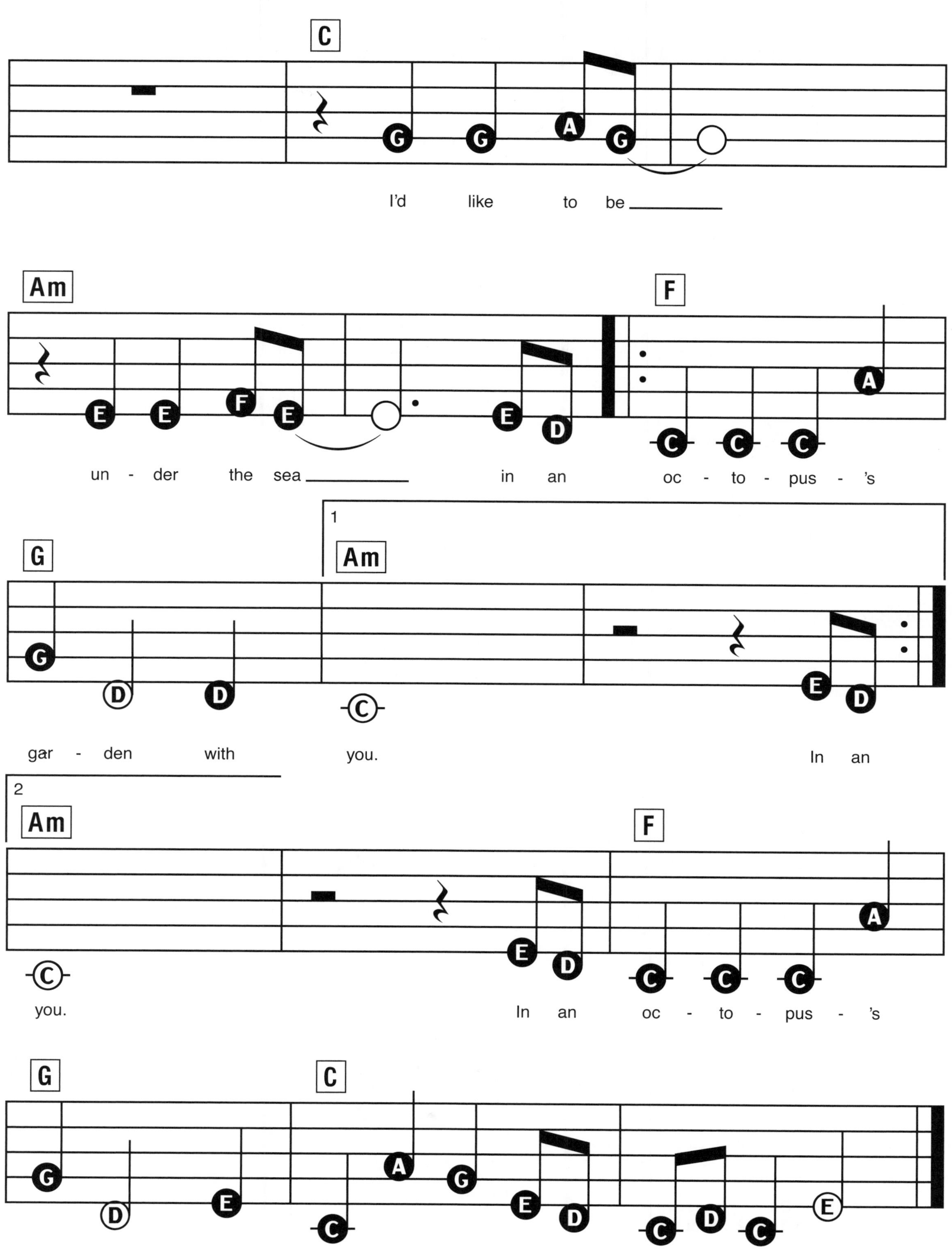
C
I'd like to be
Am
un - der the sea
in an
F
oc - to - pus - 's
G
gar - den with
1
Am
you.
In an
2
Am
you.
In an
F
oc - to - pus - 's
G
gar - den with
C
you. (Instrumental)

Oh Where, Oh Where Has My Little Dog Gone

Registration 8
Rhythm: Waltz

Words by Sep. Winner
Traditional Melody

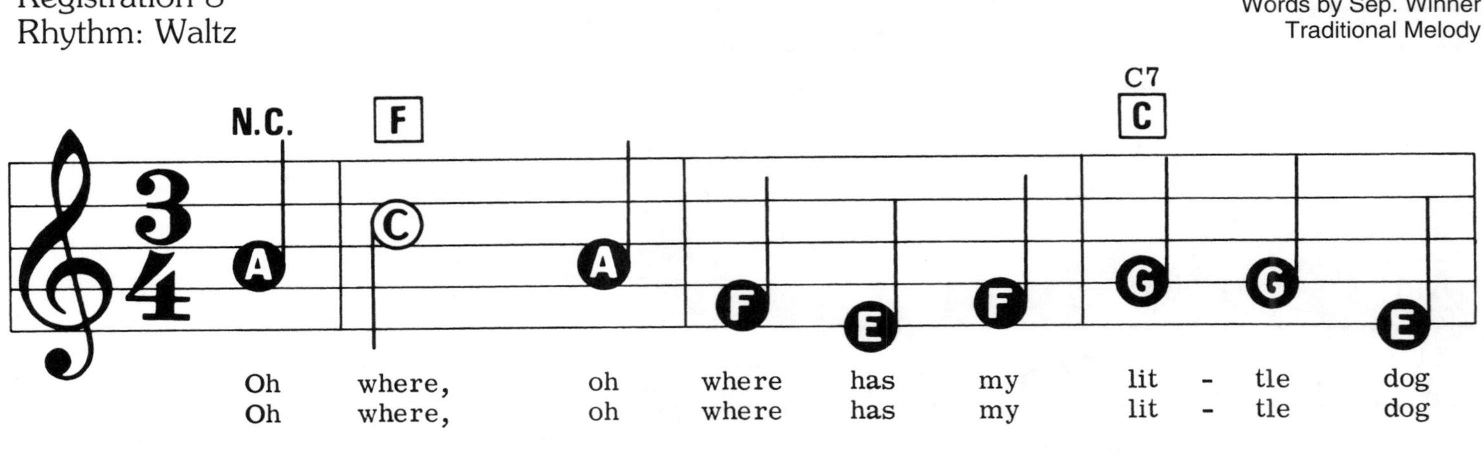

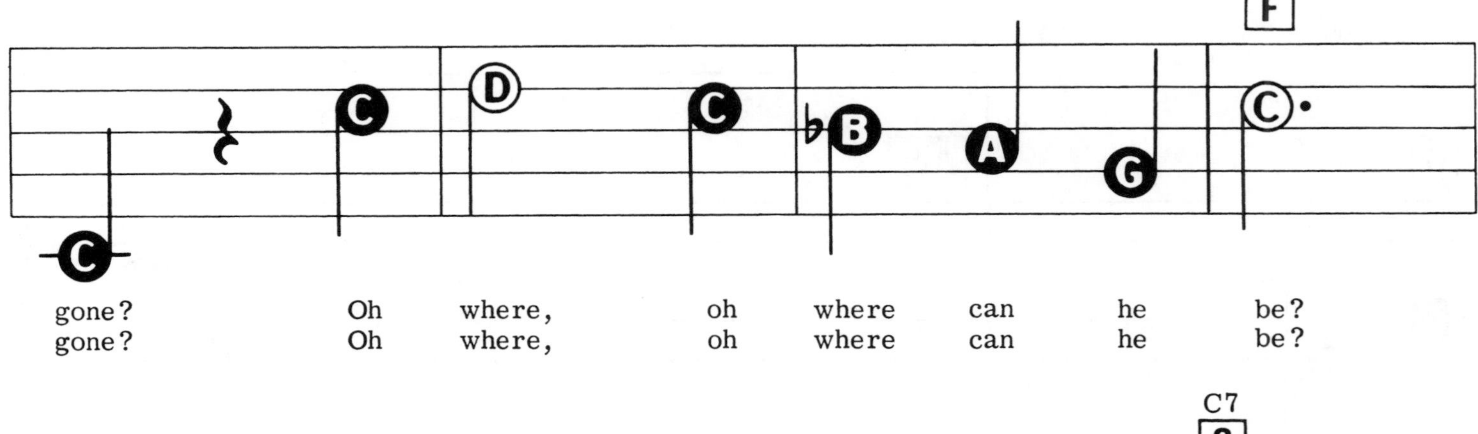

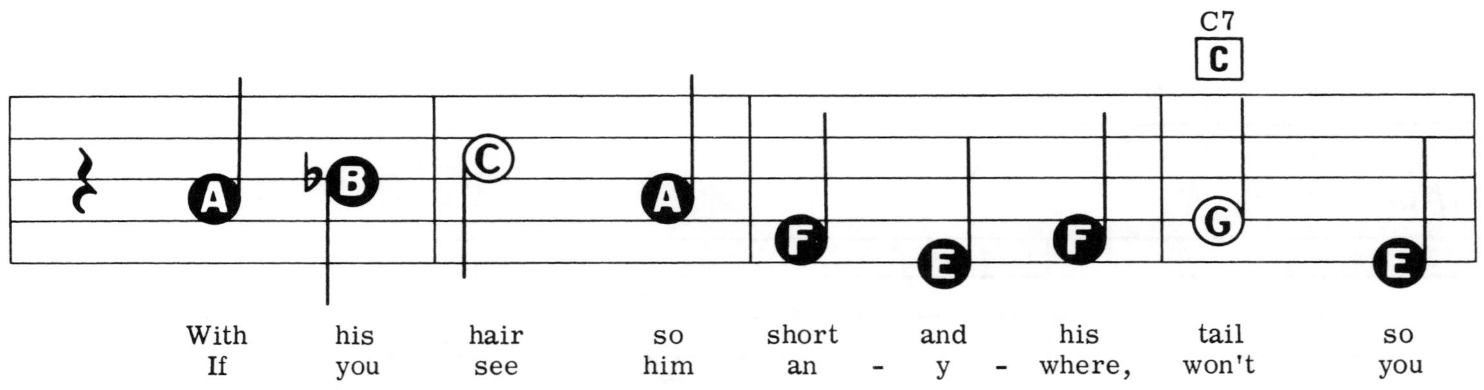

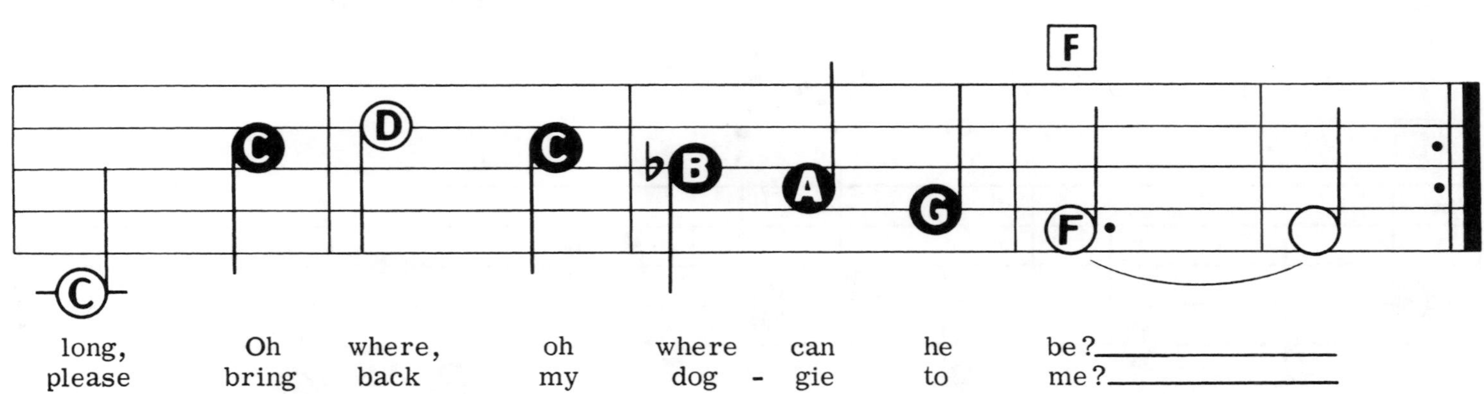

Copyright © 1977 by HAL LEONARD CORPORATION
International Copyright Secured All Rights Reserved

Over the Rainbow
from THE WIZARD OF OZ

Registration 3
Rhythm: Ballad

Music by Harold Arlen
Lyric by E.Y. "Yip" Harburg

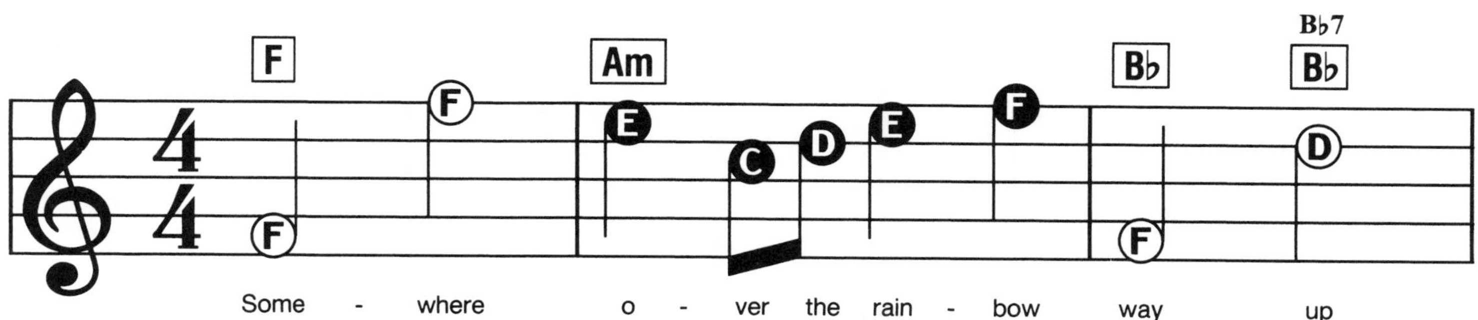

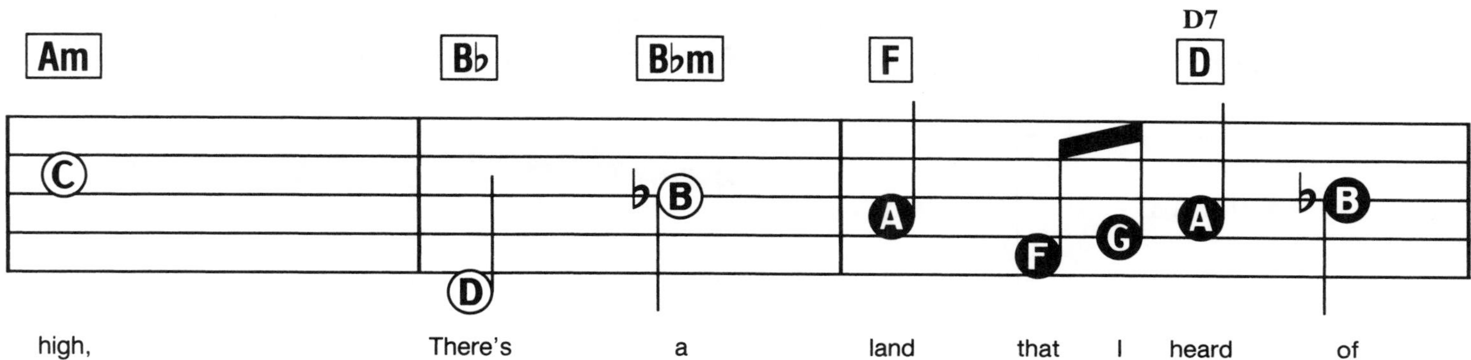

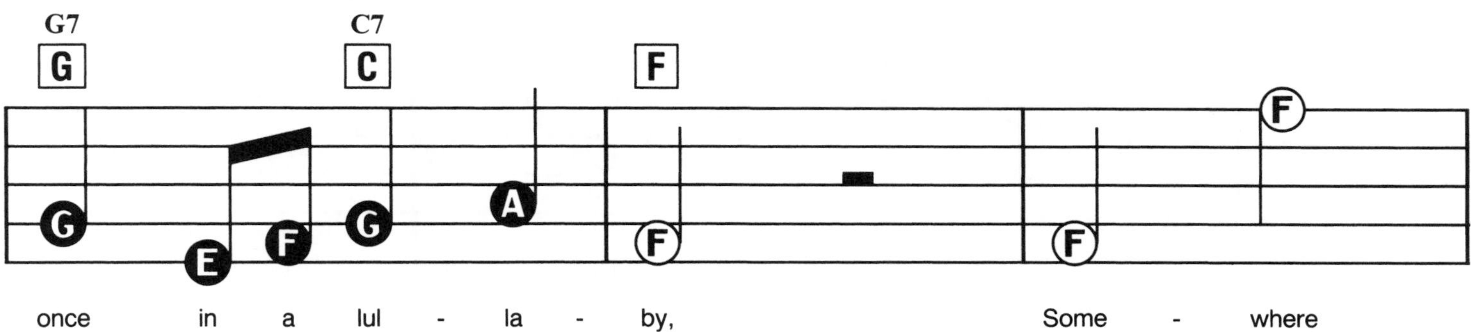

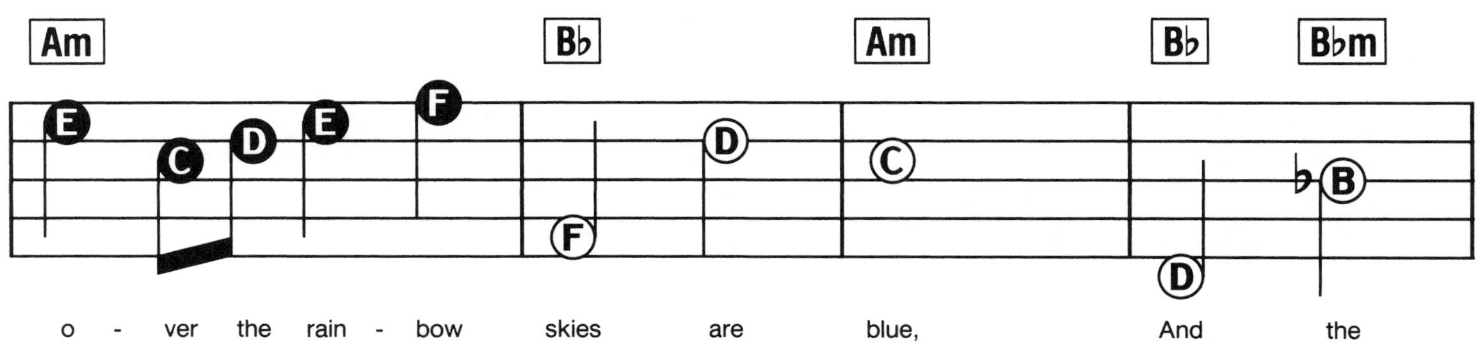

© 1938 (Renewed) METRO-GOLDWYN-MAYER INC.
© 1939 (Renewed) EMI FEIST CATALOG INC.
All Rights Administered by EMI FEIST CATALOG INC. (Publishing) and ALFRED MUSIC (Print)
All Rights Reserved Used by Permission

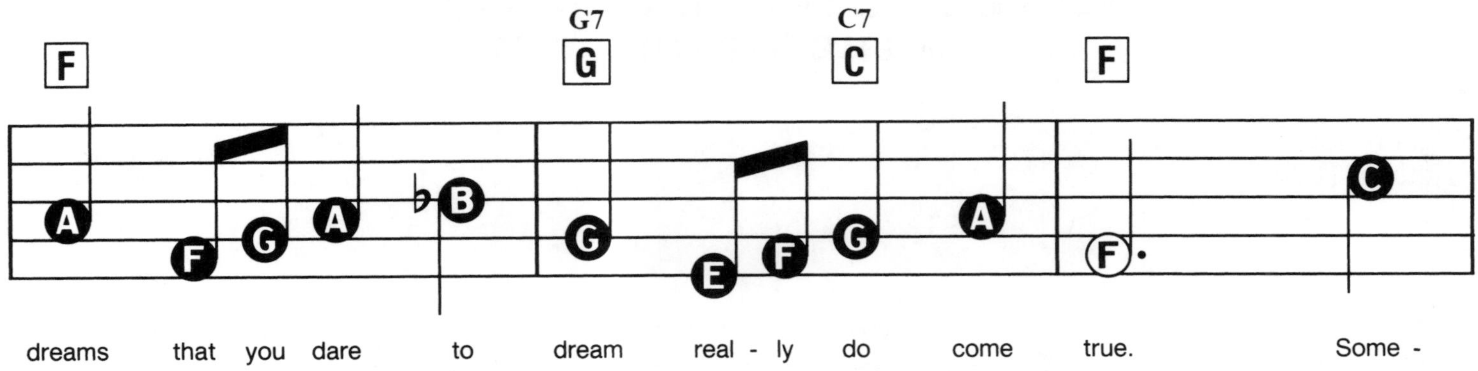
G7
C7
F
G
C
F
A
F
G
A
B
G
E
F
G
A
F
C
dreams that you dare to dream real - ly do come true. Some -

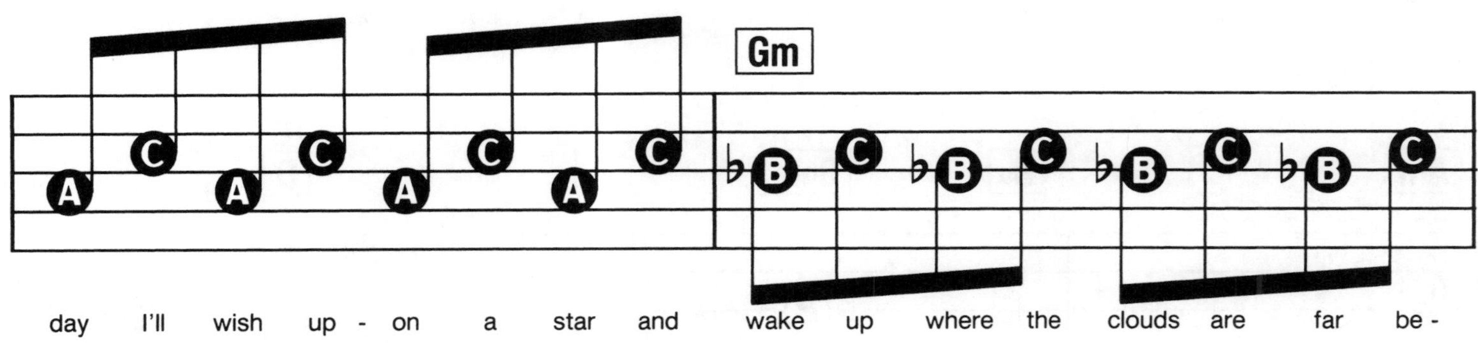
Gm
A
C
A
C
A
C
A
C
B
C
B
C
B
C
B
C
day I'll wish up - on a star and wake up where the clouds are far be -

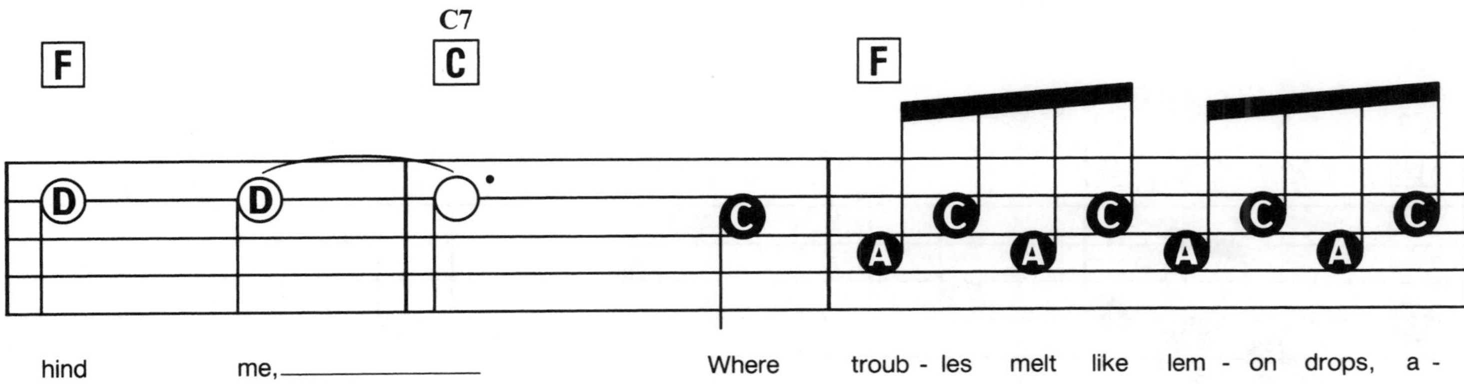
C7
F
C
F
D
D
C
A
C
A
C
A
C
A
C
hind me,
Where troub - les melt like lem - on drops, a -

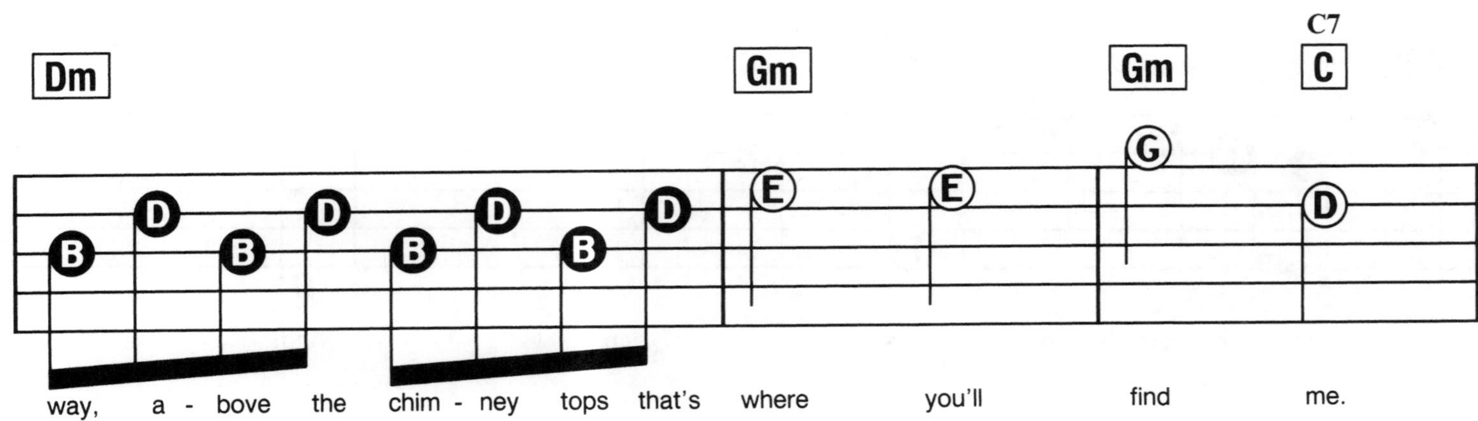
C7
Dm
Gm
Gm
C
B
D
B
D
B
D
B
D
E
E
G
D
way, a - bove the chim - ney tops that's where you'll find me.

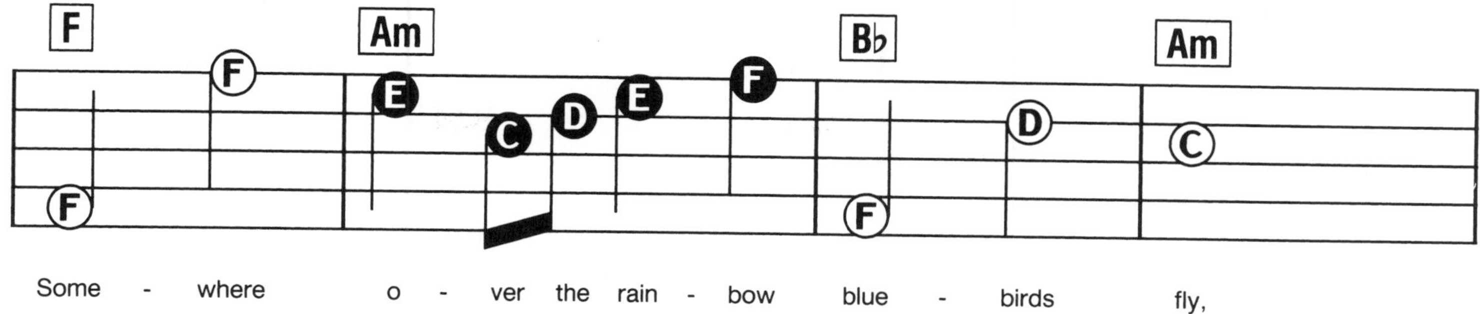
F Am B♭ Am
Some - where o - ver the rain - bow blue - birds fly,

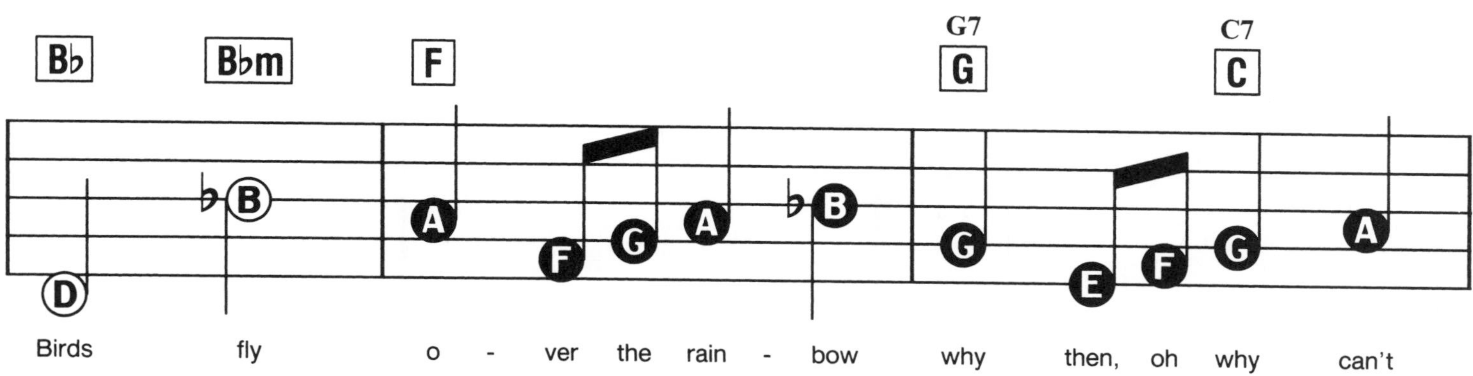
B♭ B♭m F G7 G C7 C
Birds fly o - ver the rain - bow why then, oh why can't

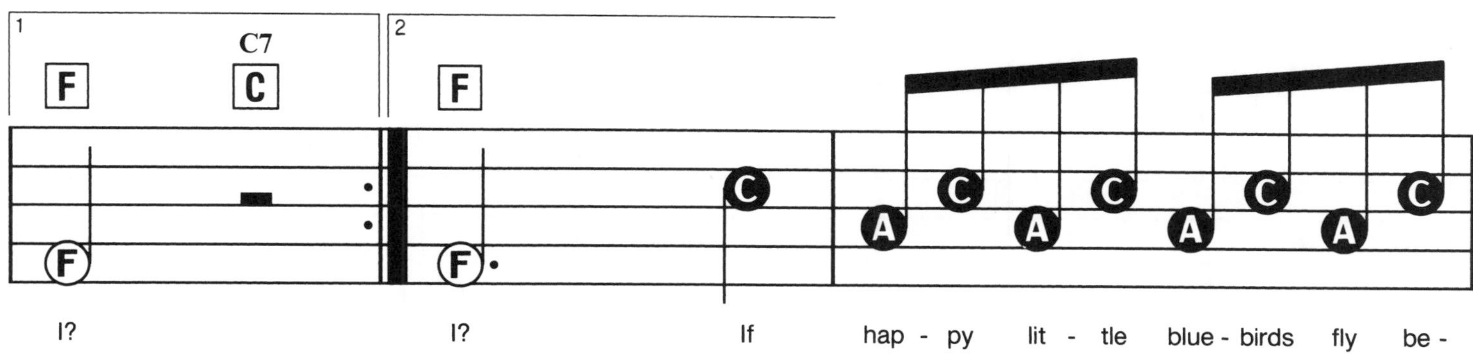
1 F C7 C
I?
2 F
I? If hap - py lit - tle blue - birds fly be -

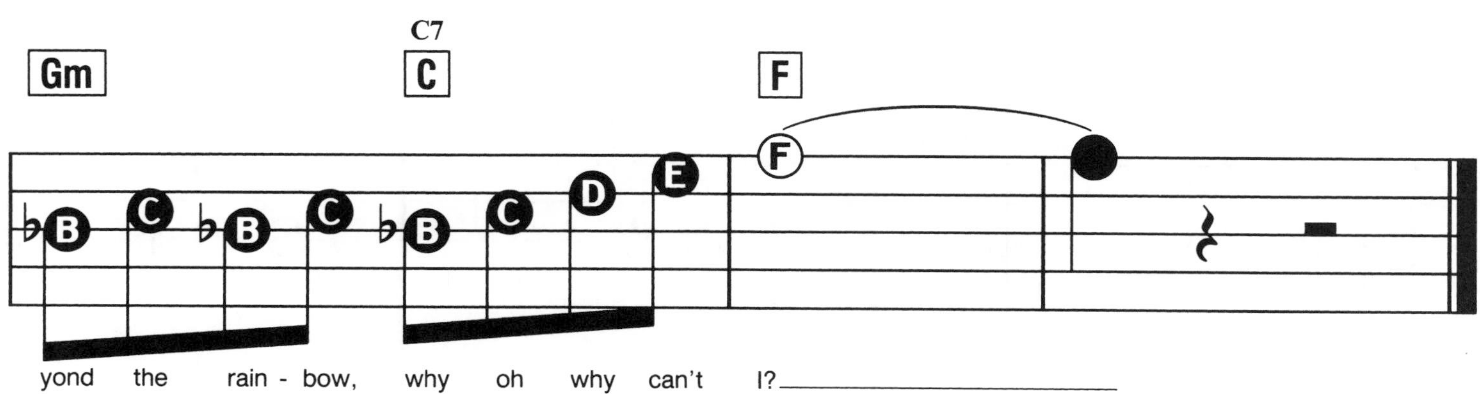
Gm C7 C F
yond the rain - bow, why oh why can't I?

Old MacDonald Had a Farm

Registration 4
Rhythm: Fox Trot

Traditional

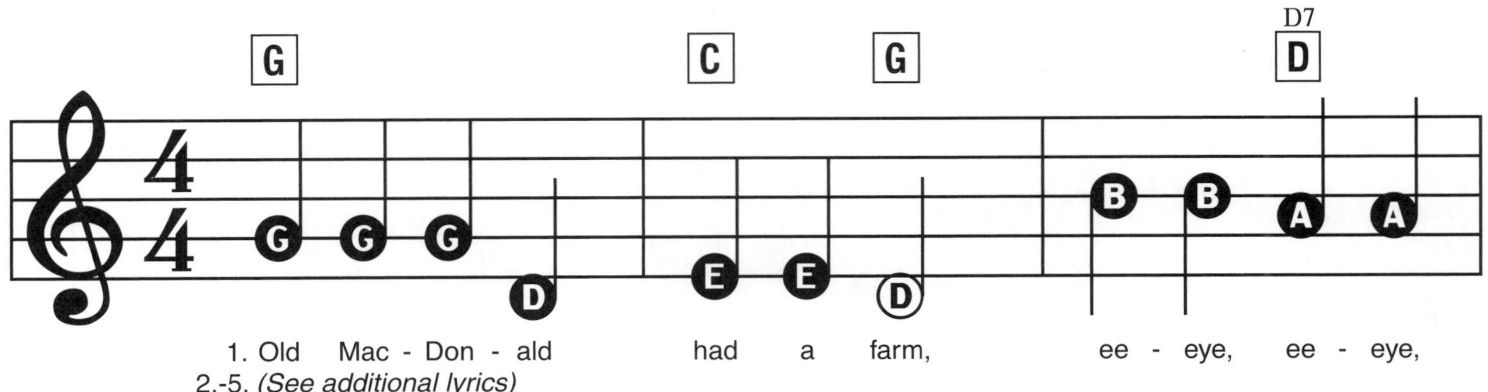

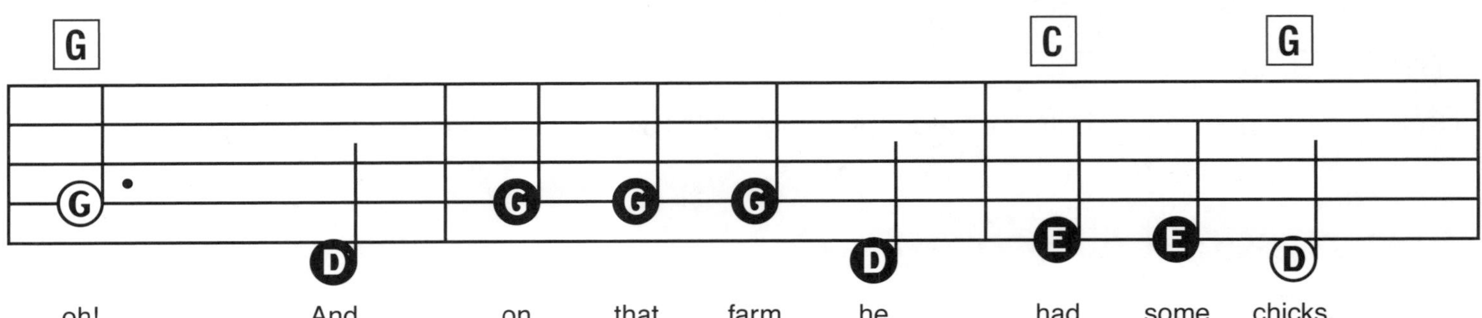

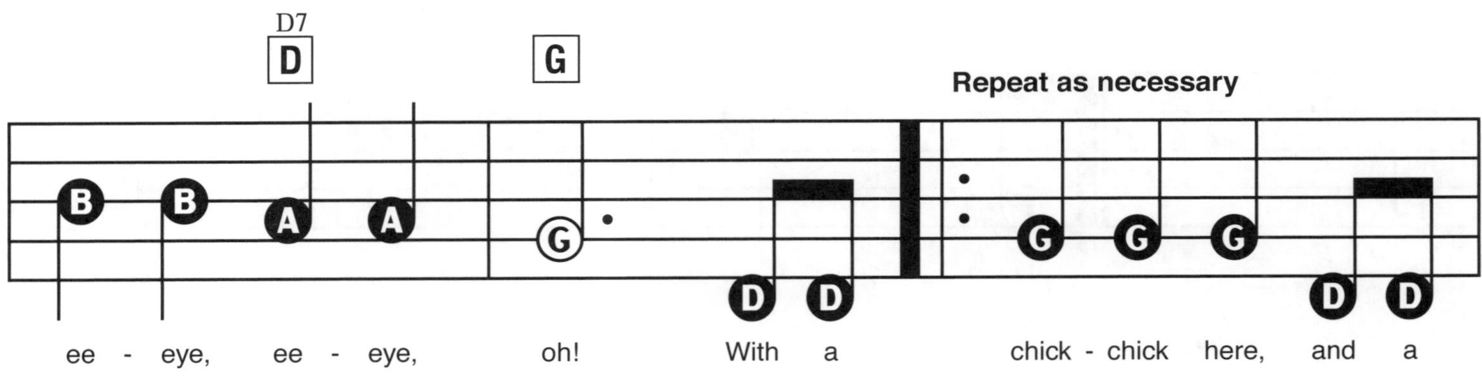

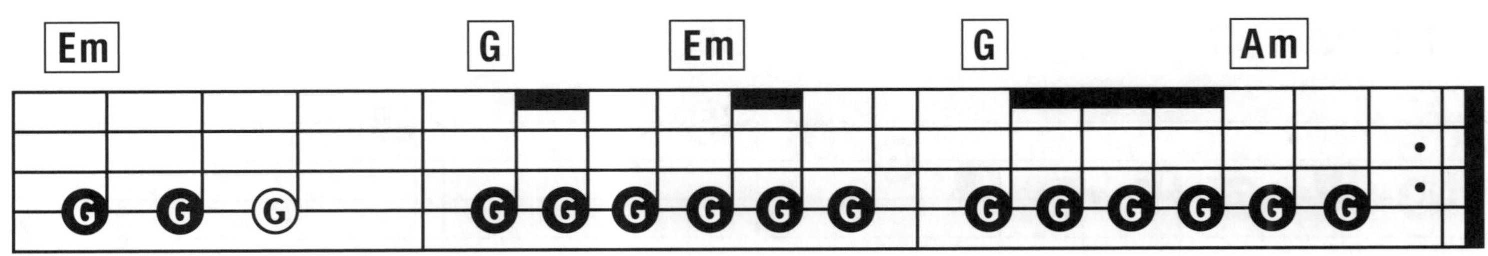

Copyright © 2012 by HAL LEONARD CORPORATION
International Copyright Secured All Rights Reserved

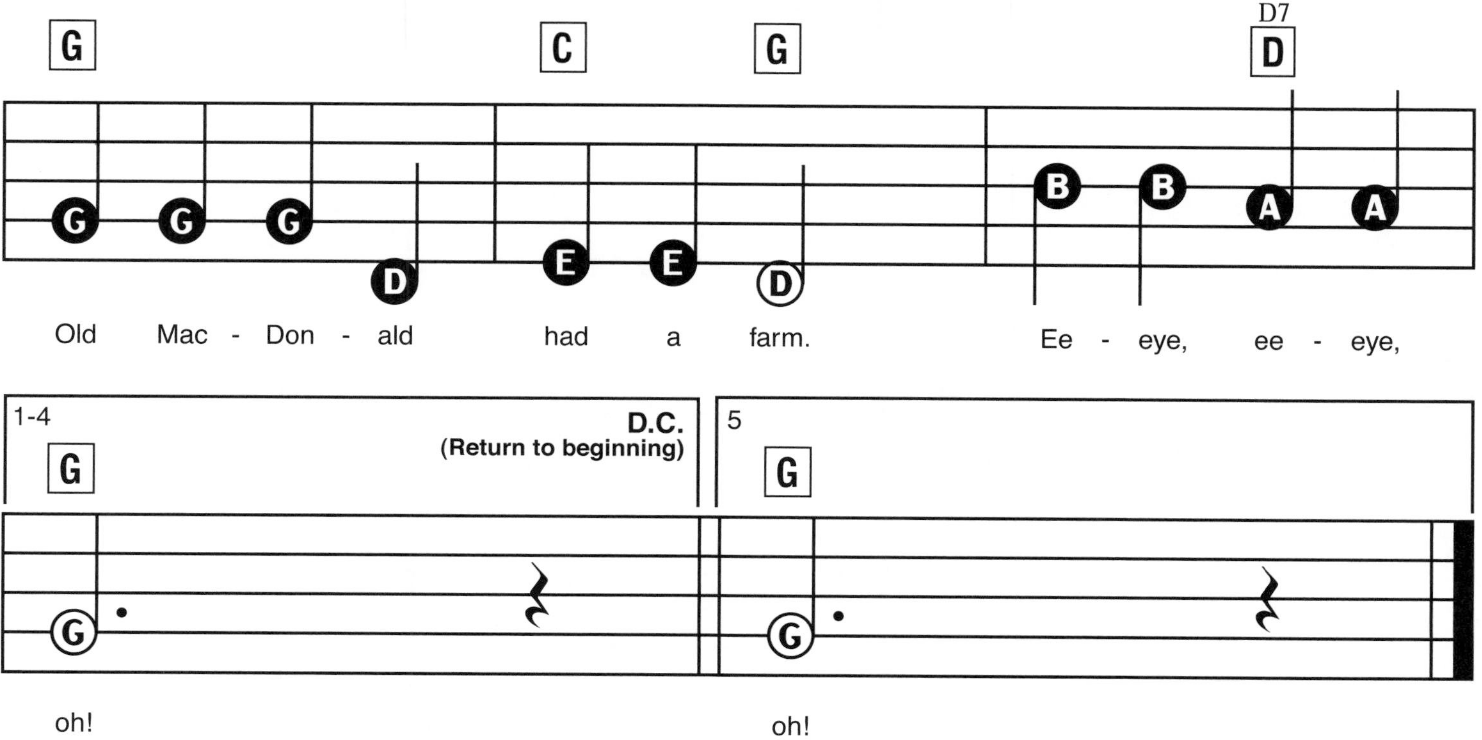

Additional Lyrics

2. Old MacDonald had a farm,
   Ee-eye, ee-eye, oh!
   And on that farm he had some ducks,
   Ee-eye, ee-eye, oh!
   With a quack-quack here and a quack-quack there,
   Here a quack, there a quack, everywhere a quack-quack.
   Chick-chick here and a chick-chick there,
   Here a chick, there a chick, everywhere a chick-chick.
   Old MacDonald had a farm,
   Ee-eye, ee-eye, oh!

3. …and on that farm he had some cows…
   With a moo-moo here and a moo-moo there,
   Here a moo, there a moo, everywhere a moo-moo,
   Quack-quack here and a quack-quack there…
   Chick-chick here and a chick-chick there…

4. …and on that farm he had some pigs…
   With an oink-oink here and an oink-oink there,
   Here an oink, there an oink, everywhere an oink-oink,
   Moo-moo here…
   Quack-quack here…
   Chick-chick here…

5. …and on that farm he had some sheep…
   With a baa-baa here and a baa-baa there…
   Oink-oink here…
   Moo-moo here…
   Quack-quack here…
   Chick-chick here…

On Top of Spaghetti

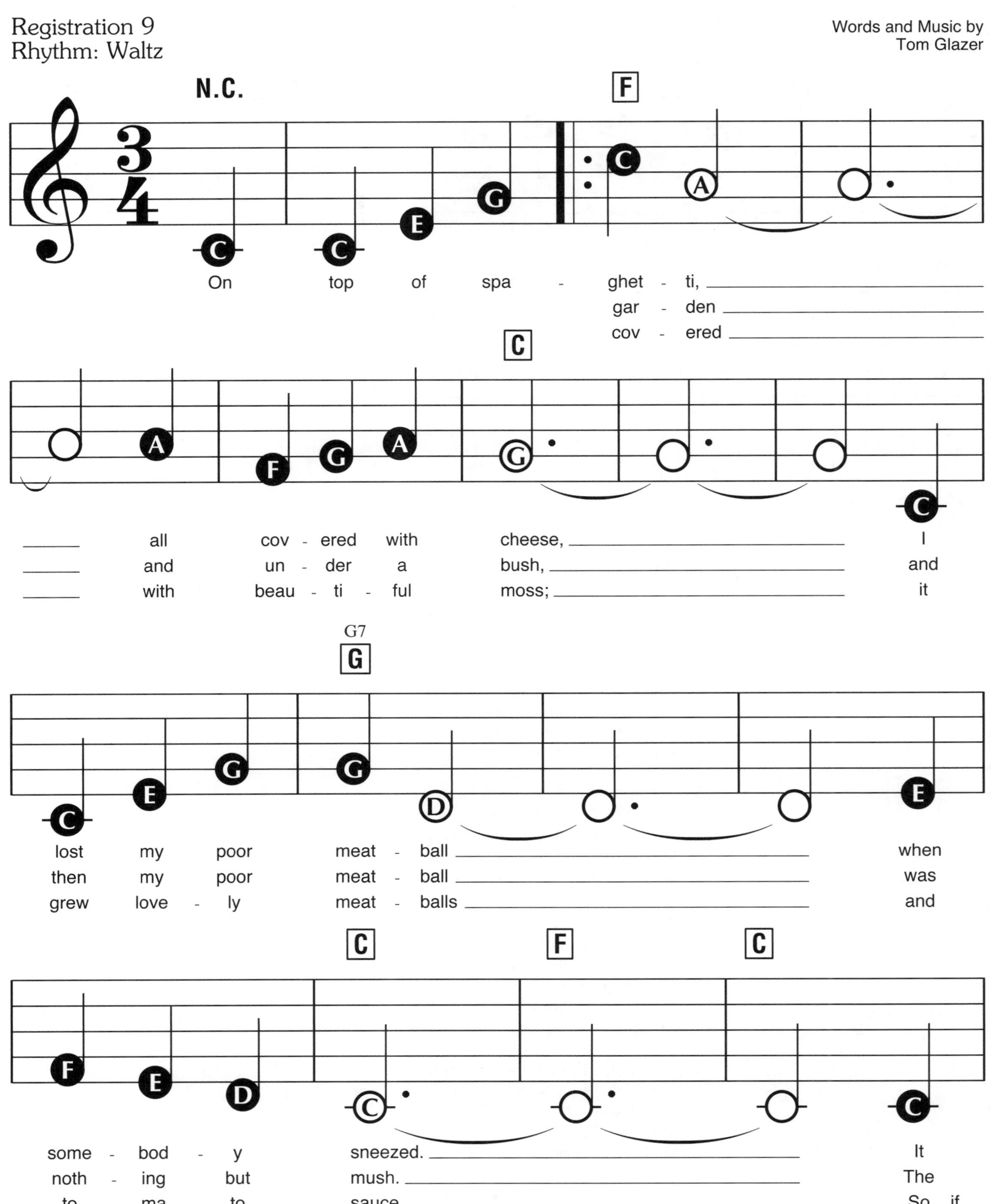

Copyright © 1963 by Songs Music Inc.
Copyright Renewed
All Rights Administered by Larry Spier Music LLC
International Copyright Secured All Rights Reserved

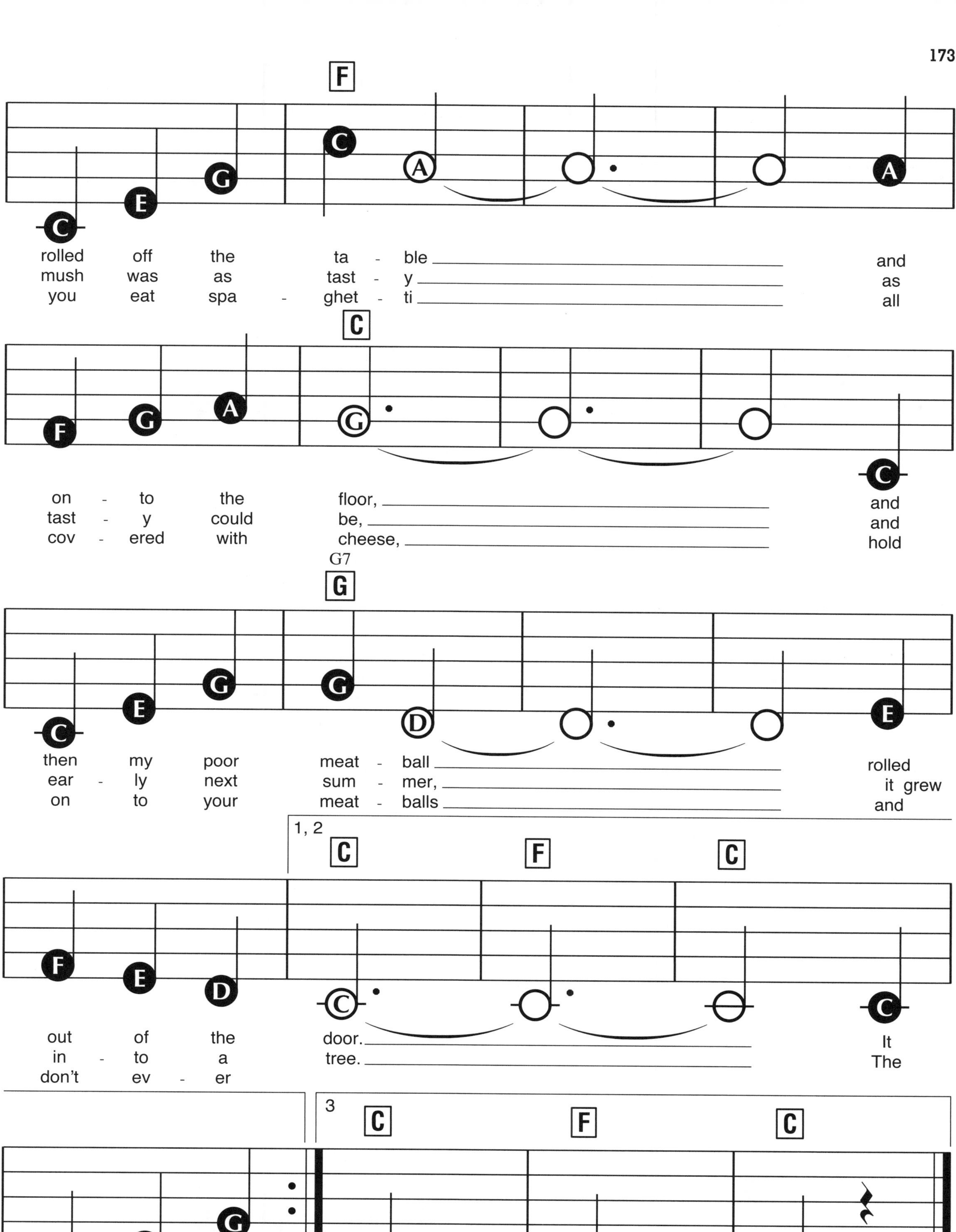
F
C E G C A A
rolled off the ta - ble and
mush was as tast - y as
you eat spa - ghet - ti all
C
F G A G C
on - to the floor, and
tast - y could be, and
cov - ered with cheese, and hold
G7
G
C E G G D E
then my poor meat - ball rolled
ear - ly next sum - mer, it grew
on to your meat - balls and
1, 2
C F C
F E D C C
out of the door. It
in - to a tree. The
don't ev - er
3
C F C
C E G C
rolled in the
tree was all
sneeze.

Once Upon a Dream
from Walt Disney's SLEEPING BEAUTY

Registration 2
Rhythm: Waltz

Words and Music by Sammy Fain
and Jack Lawrence
Adapted from a Theme by Tchaikovsky

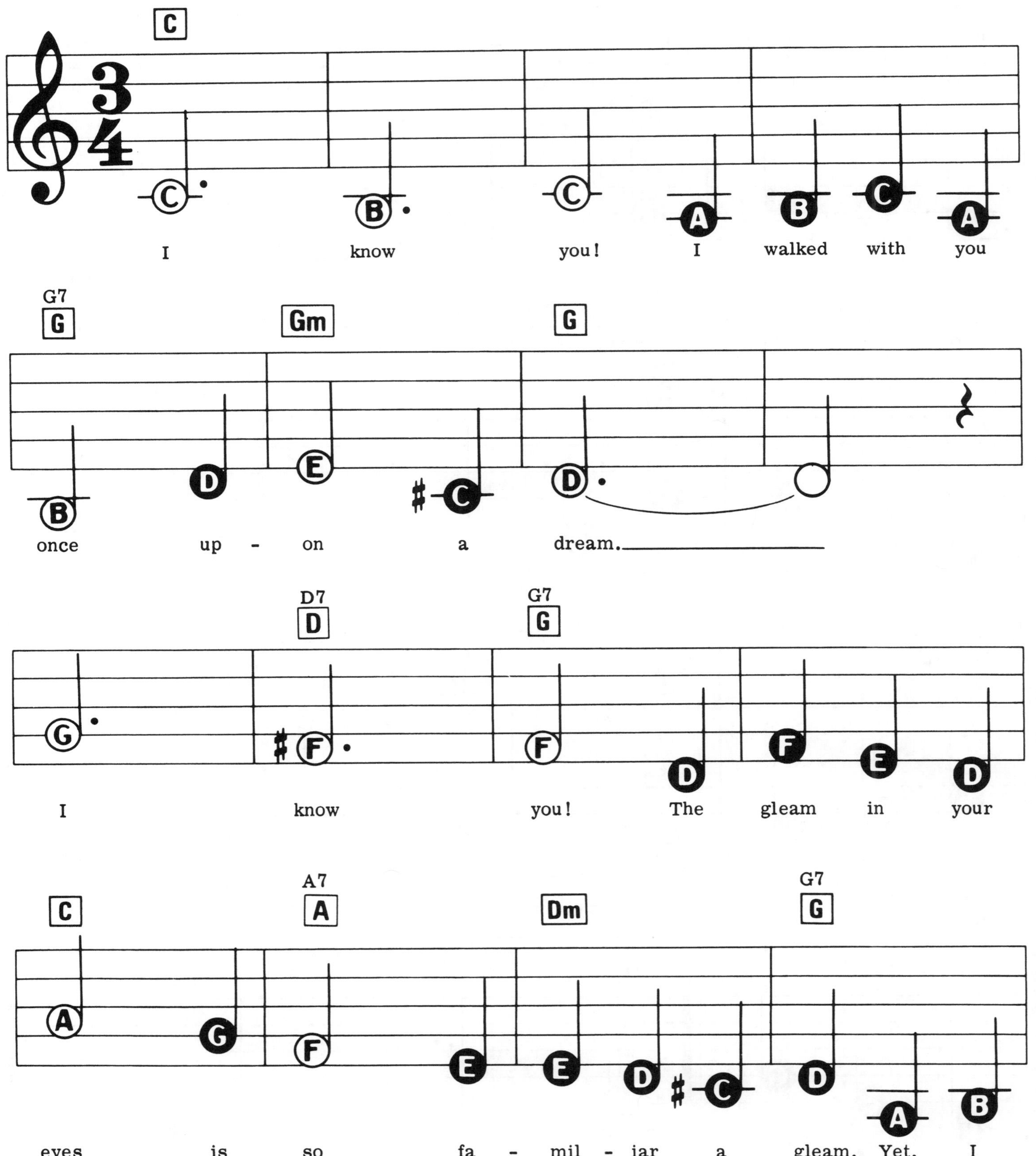

© 1952 Walt Disney Music Company
Copyright Renewed
All Rights Reserved. Used by Permission.

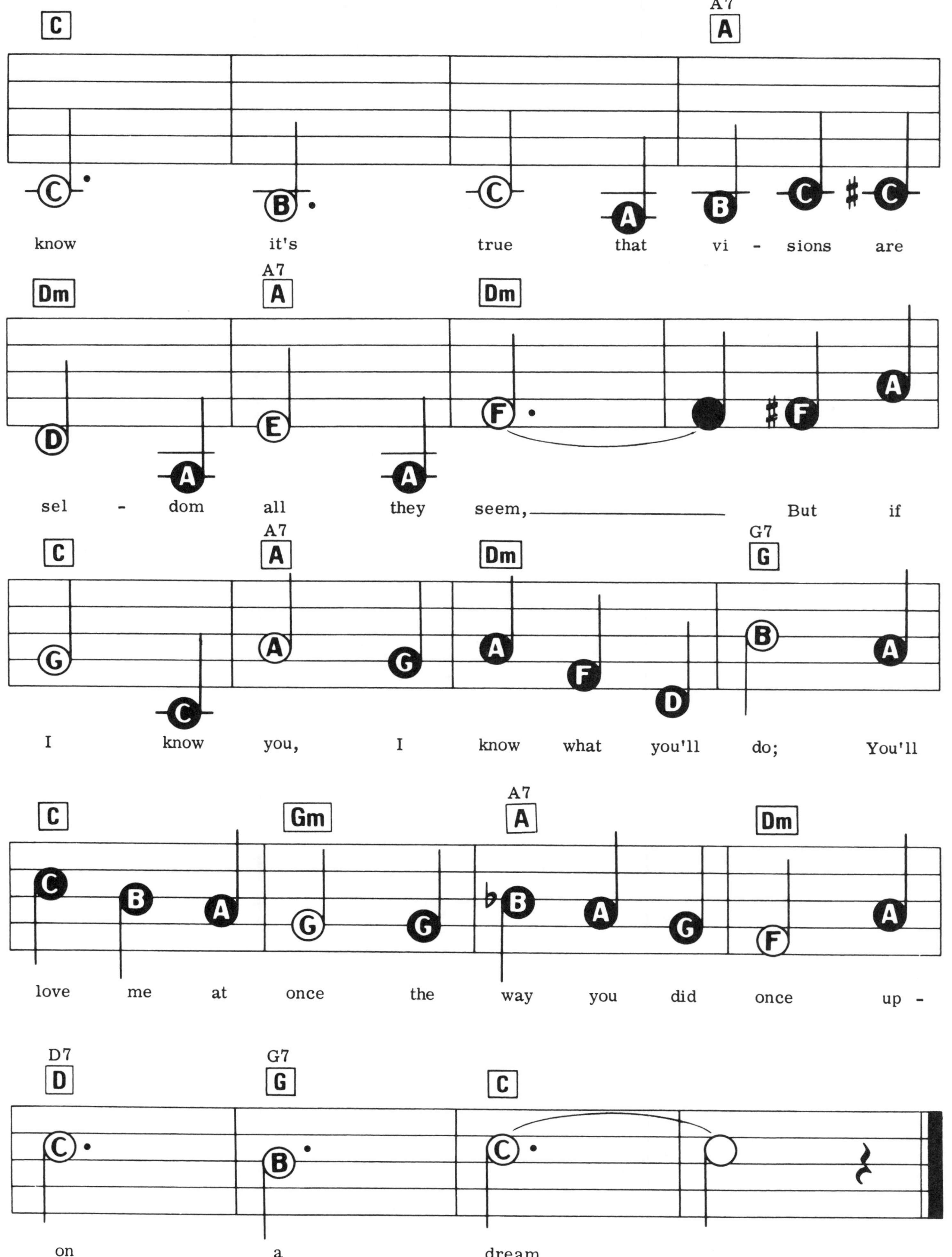
C
A7
A
know
it's
true
that
vi - sions
are
Dm
A7
A
Dm
sel - dom
all
they
seem,
But
if
C
A7
A
Dm
G7
G
I
know
you,
I
know
what
you'll
do;
You'll
C
Gm
A7
A
Dm
love
me
at
once
the
way
you
did
once
up -
D7
D
G7
G
C
on
a
dream.

Over the River and Through the Woods

Registration 8
Rhythm: 6/8 March

Traditional

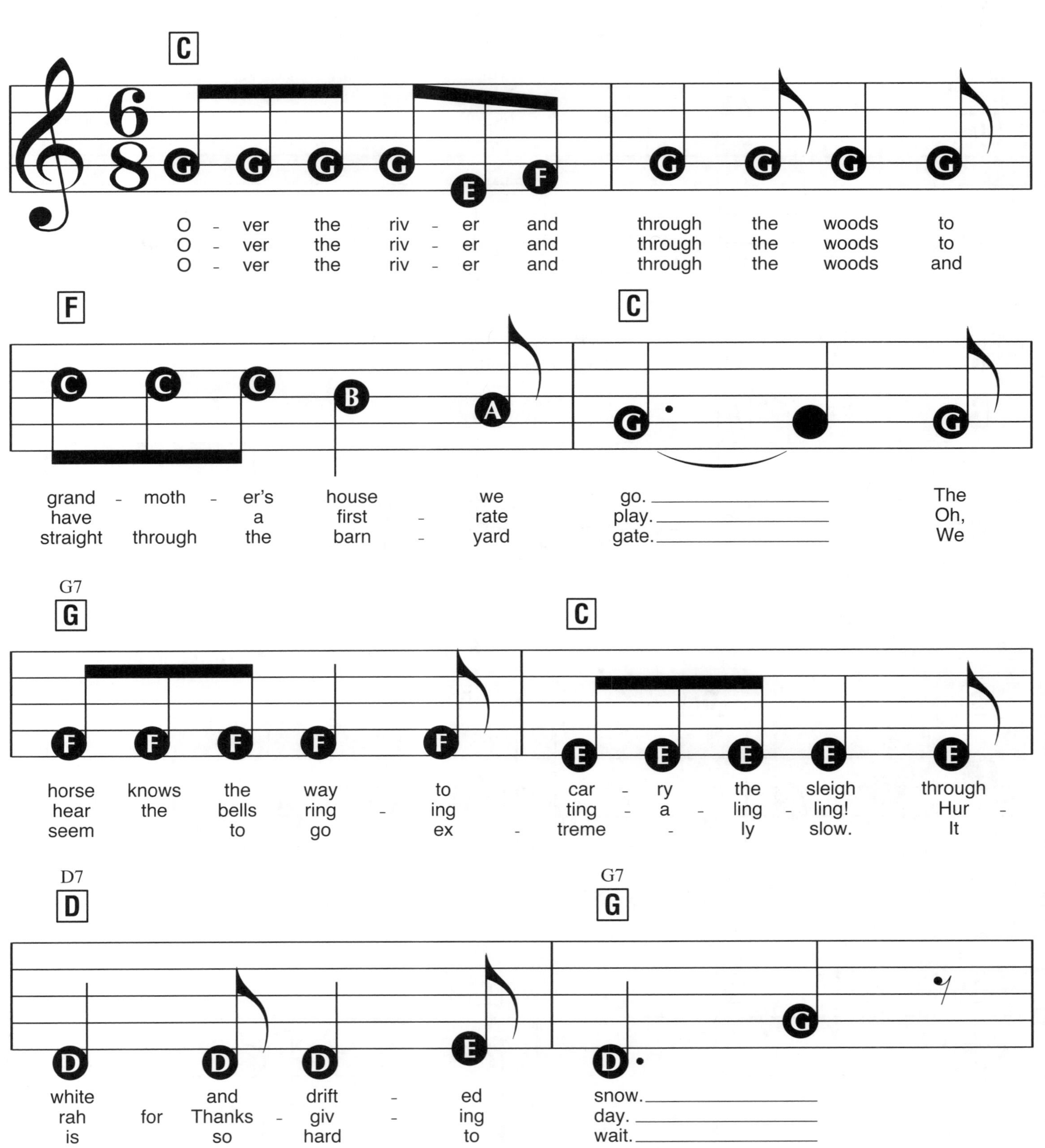

Copyright © 1989 by HAL LEONARD CORPORATION
International Copyright Secured All Rights Reserved

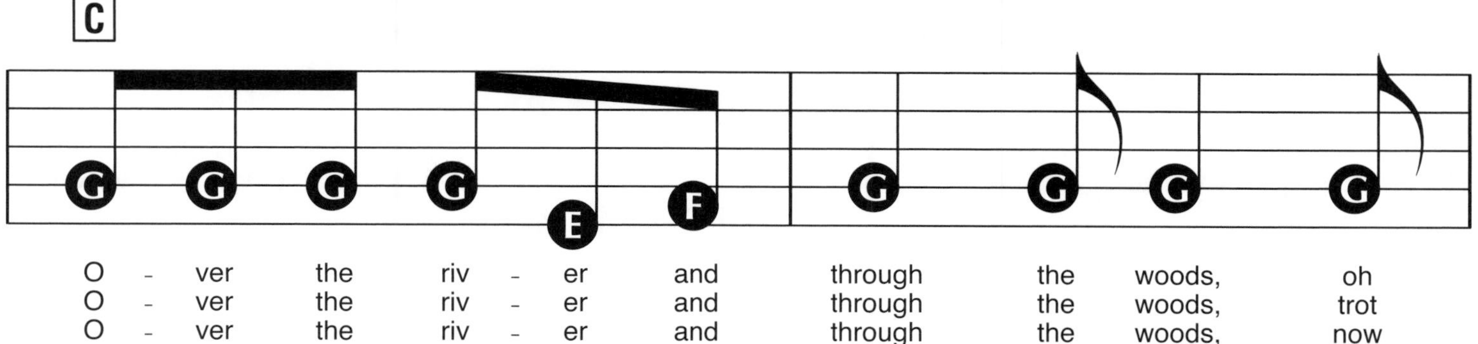
C
O - ver the riv - er and through the woods, oh
O - ver the riv - er and through the woods, trot
O - ver the riv - er and through the woods, now

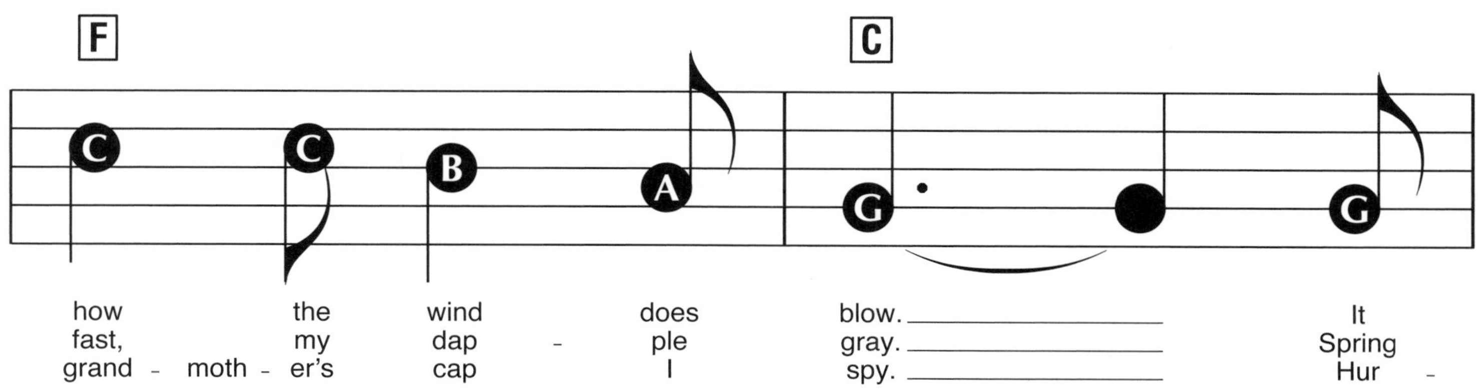
F
C
how the wind does blow. It
fast, my dap - ple gray. Spring
grand - moth - er's cap I spy. Hur -

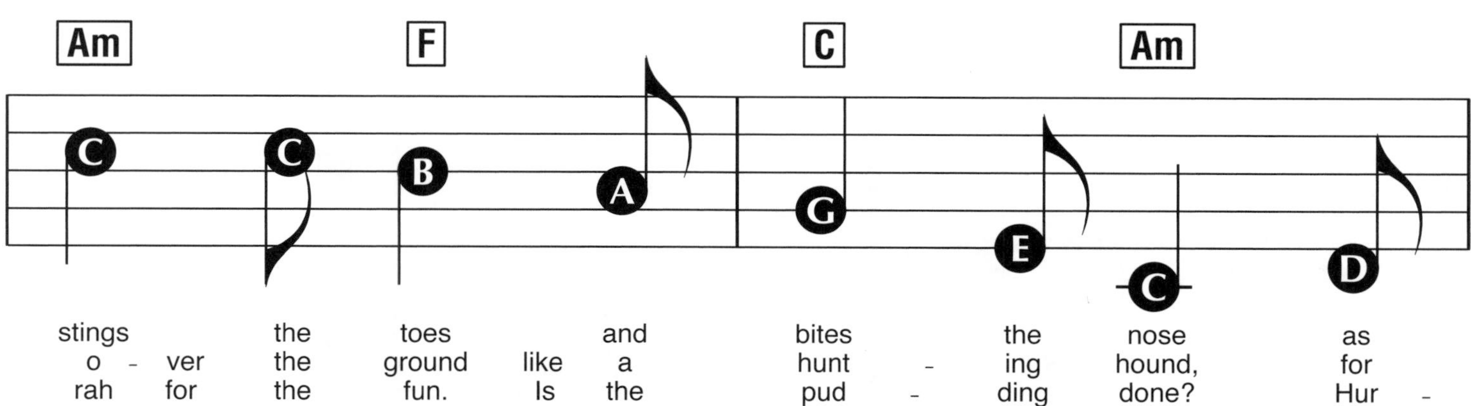
Am
F
C
Am
stings the toes and bites the nose as
o - ver the ground like a hunt - ing hound, for
rah for the fun. Is the pud - ding done? Hur -

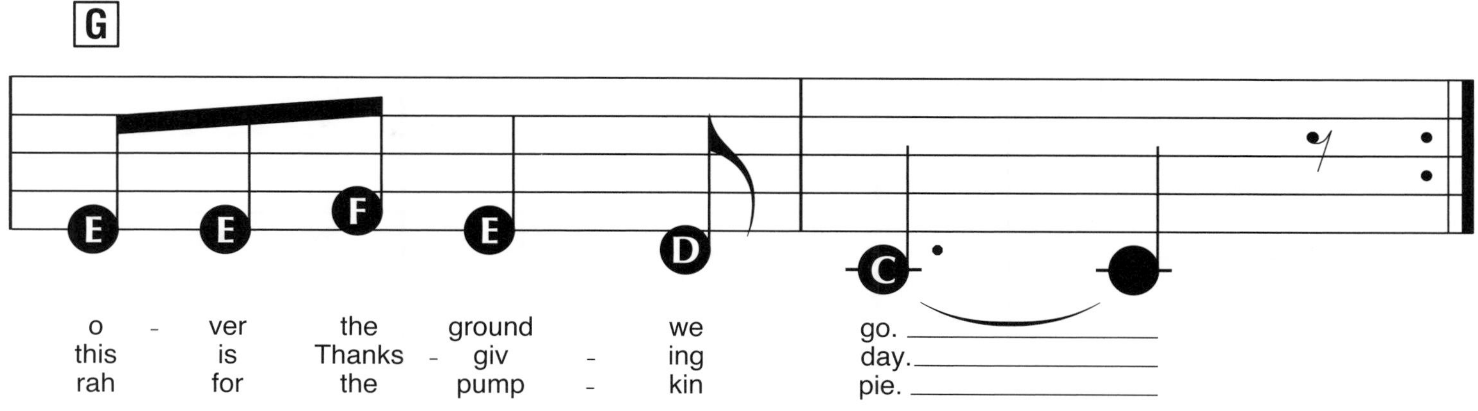
G
o - ver the ground we go.
this is Thanks - giv - ing day.
rah for the pump - kin pie.

Part of Your World

from Walt Disney's THE LITTLE MERMAID

Registration 1
Rhythm: Pops or 8-Beat

Music by Alan Menken
Lyrics by Howard Ashman

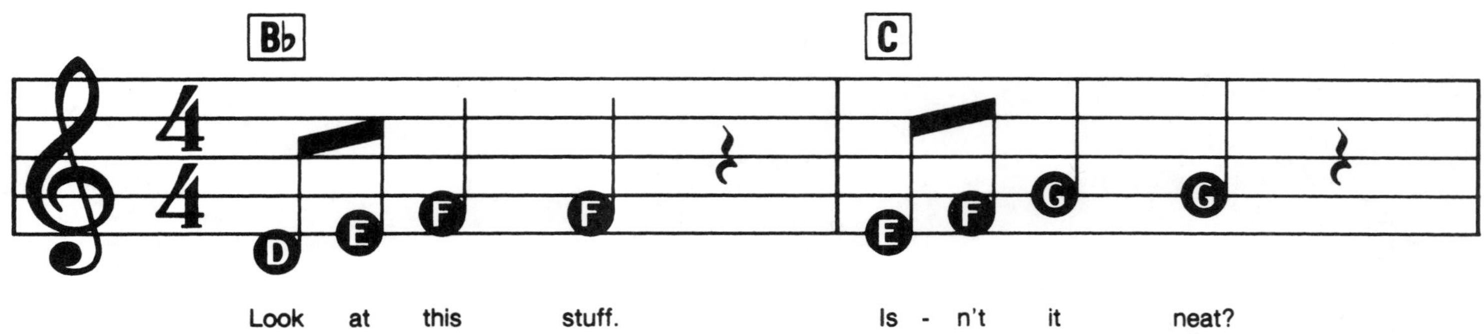

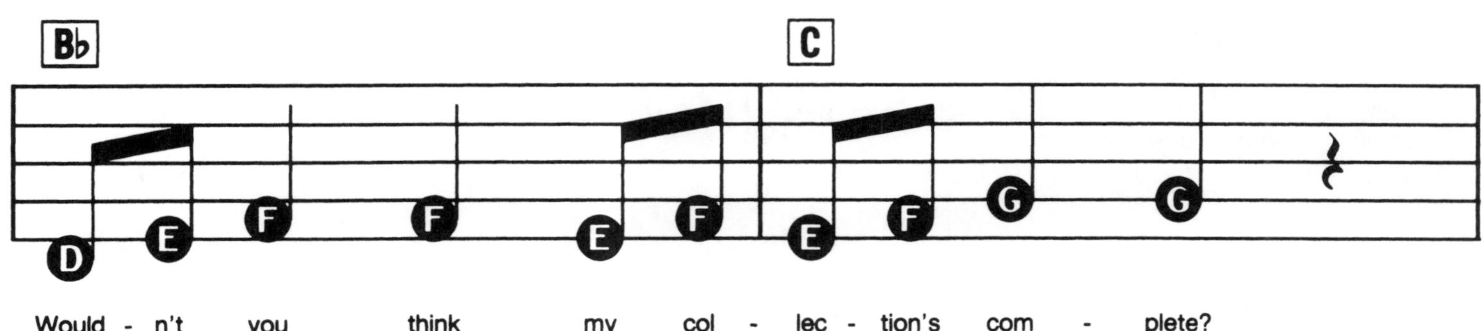

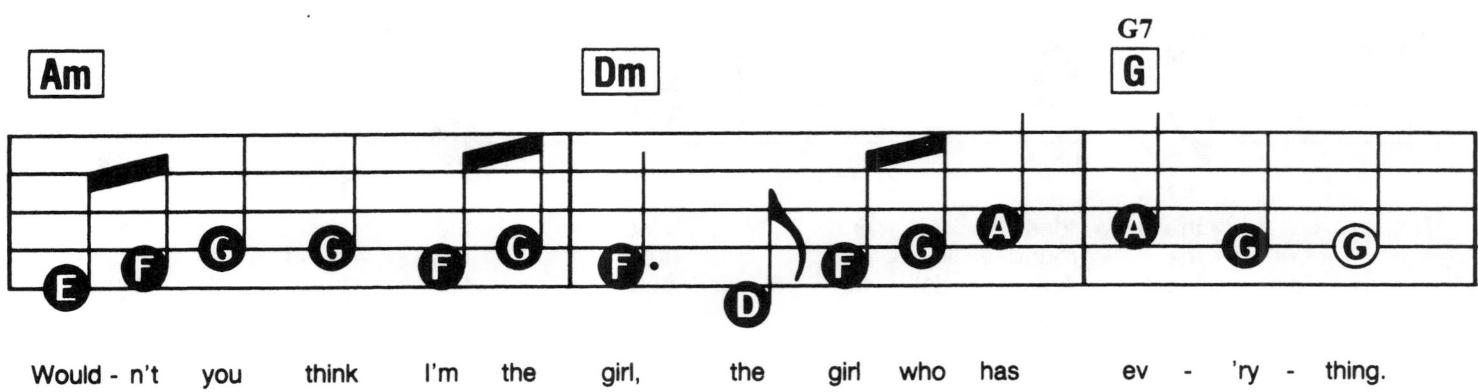

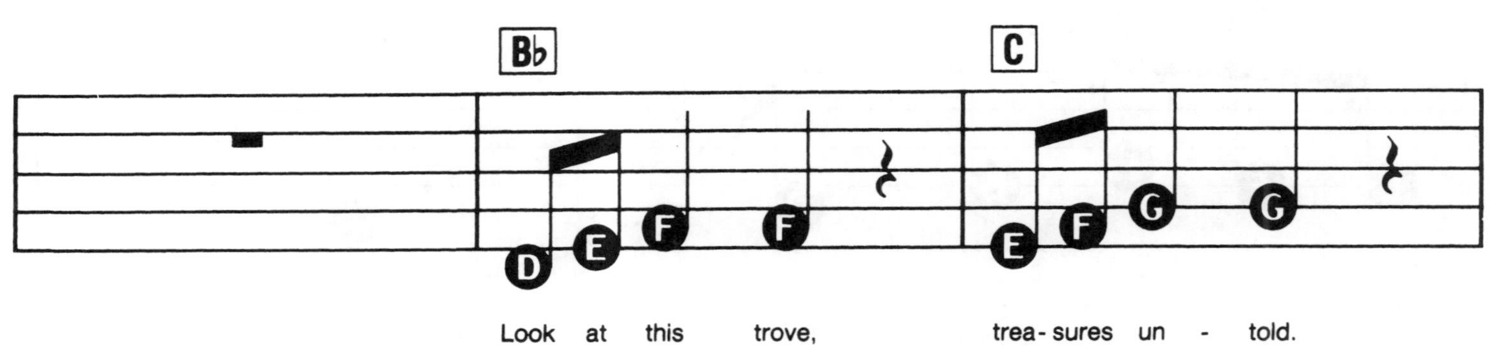

© 1988 Wonderland Music Company, Inc. and Walt Disney Music Company
All Rights Reserved. Used by Permission.

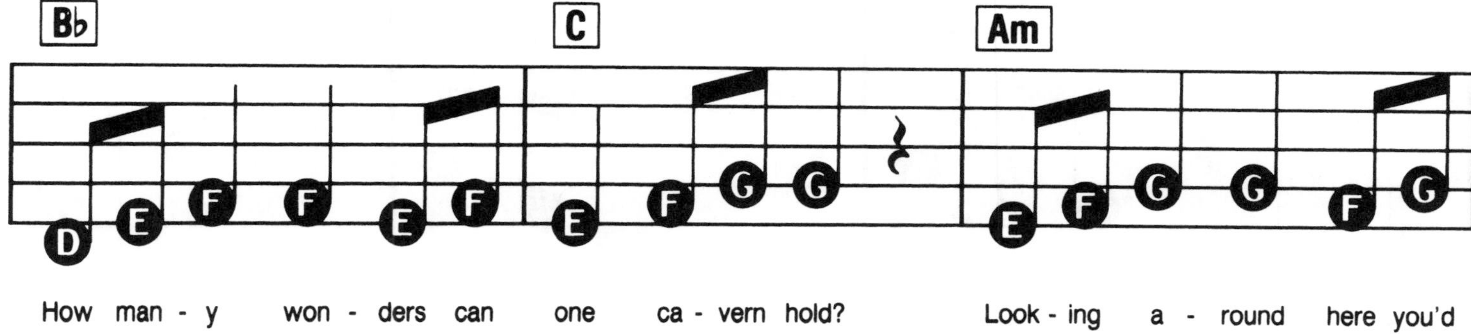
B♭
C
Am
D E F F E F E F G G E F G G F G
How man - y won - ders can one ca - vern hold? Look - ing a - round here you'd

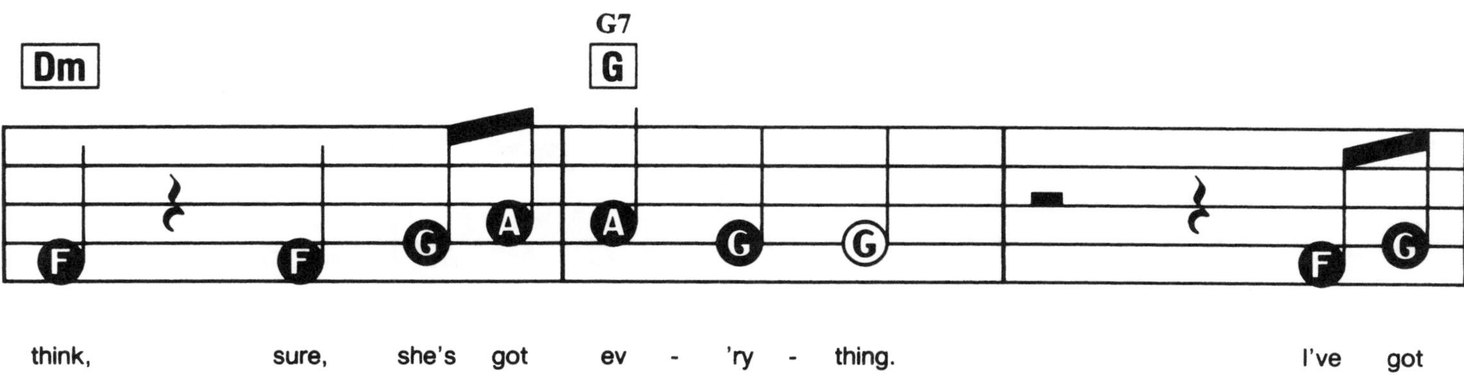
Dm
G7
G
F F G A A G G F G
think, sure, she's got ev - 'ry - thing. I've got

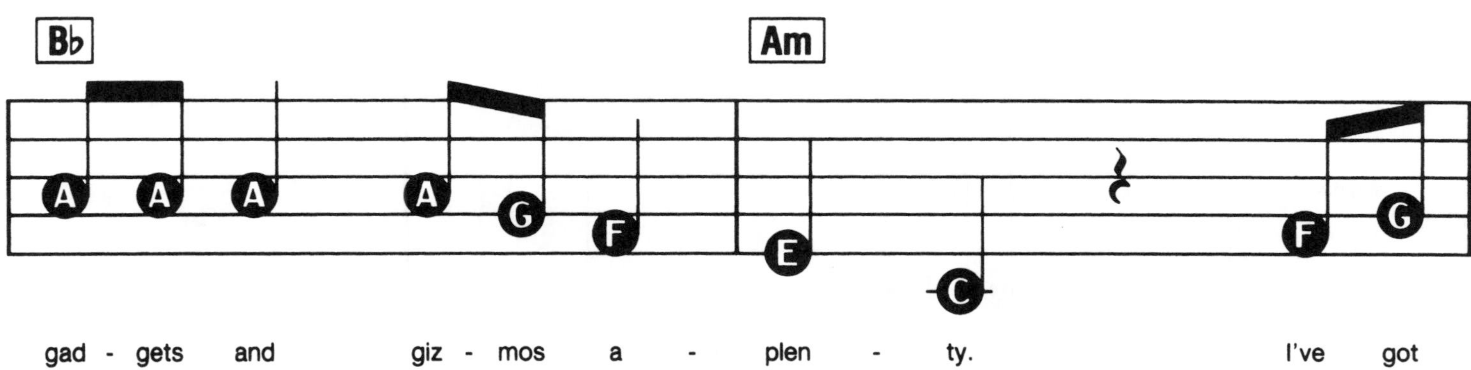
B♭
Am
A A A A G F E C F G
gad - gets and giz - mos a - plen - ty. I've got

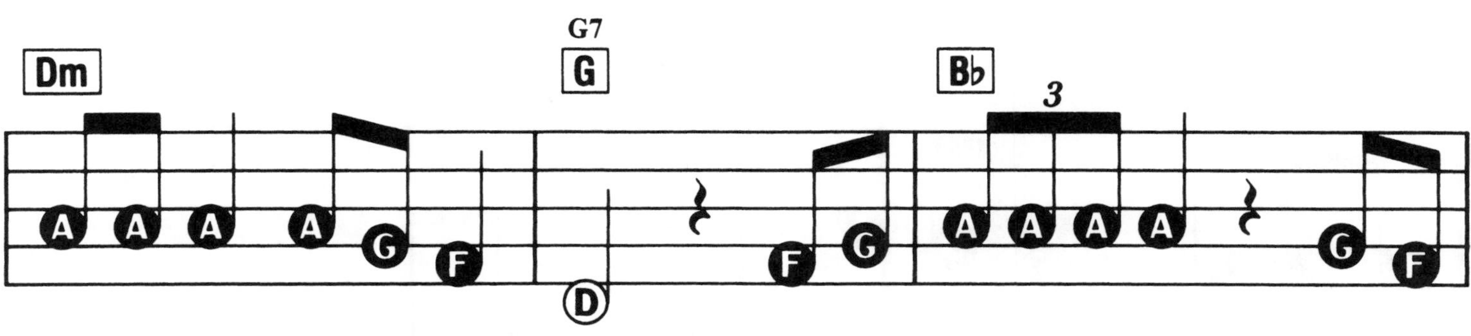
Dm
G7
G
B♭
3
A A A A G F D F G A A A A G F
who - zits and what - zits ga - lore. You want thing - a - ma - bobs, I've got

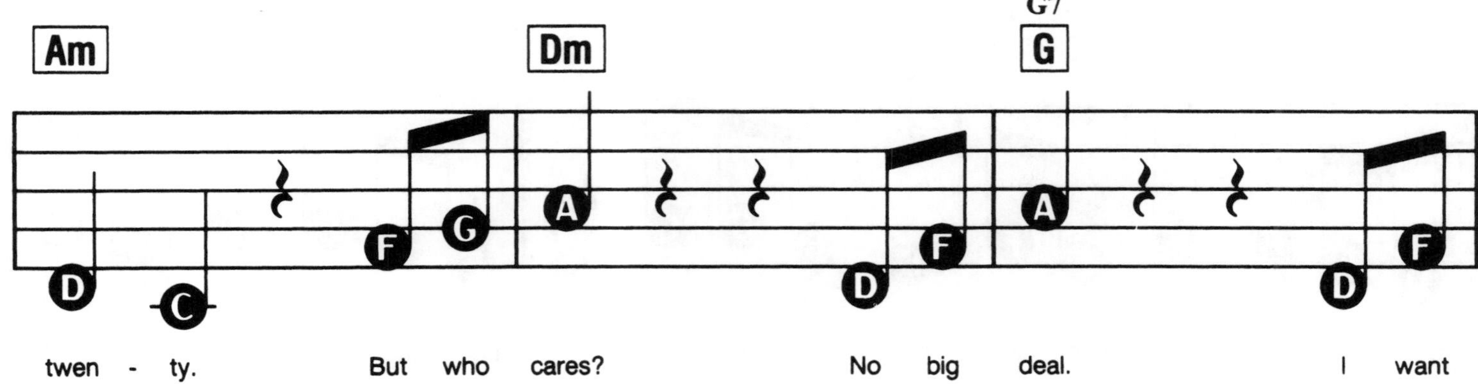
G7
Am
Dm
G
D C F G
A D F
A D F
twen - ty. But who cares? No big deal. I want

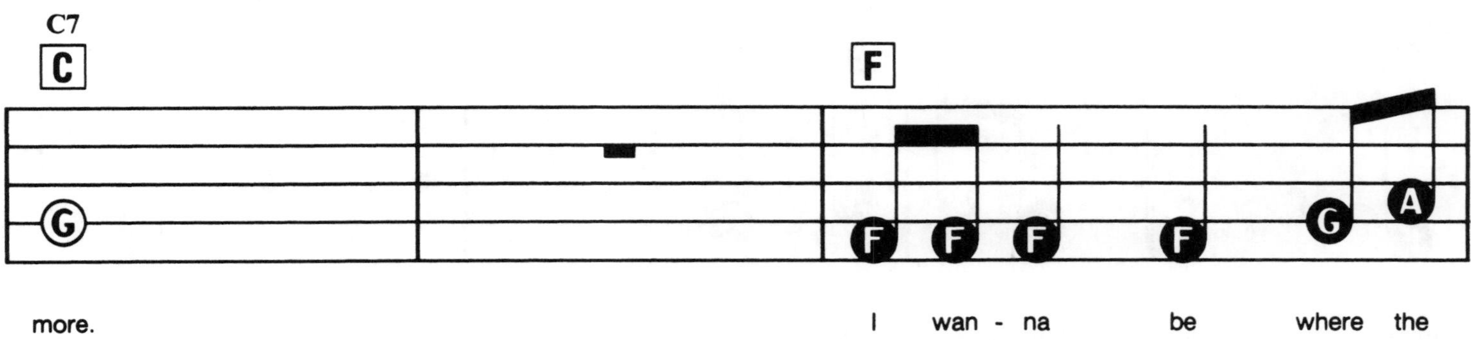
C7
C
F
G
F F F F G A
more. I wan - na be where the

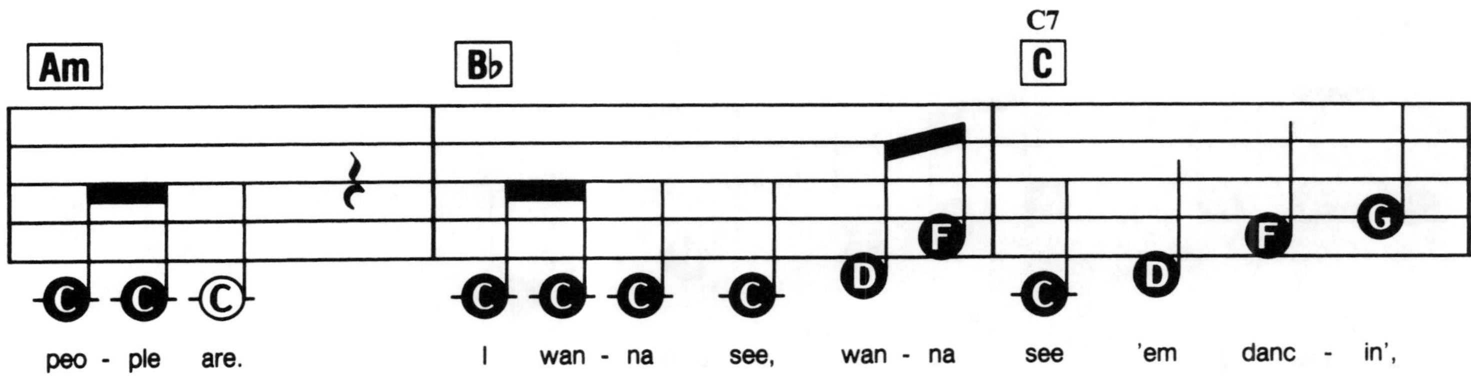
C7
Am
B♭
C
C C C
C C C C D F
C D F G
peo - ple are. I wan - na see, wan - na see 'em danc - in',

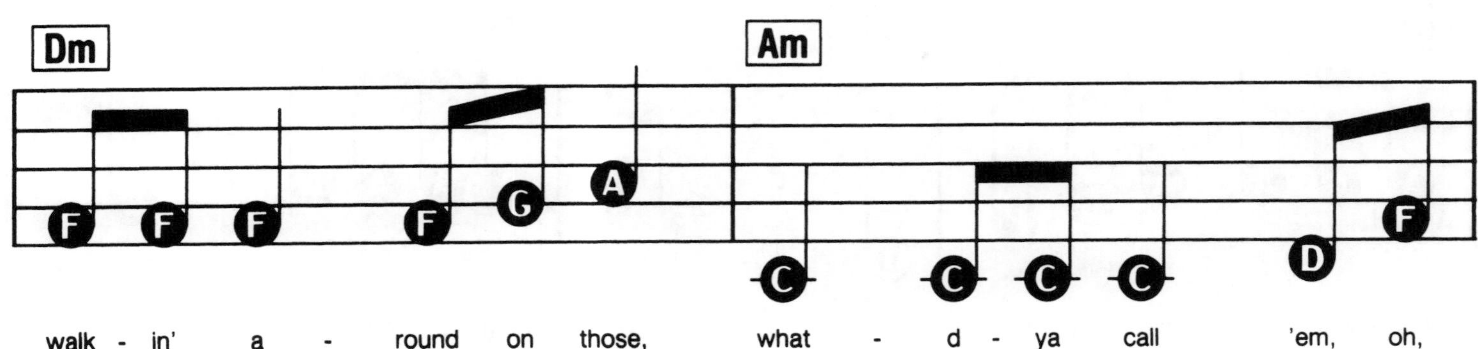
Dm
Am
F F F F G A
C C C C D F
walk - in' a - round on those, what - d - ya call 'em, oh,

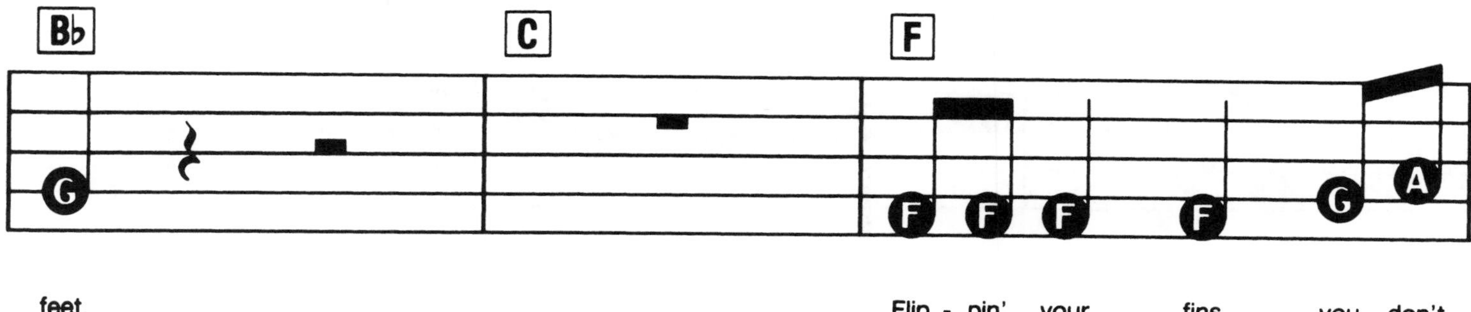
B♭
C
F
G
F F F F G A
feet.
Flip - pin' your fins you don't

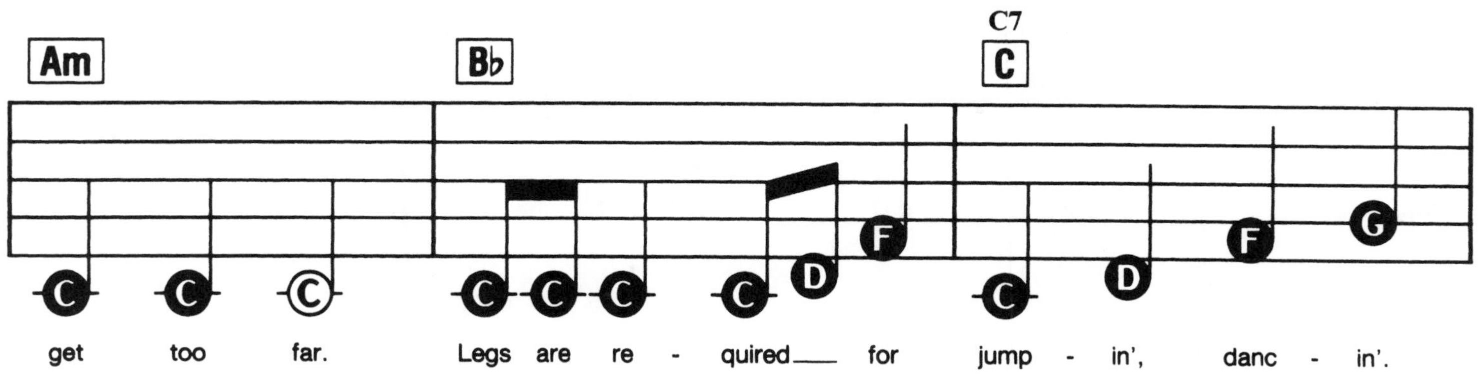
C7
Am
B♭
C
C C C
C C C C D F
C D F G
get too far.
Legs are re - quired for jump - in', danc - in'.

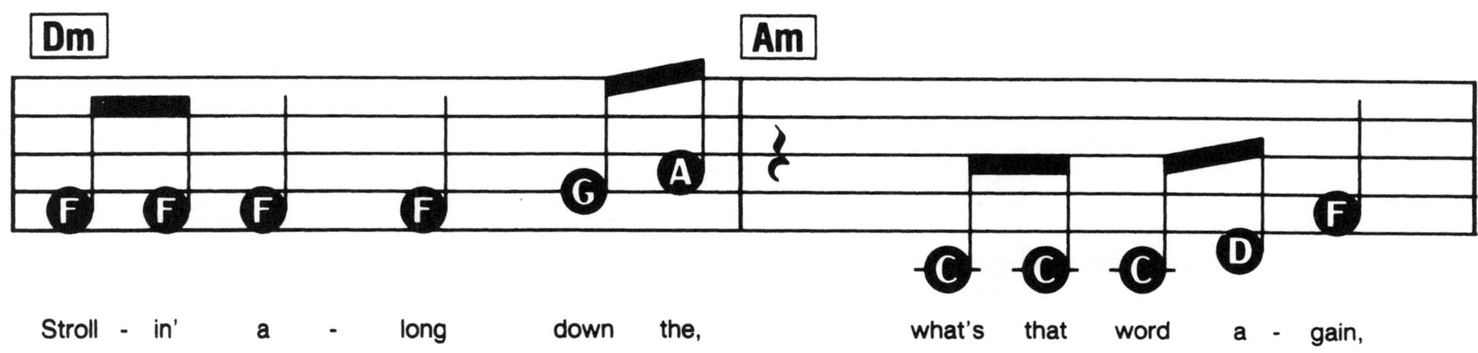
Dm
Am
F F F F G A
C C C D F
Stroll - in' a - long down the,
what's that word a - gain,

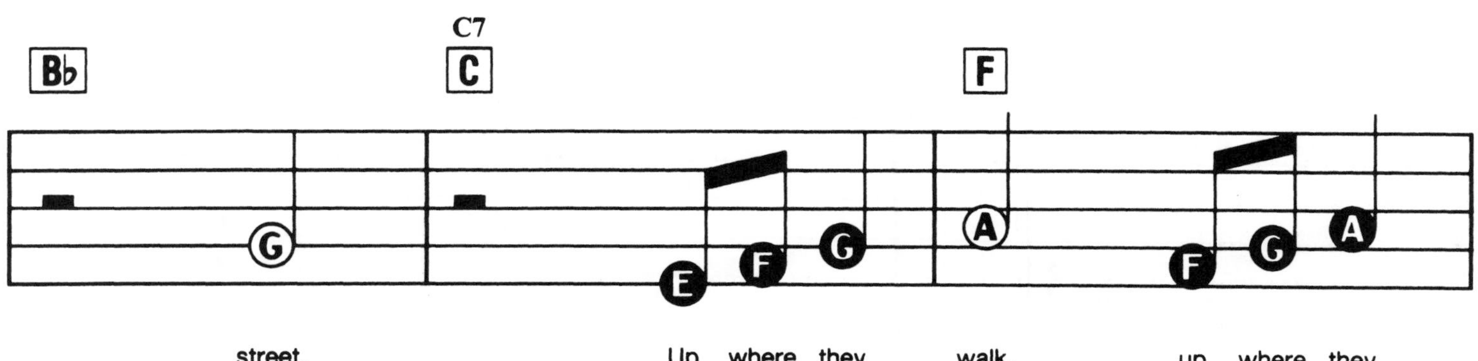
C7
B♭
C
F
G
E F G
A F G A
street.
Up where they walk,
up where they

F7 F Bb Bbm
run, up where they stay all day in the sun. Wan - der - in'
F C7 C F
free, wish I could be part of that world.
Bb C7 C
What would I give if I could live out - ta these
Am Dm Bb
wa - ters. What would I pay to spend a
C7 C Am F7 F
day warm on the sand. Bet - cha on

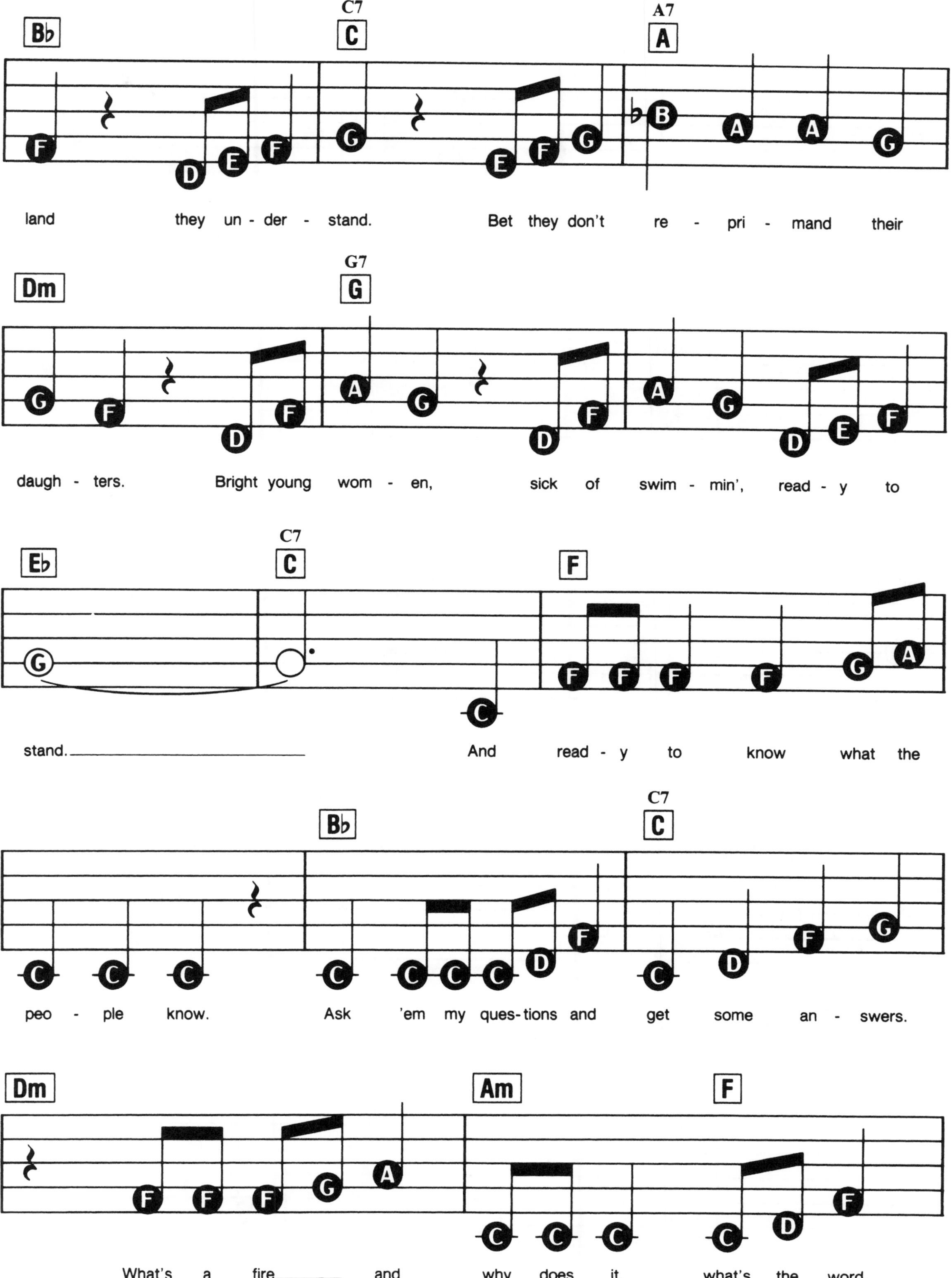
B♭ C7 C A7 A
land they un - der - stand. Bet they don't re - pri - mand their
Dm G7 G
daugh - ters. Bright young wom - en, sick of swim - min', read - y to
E♭ C7 C F
stand. And read - y to know what the
B♭ C7 C
peo - ple know. Ask 'em my ques- tions and get some an - swers.
Dm Am F
What's a fire and why does it, what's the word,

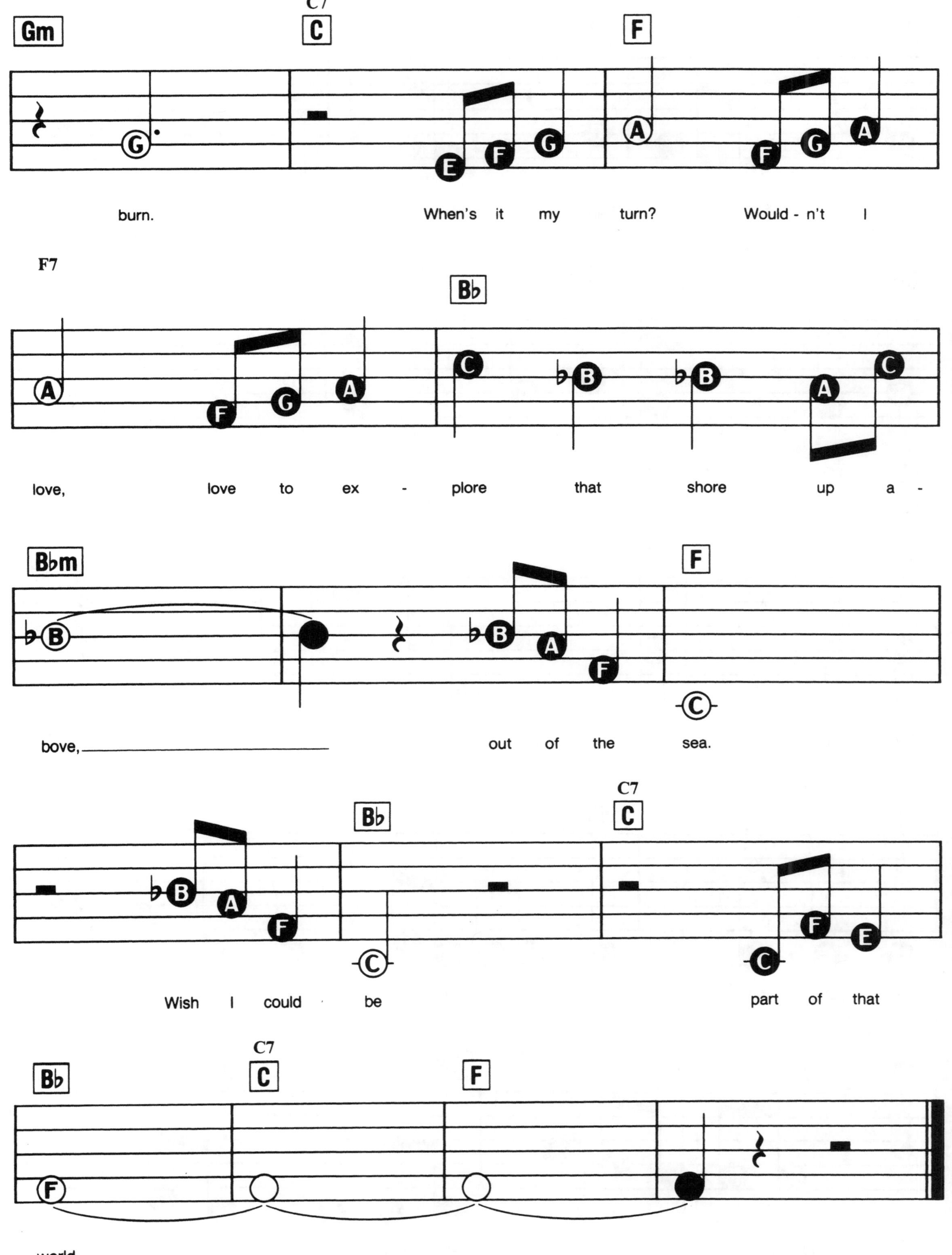
Gm C7 C F
burn. When's it my turn? Would - n't I
F7 B♭
love, love to ex - plore that shore up a -
B♭m F
bove, out of the sea.
B♭ C7 C
Wish I could be part of that
B♭ C7 C F
world.

Pop Goes the Weasel

Registration 9
Rhythm: Waltz

Traditional

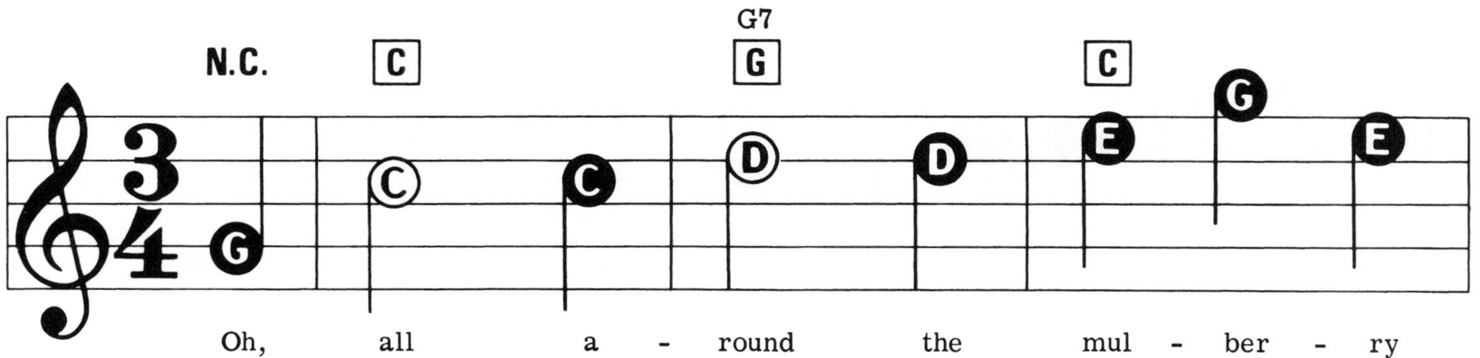

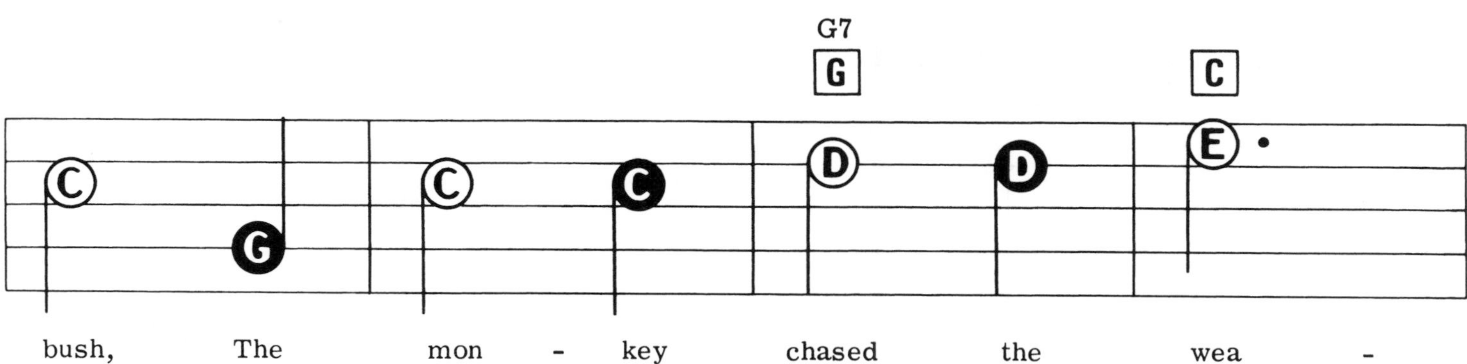

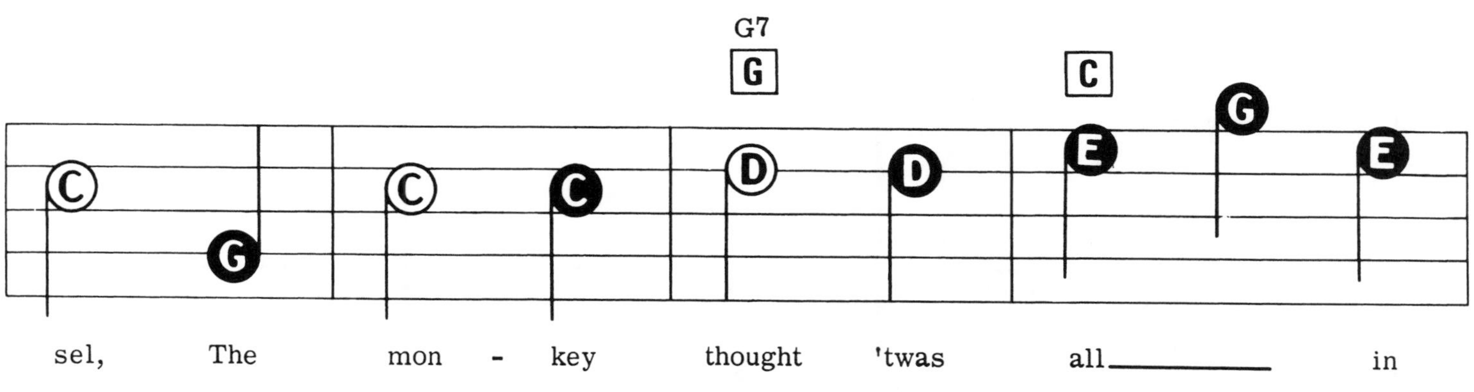

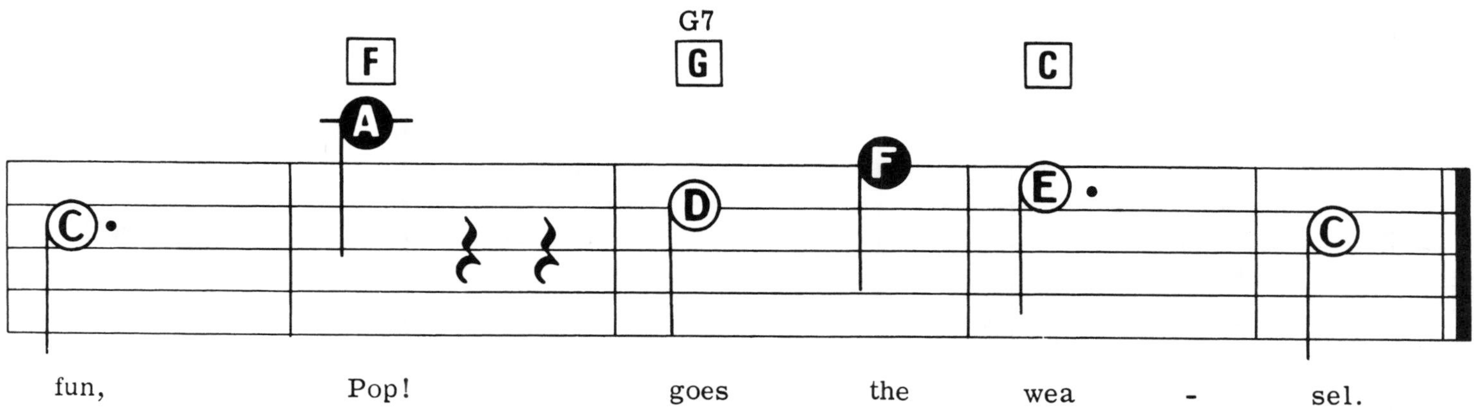

Copyright © 1977 by HAL LEONARD CORPORATION
International Copyright Secured All Rights Reserved

Peter Cottontail

Registration 1
Rhythm: Fox Trot

Words and Music by Steve Nelson
and Jack Rollins

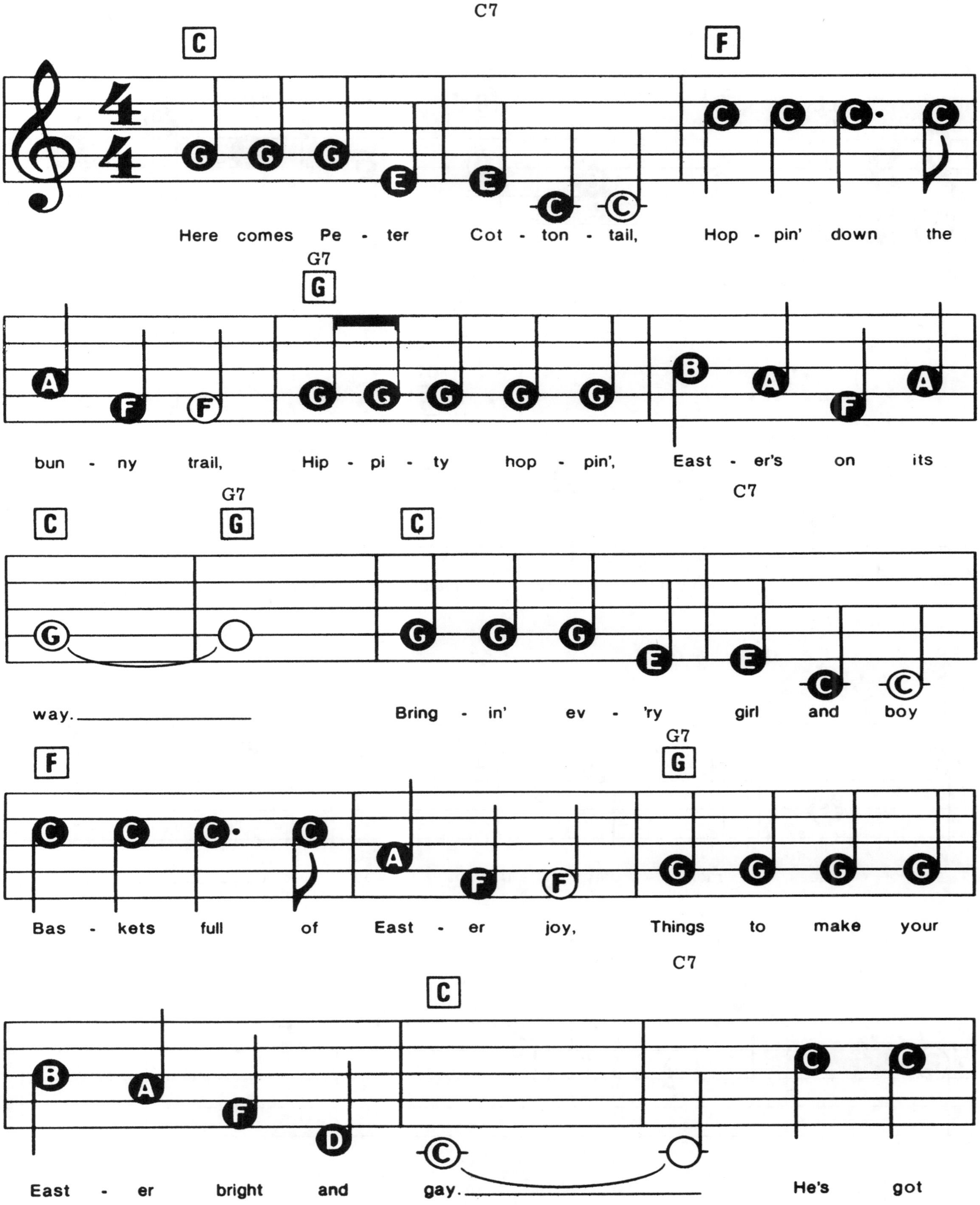

C C7 F
Here comes Pe - ter Cot - ton - tail, Hop - pin' down the

G7 G
bun - ny trail, Hip - pi - ty hop - pin', East - er's on its

C G7 G C C7
way. ___ Bring - in' ev - 'ry girl and boy

F G7 G
Bas - kets full of East - er joy, Things to make your

C C7
East - er bright and gay. ___ He's got

© 1950 (Renewed) CHAPPELL & CO., INC.
All Rights Reserved Used by Permission

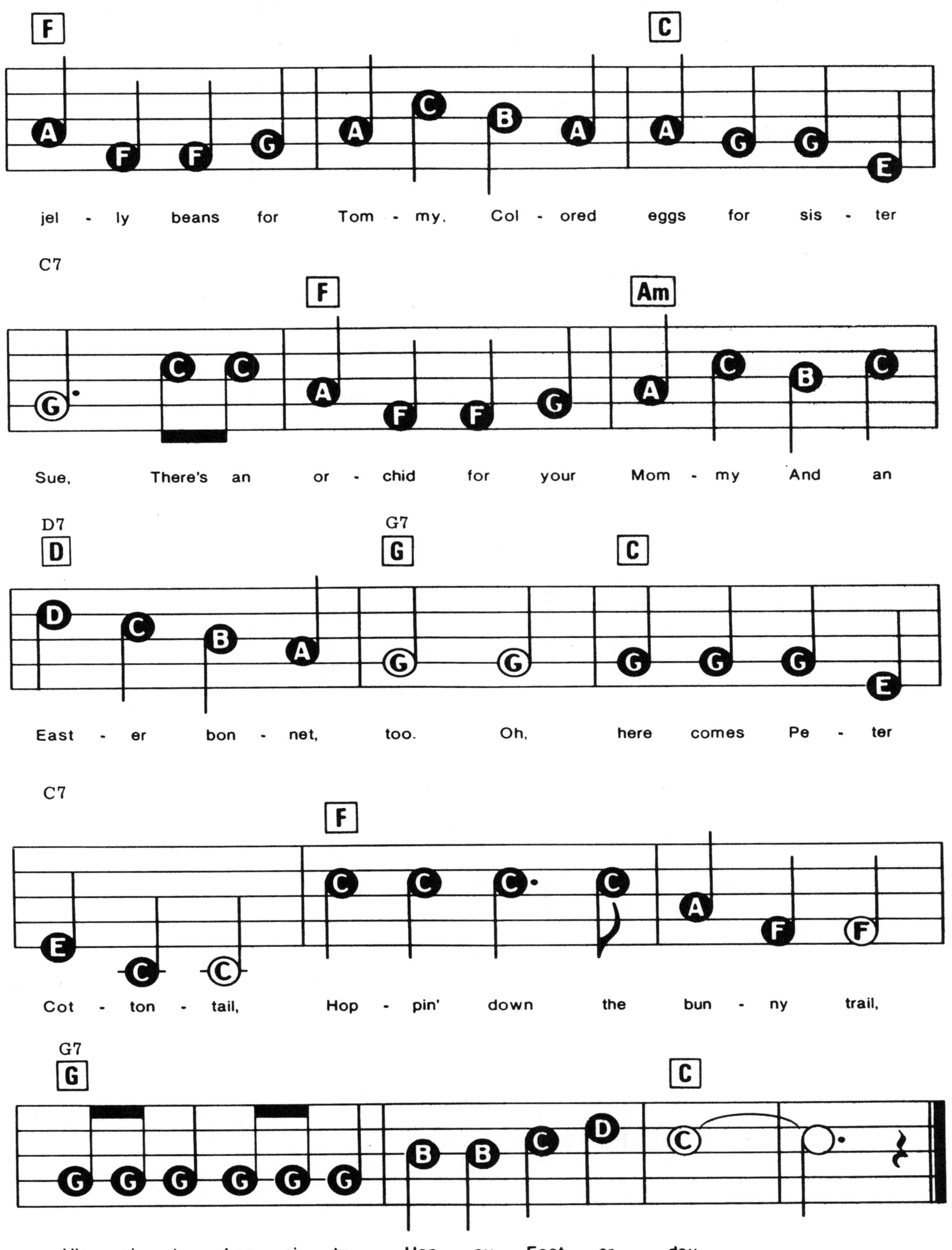
F C
jel - ly beans for Tom - my. Col - ored eggs for sis - ter
C7 F Am
Sue, There's an or - chid for your Mom - my And an
D7 D G7 G C
East - er bon - net, too. Oh, here comes Pe - ter
C7 F
Cot - ton - tail, Hop - pin' down the bun - ny trail,
G7 G C
Hip - pi - ty hop - pi - ty, Hap - py East - er day.

Puff the Magic Dragon

Registration 2
Rhythm: Swing

Words and Music by Lenny Lipton and
Peter Yarrow

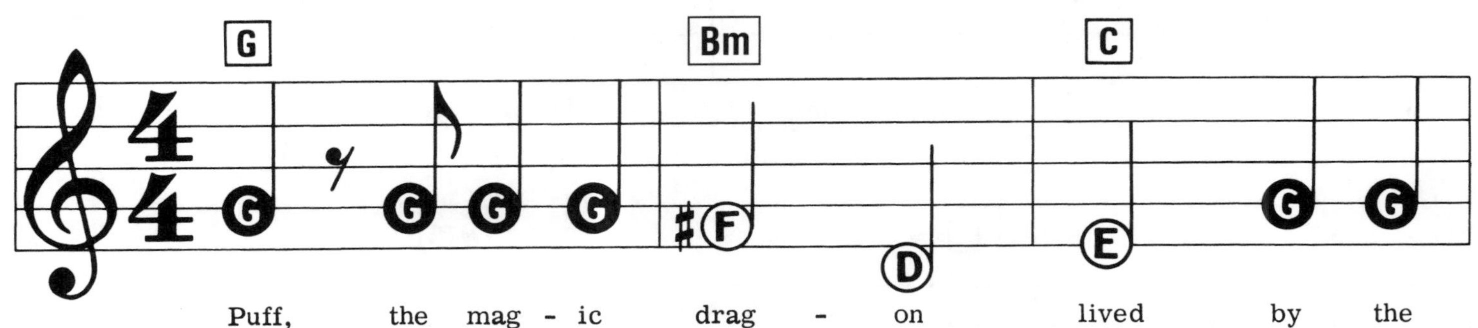

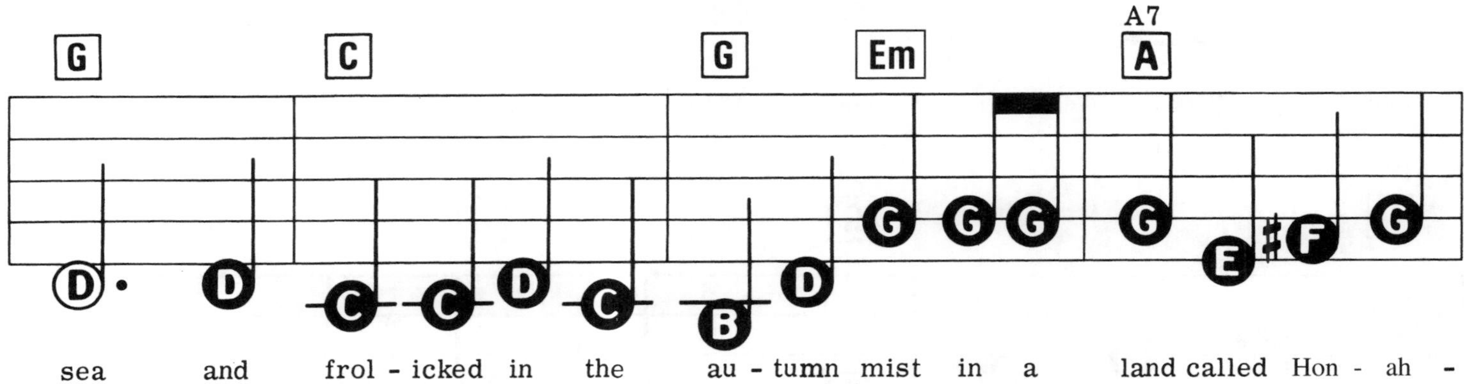

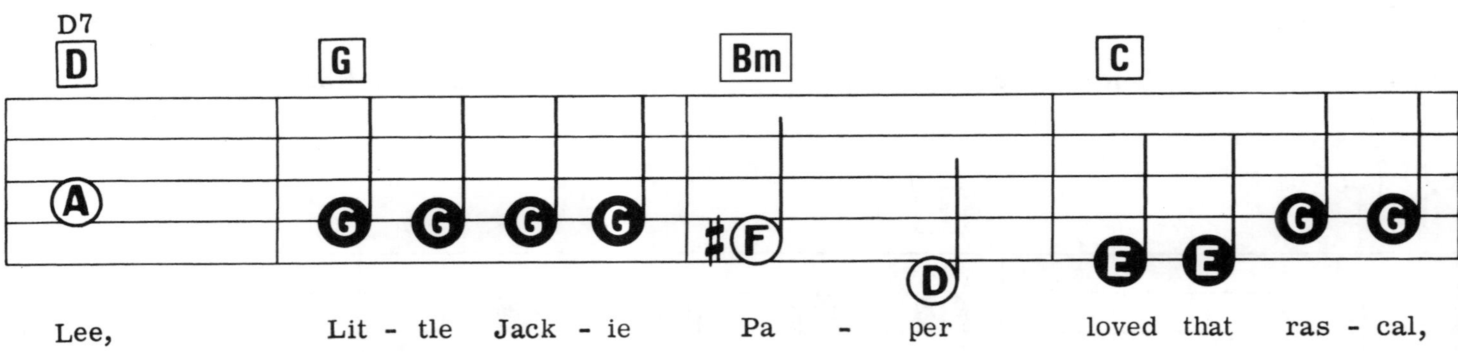

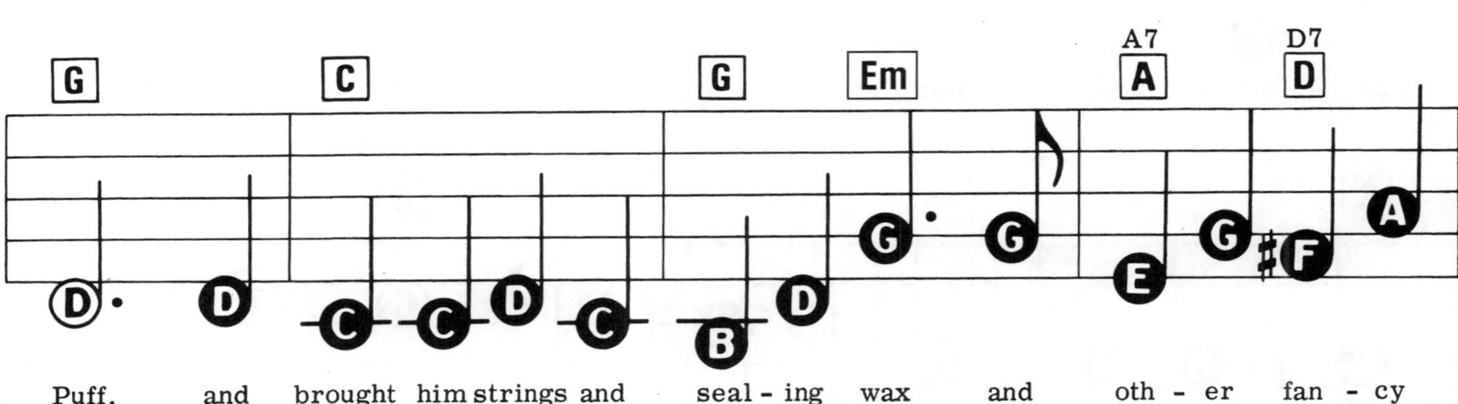

Copyright © 1963; Renewed 1991 Honalee Melodies (ASCAP) and Silver Dawn Music (ASCAP)
Worldwide Rights for Honalee Melodies Administered by BMG Rights Management (US) LLC
Worldwide Rights for Silver Dawn Music Administered by WB Music Corp.
International Copyright Secured All Rights Reserved

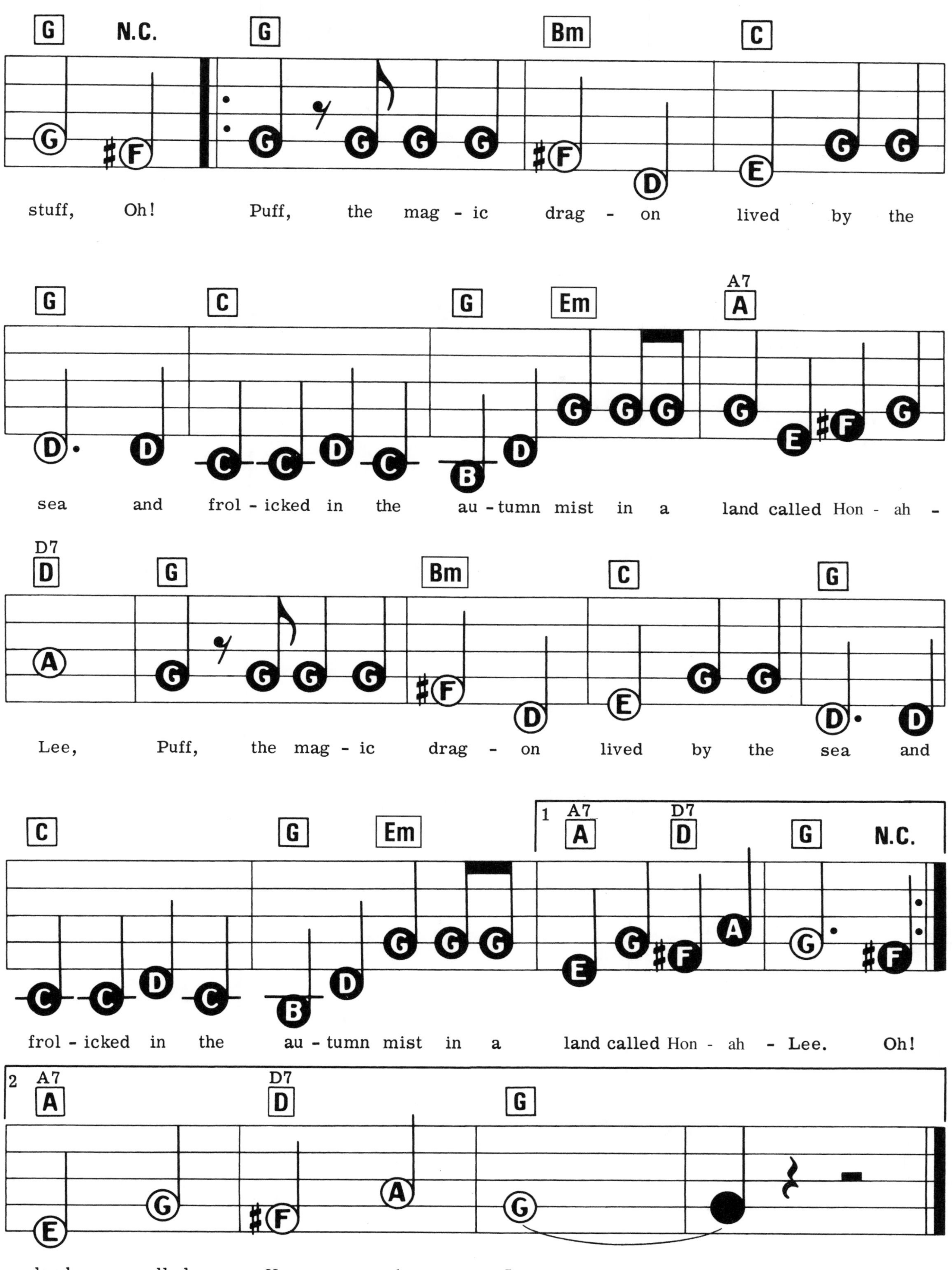
G N.C. G Bm C
stuff, Oh! Puff, the mag - ic drag - on lived by the
G C G Em A7 A
sea and frol - icked in the au - tumn mist in a land called Hon - ah -
D7 D G Bm C G
Lee, Puff, the mag - ic drag - on lived by the sea and
C G Em 1 A7 A D7 D G N.C.
frol - icked in the au - tumn mist in a land called Hon - ah - Lee. Oh!
2 A7 A D7 D G
land called Hon - ah - Lee.

Que Sera, Sera

from THE MAN WHO KNEW TOO MUCH

Registration 10
Rhythm: Waltz

Words and Music by Jay Livingston
and Raymond B. Evans

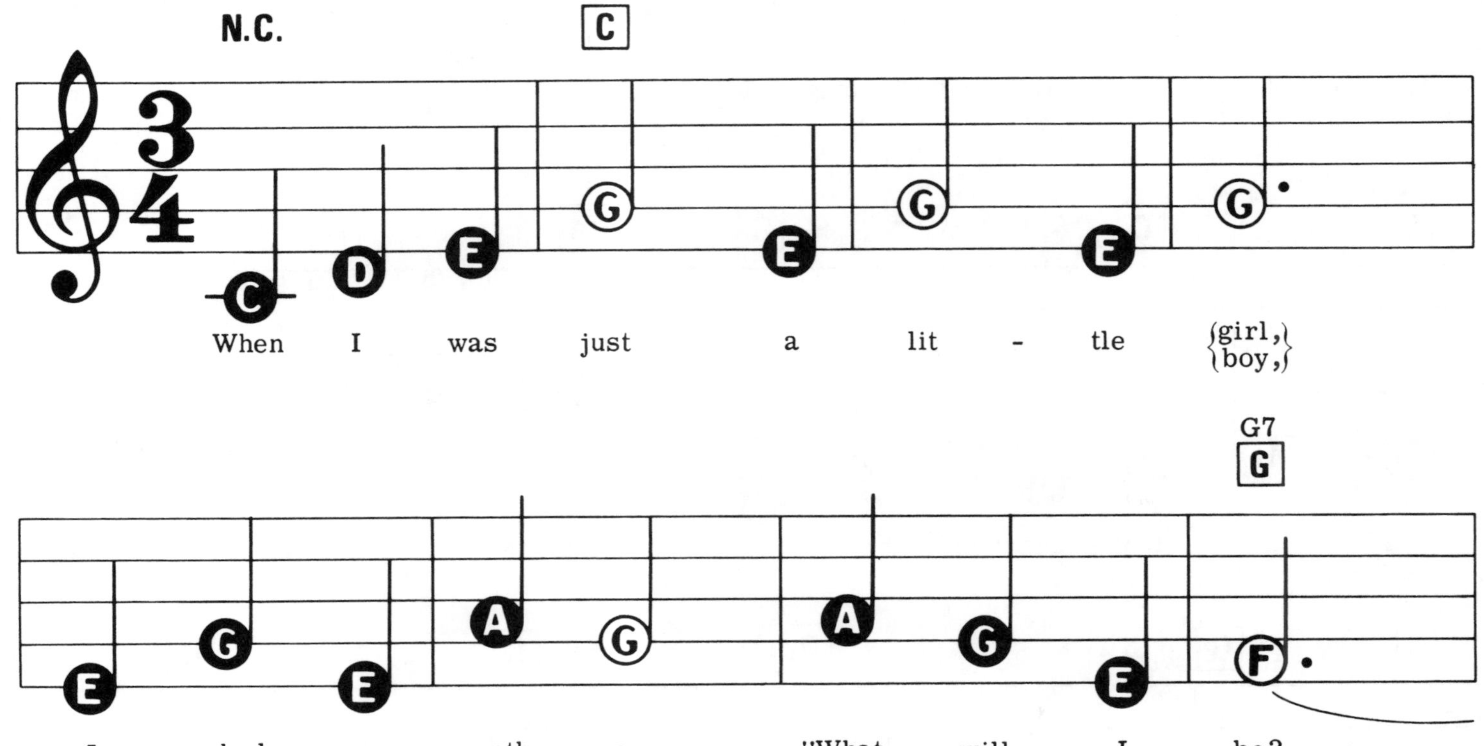

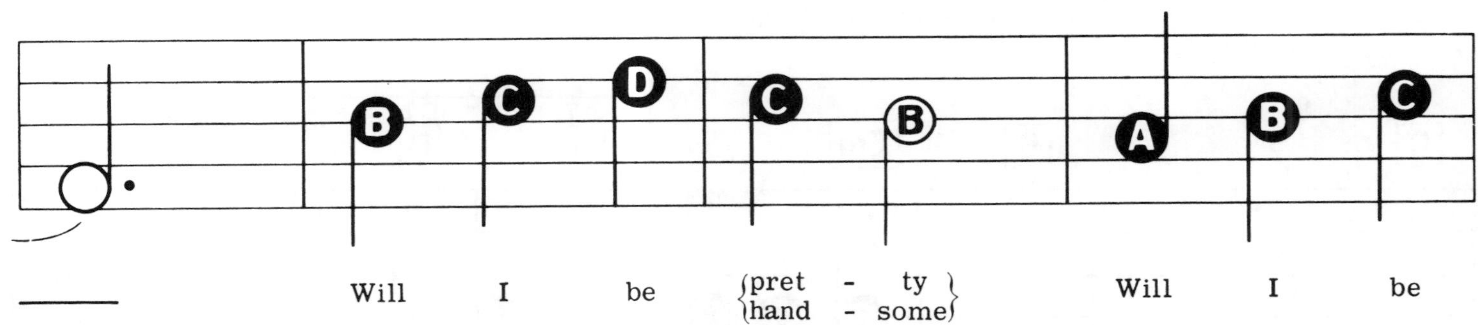

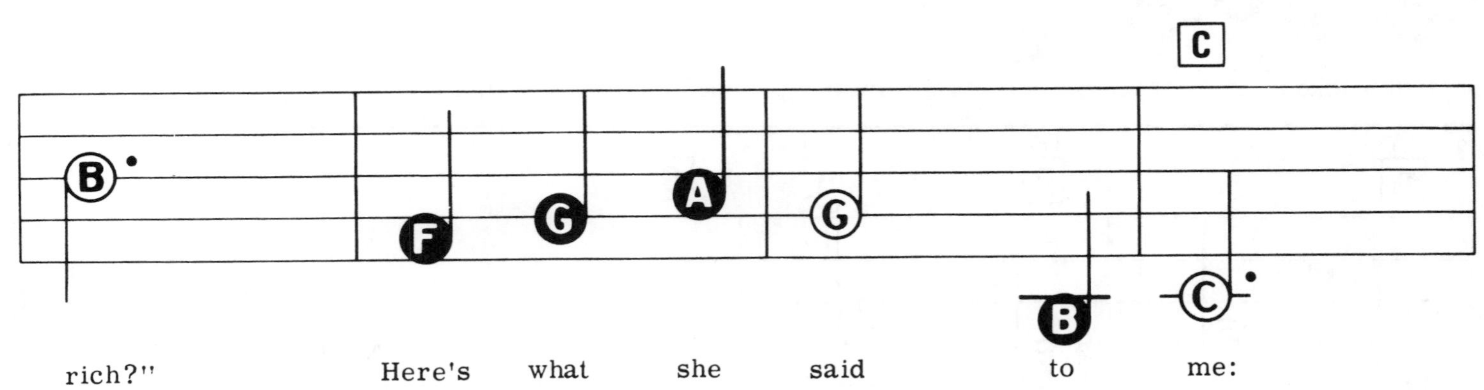

Copyright © 1955 by JAY LIVINGSTON MUSIC and ST. ANGELO MUSIC
Copyright Renewed
All Rights Reserved Used by Permission

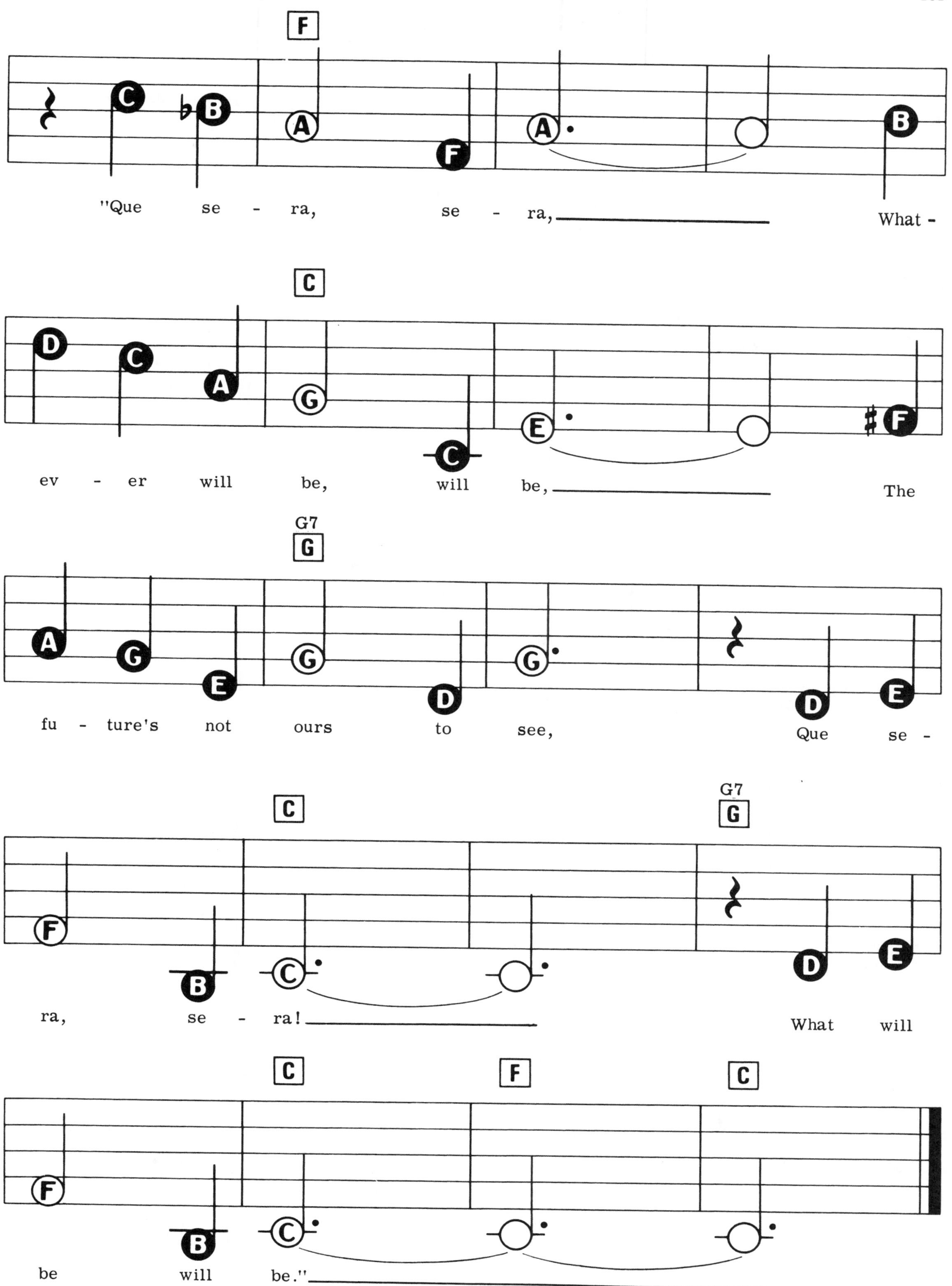
F
C
B
A
F
A
B
"Que se - ra, se - ra, What -
C
D
C
A
G
C
E
F
ev - er will be, will be, The
G7
G
A
G
E
G
D
G
D
E
fu - ture's not ours to see, Que se -
C
G7
G
F
B
C
D
E
ra, se - ra! What will
C
F
C
F
B
C
be will be."

The Rainbow Connection

from THE MUPPET MOVIE

Registration 4
Rhythm: Waltz

Words and Music by Paul Williams
and Kenneth L. Ascher

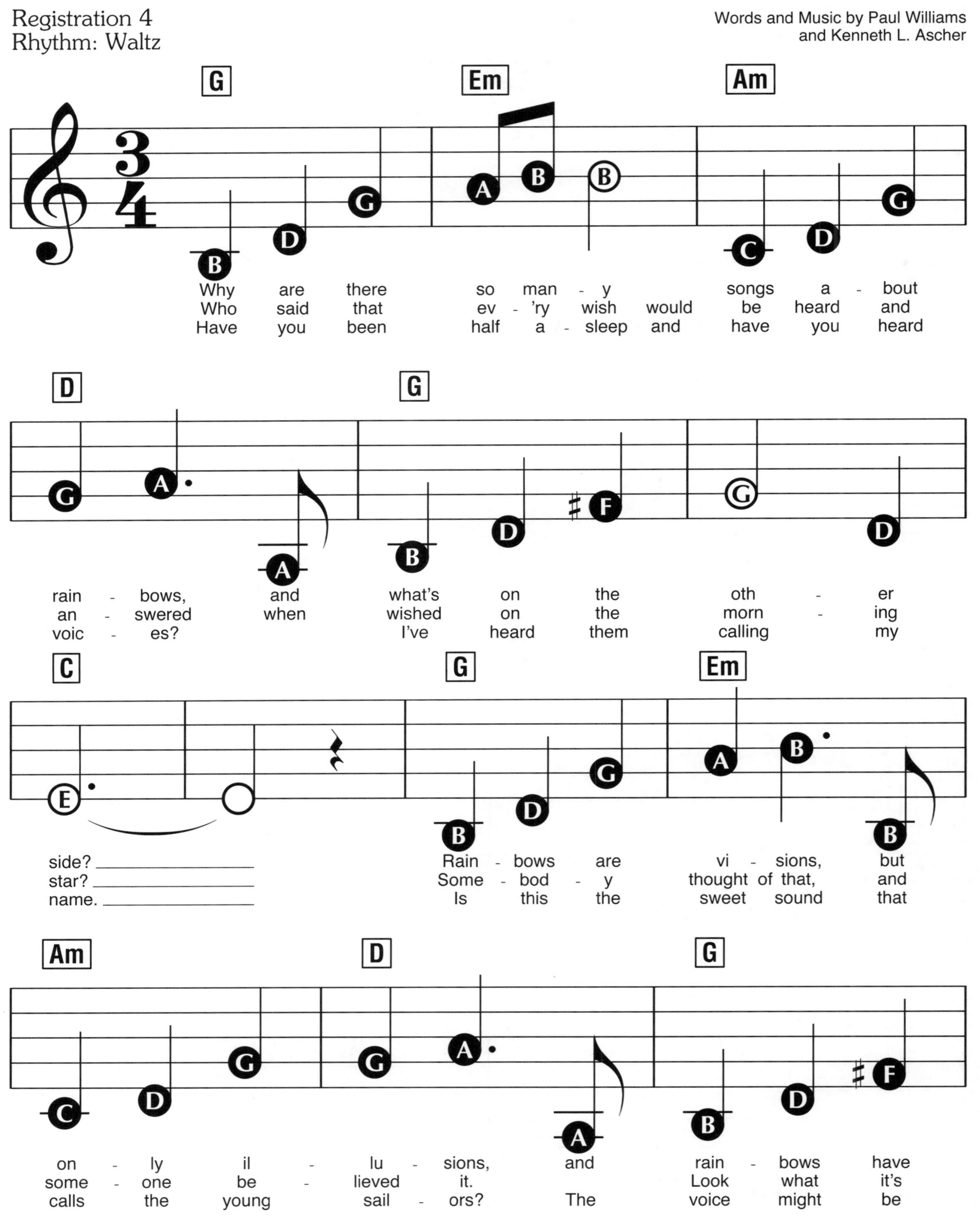

© 1979 Fuzzy Muppet Songs
All Rights Reserved Used by Permission

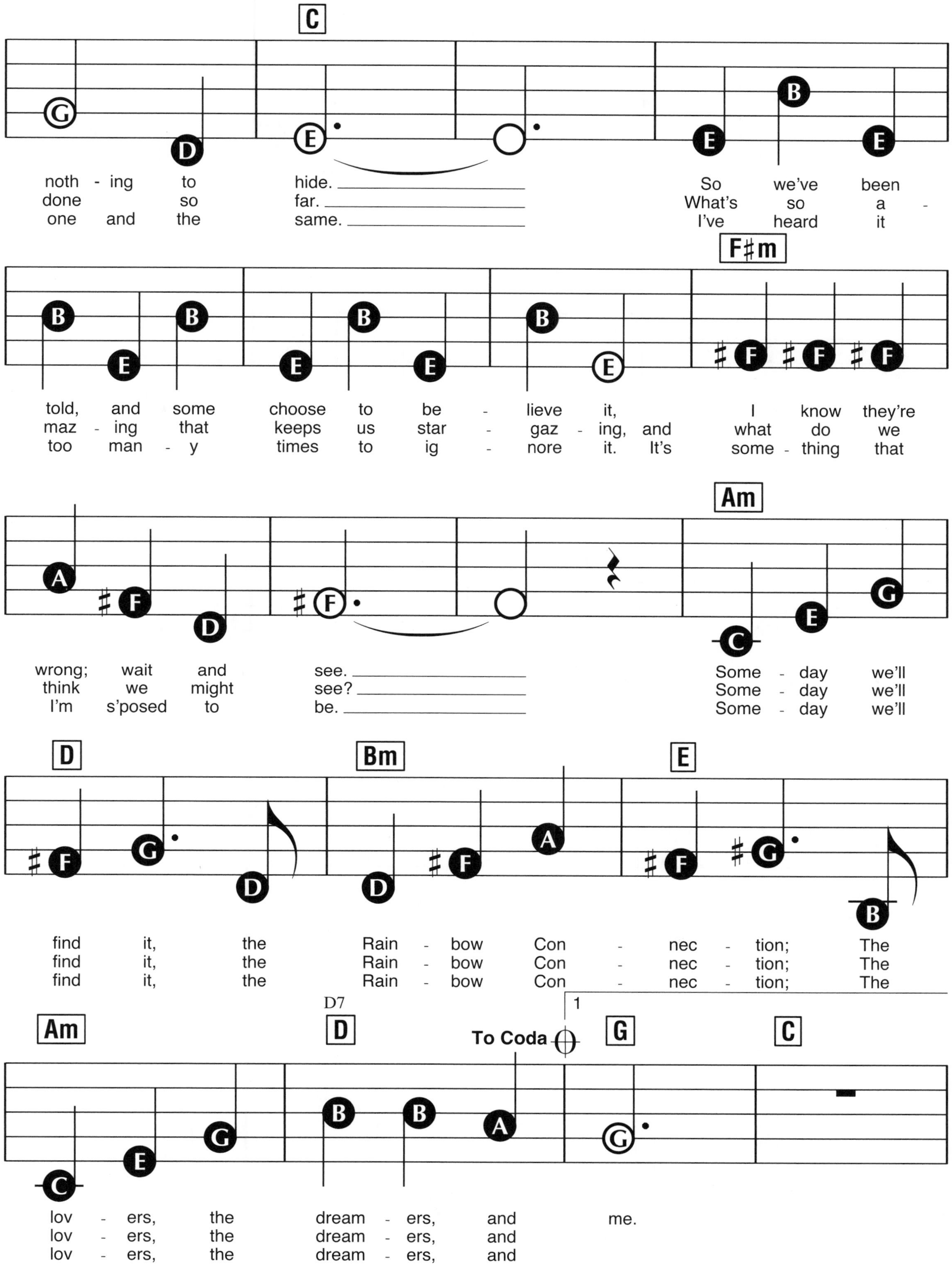
C
G D E E B E
noth - ing to hide.
done so far.
one and the same.
So we've been
What's so a -
I've heard it
B E B E B E B E
F♯m
F F F
told, and some choose to be - lieve it,
maz - ing that keeps us star - gaz - ing, and
too man - y times to ig - nore it. It's
I know they're
what do we
some - thing that
A F D F
Am
C E G
wrong; wait and see.
think we might see?
I'm s'posed to be.
Some - day we'll
D
F G D
Bm
D F A
E
F G B
find it, the Rain - bow Con - nec - tion; The
Am
C E G
D7
D
B B A
To Coda
1
G
G
C
lov - ers, the dream - ers, and me.
lov - ers, the dream - ers, and
lov - ers, the dream - ers, and

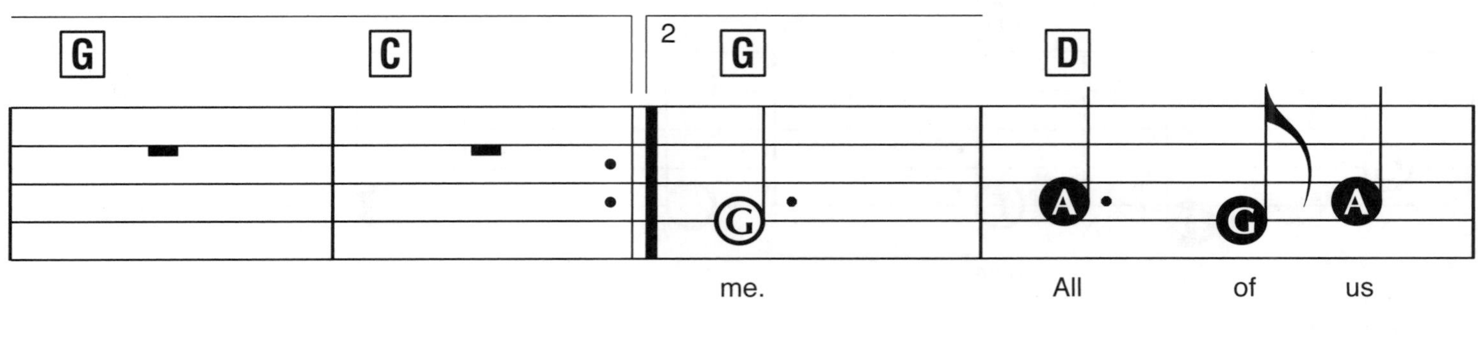
G
C
2
G
D
G
A
G
A
me.
All of us

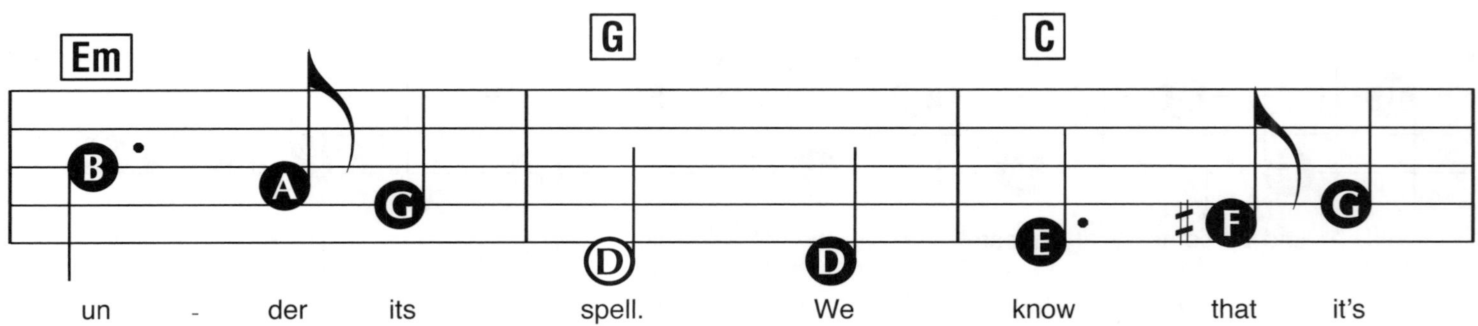
Em
G
C
B
A
G
D
D
E
♯F
G
un - der its
spell.
We
know that it's

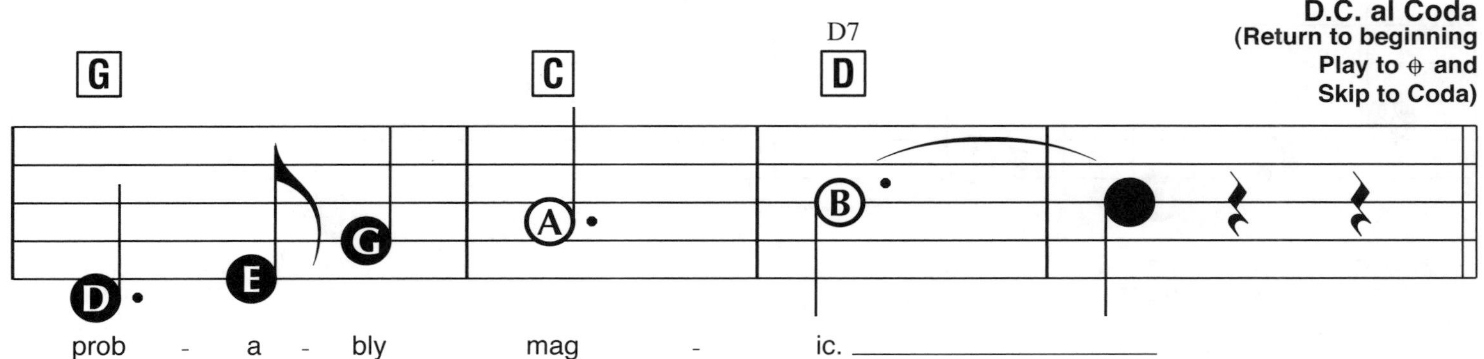
D.C. al Coda
(Return to beginning
Play to ⊕ and
Skip to Coda)
G
C
D7
D
D
E
G
A
B
prob - a - bly
mag - ic.

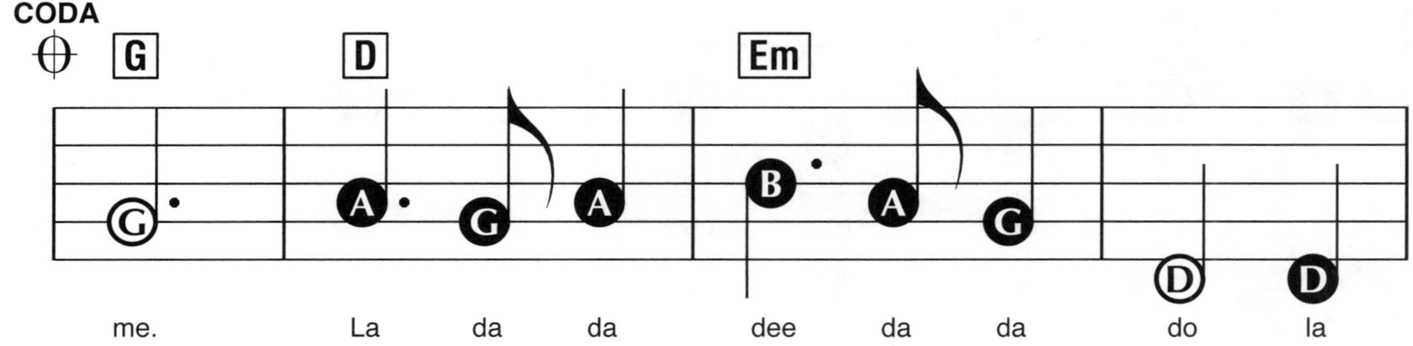
CODA
G
D
Em
G
A
G
A
B
A
G
D
D
me.
La da da
dee da da
do la

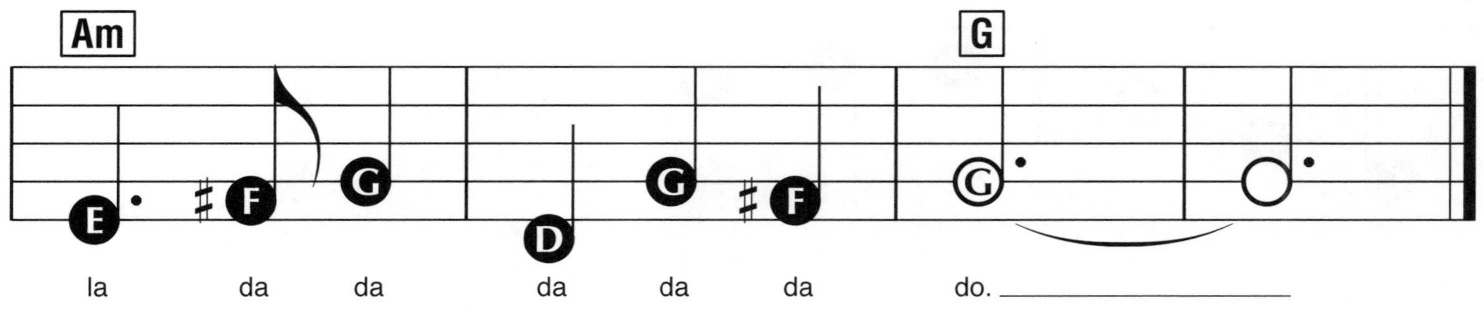
Am
G
E
♯F
G
D
G
♯F
G
la da da
da da da
do.

Row, Row, Row Your Boat

Registration 5
Rhythm: Waltz

Traditional

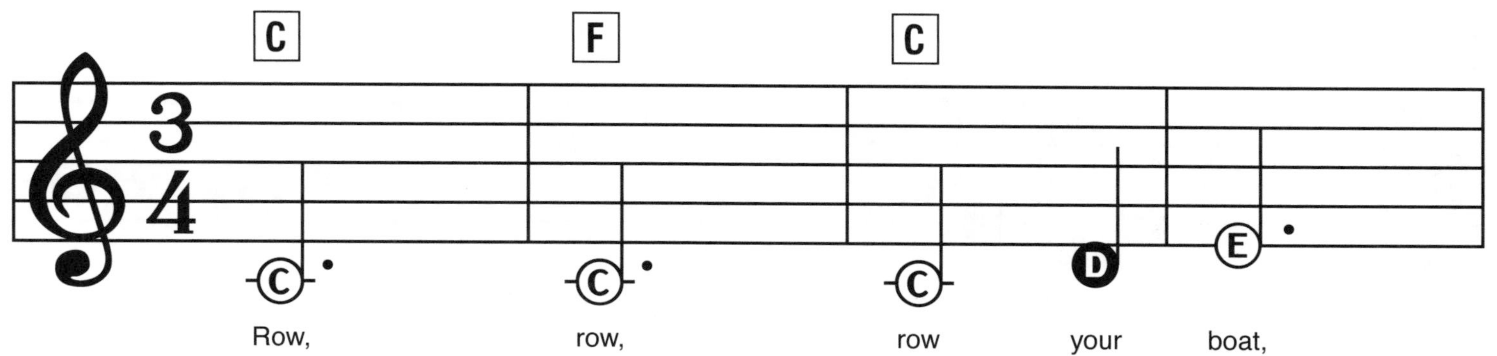

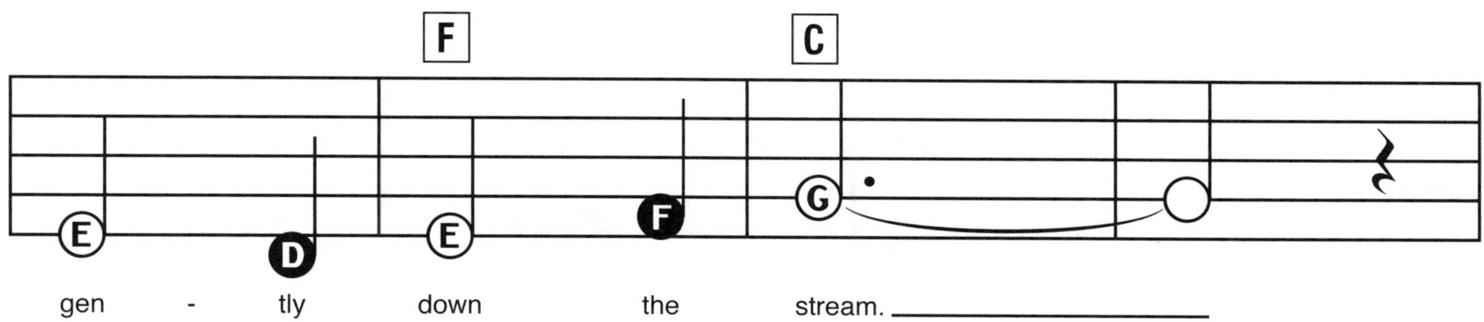

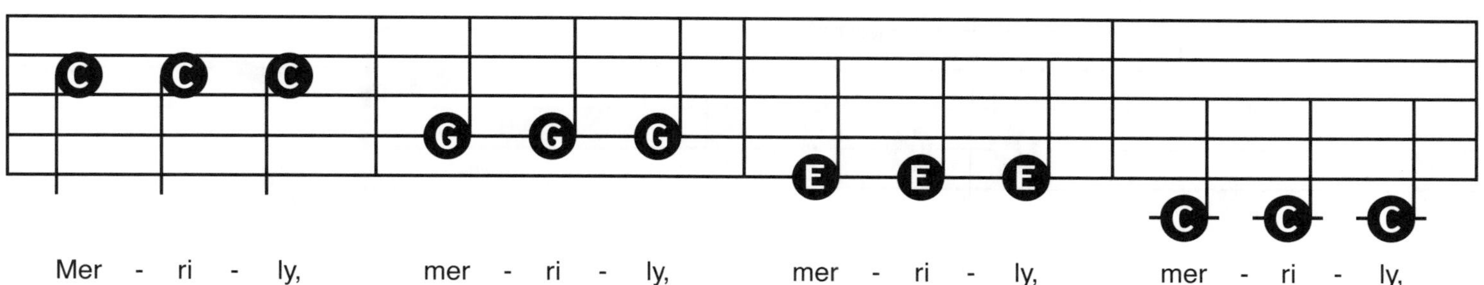

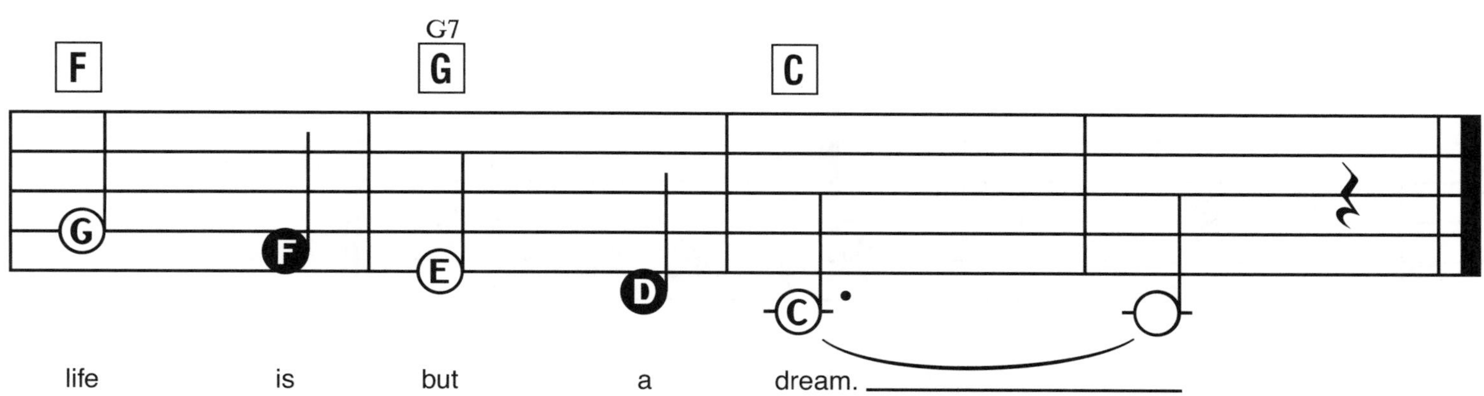

Copyright © 2012 by HAL LEONARD CORPORATION
International Copyright Secured All Rights Reserved

Rubber Duckie

from the Television Series SESAME STREET

Registration 9
Rhythm: Swing or Shuffle

Words and Music by
Jeff Moss

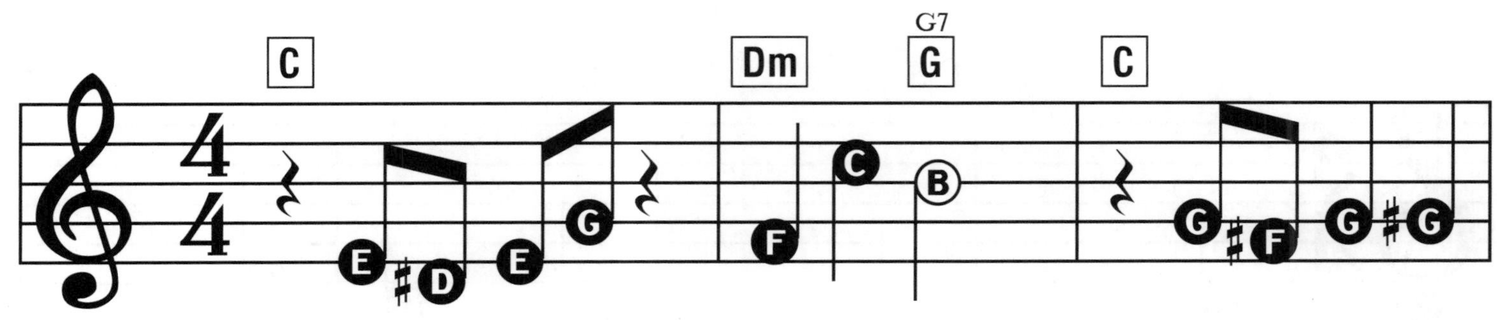

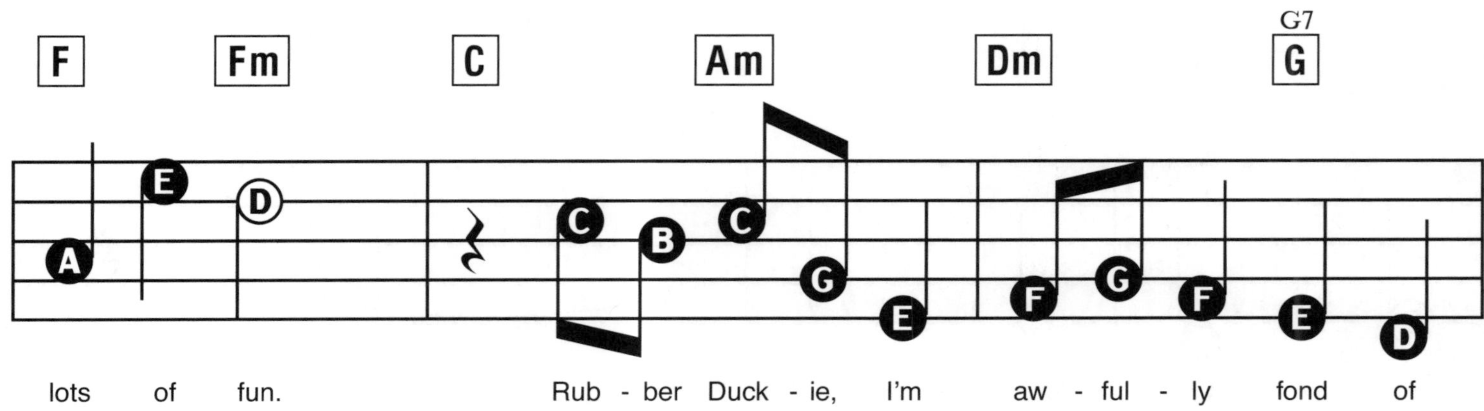

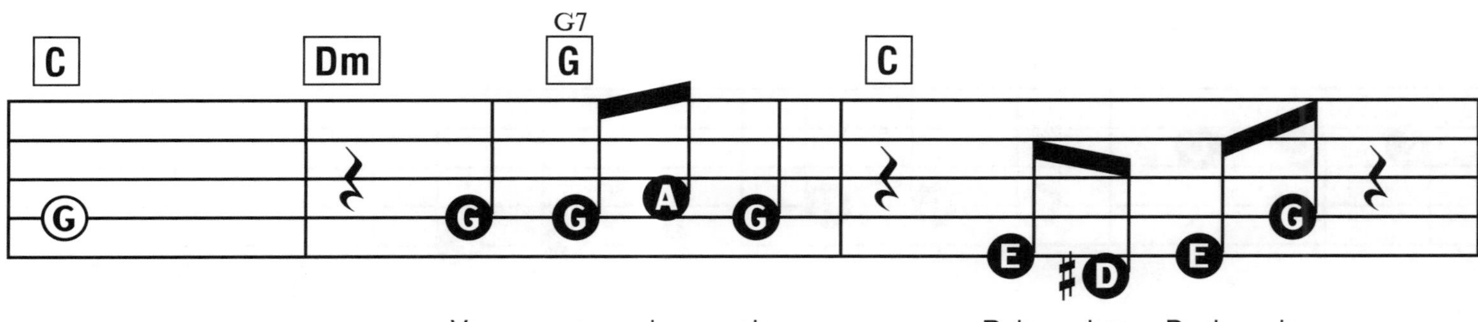

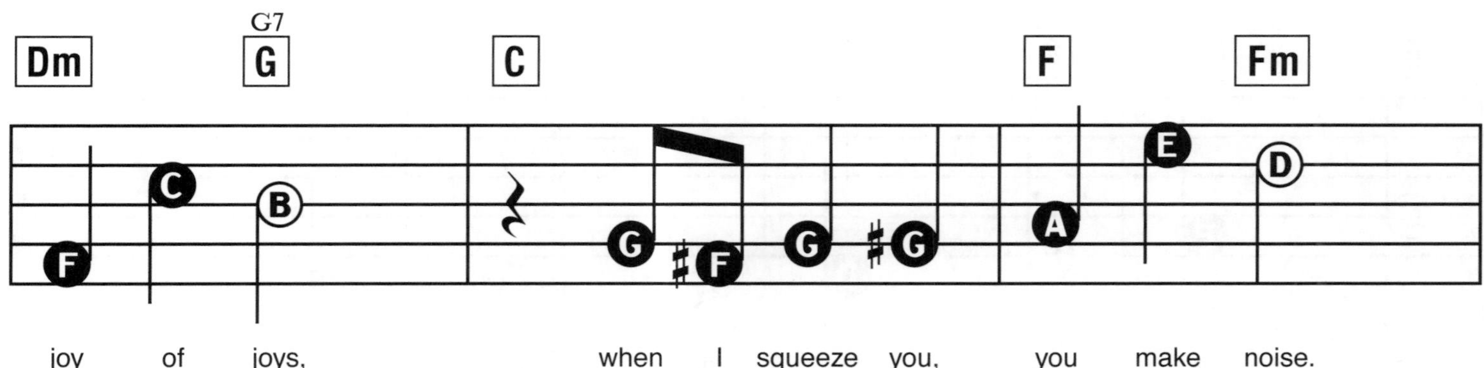

Copyright © 1970 Festival Attractions, Inc.
Copyright Renewed
International Copyright Secured All Rights Reserved

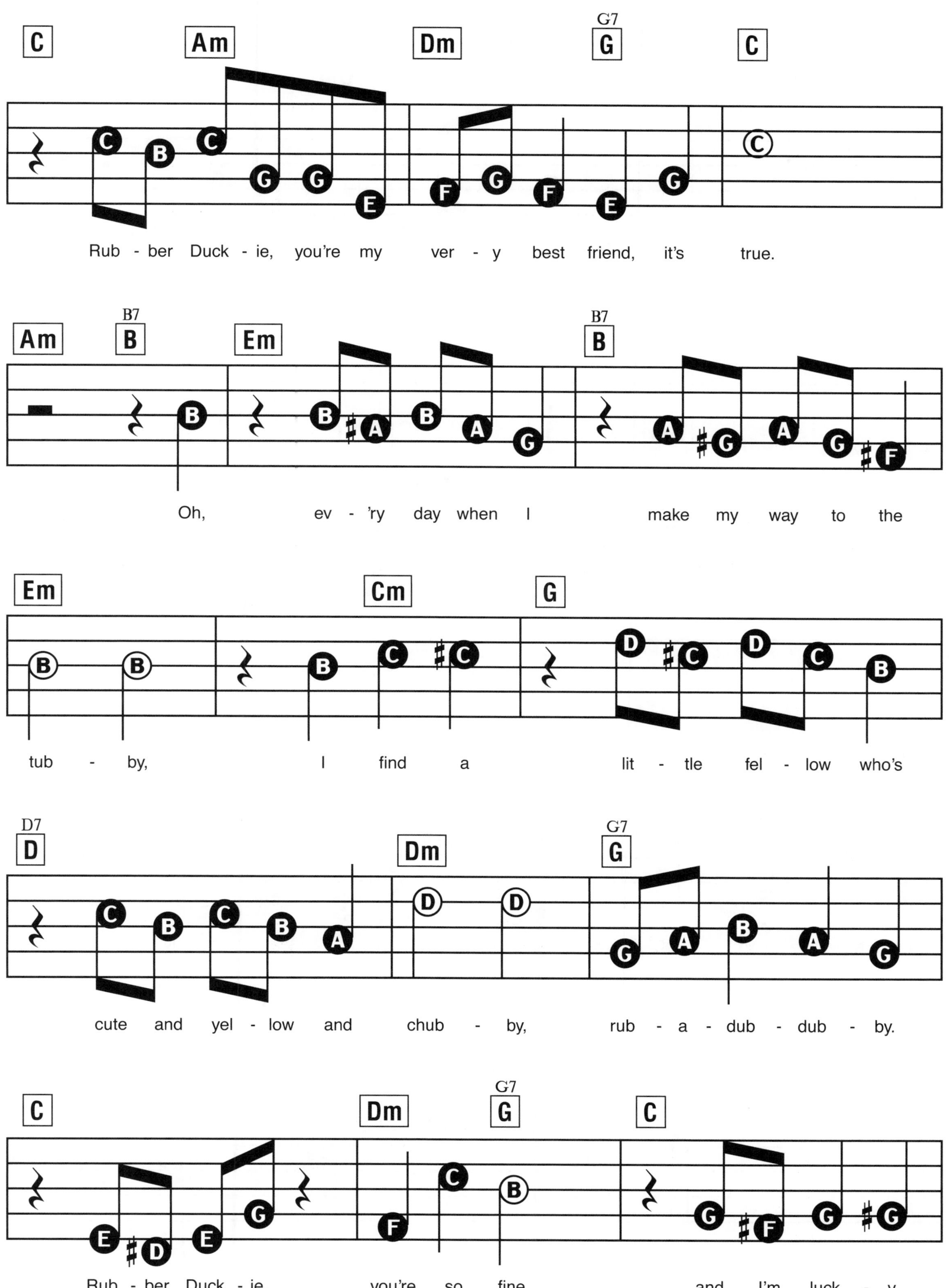
C
Am
Dm
G7
G
C
C B C G G E F G F E G C
Rub - ber Duck - ie, you're my ver - y best friend, it's true.
Am
B7
B
Em
B7
B
B B A B A G A G A G F
Oh, ev - 'ry day when I make my way to the
Em
Cm
G
B B B C C D C D C B
tub - by, I find a lit - tle fel - low who's
D7
D
Dm
G7
G
C B C B A D D G A B A G
cute and yel - low and chub - by, rub - a - dub - dub - by.
C
Dm
G7
G
C
E D E G F C B G F G G
Rub - ber Duck - ie, you're so fine, and I'm luck - y

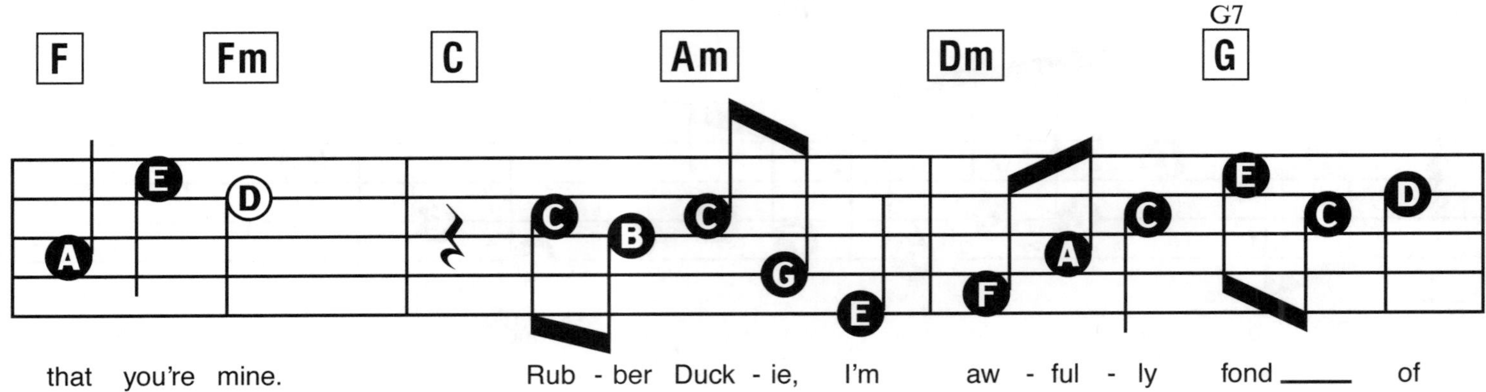
F
Fm
C
Am
Dm
G7
G
A E D C B C G E F A C E C D
that you're mine. Rub - ber Duck - ie, I'm aw - ful - ly fond of

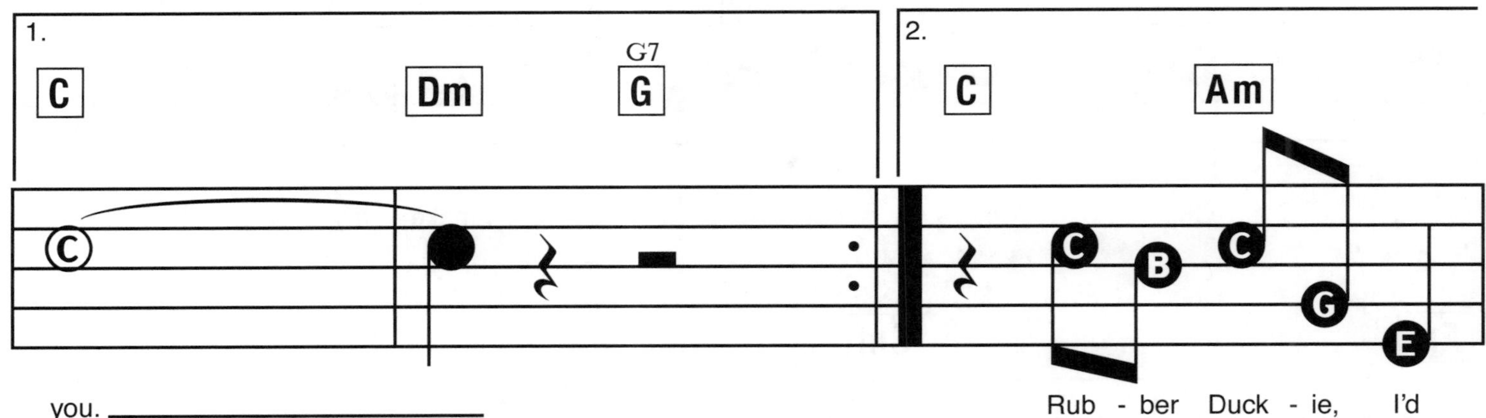
1.
C
Dm
G7
G
2.
C
Am
C C B C G E
you. Rub - ber Duck - ie, I'd

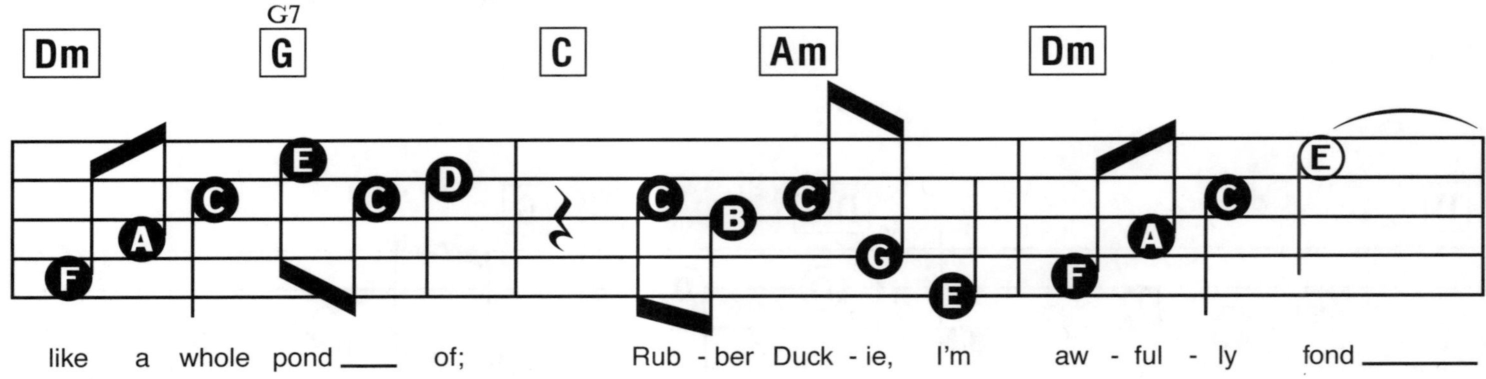
Dm
G7
G
C
Am
Dm
F A C E C D C B C G E F A C E
like a whole pond of; Rub - ber Duck - ie, I'm aw - ful - ly fond

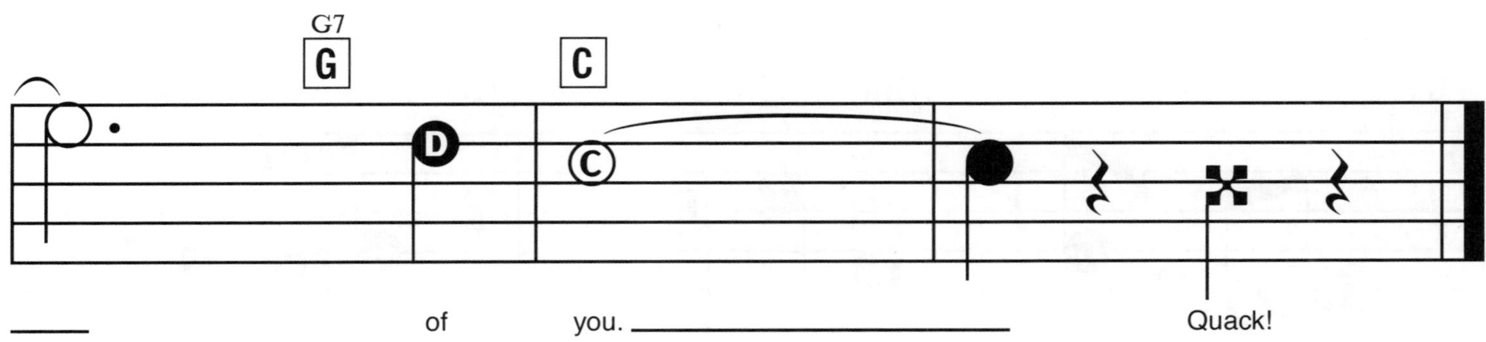
G7
G
C
D C
of you. Quack!

Splish Splash

Registration 9
Rhythm: Rock

Words and Music by Bobby Darin
and Murray Kaufman

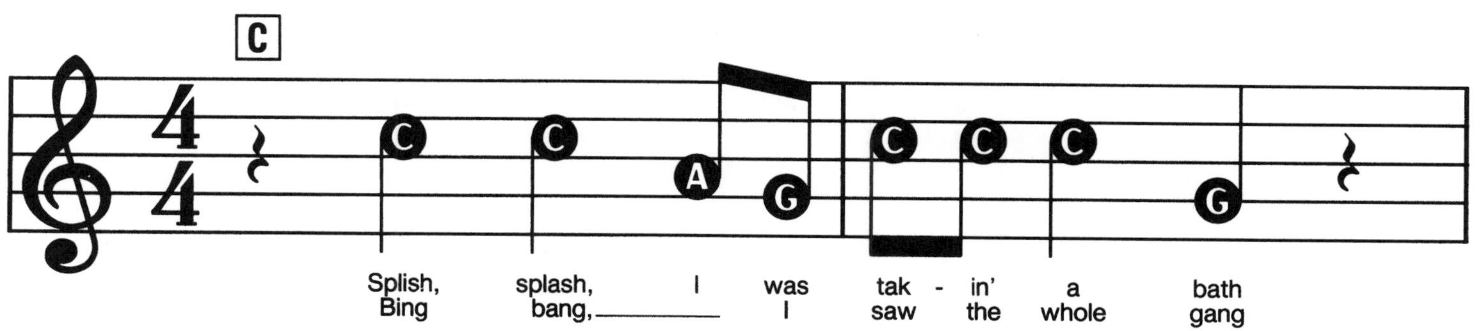

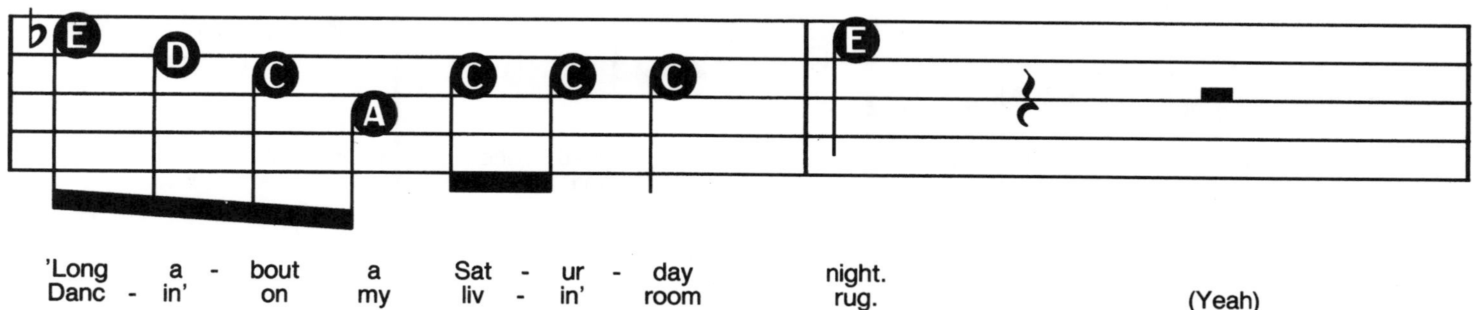

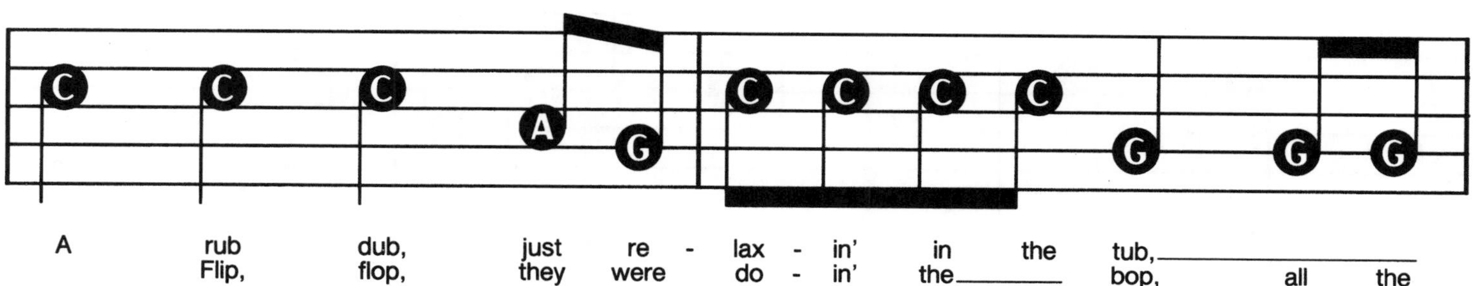

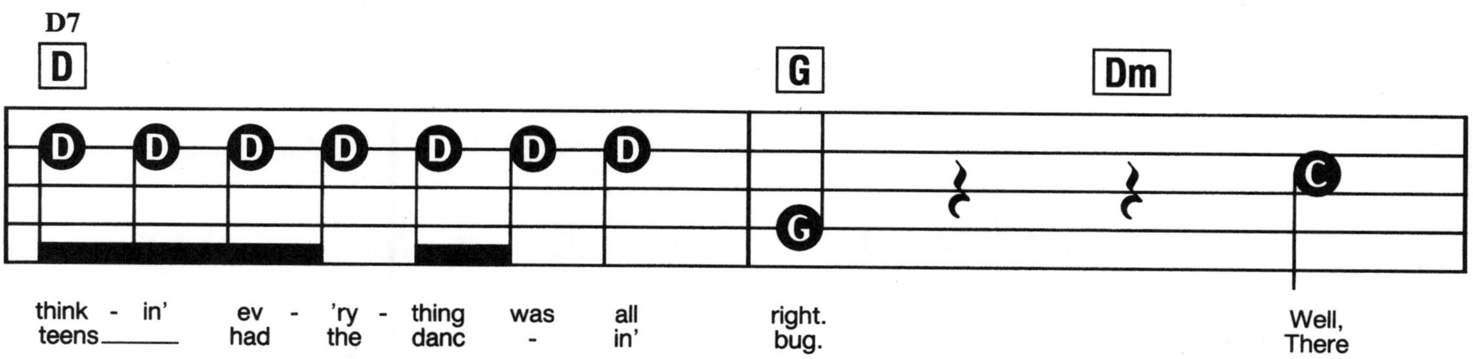

Copyright © 1958 by Unart Music Corporation
Copyright Renewed and Assigned to Alley Music Corp., Trio Music Company and EMI Unart Catalog Inc.
All Rights for Alley Music Corp. and Trio Music Company Administered by Hudson Bay Music Inc.
All Rights for EMI Unart Catalog Inc. Administered by EMI Unart Catalog Inc. (Publishing) and Alfred Music (Print)
International Copyright Secured All Rights Reserved
Used by Permission

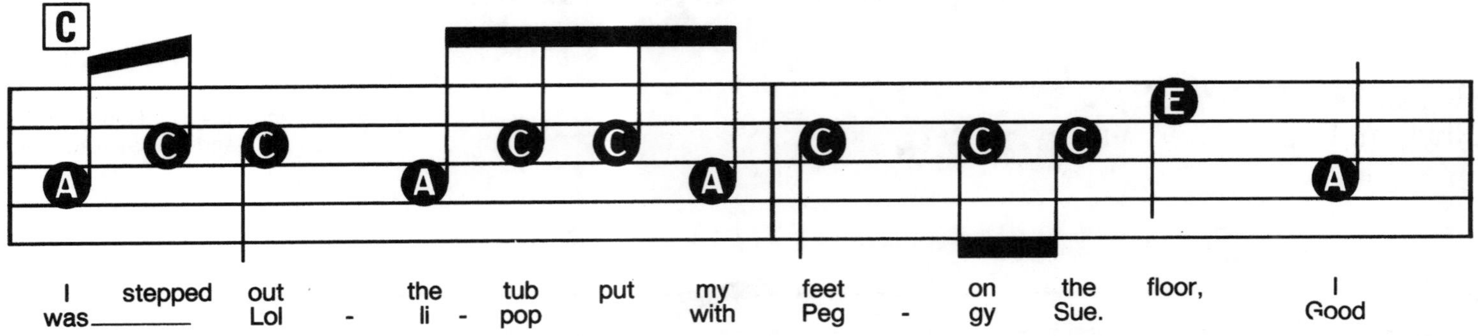
C
I stepped out the tub put my feet on the floor, I
was___ Lol - li - pop with Peg - gy Sue. Good

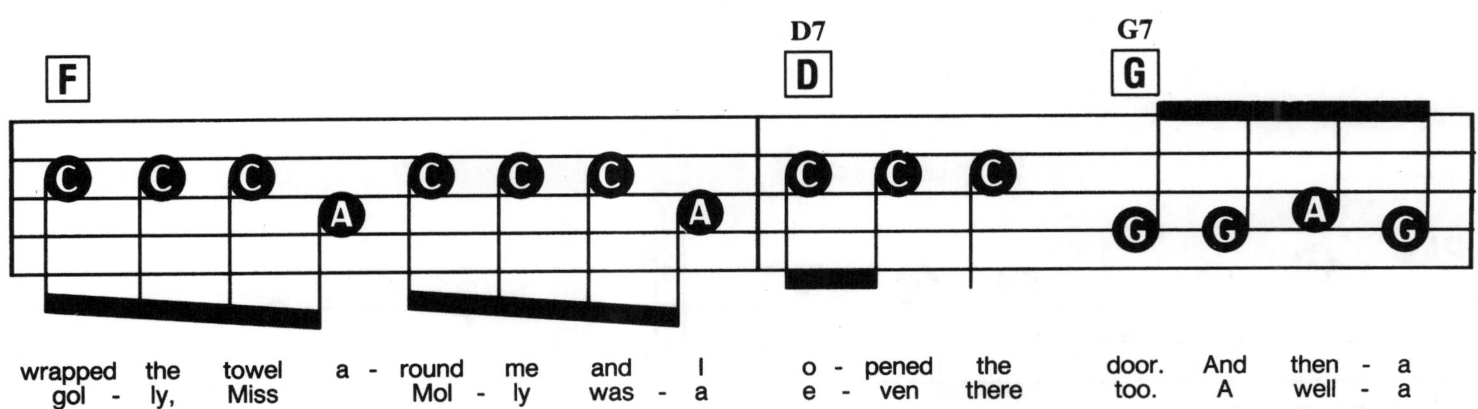
F
D7
D
G7
G
wrapped the towel a - round me and I o - pened the door. And then - a
gol - ly, Miss Mol - ly was - a e - ven there too. A well - a

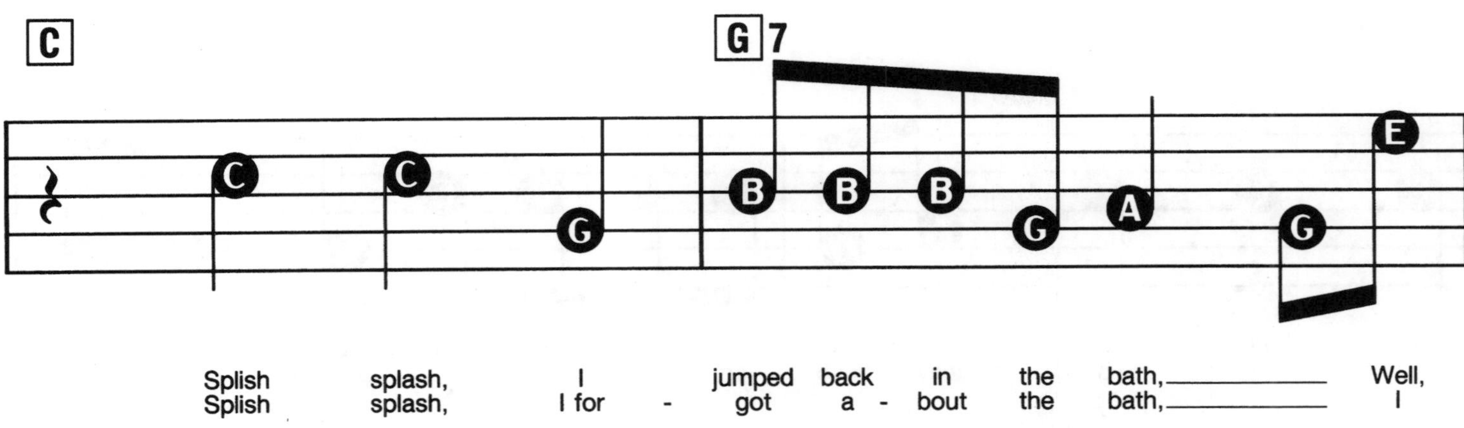
C
G7
Splish splash, I jumped back in the bath,___ Well,
Splish splash, I for - got a - bout the bath,___ I

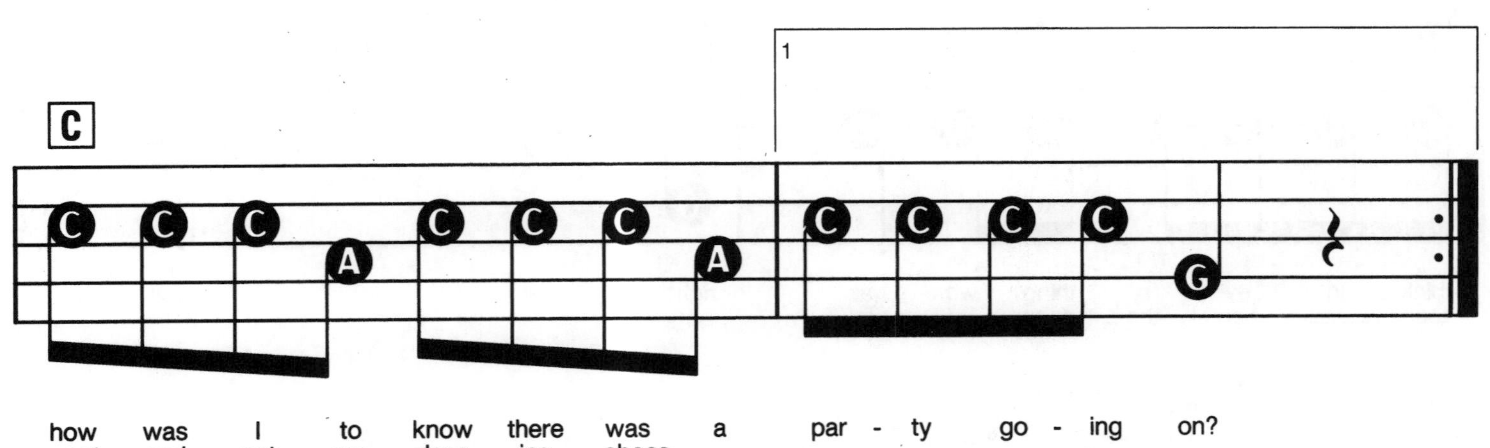
C
1
how was I to know there was a par - ty go - ing on?
went and put my danc - ing shoes___

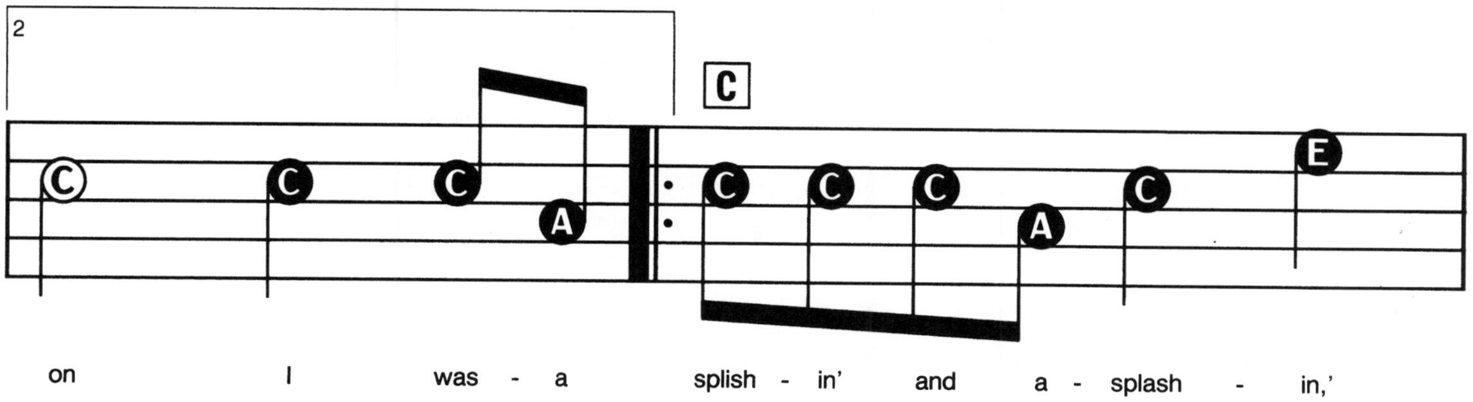
2
C
C C C A
C C C A C E
on I was - a splish - in' and a - splash - in,'

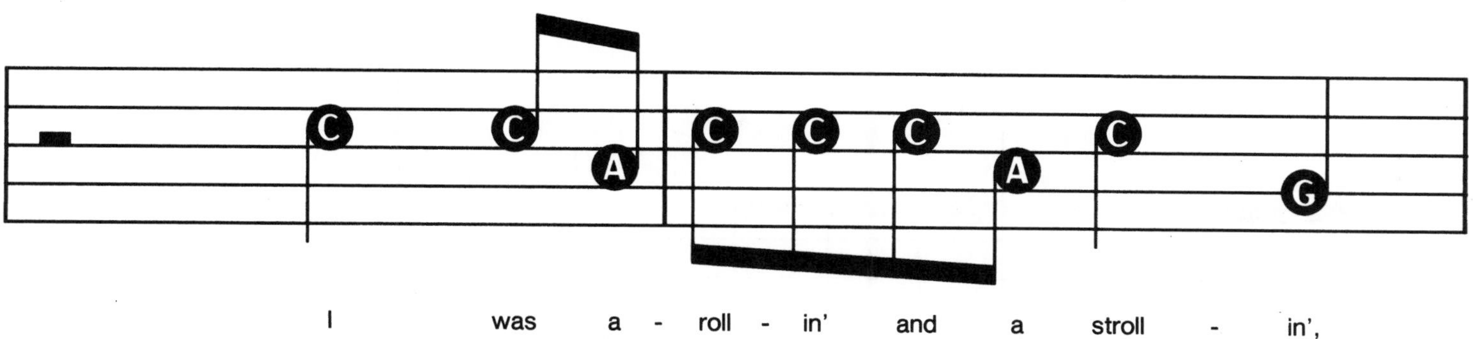
C C A
C C C A C G
I was a - roll - in' and a stroll - in',

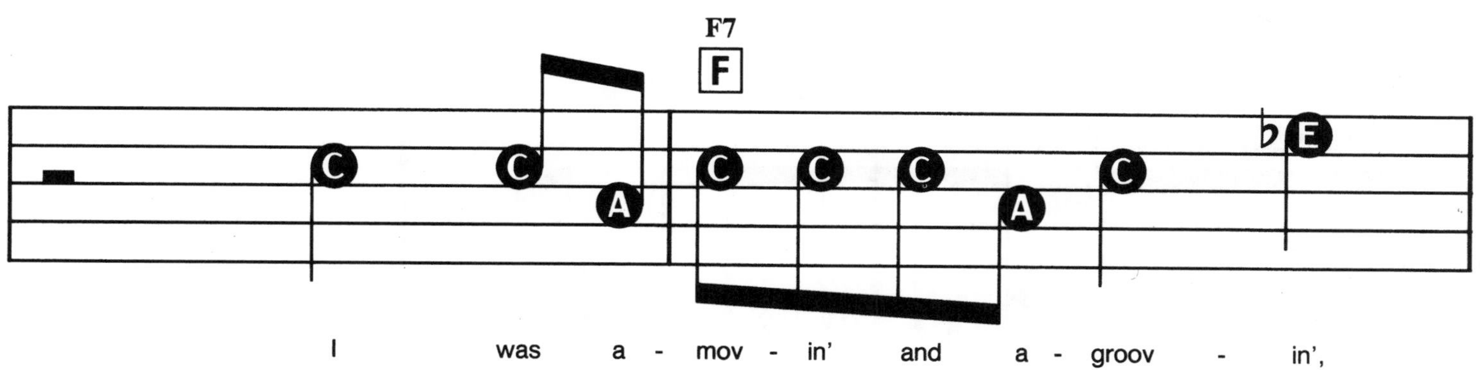
F7
F
C C A
C C C A C ♭E
I was a - mov - in' and a - groov - in',

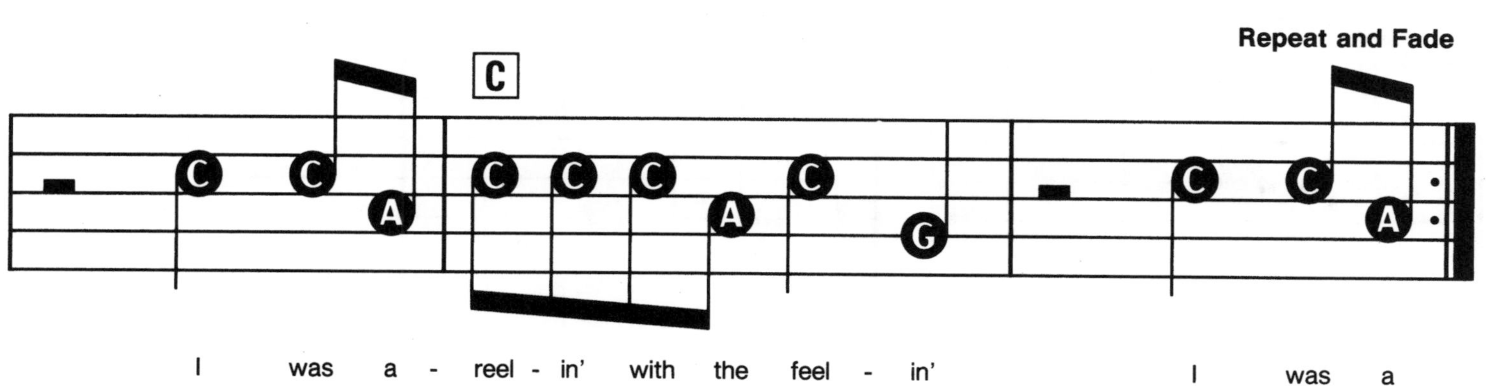
Repeat and Fade
C
C C A
C C C A C G
C C A
I was a - reel - in' with the feel - in' I was a

The Siamese Cat Song

from Walt Disney's LADY AND THE TRAMP

Registration 5
Rhythm: Folk or None

Words and Music by Peggy Lee
and Sonny Burke

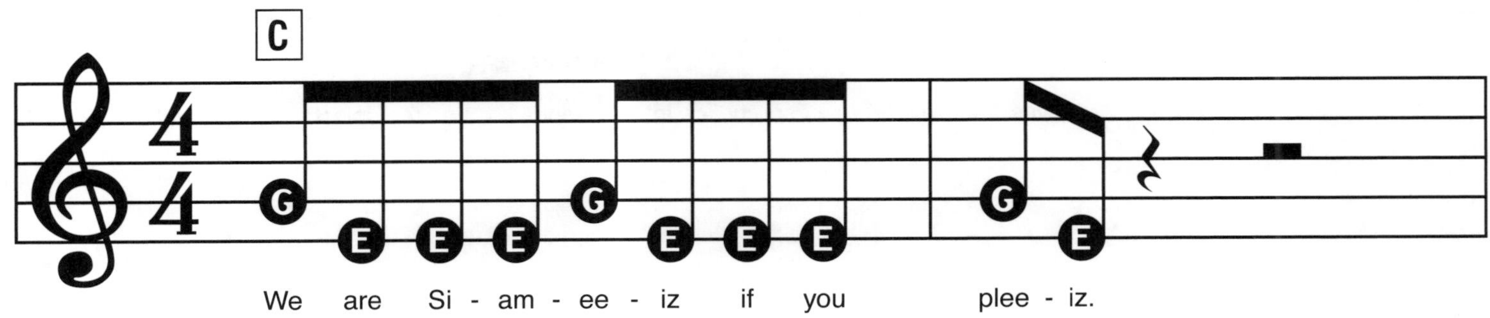

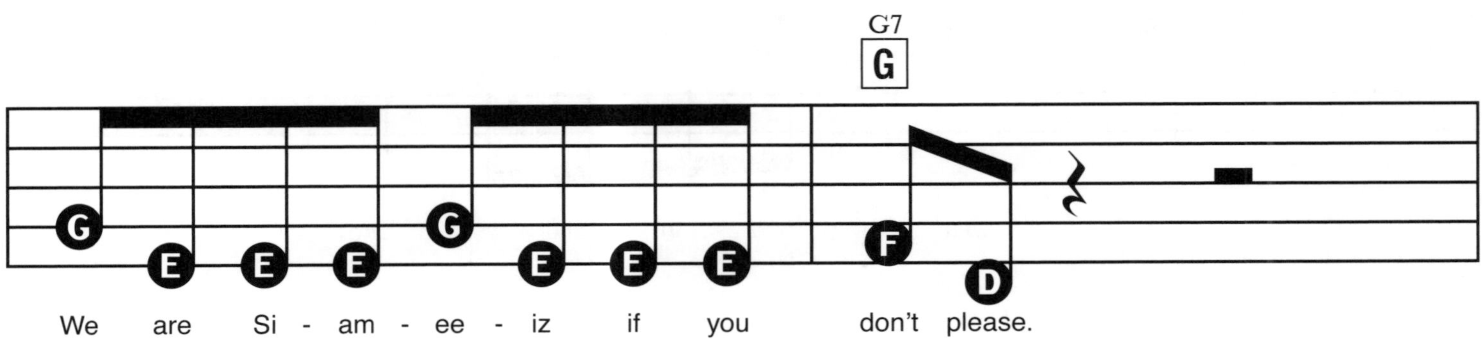

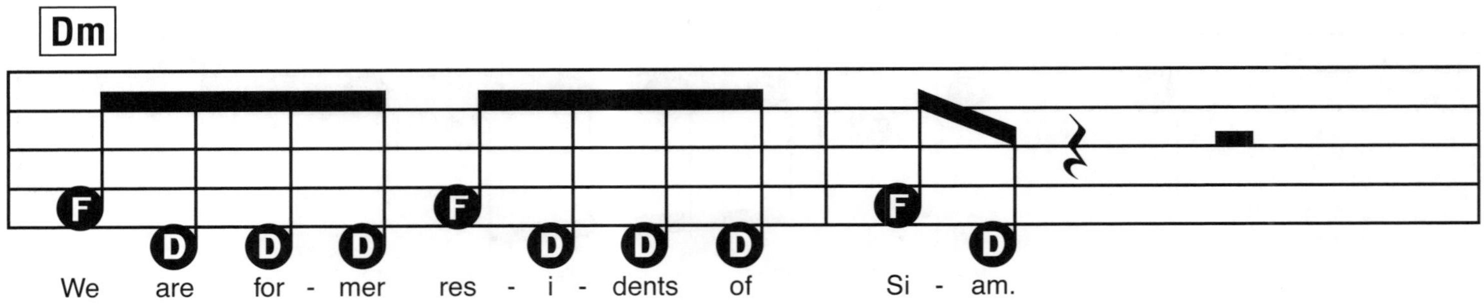

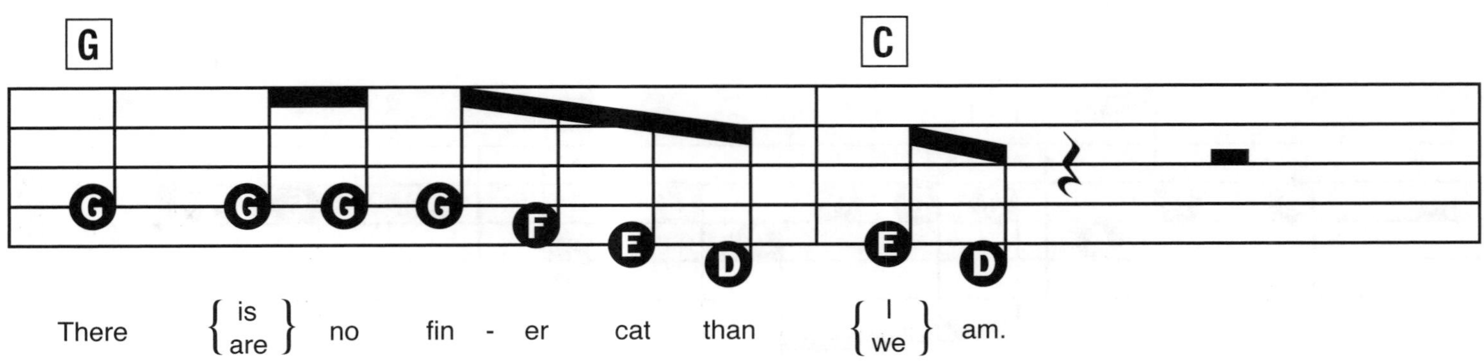

© 1953 Walt Disney Music Company
Copyright Renewed
All Rights Reserved. Used by Permission.

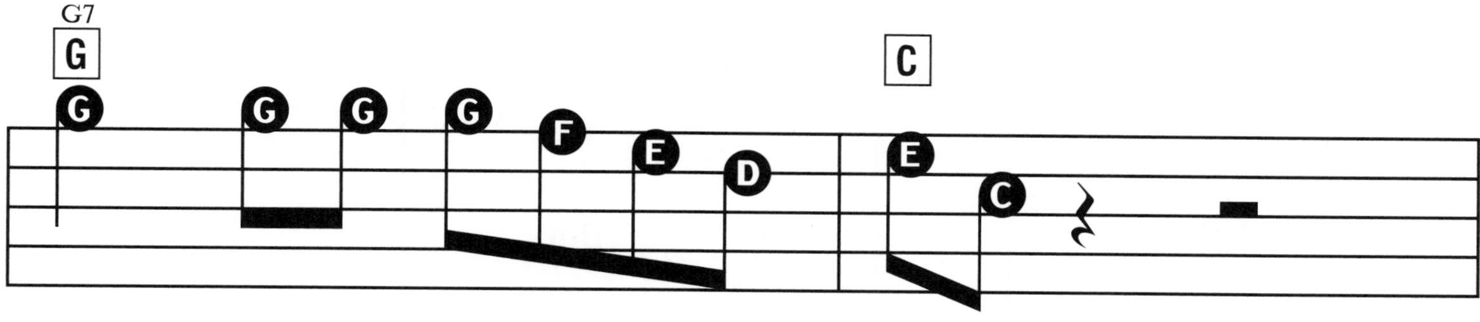

(Instrumental)

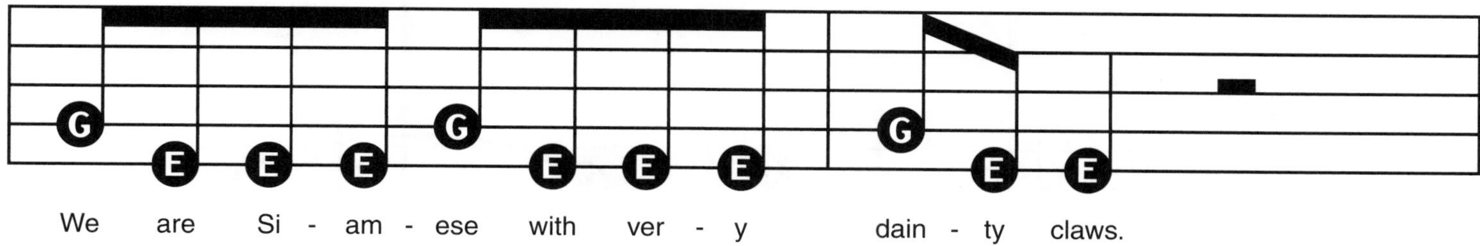

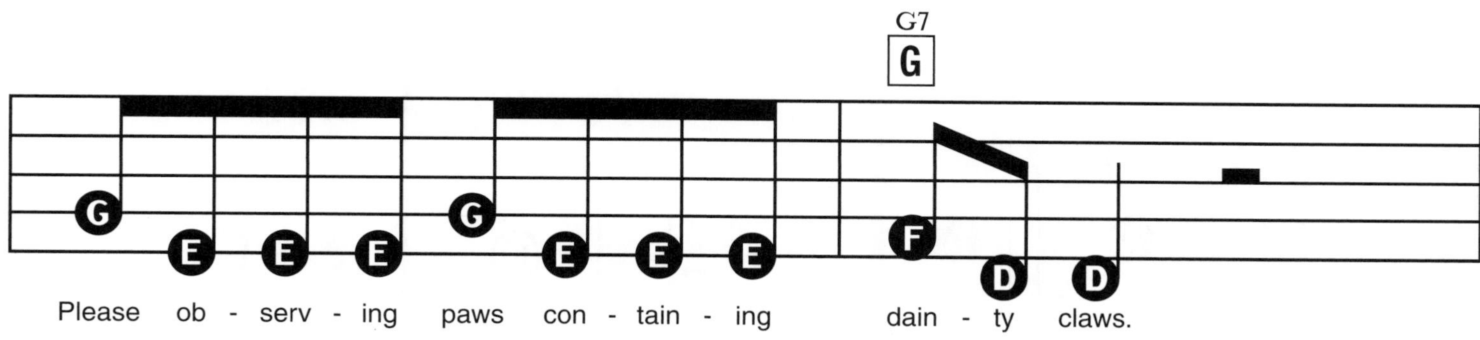

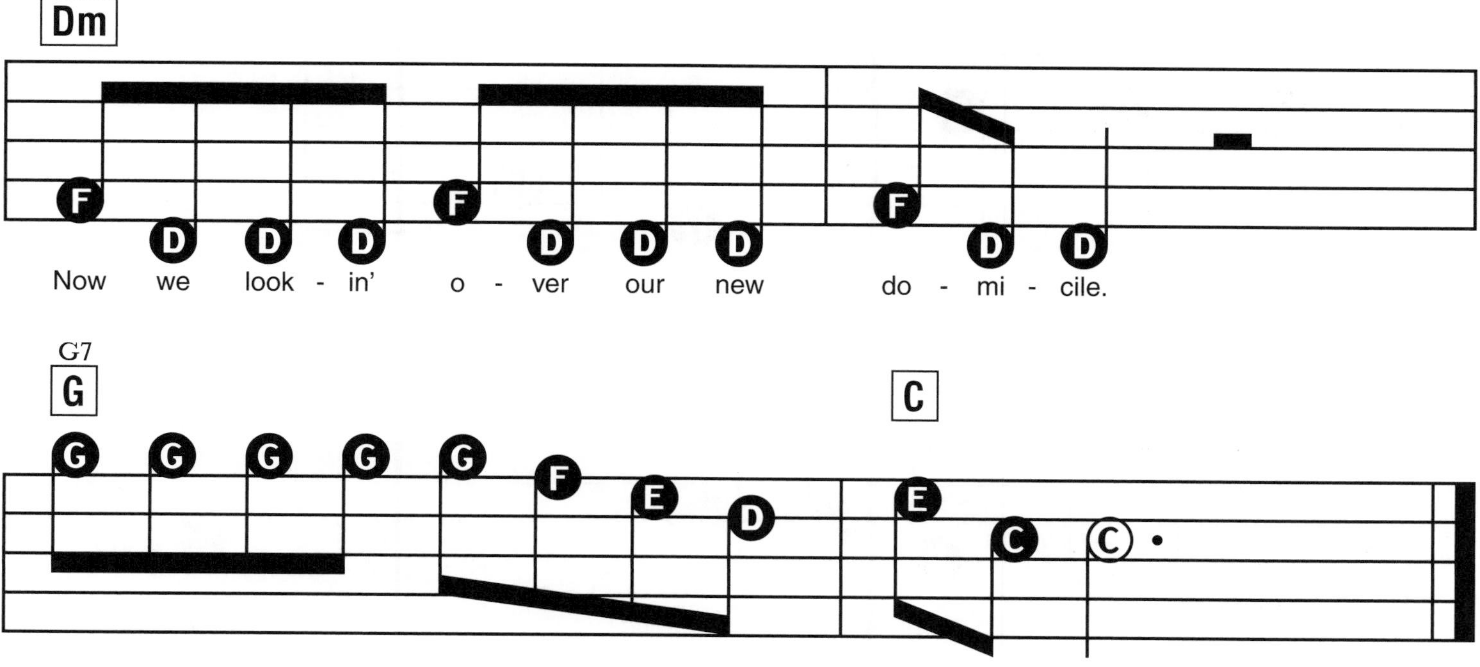

Sing

from SESAME STREET

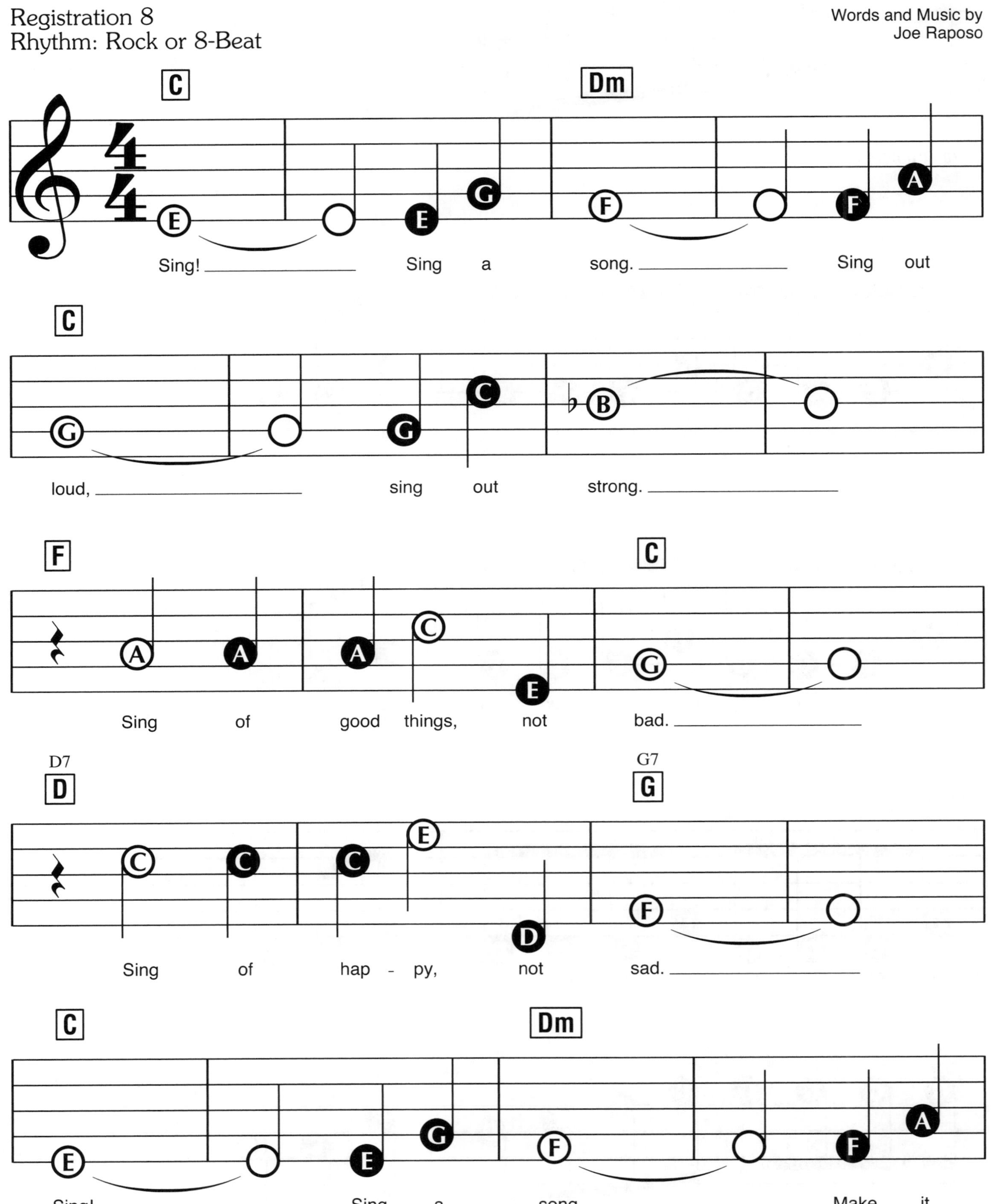

Copyright © 1971 by Jonico Music, Inc.
Copyright Renewed
All Rights in the U.S.A. Administered by Green Fox Music, Inc.
International Copyright Secured All Rights Reserved

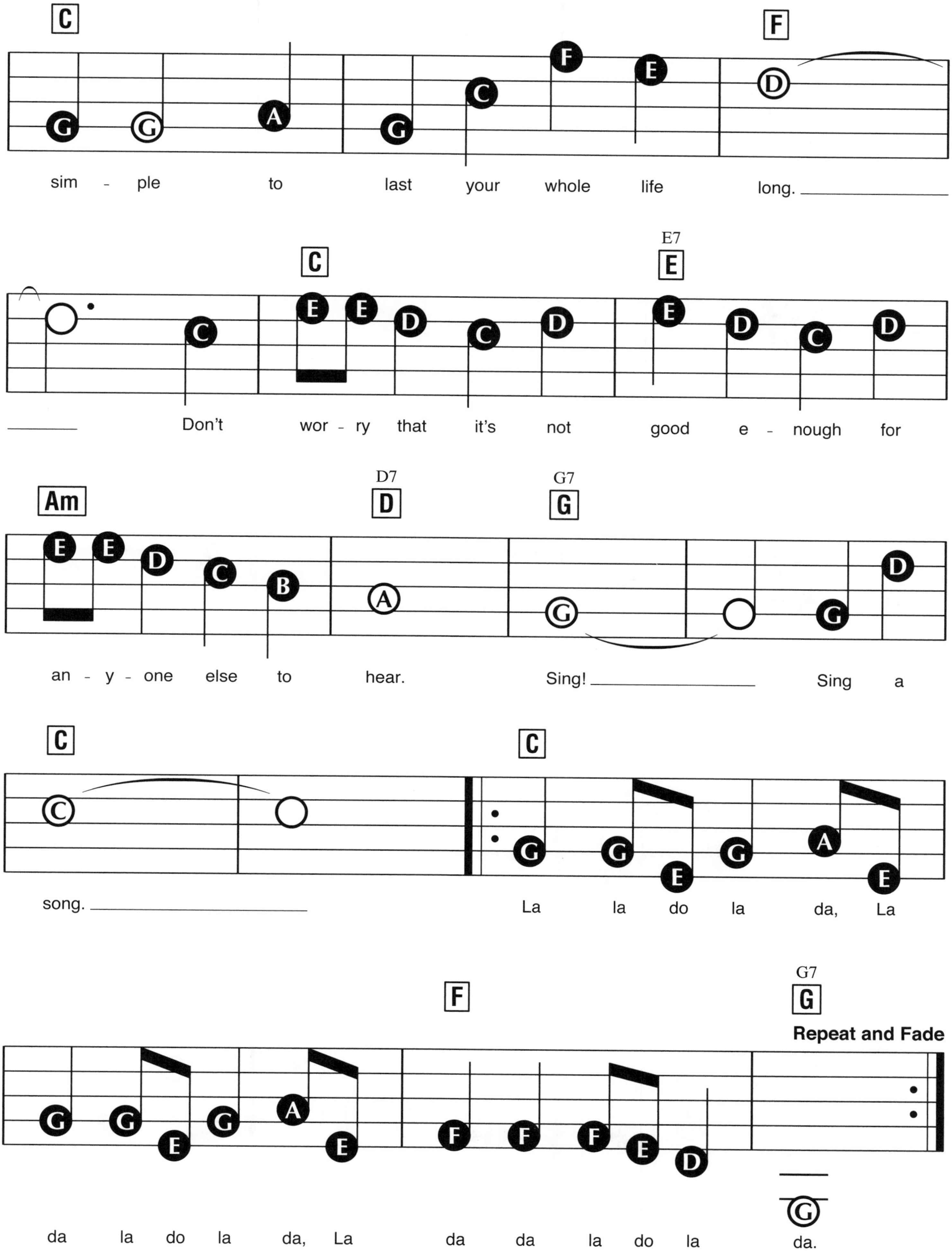
C
F
sim - ple to last your whole life long.
C
E7
E
Don't wor - ry that it's not good e - nough for
Am
D7
D
G7
G
an - y - one else to hear. Sing! Sing a
C
C
song. La la do la da, La
F
G7
G
Repeat and Fade
da la do la da, La da da la do la da.

So Long, Farewell
from THE SOUND OF MUSIC

Registration 3
Rhythm: Polka or Fox Trot

Lyrics by Oscar Hammerstein II
Music by Richard Rodgers

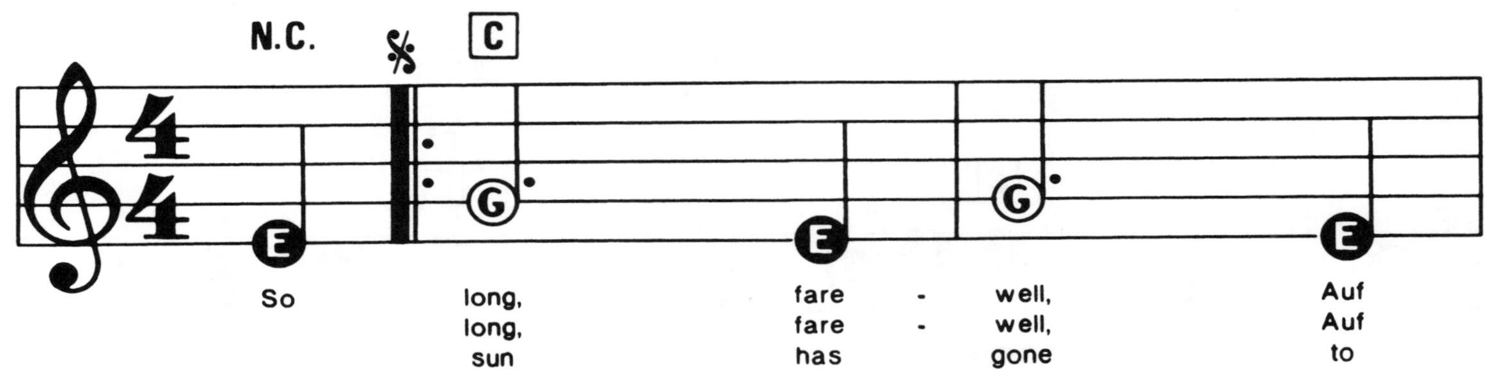

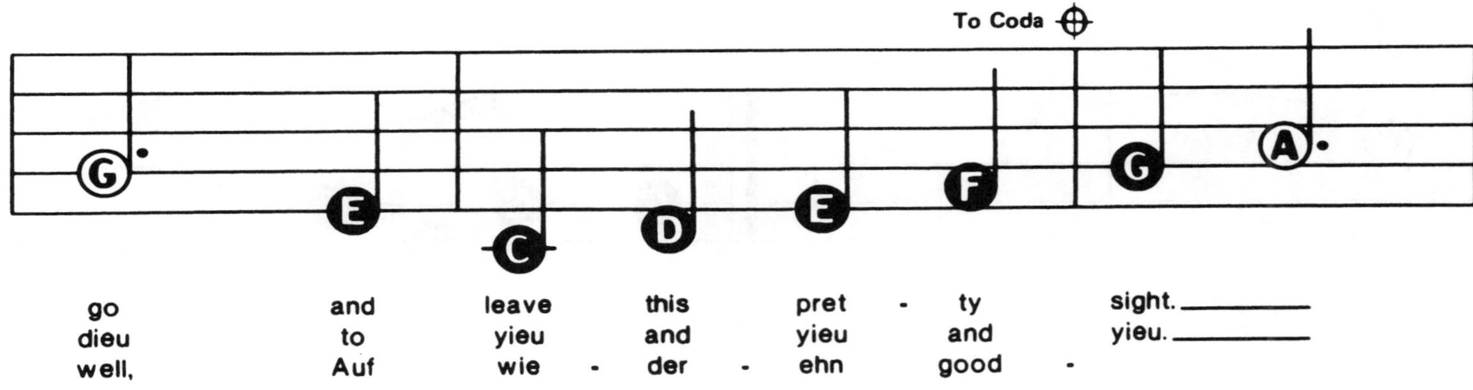

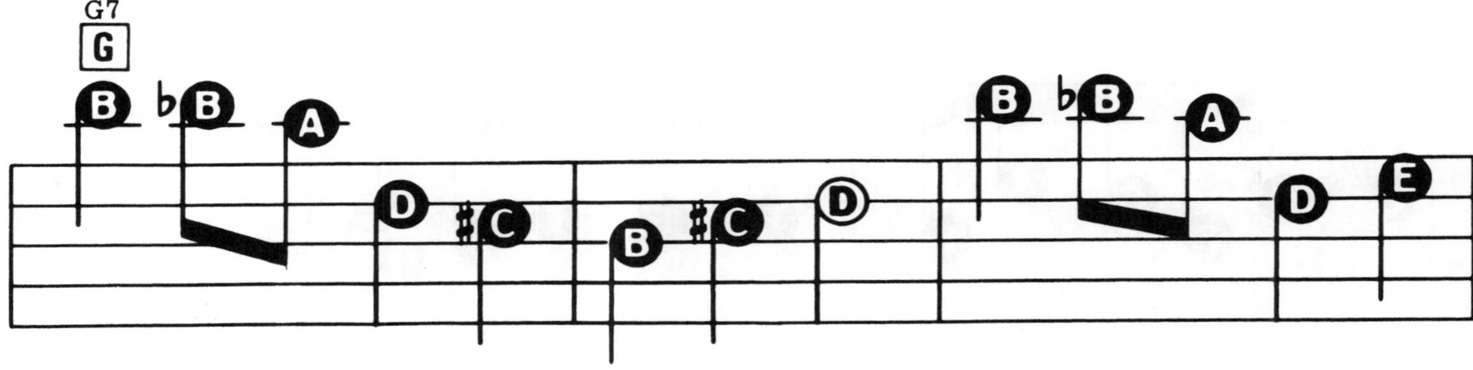

Copyright © 1959, 1960 by Richard Rodgers and Oscar Hammerstein II
Copyright Renewed
Williamson Music, a Division of Rodgers & Hammerstein: an Imagem Company, owner of publication and allied rights throughout the world
International Copyright Secured All Rights Reserved

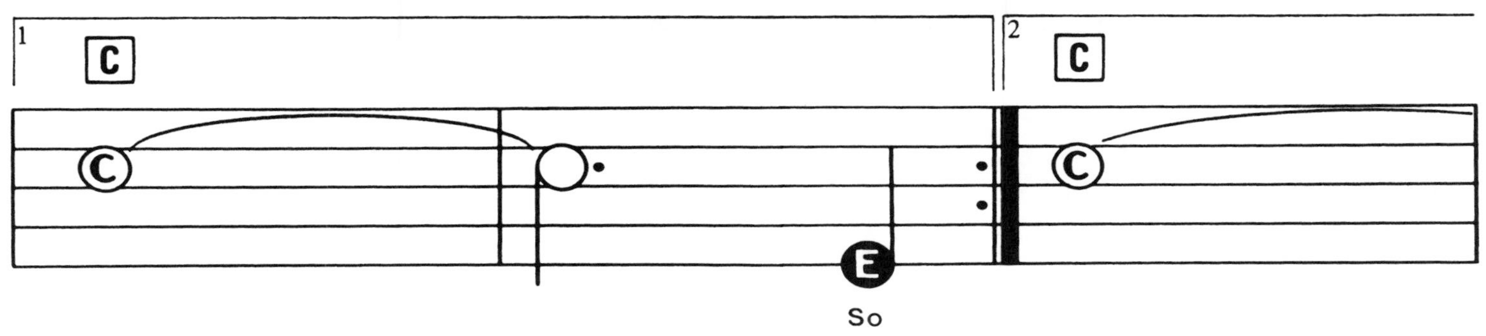
1
C
C
E
So
2
C
C

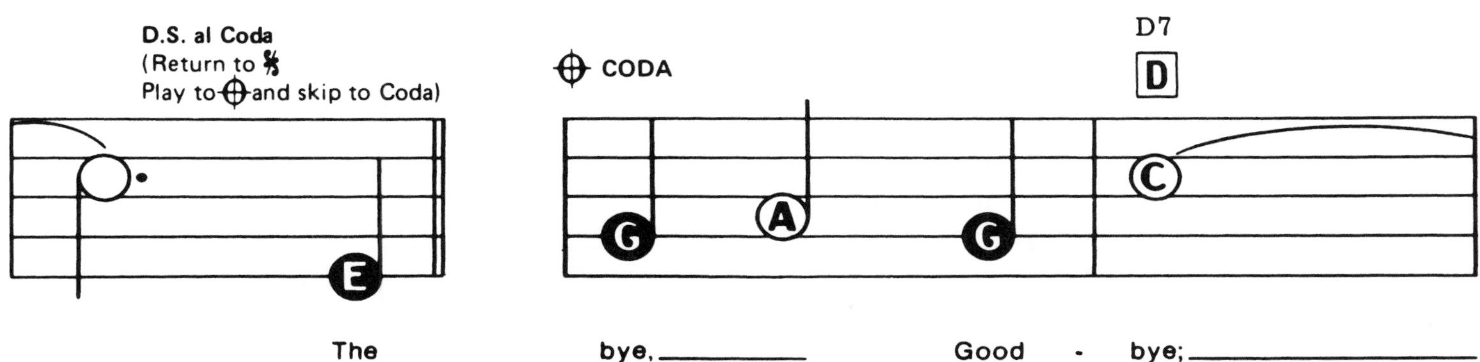
D.S. al Coda
(Return to 𝄋
Play to ⊕ and skip to Coda)
E
The
⊕ CODA
G
A
G
bye, ____ Good - bye; ____
D7
D
C

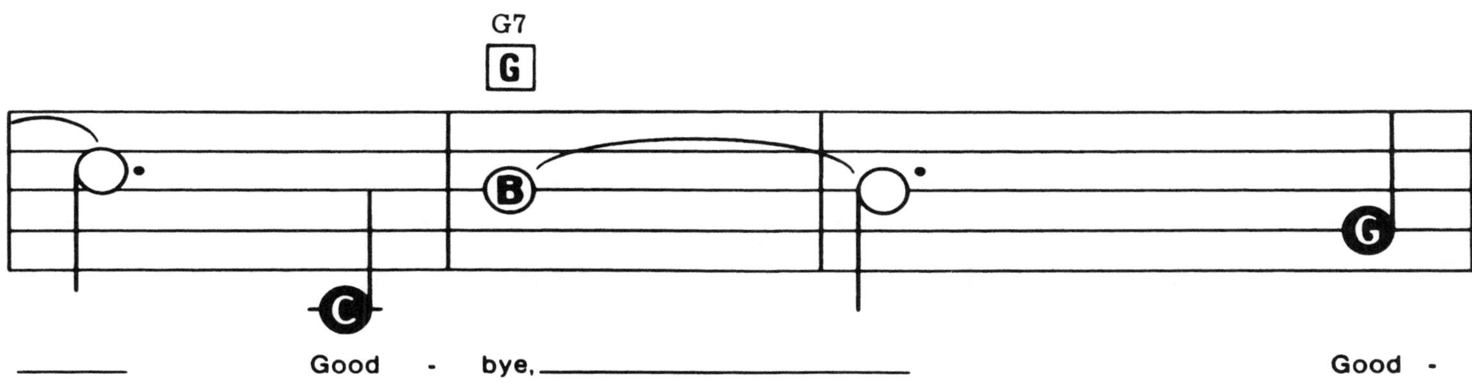
G7
G
C
B
G
____ Good - bye, ____ Good -

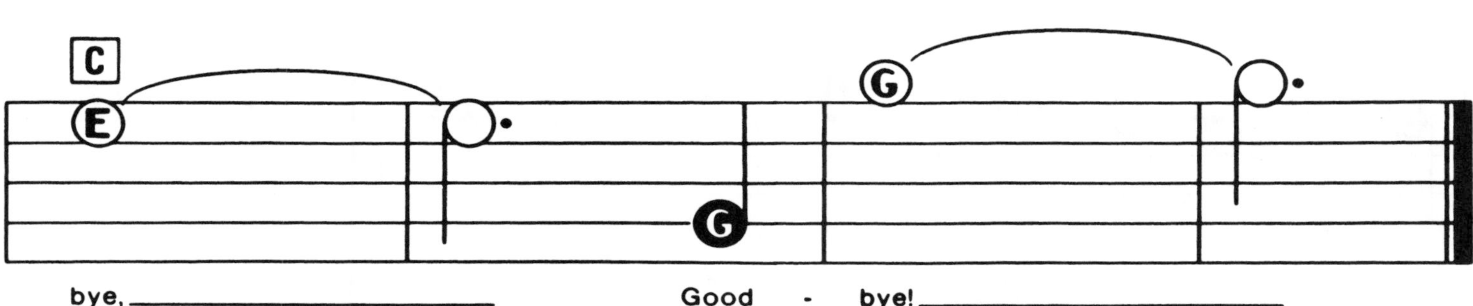
C
E
G
G
bye, ____ Good - bye! ____

A Spoonful of Sugar
from Walt Disney's MARY POPPINS

Registration 3
Rhythm: Fox Trot or Swing

Words and Music by Richard M. Sherman
and Robert B. Sherman

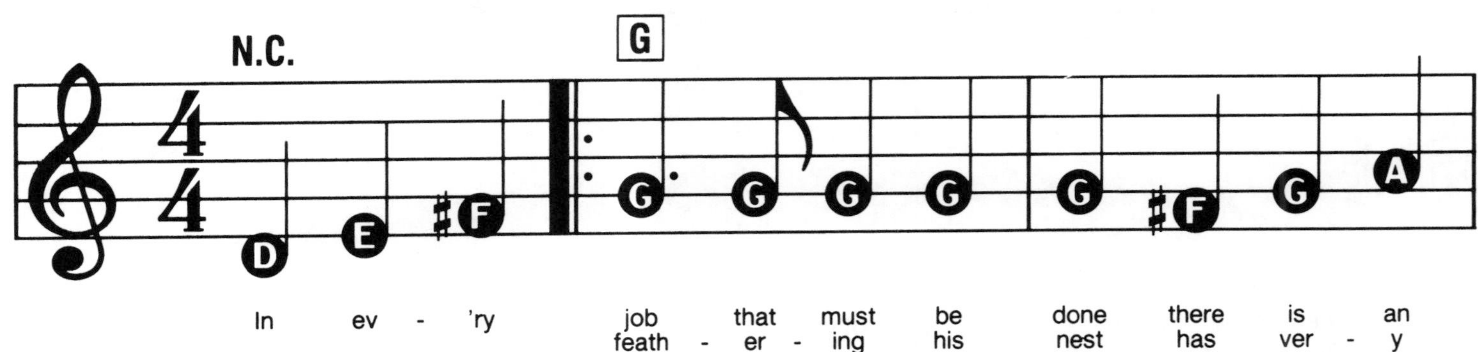

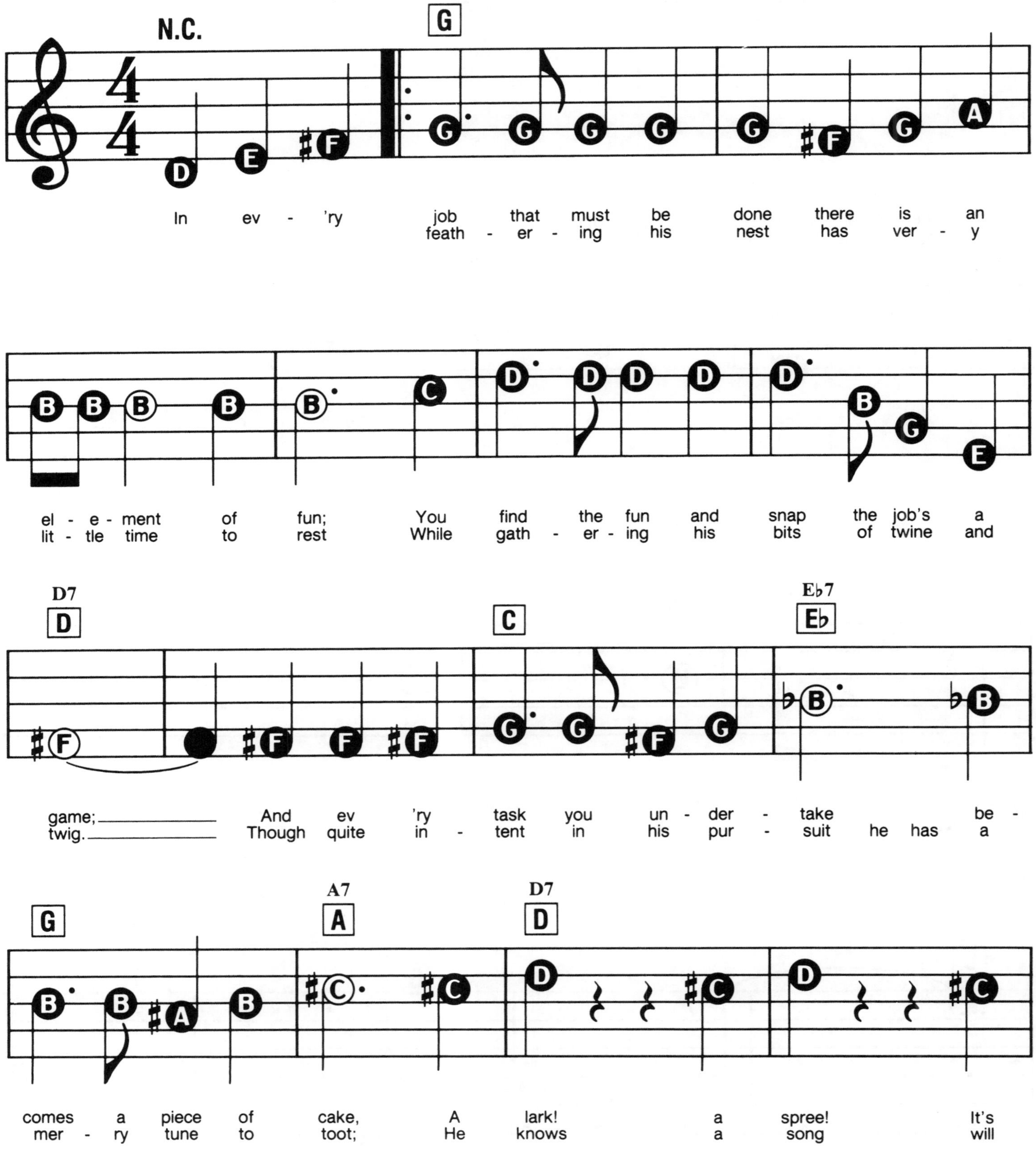

N.C.
G
In ev - 'ry job that must be done there is an
feath - er - ing his nest has ver - y
el - e - ment of fun; You find the fun and snap the job's a
lit - tle time to rest While gath - er - ing his bits of twine and
D7
D
C
Eb7
Eb
game; And ev 'ry task you un - der - take be -
twig. Though quite in - tent in his pur - suit he has a
G
A7
A
D7
D
comes a piece of cake, A lark! a spree! It's
mer - ry tune to toot; He knows a song will

© 1963 Wonderland Music Company, Inc.
Copyright Renewed
All Rights Reserved. Used by Permission.

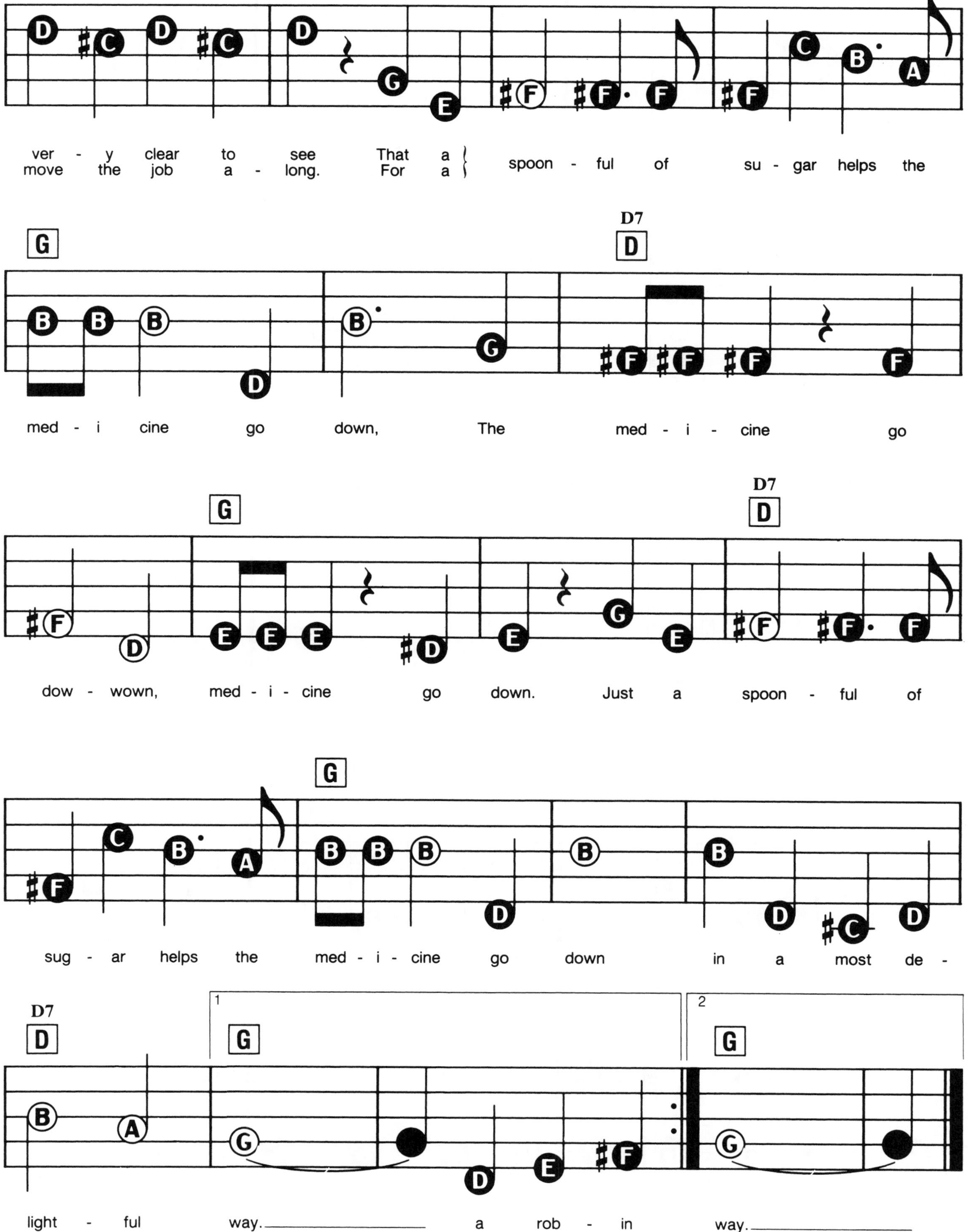
very clear to see That a
move the job along. For a
spoonful of sugar helps the
G
medicine go down, The
D7
D
medicine go
dowown,
G
medicine go down. Just a
D7
D
spoonful of
sugar helps the
G
medicine go down in a most de-
D7
D
lightful
1
G
way. a robin
2
G
way.

Supercalifragilisticexpialidocious

from Walt Disney's MARY POPPINS

Registration 2
Rhythm: Fox Trot or Swing

Words and Music by Richard M. Sherman
and Robert B. Sherman

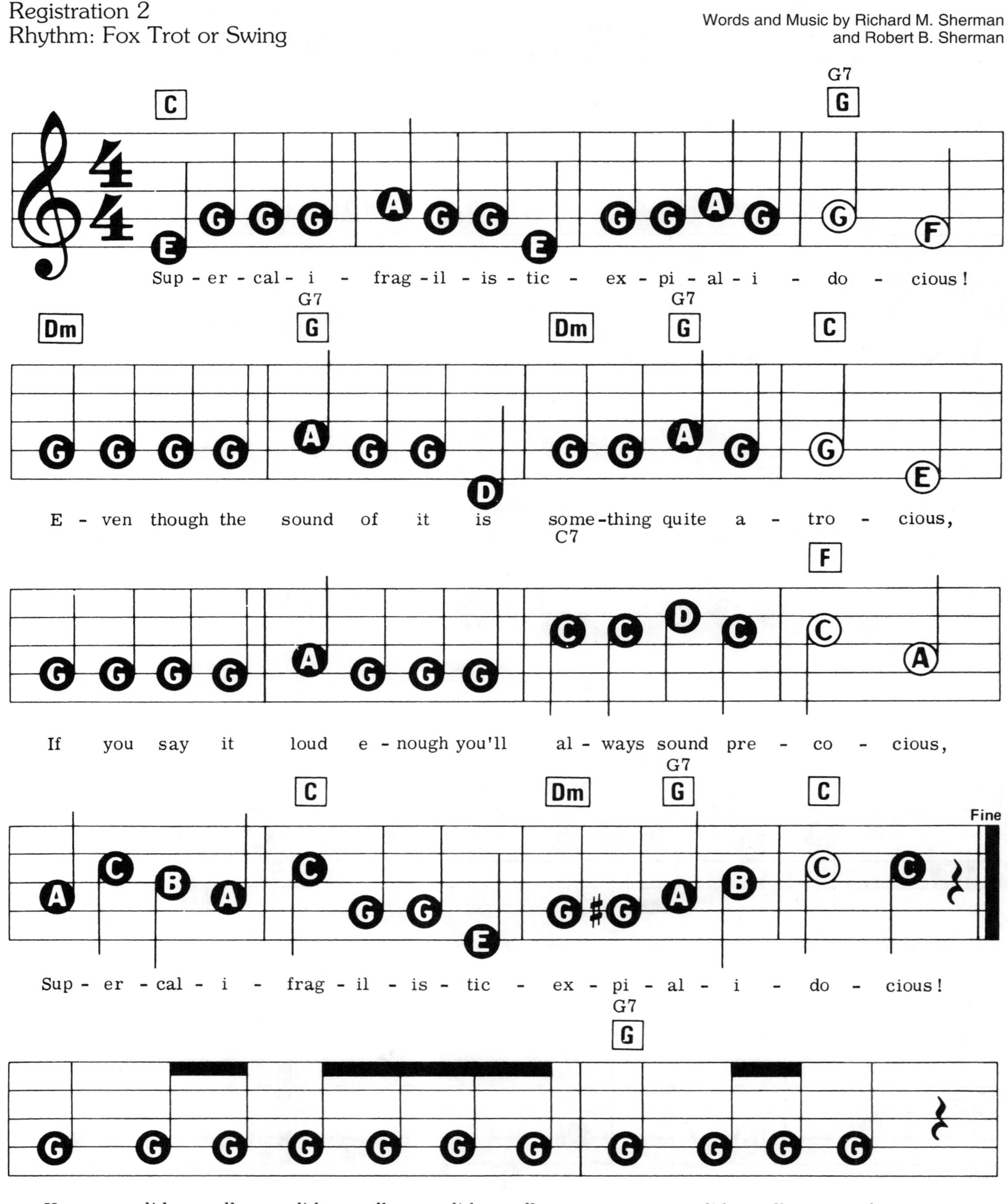

© 1963 Wonderland Music Company, Inc.
Copyright Renewed
All Rights Reserved. Used by Permission.

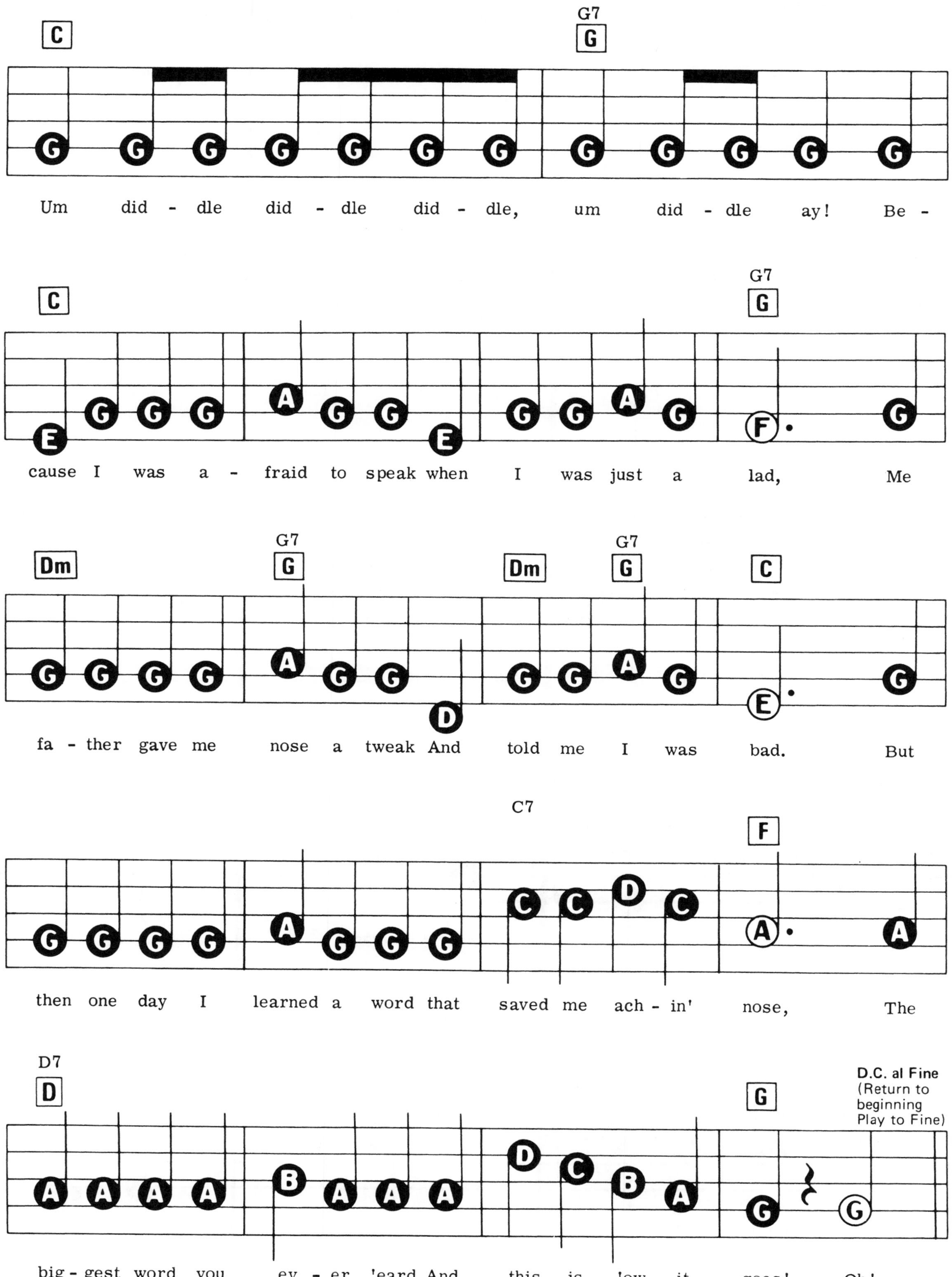
C
G7
G
G G G G G G G G G G G G
Um did - dle did - dle did - dle, um did - dle ay! Be -
C
G7
G
E G G G A G G E G G A G F G
cause I was a - fraid to speak when I was just a lad, Me
Dm
G7
G
Dm
G7
G
C
G G G G A G G D G G A G E G
fa - ther gave me nose a tweak And told me I was bad. But
C7
F
G G G G A G G G C C D C A A
then one day I learned a word that saved me ach - in' nose, The
D7
D
G
D.C. al Fine
(Return to beginning Play to Fine)
A A A A B A A A D C B A G G
big - gest word you ev - er 'eard And this is 'ow it goes! Oh!

Take Me Out to the Ball Game

Registration 9
Rhythm: Waltz

Words by Jack Norworth
Music by Albert von Tilzer

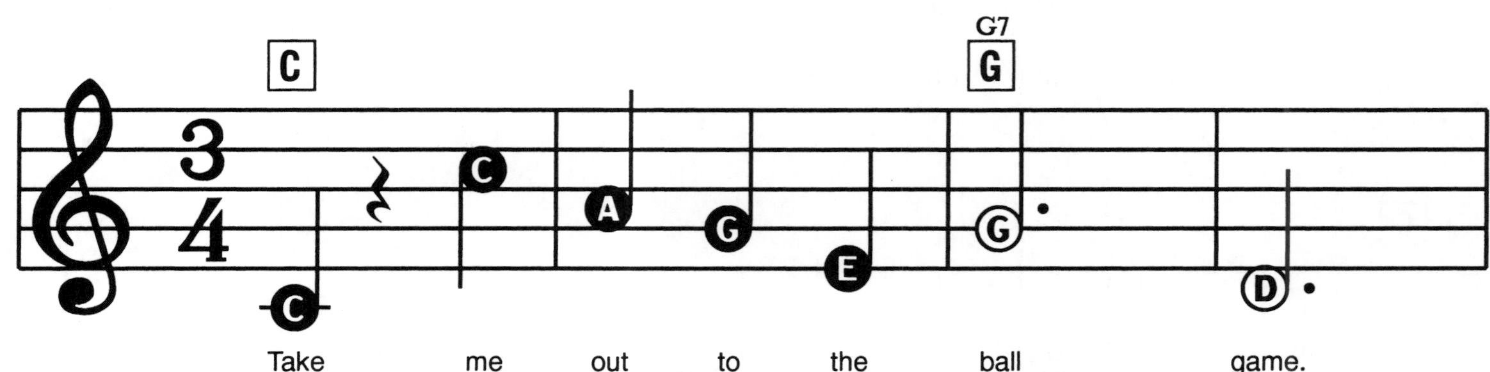

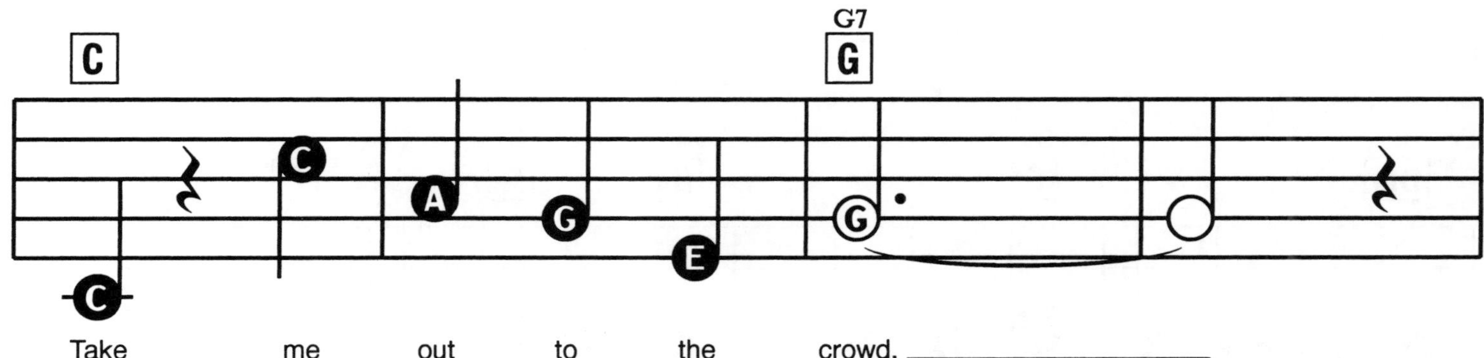

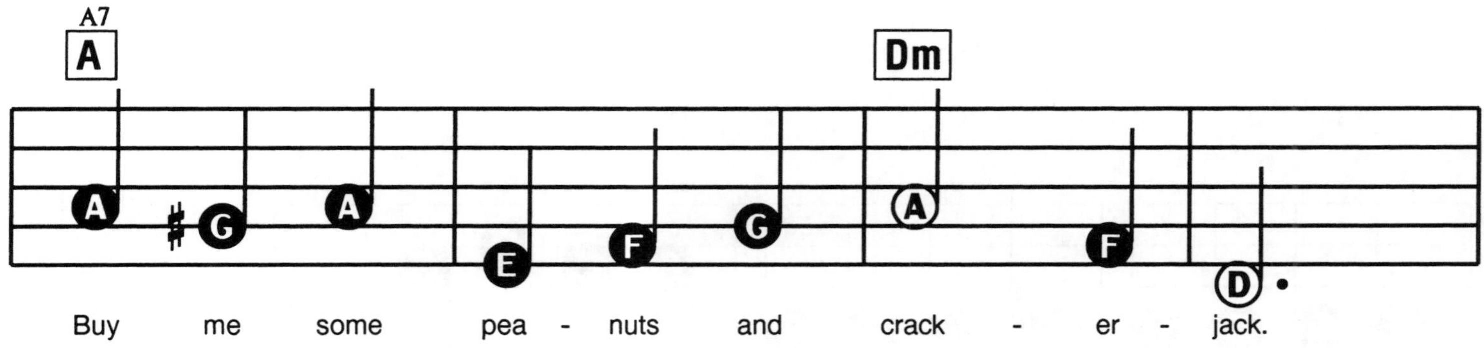

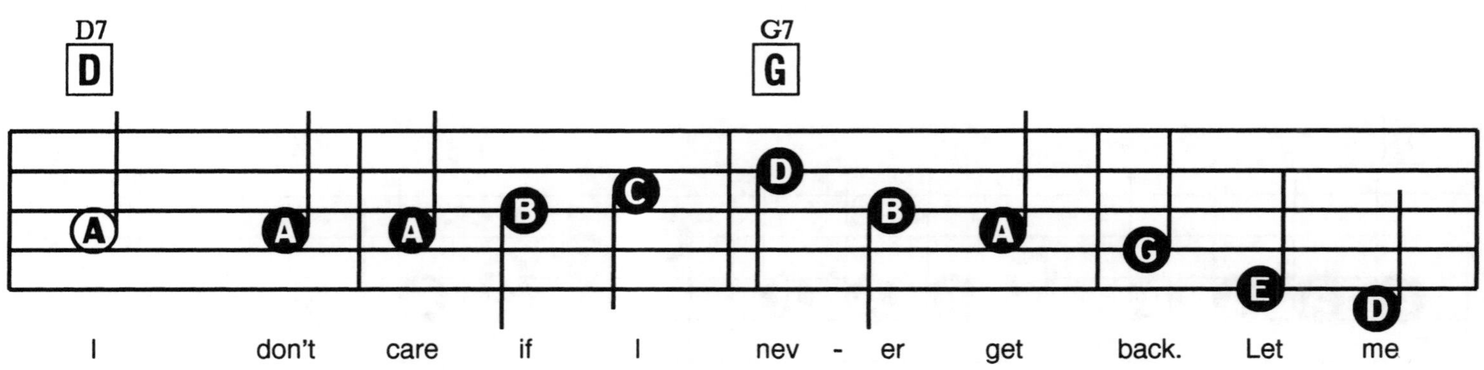

Copyright © 1994 by HAL LEONARD CORPORATION
International Copyright Secured All Rights Reserved

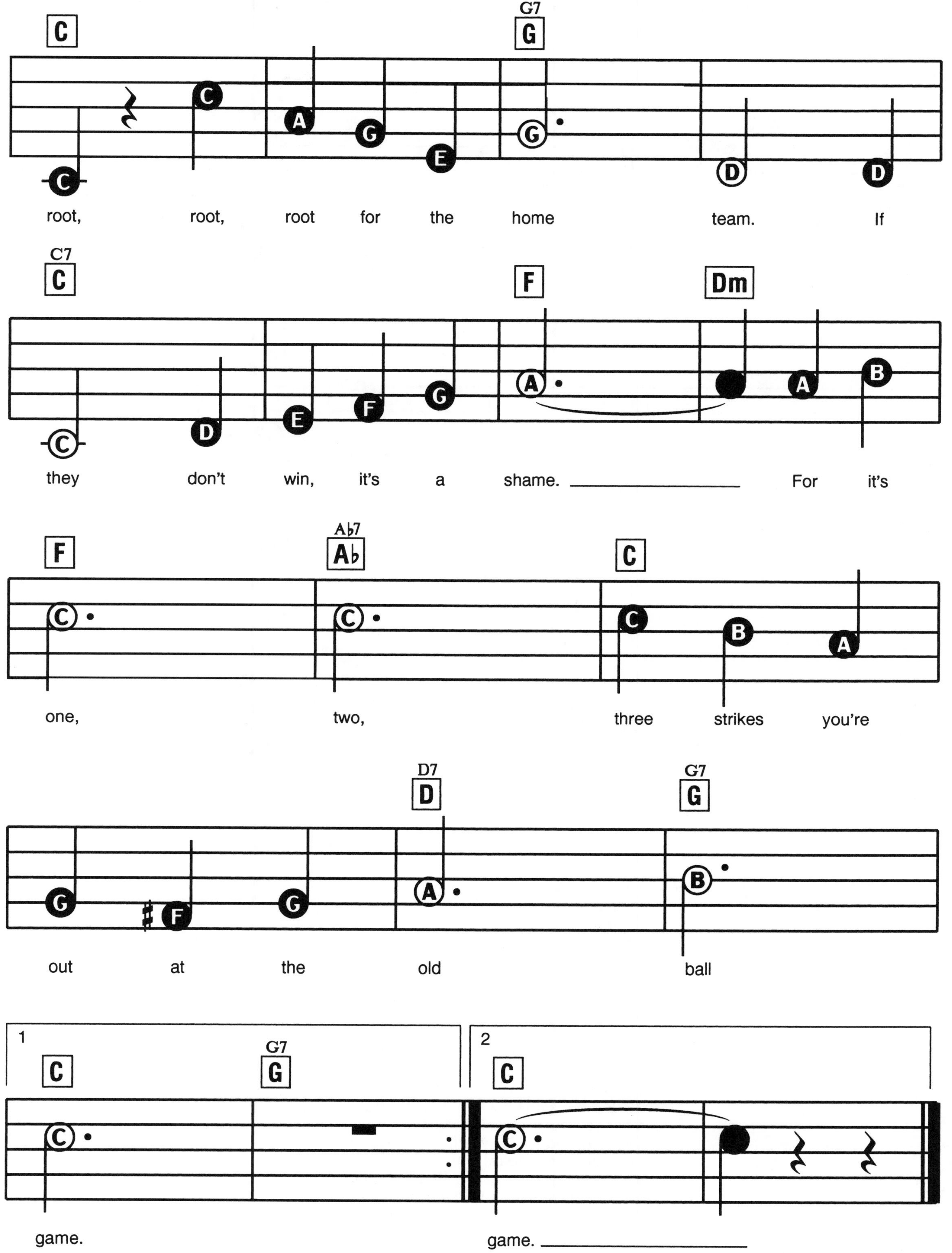
C G7 G
root, root, root for the home team. If
C7 C F Dm
they don't win, it's a shame. For it's
F A♭7 A♭ C
one, two, three strikes you're
D7 D G7 G
out at the old ball
1 C G7 G
game.
2 C
game.

There's a Hole in the Bucket

Registration 10
Rhythm: Waltz

Traditional

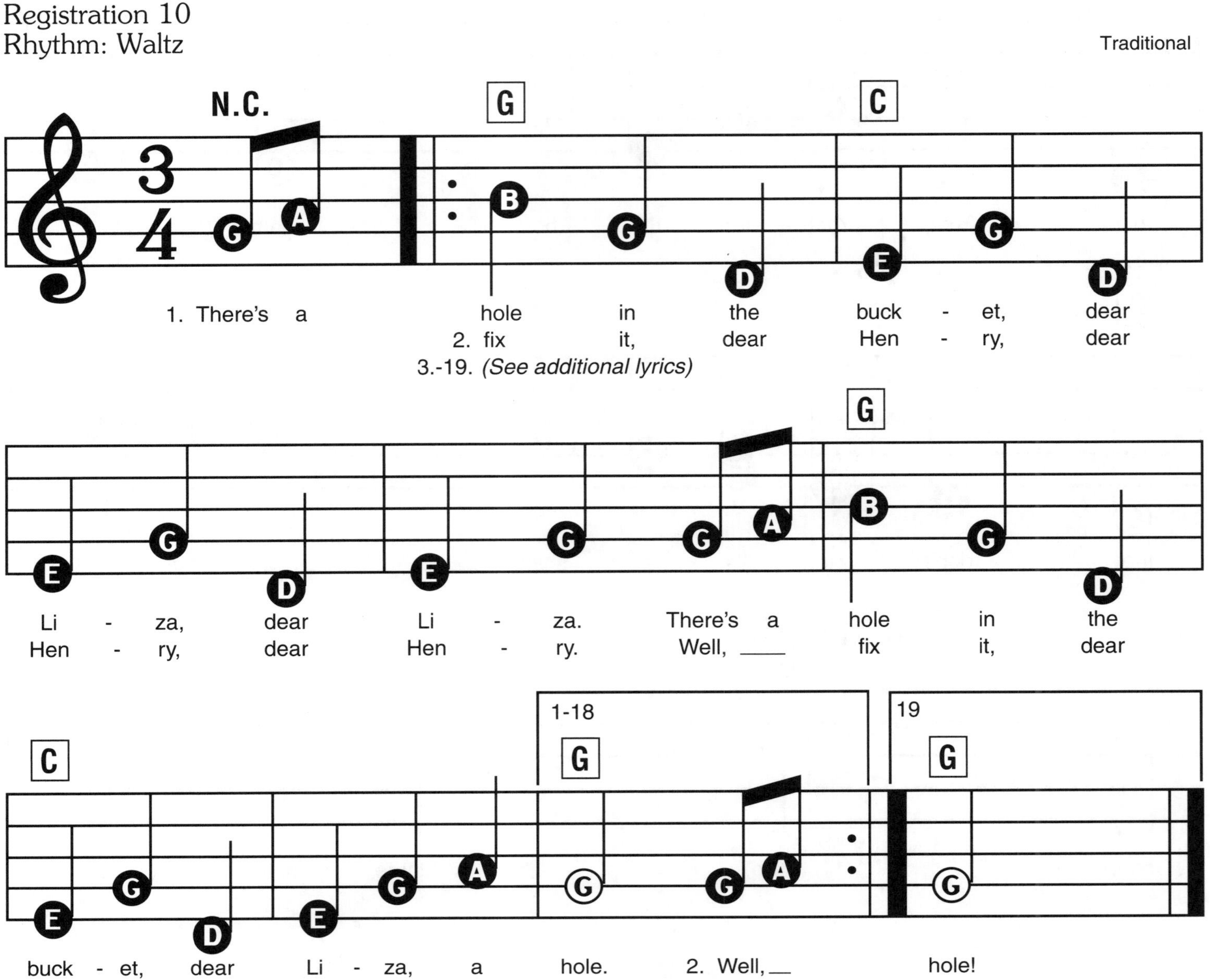

Additional Lyrics

3. With what shall I fix it, dear Liza, *etc.*
4. With a straw, dear Henry, *etc.*
5. But the straw is too long, dear Liza, *etc.*
6. Then cut it, dear Henry, *etc.*
7. With what shall I cut it, dear Liza, *etc.*
8. With a knife, dear Henry, *etc.*
9. But the knife is too dull, dear Liza, *etc.*
10. Then sharpen it, dear Henry, *etc.*
11. With what shall I sharpen it, dear Liza, *etc.*
12. With a stone, dear Henry, *etc.*
13. But the stone is too dry, dear Liza, *etc.*
14. Then wet it, dear Henry, *etc.*
15. With what shall I wet it, dear Liza, *etc.*
16. With water, dear Henry, *etc.*
17. In what shall I carry it, dear Liza, *etc.*
18. In a bucket, dear Henry, *etc.*
19. There's a hole in the bucket, dear Liza, *etc.*

Copyright © 2012 by HAL LEONARD CORPORATION
International Copyright Secured All Rights Reserved

When I'm Sixty-Four

Registration 3
Rhythm: Rock

Words and Music by John Lennon
and Paul McCartney

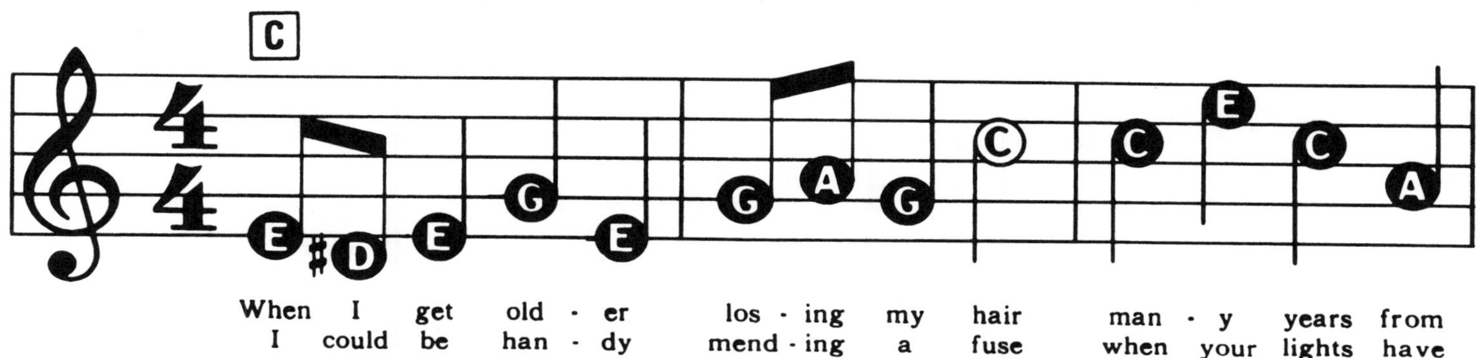

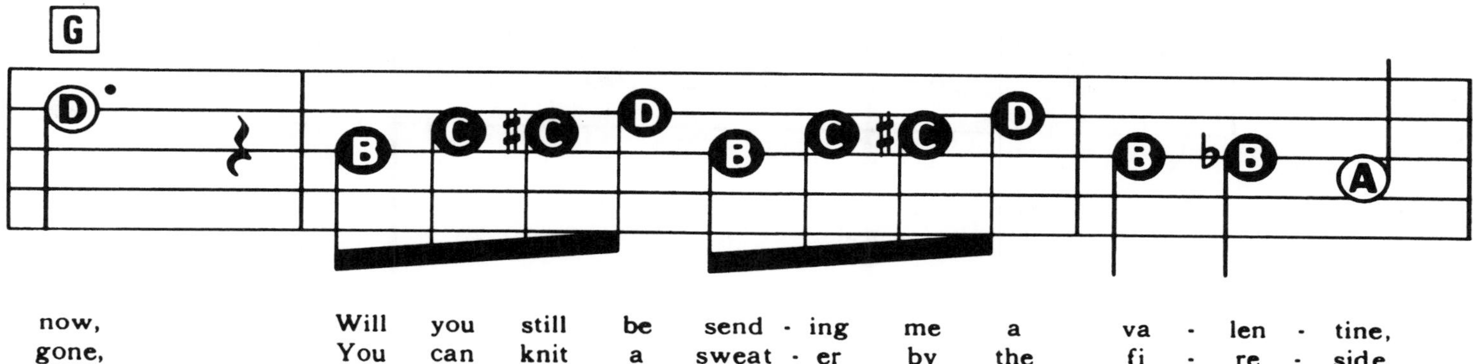

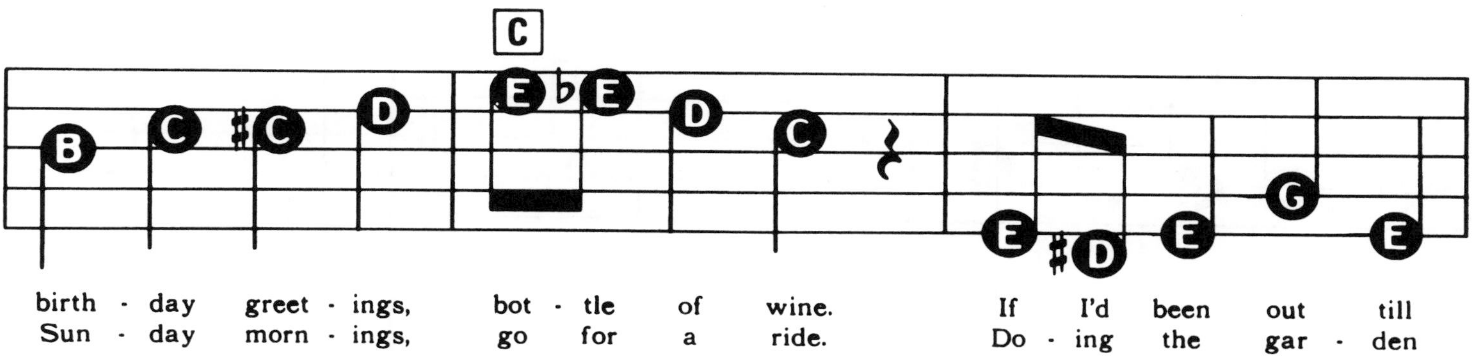

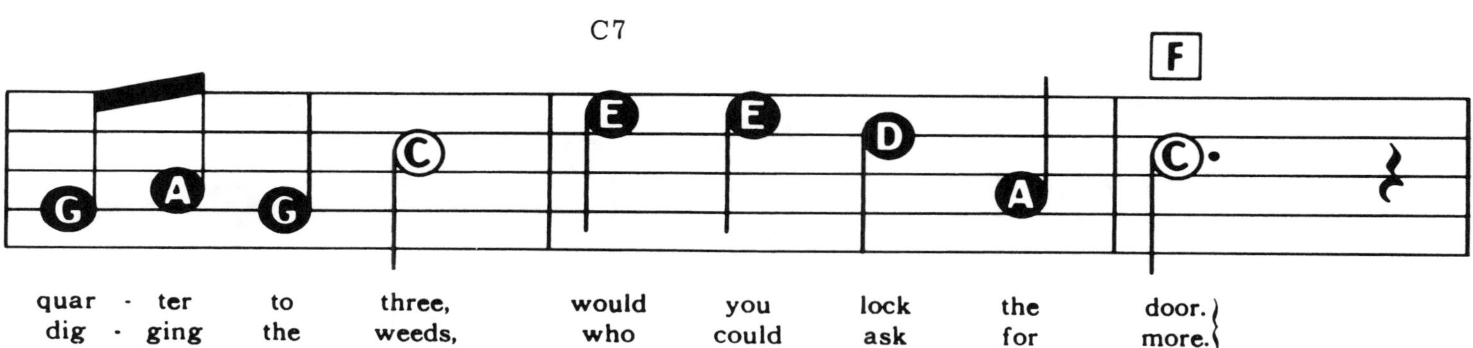

Copyright © 1967 Sony/ATV Music Publishing LLC
Copyright Renewed
All Rights Administered by Sony/ATV Music Publishing LLC, 424 Church Street, Suite 1200, Nashville, TN 37219
International Copyright Secured All Rights Reserved

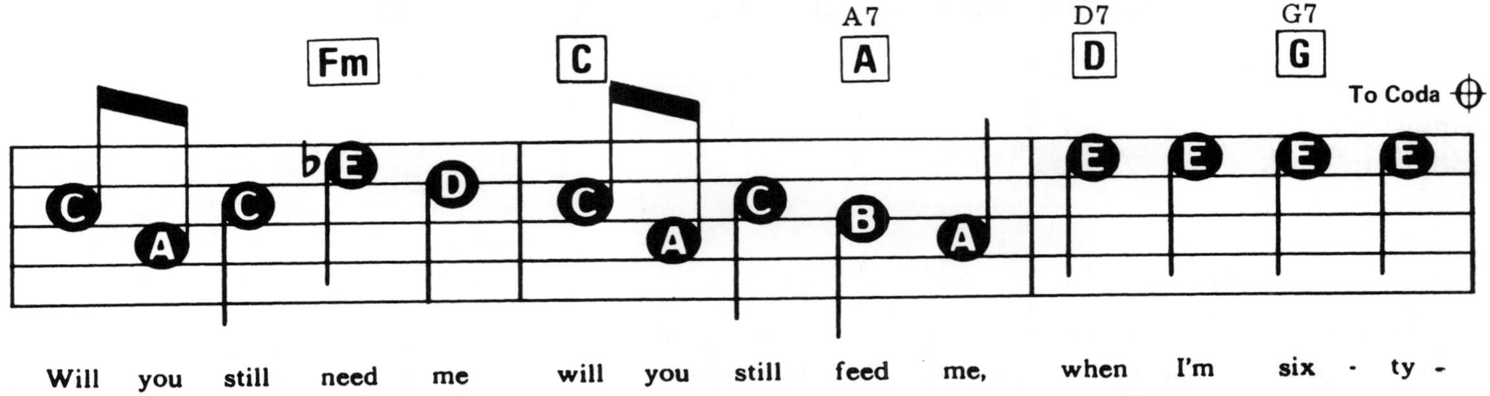
Fm
C
A7
A
D7
D
G7
G
To Coda
C A C ♭E D C A C B A E E E E
Will you still need me will you still feed me, when I'm six - ty -

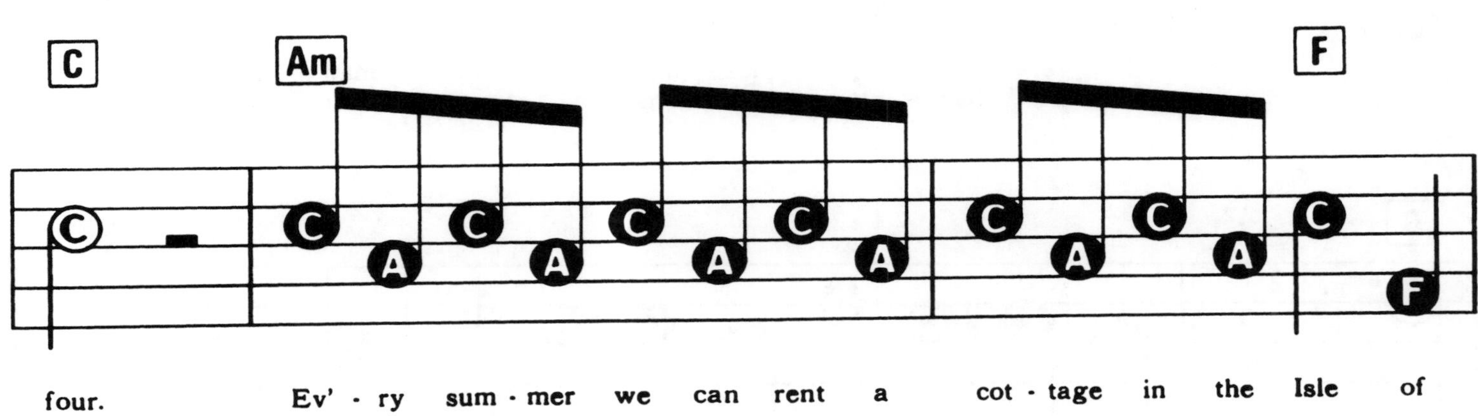
C
Am
F
C C A C A C A C A C A C A C F
four. Ev' - ry sum - mer we can rent a cot - tage in the Isle of

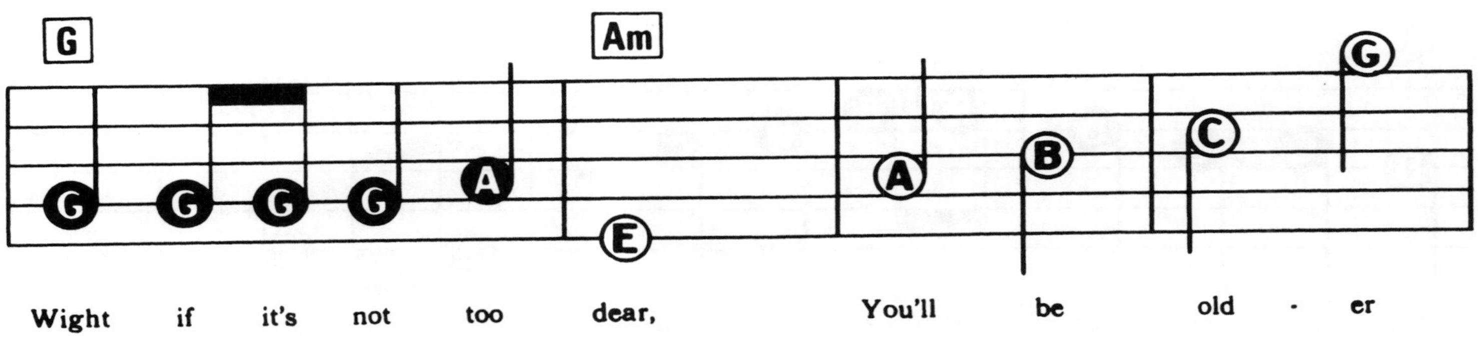
G
Am
G G G G A E A B C G
Wight if it's not too dear, You'll be old - er

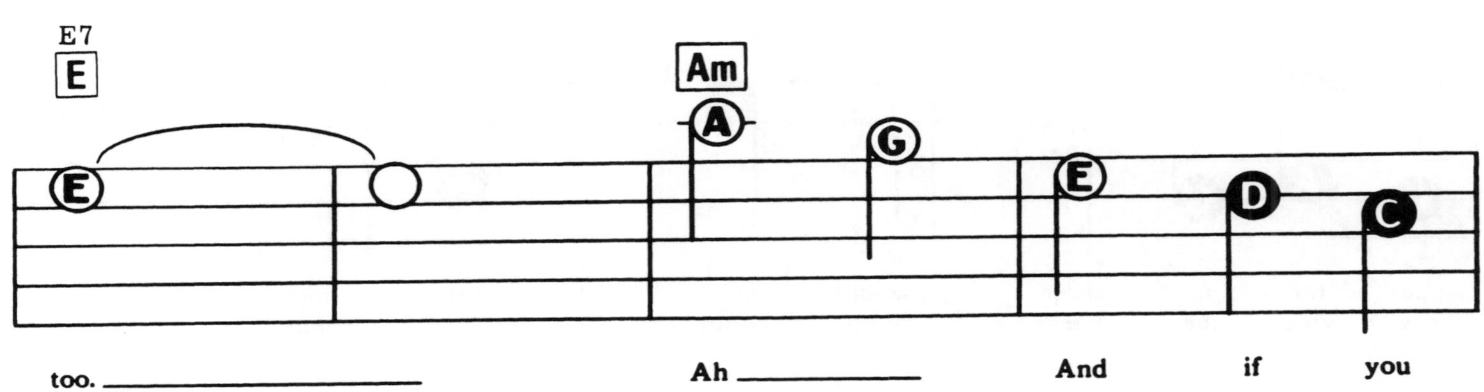
E7
E
Am
E A G E D C
too. Ah And if you

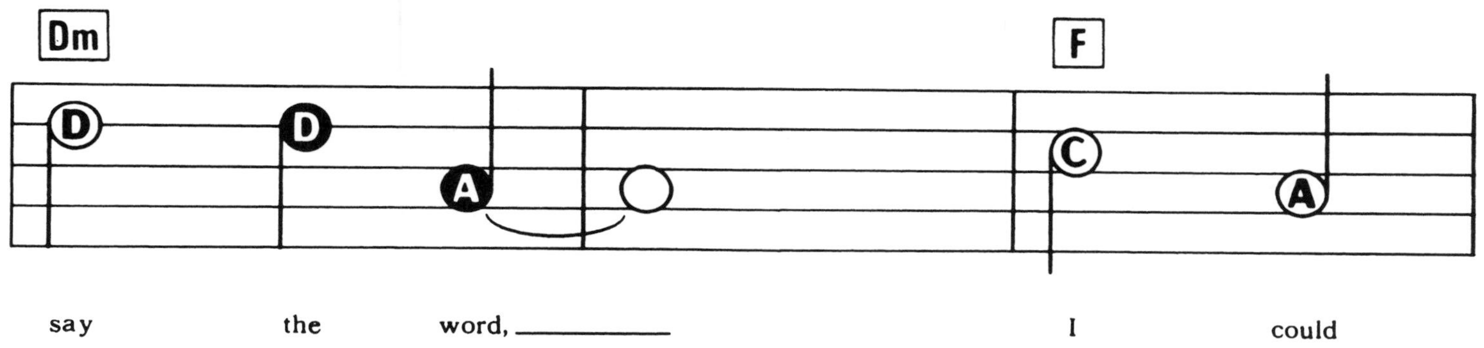
Dm
F
D
D
A
C
A
say
the
word, ___________
I
could

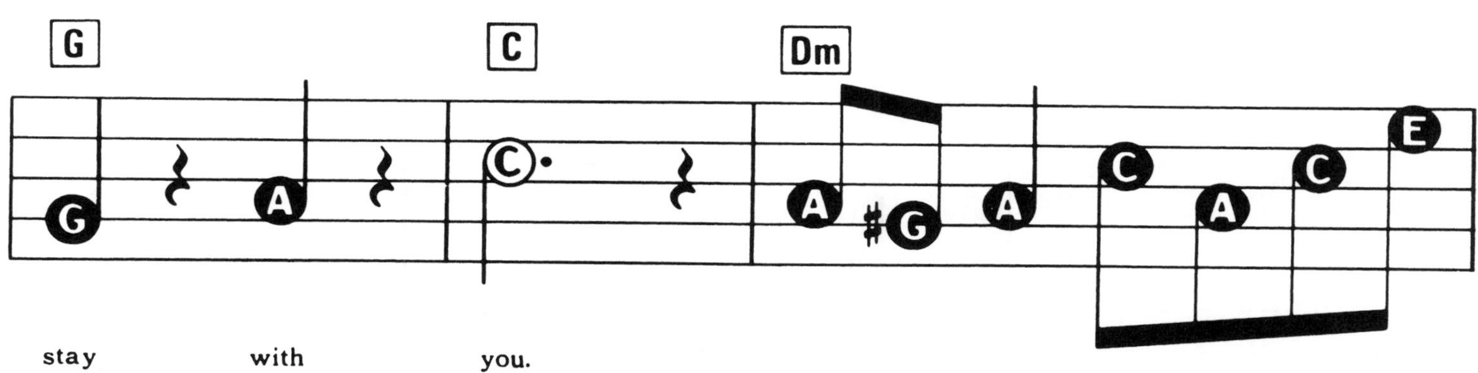
G
C
Dm
G
A
C
A
♯G
A
C
A
C
E
stay
with
you.

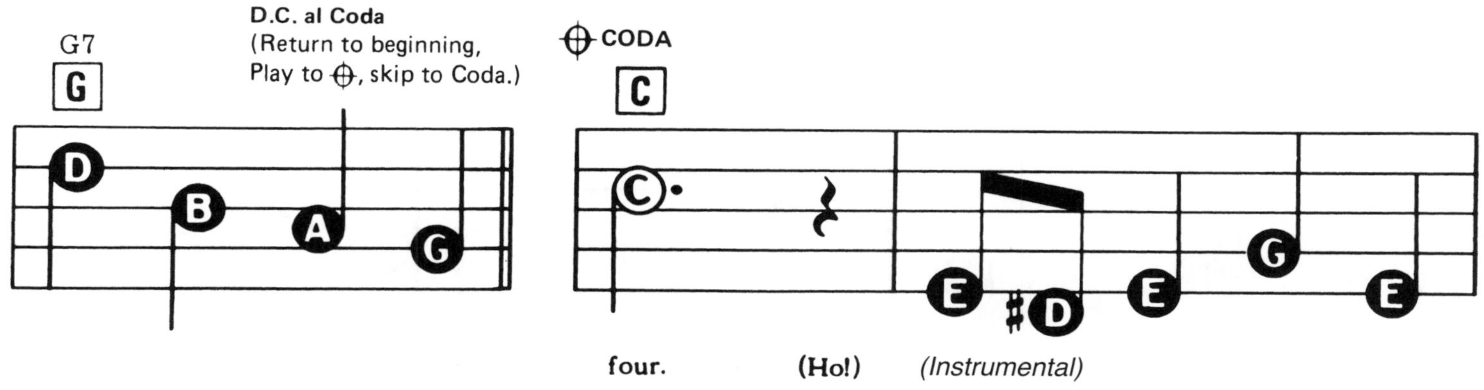
G7
G
D.C. al Coda
(Return to beginning,
Play to ⊕, skip to Coda.)
⊕ CODA
C
D
B
A
G
C
E
♯D
E
G
E
four.
(Ho!)
(Instrumental)

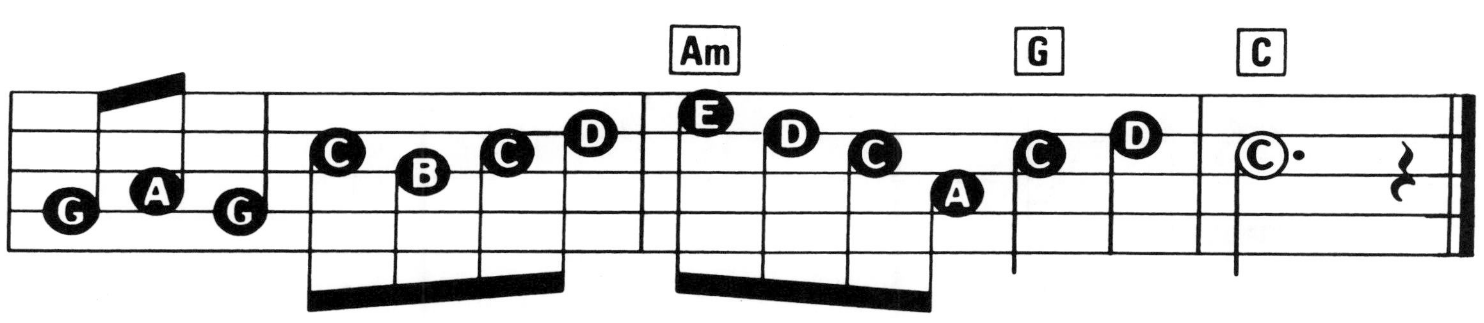
Am
G
C
G
A
G
C
B
C
D
E
D
C
A
C
D
C

This Land Is Your Land

Registration 4
Rhythm: Country or Swing

Words and Music by
Woody Guthrie

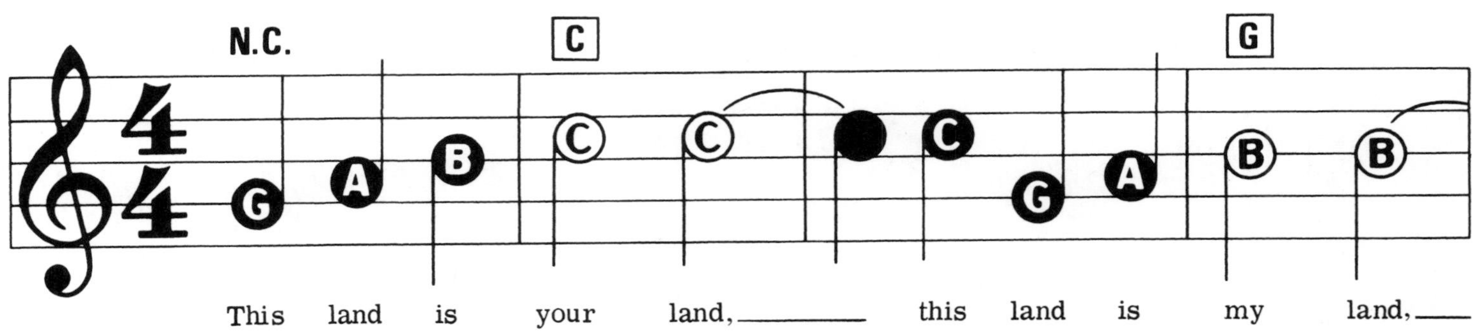

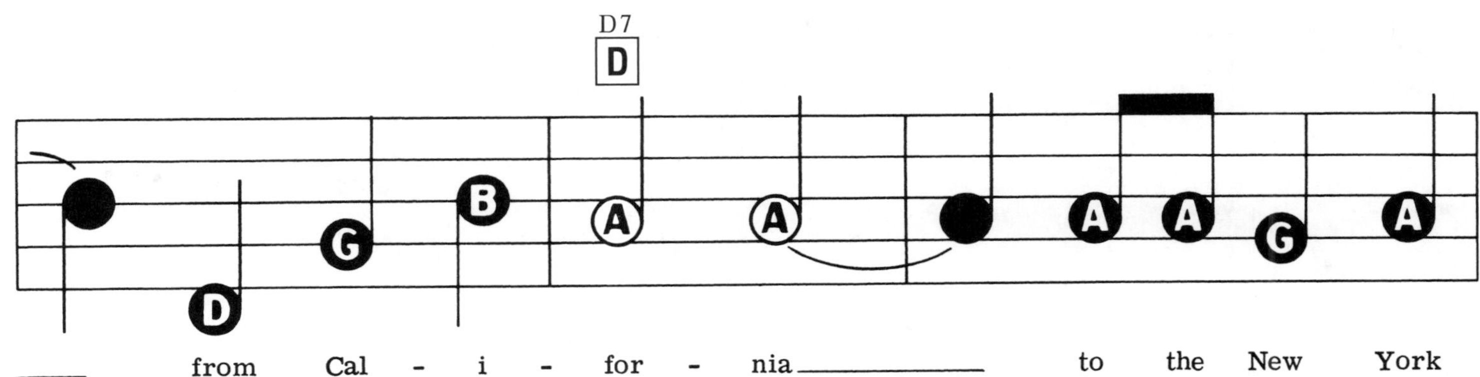

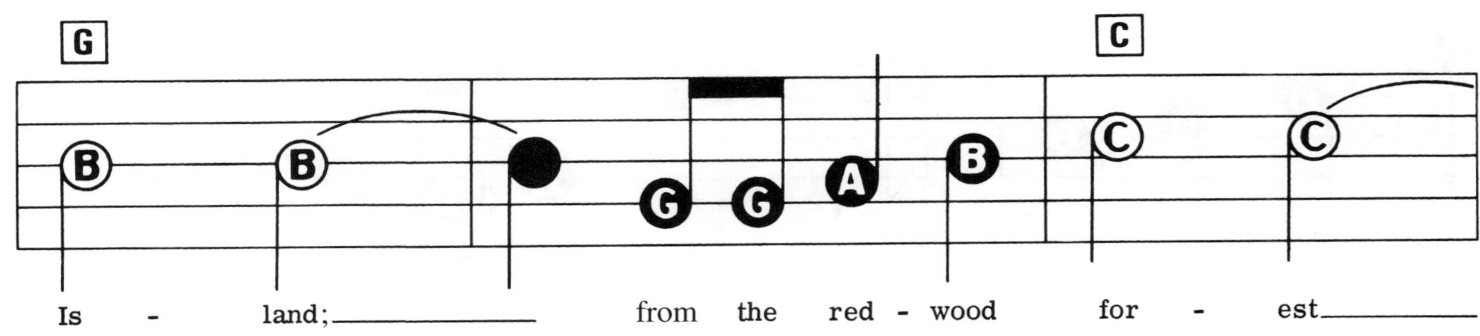

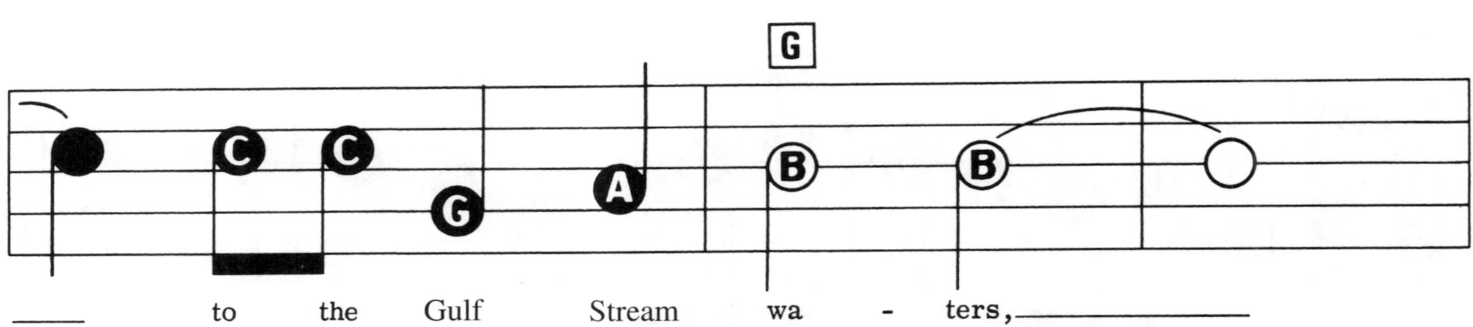

WGP/TRO - © Copyright 1956, 1958, 1970, 1972 (Copyrights Renewed) Woody Guthrie Publications, Inc. & Ludlow Music, Inc., New York, NY administered by Ludlow Music, Inc.
International Copyright Secured
All Rights Reserved Including Public Performance For Profit
Used by Permission

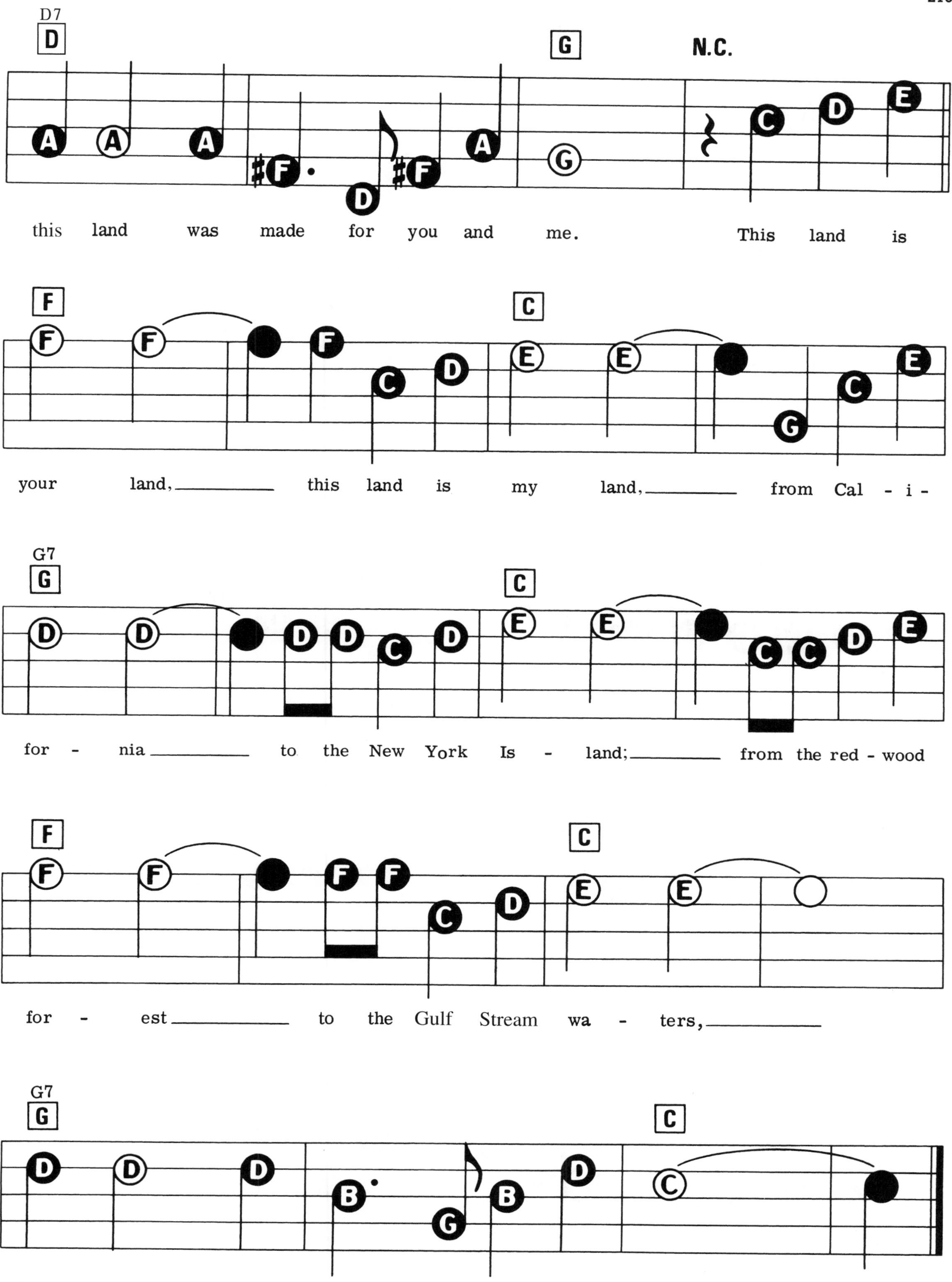
D7
D
G
N.C.
A A A F D F A G C D E
this land was made for you and me. This land is
F
C
F F F C D E E G C E
your land, this land is my land, from Cal - i -
G7
G
C
D D D D C D E E C C D E
for - nia to the New York Is - land; from the red - wood
F
C
F F F F C D E E
for - est to the Gulf Stream wa - ters,
G7
G
C
D D D B G B D C
this land was made for you and me.

This Old Man

Registration 5
Rhythm: Fox Trot

Traditional

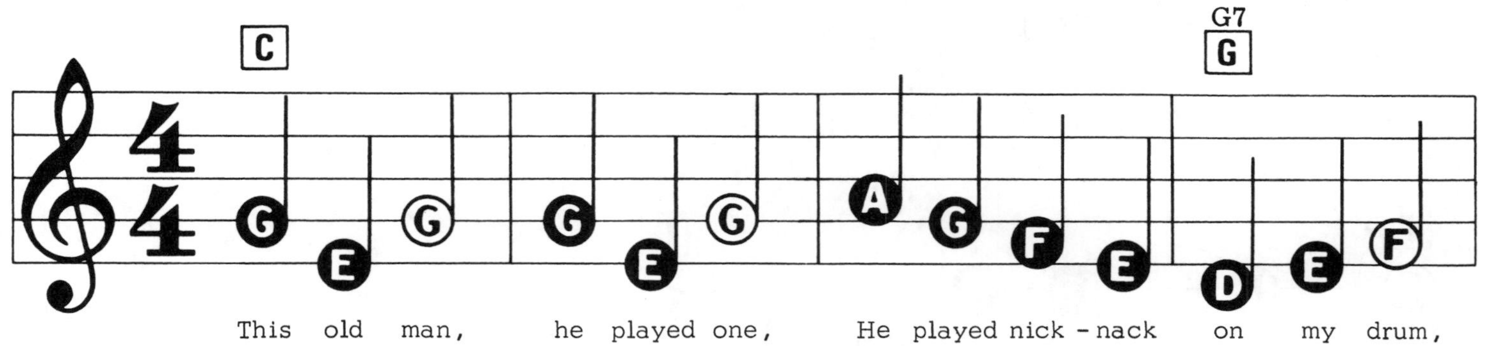

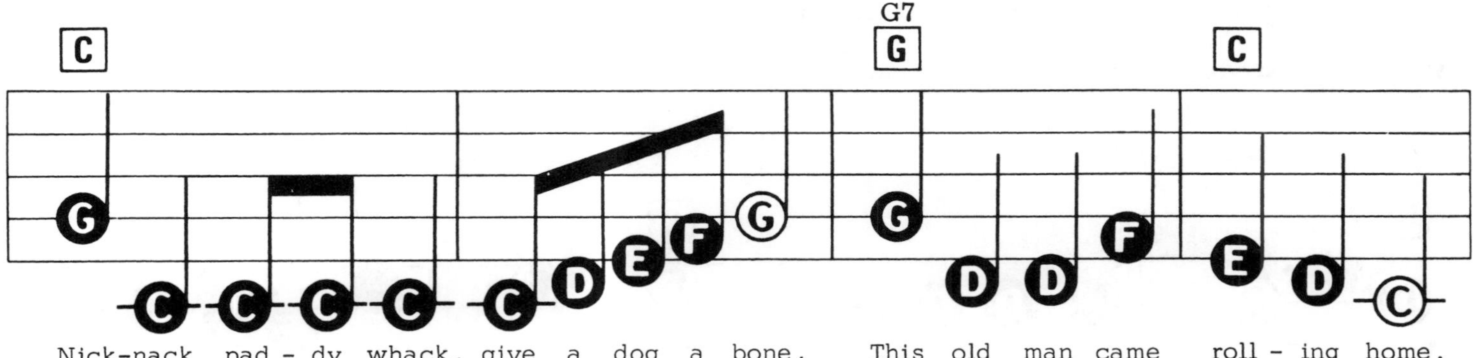

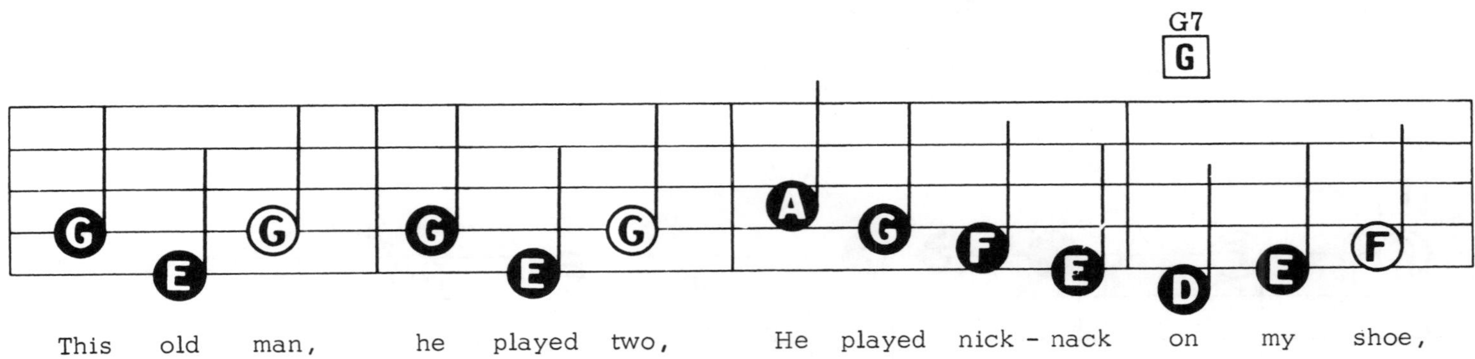

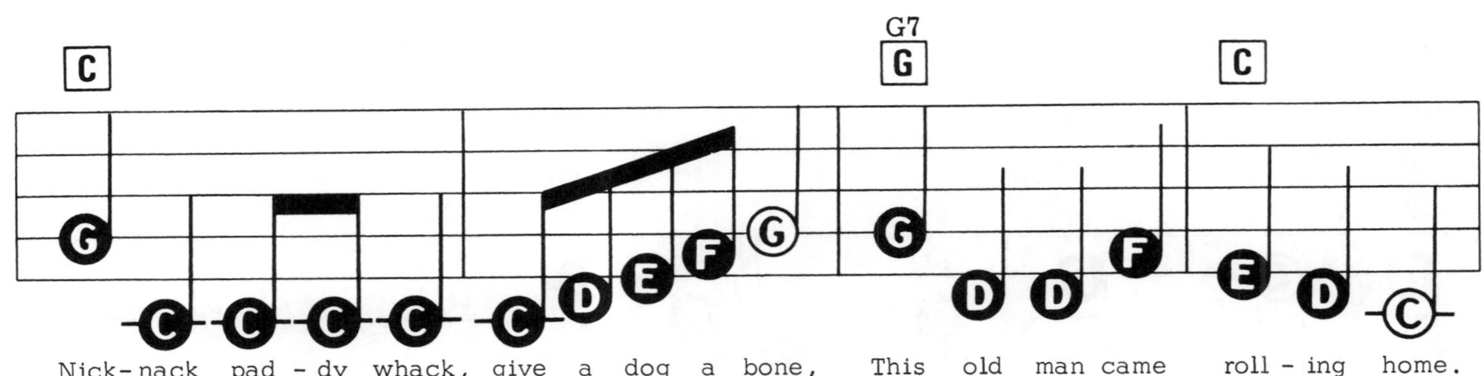

Copyright © 1978 by HAL LEONARD CORPORATION
International Copyright Secured All Rights Reserved

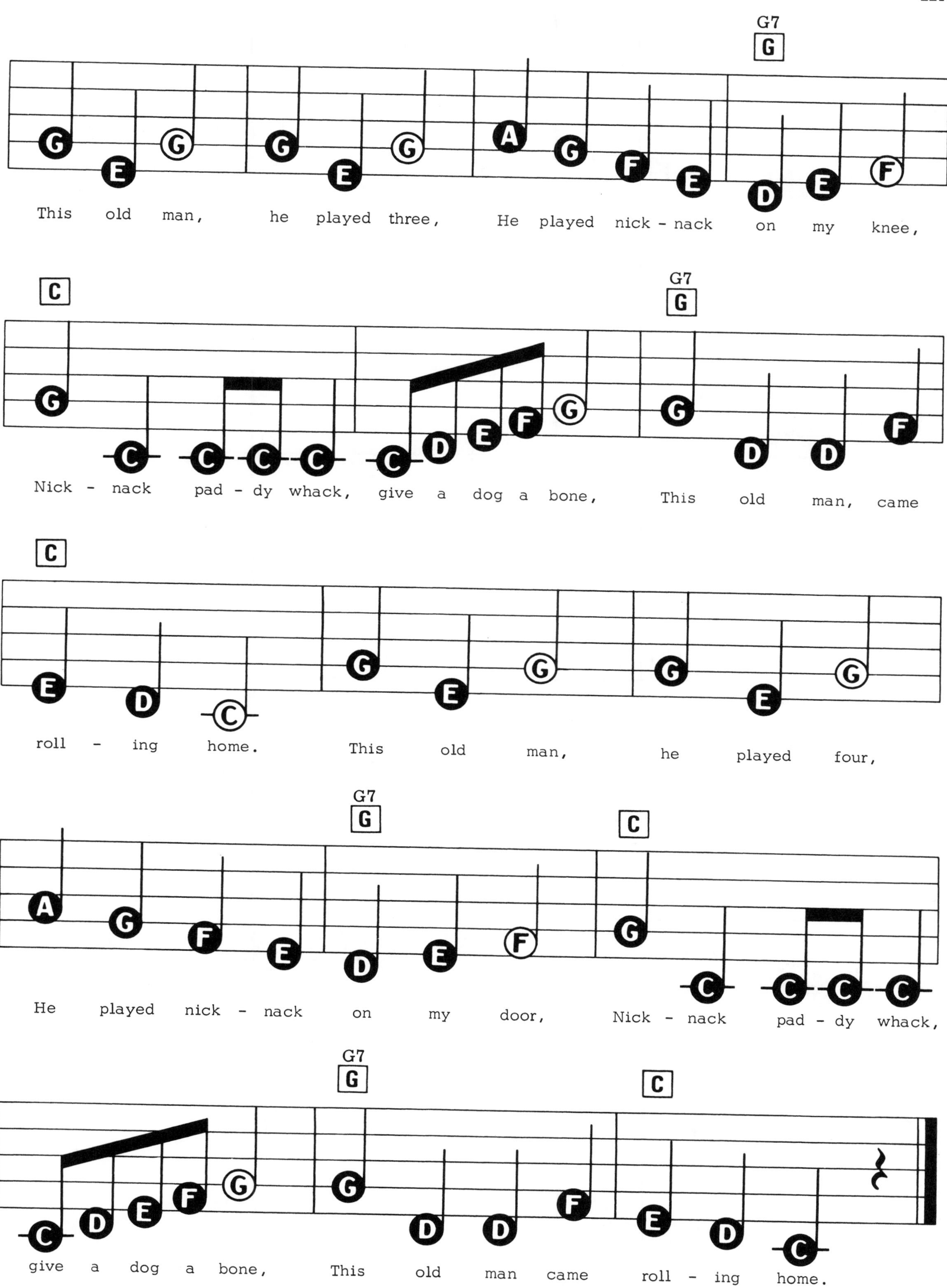
G7
G
This old man, he played three, He played nick - nack on my knee,
C
G7
G
Nick - nack pad - dy whack, give a dog a bone, This old man, came
C
roll - ing home. This old man, he played four,
G7
G
C
He played nick - nack on my door, Nick - nack pad - dy whack,
G7
G
C
give a dog a bone, This old man came roll - ing home.

Tomorrow
from the Musical Production ANNIE

Registration 1
Rhythm: Swing or Jazz

Lyric by Martin Charnin
Music by Charles Strouse

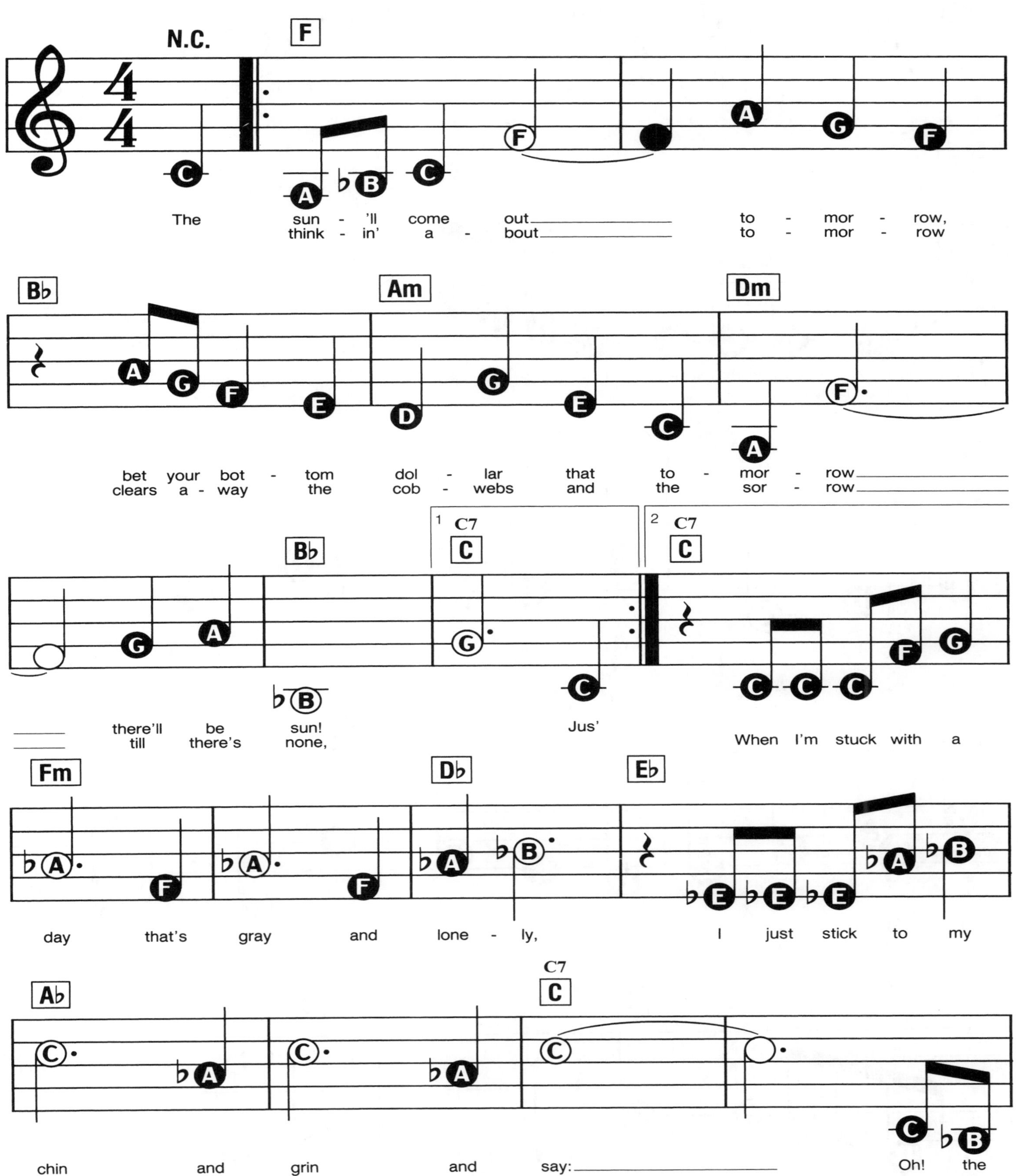

© 1977 (Renewed) EDWIN H. MORRIS & COMPANY, A Division of MPL Music Publishing, Inc. and CHARLES STROUSE PUBLISHING
All Rights for CHARLES STROUSE PUBLISHING Administered by WB MUSIC CORP.
All Rights Reserved Used by Permission

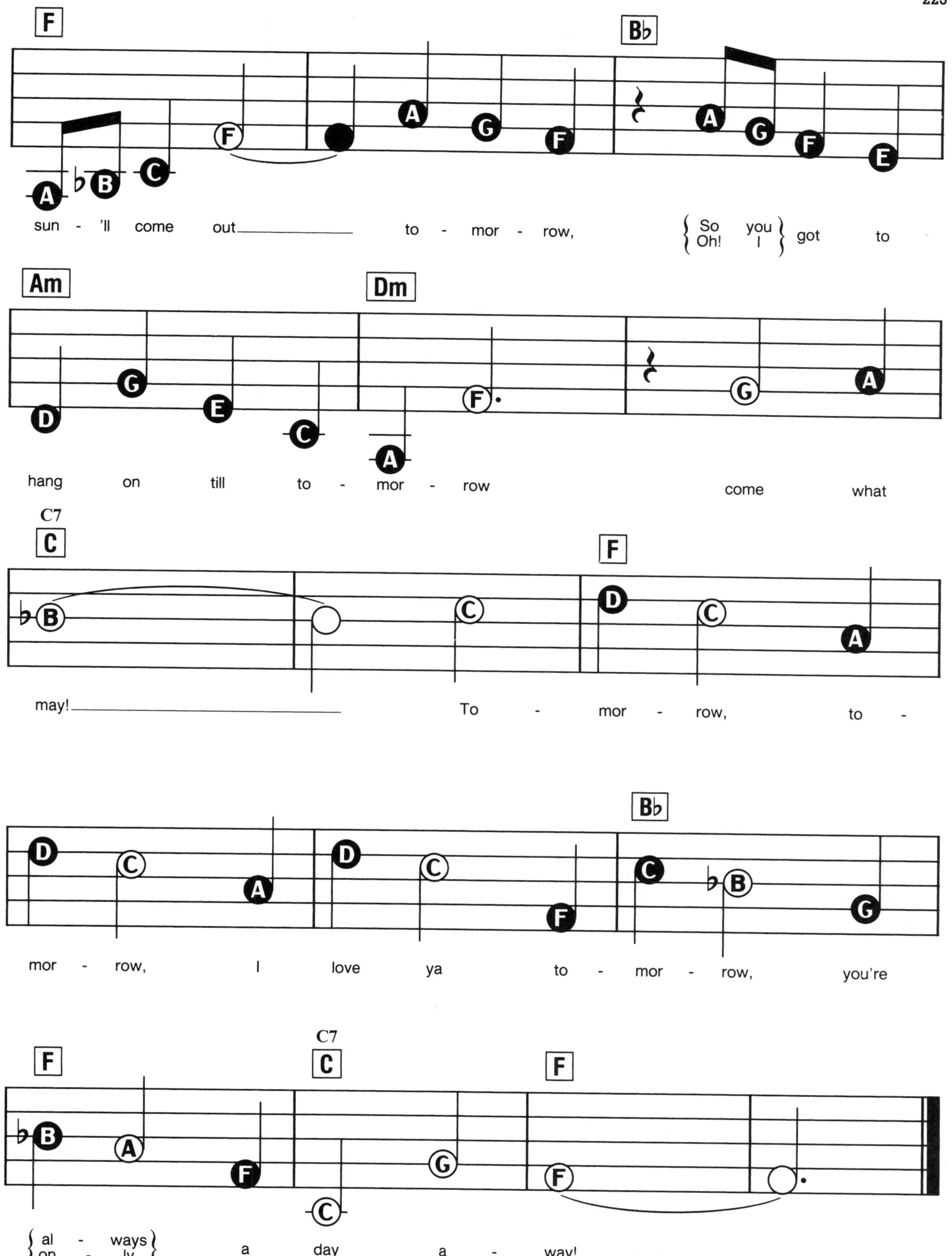
F
B♭
sun - 'll come out to - mor - row, { So you / Oh! I } got to
Am
Dm
hang on till to - mor - row come what
C7
C
F
may! To - mor - row, to -
B♭
mor - row, I love ya to - mor - row, you're
F
C7
C
F
{ al - ways / on - ly } a day a - way!

The Unbirthday Song

from Walt Disney's ALICE IN WONDERLAND

Registration 2
Rhythm: Fox Trot

Words and Music by Mack David,
Al Hoffman and Jerry Livingston

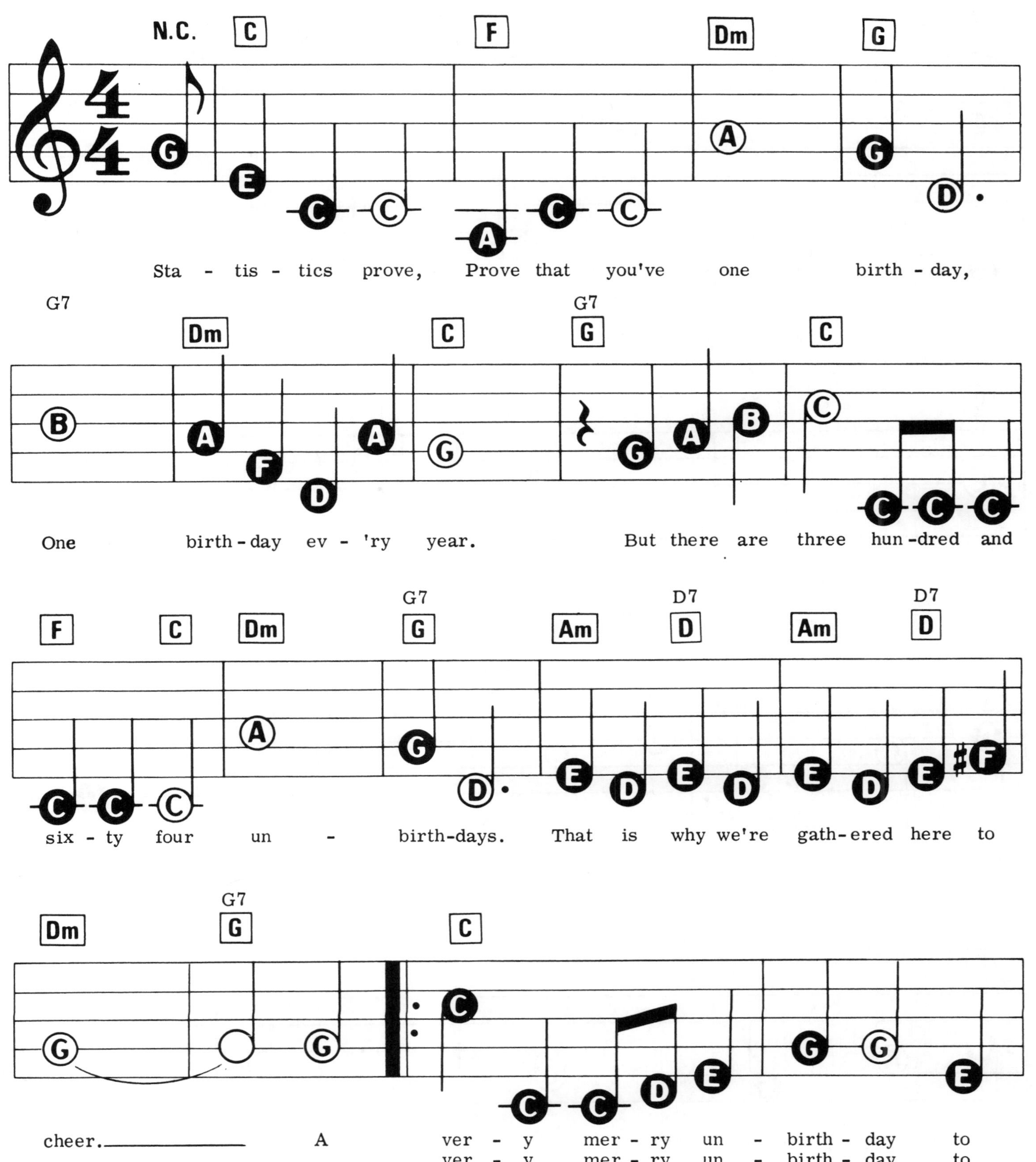

© 1948 Walt Disney Music Company
Copyright Renewed
All Rights Reserved. Used by Permission.

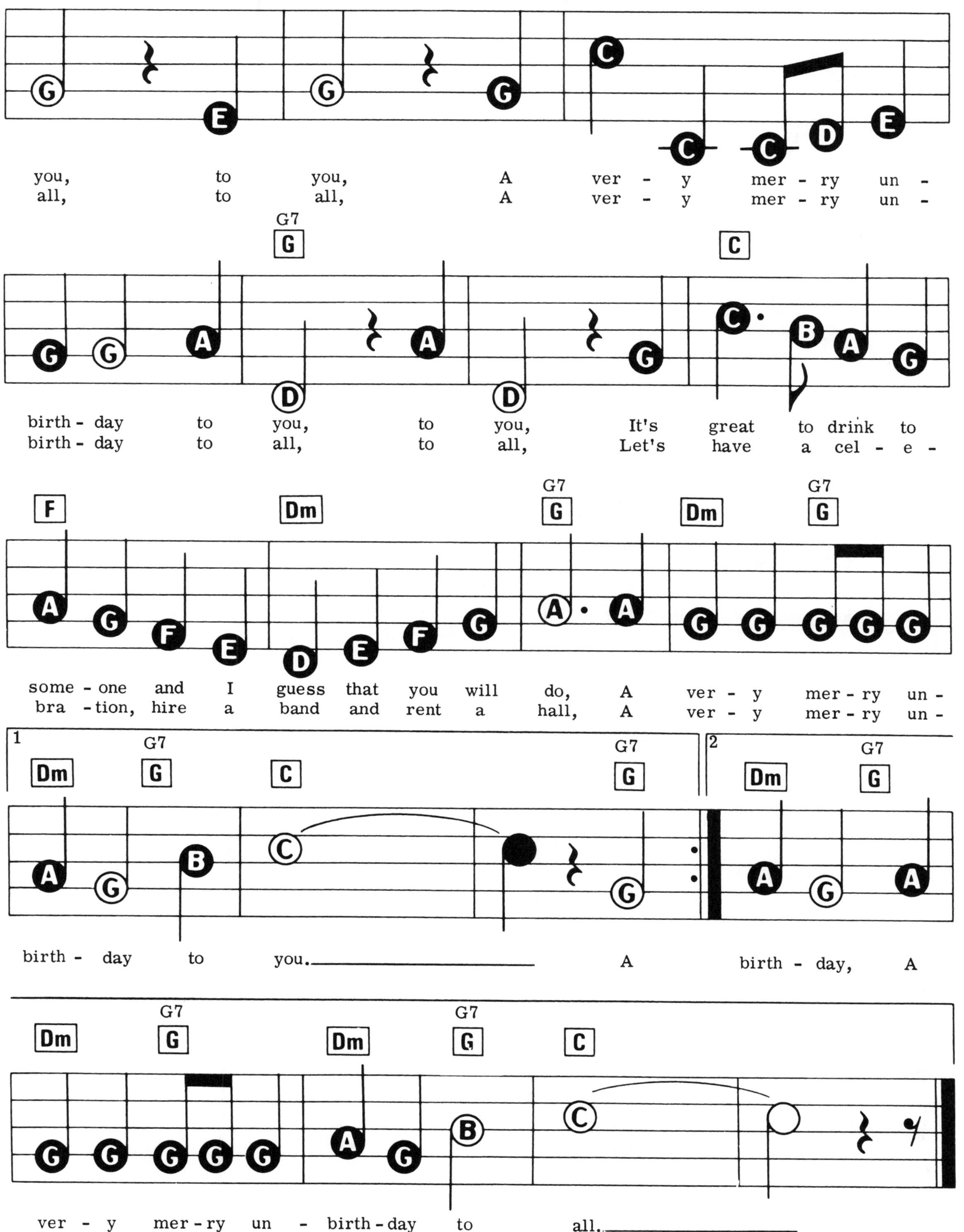
you, to you, A ver - y mer - ry un -
all, to all, A ver - y mer - ry un -
G7
G
C
birth - day to you, to you, It's great to drink to
birth - day to all, to all, Let's have a cel - e -
F
Dm
G7
G
Dm
G7
G
some - one and I guess that you will do, A ver - y mer - ry un -
bra - tion, hire a band and rent a hall, A ver - y mer - ry un -
1
Dm
G7
G
C
G7
G
2
Dm
G7
G
birth - day to you. A birth - day, A
Dm
G7
G
Dm
G7
G
C
ver - y mer - ry un - birth - day to all.

We're Off to See the Wizard

from THE WIZARD OF OZ

Registration 2
Rhythm: 6/8 March

Lyric by E.Y. "Yip" Harburg
Music by Harold Arlen

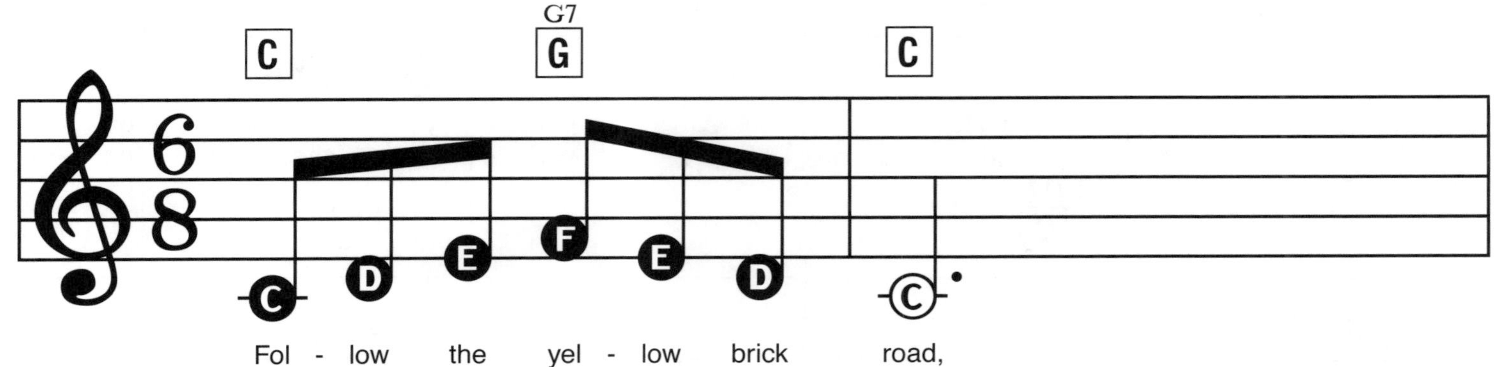

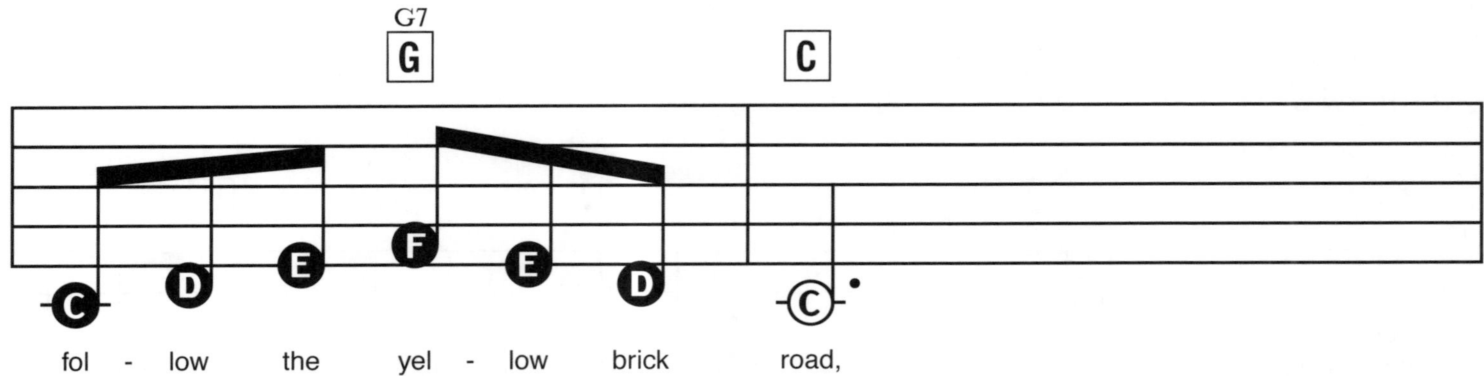

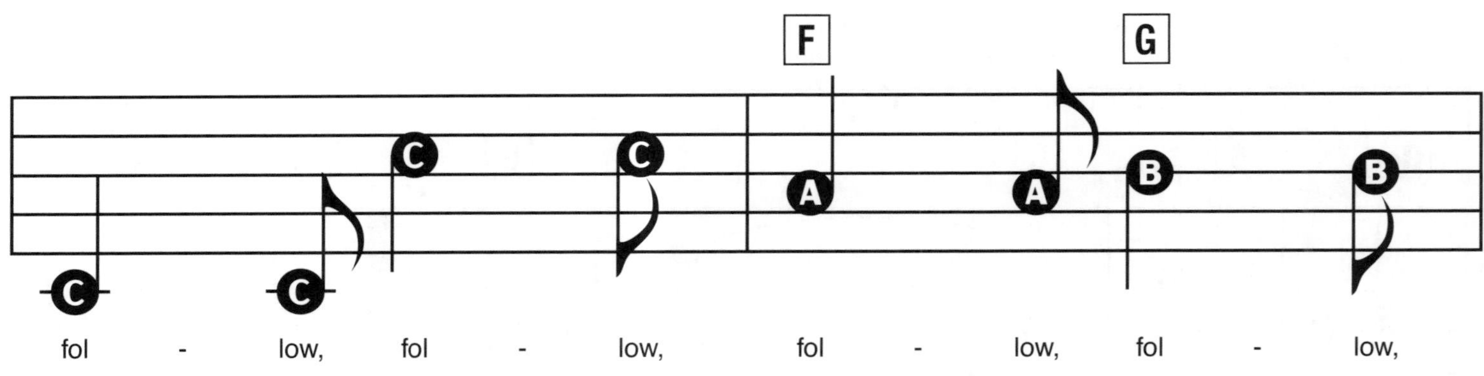

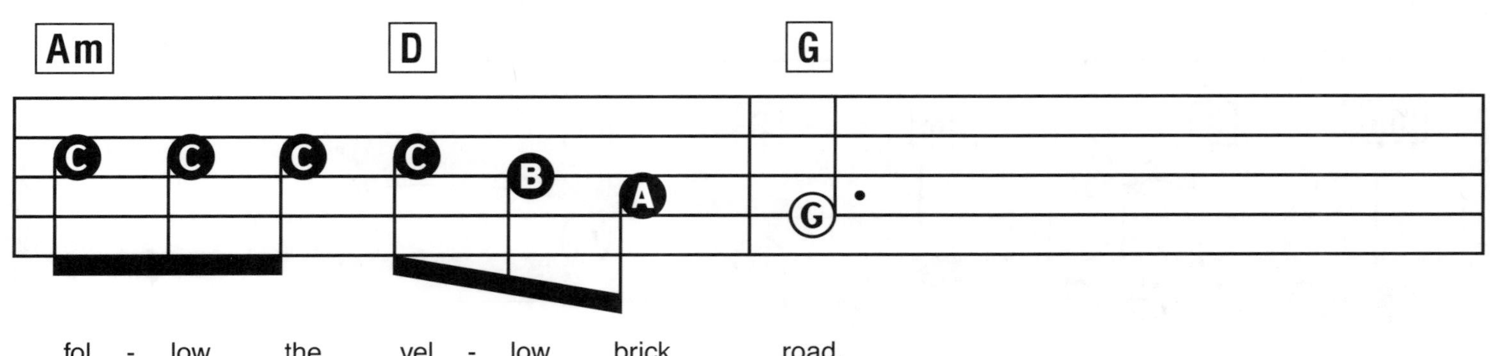

© 1938 (Renewed) METRO-GOLDWYN MAYER INC.
© 1959 (Renewed) EMI FEIST CATALOG INC.
All Rights Administered by EMI FEIST CATALOG INC. (Publishing) and ALFRED MUSIC (Print)
All Rights Reserved Used by Permission

Dm G C
A A G A B C G G G
Fol - low the rain - bow o - ver the stream,
Dm G C
F F E D D G E E D C
fol - low the fel - low who fol - lows a dream,
F G
C C C C A A B B
fol - low, fol - low, fol - low, fol - low,
D G
D D D D C A G G
fol - low the yel - low brick road. We're
C G C
C G E F G C G
off to see the wiz - ard, the

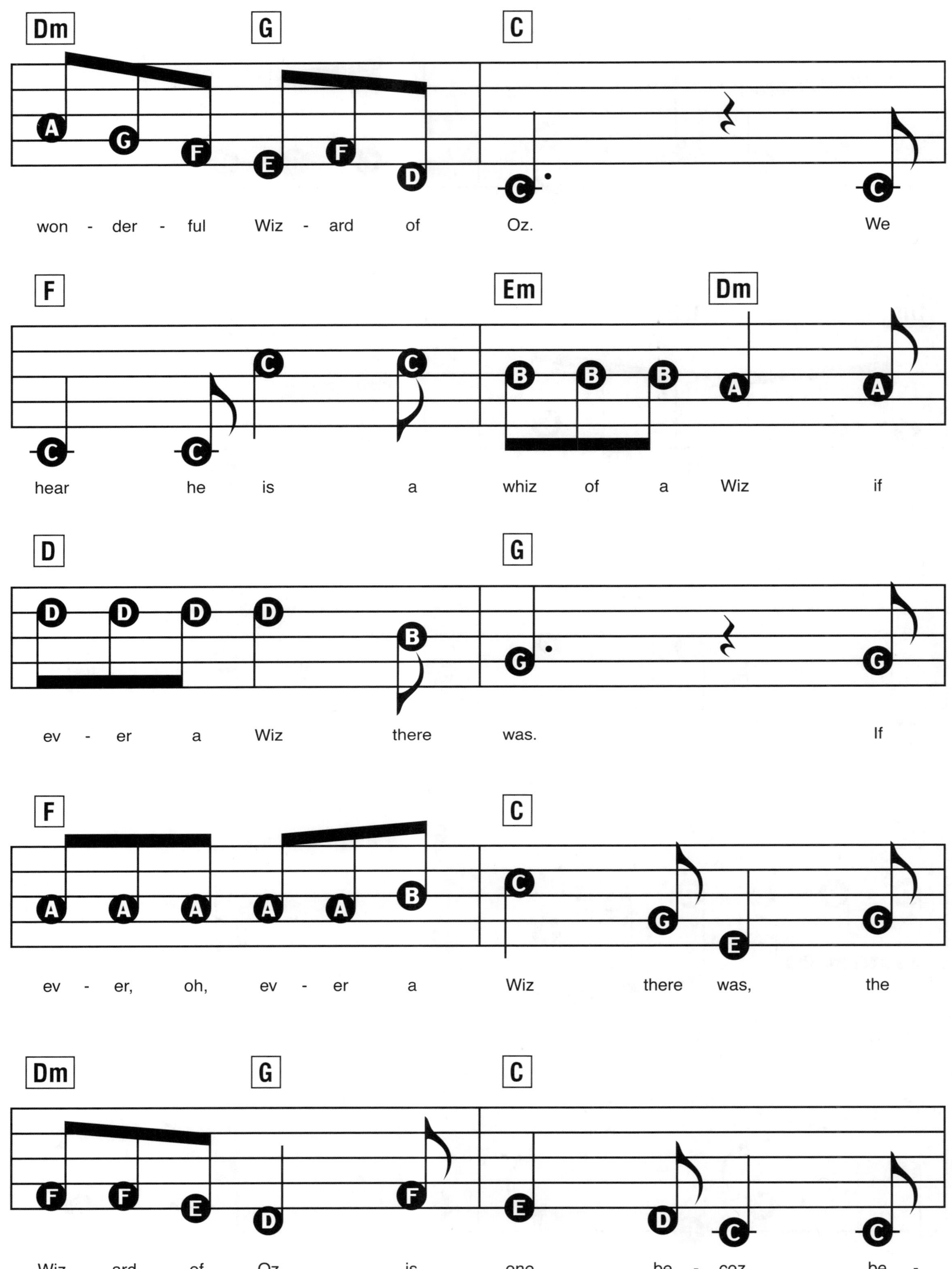
Dm
G
C
A G F E F D C C
won - der - ful Wiz - ard of Oz. We
F
Em
Dm
C C C C B B B A A
hear he is a whiz of a Wiz if
D
G
D D D D B G G
ev - er a Wiz there was. If
F
C
A A A A A B C G E G
ev - er, oh, ev - er a Wiz there was, the
Dm
G
C
F F E D F E D C C
Wiz - ard of Oz is one be - coz, be -

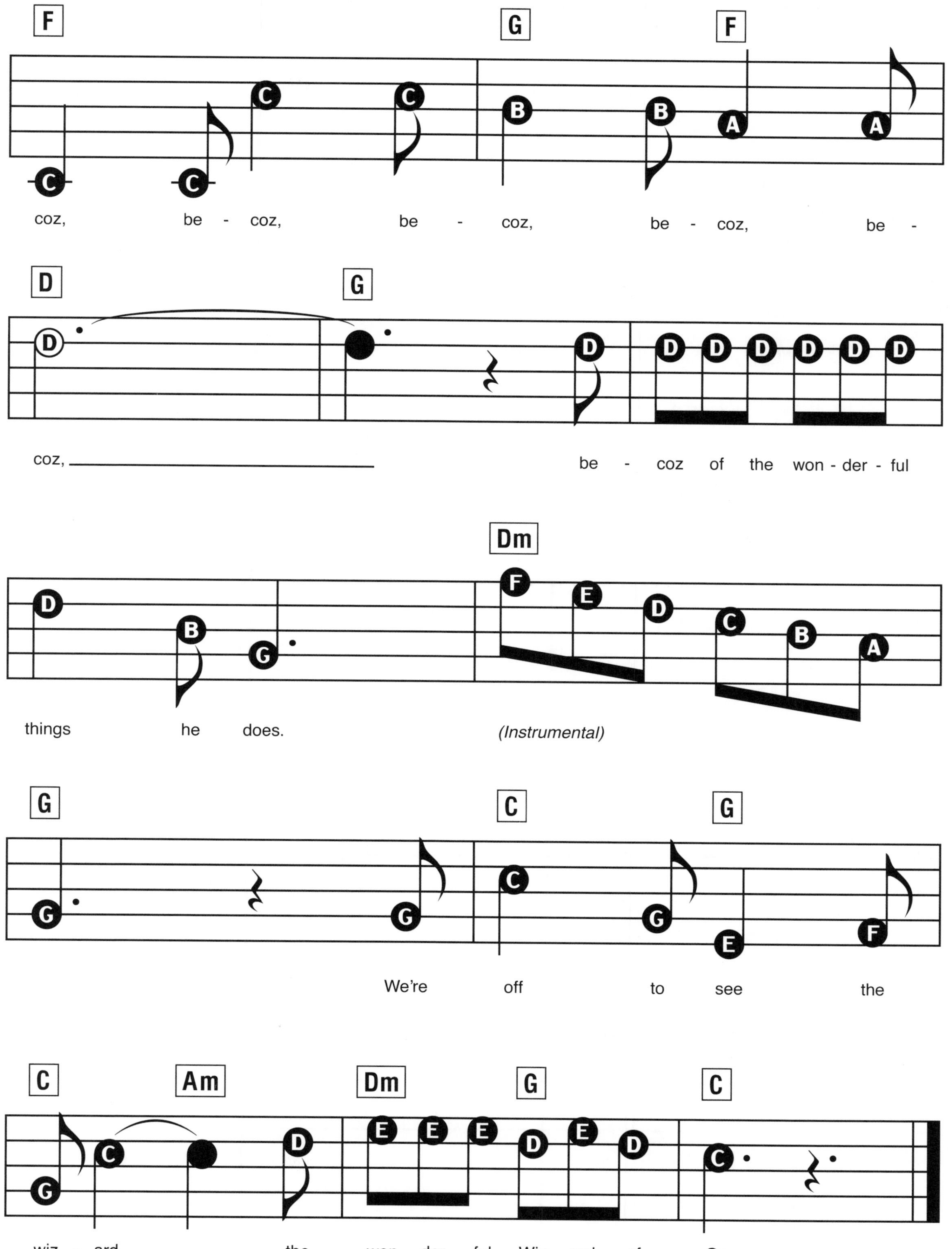
F G F
C C C C B B A A
coz, be - coz, be - coz, be - coz, be -
D G
D D D D D D D D
coz, be - coz of the won - der - ful
Dm
D B G F E D C B A
things he does. (Instrumental)
G C G
G G C G E F
We're off to see the
C Am Dm G C
G C D E E E D E D C
wiz - ard, the won - der - ful Wiz - ard of Oz.

When I Grow Too Old to Dream

Registration 10
Rhythm: Waltz

Lyrics by Oscar Hammerstein II
Music by Sigmund Romberg

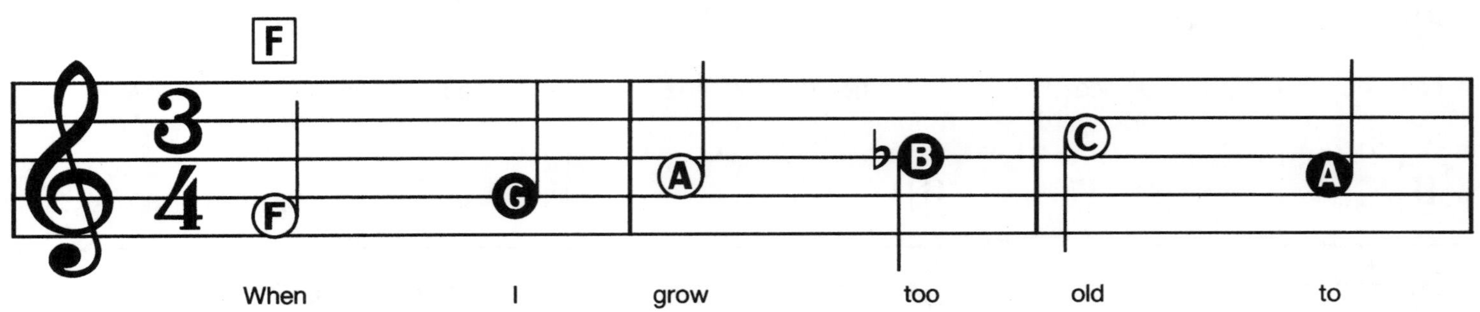

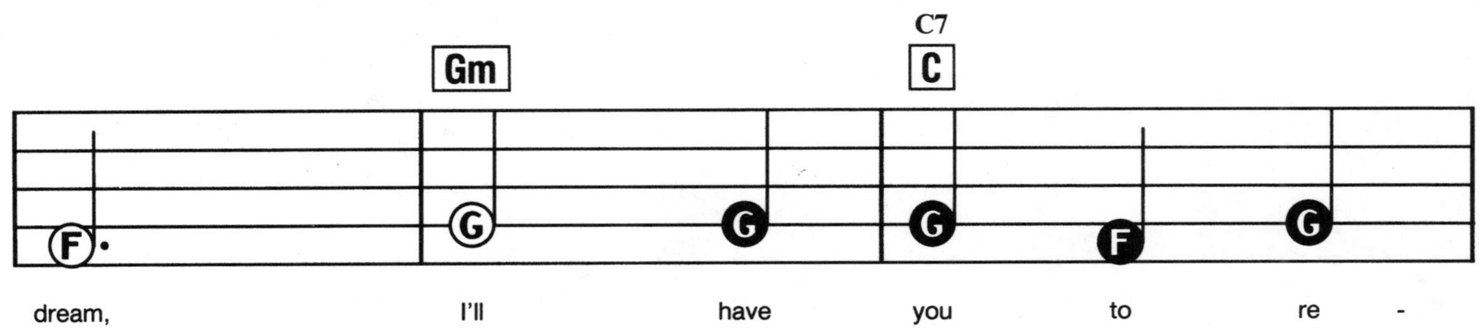

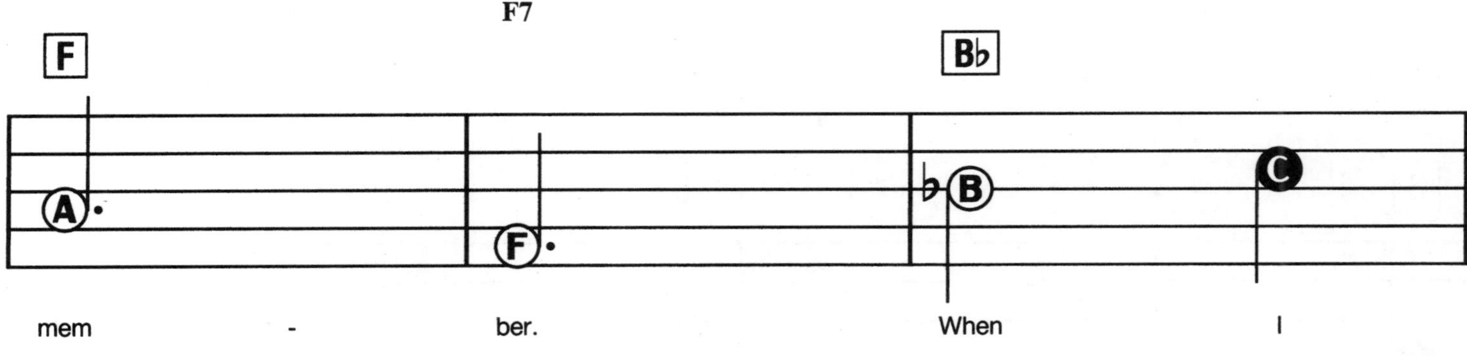

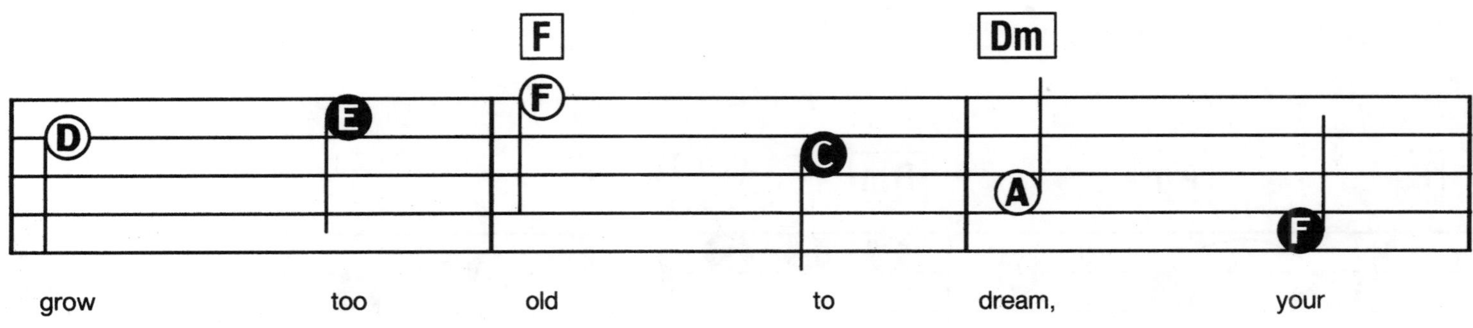

© 1934 (Renewed) EMI ROBBINS CATALOG INC.
All Rights Administered by EMI ROBBINS CATALOG INC. (Publishing) and ALFRED MUSIC (Print)
All Rights Reserved Used by Permission

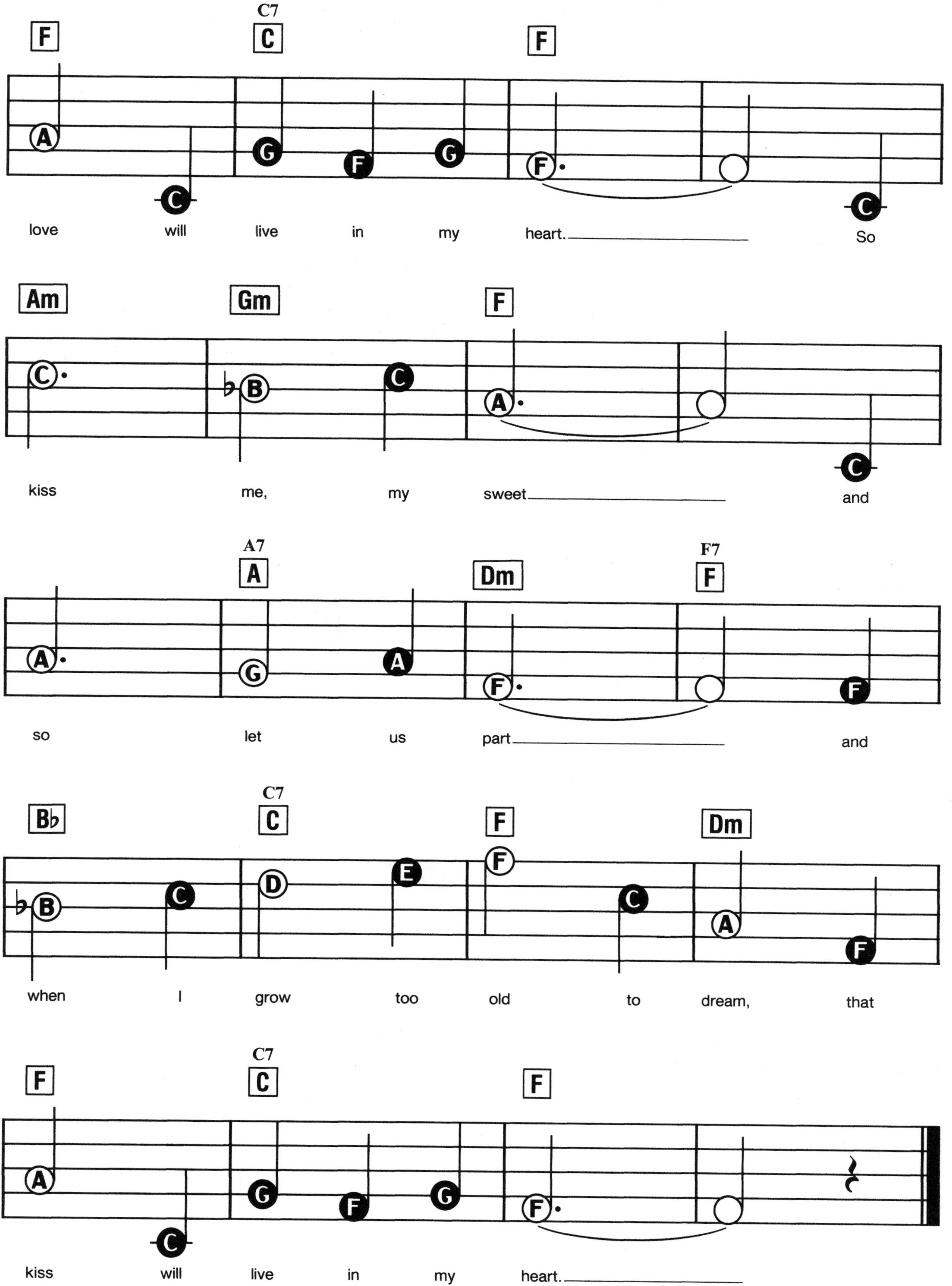
F
C7
C
F
love will live in my heart.
So
Am
Gm
F
kiss me, my sweet
and
A7
A
Dm
F7
F
so let us part
and
B♭
C7
C
F
Dm
when I grow too old to dream, that
F
C7
C
F
kiss will live in my heart.

When She Loved Me

from Walt Disney Pictures' TOY STORY 2 – A Pixar Film

Registration 8
Rhythm: Ballad or Fox Trot

Music and Lyrics by
Randy Newman

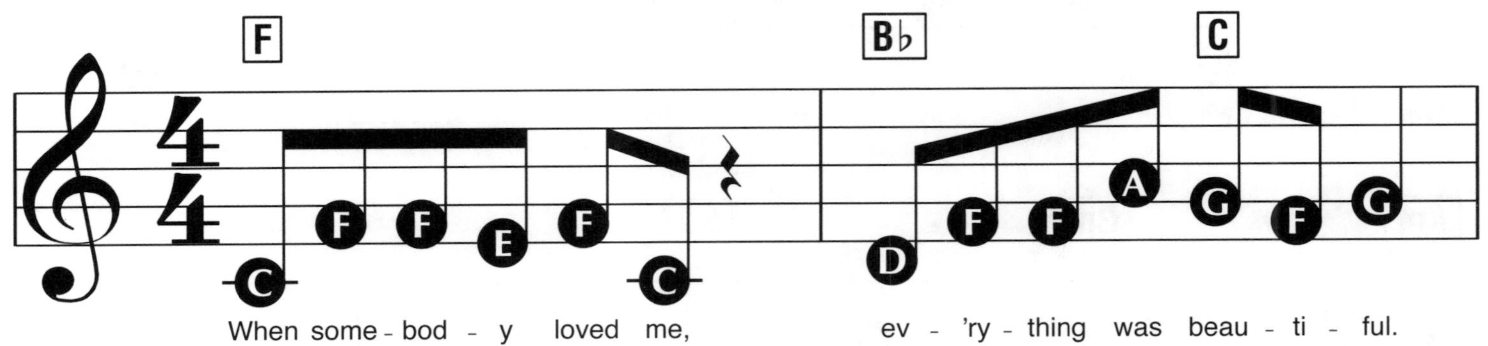

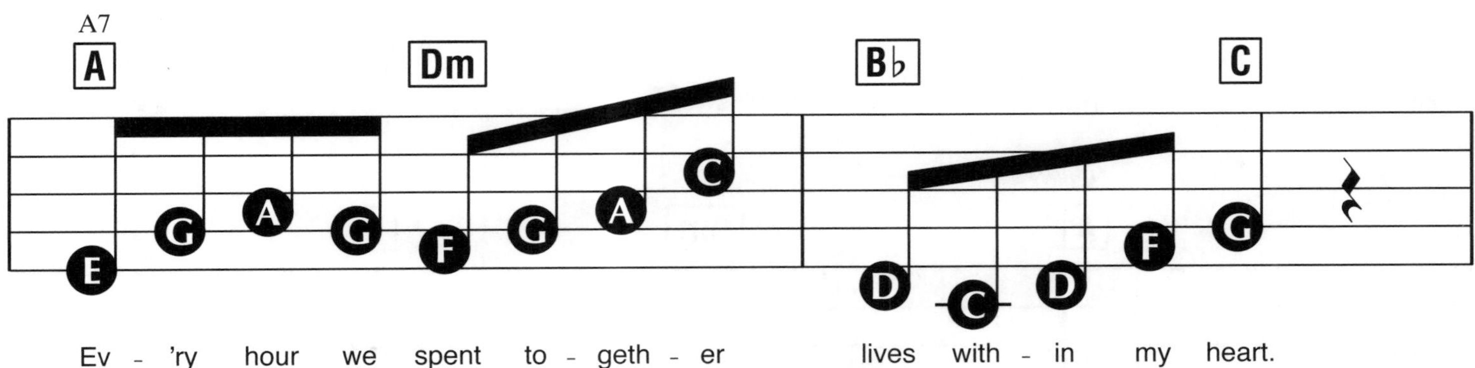

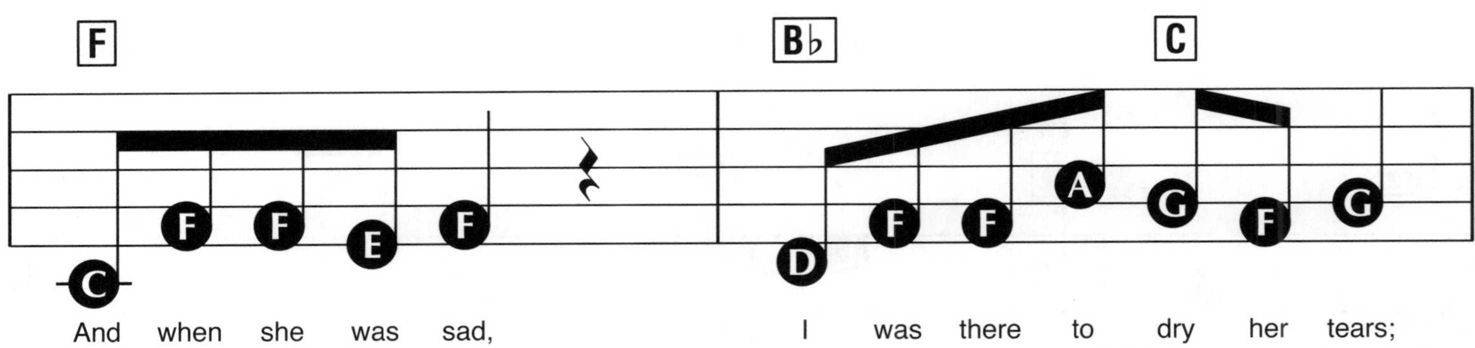

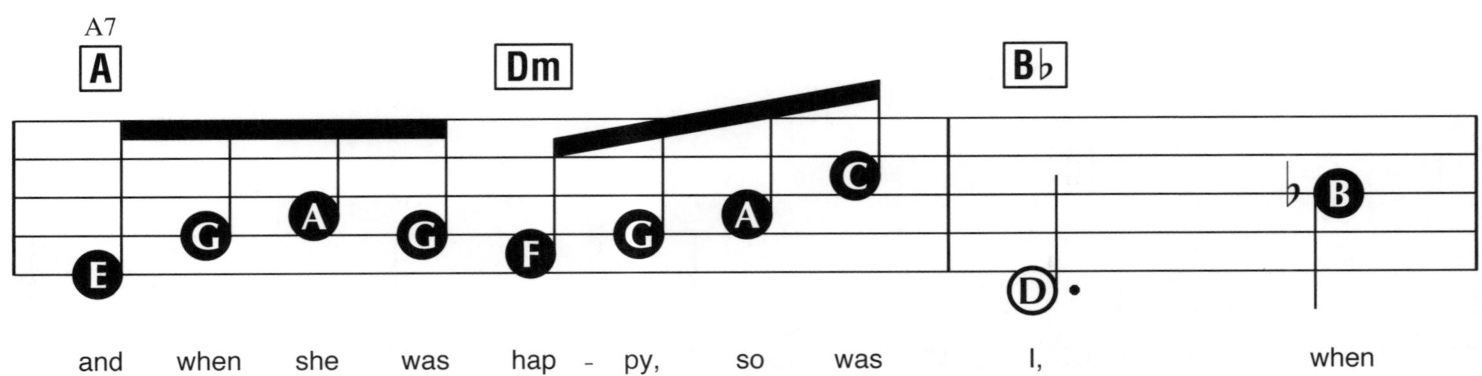

© 1999 Walt Disney Music Company and Pixar Talking Pictures
Administered by Walt Disney Music Company
All Rights Reserved Used by Permission

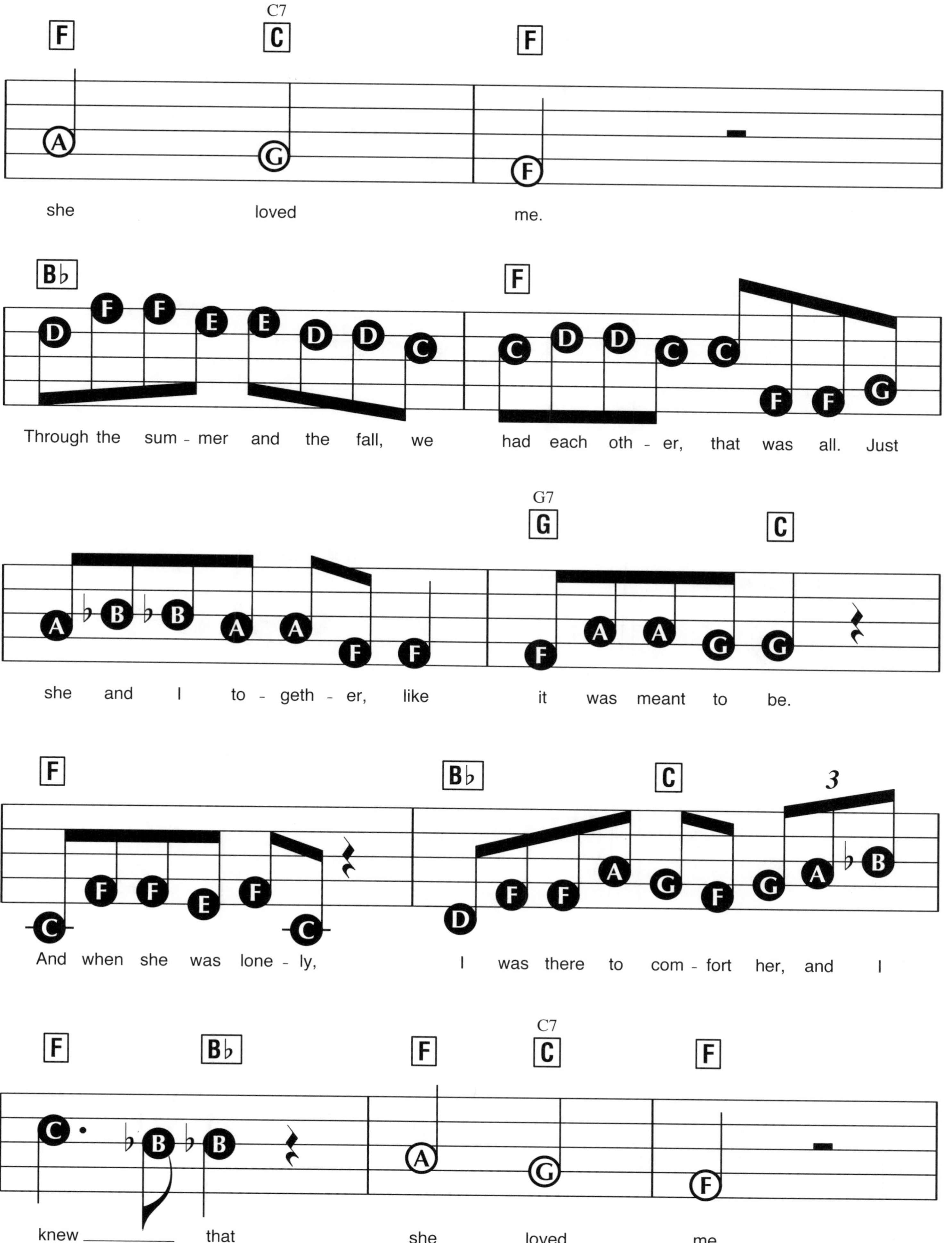
F C7 C F
she loved me.
B♭ F
Through the sum - mer and the fall, we had each oth - er, that was all. Just
G7 G C
she and I to - geth - er, like it was meant to be.
F B♭ C 3
And when she was lone - ly, I was there to com - fort her, and I
F B♭ F C7 C F
knew that she loved me.

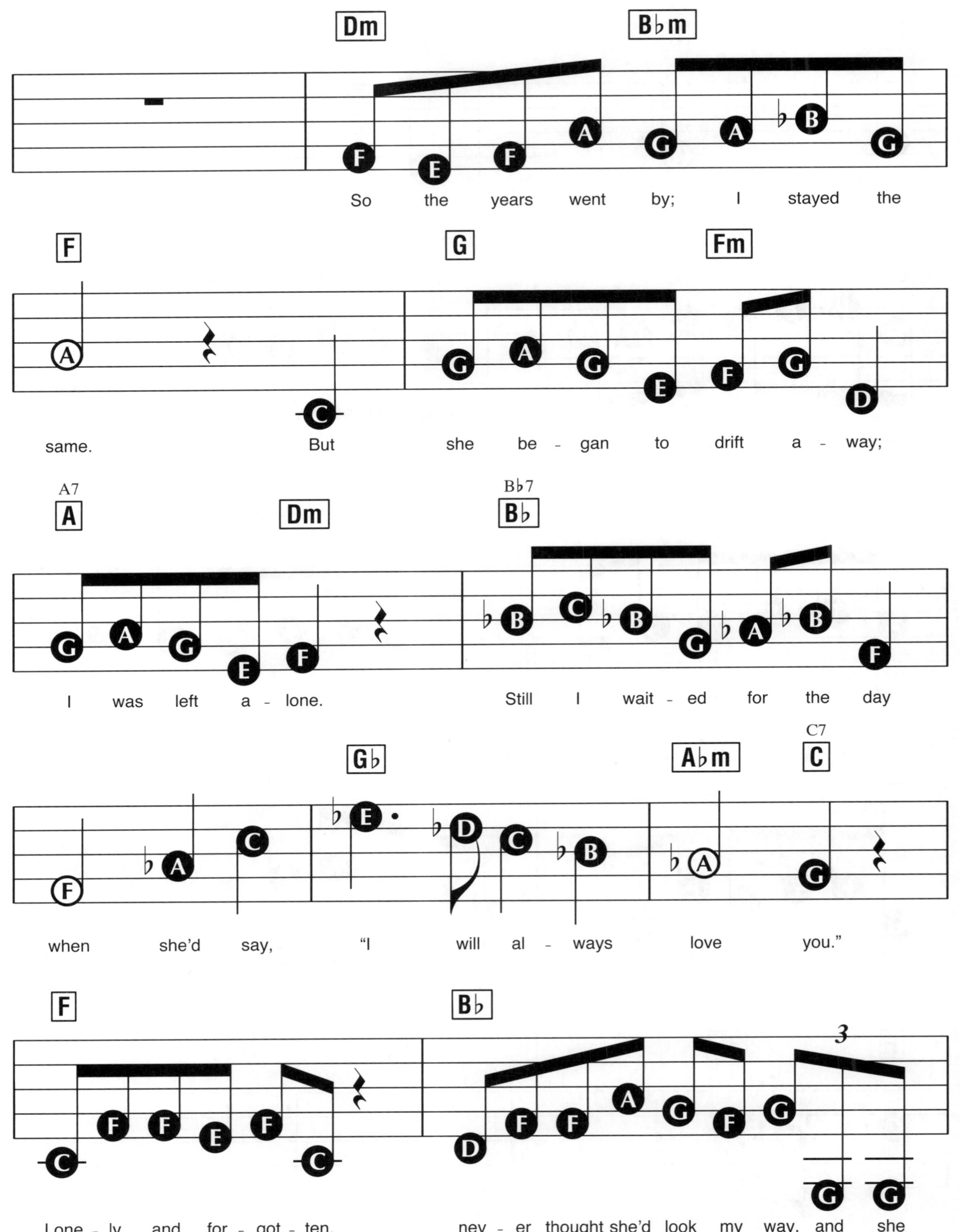
Dm
B♭m
So the years went by; I stayed the
F
G
Fm
same. But she be - gan to drift a - way;
A7
A
Dm
B♭7
B♭
I was left a - lone. Still I wait - ed for the day
G♭
A♭m
C7
C
when she'd say, "I will al - ways love you."
F
B♭
3
Lone - ly and for - got - ten, nev - er thought she'd look my way, and she

A7
A Dm B♭ C
smiled at me and held me just like she used to do, like she
F7 C7
F B♭ F C
loved me when she loved me.
F B♭ C
When some - bod - y loved me, ev - 'ry - thing was beau - ti - ful.
A7
A Dm B♭ C
Ev - 'ry hour we spent to - geth - er lives with - in my heart, when
C7
F C F
she loved me.

When You Wish Upon a Star

from Walt Disney's PINOCCHIO

Registration 1
Rhythm: Ballad

Words by Ned Washington
Music by Leigh Harline

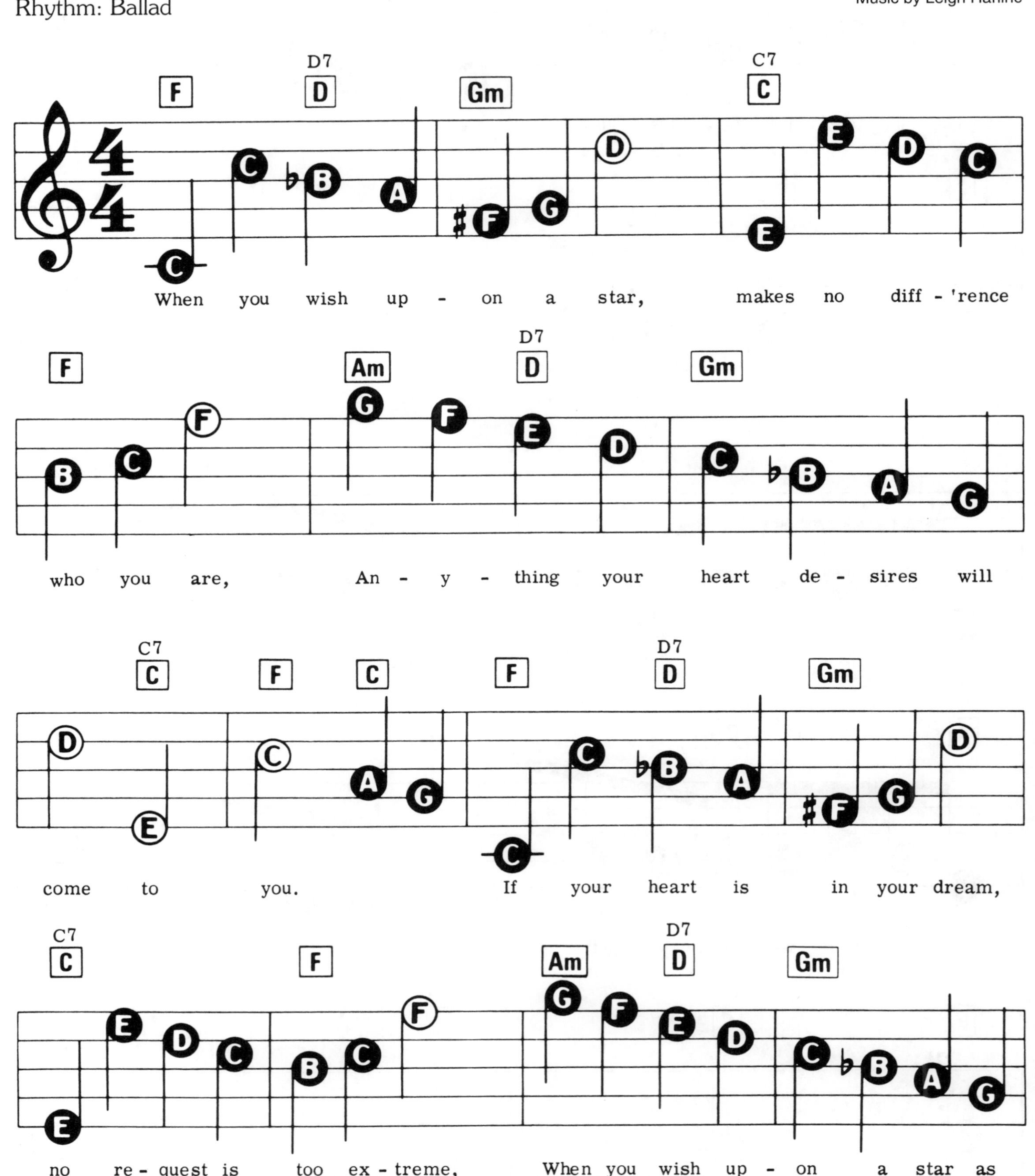

Copyright © 1940 by Bourne Co. (ASCAP)
Copyright Renewed
International Copyright Secured All Rights Reserved

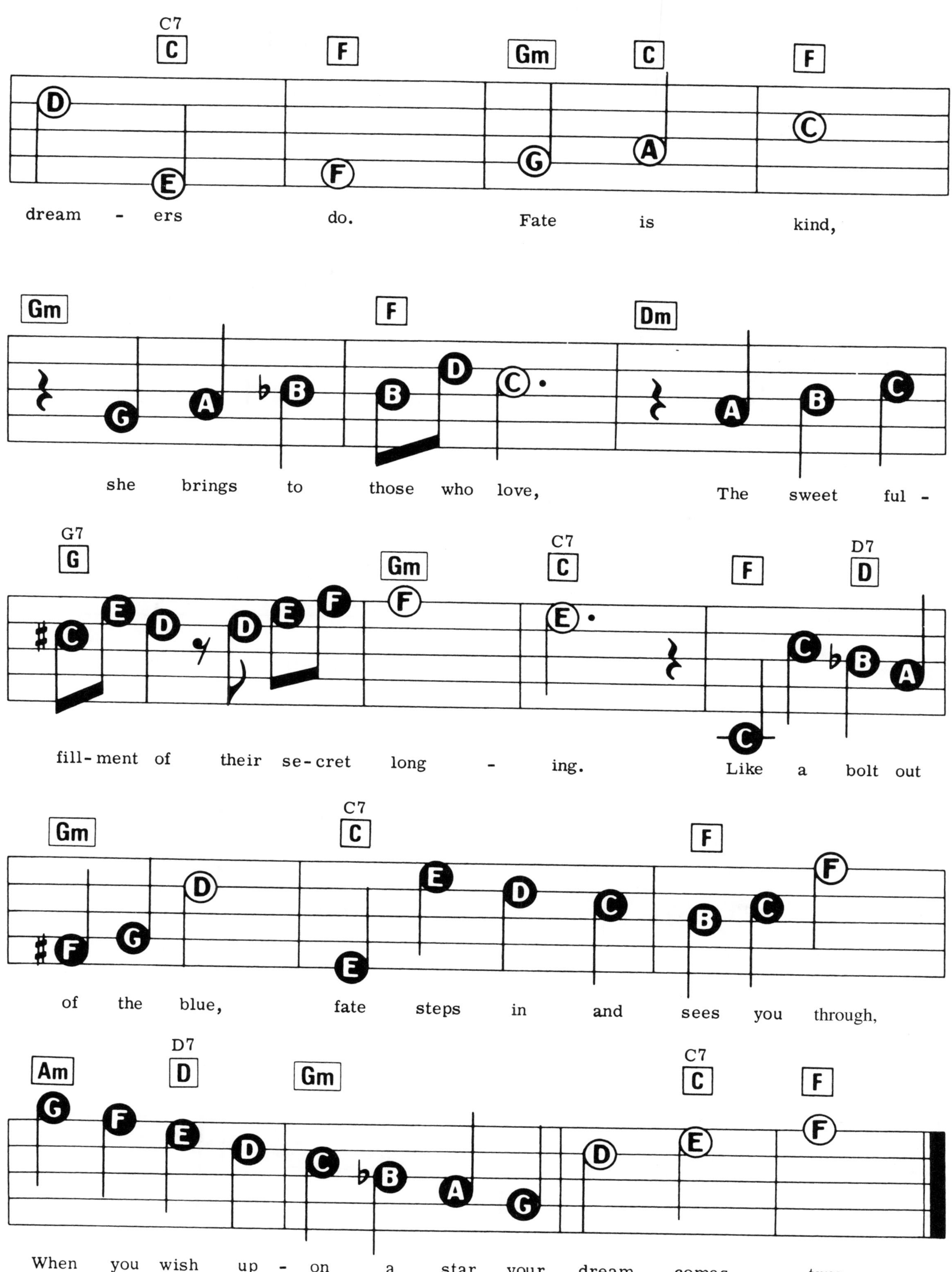
C7 C F Gm C F
dream - ers do. Fate is kind,
Gm F Dm
she brings to those who love, The sweet ful -
G7 G Gm C7 C F D7 D
fill- ment of their se- cret long - ing. Like a bolt out
Gm C7 C F
of the blue, fate steps in and sees you through,
Am D7 D Gm C7 C F
When you wish up - on a star your dream comes true.

Where Is Love?

from the Broadway Musical OLIVER!

Registration 2
Rhythm: Ballad or Fox Trot

Words and Music by
Lionel Bart

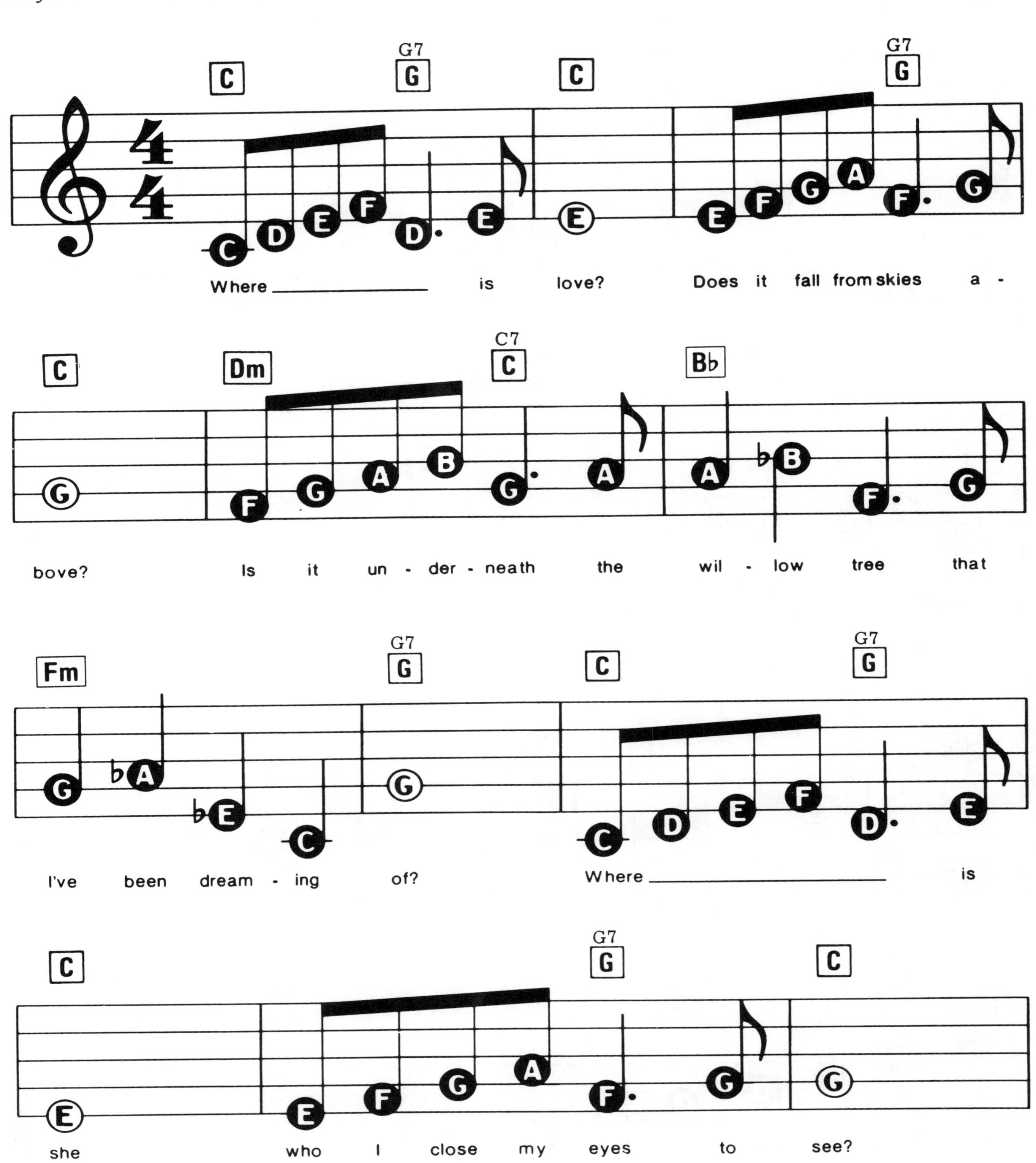

Copyright 1960 (Renewed), 1968 (Renewed) Lakeview Music Co., Ltd., London, England
TRO - Hollis Music, Inc., New York, controls all publication rights for the U.S.A. and Canada
International Copyright Secured
All Rights Reserved Including Public Performance For Profit Copyright
Used by Permission

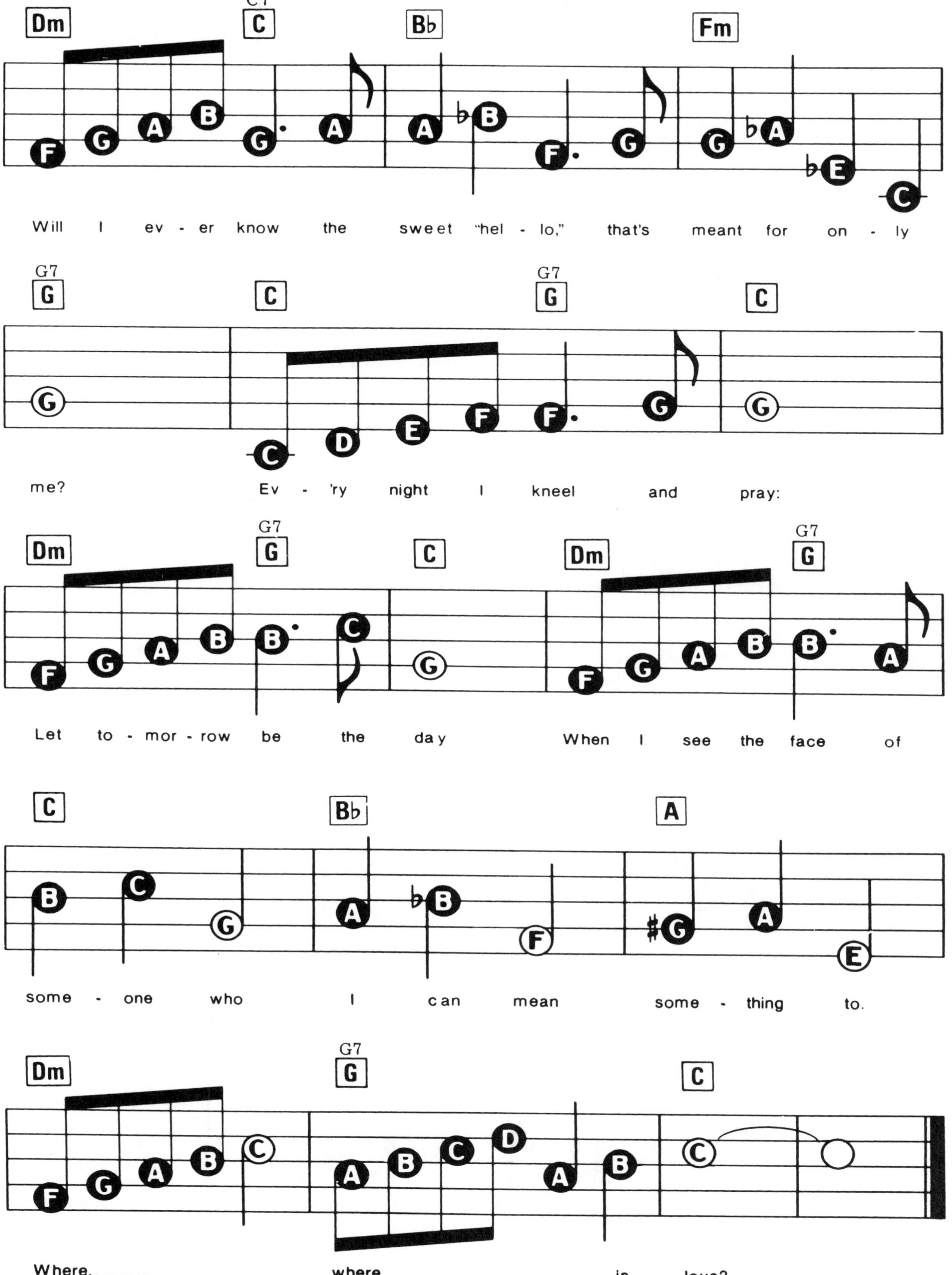
Dm C7 C B♭ Fm
Will I ev - er know the sweet "hel - lo," that's meant for on - ly
G7 G C G7 G C
me? Ev - 'ry night I kneel and pray:
Dm G7 G C Dm G7 G
Let to - mor - row be the day When I see the face of
C B♭ A
some - one who I can mean some - thing to.
Dm G7 G C
Where, where is love?

Whistle While You Work

from Walt Disney's SNOW WHITE AND THE SEVEN DWARFS

Registration 2
Rhythm: Fox Trot or Swing

Words by Larry Morey
Music by Frank Churchill

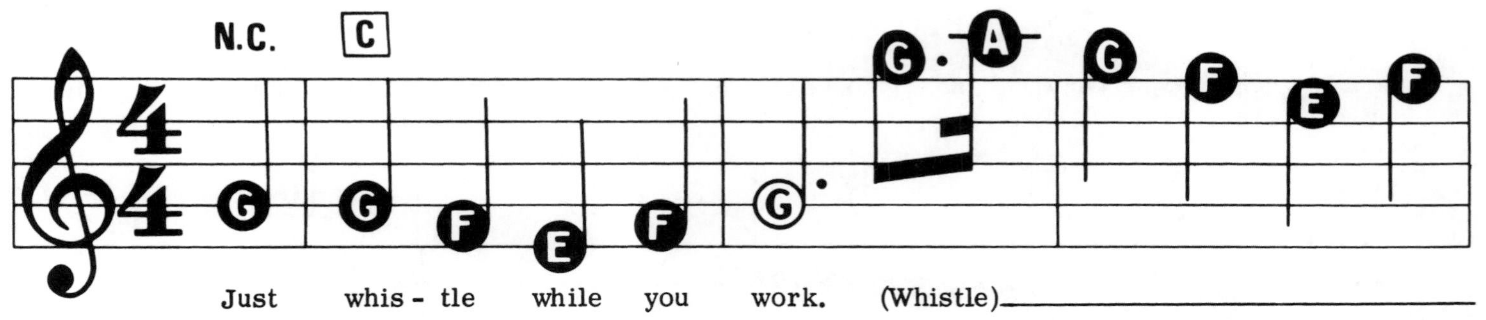

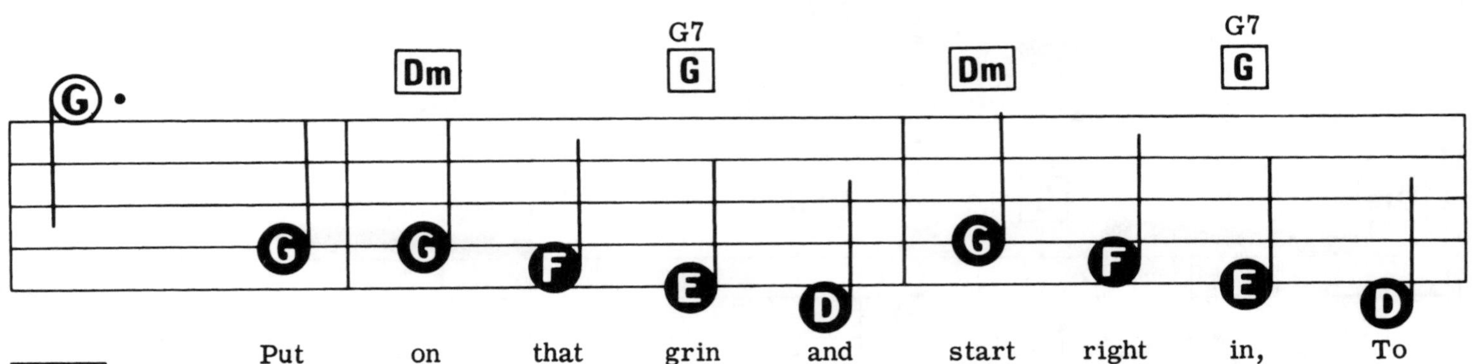

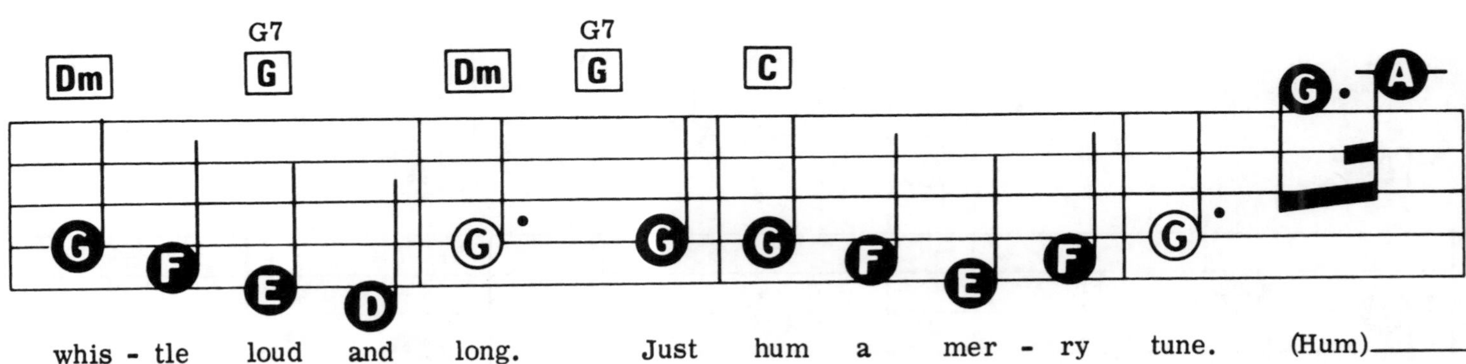

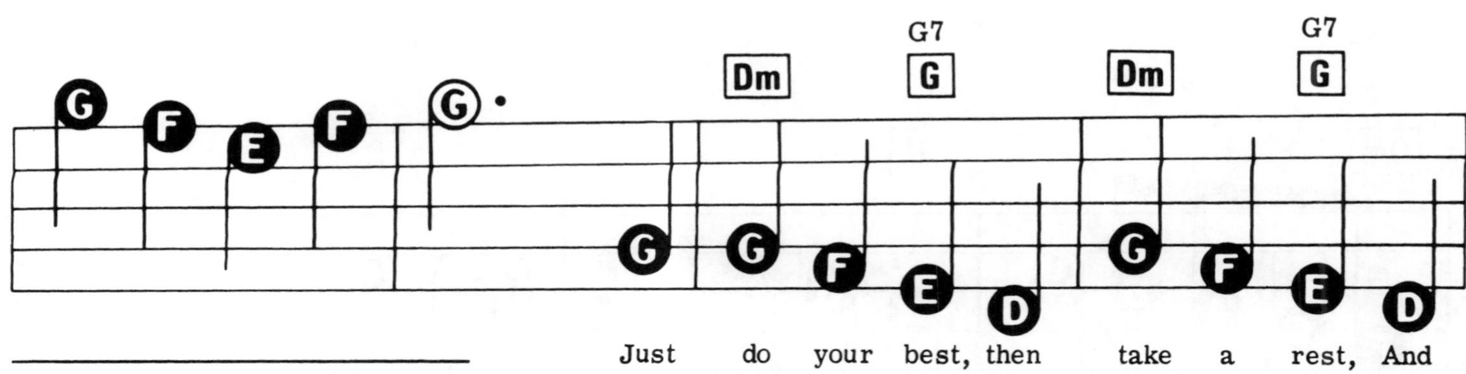

Copyright © 1937 by Bourne Co. (ASCAP)
Copyright Renewed
International Copyright Secured All Rights Reserved

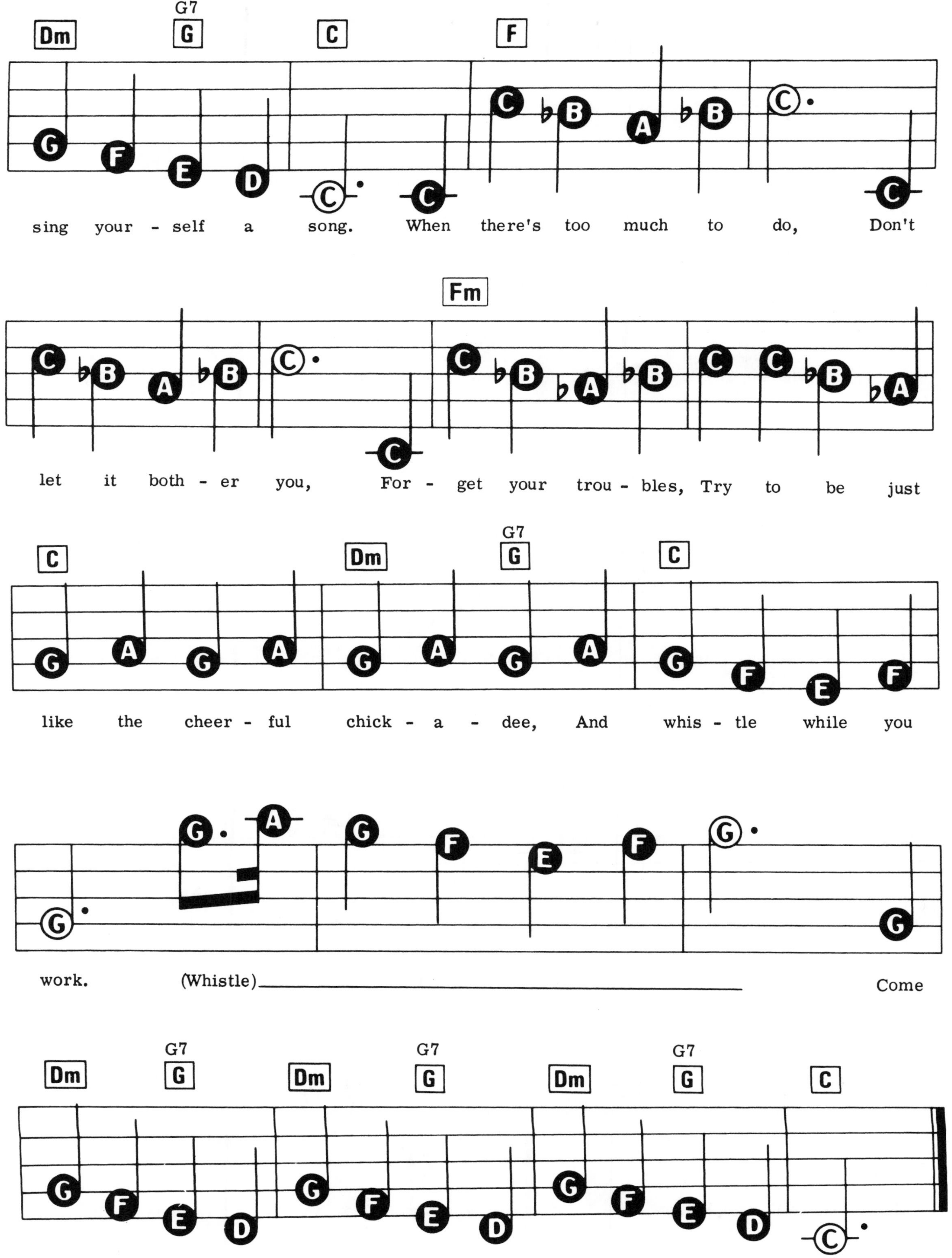
Dm G7 G C F
sing your - self a song. When there's too much to do, Don't
Fm
let it both - er you, For - get your trou - bles, Try to be just
C Dm G7 G C
like the cheer - ful chick - a - dee, And whis - tle while you
work. (Whistle) Come
Dm G7 G Dm G7 G Dm G7 G C
on, get smart, Tune up and start, To whis - tle while you work.

Who's Afraid of the Big Bad Wolf?

from Walt Disney's THREE LITTLE PIGS

Registration 4
Rhythm: Fox Trot or Swing

Words and Music by Frank Churchill
Additional Lyri by Ann Ronell

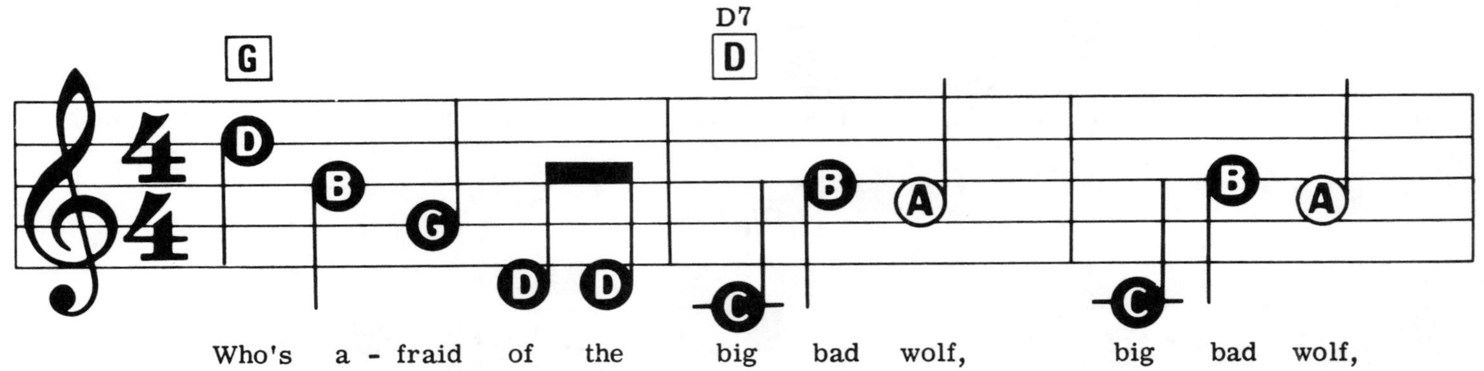

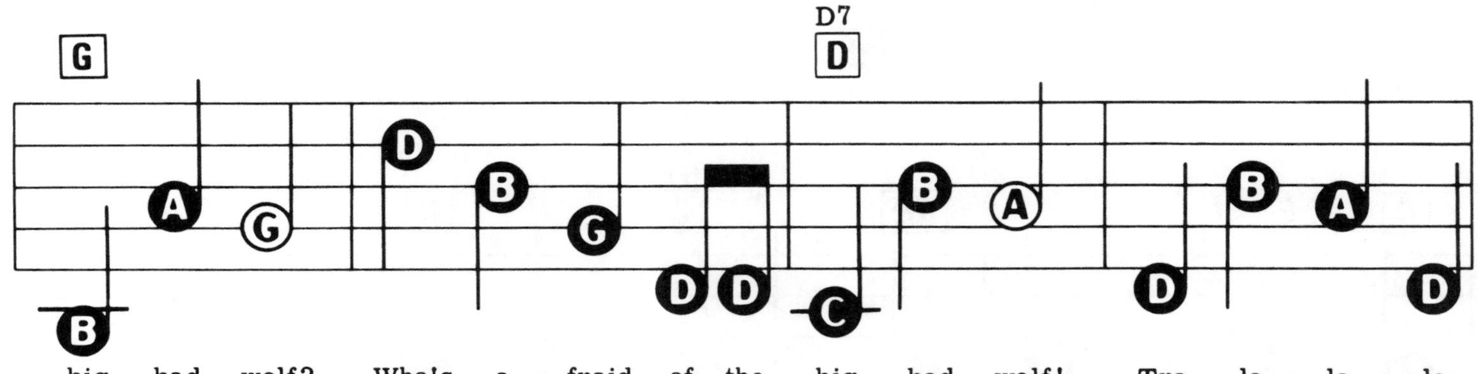

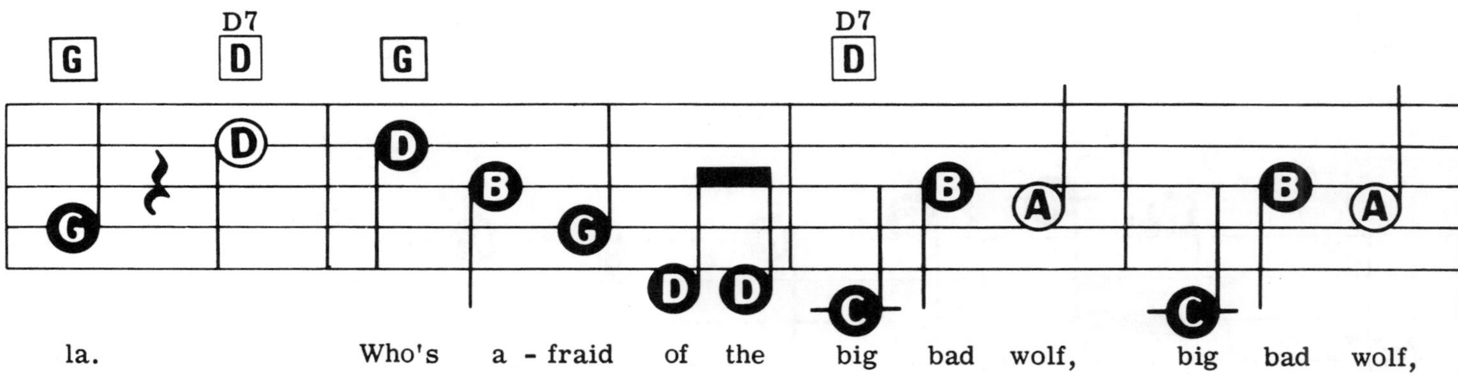

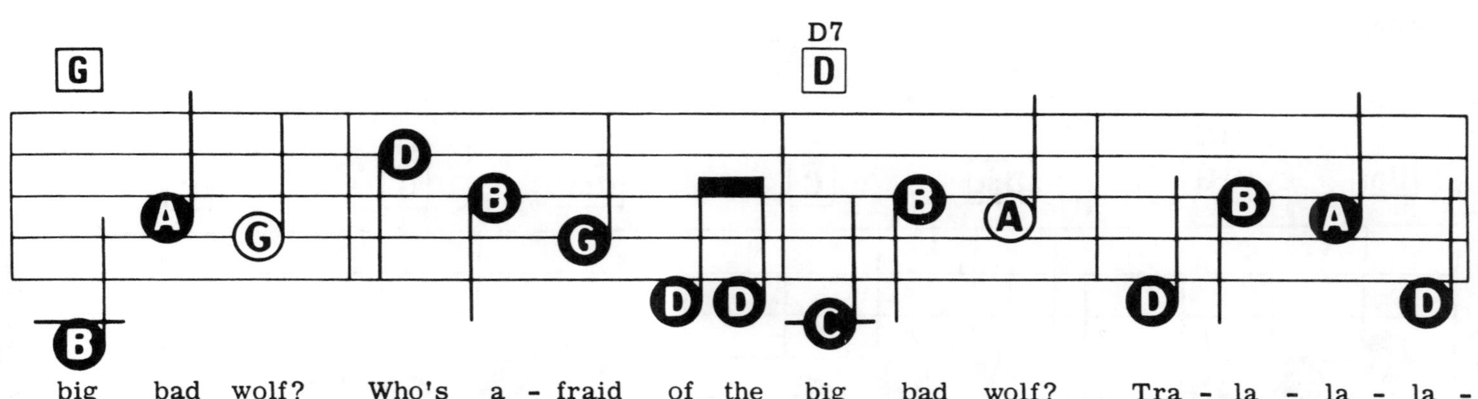

Copyright © 1933 by Bourne Co. (ASCAP)
Copyright Renewed
International Copyright Secured All Rights Reserved

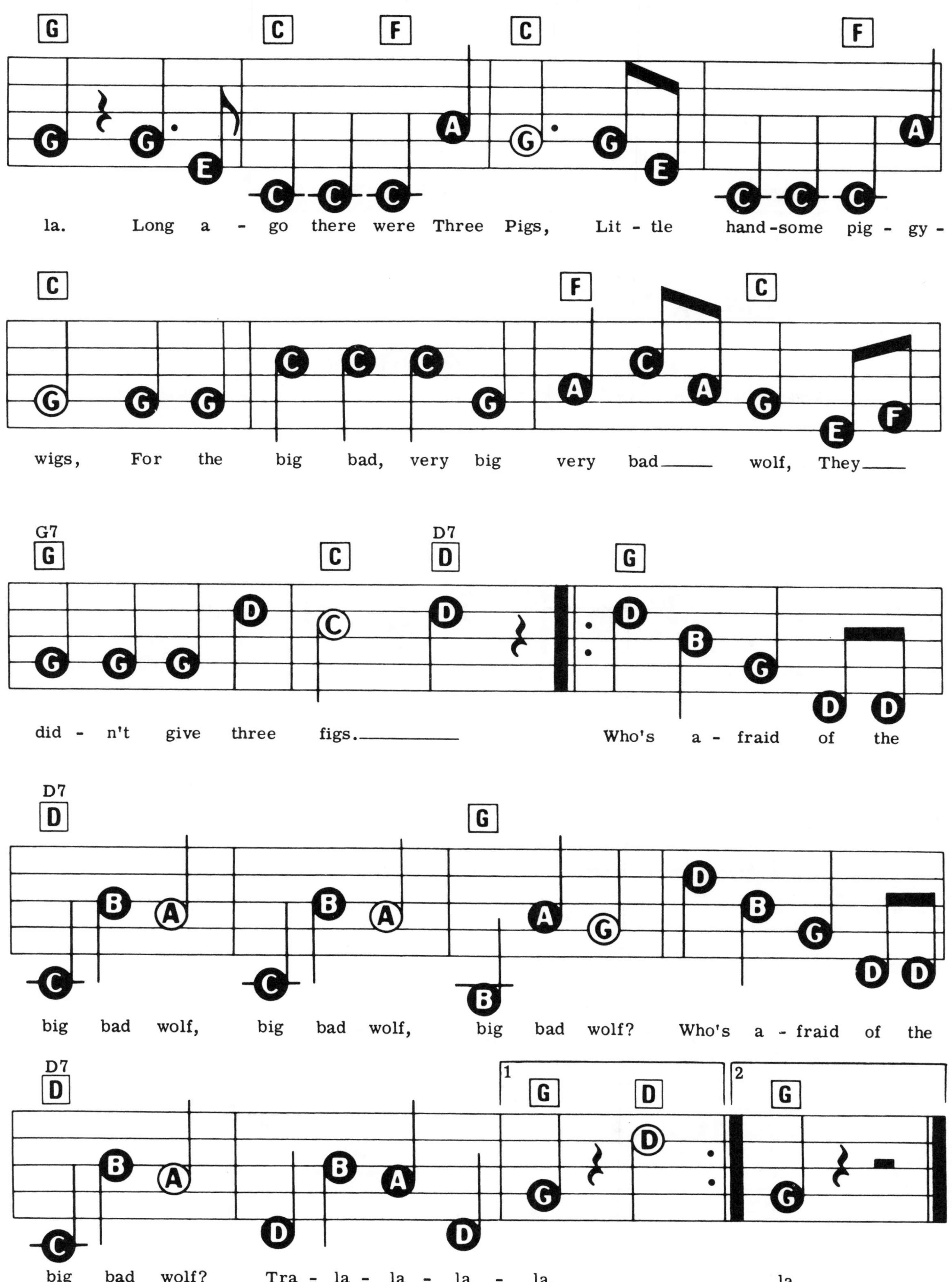
la. Long a - go there were Three Pigs, Lit - tle hand-some pig - gy -
wigs, For the big bad, very big very bad wolf, They
did - n't give three figs.
Who's a - fraid of the big bad wolf, big bad wolf, big bad wolf?
Who's a - fraid of the big bad wolf? Tra - la - la - la - la.
la.
G7
D7
D7
D7
1
2

A Whole New World

from Disney ALADDIN

Registration 1
Rhythm: 8-Beat or Pops

Music by Alan Menken
Lyrics by Tim Rice

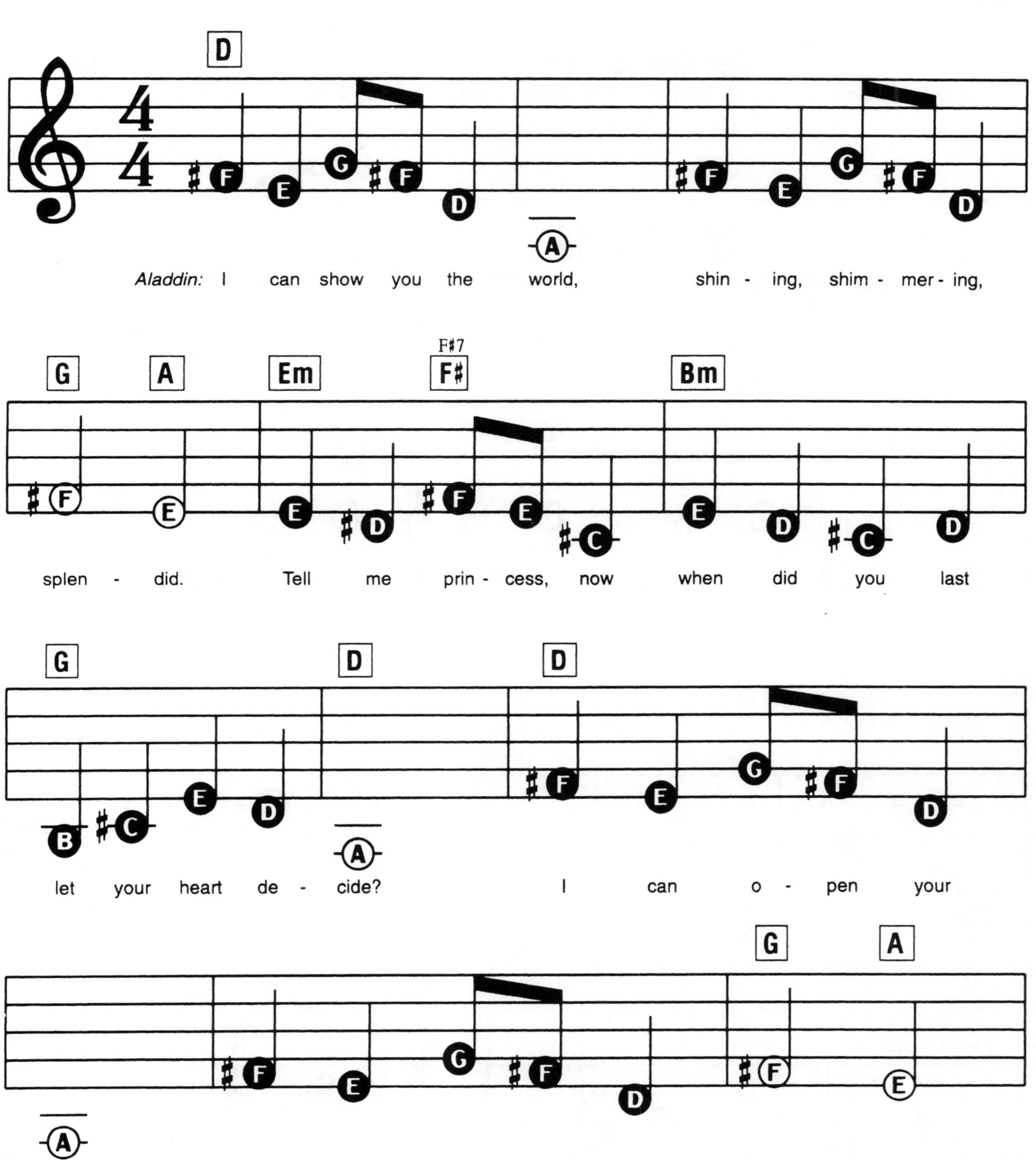

© 1992 Wonderland Music Company, Inc. and Walt Disney Music Company
All Rights Reserved. Used by Permission.

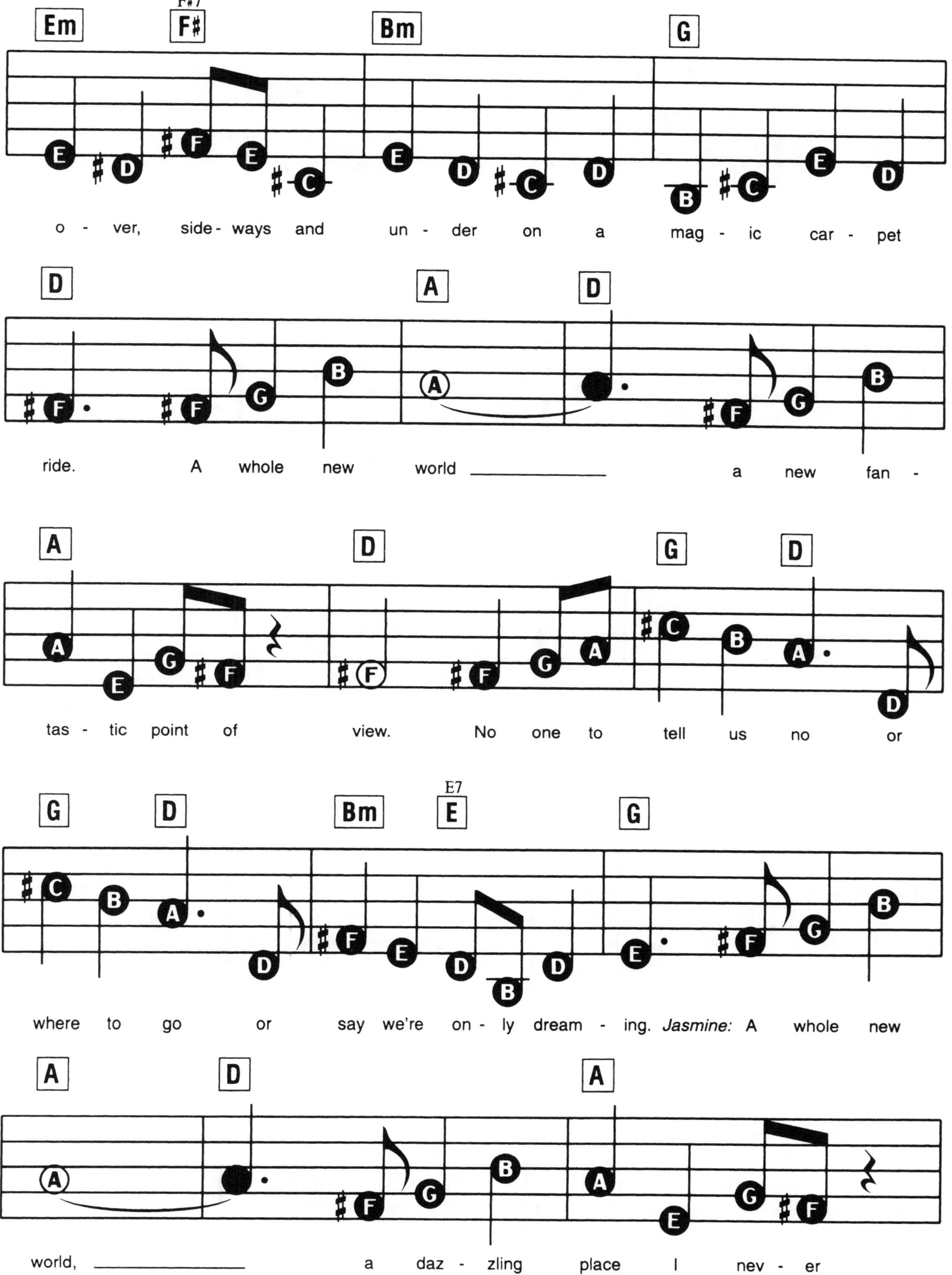
Em
F#7
F#
Bm
G
E
D
F
E
C
E
D
C
D
B
C
E
D
o - ver, side- ways and un - der on a mag - ic car - pet
D
A
D
F
F
G
B
A
F
G
B
ride. A whole new world a new fan -
A
D
G
D
A
E
G
F
F
F
G
A
C
B
A
D
tas - tic point of view. No one to tell us no or
G
D
Bm
E7
E
G
C
B
A
D
F
E
D
B
D
E
F
G
B
where to go or say we're on - ly dream - ing. Jasmine: A whole new
A
D
A
A
F
G
B
A
E
G
F
world, a daz - zling place I nev - er

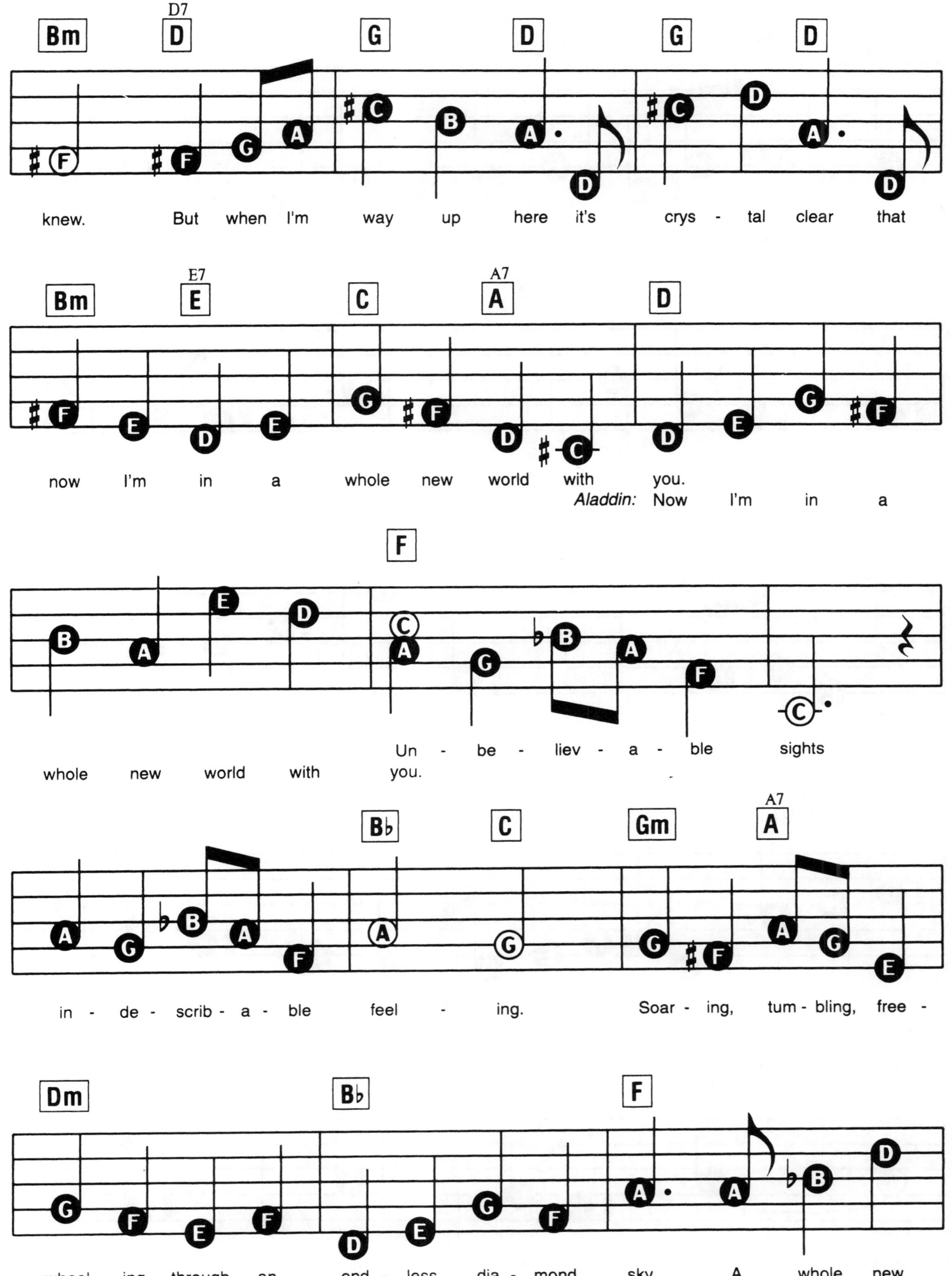
Bm
D7
D
G
D
G
D
knew. But when I'm way up here it's crys - tal clear that
Bm
E7
E
C
A7
A
D
now I'm in a whole new world with you.
Aladdin: Now I'm in a
F
whole new world with you.
Un - be - liev - a - ble sights
B♭
C
Gm
A7
A
in - de - scrib - a - ble feel - ing. Soar - ing, tum - bling, free -
Dm
B♭
F
wheel - ing through an end - less dia - mond sky. A whole new

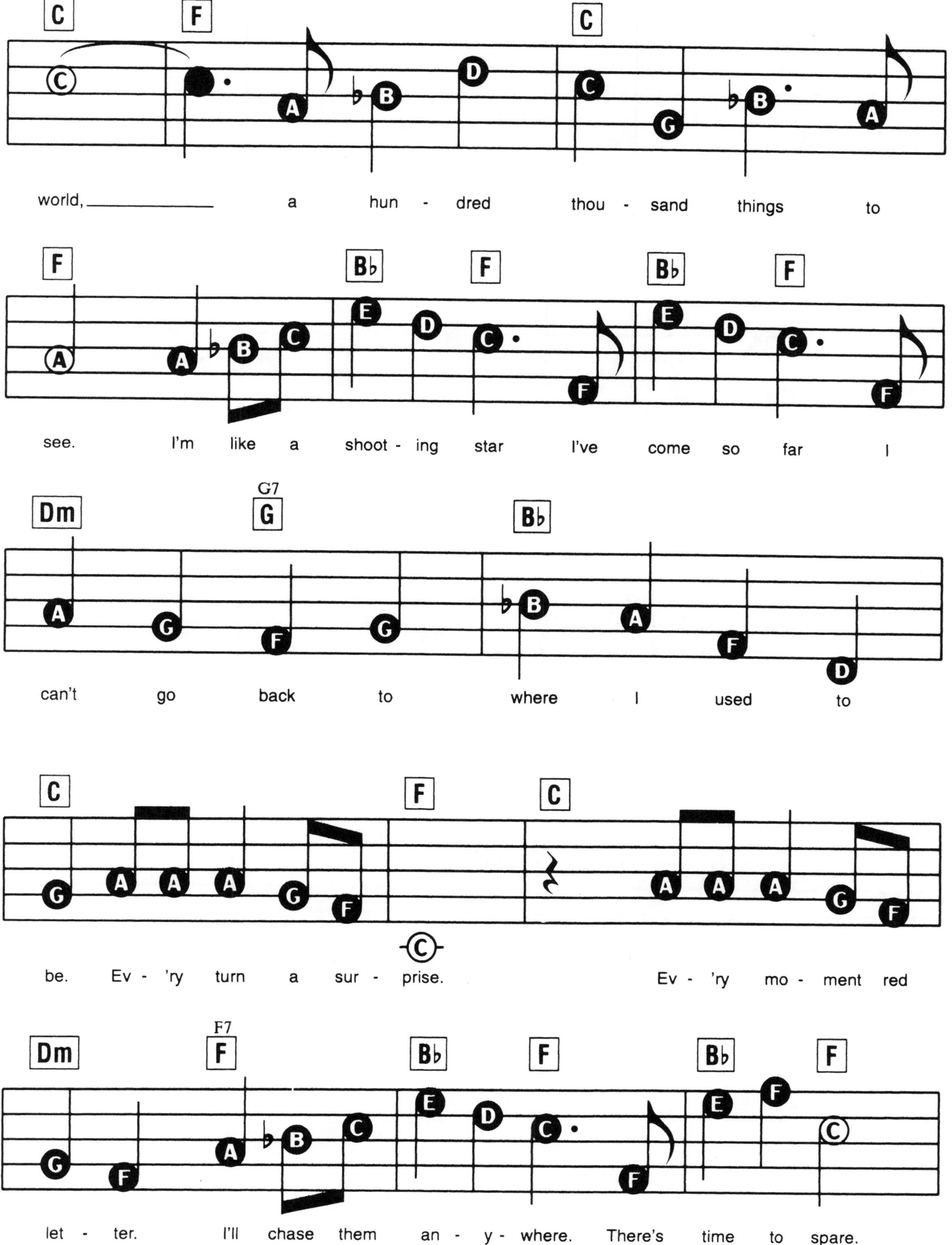
C F C
world, ___ a hun - dred thou - sand things to
F B♭ F B♭ F
see. I'm like a shoot - ing star I've come so far I
Dm G7 G B♭
can't go back to where I used to
C F C
be. Ev - 'ry turn a sur - prise. Ev - 'ry mo - ment red
Dm F7 F B♭ F B♭ F
let - ter. I'll chase them an - y - where. There's time to spare.

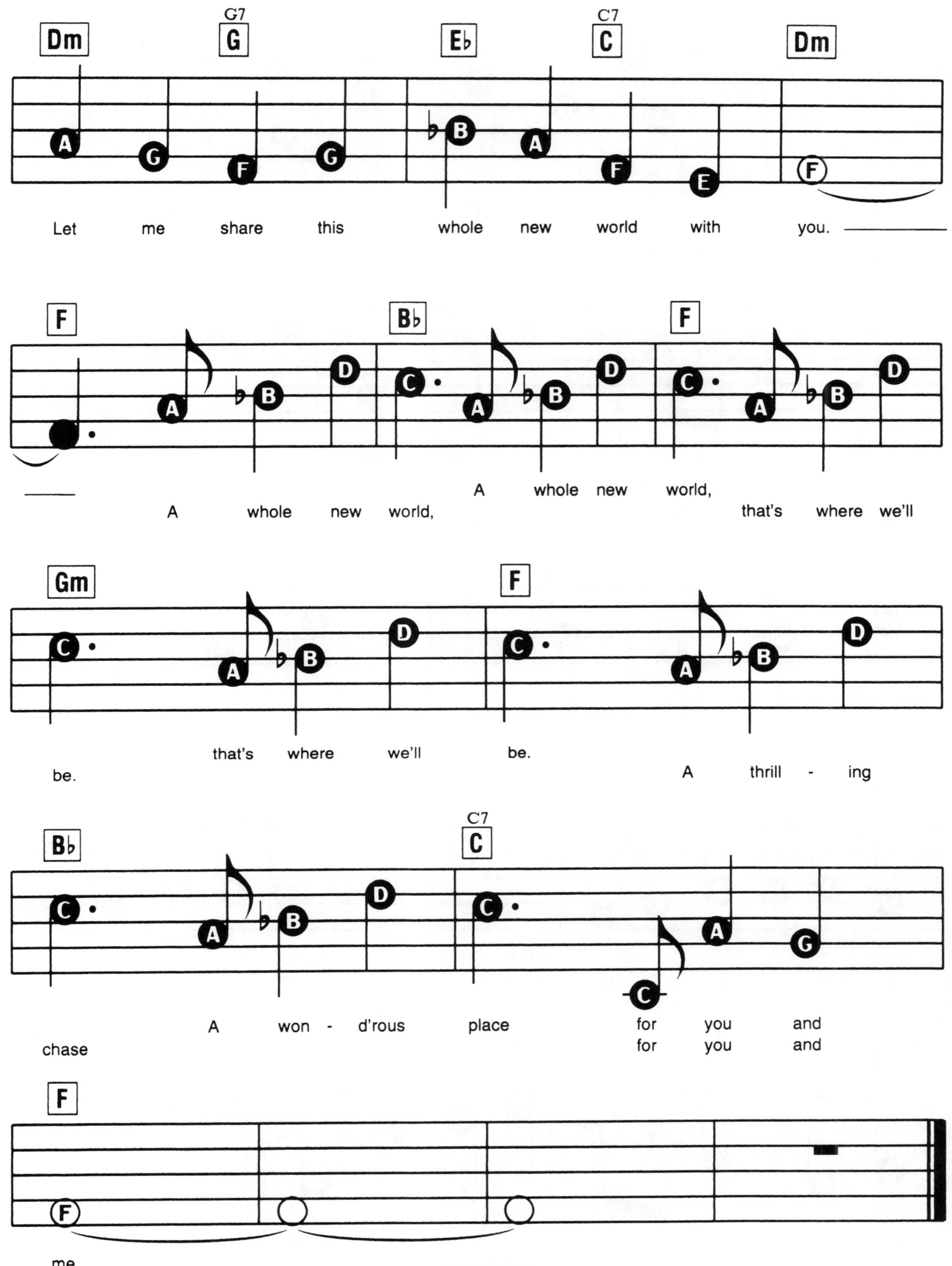
Dm G7 G Eb C7 C Dm
Let me share this whole new world with you.
F Bb F
A whole new world, A whole new world, that's where we'll
Gm F
be. that's where we'll be. A thrill - ing
Bb C7 C
chase A won - d'rous place for you and for you and
F
me. me.

You Are My Sunshine

Registration 4
Rhythm: Fox Trot

Words and Music by
Jimmie Davis

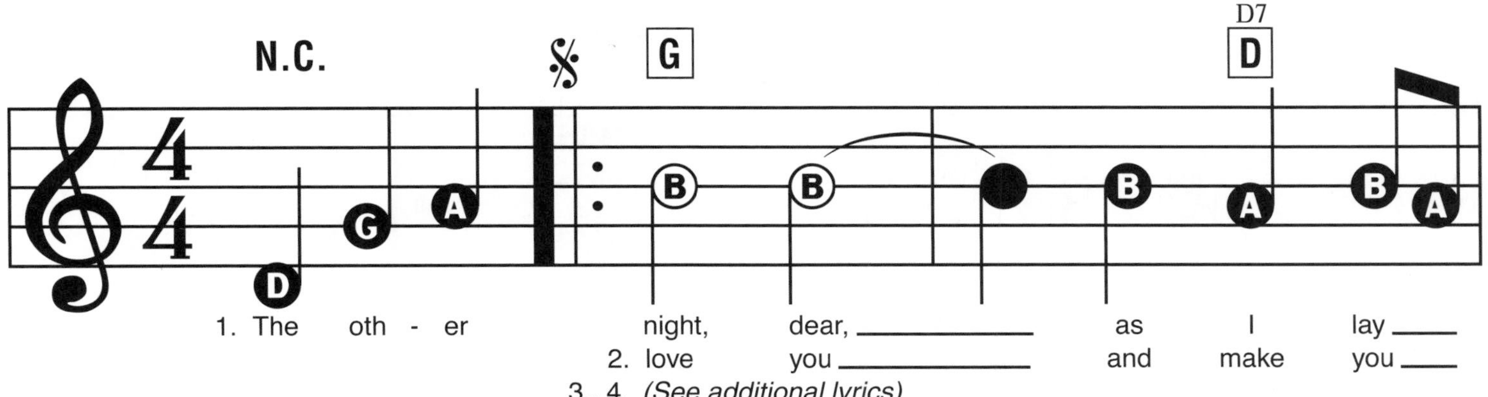

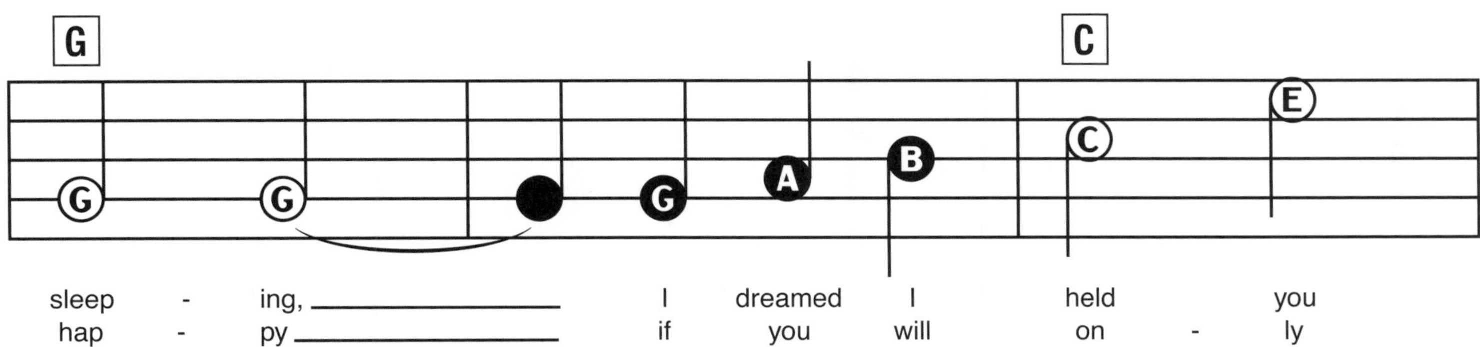

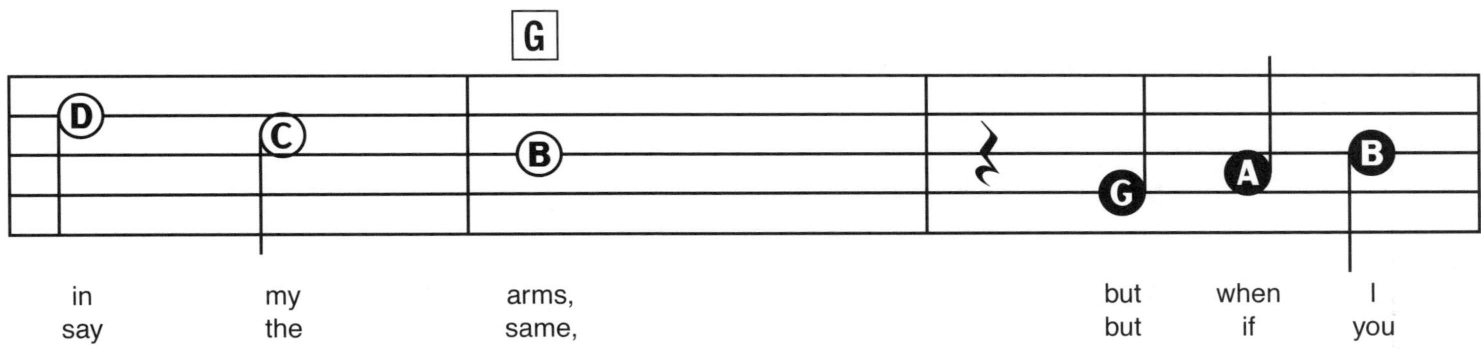

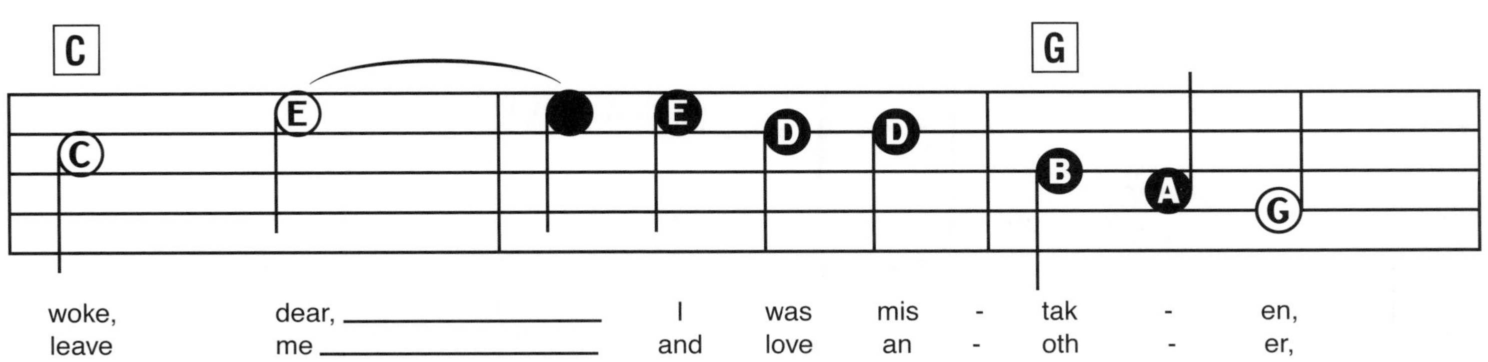

Copyright © 1940 by Peer International Corporation
Copyright Renewed
International Copyright Secured All Rights Reserved

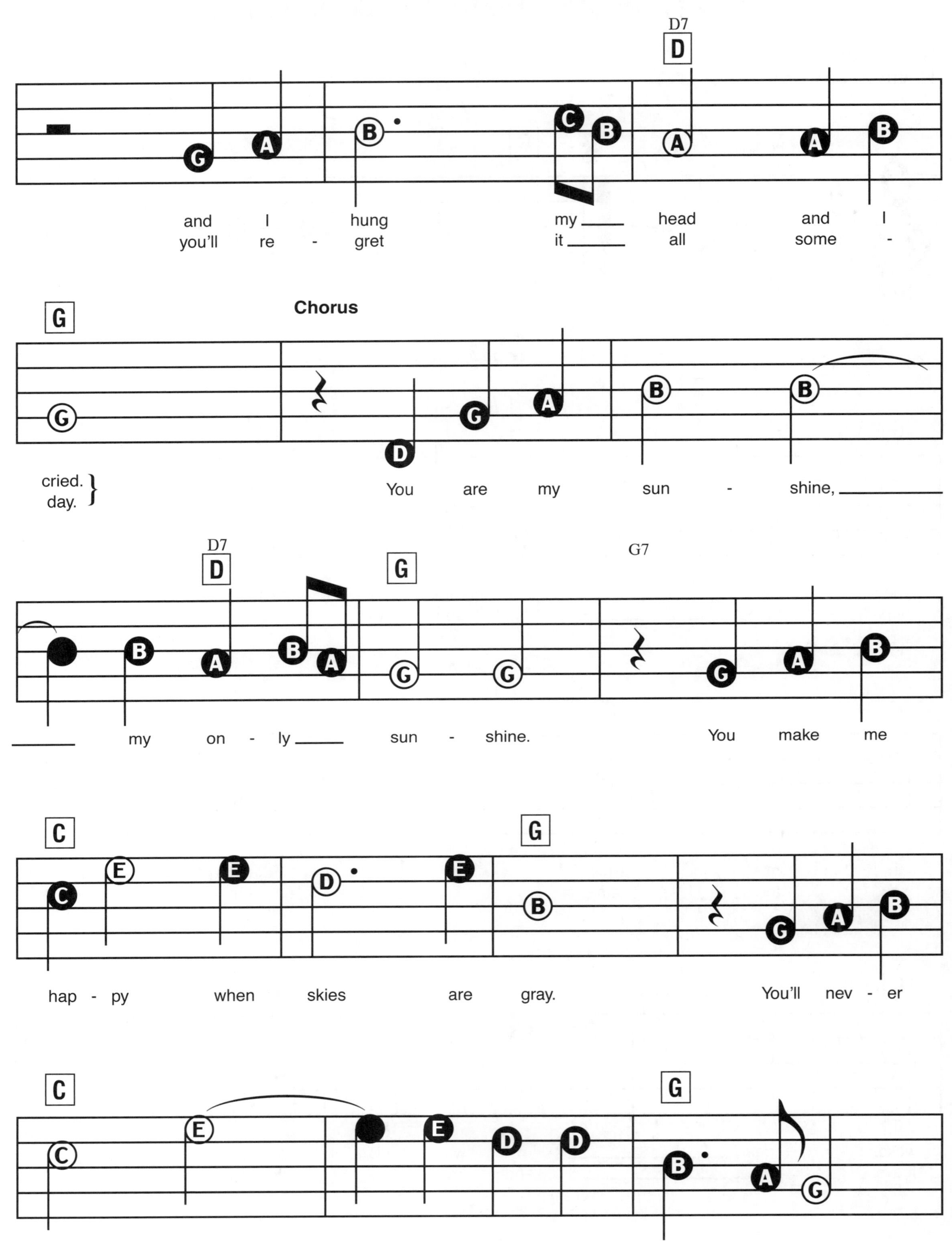
D7
D
G
and I hung my head and I
you'll re - gret it all some -
G
Chorus
cried.
day.
You are my sun - shine,
D7
D
G
G7
my on - ly sun - shine.
You make me
C
G
hap - py when skies are gray.
You'll nev - er
C
G
know dear, how much I love you.

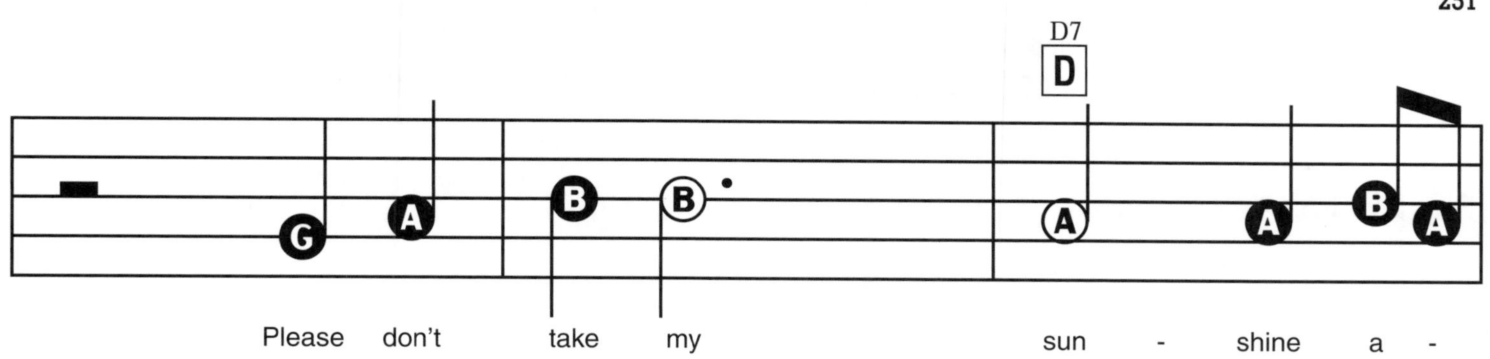

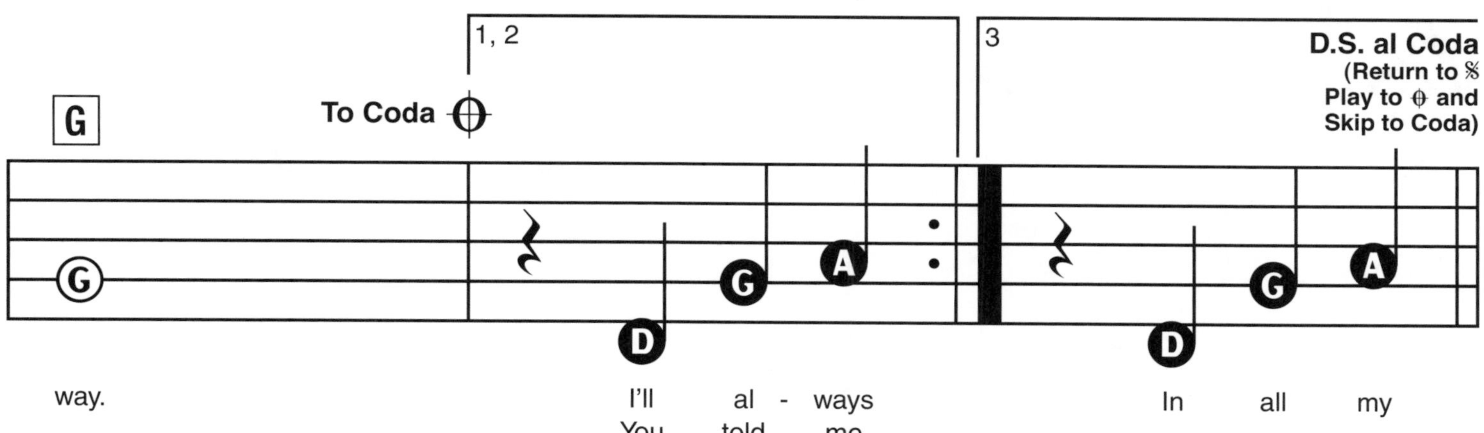

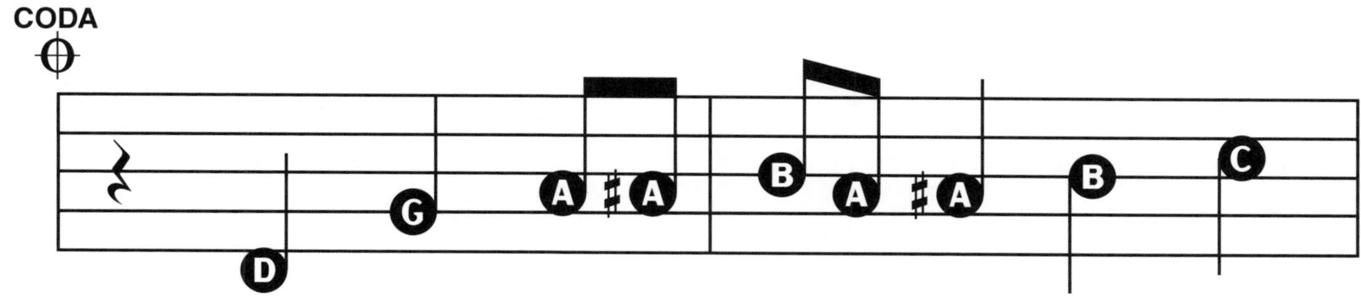

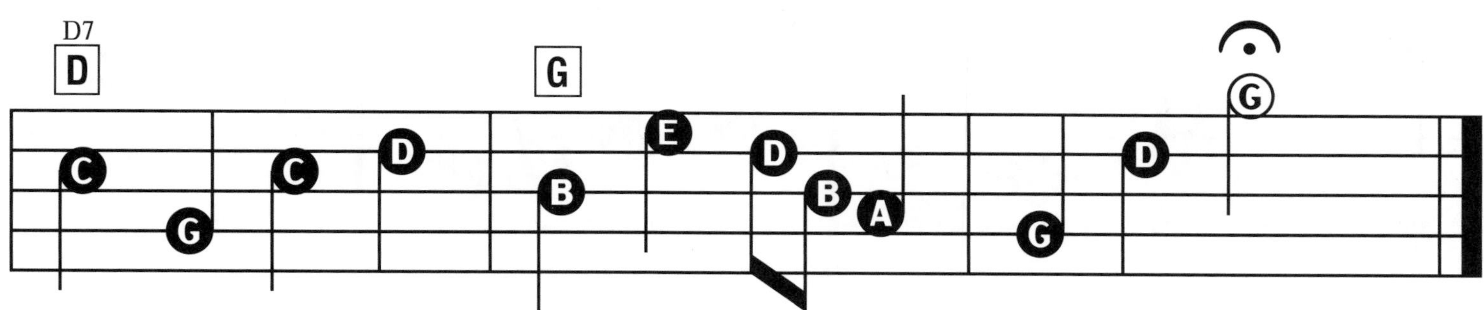

Additional Lyrics

3. You told me once, dear, you really loved me
And no one could come between,
But now you've left me to love another.
You have shattered all of my dreams.
Chorus

4. In all my dreams, dear, you seem to leave me.
When I awake my poor heart pains.
So won't you come back and make me happy?
I'll forgive, dear; I'll take all the blame.
Chorus

Winnie the Pooh

from Walt Disney's THE MANY ADVENTURES OF WINNIE THE POOH

Registration 2
Rhythm: Fox Trot or Ballad

Words and Music by Richard M. Sherman
and Robert B. Sherman

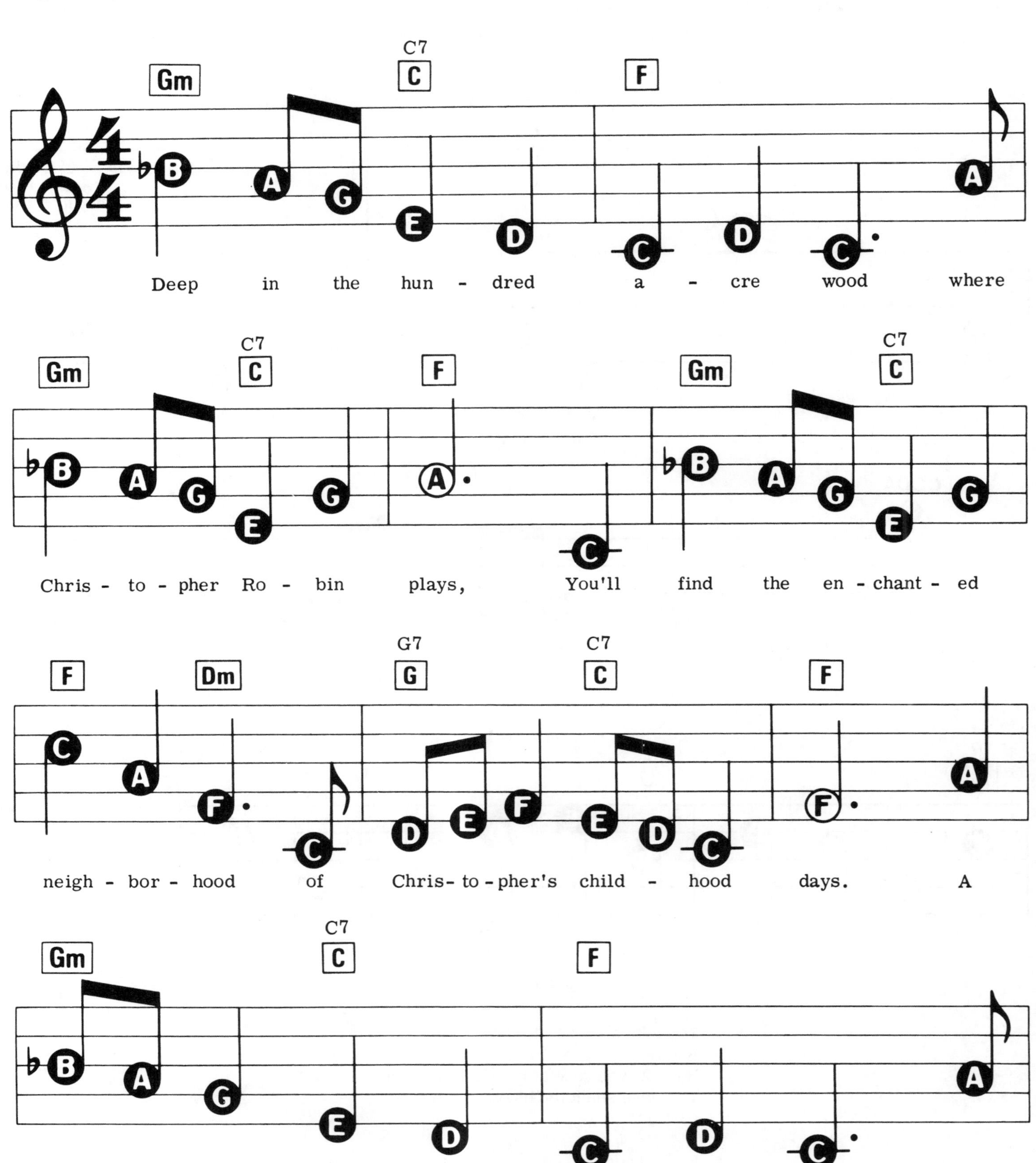

© 1963 Wonderland Music Company, Inc.
Copyright Renewed
All Rights Reserved. Used by Permission.

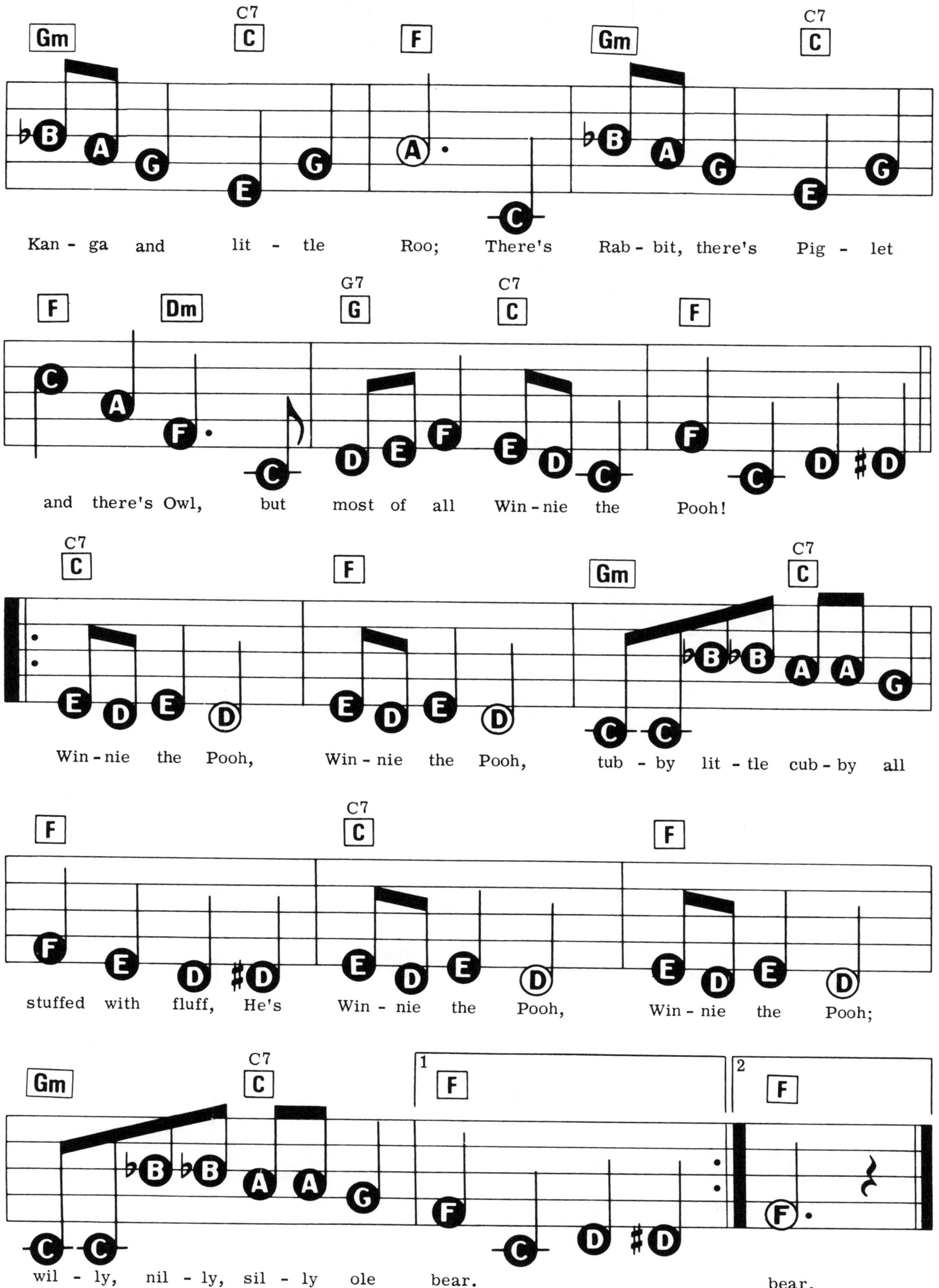
Gm
C7
C
F
Gm
C7
C
Kan - ga and lit - tle Roo; There's Rab - bit, there's Pig - let
F
Dm
G7
G
C7
C
F
and there's Owl, but most of all Win - nie the Pooh!
C7
C
F
Gm
C7
C
Win - nie the Pooh, Win - nie the Pooh, tub - by lit - tle cub - by all
F
C7
C
F
stuffed with fluff, He's Win - nie the Pooh, Win - nie the Pooh;
Gm
C7
C
1
F
2
F
wil - ly, nil - ly, sil - ly ole bear. bear.

Won't You Be My Neighbor?
(It's a Beautiful Day in the Neighborhood)
from MISTER ROGERS' NEIGHBORHOOD

Registration 8
Rhythm: Swing or Shuffle

Words and Music by
Fred Rogers

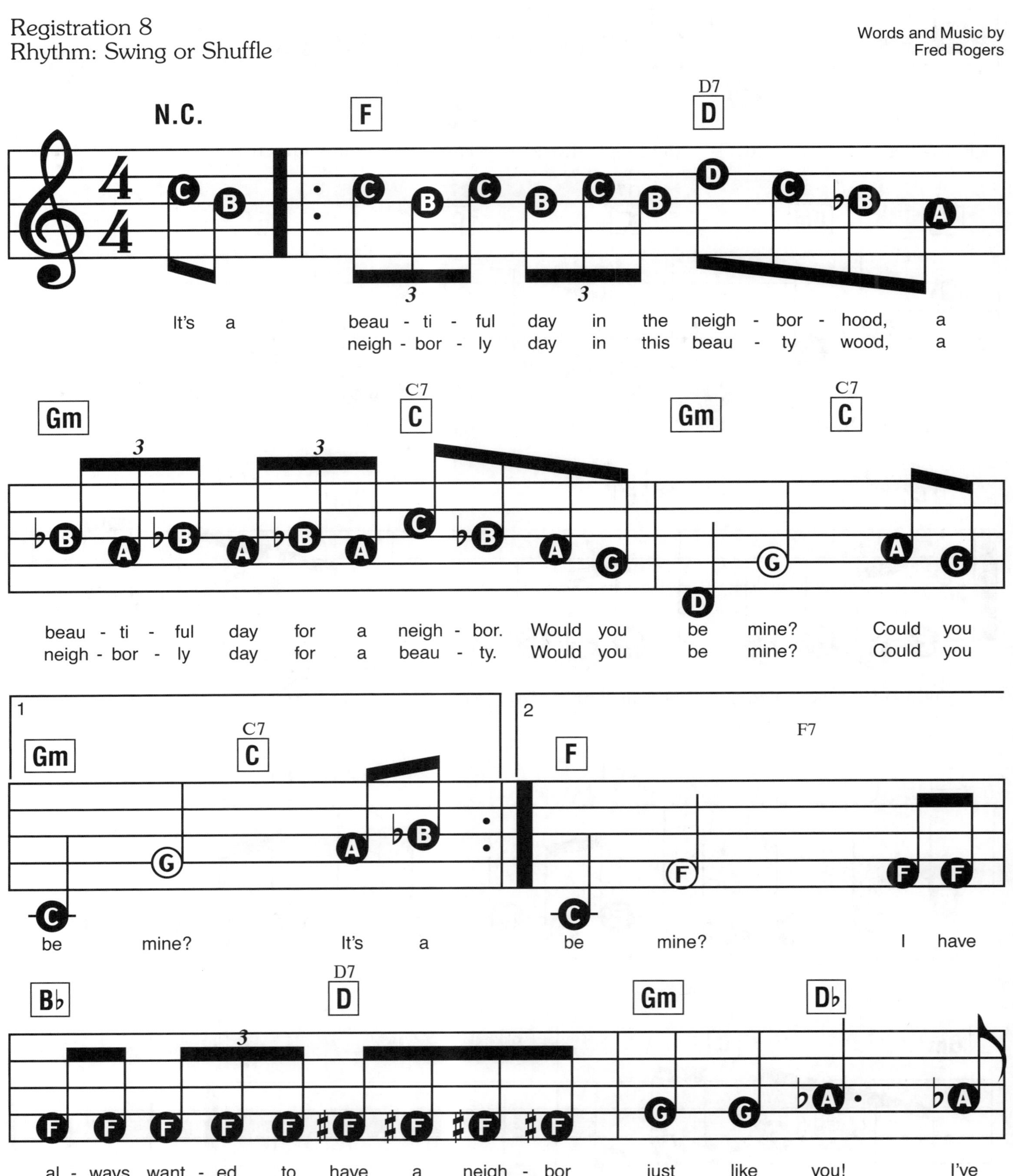

Copyright © 1967 by Fred M. Rogers
Copyright Renewed
International Copyright Secured All Rights Reserved

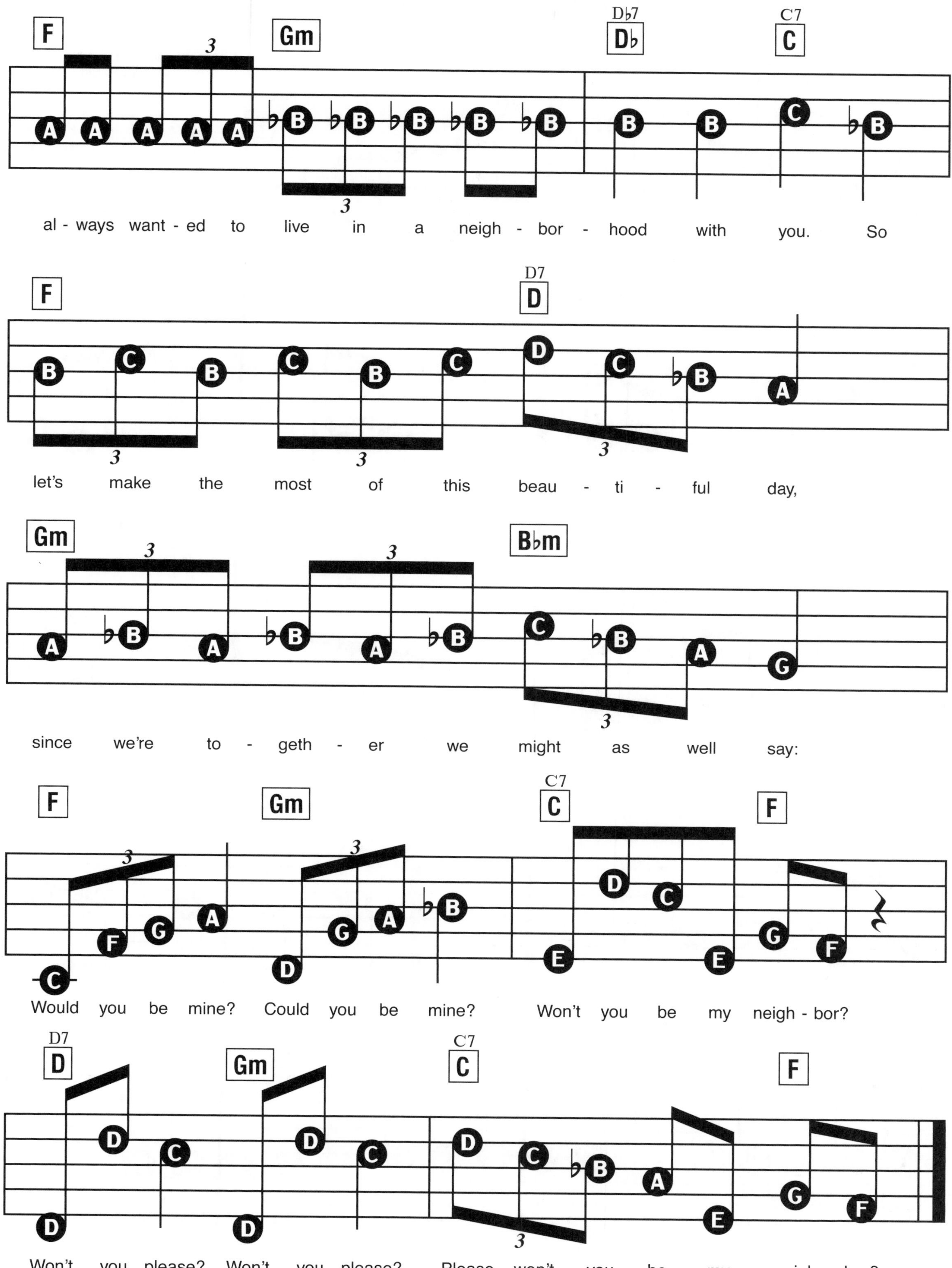
F Gm D♭7 D♭ C7 C
al - ways want - ed to live in a neigh - bor - hood with you. So
F D7 D
let's make the most of this beau - ti - ful day,
Gm B♭m
since we're to - geth - er we might as well say:
F Gm C7 C F
Would you be mine? Could you be mine? Won't you be my neigh - bor?
D7 D Gm C7 C F
Won't you please? Won't you please? Please won't you be my neigh - bor?

Yellow Submarine

Registration 2
Rhythm: 8-Beat or Rock

Words and Music by John Lennon
and Paul McCartney

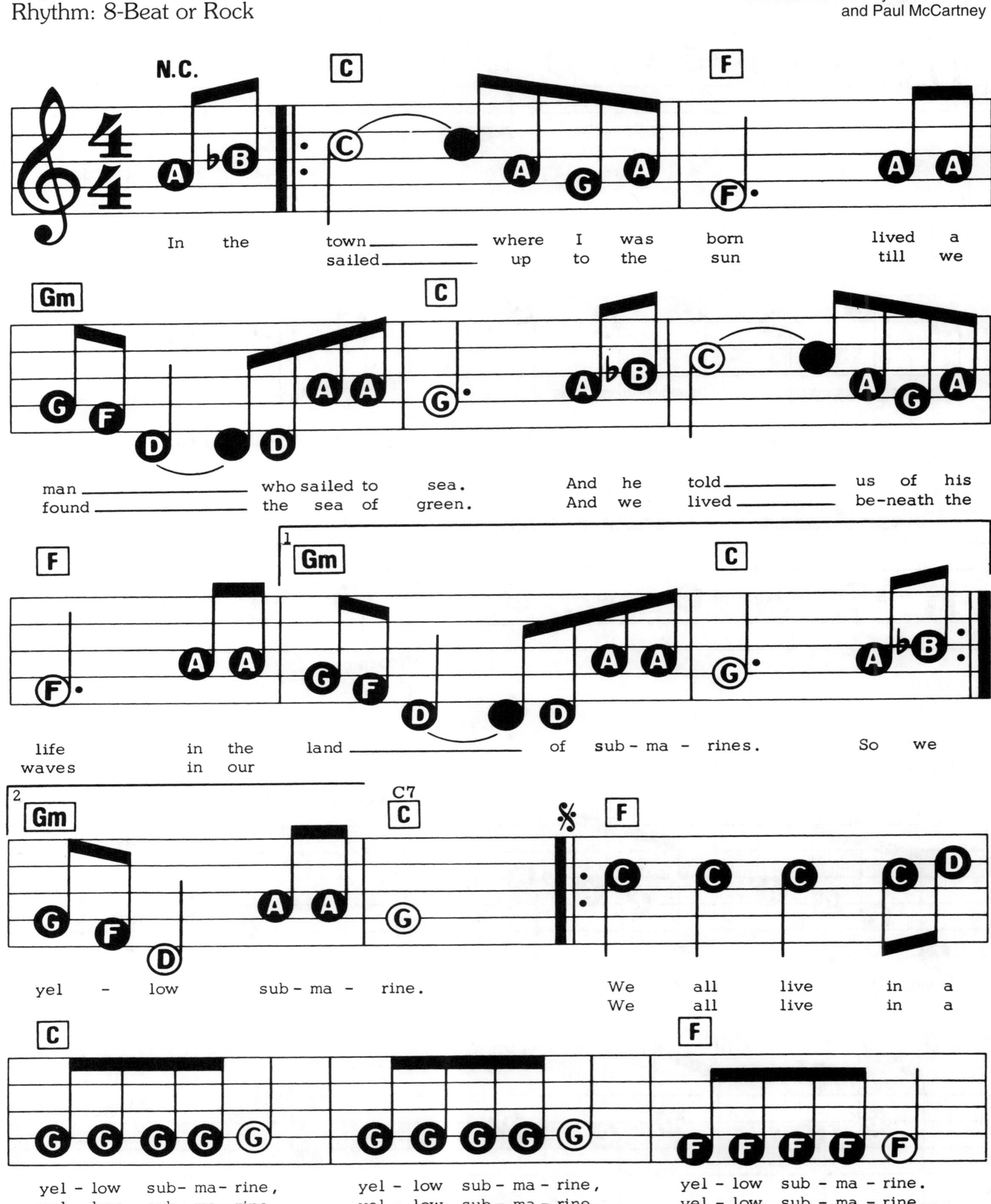

Copyright © 1966 Sony/ATV Music Publishing LLC
Copyright Renewed
All Rights Administered by Sony/ATV Music Publishing LLC, 424 Church Street, Suite 1200, Nashville, TN 37219
International Copyright Secured All Rights Reserved

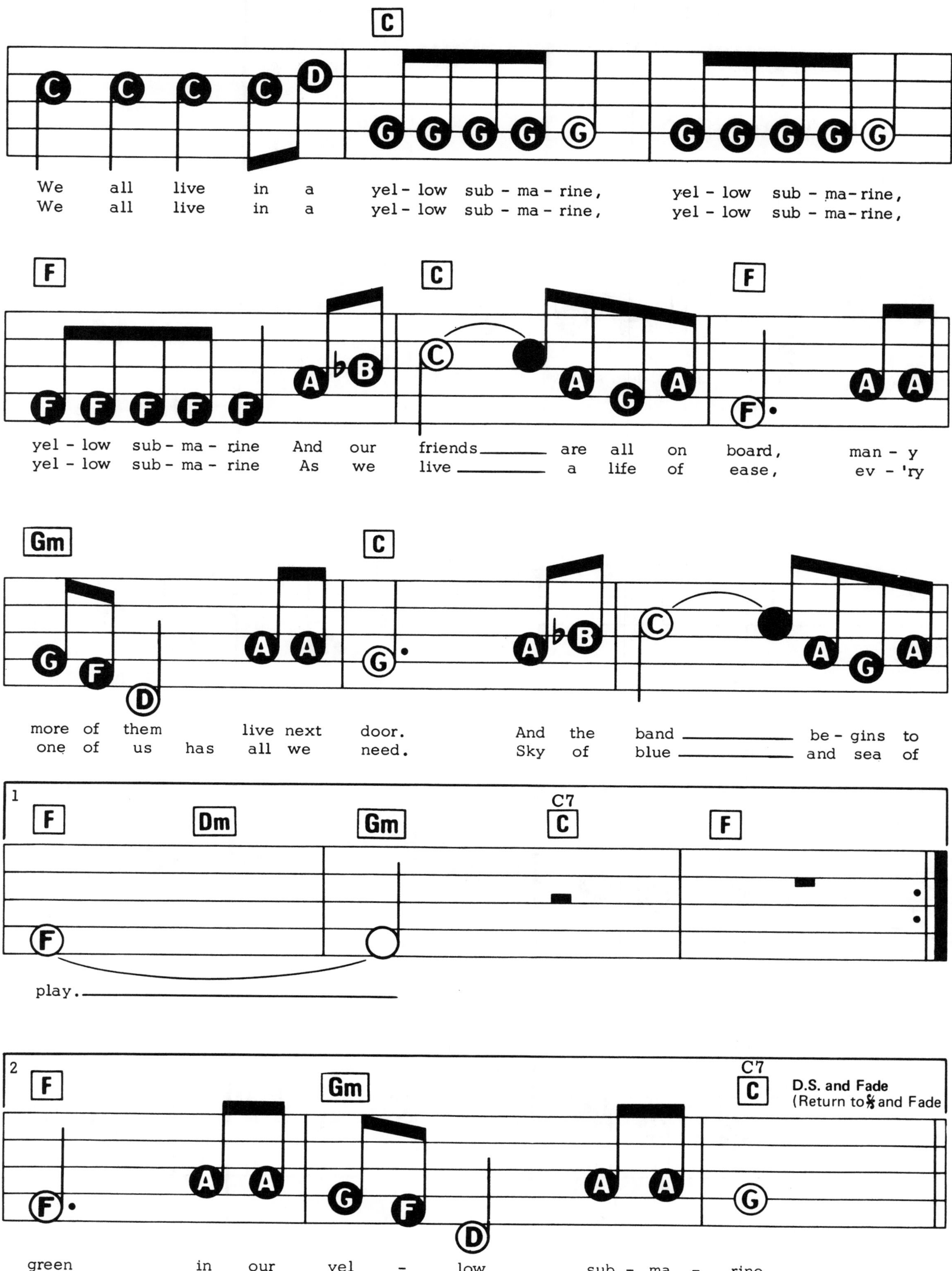
C
We all live in a yel-low sub-ma-rine, yel-low sub-ma-rine,
We all live in a yel-low sub-ma-rine, yel-low sub-ma-rine,
F C F
yel-low sub-ma-rine And our friends are all on board, man-y
yel-low sub-ma-rine As we live a life of ease, ev-'ry
Gm C
more of them live next door. And the band be-gins to
one of us has all we need. Sky of blue and sea of
1
F Dm Gm C7 C F
play.
2
F Gm C7 C
D.S. and Fade
(Return to 𝄋 and Fade
green in our yel-low sub-ma-rine.

Zip-A-Dee-Doo-Dah

from Walt Disney's SONG OF THE SOUTH

Registration 8
Rhythm: Fox Trot or Swing

Words by Ray Gilbert
Music by Allie Wrubel

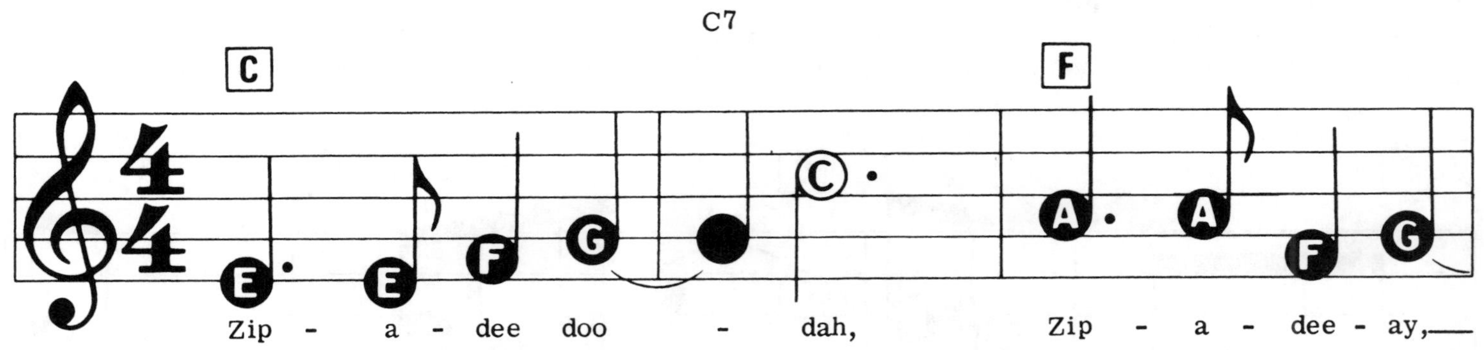

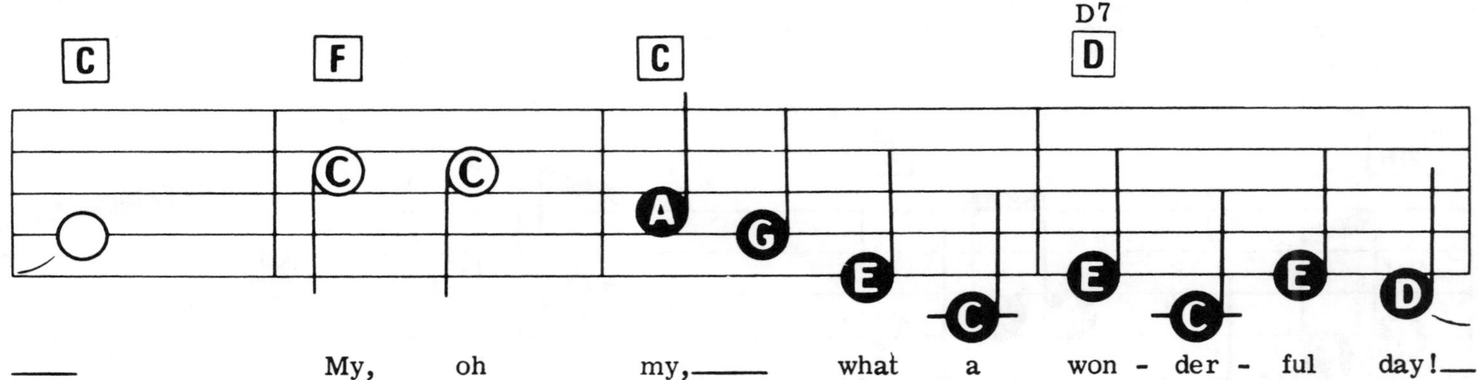

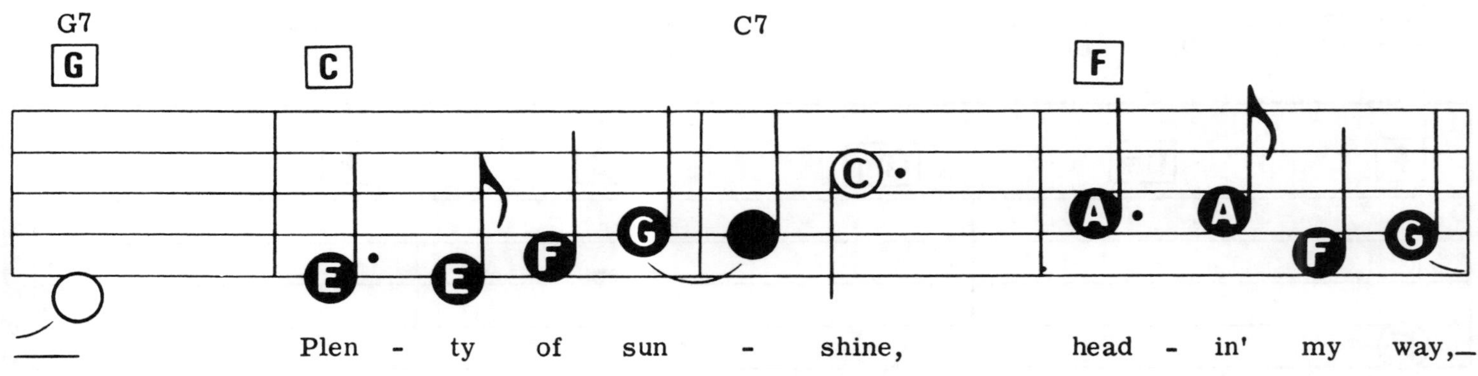

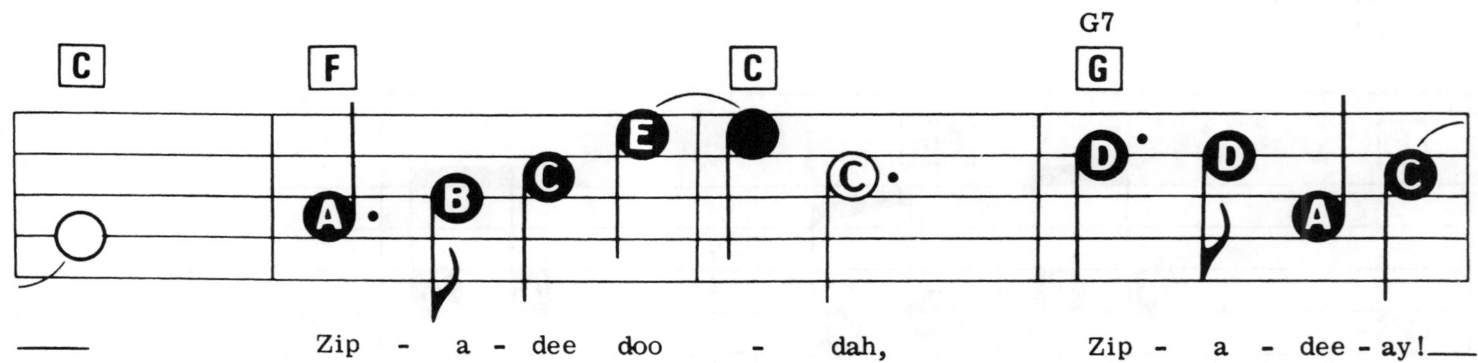

© 1945 Walt Disney Music Company
Copyright Renewed
All Rights Reserved. Used by Permission.

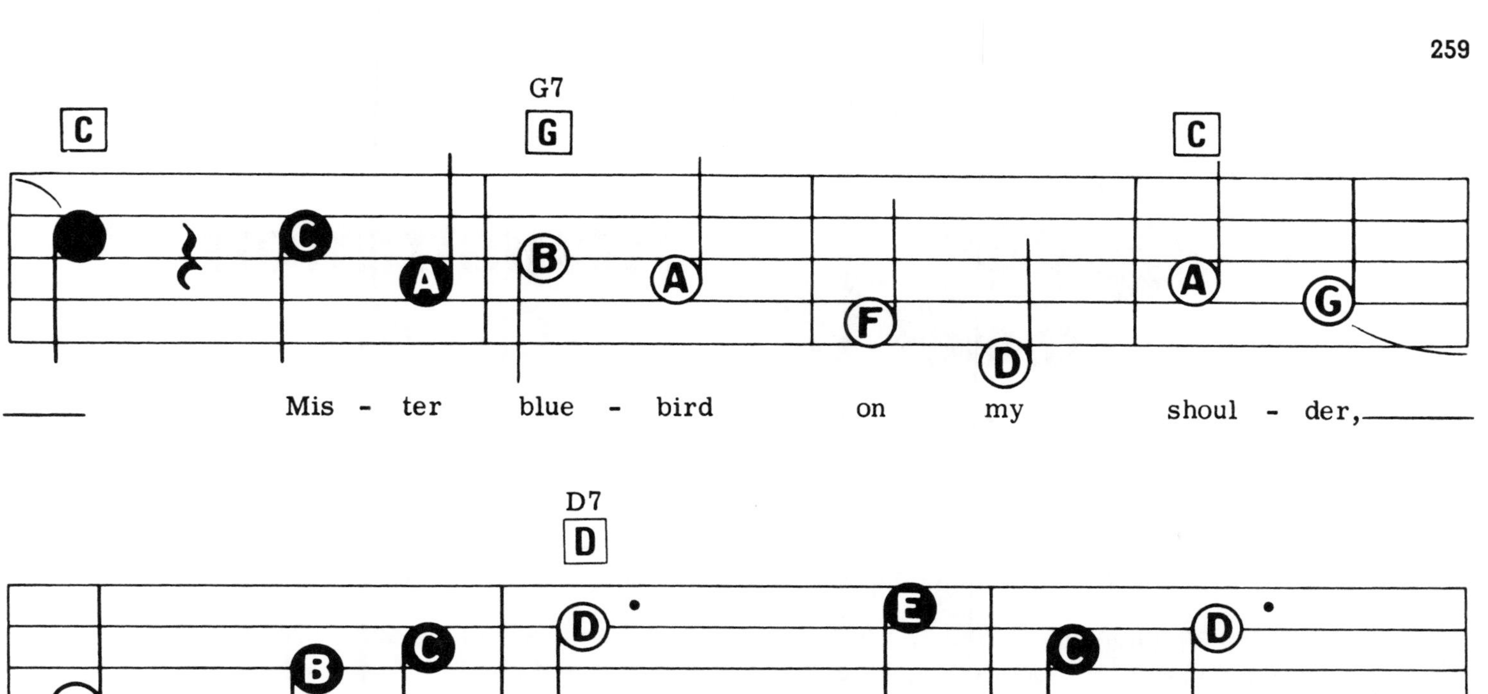
C
G7
G
C
C A B A F D A G
Mis - ter blue - bird on my shoul - der,

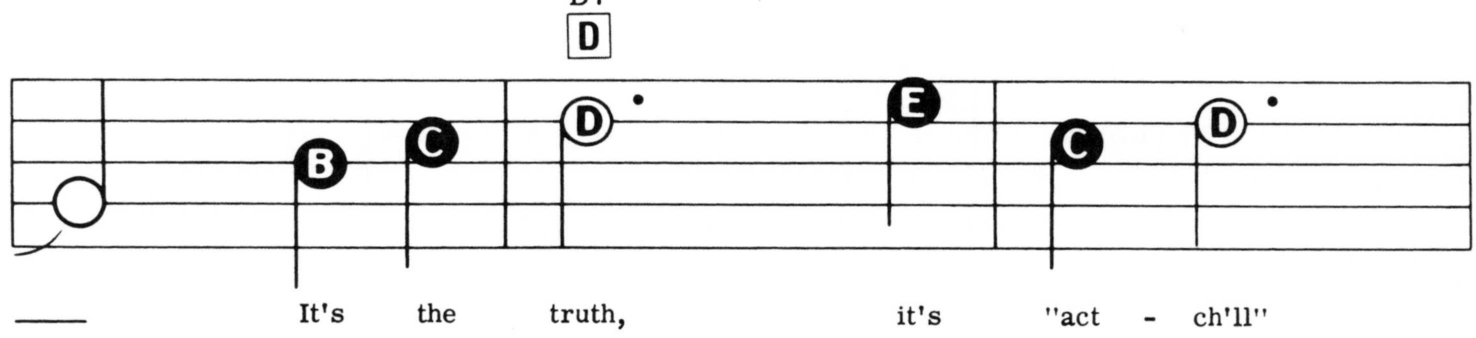
D7
D
B C D E C D
It's the truth, it's "act - ch'll"

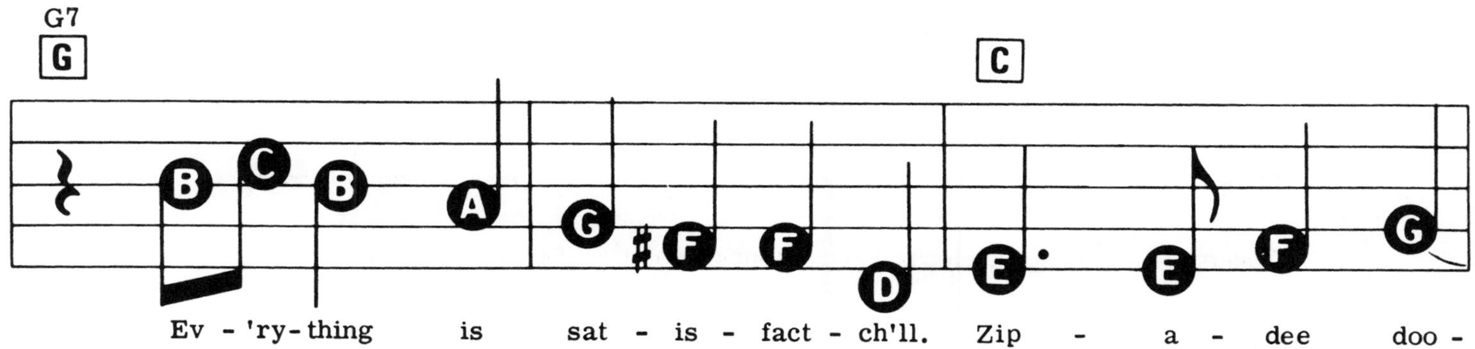
G7
G
C
B C B A G F F D E E F G
Ev - 'ry - thing is sat - is - fact - ch'll. Zip - a - dee doo -

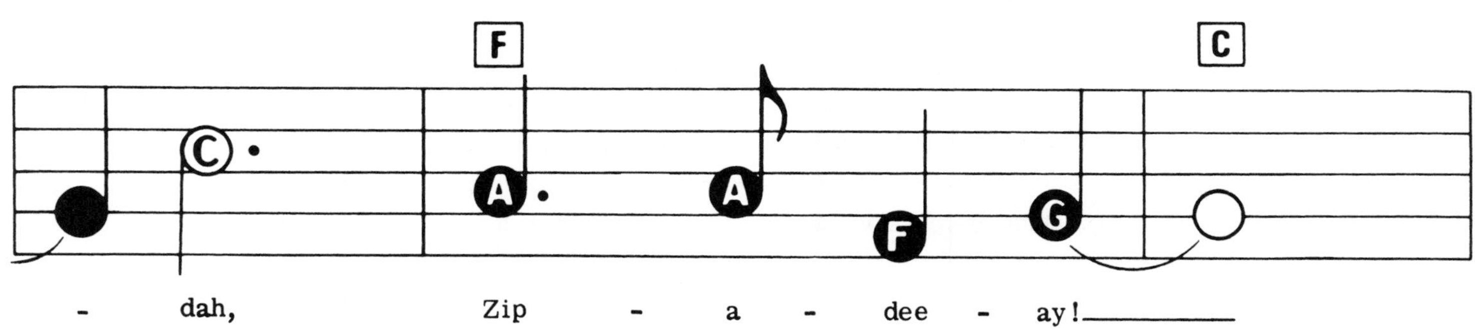
F
C
C A A F G
- dah, Zip - a - dee - ay!

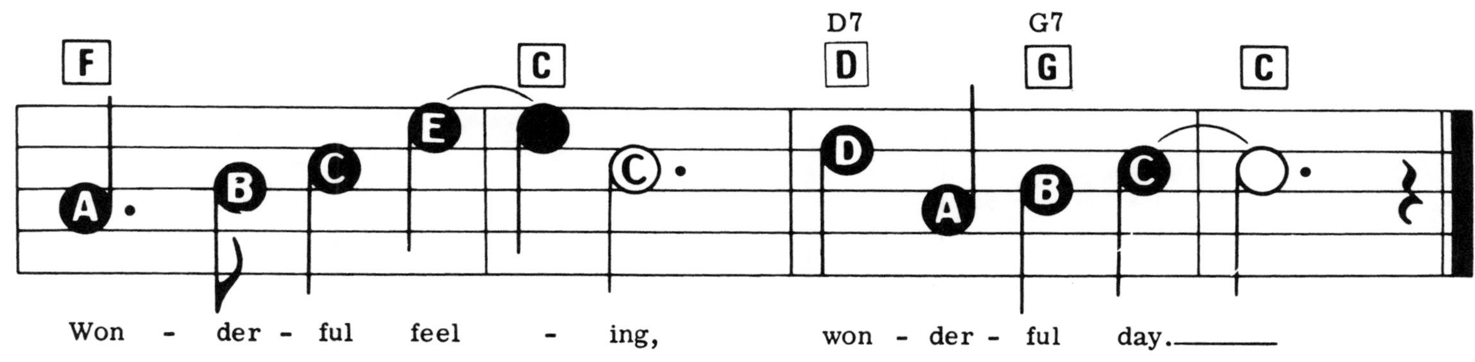
F
C
D7
D
G7
G
C
A B C E C D A B C
Won - der - ful feel - ing, won - der - ful day.

Registration Guide

- Match the Registration number on the song to the corresponding numbered category below. Select and activate an instrumental sound available on your instrument.
- Choose an automatic rhythm appropriate to the mood and style of the song. (Consult your Owner's Guide for proper operation of automatic rhythm features.)
- Adjust the tempo and volume controls to comfortable settings.

Registration

1	Mellow	Flutes, Clarinet, Oboe, Flugel Horn, Trombone, French Horn, Organ Flutes
2	Ensemble	Brass Section, Sax Section, Wind Ensemble, Full Organ, Theater Organ
3	Strings	Violin, Viola, Cello, Fiddle, String Ensemble, Pizzicato, Organ Strings
4	Guitars	Acoustic/Electric Guitars, Banjo, Mandolin, Dulcimer, Ukulele, Hawaiian Guitar
5	Mallets	Vibraphone, Marimba, Xylophone, Steel Drums, Bells, Celesta, Chimes
6	Liturgical	Pipe Organ, Hand Bells, Vocal Ensemble, Choir, Organ Flutes
7	Bright	Saxophones, Trumpet, Mute Trumpet, Synth Leads, Jazz/Gospel Organs
8	Piano	Piano, Electric Piano, Honky Tonk Piano, Harpsichord, Clavi
9	Novelty	Melodic Percussion, Wah Trumpet, Synth, Whistle, Kazoo, Perc. Organ
10	Bellows	Accordion, French Accordion, Mussette, Harmonica, Pump Organ, Bagpipes

FOR ORGANS, PIANOS & ELECTRONIC KEYBOARDS

E-Z PLAY® TODAY PUBLICATIONS

The E-Z Play® Today songbook series is the shortest distance between beginning music and playing fun! Check out this list of highlights and visit www.halleonard.com for a complete listing of all volumes and songlists.

Item	Title	Price
00102278	1. Favorite Songs with 3 Chords	$7.99
00100374	2. Country Sound	$8.95
00100167	3. Contemporary Disney	$16.99
00100382	4. Dance Band Greats	$7.95
00100305	5. All-Time Standards	$7.99
00100428	6. Songs of The Beatles	$10.99
00100442	7. Hits from Musicals	$7.99
00100490	8. Patriotic Songs	$8.99
00100355	9. Christmas Time	$7.95
00100435	10. Hawaiian Songs	$7.95
00137580	11. 75 Light Classical Songs	$19.99
00110284	12. Star Wars	$7.99
00100248	13. Three-Chord Country Songs	$12.95
00100300	14. All-Time Requests	$8.99
00100370	15. Country Pickin's	$7.95
00100335	16. Broadway's Best	$7.95
00100415	17. Fireside Singalong	$14.99
00149113	18. 30 Classical Masterworks	$8.99
00137780	19. Top Country Songs	$12.99
00102277	20. Hymns	$7.95
00100570	22. Sacred Sounds	$7.95
00140724	25. Happy Birthday to You and Other Great Songs	$10.99
14041364	26. Bob Dylan	$12.99
00001236	27. 60 of the World's Easiest to Play Songs with 3 Chords	$8.95
00101598	28. Fifty Classical Themes	$9.95
00100135	29. Love Songs	$7.95
00100030	30. Country Connection	$8.95
00100253	34. Inspirational Ballads	$10.95
00100254	35. Frank Sinatra – Romance	$8.95
00100122	36. Good Ol' Songs	$10.95
00100410	37. Favorite Latin Songs	$7.95
00119955	40. Coldplay	$10.99
00100425	41. Songs of Gershwin, Porter & Rodgers	$7.95
00100123	42. Baby Boomers Songbook	$9.95
00100576	43. Sing-along Requests	$8.95
00102135	44. Best of Willie Nelson	$10.99
00100460	45. Love Ballads	$8.99
00156236	46. 15 Chart Hits	$12.99
00100007	47. Duke Ellington – American Composer	$8.95
00100343	48. Gospel Songs of Johnny Cash	$7.95
00102114	50. Best of Patsy Cline	$9.99
00100208	51. Essential Songs – The 1950s	$17.95
00100209	52. Essential Songs – The 1960s	$17.95
00100210	53. Essential Songs – The 1970s	$19.95
00100342	55. Johnny Cash	$10.99
00137703	56. Jersey Boys	$10.99
00100118	57. More of the Best Songs Ever	$17.99
00100285	58. Four-Chord Songs	$10.99
00100353	59. Christmas Songs	$8.95
00100304	60. Songs for All Occasions	$16.99
00102314	61. Jazz Standards	$10.95
00100409	62. Favorite Hymns	$6.95
00100360	63. Classical Music (Spanish/English)	$7.99
00100223	64. Wicked	$9.95
00100217	65. Hymns with 3 Chords	$7.99
00100218	67. Music from the Motion Picture Ray	$8.95
00100449	69. It's Gospel	$7.95
00100432	70. Gospel Greats	$7.95
00100117	72. Canciones Románticas	$7.99
00147049	74. Over the Rainbow & 40 More Great Songs	$12.99
00100568	75. Sacred Moments	$6.95
00100572	76. The Sound of Music	$9.99
00100489	77. My Fair Lady	$7.99
00100424	81. Frankie Yankovic – Polkas & Waltzes	$7.95
00100286	87. 50 Worship Standards	$14.99
00100287	88. Glee	$9.99
00100577	89. Songs for Children	$7.95
00290104	90. Elton John Anthology	$16.99
00100034	91. 30 Songs for a Better World	$8.95
00100288	92. Michael Bublé – Crazy Love	$10.99
00100036	93. Country Hits	$10.95
00100139	94. Jim Croce – Greatest Hits	$8.95
00100219	95. The Phantom of the Opera (Movie)	$10.95
00100263	96. Mamma Mia – Movie Soundtrack	$7.99
00109768	98. Flower Power	$16.99
00100125	99. Children's Christmas Songs	$8.99
00100602	100. Winter Wonderland	$8.95
00001309	102. Carols of Christmas	$7.99
00119237	103. Two-Chord Songs	$9.99
00147057	104. Hallelujah & 40 More Great Songs	$12.99
00139940	106. 20 Top Hits	$12.99
00100256	107. The Best Praise & Worship Songs Ever	$16.99
00100363	108. Classical Themes (English/Spanish)	$6.95
00102232	109. Motown's Greatest Hits	$12.95
00101566	110. Neil Diamond Collection	$14.99
00100119	111. Season's Greetings	$15.99
00101498	112. Best of The Beatles	$19.99
00100134	113. Country Gospel USA	$10.95
00101612	115. The Greatest Waltzes	$9.99
00100136	118. 100 Kids' Songs	$12.95
00100433	120. Gospel of Bill & Gloria Gaither	$14.95
00100333	121. Boogies, Blues and Rags	$7.95
00100146	122. Songs for Praise & Worship	$8.95
00100001	125. Great Big Book of Children's Songs	$14.99
00101563	127. John Denver's Greatest Hits	$10.99
00116947	128. John Williams	$10.99
00140764	129. Campfire Songs	$10.99
00116956	130. Taylor Swift Hits	$10.99
00102318	131. Doo-Wop Songbook	$10.95
00100306	133. Carole King	$9.99
00001256	136. Christmas Is for Kids	$8.99
00100144	137. Children's Movie Hits	$7.95
00100038	138. Nostalgia Collection	$14.95
00100289	139. Crooners	$19.99
00101956	140. Best of George Strait	$12.95
00101946	143. The Songs of Paul McCartney	$8.99
00140768	144. Halloween	$10.99
00147061	147. Great Instrumentals	$9.99
00101548	150. Best Big Band Songs Ever	$16.95
00100152	151. Beach Boys – Greatest Hits	$9.99
00101592	152. Fiddler on the Roof	$9.99
00140981	153. Play Along with 50 Great Songs	$14.99
00101549	155. Best of Billy Joel	$12.99
00100315	160. The Grammy Awards Record of the Year 1958-2010	$16.99
00100293	161. Henry Mancini	$9.99
00100049	162. Lounge Music	$10.95
00100295	163. The Very Best of the Rat Pack	$12.99
00101530	164. Best Christmas Songbook	$9.99
00101895	165. Rodgers & Hammerstein Songbook	$9.95
00149300	166. The Best of Beethoven	$8.99
00149736	167. The Best of Bach	$8.99
00100148	169. A Charlie Brown Christmas™	$10.99
00101900	170. Kenny Rogers – Greatest Hits	$12.99
00101537	171. Best of Elton John	$9.99
00100321	173. Adele – 21	$10.99
00100149	176. Charlie Brown Collection™	$9.99
00102325	179. Love Songs of The Beatles	$10.99
00149881	180. The Best of Mozart	$8.99
00101610	181. Great American Country Songbook	$12.95
00001246	182. Amazing Grace	$12.99
00450133	183. West Side Story	$9.99
00100151	185. Carpenters	$10.99
00101606	186. 40 Pop & Rock Song Classics	$12.95
00100155	187. Ultimate Christmas	$18.99
00102276	189. Irish Favorites	$7.95
00100053	191. Jazz Love Songs	$8.95
00101998	192. 65 Standard Hits	$15.95
00123123	193. Bruno Mars	$10.99
00124609	195. Opera Favorites	$8.99
00101609	196. Best of George Gershwin	$14.99
00100057	198. Songs in 3/4 Time	$9.95
00119857	199. Jumbo Songbook	$24.99
00101539	200. Best Songs Ever	$19.99
00101540	202. Best Country Songs Ever	$17.95
00101541	203. Best Broadway Songs Ever	$17.99
00101542	204. Best Easy Listening Songs Ever	$17.99
00101543	205. Best Love Songs Ever	$17.95
00100059	210. '60s Pop Rock Hits	$12.95
14041777	211. The Big Book of Nursery Rhymes & Children's Songs	$12.99
00126895	212. Frozen	$9.99
00101546	213. Disney Classics	$14.95
00101533	215. Best Christmas Songs Ever	$19.95
00131100	216. Frank Sinatra Centennial Songbook	$19.99
00100156	219. Christmas Songs with 3 Chords	$9.99
00102080	225. Lawrence Welk Songbook	$9.95
00101935	232. Songs of the '60s	$14.95
00101936	233. Songs of the '70s	$14.95
00101581	235. Elvis Presley Anthology	$15.99
00290170	239. Big Book of Children's Songs	$14.95
00100158	243. Oldies! Oldies! Oldies!	$10.95
00100041	245. Best of Simon & Garfunkel	$8.95
00100296	248. The Love Songs of Elton John	$12.99
00102113	251. Phantom of the Opera (Broadway)	$14.95
00100203	256. Very Best of Lionel Richie	$8.95
00100302	258. Four-Chord Worship	$9.99
00100178	259. Norah Jones – Come Away with Me	$10.99
00100063	266. Latin Hits	$7.95
00100062	269. Love That Latin Beat	$7.95
00101425	272. ABBA Gold – Greatest Hits	$9.99
00102248	275. Classical Hits – Bach, Beethoven & Brahms	$6.95
00100186	277. Stevie Wonder – Greatest Hits	$10.99
00100237	280. Dolly Parton	$9.99
00100068	283. Best Jazz Standards Ever	$15.95
00100244	287. Josh Groban	$12.99
00100022	288. Sing-a-Long Christmas	$12.99
00100023	289. Sing-a-Long Christmas Carols	$10.99
00102124	293. Movie Classics	$9.95
00100303	295. Best of Michael Bublé	$12.99
00100075	296. Best of Cole Porter	$7.95
00102130	298. Beautiful Love Songs	$7.95
00001102	301. Kid's Songfest	$10.99
00110416	302. More Kids' Songfest	$12.99
00102147	306. Irving Berlin Collection	$14.95
00102182	308. Greatest American Songbook	$9.99
00100194	309. 3-Chord Rock 'n' Roll	$8.95
02501515	312. Barbra – Love Is the Answer	$10.99
00100197	315. VH1's 100 Greatest Songs of Rock & Roll	$19.95
00100080	322. Dixieland	$7.95
00100277	325. Taylor Swift	$10.99
00100092	333. Great Gospel Favorites	$7.95
00100278	338. The Best Hymns Ever	$19.99
00100280	341. Anthology of Rock Songs	$19.99
00102235	346. Big Book of Christmas Songs	$14.95
00100095	359. 100 Years of Song	$17.95
00100096	360. More 100 Years of Song	$19.95
00100103	375. Songs of Bacharach & David	$7.95
00100107	392. Disney Favorites	$19.99
00100108	393. Italian Favorites	$7.95
00100111	394. Best Gospel Songs Ever	$17.95
00100114	398. Disney's Princess Collections	$12.99
00100115	400. Classical Masterpieces	$10.99

7777 W. Bluemound Rd. P.O. Box 13819 Milwaukee, WI 53213

Prices, contents, and availability subject to change without notice.